Blogging
ALL-IN-ONE
FOR
DUMMIES®

by Susan Gunelius

WILEY

Wiley Publishing, Inc.

Blogging All-in-One For Dummies®

Published by
Wiley Publishing, Inc.
111 River Street
Hoboken, NJ 07030-5774

www.wiley.com

Copyright © 2010 by Wiley Publishing, Inc., Indianapolis, Indiana

Published by Wiley Publishing, Inc., Indianapolis, Indiana

Published simultaneously in Canada

For general information on our other products and services, please contact our Customer Care Department within the U.S. at 877-762-2974, outside the U.S. at 317-572-3993, or fax 317-572-4002.

For technical support, please visit www.wiley.com/techsupport.

Wiley also publishes its books in a variety of electronic formats. Some content that appears in print may not be available in electronic books.

Library of Congress Control Number: 2010926837

ISBN: 978-0-470-57377-8

Manufactured in the United States of America

10 9 8 7 6 5 4 3 2 1

WILEY

About the Author

Susan Gunelius is a marketing expert with nearly 20 years of experience who added blogging to her skill set as an extension of her career as an author and freelance writer. Her marketing background and writing experience allowed her to quickly learn and leverage the blogosphere as a tool for personal and professional growth.

Today, Susan is a professional blogger authoring several blogs for various small and large companies as well as her own company blog at www.key splashcreativeconversations.com. She is the Guide to Web Logs for About.com, a New York Times company, (http://weblogs.about.com), and she owns one of the leading blogs for business women, www.womenon business.com, which was recognized as a finalist for Best Blog by the 2009 Stevie Awards for Women in Business.

Susan spent the first decade of her career managing and executing marketing programs for some of the largest companies in the world, including divisions of AT&T and HSBC. In 2004, she left the corporate world and shortly thereafter, began a career as a freelance writer, copywriter, author, professional blogger, and marketing and branding consultant. In 2008, she opened KeySplash Creative, Inc. (www.keysplashcreative.com), and as the President of KeySplash Creative, she offers marketing and writing services to clients around the world.

Susan is a columnist for Entrepreneur.com and ForbesWoman.com and her marketing-related articles have appeared on Web sites such as MSNBC.com, FoxBusiness.com, WashingtonPost.com, BusinessWeek.com, TheStreet.com, SmartMoney.com, Yahoo! Small Business, Yahoo! Finance, and more. Additionally, she is the author of *Google Blogger For Dummies* (Wiley), *Building Brand Value the Playboy Way* (Palgrave Macmillan), *Harry Potter: The Story of a Global Business Phenomenon* (Palgrave Macmillan), *Kick-ass Copywriting in 10 Easy Steps* (Entrepreneur Press), and Spread the Word: Social Media Marketing in 30 Minutes a Day (McGraw-Hill).

You can learn more about Susan Gunelius at www.keysplashcreative.com and connect with her on Twitter (www.twitter.com/susangunelius), Facebook (www.facebook.com/susangunelius), and LinkedIn (www.linkedin.com/in/susangunelius).

Dedication

To my husband, Scott, for picking up the pieces without complaint while I write. I couldn't do this without you.

Author's Acknowledgments

I want to acknowledge my husband, Scott, first and foremost for truly being the best husband and father, and my children, Brynn, Daniel, and Ryan, for always making me smile, even after a long day in front of my computer.

I want to also acknowledge my parents, Bill and Carol Ann Henry, for babysitting when I'm pressed to meet a deadline and for listening to me ramble on when I'm overly stressed.

I want to thank Amy Fandrei, Nicole Sholly, Jennifer Webb, and everyone at Wiley for helping to make this book a reality, and I want to thank my agent, Bob Diforio, for listening to me and watching out for me.

I also want to thank all the bloggers out there, especially the ones I've learned from and gotten to know over the past few years. Without all of you, the blogosphere would be a very boring place.

And of course, it's no fun blogging if no one is reading, so thank you to everyone who reads my blogs!

Publisher's Acknowledgments

We're proud of this book; please send us your comments at http://dummies.custhelp.com. For other comments, please contact our Customer Care Department within the U.S. at 877-762-2974, outside the U.S. at 317-572-3993, or fax 317-572-4002.

Some of the people who helped bring this book to market include the following:

Acquisitions, Editorial

Project Editor: Nicole Sholly

Acquisitions Editor: Amy Fandrei

Copy Editor: Virginia Sanders

Technical Editor: Roberta Rosenberg

Editorial Manager: Kevin Kirschner

Editorial Assistant: Amanda Graham

Sr. Editorial Assistant: Cherie Case

Cartoons: Rich Tennant
(www.the5thwave.com)

Composition Services

Project Coordinator: Patrick Redmond

Layout and Graphics: Carl Byers,

Proofreaders: Cara L. Buitron, John Greenough

Indexer: Valerie Haynes Perry

Publishing and Editorial for Technology Dummies

   Richard Swadley, Vice President and Executive Group Publisher

   Andy Cummings, Vice President and Publisher

   Mary Bednarek, Executive Acquisitions Director

   Mary C. Corder, Editorial Director

Publishing for Consumer Dummies

   Diane Graves Steele, Vice President and Publisher

Composition Services

   Debbie Stailey, Director of Composition Services

Contents at a Glance

Table of Contents

Introduction

*E*ach person who creates a blog is unique, and therefore, each blog is unique. There are almost no boundaries to entering the *blogosphere* (the online blogging community made up of bloggers from around the world, creating user-generated content as part of the social Web.), and everyone is welcome to the party. Blogging is an amazing way to connect with people, promote a business, establish yourself as an expert in your chosen field, make money, or simply to share content with friends and family. The choice is yours!

However, the blogosphere might be open to anyone, but many people are confused and intimidated by the terminology, technology, and rules of the blogosphere. Truth be told, most bloggers dive in and learn as they go, but in case you prefer to have a guide on hand to walk you through the theories, tools, and processes to create, publish, and maintain a blog, *Blogging All-in-One For Dummies* offers exactly that — a complete guide to blogging, all in one place.

About Blogging All-in-One For Dummies

Blogging All-in-One For Dummies provides a clear and concise introduction to all the terms, theories, and processes you need to understand how to not only join the blogosphere, but to also meet your individual goals for your blog. The following list highlights some of the information you can better understand and apply to your blogging experience as you read this book — you find out how to

- ✦ Find blogs to read

- ✦ Choose a topic and write blog posts

- ✦ Pick a domain name and identify the parts of a blog

- ✦ Follow the rules of the blogosphere

- ✦ Create a niche blog

- ✦ Develop a business blog

- ✦ Select a blogging application, using detailed descriptions of the most popular blogging applications — WordPress, Blogger, and TypePad

- ✦ Write with search engine optimization in mind

- ✦ Analyze your blog's performance

- ✦ Find and edit images for your blog

- ✦ Create a blog feed

+ Use an offline blog editor

+ Create a podcast or vlog

+ Promote and grow your blog

+ Make money from your blogging efforts

+ Microblog with Twitter

Blogging can be fun. It can also be lucrative and help you meet a wide variety of goals, from growing a business to building relationships with a global audience. The choice is yours, and *Blogging All-in-One For Dummies* can help you get started on the path to blogging success, regardless of your personal or professional goals.

Foolish Assumptions

Blogging All-in-One For Dummies is written primarily for a beginner audience — people who have never blogged before. However, I'm assuming you know a few things before you start reading this book:

+ You know how to access and surf the Internet using a Web browser on your computer.

+ You have a general understanding of what a blog is, or you've seen a blog online before.

+ You want to start your own blog, or you want to find out more about blogging to enhance your existing blog.

Understand that if you are a skilled blogger with a deep understanding of the tools and theories of the blogosphere, then many of the topics discussed in this book are likely to be very rudimentary for you. However, even the most seasoned bloggers admit they don't know everything about blogging and the social Web, or at the very least, they haven't thought of something in a certain way before. For example, you may have been blogging for years, but now you want to learn more about a different tool or niche. In other words, even skilled bloggers can find plenty of tips and techniques in this book that could come in handy or make their lives easier.

Conventions Used in This Book

It's time to review the technical aspects of how this book is laid out. Watch for **bold text** included within step-by-step instructions. This text directs you to enter specific text on your computer screen. Terms or words specific to blogging are *italicized* when they're first introduced, and I give you definitions for them. Also, note that Web site addresses (URLs) and e-mail addresses are in monofont so they stand out from regular text.

What You Don't Have to Read

Blogging All-in-One For Dummies is divided into eight minibooks. Each minibook (and each chapter within a minibook) is capable of standing on its own. Therefore, you can pick and choose to read specific minibooks or specific chapters to meet your needs and skip those minibooks and chapters that don't apply.

It's important to point out that reading the book from start to finish gives you a complete introduction to blogging and positions you to start your blog successfully and with fewer problems in the future. However, it's entirely up to you to decide how you want to use this book. Just as there really is no wrong way to blog, there's no wrong way to read this book.

How This Book Is Organized

Blogging All-in-One For Dummies is divided into eight minibooks. Each minibook tackles a broad topic related to blogging, from discovering what a blog is to monetizing a blog and everything in between — this book has a section on nearly every blogging subject. Here's a description of each minibook, so you can identify the ones that are likely to be most helpful to you.

Book 1: Joining the Blogosphere

Book I starts from the very beginning with an introduction to the fundamental principles of blogging. You find out what blogs are and why people blog. You also get guidance on finding blogs to read and making the decision to start your own blog.

After the introduction, you start to get your hands dirty. This minibook explains how to pick a blog topic, write blog content, choose a domain name, and understand the bits and pieces that make up a blog. Importantly, you also find out the written and unwritten rules and ethics of the blogosphere. If you want to be a welcome member of the blogosphere, make sure you know and follow the rules discussed in this minibook.

Book 11: Niche Blogging

Niche blogging has become more and more popular in recent years as the blogosphere gets more crowded. Book II explains what niche blogs are, how to choose a niche, and how to start your own niche blog. You also find out how to write content for a niche blog. Although many of the guidelines of writing a blog discussed in Book I apply to niche blogs, there are even more considerations that niche bloggers need to think about when they write blog posts. This minibook tells you how to set up your niche blog for success.

Book III: Corporate and Business Blogging

Blogging for business is becoming a strategic imperative for large organizations and a competitive differentiator for small companies. No matter what business you're in, a blog can help you with both tangible and intangible benefits. This minibook teaches you how starting a business blog can benefit your company. You also find out about companies that are effectively using business blogs, so you can benchmark them for your own efforts. Furthermore, you find out how to create your own business blog marketing plan, choose business bloggers, and write your business blog. Finally, you discover how to blog safely so you keep yourself and your company out of trouble.

Book IV: Choosing a Blogging Application

With so many blogging applications and tools to choose from, it can be hard for beginner bloggers to know where to begin. This minibook explains what blogging applications and blog hosts are and helps you select the best choices for you to help you meet your goals. You also get a more detailed introduction to three of the most popular blogging applications — WordPress, Blogger, and TypePad.

Book V: Blogging Tools

There's a never-ending list of blogging tools that you can use to extend and enhance your blog. This minibook introduces you to some of the most commonly used tools to help you with handling search engine optimization, analyzing your blog's performance, editing and finding images, and understanding and creating blog feeds. You also find out about the benefits of using an offline blog editor as well as how to create an audio blog post (called a *podcast*) or a video blog post (called a *vlog*).

Book VI: Promoting and Growing Your Blog

Many bloggers have goals to develop a popular and well-trafficked blog. If you're one of those bloggers, than Book VI is a chapter you need to read. You find out the secrets of blogging success, how to build a community, and how to market your blog through social networking, social bookmarking, guest blogging, blog contests, and blog carnivals.

Book VII: Making Money from Your Blog

If you want to make money from your blog, then Book VII is for you! This chapter tells you all about blog advertising, including contextual ads, text link ads, impression ads, affiliate ads, feed ads, and direct ads. This minibook explains publishing ads on your blog as a monetization tactic, as well as publishing sponsored reviews and paid posts, selling merchandise, and a variety of indirect monetization opportunities.

Book VIII: Microblogging with Twitter

Microblogging has exploded in popularity, and Twitter is the most commonly used microblogging tool. Book VIII introduces you to microblogging and Twitter. You find out how to create your Twitter profile, follow other users, write and publish tweets, and more. This minibook also covers Twitter terminology, so you can speak the language, too. Finally, you find out about some of the most popular third-party Twitter applications, which you can use to enhance your Twitter experience.

Glossary

Not sure what a word used in this book means? Check the glossary for layman's definitions to many of the terms used by members of the blogosphere.

Icons Used in This Book

All *For Dummies* books include helpful icons that highlight valuable information, tips, tricks, and warnings:

Points out helpful information that's likely to save you time and effort.

Alerts you of lurking danger. This icon tells you to pay attention and proceed with caution.

Highlights techie-type information nearby. If you're not feeling highly technical, you can skip this information; if you're brave, the information next to the Technical Stuff icons throughout this book can be very helpful.

Marks a point that's interesting and useful, which you probably want to remember for future use.

Where to Go from Here

It's up to you! You can read this book in any order you choose. Each chapter is modular, meaning each chapter can stand on its own. Of course, reading the book from start to finish provides you with a complete and thorough introduction to blogging, but, depending on your goals and experience, the number of chapters you read and the order in which you read them will vary.

Bottom-line, blogging is fun, and each blogger's goals are completely different. Just because someone else is doing XYZ on his blog, doesn't mean that XYZ is right for your blog. Use this book as a guide to help you understand the theories, tactics, strategies, and tools of the blogosphere, and then apply them to your blog in the best way to meet *your* needs.

Now it's time to start blogging!

Book I

Joining the Blogosphere

The 5th Wave   By Rich Tennant

"He should be all right now. I made him spend two and a half hours reading prisoner blogs on the state penitentiary web site."

Contents at a Glance

Chapter 1: Joining the Blogosphere

The term *blog* has become part of common vernacular. What was once thought of as a fad has become an integral part of the social, media, and business worlds. It seems like everyone knows someone who writes or reads a blog. In fact, many people read blogs and don't even realize it! Today, blogs can look just like traditional Web sites. In fact, some of the most popular online destinations are blogs, which shows just how far the fad has actually come.

According to the popular research report, The State of the Blogosphere 2008, published by Technorati.com (a popular blog search tool), there were over 184 million blogs by the end of 2008, and that number continues to grow each day. Why? It's simple. There are virtually no barriers to entry. Just about anyone can create a blog, for free and with very little technical abilities, and have a place on the Web to publish anything he or she wants. (Of course, there are unwritten rules of the blogging community, called the *blogosphere,* which you can find out about in Chapter 4 of this minibook.)

The inherent draw of blogging is the opportunity it provides for anyone with access to a computer and the Internet to publish content online. They can make that content available to a global audience or to a select few. The choices are made by each individual blogger. Again, when you start a blog, you become the leader of your own mini media outlet.

As you read, keep in mind that different people have different goals for their blogs, and for that reason no two blogs are alike. You find out more about why people blog later in this chapter. For now, just remember not to judge a blog by its cover. A blog is what the author makes of it, and that's where this book comes into action. There are few rights and wrongs to blogging, but you can't begin to understand why that's true until you dive in and join the blogosphere!

Welcome to the Blogosphere

Blogs have been around for over a decade, but they've come a long way since their inception. There was a time in the early days of the Internet when Web sites were fairly static destinations for information. As new ways evolved for people without extensive technical knowledge to develop their own Web presences, blogging was born.

The term *blog* is a fusion of the words *Web* and *log* and is sometimes still referred to as *weblog.* Originally, blogs were simple online diaries where people posted the daily events of their lives. Typically, people wrote blogs to keep friends and family connected. For example, a woman might update her online diary with information about her journey through pregnancy to share the events with her family and friends across long distances. Just as the telephone brought people closer than ever a century earlier, blogs brought people from around the world together at the end of the 20th century.

In the beginning

Blogs began as very rudimentary Web pages that looked like little more than a lengthy narrative of text (and possibly some pictures), sometimes with entry dates acting as content separators, just as the pages of a hard copy diary or journal might look. Early blogs didn't include the social element that today's blogs offer through the commenting feature, which allows two-way conversation to take place. In this sense, early blogs were still a one-sided conversation and evolved during the transitional period of the growth of the World Wide Web.

Not only was the layout of the content simple, but the overall design was as well. More technical knowledge was required to create a blog in 1994, such as HTML coding skills or access to expensive software that would allow people to create their own Web pages. Therefore, some folks might argue that blogging as we know it today didn't actually begin until 1999, when hosted blogging applications — such as LiveJournal.com and Blogger.com — debuted and made blogging accessible, easy, and free to the masses.

It wasn't until 2002–2003 that blogging became popular among broad audiences. According to Technorati's State of the Blogosphere 2008 report, the number of blogs grew from under 200,000 in 2003 to over 184 million in 2008. Suddenly, what was originally viewed as a tool for personal communication turned into an alternative media channel: Journalists, politicians, businesses, and experts in a wide variety of industries and fields started their own blogs and gained notoriety and popularity because of them.

Blogs today

What was once considered an ancillary or fun way to get online has turned into an essential tool to many. Today, blogs are competing with mainstream media in delivering news and information faster and more accurately than ever before.

For example, the news of Michael Jackson's death first appeared on a celebrity gossip blog, TMZ.com. (Figure 1-1 shows the article on TMZ.com.) Traditional news media organizations, such as CNN.com, were hours behind the blog in verifying the accuracy of the TMZ.com report.

Similarly, news of rebellion in Iran that followed the 2009 presidential election in that country spread through individuals updating the world from inside Iran via Twitter (the most popular microblogging tool), not from traditional news media. A scheduled shut down of Twitter.com for routine maintenance was cancelled so as not to interrupt the spread of information through the site about the fallout from the Iranian election.

Figure 1-1:
The news
of Michael
Jackson's
death
was first
reported by
the TMZ.
com blog.

Blogs have come a long way in terms of design and use. No longer are they simple online diaries. Today, blogs are used for a myriad of reasons, from sharing information with friends and families, to spreading political news, to promoting a business, to making money, and everything in between. The opportunities are endless.

In fact, many business Web sites are built using a blogging application, such as WordPress.org, rather than more traditional Web design techniques. Why? Because blogs are very easy for business owners to update and modify without incurring huge investments in redesigns. Blogging applications are so easy to use and customize that users can create just about any kind of Web site they want with them — not just online diaries.

What is a blog?

Today's blogs can have many different forms, but the following elements make up the traditional model of a blog:

- ✦ **Posts:** A blog is a Web site that consists of entries (called *posts*) that appear in reverse chronological order, so the most recent appears at the top of the page.

- ✦ **A commenting feature:** A blog includes a comment feature that allows readers to publish their own comments on the posts they read. Comments provide interactivity, discussions, and relationship-building opportunities between the blogger and his community of readers.

- ✦ **Links:** The links in a blog allow readers to find more information either within the blog or on other blogs and Web sites. Links provide another interactive tool and allow the blogger to build relationships with other bloggers and Web site owners by sending traffic to their sites.

- ✦ **Archives:** A blog includes an archive of all posts published on that blog since its inception, making it very easy to find older posts.

Blogs are highly social tools designed to build relationships and network. With a blog, you can connect with people around the world from the comfort of your own home.

Blogs have evolved to come in several forms. For example, blogs can include written entries, which is the most common form of blogging. However, blogs can also consist of photo entries (called *photo blogs*), videos (called *vlogs*), or audio content (called *podcasts*). In fact, blogs could include a combination of *each* of those types of entries.

The uniqueness of blogs comes from the voices of the people writing them and how they choose to use the additional blogging application functionality and blogging tools available to them to make their blogs stand out from the crowd. A blogger's creativity typically stems from why he blogs in the first place.

Finding Out Why People Blog

The best part about blogging is anyone can do it! Young or old, male or female, it doesn't matter. If you have a desire to get your voice heard online, whatever the reason, you can do it with a blog. You are your own boss when it comes to your blog.

There are many types of blogs as well. For example, some of the common types of blogs are

- ✦ **Personal blogs:** These blogs are written by individuals about topics of a personal nature such as their likes and dislikes, hobbies, opinions, and so on.

✦ **Business blogs:** These blogs are written for a business for the purpose of growing the business, connecting with consumers, networking, and so on.

✦ **Corporate blogs:** Corporate blogs are a form of business blogs that are owned by large corporate entities.

✦ **Nonprofit blogs:** Many nonprofit organizations publish blogs to share information about causes, gain support, and solicit donations.

✦ **News and information blogs:** These blogs share information, news, current events, and so on about topics such as popular culture, entertainment, sports, and so on.

✦ **Expert blogs:** These blogs are written by people who are experts in their fields and share their knowledge through their posts.

✦ **Entertainment and fan blogs:** These blogs are written by individuals or organizations about celebrities, sports, music, and so on.

✦ **Niche blogs:** Niche blogs are written about *very* specific topics of the blogger's choosing.

Blogs can be written on just about any subject. They can be written in a multitude of languages, and they can be updated as often as you want. Of course, if you have goals to make money, build your business, increase Web traffic, and so on with your blog, you ought to know some tricks of the trade that can help you be a successful blogger (some are mentioned at the end of this chapter), but for now, it's important to understand the open nature of the blogosphere.

Some of the most popular topics being blogged about are related to entertainment, technology, and business, but you can write on any topic you're passionate about. You'd be surprised how many people around the world are interested in the same things that you love!

Blogging for fun

Millions of blogs are written by people who have few goals for their blogs other than to have fun. They might just be connecting with family and friends or using the blogosphere as a place to share their opinions simply because they love to write those opinions down somewhere. Interestingly, many blogs that people write just for fun become incredibly popular, turning the bloggers behind them into Web stars.

Bloggers like Heather Armstrong, of Dooce.com (shown in Figure 1-2); Mario Lavandeira, of PerezHilton.com; and Gary Vaynerchuk, of Wine Library TV (http://tv.winelibrary.com) all started their blogs for fun, because they loved the topics they wrote about or simply wanted to document a part of their lives or opinions. Today, all three are minor celebrities both online and offline.

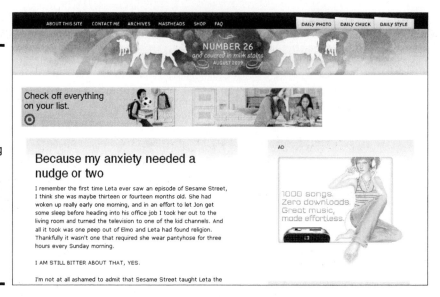

Figure 1-2: Heather Armstrong, of Dooce. com, rose to stardom after getting fired from her job based on something she wrote on her personal blog.

Blogs written for fun are typically very personal in nature, but, as with all aspects of blogging, a few set rules apply. People often write about the following ten topics on personal blogs, but remember, the topic you blog about is up to you. With that in mind, this list is not exhaustive.

✦ **Entertainment:** Celebrity gossip, fan clubs, movie reviews, book club discussions, music, personal writing, personal videos, personal photos, and so on

✦ **Sports:** Favorite teams, local sports, children's sports, exercise, and so on

✦ **Parenting:** Pregnancy, home-schooling, humor, raising babies, pre-schoolers, teens, and so on

✦ **Photography:** Travel, people, landscape, and so on

✦ **Personal health:** Dieting, medical battles, pain management, nutrition, and so on

✦ **Creativity:** Your own writing, art, music, and so on

✦ **Travel:** Documenting your vacations and other travels locally and around the world

✦ **Current events:** Your views on current events of any kind

✦ **Hobbies:** Cooking, crafts, auto maintenance, home repairs, and so on

✦ **Pets:** Your own pets, breeding, competitions, grooming, and so on

The list of blog topics could go on and on, but the take away is this: Any blog topic is okay as long as you're passionate enough about the subject to want to keep writing about it. Of course, it also helps if you have at least a basic knowledge of your blog's topic.

Check out Chapter 2 in this minibook to find out more about choosing a blog topic.

Blogging for networking

Many people decide to start a blog simply to meet other people with similar interests. This type of networking can be for personal or professional reasons. People who blog for networking define their success by the communities that develop around their blogs through comments, links, and even e-mails.

WomenOnBusiness.com, shown in Figure 1-3, is an example of a blog written for networking purposes. The community of business women that frequent the Women On Business blog do so for common reasons: to meet, communicate with, and build relationships with their peers around the world.

Figure 1-3:
Women On Business is a blog for business women to network with and learn from each other.

The following are three more examples of very different networking blogs that you can take a look at to see how they compare. The blogs differ depending on the blogger's goals:

✦ **The Leaky Cauldron (`www.the-leaky-cauldron.org`):** This blog began as a simple fan blog but has turned into one of the biggest and most vibrant online communities of *Harry Potter* fans. Users comment on posts, submit content, and more.

✦ **SEOmoz (`www.seomoz.org`):** This blog is one of the most vocal communities of search engine optimization experts who share their knowledge with each other and the wider audience of readers.

✦ **MacRumors.com (`www.macrumors.com`):** This blog has become a vocal community of Apple product enthusiasts.

Blogging for exposure

Many celebrities, authors, and businesspeople blog to increase their online exposure. In other words, the primary goal of these bloggers is to get their name in front of a wider audience than they could achieve with a static Web site (or no Web presence at all). These blogs often include updates about the blogger's career or business with some promotional content peppered in between knowledge-based or opinion posts.

A unique example of a blogger who writes for exposure is celebrity blogger Wil Wheaton, who was actually an early adopter of blogging. His blog, WWdN: In Exile, is a mix of great writing and information about his career, as shown in Figure 1-4, and can be found at `http://wilwheaton.typepad.com`.

Figure 1-4: Wil Wheaton is a popular celebrity blogger who writes for increased exposure and for fun, which is a rare combination.

Blogging for business

You can find many types of business-related blogs on the Web. Whether a blogger is trying to share his knowledge of business, boost sales for his business, or indirectly promote his business, a blog is a great way to reach those goals. I discuss business blogging in detail in Book III.

The KeySplash Creative Conversations blog (`http://keysplashcreative.com/category/blog`; see Figure 1-5), owned by KeySplash Creative, Inc., is an example of a small business blog used as a tool to share knowledge and indirectly promote that business to a wider audience.

Figure 1-5:
KeySplash
Creative
Conver-
sations is
the business
blog of
KeySplash
Creative,
Inc.

Finding and Reading Blogs

One of the best ways to determine whether you should join the blogosphere and whether you can be successful as a blogger is to find and read other blogs. Paramount to being a good blogger is understanding what other people are saying and doing across the blogosphere, particularly within the topic you ultimately choose to blog about.

Why read other blogs?

If you didn't know how to swim, would you jump into a pool of water before trying to learn how to swim? If your answer is "no," you're very smart. The same concept holds true for blogging: Just because anyone can do it, that doesn't mean anyone *should* do it.

First, you should find out how it (swimming or blogging) works and take a look at what else is going on around you (in the pool or blogosphere). You need to check out your surroundings. If you see the person next to you flailing her arms barely keeping her head above water, it's unlikely you would want to copy her technique when you get in the pool. Again, the same holds true in blogging. Take some time to look around, read blogs, see what you like and what you don't like, and then apply those techniques to your own blog.

As with anything else in life, a book and proper instruction can only take you so far until you finally do have to jump in and get started. Just make sure you're prepared first. Think of this book as your life preserver.

Finding blogs

Fortunately, several search tools are available to help you find blogs and specific blog posts about the topics of your choice, and I cover three such tools in the following sections. However, it's very important to understand that no search tool is perfect. In fact, more people complain about the relevancy of search results than applaud it, but based on the massive scale of the Web (Google indexes 1 trillion pages as of the company's report in June 2008), it's not surprising that search results leave something to be desired overall.

Blog search tools are imperfect at best, but they're better than nothing. You can also ask your friends and colleagues about their recommendations for blogs they enjoy.

The more time you spend reading other blogs, the more cool blogs you'll stumble upon accidentally, and that's where the power of links and networking across the blogosphere becomes apparent. You need someplace to start though, and blog search tools are the best starting point to find blogs.

Technorati

Technorati has long been considered the best blog search site. The reason might just be because Technorati was the first site to index blog posts and pages fairly well. Today, it's debatable whether Technorati is as valuable as it once was, but until the debate comes to a conclusion, the site is still considered a go-to place for blog searches.

One of the unique things about Technorati is that blog owners can claim their blogs on Technorati and provide additional information about those blogs. Doing so makes it easier for Technorati to include entire blogs within its search results as opposed to simply searching individual blog posts as other blog search tools do.

Follow these steps to find blogs about specific topics using Technorati.com:

1. **Visit www.technorati.com/search, shown in Figure 1-6.**

2. **Enter your search term in the Blog Search text box provided.**

Be sure to use the text box with the Search button and the drop-down lists, not the text box above that.

3. **Select the A Lot of Authority option from the drop-down list on the left beneath the Blog Search text box.**

Selecting A Lot of Authority means that more popular blogs should be returned in your search results. Technorati believes that blogs with more incoming links are publishing better content more often, so those blogs get higher authority rankings.

4. **Select your language from the drop-down list on the right beneath the search term box.**

This step ensures that blogs written in languages other than your own are left out of your search results.

5. **Click the Search button.**

Your results are displayed, as shown in Figure 1-7. However, these results show blog *posts* that use your search term, not entire blogs about that term.

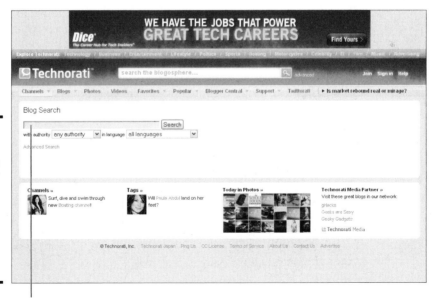

Figure 1-6:
Enter your blog search term in the text box provided on the Technorati search page.

Enter your blog search term here.

Figure 1-7:
Technorati
first
provides
results for
blog posts
that include
your search
term.

6. **Click the drop-down list on the far left in the green bar directly above your results and select the Search Blogs option.**

   Your search is now restricted to entire blogs about your search term rather than individual posts.

7. **Click the Go button.**

   Your search results are displayed, as shown in Figure 1-8.

Notice that the results provided in this example include some of the most popular Twitter blogs, including Twitter's official blog. However, this isn't always the case. Again, Technorati's search results leave a lot to be desired, but they do provide a starting point for your trip across the blogosphere.

Follow the links for several of the top results from your Technorati search (particularly those with high authority rankings). If those sites appear to be relevant when you review them, dig deeper within those blogs for more information and follow the links you find to other sites. You'll be surprised at where the links might take you and the wealth of information and great blogs you'll find.

IceRocket

IceRocket is a popular blog search tool, but, unlike Technorati, you can use it to search only for blog posts, not entire blogs about specific topics. The advanced search tools are useful if you know specifically what you're looking for, but when you're first joining the blogosphere and looking for blogs dedicated to specific topics, the IceRocket advanced search tools aren't particularly helpful.

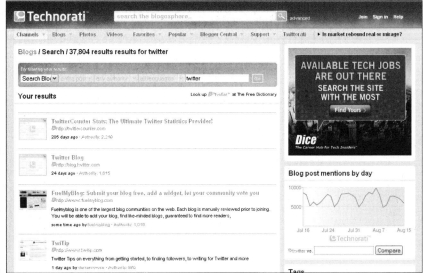

Figure 1-8:
Technorati
displays
results for
entire blogs
about your
search term.

IceRocket does offer an advantage in that you can narrow your search by date ranges. For example, instead of simply searching for all blog posts that mentioned your search term anytime, you can search for blog posts that mentioned the search term in the last month, week, or day.

To find content on IceRocket, follow these steps:

1. **Visit www.icerocket.com (shown in Figure 1-9) and enter your search term into the search box in the center of the page.**

Notice the tabs above the Search box. The Blogs tab is the default setting, meaning IceRocket searches blog content for your search term unless you select a different tab.

2. **Click the Search button.**

Your results are displayed, as shown in Figure 1-10.

3. **In the left sidebar, click the Past Week link to narrow your search.**

Narrowing your search to the past week ensures that only blogs that are actively talking about your search term are included in your list of results. You can try different date links (your options are Today, Past Week, Past Month, and Anytime) or enter your own date range to see how the results change. To enter your own date range, select the Choose Dates link in the left sidebar. Text boxes appear beneath the Choose Dates link where you can enter your desired start and end dates and then click the Proceed button beneath the text boxes to narrow your search. Note that when you narrow your search using the links and functions in the left sidebar, your search results are updated immediately to fit that criteria.

4. Select your language from the drop-down list in the left sidebar.

Your search results are automatically updated, as shown in Figure 1-10.

Figure 1-9:
Enter your
search term
into the
IceRocket
search box.

Figure 1-10:
IceRocket
displays
your search
results.

Google Blog Search

Google's blog search tool is becoming the go-to place for blog searches, but it still isn't perfect. You can't search for entire blogs related to a search term. Instead, only specific blog posts that use that search term are provided in the search results. However, at the top of the page for most search results, you can find a small list of blogs about the search term, and this neat feature makes Google a best of both worlds created by Technorati and IceRocket.

Like IceRocket, Google Blog Search has a number of useful advanced search tools, but until you know specifically what you're looking for, they won't help you much. Also, Google Blog Search offers the same advantage as IceRocket in that you can narrow your search using date ranges, which is useful for finding current results.

Book I
Chapter 1

Joining the
Blogosphere

To find blog content using Google Blog Search, here's what you do:

1. **Visit `http://blogsearch.google.com`, shown in Figure 1-11, and enter your search term into the search box.**

Google searches its index for pages that mention your search term.

2. **Click the Search Blogs button to the right of the search box.**

Your search results are displayed, as shown in Figure 1-12. A small list of blogs related to your search term is presented at the top of the search results followed by a list of blog posts that mentioned your search term.

Figure 1-11:
Enter your search term in the search box on Google Blog Search.

3. **Click the Past Week link in the left sidebar to narrow your search results.**

   Doing so ensures that only current blog posts that mention your search term in the past week are returned in your search results rather than all results published anytime.

   When you click the link, your results are updated, as shown in Figure 1-13.

Figure 1-12: Google first displays all search results published anytime for your search term.

Figure 1-13: Google Blog Search provides blog and blog posts results.

Deciding to Start a Blog

To many people, the decision of whether to start a blog is a difficult one because it seems like a daunting task and a big commitment. Truth be told, starting a blog is one of the easiest things you can do. Don't think of the larger picture. Instead, start small, and you'll be surprised how quickly you get up to speed, grow your blog, connect with new people, and start enjoying yourself.

The key is to define the reasons why you want to start a blog so you can then determine the best path to meet your goals. Read on to find out about the pros and cons of blogging before you decide to become a blogger.

Blogging benefits

Ask any two bloggers what they think are the benefits to publishing their blogs, and it's highly likely that you'll get two very different answers. That's because all bloggers have their own reasons for blogging and derive their own benefits from it.

The following are ten ways blogging can benefit you, depending on your goals:

+ **Have fun and express yourself.** If you have something you want to say, blogging is an enjoyable way to do it.

+ **Connect with people.** Whether you want to communicate with family, friends, colleagues, or strangers, a blog can make it happen.

+ **Find people like you.** Maybe you just want to find people who share your views on life or a specific subject. You'd be surprised how many other people are traveling across the blogosphere waiting to be found.

+ **Have a creative outlet.** If you love painting, photography, architecture, or any other creative activity, a blog is a great place to share your work and ideas.

+ **Learn.** A big part of blogging is reading other blogs, communicating with people, and publishing updated content. What better way is there to make the learning process fun and ongoing?

+ **Make a difference.** If you feel strongly about a particular issue, then a blog is a great place to talk about it and gather people to rally around it with you.

+ **Help people.** If you have specific knowledge on a topic, why not share it and help other people learn and grow?

+ **Promote yourself or your business.** If you have a product, service, or business, a blog is a perfect place to talk about it directly or indirectly.

✦ **Establish yourself as an expert.** Blogging is a great way to share your knowledge in a field or industry in which you want to be known as an expert. Whether you're looking for a career boost or trying to pick up speaking engagements, a blog offers a destination to share your expertise with the world.

✦ **Make money.** Many people blog simply to make some extra money through advertising, reviews, and more.

Blogging repercussions

Blogging isn't all fun and love. There are negatives to joining the blogosphere, and you should consider them before you start a blog. Check out the following list of blogging cons:

✦ **Privacy issues:** Blogs are visible to everyone with access to the Internet.

It's highly probable that anyone can find out your address, phone number, and more by doing a simple Google search. Therefore, as long as you're not publishing anything too personal or slanderous to another person or entity on your blog, it's unlikely that you have to worry about privacy issues simply because you write a blog. However, it's important to remember that public blogs are visible to anyone. You might not want to publish those pictures of you and your friends partying on a blog that your boss can find. Remember what happened to Heather Armstrong, of Dooce.com, mentioned earlier in this chapter. The content on her personal blog caused her to get fired from her job. With that in mind, publish content with the knowledge that a wider audience than you can imagine might stumble upon your blog.

✦ **Time commitment:** Successful blogging can require a big time commitment. You have to find subjects to write about, update your blog regularly, respond to comments, read other blogs and comment, and more. Of course, your success is dependent on that time commitment, so you need to determine how much time is enough to invest toward reaching your blogging goals.

✦ **Technological demands:** The blogosphere, the Internet, and technology are constantly changing. Although blogging doesn't require a degree in computer science, you will find greater success if you continue to learn and adopt new tools.

✦ **Writing requirements:** Blogging requires writing, so if you don't like to write, blogging will undoubtedly be a grueling chore for you. Furthermore, people don't like to read blogs that are poorly written. You don't need to be Shakespeare, but you should be able to put together a coherent, grammatically correct sentence. If you can't, brush up on your writing skills before you start blogging.

✦ **Patience concerns:** Blogging success doesn't happen overnight. You need to be prepared to make a long-term commitment to your blog. Without patience, you're likely to abandon your blog too soon.

✦ **Social pressures:** Blogging is a two-way street. If you don't interact with your audience members, they'll leave and find someone who values their input. It's not much fun to blog alone.

✦ **Some people won't like you:** The online world is filled with all kinds of people, and they won't all like you. Unfortunately, many of those people never learned the old adage, "if you don't have anything nice to say, don't say anything at all." To make matters worse, some people, often called *trolls,* enjoy visiting blogs and making nasty comments for no reason other than to stir up trouble. As a blogger, you need to be prepared to read negative things said about you on your blog and on other sites without getting overly concerned about them.

Blogging success secrets

The preceding section tells you about the repercussions and negatives of blogging, but how can those very same things be turned around into the secrets of successful blogging? It's simple! Take a look at the following list to see what I mean.

Successful bloggers . . .

✦ **Write a lot:** The best blogs are updated frequently with fresh, relevant, and interesting content.

✦ **Are passionate:** That passion and their unique personalities shines through in their writing styles.

✦ **Love to read:** The best bloggers spend a lot of time surfing the Web and reading (and commenting) about their blog topics.

✦ **Are very social:** The best bloggers care about their audience and take time to interact with them and show them that their opinions are truly valued.

✦ **Are thick-skinned:** Insults roll off the best bloggers' backs and are forgotten quickly.

✦ **Like to take risks:** New technology means new opportunities, and the best bloggers dive right in.

✦ **Love to learn:** The best bloggers realize they don't know it all.

✦ **Are comfortable speaking their minds:** The best blogs are written by people who are not afraid to express their opinions to the online audience and then discuss those opinions in an open and professional matter with both proponents and opponents.

Setting your goals

Now that you know the good, the bad, and the ugly about blogging, it's time to think about what you want to get out of your blogging experience. Consider both the short- and long-term objectives for your blog because they can have a significant effect on the path you take in joining the blogosphere.

Start by creating a plan to get your blog up and running, but don't try to do everything at once. Take your time, learn as you go, and in no time at all, you'll be an active and welcome member of the blogosphere!

Chapter 2: Preparing to Start and Write a Blog

In This Chapter

✔ Picking your blog topic

✔ Writing in your own voice

✔ Knowing what to write about

✔ Writing blog posts that readers will enjoy

✔ Understanding blogging frequency

✔ Finding stuff to write about

*A*fter you make the decision to start a blog, you need to take some time to do some planning. What do you want to blog about? How often should you publish posts? What writing style should you use? These are all questions that every blogger needs to consider. This chapter walks you through the basics, so you can start with a confident plan of action in mind.

Of course, if you're simply blogging for fun, your planning process doesn't have to be as detailed as it would be if you intend to blog to build your business, make money, or establish yourself as an expert in your field or industry. However, if you have greater goals then simply blogging for personal enjoyment, investing time into understanding the *process* of blogging before you get started can save both time and frustration later.

Choosing a Topic

The first step to starting a blog is choosing your blog's topic. Most blogs are dedicated to a particular subject. For example, you can find blogs about entertainment, crafts, sports, business, and many other topics. Chapter 1 of this minibook provides a variety of blog topic ideas, some of which I discuss later in this chapter as well.

Take some time to surf the blogosphere and find out what kind of blogs are already out there. Does it matter to you, based on your long-term blogging goals, if there are already a lot of popular blogs written about your topic of choice? Does competition for traffic affect your objectives? You need to ask yourself these questions before you finalize your blog topic selection.

For example, technology and gadgets are extremely popular blog topics. Several of the most popular blogs online are about technology and gadgets, such as TechCrunch (`www.techcrunch.com`), Gizmodo (`www.gizmodo.com`), and Engadget (`www.engadget.com`), which is shown in Figure 2-1. If you're considering technology and gadgets as the topic of your blog, you need to decide whether that kind of heavy-hitting competition is a problem for you before you start your blog.

Reviewing popular blog topics

Technorati, one of the most popular blog search tools, keeps a continually updated list of the top 100 blogs (see Figure 2-2), according to its ranking system. You can find the list at `www.technorati.com/pop/blogs`. This list is a great place to begin your analysis of popular blog topics because not only are these blogs getting a lot of traffic, but a lot of other blogs and Web sites are linking to them as well, making it safe to assume that people like the content they find on these blogs.

Don't waste time reinventing the wheel. Instead, start reading popular blogs to find out what draws people to them. Then emulate those techniques on your own blog as appropriate.

Looking through Technorati's list of the top 100 blogs, you can see that several topics are represented, with entertainment, technology, and politics making up a large percentage. It's very true that those are some of the most popular blog topics, but you have many other topics to choose from as well.

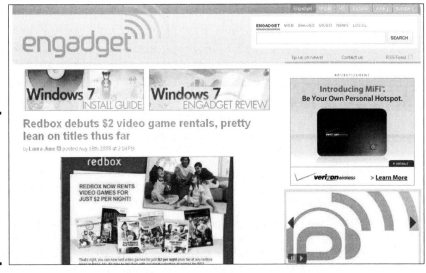

Figure 2-1: Engadget is one of the most popular blogs about gadgets and consumer electronics.

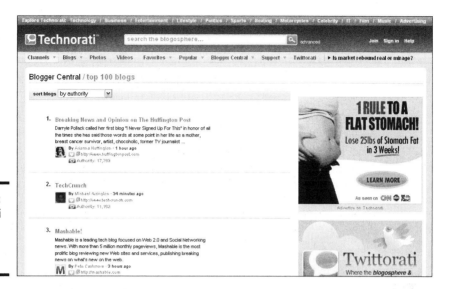

Figure 2-2:
Technorati
maintains
a Top 100
Blogs list.

Take a look at this list for more popular blog topics:

+ **Celebrities:** Some of the most popular blogs are about celebrity gossip and information for fans.

+ **Movies:** Many bloggers write movie reviews and about news related to the production of upcoming movies.

+ **Television:** You can find many fan blogs dedicated to favorite television programs.

+ **Sports:** Many sports fans have blogs dedicated to their favorite sport, team, player, and so on. People even write blogs about local sports, their children's teams, or teams they play on recreationally.

+ **Business:** People blog about every business-related topic you can imagine — from marketing to taxes, small business to the corporate world, and everything else in between.

+ **Politics:** There is almost no political topic that is off limits in the blogosphere.

+ **Hobbies:** Many people are very passionate about their hobbies. Whether they surf, cook, skydive, or knit, they can find a place to share their ideas and opinions in the blogosphere.

+ **Current events and news:** Breaking news and current events are popular blog topics for people who like to be the first to spread the word or simply like to lead conversations about what's happening around their towns, their countries, or even the world.

✦ **Personal opinion:** Anything goes (within reason, of course) on a personal opinion blog. Use your imagination!

✦ **Travel:** Whether people travel professionally or just for fun, or even if they simply wish they could travel, the blogosphere provides them with a place to talk about it.

At the time of this book's writing, the top blog according to Technorati is The Huffington Post (`www.huffingtonpost.com`), shown in Figure 2-3, which focuses on breaking news and opinions.

Determining the best topic for your blog

Considering all the topics you could write about on your blog can be overwhelming. Take a deep breath. There are ways to pick the *best* topic for you to write about on your blog.

Blog about a topic you love

First, you need to think about the subjects that you feel passionately about. When you blog, you need to be able to write about that topic *a lot.* That means you shouldn't pick a topic that you're likely to get bored with quickly. There's not much point in starting a blog that you're going to abandon in three months because you're already tired of the subject matter. Instead, pick a topic that you know you'll be able to write about for many, many months (and possibly years) to come.

Blogging takes a lot of effort and a big time commitment if you want to become a successful blogger. With that in mind, you need to be certain that you really, really love your chosen topic before you get started.

Figure 2-3:
The news and opinion blog The Huffington Post made it to the top of Technorati's Top 100 Blogs list.

Blog about a topic you like to talk about with other people

An inherent and powerful feature of blogs is the commenting feature, which invites readers to provide their own thoughts related to the posts you publish. To be a successful blogger, you need to engage your readers by showing them you value their opinions. Whether or not they agree with you, you need to actively join the conversation by responding to their comments and creating an ongoing dialogue.

In simplest terms, if you don't want to debate anyone about your blog topic and don't want to hear anyone else's opinions but your own, you should probably look for another topic. A blog is only as successful as the community that develops around it, and that community grows through the conversations that take place on the blog.

Unfortunately, the commenting feature inherent to blogs opens up your blog to spam and rude comments. You should delete these comments in order to ensure the user experience on your blog is a positive one. (For more about handling comments, see Chapter 2 of Book VI.)

Blog about a topic you like researching and reading about

An important part of being a successful blogger is staying abreast of what's happening with your blog topic. You need to be willing to keep reading and discovering new things about your topic. Doing so will give you ideas for blog posts, keep your blog fresh, help you network with other bloggers, and help you build relationships with both your readers and other bloggers.

The best bloggers don't claim to know all there is to know about their blog topics. That's why they embrace the social aspect blogging provides by actively engaging in conversations with their readers and other bloggers through the commenting and linking features blogs offer.

Going broad or staying focused

As the blogosphere gets more crowded, it's important to determine whether you want to blog about a broad topic, which could mean your blog will have a lot of competition from similar sites, or whether you want to blog about a more specific subject, which could mean a smaller potential audience. Only you can choose which option will better help you meet your blogging goals.

Blogger Buster (`www.bloggerbuster.com`), shown in Figure 2-4, is an example of a blog about a focused topic: how to use the features and functionality of the Blogger.com blogging application. On the other hand, the About.com: Blogging blog (`http://weblogs.about.com`) is about a broad topic: blogging. This blog and the corresponding articles are devoted to all things blog-related, from writing to technological tools, promoting to making money, and every other blogging topic you can think of.

Figure 2-4:
Blogger
Buster is
an example
of a blog
focused on
a narrow
topic.

You can find out more about blog specificity (called *niche* blogging) and the pros and cons of focused versus broad blogging in Book II.

Choosing Your Voice

One of the reasons people enjoy writing and reading blogs is the personality behind them. Each blogger has a unique writing style and personality that shines through their blog posts. That unique element is called the blogger's voice, and it's something you need to consider before you begin writing your own blog.

Do you want the tone of your blog to be professional or humorous? Do you want a journalistic tone or a personal diary tone? The answers to these questions determine the writing style you should use on your blog. For example, you can write in a highly professional manner, as if you're writing business communications. Alternatively, you might write in a personal manner, exactly the way that you speak. You may even decide to combine both extremes and find a happy medium. The choice is yours, but your style should stay consistent in every post and match your blog's topic and content.

The next step is to inject your personality into that style. That's what makes your blog stand out from the crowd. Of course, the persona you take on in your blog could be completely fabricated, and that's just fine. Daniel Lyons, author of the popular The Secret Life of Steve Jobs blog (`www.fakesteve.blogspot.com`), shown in Figure 2-5, did exactly that. He writes his blog as if he were Steve Jobs, and readers love it for its satirical humor.

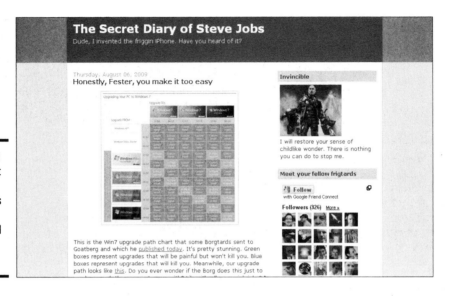

Figure 2-5:
The Secret
Life of
Steve Jobs
blog has a
unique and
humorous
voice.

Together, writing style and personality define your blog's unique voice, and it's that voice, coupled with great content, that keeps readers coming back for more.

A specific personality should shine through your writing, connecting your readers to you and making them feel like they know you personally.

Deciding What to Write About

After you've chosen your blog's topic, you need to decide what to write about in your blog posts. It's your blog, so you can write about whatever you want. (Of course, keep it within reason; read the next section for cautionary information.) The key to success is choosing subjects that you're passionate about (so your personality shines through) and that other people are likely to be interested in, too.

Don't be afraid to get creative, and don't feel bound to your blog's topic. Although relevant content should certainly dominate your blog posts, it's acceptable to inject an unrelated post on occasion. Doing so lets your readers get to know you a little bit better by introducing them to another aspect of your life or another subject that interests you.

Read "Understanding Types of Blog Posts" and "Finding Blog Post Ideas" later in this chapter for more information about what to write about on your blog.

Knowing What Not to Write About

Although the rules of the blogosphere are primarily unwritten, there are topics and content you might want to consider not writing about on your blog. For example, if you're not up for debate and name-calling, you should steer clear of blog topics that invite that kind of behavior. (Highly political blogs often lead to passionate dialogue.)

Manners count online, too. Just because you can hide behind your computer doesn't mean you should forget to be courteous, polite, and professional on your blog and in related communications.

Exercise some caution as you write your blog content. Avoid writing anything that might be considered slanderous. Whether you mention another person, a product, or a company on your blog, keep in mind that the world can see what you publish. It's okay to provide your opinions, but don't cross the line into slandering anyone or anything.

Also, think about sensitive topics before you write about them. Although you might not think much about religion, for example, millions of people around the world are very devoted to their religions. Think twice before you write about a subject that you don't know much about but other people are passionate and vocal about.

Writing Great Blog Posts

An essential part of your blogging success is publishing great content, and this holds true no matter what type of blog you write or what goals you have for your blog. (You can find some specific tips for writing posts for niche blogs and business blogs in Chapter 4 of Book II and Chapter 4 of Book III, respectively.) That means your posts must be well written, interesting, and entertaining. The first step to writing great blog content is injecting your personality into your posts. (Read the earlier section, "Choosing Your Voice," for details.) Your blog post should not only interest your readers, but also encourage them to talk more about it by leaving a comment, writing and linking to your post from their own blogs, and return to your blog to read more of your content in the future.

Writing meaningful and interesting content

Select blog post topics that are meaningful and interesting to your blog's audience. If people aren't interested in the posts you're writing on your blog, they're unlikely to keep reading or ever return. Always consider your audience before you write a new blog post.

Staying consistent

Consistency matters in terms of your topic and your voice. People return to your blog because they want to hear more from you. They're building a relationship with you because they like what you have to say and how you say it. Don't confuse them by changing your subject matter or tone on the fly. Your blog content needs to meet the expectations that your audience creates for you and your blog over time.

Being honest

Be honest in your blog posts. People want to feel comfort in returning to your blog and relying on your content. They're building trust with you, as people do in any relationship. Don't destroy that trust by lying to your audience. You'll probably get caught.

Citing sources

Cite your sources, link to them, and build relationships with them if possible. Doing so is not only the right thing to do ethically, but it also helps you network with peers and give your readers more sources for great content. The blogosphere has plenty of room for healthy competition. Sharing great sources with your readers is a good thing. If you continue to write great, consistent content, you shouldn't have to worry about losing readers to the sources you cite in your own blog posts.

Using images

Use images as appropriate, and cite their sources. Images make your posts visually appealing and can draw a reader in to read more. Just be sure to use images that are actually relevant to your content and that you hold appropriate copyright licenses. (Read Chapter 4 in this minibook for more information about copyrights.)

Writing for the Web

Write in a Web-friendly style. That means writing in short paragraphs, using headings to separate text and to provide visual relief, and using bulleted or numbered lists. Web pages with a lot of white space are far easier to read (or even skim) than text-heavy pages. Your goal is to get people to read your content (skimming is perfectly fine, too), not click away because they're bombarded with more text than they can process.

Understanding Types of Blog Posts

Blog posts come in many flavors, some more popular than others. It's your blog, so you can write any type of post you want. However, it's good to understand what some of the most popular types of blog posts are, so you can meet readers' expectations and give them a format they're already familiar with and possibly looking for.

Take a look at my explanations of types of blog posts:

+ **Lists:** Lists are one of the most popular types of blog posts. People love lists! For example, posts that promise *Top 10 or 20 Mistakes to Avoid* are often too irresistible for readers to bypass. The List Maven (`www.the listmaven.com`), part of the b5media network of blogs, is an example of a blog made up entirely of list posts, as shown in Figure 2-6.

+ **Current events:** Do some research and find out what's going on in the world related to your blog topic and then publish a post about those events.

+ **Tips:** People love to get insider tips or expert tips. If you have a specialized knowledge, share it through a blog post where you provide that knowledge as a series of tips.

+ **Reviews:** Bloggers are considered to be online influencers and a powerful source of word-of-mouth marketing. The reason is simple. Research shows that people trust other people more than they trust traditional advertising. You can review anything related to your blog topic in your blog posts, and your readers are likely to be happy to read that content and possibly share it with other people.

Figure 2-6: All posts published on The List Maven blog are lists.

✦ **Recommendations:** Similar to reviews, recommendation posts allow you to share your favorites or preferred things related to your blog topic without providing complete reviews.

✦ **How-to:** People love to learn how to do something, and how-to posts are very popular. How-to posts can even include images to demonstrate the steps provided in your blog post.

✦ **Polls:** Get your readers involved by creating a poll and asking them to vote. People love polls! Use a tool like PollDaddy (`www.polldaddy.com`) or SurveyGizmo (`www.surveygizmo.com`) to create polls about anything you want.

✦ **Interviews:** Interview someone related to your blog's topic and publish another perspective on your blog. You can contact people via e-mail, telephone, and so on to request their participation in an interview to be published on your blog. You'd be surprised how many people will welcome the exposure your interview can bring them.

✦ **Contests:** Hold a contest and offer a small prize. People love to win things. You can find out more about blog contests in Chapter 6 of Book VI.

✦ **Videos:** Make a video and publish it in a blog post. Online video is getting more popular every day. You can find out more about video blogging (vlogging) in Chapter 7 of Book V.

✦ **Podcasts:** If you're not comfortable appearing in a video, why not try audio? Podcasts add another dimension of interactivity to your blog. You can find out more about creating podcasts in Chapter 6 of Book V.

✦ **Guest posts:** Approach another blogger or expert in your topic and ask that person to write a guest post for your blog. You can find out more about guest blogging in Chapter 5 of Book VI.

Avoiding Blogger's Block and Finding Blog Post Ideas

Blogger's block occurs when a blogger can't think of anything to write about on his blog. It's very common, and every blogger experiences it at one time or another. Some days, you just feel less inspired than others. Don't despair, though: You can try some tricks to get your creative juices flowing. Take a look at the sidebar for tips to get past blogger's block.

If you have trouble moving beyond blogger's block, you need to invest more time into finding post ideas. Fortunately, there are many sources available to bloggers to help them find blog post fodder.

Tricks to cure blogger's block

It's inevitable. One day you'll sit down at your computer to write a blog post, and you won't be able to think of anything to write about. Try the following tricks to cure blogger's block:

- Walk away from your computer. Do something else. When you return to your computer later, you might be in a completely different frame of mind, and blog post ideas might be easier to come by.

- If a break doesn't help, try turning on some music or surfing the blogosphere to read about your blog topic simply for pleasure. A blog post idea might strike you when you're not trying so hard to think of one.

- You can also contact your peers or friends who enjoy talking about your blog topic and start a conversation. You never know what kinds of blog post ideas might come from a casual conversation.

- Many bloggers swear by deep-breathing exercises or physical exercise (such as yoga) to regain focus and get the mind flowing freely again.

- If all else fails, grab a candy bar, a beer, or whatever your favorite personal indulgence is and enjoy. I know I always think more clearly after some chocolate!

Take a look at the following list for some popular ways to find blog post ideas:

- ✦ **Read your favorite blogs.** No doubt there's hot material to be found on the blogs that you enjoy reading. It's not okay to copy, but it is okay to get inspiration from other blogs. The trick is to write about the topic in your own way, with your own voice, and share your own opinions.

- ✦ **Visit social bookmarking sites.** Sites such as Digg (`http://digg.com`), StumbleUpon (`www.stumbleupon.com`), Reddit (`www.reddit.com`), and Yahoo! Buzz (`http://buzz.yahoo.com`) provide people with places to save Web pages they enjoy online rather than locally on their computer hard drives through their browser tools. Social bookmarking also makes it easy to share Web pages with other people. (That's what makes them social.) For example, conduct a search on one of these social bookmarking sites using a term related to your blog's topic, and see what comes up. You can find out more about social bookmarking in Chapter 4 of Book VI.

- ✦ **Look at Google Trends.** Google Trends (`www.google.com/trends`) provides a list of the most-searched-for search terms, as shown in Figure 2-7. The list is updated continually. If a term is being searched for, it's safe to assume people are interested in it, and it could make a great blog post idea!

Figure 2-7:
Google
Trends
provides a
snapshot of
the most-
searched-
for terms on
Google.

✦ **Read news sites.** Take a look at news sites (local, regional, national, or global), which may have breaking stories related to your blog topic that you could write about on your blog.

✦ **Conduct a blog search.** Using blog search sites, such as Technorati (`www.technorati.com`), IceRocket (`www.icerocket.com`) or Google Blog Search (`www. blogsearch.google.com`), search blog posts for the past day using a search term related to your blog topic. The results of your search show you what other bloggers, who you might not know, are writing about. You just might find a blog post idea and a great blog to start following! You can find out how to conduct blog searches in more detail in Chapter 1 of this minibook.

Determining How Often to Publish Blog Posts

The frequency with which you publish posts on your blog depends on your goals for your blog. If you're blogging for fun and don't care how many people are reading your blog, you can publish as frequently or infrequently as you want. However, if you want to grow your blog and become a successful blogger, you need to publish with greater frequency.

Of course, the quality of your content is critical to your blog's success, but without fresh content, people won't have much incentive to return to your blog or tell other people about it. One great post just doesn't get the job done if you want to grow your blog. What's the point in returning to your blog if the content never changes? The more frequently you publish good blog posts, the more reason there is for people to return again and again.

Frequent blog updates can also help with search engine optimization (which I discuss in Chapter 1 of Book V) because each new blog post is a new entry point for search engines to find your blog. More entry points give people more chances to find your blog through a Google search, for example.

When you know how much you want your blog to grow and how quickly, you can determine how often you need to publish new blog posts. For maximum growth, you should publish multiple blog posts per day (at least three to five posts per day). For steady growth, publish at least one new blog post per day. If growth isn't that important to you, but you don't want to be the only person reading your blog, try to publish a new blog post every few days so you have fresh content up two to three times per week. Finally, if growth means absolutely nothing to you, you can publish new blog posts whenever you want and as infrequently as you want.

Remember, blogging success is directly tied to your goals for your blog and your commitment to investing time into your blog. Write great content in your own voice, be social, and make sure your content is fresh. In time, your blog will grow organically.

Chapter 3: Blogging Basics

In This Chapter

✔ **Understanding domain names**

✔ **Selecting a domain name**

✔ **Buying a domain name**

✔ **Getting to know the parts of a blog**

*A*fter you select your topic and commit to starting a blog, you need to choose a domain name for your blog and get a clear understanding of the various parts of a blog. Starting a successful blog on the right foot takes a bit of prep work.

This chapter teaches you everything you need to know about domains and the parts of a blog, so you're completely educated and ready to get into the nitty-gritty technical part of creating your blog.

Choosing a Domain Name

Your blog's domain name is the unique part of your blog's Uniform Resource Locator (URL), which is connected to your blog only. Your URL is your blog's complete Web address that people type into their browser search bars to find your site. Take a look at the format of the following URL:

```
http://www.google.com
```

The parts of the URL are as follows:

1. **Access protocol:** The `http://` represents the access protocol, Hypertext Transfer Protocol, in the above URL example used to send and retrieve information across the Web.

2. **Domain name:** `www.google.com` represents the domain name in the URL example — a unique identifier and extension. In the example, `www.` stands for World Wide Web, `google` is the unique identifier, and `.com` is the domain name extension.

In the early days of the Internet, `.com` was one of the only domain name extension options, representing commercial Web sites. Additional extensions such as `.gov`, `.org`, and `.edu` came along to help distinguish between different types of Web sites that debuted online: government, nonprofit, and education/schools, respectively.

Before you can start your blog, you need to choose a domain name for it. The type of domain and the process you follow to get it depends on the blogging application you choose. However you go about getting a domain name for your blog, you need to think of one. In fact, you should come up with a list of options, because it's highly likely your first choice is already taken. The Web is a crowded place, and many people purchase domains for the sole purpose of selling them for a profit in the future. Finding an available domain name that you like can be a challenging task.

Understanding the types of domain names and extensions

If you decide to use a blogging application that provides hosting for your blog (meaning you don't have to purchase a hosting account through a separate company to store your blog data), choosing a domain name is a simple process. However, if you host your blog content through a third-party Web host, you need to purchase your own domain and associate it with your hosting account and blog. Book IV discusses domain names as they relate to specific blogging applications in detail.

For now, take a look at the following list of popular domain name extensions in the United States, because choosing the unique identifier for your domain name is only half of the struggle.

Bloggers outside of the United States have different domain extensions available to them, typically identified by a letter combination that represents their country.

+ `.com`: This is the most common and most well-known domain extension. As such, it's typically the first extension people add to domains when they type them into their browser search bars. However, this habit is breaking as more and more popular blogs and Web sites launch using alternative extensions. It can be very difficult to find an available domain name that you like with the `.com` extension, but it's not impossible if you get creative.

+ `.net`: This domain extension is getting more and more popular as the second choice behind `.com`. Many of the most popular blogs and Web sites use the `.net` extension, such as the highly popular blog about blogging by Darren Rowse, ProBlogger (`www.problogger.net`), shown in Figure 3-1.

+ `.org`: Although this extension was once restricted to nonprofit organizations, today, anyone can register a domain using `.org`.

Figure 3-1:
Darren Rowse's popular blog about blogging, ProBlogger, uses the .net domain extension.

✦ .info: This is a newer domain extension, but it's growing in popularity. Unfortunately, spammers have a tendency to target blogs using this extension, so you might want to check the availability of your chosen domain using other extensions before you settle on .info.

✦ .me: This domain extension is very new and can be used by anyone for any type of site.

✦ .name: This domain extension is restricted to people who want to register their own names only. If you register a name with the .name extension that does not belong to you, you might be required to give up that domain in the future.

✦ .tv: This domain is typically used by Web sites and blogs that publish video content.

✦ .biz: This domain extension is restricted to businesses.

✦ .edu: Only schools are allowed to use a .edu domain.

✦ .gov: This domain can be used only by government agencies.

✦ .jobs: Only companies actively publishing open job listings (no third-party job listings allowed) can use this domain.

✦ .mil: This domain is reserved for United States military use.

✦ .mobi: This domain is for Web sites that are compatible with mobile devices.

✦ .pro: Only licensed or certified lawyers, accountants, and engineers in the United States, United Kingdom, Canada, or France can use this domain.

Some domain extensions require you to pay an additional fee for registration. Read the fine print before you make your final purchase.

The domain extension you choose depends greatly on the domain name you want to use and the availability of that name.

Creating a domain name and making sure it's available

When it comes to naming your blog, you have to balance two factors: the creative factor of coming up with a great name and the practical factor of making sure the domain name is available for you to use.

As you do your setup, you're going to go one of two ways:

✦ **Hosted account domain name:** If you blog with WordPress, Blogger, TypePad, or another provider that hosts your blog content online for you, you aren't required to purchase your own domain name. Instead, a free domain name is available to you, which uses the provider's extension by default (for example, `domainname.wordpress.com`, `domain name.blogspot.com`, or `domainname.typepad.com`). You *do* get to choose the unique name that appears before the domain extension.

✦ **Purchased domain name:** If you aren't blogging with a provider that gives you a domain name, you need to purchase your own.

Keep in mind that you can give your blog a boost in credibility by demonstrating that you're committed enough to your blog to spend money and effort on obtaining your own unique Web address for it.

If you need to or want to purchase your own domain name for your blog, you need to start by creating a list of domain names you'd like to use. After you make your list of first choices, consider the alternative extensions you'd accept if your first isn't available. Also, think of ways you can creatively enhance your chosen domain name to make it more unique and thus more likely to be available. Most domain name registrars offer a search tool that delivers both availability of your chosen domain as well as alternative domain options. Several domain name registrars are discussed in greater detail later in this chapter.

Following are suggestions to enhance your domain name to broaden your search and increase the odds of the name being available for use with a common extension such as `.com` or `.net`. People are comfortable with those extensions and likely to use them when searching for your blog if they aren't already aware that your domain uses a less common extension.

✦ **Get creative.** If the domain name you want is intuitive and obvious, consider using something more creative.

✦ **Add an article.** Such words as *the* or *a* can do the trick when it comes to making an unavailable domain available.

✦ **Add prefixes or suffixes.** Sites such as Engadget (www.engadget.com) and Friendster (www.friendster.com) are examples of domains that include prefixes and suffixes to make them unique.

✦ **Use a superlative.** Try using such words as *best* or *fastest* in your domain name.

✦ **Add an adjective.** Just as you can try using superlatives, try adding descriptive words into your domain name.

✦ **Add a hyphen.** If your desired domain is more than one word, try adding a hyphen between those words.

✦ **Use plurals.** Is there a word in your domain that you can change from singular to plural? Give it a try!

✦ **Make up a word.** Many blogs and Web sites use words that aren't in the dictionary, such as Squidoo (www.squidoo.com), which is shown in Figure 3-2. If you find yourself at a dead end, make up your own word and use it in your domain and as your blog's title. If nothing else, your blog will have instant branding!

After you choose your domain name, changing it can cause a lot of problems. Old links to your blog won't work, your Google search rankings will drop, and more. Pick your domain name with great care and be sure it's one you can live with for the life of your blog in order to avoid problems later.

Figure 3-2:
Squidoo is
an example
of a Web
site with
a name
and corre-
sponding
domain
name that
isn't in the
dictionary.

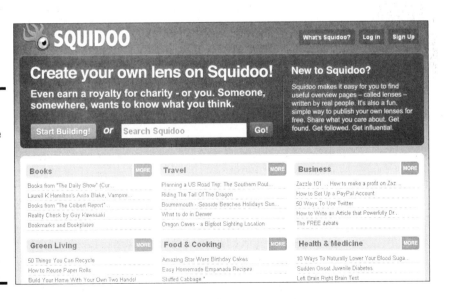

Finding a domain name that you like can be challenging. Even if you use a blogging application that doesn't require you to purchase your own domain name, finding an available domain through those sites is still a challenge. For example, millions and millions of blogs are hosted on Blogger, which means millions and millions of domain names with the provided `.blogspot.com` extension are already taken. Take your time, don't get frustrated, and be prepared to not get the first, second, or even the tenth domain name of your choice. Eventually though, you'll find a domain name that's available and suitable for your blog.

Buying a domain name

A *domain name registrar* is a Web site that enables you to purchase your own, unique domain name. Many sites allow you to purchase a domain name, but not all domain name registrars are alike. For example, they charge different fees that can vary based on the length of your contract or the domain name extension you choose. Be sure to read all the fine print before you make your final purchase, and do some comparison shopping before you commit to a vendor.

When you do find an available domain name that you're happy with, be prepared to purchase it immediately. It's not uncommon to find an available domain name one minute and then find it's gone a few minutes later. With that in mind, do your research on current pricing plans and discounts *before* you actually search for available domain names, or you could waste a lot of time. Select the domain registrar you want to make your purchase through and then conduct your search on that site.

Following is a brief list of popular Web sites where you can search for and purchase domain names. This list is *not* exhaustive, and companies and offers change all the time. Do your research when you're ready to find your domain, so you're certain to get the best deal from the best company at that time.

✦ **BlueHost:** (`www.bluehost.com`) BlueHost is a popular blog host. You can also purchase domain names from BlueHost.

✦ **Go Daddy:** (`www.godaddy.com`) Go Daddy has been around for a long time and is a popular site for hosting and domain name registration. Take a look at Figure 3-3 to see how easy it is to search for a domain name from the Go Daddy home page. Also take note of the various offers marked SAVE! beneath the domain search box in the center of the page. That should give you an idea of the many types of fees and discounts you need to review to be able to accurately compare pricing from one domain registrar to another.

✦ **Host Gator:** (`www.hostgator.com`) Host Gator is another commonly used site for purchasing both blog hosting and domain names.

Figure 3-3: Go Daddy makes it easy to search for domains directly from the site's home page.

Check all the pricing and check it again before you commit to purchasing a domain name. Compare pricing from several providers to ensure you're getting the best deal.

Identifying the Basic Elements of a Blog

Although the content of every blog is unique, most blogs have specific elements in common. Of course, as with most aspects of blogging, there are exceptions to every rule: Even though most blogs include elements such as sidebars, footers, and archives, those elements are not mandatory. It's up to individual bloggers to choose and include the blog elements that provide the user experiences they want to deliver.

Furthermore, blogs vary in the way they're laid out. In other words, the design of the blog can affect where elements appear on your screen. The flexible layout is one of the best parts about blogging. So even though there are commonly accepted places to find specific elements of a blog, there are no rules set in stone. The look and feel of your blog are entirely up to you.

Home page

Your blog's home page is the primary landing page that people arrive at when they visit your blog's top-level domain. In other words, it's the most popular starting point for a readers' journey through your blog's content. Figure 3-4 shows an example of a well-designed and simple three-column blog home page, Copyblogger (www.copyblogger.com), where it's easy to find useful information without feeling intimidated.

Figure 3-4:
Copyblogger, by Brian Clark, offers an inviting home page.

Your most recent blog posts typically appear first, in reverse chronological order, as the main focal point of your home page. Blogs are usually divided into columns of content (two- and three-column blog formats are most common) with your blog posts appearing in the widest column. Additional content on the home page can include links and the various elements described throughout the remainder of this chapter.

However, in recent years, there has been an explosion in blog design options. Today's blogs can use home pages that replicate popular news sites' layouts (sometimes referred to as *magazine layouts*), or specific layouts for portfolios or photography. Bloggers have more choices than ever, so don't be surprised if a blog you visit doesn't have a simple home page layout or looks more like a Web site than a blog.

As a beginner blogger, you should strongly consider keeping things simple in terms of your blog's home page layout. More complicated blog layouts often require more work in terms of formatting, updating, and so on. Unless you're prepared for those technological challenges, stick with more traditional two- or three-column blog layouts.

The important point to remember when creating your blog is that your home page is your blog's welcome page. Think of it like the exterior of a home. It can either have curb appeal or turn visitors off. Make sure your blog's home page has curb appeal.

Don't try to fit every piece of information you want to share with your visitors on your home page or it will get cluttered and become difficult for your audience to read. Instead, try to create a clean home page with useful information and easy-to-follow links.

About or profile page

The About page of your blog is simply a biography or description of who you are and why you're writing your blog. Readers like to know more about the person behind the blog, particularly if your blog offers advice or professional opinion. Your audience needs to believe that you're qualified to be writing your blog.

Remember that an essential part of becoming a successful blogger is developing relationships with your readers. The strength of a blog comes from the community that evolves around it. Don't cheat your audience. Instead, take the time to write a thorough profile page that shares information about your experience, credentials, and reasons for taking the time to write your blog.

Some bloggers' profile pages are very long with professional and personal information included in rich detail. Others are short and to the point. Either approach can work depending on your goals for your blog. Figure 3-5 offers an example of a succinct yet effective About page for Randa Clay's blog (`http://randaclay.com`).

It's also important that your profile page is easily accessible. Don't make your readers try to hunt down information about you. Reach out to them and make it easy for them to get to know you by making your profile page a prominent part of your blog.

Keep in mind that some blogs have two About pages. One talks about the blog itself, and the other talks about the blogger. It's up to you to decide whether you want two About pages or one, but most blogs use the single-About-page approach.

Posts

All blogs include posts. The exception occurs when someone uses a blogging application to create a more traditional Web site, but then it could be argued that those sites aren't really blogs at all. The essential element that makes a Web site a blog is the post feature, where entries appear in reverse chronological order. Therefore, it's safe to say that all blogs, in the traditional sense, include posts.

Each entry that you write and publish on your blog is called a *post.* Those posts are typically displayed on your blog's home page in the order that you published them with the most recent appearing at the top of the page. A certain number of posts appears on the home page, depending on the settings you choose within your blogging application. You can find older posts by clicking a link that appears at the bottom of the posts on the home page and each subsequent page. (The link is usually labeled as Previous Posts, Previous Entries, or something similar.) You can also find older entries by using the archive and category features of your blog, as described later in this chapter.

Your blog posts typically include a few common elements, including an author byline, date, title, the post content, links, images, and comments. A sample blog post is shown in Figure 3-6, so you can see the various elements in detail.

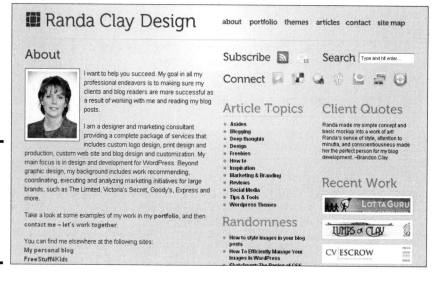

Figure 3-5: Randa Clay uses a simple, effective About page on her blog.

Figure 3-6: A typical blog post.

The blog post column typically takes up about 75 percent of the width of your blog's screen space.

Comments

Comments are what make blogs interactive. If your blog posts are the heart of your blog, comments are the veins and arteries pumping blood to and from your blog's heart. Blogging is meant to be a social tool. If it were intended to be one-sided, it wouldn't be much different from a traditional Web site aside from frequent updates being published. A regular Web site could publish frequent updates, too, but it doesn't offer the interactivity and conversation that blogs do thanks to commenting.

Comments appear at the end of a blog post. Most bloggers allow anyone to leave a comment, using the comment moderation tool in their blogging applications to filter inappropriate and spam comments before they're actually published. You can read more about comment moderation in Chapter 2 of Book VI.

People like to offer their own opinions, and blog commenting allows them to do exactly that. Commenting helps them feel involved and part of the community on your blog. That's a powerful thing when it comes to growing your blog. However, it's important to acknowledge the people who leave comments on your blog and show them you value them by responding to those comments and engaging the people who leave them. That's how you build relationships with your readers.

As your blog grows, so too will the number of comments your posts receive. Figure 3-7 shows an example of a blog post with comments. Don't be discouraged if your blog doesn't get a lot of comments. If you stay committed, keep writing, and continue interacting with the people who do leave comments on your posts, eventually more comments should come. Patience is key to your blog's success and growing your blog's community.

Categories or labels

Depending on the blogging application that you use, you might be able to categorize your blog posts (as WordPress lets you do) or attach labels to them in an informal categorization system (as with Blogger). Regardless of the specific functionality available to you, the end result is similar. Categories (or labels) create an easy way for readers to find old content related to specific topics.

Most bloggers include a list of categories (or labels) in their blog's sidebar, making it extremely easy for readers to find additional content of interest. For example, KeySplash Creative Conversations (`http://keysplash creativeconversations.com`) is a blog about marketing, copywriting, and branding. Figure 3-8 shows the categories used for posts on that blog, which make it quick and easy for readers to find additional information and older posts.

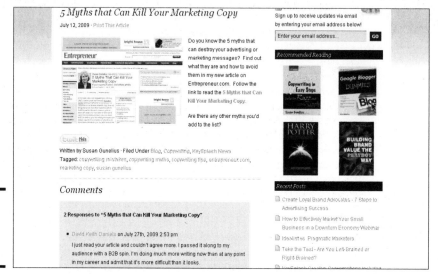

Figure 3-7:
A blog
post with
comments.

Figure 3-8:
The list of
categories
for
KeySplash
Creative
Conver-
sations.

Make sure you take the time to categorize or label your blog posts well, so readers have no trouble finding older blog posts.

Use labels and categories that are intuitive. Consider what term you would search for in order to find the type of content in your blog posts; then label or categorize your content to match.

Sidebar

Sidebars give your blog flexibility. Although you can have a blog with just one column that includes your blog posts, it's not common. More often, people use a two- or three-column format where sidebars appear to the left and/or right of the blog post column. It's easy to fall into the trap of filling your sidebars with as many elements as you can possibly squeeze into them, such as ads, links, and so on. However, your sidebars should offer information and links that are truly useful to your readers. If an element doesn't add value to the user experience, leave it out of your sidebar.

Just because you have space that can be filled in your blog's sidebar, that doesn't mean you have to fill it. Less is more.

Perhaps the biggest trap bloggers fall into when creating their blogs' sidebars is related to advertising. If you decide to include ads in your blog's sidebar to make money, then it's easy to clutter your sidebar with every kind of ad you can get access to. That's a huge mistake though. Blogs that are covered in ads create a negative user experience. Instead, try testing just a few ads in your sidebars. Analyze the results and then pick and choose the advertising opportunities that make the most sense for your blog, your audience, and your revenue goals. You can learn all about blog monetization, including advertising, in Book VII.

To get you started in building your blog's sidebar, following is a list of some of the most common sidebar elements that bloggers use, which you might want to include in your own sidebar:

✦ A link to your About or Profile page

✦ Your picture

✦ Your contact information

✦ Links to your Twitter, Facebook, or LinkedIn profiles

✦ Your blog's subscription information

✦ A list of categories or labels

✦ Links to your blog archives by date

✦ Ads

✦ A blogroll (essentially, a list of links to other blogs you like)

✦ A list of links to recent comments on your blog

✦ A list of links to your recent blog posts

✦ A list of links to your popular blog posts

You can see a partial sidebar sample from Women On Business (`www.women onbusiness.com`) in Figure 3-9.

Archives

It's easy for readers to find your recent posts by looking at your blog's home page or clicking through to the first few pages of content, but what if they want to see what you were talking about a month ago or a year ago? That would take a lot of clicking. That's where the archive feature in blogging applications comes in handy.

The blog archive feature makes it simple for readers to find and read your older posts by date. Most archives are divided by year, month, or week. You can display your archive links in your blog's sidebar, as shown in Figure 3-10.

Figure 3-9:
A partial
blog
sidebar.

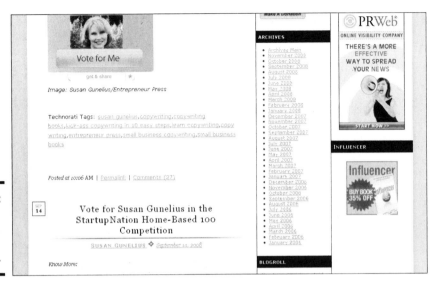

Figure 3-10:
This blog's archives appear in the sidebar.

Archives are useful for search engine optimization because all the blog posts you've ever written on your blog live online through your blog archives. That means that every post is an entry point to your blog for search engines to find your content. Frequently updated blogs that have been around for years can have thousands of entry points!

Header

Your blog's header can be loosely compared to a newspaper masthead. It's the area that stretches across the top of every page of your blog and typically includes your blog's name, an image, and possibly a slogan or short description of your blog. Your blog's header is what brands your blog and tells people where they are when they arrive on your site. Think about it: Would you know you were on the *New York Times* Web site if the header at the top of the page didn't tell you so? Most people wouldn't know. The same principle holds true for your blog.

That's why taking the time to create a great header is important. Try to make your header distinct. Use a font that's easy to read and an image that you own or are allowed to use based on its copyright license, described in more detail in Chapter 4 of this minibook.

Depending on the template that you use to create your blog or if you hire a designer to help you create your blog, you may be able to include additional elements in your blog's header. Some people include a search bar, subscription area, or ads in their blog's header. Figure 3-11 shows the header for Women On Business (www.womenonbusiness.com), which includes a title and graphic above the navigation bar at the top of the page.

Figure 3-11: A sample blog header.

Your blog's header appears at the top of every page on your blog and is the primary element people notice first anytime they visit your blog. Make it unique so people remember it and grow to recognize it.

Footer

A blog footer typically spans across the bottom of the screen on all pages of your blog. Although it's not essential to include a footer in your blog's design, it's a great place to put copyright information. In fact, some people use the space in their footer for far more than just disclaimers and legalese.

Following are some suggestions of elements to include in your blog's footer:

✦ Copyright and disclaimer statements

✦ Link to your e-mail address

✦ Your contact information such as your phone number or address (This is primarily useful for business blogs.)

✦ Ads

✦ Links to other resources within or outside of your blog

✦ Links to your social networking, bookmarking, and Twitter profiles

✦ Feeds from other blogs you write or enjoy

As always, it's important to keep in mind that there are no set rules related to formatting a blog footer. Use that space to help you meet your blogging goals and create a better user experience. Check out the blog footer for Performancing (`http://performancing.com`) in Figure 3-12 for some creative ways to fill a blog footer.

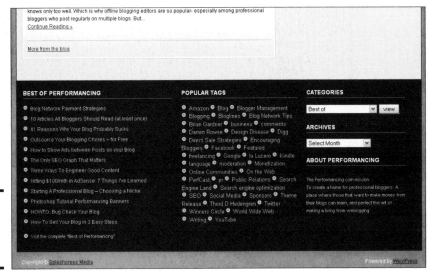

Figure 3-12:
An example
of a blog
footer.

Not all of your blog readers are going to scroll through to the bottom of your blog pages to find and read your footer information. In fact, very few of them probably will do so. Therefore, don't put critical information that you really want your readers to see in your blog's footer. Save that space for ancillary information you want to share that isn't essential to meeting your goals.

Blogroll or links

Depending on what blogging application you choose, you have the option to include a blogroll or list of links in your blog's sidebar (or footer, depending on your blog's template layout). A blogroll (or link list) is a list of links to other blogs that you like and recommend to your readers.

In the early days of blogging, blogrolls were powerful tools that directly led to increased traffic. There were a few reasons for this phenomenon. First, getting your blog's link listed on other blogs meant that other people who read those blogs might notice the link, follow it, and start reading your blog, too. If the blogger linking to you in his blogroll has a popular, well-trafficked blog, the number of click-throughs to your blog could be quite high. Second, each incoming link to your blog is weighted as a positive in Google's search algorithm. In other words, having more incoming links (particularly from popular Web sites and blogs) means your blog is ranked higher by Google, driving your pages up higher in related keyword searches. Higher rankings provide the potential for more search traffic.

Today, the power of blogrolls isn't what it once was. For example, there are companies that pay for links in blogrolls, which diminishes the value of them to readers. Many blogrolls are created and forgotten — making the links in them less than useful to people as time passes — and links break or the content on blogs becomes outdated. Also, originally, adding links to a blogroll was considered a reciprocal practice. If you added someone's blog to your blogroll, you could contact her to let her know, and she would almost always link back to you. It was an unwritten rule of blog etiquette. That rule doesn't necessarily apply today. In fact, many blogs don't even include blogrolls anymore.

However, blogrolls can still be a good networking tool, and if you're truly sharing links to blogs that you think your readers can benefit from and enjoy, it's an element you can provide as an added benefit. In other words, a useful blogroll certainly can't hurt your blog, and it may even help it. Figure 3-13 shows a sample blogroll from Women On Business (`www.womenonbusiness.com`).

Many bloggers call their blogrolls by an entirely different name these days. For example, you might see a list of links that would have been referred to as a blogroll a few years ago now labeled as Resources or Helpful Links.

Figure 3-13:
This blogroll includes plenty of links.

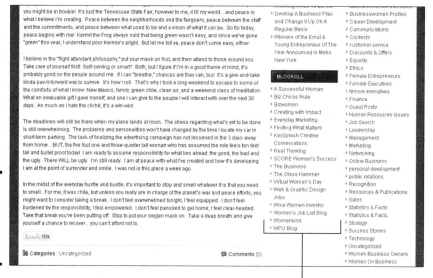

Blogroll

Trackbacks or backlinks

Depending on the blogging application you choose, you might be able to include trackback (WordPress or TypePad, for example) or backlink (Blogger) functionality in your blog posts. In simplest terms, a *trackback* is a virtual shoulder tap telling another blogger that you linked to one of his posts in one of your own posts. *Backlinks* from blogs hosted by Blogger work *only* on other Blogger-hosted blogs. Backlinks appear as a Links list below the blog post comments.

If you want your blog to grow and be successful, it's important that you take the time to turn on the trackback or backlink functionality within your blog settings and then actively use it. Doing so lets other bloggers know you liked their content enough to link to it, thereby promoting it on your blog, too. By linking to another blogger's content, you could help to boost his traffic *and* yours because the process of trackbacks and backlinks automatically leaves a reciprocal link on the blog post you linked to (assuming the other blogger has the functionality activated on his blog as well). Figure 3-14 shows track-back links on a post from Seth Godin's TypePad blog (`www.sethgodin.typepad.com`), which appear grouped together below the post but before the comments section.

You can find out more about trackbacks and backlinks as they relate to specific blogging applications in Book IV.

Trackbacks appear chronologically and mixed with other comments on WordPress blog posts.

Pings

A *ping* is a signal sent from one Web site to another to ensure that the other site exists. Pings are also used to notify sites that receive information from ping servers of updates to a blog or Web site. When you create your blog, you have the opportunity to enable pings within your blog settings.

Each time you publish a new blog post, sites such as Google, Technorati, and other search indexers are pinged, letting them know your new post exists. Pings are meant to speed up the process of getting your new posts indexed by major search engines, so your content is available to display within keyword search results as soon as possible.

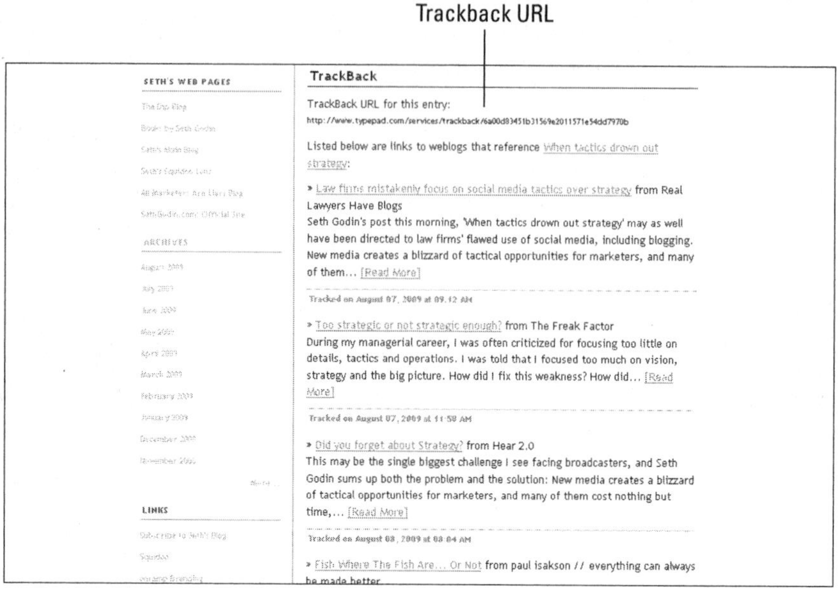

Trackback URL

TrackBack

TrackBack URL for this entry:
http://www.typepad.com/services/trackback/6a00d8345lb3l569e2011571e54dd7970b

Listed below are links to weblogs that reference *When tactics drown out strategy*:

» *Law firms mistakenly focus on social media tactics over strategy* from Real Lawyers Have Blogs
Seth Godin's post this morning, 'When tactics drown out strategy' may as well have been directed to law firms' flawed use of social media, including blogging. New media creates a blizzard of tactical opportunities for marketers, and many of them... [Read More]

Tracked on August 07, 2009 at 09:12 AM

» *Too strategic or not strategic enough?* from The Freak Factor
During my managerial career, I was often criticized for focusing too little on details, tactics and operations. I was told that I focused too much on vision, strategy and the big picture. How did I fix this weakness? How did... [Read More]

Tracked on August 07, 2009 at 11:58 AM

» *Did you forget about Strategy?* from Hear 2.0
This may be the single biggest challenge I see facing broadcasters, and Seth Godin sums up both the problem and the solution: New media creates a blizzard of tactical opportunities for marketers, and many of them cost nothing but time,... [Read More]

Tracked on August 03, 2009 at 08:04 AM

» *Fish Where The Fish Are... Or Not* from paul isakson // everything can always be made better

SETH'S WEB PAGES
The Dip Blog
Books by Seth Godin
Seth's Main Blog
Seth's Squidoo Lens
All Marketers Are Liars Blog
SethGodin.com (Official Site)

ARCHIVES
August 2009
July 2009
June 2009
May 2009
April 2009
March 2009
February 2009
January 2009
December 2008
November 2008

LINKS
Subscribe to Seth's Blog
Squidoo
my amp Scienta

Figure 3-14:
A trackback
link on a
TypePad
blog post.

Many services claim to be able to help you with setting up pings with a long list of sites. Also, you might hear that it's necessary to visit a long list of sites individually to manually set up your blog's ping service. Don't be fooled. Configuring the ping functionality within your blog's settings is enough to notify all the major sites when you publish new content.

Tags

In WordPress, tags are used for search engine optimization purposes. In simplest terms, when you write a new blog post using WordPress, you can input keywords as *tags,* which sites such as Technorati use to index your content. Additionally, because tags appear as links on your blog post, Google includes them in its indexing process. Either way you look at it, tags can only help your blog posts get found — as long as you don't overstuff keywords in your blog post tags that is. Figure 3-15 shows what tags look like on a WordPress blog post.

Depending on the blog template design, tags can appear in different locations such as at the top or bottom of a blog post.

Figure 3-15:
You can find the tags at the bottom of this WordPress blog post.

Bunches of tags

Template or theme

Every blog is built on a template, which designers and bloggers customize to create their own blogs' unique looks. Depending on the blogging application you use, your blog's layout could be called a *template* (Blogger) or a *theme* (WordPress), but either way, the concept is the same.

Many free templates are available to bloggers, which anyone can use. You can also find premium templates that are offered for a fee, making them both much rarer than the scores of free templates available online and, typically, more customizable. Some bloggers invest in having a custom template created so their blogs look completely original.

Templates usually include one, two, or three columns, with the blog posts taking up the majority of the space (approximately 75 percent). There are also unique templates for magazine-style sites, portfolios, and more. Long story short, you have tons and tons of choices when it comes to blog design. The template you ultimately use depends on your technical skills for updating and your budget. Figure 3-16 shows the popular, premium Thesis theme for WordPress from DIYthemes (www.DIYthemes.com).

Figure 3-16:
The
premium
Thesis
theme for
self-hosted
WordPress
blogs.

Remember, the type of template you decide to use on your blog is entirely up to you. Choose a template that provides the basic look and feel you want your blog to communicate to readers. You can find out more about finding and choosing a template for your blog based on your chosen blogging application in Book IV.

Chapter 4: Blogging Rules and Ethics

In This Chapter

- ✔ Avoiding trouble
- ✔ Finding out about copyrights and fair use
- ✔ Understanding Creative Commons licenses
- ✔ Attributing sources
- ✔ Creating comment and privacy policies
- ✔ Writing legal language and disclaimers

Although you won't find any formal rules and regulations related specifically to blogging, there are laws that extend to your blog's content and widely accepted practices that you should be aware of and adhere to throughout your life as a blogger. Those guidelines can extend from common courtesy and avoiding doing things that can be perceived as spam all the way to acts punishable by law, such as plagiarism.

This chapter points you in the right direction by highlighting some of the biggest things you should avoid doing on and off your blog as well as offering tips for how to do things the right way (or at least the way that other bloggers and blog readers prefer). If you want to be a welcomed member of the blogosphere, you need to fully understand the topics in this chapter.

Avoiding Blogging Don'ts

The safest path to follow as a blogger is to remember your manners. Just as if you were a magazine or newspaper publisher, the information you publish online through your blog must follow similar ethical and legal codes of conduct. Those codes relate to plagiarism, libel, and more.

Many bloggers, particularly in the United States, argue that laws related to free speech give them the right to write and publish anything they want on their blogs. However, freedom of speech should not be used as an excuse to publish content that could be hurtful to another person or entity. That's where bloggers need to dance the fine line between staying within the law and within ethical limitations while still freely publishing their thoughts and opinions. Remember your manners, and you should be okay.

With that in mind, the blogging don'ts that I discuss in the following sections are some of the biggest. Violate them at your own risk!

Don't plagiarize (Get permissions!)

Just as your teacher told you in your high school English class, plagiarism is wrong and punishable by law. Don't copy content from any other source and simply republish it on your blog. If you find another blog post or article online or offline that you want to write about on your blog, write your own original content about that subject.

If you believe someone has copied content from your blog, you can test your suspicions by using a site like Copyscape (www.copyscape.com), shown in Figure 4-1, which allows you to enter the URL of a page on your blog and do a search to determine whether the text on that page appears anywhere else online.

If you decide to copy a portion of another blog post or article on your blog or use an image that you find elsewhere on the Web within one of your blog posts, it is likely that you'll need to obtain permission to do so based on the type of copyright license attached to that content or image. (I discuss copyrights later in this chapter in detail, in the section "Understanding Copyright and Fair Use.") The safest route to take if you're not certain whether you're allowed to republish content or an image on your blog is to contact the owner and request permission to do so. If you can't obtain written permission, don't use the content or image.

Figure 4-1:
Copyscape allows you to determine whether your blog content has been copied elsewhere on the Web.

Don't commit libel against someone or something

Publishing libelous statements about another person or entity is illegal. In simplest terms, *libel* is written words that are intended to destroy or negatively impact a person or entity's reputation in front of a broad audience. Although your blog is your own place in the online world and it's permissible to publish your opinions on your blog, it's not okay to publish hateful or highly disparaging content, which could be considered libelous.

Most blogging applications include rules of conduct within their terms of use agreements notifying bloggers that blogs including libelous, hateful, or similar content will be deleted (if they're found or someone reports them). Similarly, search engines try to find and eliminate from indexing processes those sites with this kind of content on them. Long story short, a blog with content that could be construed as libelous might not have a long life and could lose all search traffic — not to mention the fact that the blogger could get in trouble with the law. The best course of action is to keep your more extreme opinions to yourself.

Many bloggers have been fired from their jobs because of negative content published on their personal blogs about their employers. Be careful what you write about on your blog! You never know who might be looking.

Don't spam through comments

Many people publish comments on blogs for no reason but to drive traffic to their own blogs and Web sites through the links included in their comments. When you leave a comment on a blog post, there is a field in the comment form where you can include a link back to your own blog. Doing so is perfectly acceptable and even expected.

Comment spam comes in two flavors:

✦ **Irrelevant comments:** Comment spam can come from people who leave useless or completely irrelevant comments on a blog post for the sole purpose of getting their link to show up in the comment section of the post.

✦ **Comments stuffed with links:** Comment spam can come from people who leave a useful comment but also include several links, which could be relevant or irrelevant. Leaving an additional useful link within a comment is perfectly acceptable, but stuffing comments with a list of links is not, whether or not those links are related to the topic of the corresponding post. Some comments stuffed with links are quite obviously spam, such as the one shown in Figure 4-2.

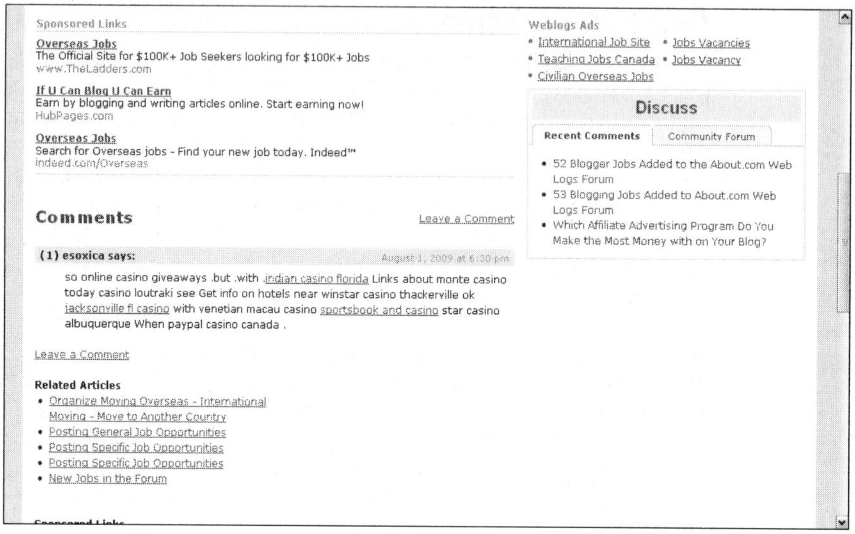

Figure 4-2:
An example
of comment
spam.

Be sure to avoid leaving comments on other blog posts that could be viewed as spam. Doing so can get you blacklisted within the minds of other bloggers who will think of you as little more than a spammer.

It's also important to reduce comment spam on your own blog to enhance the user experience by creating a comment policy, as discussed in the "Creating a Comment Policy" section later in this chapter. Also, you can reduce spam through comment moderation, which I discuss in Chapter 2 of Book VI.

Don't publish spammy posts

Just as blog comments can be spam, so can blog posts or entire blogs. If your blog posts include nothing more than one promotional message after another or if your blog is covered in ads with little to no useful information, readers (and search engines) will identify it as spam. Readers have no reason to return to a blog that offers no meaningful content. Just as you wouldn't want to sit in front of a television all day and watch nothing but commercials, no one wants to read a blog that includes nothing but ads or promotional posts.

It's absolutely fine to include ads and promotional posts on your blog, but they should be identified as such for full transparency and disclosure. They should also be limited in quantity. The part of your blog that will convince people to return again and again is the content that you write, not the ads that you publish.

Don't steal bandwidth

Bandwidth is a measure of digital data consumption. Stealing bandwidth happens when you publish something on your blog, such as an image, without uploading that image to your own blog hosting account first. Instead, you simply publish the link code from the original blog or Web site where you found the image. Doing so allows the image to appear in your blog post, but that image still resides on the originating site's hosting account. Anytime the image loads on your blog, the originating site serves it, meaning you're blog is using the originating site's bandwidth each time a visitor views the image on your blog.

For every piece of content (written, image, audio, video, and so on) that you publish on your blog, a bit of space is used up from your hosting account. Most blogs and Web sites have a limited amount of hosting space that the blogger pays for each month (or uses up each month, in the case of some free blogging accounts). Bloggers and Web site owners can be charged more if the amount of times that their content is accessed increases dramatically (such as when other bloggers use images without saving them to their own hosting accounts first).

Long story short, you wouldn't like it if you had to pay extra because other people were stealing your bandwidth, so don't do it to other bloggers and Web site owners. Instead, copy the picture you want to use (being certain you have permission to do so first), save it to your hosting account, and then insert it into your blog post. (See Book IV for details on how to make a blog post.)

Providing Attribution

When you find a great article or blog post and write about it on your blog, you should provide attribution to your source. Not only is it ethical to do so, but if you cite and provide a link to the original source, that other blog or Web site could get a trackback or backlink (as described in Chapter 3 of this minibook). The blog or Web site owner can also see traffic coming from your blog through his own research into his site statistics (discussed in Chapter 2 of Book V). Either way, providing attribution to sources within your blog posts could put your blog on another blogger's radar screen and lead to additional traffic to your blog. You can provide attribution by simply linking text within your blog post to your source, or you can provide a more formal attribution at the end of your blog post.

Furthermore, if you copy a specific quote from another source, it's imperative that you identify the quote as such and attribute the original source to avoid being accused of plagiarism. The same holds true for using images that you find from other sources. You should obtain permission to use them (unless they have a copyright license attached to them that allows you to republish them without first obtaining permission) and provide appropriate attribution to the source within your blog post.

Figure 4-3 shows an image used on a blog with permission and proper attribution.

Figure 4-3: Always provide attribution to your sources.

Attribution for an image

Understanding Copyright and Fair Use

The rules of copyright are a bit blurred in the online world, but the safest path to follow is one that errs on the side of being more conservative. Copyrights protect an author, artist, photographer, musician, or creator from having his or her original work stolen or misused without permission. If you didn't create a piece of content on your blog, someone else holds the copyright to it. Copyrights are enforceable by law, so before you use text, images, video, or audio on your blog, be certain a copyright license is attached to it that allows you to use it without asking formal permission to do so. If you're uncertain, ask permission before you use it.

The blurred lines of copyright come into play around the concept of *fair use* as it applies to copyright laws. If you're republishing content on your blog that someone else owns for the purpose of providing criticism, commentary, education, reporting, training, or research, you may not be required to seek permission to reuse that material on your blog thanks to a legal loophole called fair use. However, the lines of fair use are highly debatable. The safest course of action is to ask permission if you're unsure whether you can republish content on your blog within the bounds of copyright law, and of course, always provide attribution to your source, as described in the preceding section.

Using Creative Commons Licenses

Creative Commons licenses are designed to give the owners of original work a way to share that work more freely (and allow other people to build on that work) by protecting the owner of the original licensed work without applying a full and highly restrictive copyright to it. In other words, a Creative Commons license allows other people to use the owner's work, but restrictions can be attached depending on the type of Creative Commons license the owner applies to that work. The licenses were created by the nonprofit organization Creative Commons (`http://creativecommons.org`).

Six types of Creative Commons licenses exist, and each has different rules of use attached to it as well as attribution requirements. Following are brief descriptions of each license type:

✦ **Attribution:** This is the most flexible Creative Commons license: It allows anyone to reuse, revise, and build on an original work both noncommercially and commercially. The only requirement is that the license owner is provided proper credit for the original work. Bloggers can do this by citing the source.

✦ **Attribution Noncommercial:** This license works exactly the same as the Attribution license does with one restriction: The person who reuses the original work must *not* do so for commercial purposes.

✦ **Attribution No Derivatives:** This license works almost the same as the Attribution license except that the original work that is reused cannot be changed in any way. It must be used in its entirety.

✦ **Attribution No Derivatives Noncommercial:** This license works almost exactly the same as the Attribution No Derivatives license, but works cannot be reused for commercial purposes of any kind.

✦ **Attribution Share Alike:** This license works the same as the Attribution license except that anyone who reuses an original work with the Attribution Share Alike license must license their new work with an Attribution Share Alike license as well.

✦ **Attribution Share Alike Noncommercial:** This is the most restrictive type of Creative Commons license. It works almost the same way that the Attribution Share Alike license does, but new creations that use the original licensed work may not be used for commercial purposes.

In Figure 4-4, you can see the About Licenses page of the Creative Commons Web site (`http://creativecommons.org/about/licenses`) and the four icons that represent how the different licenses work.

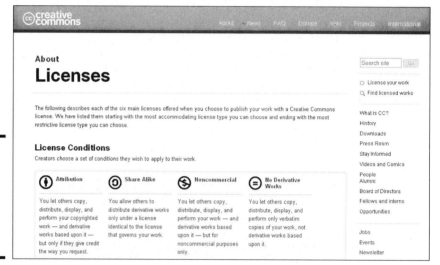

Figure 4-4:
The About Licenses page of the Creative Commons Web site.

It's a good idea to obtain a Creative Commons license for your blog content and then include information about that license in your blog's footer.

Creative Commons licenses are becoming more and more popular for images used online. There are Web sites set up so you can do searches specifically for images with Creative Commons licenses attached to them. When you're ready to look for images that you can use on your blog without violating copyright laws or going through a lengthy process to obtain permissions, take a look at Chapter 3 of Book V: That chapter contains a list of sources for finding images with Creative Commons licenses.

Disclosing Your Policies

Creating some policies for your blog is a good way to set reader expecta-tions and protect yourself from unlikely but possible legal entanglements. For example, if someone plagiarizes your content or accuses you of selling his or her e-mail address, having clear and published policies that show how you handle copyright and privacy issues would be very important. Following are three of the most common policies published on blogs:

✦ **Comment policy:** Describes what comments are inappropriate and how they're moderated

✦ **Privacy policy:** Describes what information is collected about visitors and how that information is used.

✦ **Terms and Conditions of Site Use page:** Describes legal info about your blog, such as copyrights, availability, and warnings.

Creating a comment policy

What makes blogs interactive and social is the commenting feature, wherein readers can leave comments about the posts they read. However, some people in the world either have nothing nice to say or find the need to say hateful things. Try not to take offense at the rude comments left on your blog posts. The blogosphere has a special name for people who leave hateful and obnoxious comments on blogs for no reason other than to stir up trouble: *trolls.*

It's your blog, and you can delete any comment you want, but keep in mind that even if you don't like what someone has to say, an alternative viewpoint (stated in a courteous manner) can add to the conversation on your blog. In time, your loyal readers might even step up to the plate and defend your statements from your opponents. The key to successfully balancing the process of publishing and deleting comments is to create a *comment policy* that states exactly what kind of comments will be deleted or edited before they're published. By publishing a comment policy on your blog, you're protecting yourself from accusations of controlling the conversation on your blog.

You can write your blog comment policy in a friendly or professional tone as long as your rules are clear. You may want to cover the following points in your comment policy for *any* sort of blog:

✦ **Hateful or attacking language:** You can include a rule that says comments that are hateful in nature or attack other visitors will be deleted.

✦ **Spam:** Be sure to include a statement that says all comments that are considered to be potential spam will be deleted.

✦ **Editing and Deleting:** Include language that says you reserve the right to edit or delete all comments that are off-topic, offensive, or detract from the blog community discussion.

Sometimes it's hard to tell whether a comment is legitimate. If you prefer to err on the side of caution, delete comments that could be spam even if you're not certain. By including a reference to how *potential* spam comments are handled on your blog, you're protecting your right to delete those comments and warning readers to be sure to write useful comments that can't be perceived as spam. To make your guidelines related to spam comments even clearer, you can include examples of the types of comments that you consider spam and could be deleted within your comment policy.

The following are some other items you might want to cover in your comment policy, but these items depend more on the type of blog you have and want to maintain:

+ **Profanity:** You can include a statement saying comments that include profanity will be edited to remove potentially offensive language.

+ **Links:** You can include a statement warning visitors that comments containing more than a specific number of links (such as three links) will automatically be detected as spam and deleted. (Typically, you can configure this setting within your blogging application.)

These lists are by no means complete. I recommend reading comment policies from different blogs to see whether you can find other points you want to add to your own.

Figure 4-5 shows an example of a blog comment policy. The example is from the Freelance Writing Jobs blog (`www.freelancewritinggigs.com`).

Figure 4-5:
A blog comment policy.

Writing a privacy policy

It's a good idea to include a privacy policy on your blog, particularly if you display ads. A *privacy policy* is intended to communicate to blog readers how their behavior on your blog (paths taken, links clicked, and so on) will be tracked and how any personal information provided on your blog (such as e-mail addresses in comments or forms and so on) will be used. You can provide a link to your privacy policy in your blog's footer. The policy can provide details about any information that's collected about visitors and their behaviors on your blog, confirmation that you won't sell any private information given on your blog, and acknowledgement that your site tracks visitors' behavior through the use of an automated Web tracking tool called *cookies.* (If you participate in ad programs or track your blog usage statistics as described in Chapter 2 of Book V, your blog probably uses cookies for tracking.)

Basically, you want readers of your blog to know that any personal information they provide won't be sold to marketers who will start cluttering their e-mail inboxes with offers. You also want to warn them that their behavior on your blog (links they click, the amount of time they spend on your site, and so on) is recorded. Figure 4-6 shows an example of a simple yet effective blog privacy policy.

**Book I
Chapter 4**

Blogging Rules and Ethics

> The following principles apply to the personally identifying information we ask for and that you provide. "Personally identifying information" is information that individually identifies you, such as your name, physical address or email address.
>
> Data collection
>
> **www.cropperscottage.net** collects limited non-personally identifying information your browser makes available whenever you visit a website. This log information includes your Internet Protocol address, browser type, the date and time of your access and one or more cookies that may uniquely identify your browser. We use this information to operate, develop and improve our services.
>
> Some of our services require you to register for an account. **www.cropperscottage.net** asks you for some personal information in order to create an account (typically your name, email address, and a password for your account) and we will use that information to provide the service.
>
> Cookies
>
> Upon your first visit to **www.cropperscottage.net**, a cookie is sent to your computer that uniquely identifies your browser. A "cookie" is a small file containing a string of characters that is sent to your computer when you visit a website.
>
> We use cookies to improve the quality of our service and to better understand how people interact with us. **www.cropperscottage.net** does this by storing user preferences in cookies and by tracking user trends and patterns of how people access our site.
>
> Most browsers are initially set up to accept cookies. You can reset your browser to refuse all cookies or to indicate when a cookie is being sent. However, some **www.cropperscottage.net** features or services may not function properly without cookies.
>
> Information Sharing
>
> We will not sell, disclose or lease our member's personal information to any other entity, unless this information is required by Law Enforcement Agency's.
>
> If you have any questions regarding our privacy policy, please e-mail us.

Figure 4-6:
A simple
blog privacy
policy.

Providing a privacy policy on your blog is not a requirement unless you participate in an ad program that *does* require it.

Developing a Terms and Conditions of Site Use page

A *Terms and Conditions of Site Use* page is the right place to provide disclaimers and warnings about your blog. It's a way to protect yourself and your blog's content from potential problems such as copyright infringement. A Terms and Conditions of Site Use page isn't a requirement, but if you do decide to use one, a common place to link to it is in your blog's footer.

Your blog's Terms and Conditions of Site Use page can include the following elements:

✦ **Copyright information:** Include both *your* blog's copyrights as well as information on who to contact if a reader finds content on your blog that he believes violates copyright laws.

✦ **Site availability:** Include information that protects you if, for some reason, your blog is unavailable at any given moment. For example, sometimes your blog hosting company could have a server problem, or you might need to disable your blog for maintenance.

✦ **Warnings:** Include warnings as appropriate. For example, you might want to include a warning for visitors under 18 years of age if your blog uses profanity or material offensive to children.

✦ **Link responsibilities:** Include language that tells readers you're not responsible for the content on other sites that readers are led to through links on your blog, nor are you responsible for the availability of those sites.

These are just a few examples of statements you can include in your Terms and Conditions of Site Use page for your blog. The idea is to present any and all information on this page that's needed to protect you from potential negative accusations or legal entanglements.

Book II

Niche Blogging

The 5th Wave   By Rich Tennant

"Hi all. Turns out that the rash I posted about last night is contagious..."

Contents at a Glance

Chapter 1: Understanding Niche Blogging

In This Chapter

✔ Understanding niche blogging

✔ Finding niche blogs

✔ Discovering the secrets of niche blogging success

✔ Uncovering the negatives of niche blogging

The blogosphere is a crowded place with millions of blogs and bloggers competing for readers, advertising dollars, and links every day. How can a brand-new blogger compete with bigger, established blogs? Certainly blog marketing and promotion, building relationships, and engaging readers are ways to boost your blog traffic, but before you even start your blog, you might consider another strategy to becoming a successful blogger: defining your blog's niche.

A *niche blog* is one that focuses on a very specific topic. That topic needs to be popular enough to be capable of drawing a sufficient audience to make maintaining the blog worthwhile to the blogger, but it also needs to be small enough to make it appear to be no competition to the larger, well-established blogs and bloggers.

Niche blogs can grow to be very popular simply because the bloggers behind them provide specific information that a highly targeted audience wants. They usually fill a void that other, larger blogs are missing but audiences want. This chapter explains how to find a niche, decide whether niche blogging is right for you, and how to position a niche blog for success.

Determining What Makes a Niche Blog

A niche blog is a highly focused blog. All content and conversations on a niche blog are centered on a single, specific subject. The audience for a niche blog is typically very connected to the topic and often quite vocal about it. In short, niche blogs deliver content gems that people want but struggle to find among all the information on broad-topic blogs.

Niche bloggers understand their audiences. They know readers come to their blogs for specific content, and they don't disappoint. Niche bloggers strive to continually meet the expectations of their audiences. They keep track of what other bloggers who write about their subject matter in a broader sense are publishing, and they fill the gaps.

Niche blogs have an amazing opportunity to attract and create very loyal readers simply because the audience is already connected to and passionate about the subject matter. If they like the blogger's voice and content as it relates to that subject matter, the blogger is poised for success.

Finding Niche Blogs

Searching for niche blogs is actually very easy because you can search for them using traditional blog search tools (discussed in more detail in Chapter 3 of this minibook) using very specific keyword phrases. Instead of sifting through hundreds of pages of results for a broad search term such as *parenting,* you can find niche blogs about a more specific subject using a search term such as *parenting triplets* or *potty training.* The more specific you get with your search terms, the better your chances are of finding a blog about the niche you have in mind.

Blog readers find blogs about specific subjects in exactly the same way, which is why it's important to do some keyword research before you choose your blog's niche to get an idea of its popularity. You can find out about keyword research as it relates to niche blogging in detail in Chapter 3 of this minibook.

The following sections provide examples of five different kinds of niche blogs related to five very different subjects: politics, business, making money from home, fashion, and cars. Take a look at the examples to see how researching existing niche blogs can provide you with new insight into the opportunities niche blogging presents in terms of creativity, readership, networking, and monetization.

Capitol Annex

Capitol Annex is shown in Figure 1-1 and is a great example of a niche blog that was created using a well-thought-out niche-blogging strategy. Vince Leibowitz realized that many blogs published content about Texas politics, a subject he is passionate about, but most of those blogs provide information on national, state, and local politics as well as other topics. He saw a void, wherein Texas state politics were not being covered in the way he wanted them to be, and he believed he could fill that gap. He also believed an audience existed for that specific information. Leibowitz started his blog, Capitol Annex (`http://capitolannex.com`), which is dedicated to Texas politics at the state level, and today, he has a following of loyal readers as a result.

Glass Hammer

You can find many business blogs online as well as many leadership blogs. However, there are not many blogs dedicated to women business leaders online. Nor are there many blogs dedicated specifically to women executives working in the business fields of law and finance. Glass Hammer (www.glasshammer.com), shown in Figure 1-2, fills that gap and has a powerful following of women in business who look to the blog to provide the information they're interested in. It's a perfect example of a niche blog.

Figure 1-1:
Capitol
Annex is a
niche blog
focused on
Texas state
politics.

Figure 1-2:
Glass
Hammer is
a niche blog
for women
business
executives
working
in law and
finance.

Melodee's Virtual Assistant Blog

There are many blogs online about working from home. How can a blogger turn such a broad topic into a niche blog? Simple: Choose a very specific subject within the broader topic of making money from the comfort of your own home. Melodee's Virtual Assistant Blog (`www.short-termsolutions.com/vablog`), shown in Figure 1-3, is an example of doing exactly that. Rather than trying to cover all aspects of working from home, this blog focuses on providing advice to people who want to start a successful virtual assistant business.

The Purse Blog

Fashion and beauty are popular blog topics, but there are many ways to find a niche within those broader topics. The Purse Blog (`www.purseblog.com`), shown in Figure 1-4, provides a great example. This blog is dedicated to purses — everything and anything related to luxury-brand women's handbags. This blog has a large, focused audience for the content as well as profitable niche advertising opportunities.

67 Mustang Blog

Many blogs are written about cars, and many blogs are written about specific brands of cars. Car enthusiasts are typically very loyal to their brands and are looking for great blogs about those brands of cars. Figure 1-5 shows the 67 Mustang Blog (`www.67mustangblog.com`), which takes the niche blogging concept a step further by focusing on the blogger's journey to restore his 1967 Ford Mustang with a bit of broader Ford Mustang–related content thrown in for flavor.

Figure 1-3: Melodee's Virtual Assistant Blog turns the broad topic of working from home into a niche.

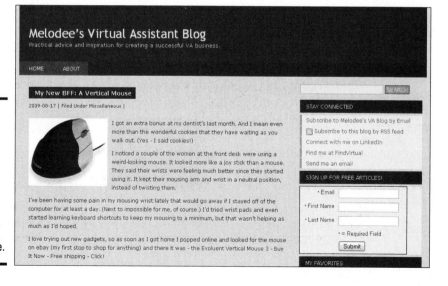

Figure 1-4: The Purse Blog is all about women's handbags and nothing else.

Figure 1-5: The 67 Mustang Blog follows the restoration of a blogger's beloved car.

Finding Out What Makes Niche Blogs Successful

The success of niche blogs comes primarily from the voices of the bloggers behind them. Typically, the niche blogger is either an expert in his niche or feels extremely strongly about it, which gives his blog a unique perspective.

However, it doesn't matter how strongly you feel about a topic: Your blog won't succeed if there aren't other people in the world who are equally interested in that topic.

The key to writing a successful niche blog is finding a topic you love that other people are equally passionate about.

For example, many people write blogs about animals. Fewer bloggers write blogs about dogs, and fewer write blogs about a specific breed of dogs such as the Basset Hound. Going a step further, even fewer blogs are written about training Basset Hounds. Notice how the subject matter of the blogs I describe here gets more and more focused and thus becomes about more-specific niches. That's the same strategy you need to use in identifying the right niche topic for your blog. Take a look at the broader topic and keep narrowing it down until you find the best niche for your blog. You can find out more about choosing a niche blog topic in Chapter 3 of this minibook.

Successful niche bloggers position themselves as the go-to people for their specific topics. Establishing yourself as an expert in your blog's topic could be as easy as listing your education, experience, and other credentials in your profile or biography published on your blog. For example, if you write a blog about pregnancy and you're an obstetrician, your authority is easy to establish.

If you don't have any official credentials, don't despair. You can still position yourself as an expert by publishing authoritative content that's both meaningful and useful. Take some time to showcase your knowledge off of your blog as well by writing guest posts or articles about your blog topic on other blogs and Web sites, participating in online forums and social networks where you can share your expertise with more people. Consider teaching courses or speaking at events where your knowledge can be highlighted. In other words, if you don't have credentials when you start your niche blog and you want your blog to grow and be successful, you should make an effort to create them. Don't be afraid to think out of the box and pursue unique opportunities to establish your expertise both on and offline.

Patience is paramount when it comes to building a niche blog. Successful niche bloggers start small in terms of topic and scope. Over time and with patience and persistence their reputation and blog traffic grows.

Because a niche blog is highly focused on a specific topic, you need to be certain you're very passionate about that topic to ensure you'll be able to write about it for a long period of time without getting dry or repetitive. (See Chapter 2 of this minibook for more about finding your focus.)

A great example of a niche blogger's success comes from Gayla Baer of MomGadget (`http://momgadget.com`), shown in Figure 1-6, who started her blog in 2000 as a step in building a career working from home. Her blog evolved to sharply focus on reviewing and discussing gadgets that make mothers' lives easier. Gayla got the idea for her blog after attending a baby shower and seeing how excited she and the other attendees got about the various gadgets the expectant mother received to ease the transition to parenthood.

The origins of Gayla's success can be attributed to her ability to recognize a niche, capitalize on it, and develop her online presence as an expert in her blog's topic with a large audience of followers. By establishing her niche, she was ultimately able to grow in a new direction just as businesses broaden their product lines after they find success in their core competencies.

Over the years, MomGadget grew in scope to include content about broader family-related topics as well as working-from-home tips based on her own blogging experience; however, without establishing her niche audience first, it would have been extremely difficult for Gayla to find success competing against broader topic blogs with deeper pockets and wider reach. By developing her core audience first, she was able to introduce new topics to her loyal followers while continuing to meet their existing expectations, thereby growing her blog exponentially. The trick is to find your niche and build a following around it *before* you try to expand in broader directions.

**Book II
Chapter 1**

**Understanding
Niche Blogging**

Figure 1-6:
Mom-
Gadget's
success
came from
exploiting
a niche
and then
adapting
content
for a wider
audience
over time.

Benefiting from the Positives of Niche Blogging

As with any online endeavor you pursue, niche blogging offers both positives and negatives. It's critical that you take the time before you start your blog to weigh those positives and negatives and make an educated decision as to whether niche blogging is right for you and your goals. Don't just think of your blogging goals today or next month. Instead, look a few years into the future and determine where you want your blog to take you between now and then. Your blog topic could greatly affect your ability to reach those goals.

The following sections give you a good idea of the primary advantages of niche blogging, but don't stop there. Also read the later section, "Identifying the Drawbacks to Niche Blogs," so you're aware of the negatives, too.

Loyal readers

The people who find your blog and like what they read on it are more apt to return and become loyal readers simply because they're likely to have a vested interest in the subject matter. The reason is simple. If visitors are interested in your niche topic and know they can count on you to write relevant posts in a voice they enjoy time and again, they'll want to come back and read more from you. It follows the principle that if you give people what they want, they'll want more from you.

There's a reason why bloggers who write about specific celebrities (and write frequent, relevant posts) typically draw large and loyal audiences: People who are interested in those specific celebrities can never get enough information about them. They want to talk about those celebrities and share their thoughts about those celebrities with other people. You can use the same principles to create loyal readers on your own blog by focusing on a niche people feel strongly about.

Less competition

As discussed earlier in this chapter, niche blogs have less competition by definition. Larger, successful blogs aren't likely to focus on a specific subject that's likely to attract a smaller, targeted audience. Instead, their focus is on providing broad content and attracting a wide audience. However, many people visit broad topic blogs looking for specific types of information. That's where the power of niche blogs comes into play — in providing that specific content consistently and accurately.

Think of it this way — if you want to get information about college football teams in Florida, would you visit a blog that covers *all* college football teams where you're likely to have to sort through dozens of unrelated posts to find what you're looking for? Or would you prefer to visit a blog that is dedicated to talking about college football teams *only* in the state of Florida? Most likely, you answered the latter because you'd save time and find more relevant information on that niche blog than you would on the broad-topic blog.

You can apply the same principles to your own niche blog by identifying the specific segments of the broader audience and delivering the information that one of those segments is looking for. Larger, broad topic blogs are unlikely to care what you write about on your niche blog because they don't view the smaller audience segment as a threat. In other words, if you steal some of their audience members, the small size is unlikely to affect them (at least that's what they hope). Also, the larger blog might actually recognize you as an expert in that niche over time and use you as a resource, providing you with another way to boost your blog traffic.

**Book II
Chapter 1**

**Understanding
Niche Blogging**

The blogosphere is a big and wide-open place. Instead of competing with other blogs, particularly popular blogs, find your niche and exploit it. Network with those bigger bloggers and become the go-to person for your niche.

Long-tail search engine optimization

Search engine optimization (SEO) is discussed in detail in Chapter 1 of Book V, but I would be remiss if I didn't mention it here. *Long-tail* search engine optimization is based on very specific keyword phrases. For example, instead of simply searching for *Italian recipes* in your preferred search engine, you could search for a targeted phrase such as *easy Italian meatballs recipes*, which would yield comparatively specific results.

Because a niche blog focuses on a specific topic, you can optimize your posts and pages for those targeted keyword phrases and drive more targeted traffic to your blog. People who are searching for a specific keyword phrase that matches the content on your site are far more likely to be satisfied when they find your blog, read more content there, and return again later than they would be if they arrived there following a broad search.

Many large Web sites and blogs spend a lot of money trying to derive benefits from long-tail search engine optimization. Those opportunities are inherent in niche blogging.

Recognition and exposure

As a niche blogger, your name may become closely associated with your blog's topic. In effect, you could become known as an expert and called upon to provide opinions, speak at events, and much more as a result of the content you write on your niche blog. Many broad-topic bloggers try to be everything to everyone, but few succeed. By virtue of being a niche blogger, you potentially position yourself as an expert in your field.

Many bloggers have gone from obscurity to online and offline celebrity status thanks to their niche blogs. For example, Wendy Piersall of Sparkplugging (www.sparkplugging.com), shown in Figure 1-7, started her blog (originally called eMoms at Home) about and for mothers working from home as a hobby. Today, she's a highly sought-after social media speaker viewed as an expert in both blogging and working from home.

Targeted advertising opportunities

Niche blogs attract targeted audiences, and smart advertisers want to match their ads with those targeted audiences. That means niche blogs can be very attractive to advertisers who share similar consumer audiences for their products. Not only do advertisers want to purchase ad space on blogs where they can connect with a targeted audience, but they're often willing to pay more for that space.

Think of it this way: If Mattel wants to advertise a new Barbie product, and the company had the choice to advertise to a smaller audience on a blog for mothers of grade school children or a blog about parenting in general, which is likely to offer a better return on their investment? Certainly, the larger, broader site might lead to more people clicking the ad overall, but the smaller, niche site is more likely to lead to more sales per click. At the end of the day, more sales per click are often worth far more to advertisers than more clicks with fewer sales.

Figure 1-7: Wendy Piersall rose from obscurity to become a blogging celebrity through her blog Sparkplugging.

Identifying the Drawbacks to Niche Blogs

Now that you understand the positives of niche blogging, it's time to look at the negatives. Unfortunately, the news about niche blogging isn't all good, but if you understand the potential drawbacks before you dive in, you can better position yourself for success as a niche blogger in the long term. By no means are the negatives of niche blogging insurmountable. On the contrary, they can all be overcome with dedication and patience.

Lower traffic and a smaller audience

By nature of the word *niche,* niche blogs appeal to a smaller audience than broad-topic blogs. That's not necessarily a bad thing though, as you discover in the previous sections. However, it can be difficult for new bloggers to make that distinction. Many bloggers join the blogosphere with dreams of attracting thousands of visitors to their blogs each month. The truth of the matter is that it takes the vast majority of bloggers a long time to attract that kind of traffic to their blogs.

Book II
Chapter 1

**Understanding
Niche Blogging**

Furthermore, niche blogs can have difficulties achieving high rankings on search engines for broad and common search phrases, because the competition for those broad search phrases is so high. Trying to compete with big sites for higher search rankings on common search terms can be a daunting and time-consuming task. Investing your time into maximizing your niche search term traffic is often a more successful strategy to pursue.

On the flip side, when you attract large numbers of visitors to your blog, it's likely that many of them won't stay long, and they're even less likely to return. The key to developing a successful blog is attracting and retaining a loyal audience of readers. Niche blogs might appeal to a smaller audience, but they're typically a very loyal audience. If you can live with a smaller audience, niche blogging might be right for you.

The startup curse

As with all new things, a niche blog might be niche today, but it could become the cool, popular thing next month. Remember when Twitter wasn't even a real word? Today, it's *the* cool and popular thing to do online. What started as a niche tool grew into a must-use tool at record speed. The same thing can happen with niche blog topics.

For example, you might have an idea to write a blog about a specific niche topic that no one else is currently writing about online. Sure, other bloggers might mention your niche topic in their broad blog, but no one is covering it exclusively. You recognize the opportunity and jump on it only to find in six months that your niche topic has become the cool, popular thing online. Competition soars before you have a chance to truly position yourself as the go-to place for information related to your niche topic. Other bloggers with greater influence, reach, and time usurp your position and become the go-to places for your niche, leaving you and your blog behind. That's a risk that all niche bloggers take, and it's up to you to determine how much effort you're willing to put into your blogging success and into creating contingency plans in case this happens to you.

The disappearing niche

A hot niche today could become obsolete tomorrow. Make sure you choose a niche that has staying power. For example, blogs about popular television shows that go off the air may have been hot while the program was going strong, but what happens to them when the show ends? What does the blogger do then? If you're looking for long-term blogging success, it's best not to tie your fate to a topic that might not be around one day. Instead, make sure you're in control by choosing a niche topic that is timeless or can morph into something else if the key element fades.

Niche fan blogs are a perfect example of mayfly blog topics. For example, blogs about upcoming sporting events, such as the next Olympic Games, can become obsolete as soon as the event is over. As another example, consider *The X-Files,* which was a highly popular television show with a strong fan following. Many of these fans created blogs to share their love of the program. When *The X-Files* went off the air in the late 1990s, the conversations died and so did most of the blogs. Others such as XFilesNews (www.xfilesnews. com), shown in Figure 1-8, continued to provide updates related to the show and actors, but the content dwindled in frequency as did the traffic.

Figure 1-8: Niche blogs, such as XFilesNews, can be dependent on the lifespan of their topics.

Fewer advertising opportunities

Although niche blogs can attract targeted advertisers who are willing to pay more to connect with the specific audiences niche blogs attract, fewer advertising opportunities are available to niche bloggers overall. There is a very simple reason for this.

Many advertisers (particularly small and mid-size company advertisers) don't understand that the return on investment in connecting with a highly targeted audience that matches their best customer's demographic profile will be higher than the return on investment they get from connecting with a larger, less-targeted audience (if their goal is to make sales rather than just raise awareness of their products and services).

Because niche sites attract fewer visitors overall than larger, broad topic blogs, it can be harder for an advertising manager to convince her leadership team of the value of advertising on a more targeted site than it is to sell them on the benefits of advertising to one of those larger blogs. It's unfortunate, but it's a gap in thinking that can be difficult for advertisers to overcome.

As such, even though your site might attract 1,000 readers who are obviously extremely interested in your niche topic and might be the *perfect* audience for an advertiser's messages, that advertiser might still choose to place its ad on a broad site that receives 10,000 visitors instead. The reason for this is simply because the decision makers on the advertiser's side can't get beyond the traffic numbers to fully understand who the audience members behind those numbers are and what they want and need.

The best option for niche bloggers is to test advertising opportunities and rates. Research what your competitors are doing (if you can find any) and test similar advertising opportunities. In time, you'll find a mix that works for you, and as your traffic increases thanks to your persistence and patience, additional advertising opportunities will undoubtedly present themselves to you.

Chapter 2: Benefiting from a Niche Blog Approach

In This Chapter

✔ **Harnessing the power of focus**

✔ **Getting traffic and an audience**

✔ **Becoming an expert**

✔ **Networking and growing your online presence**

Starting a niche blog and staying inspired and focused on a single topic can be challenging. It's easy to get bored or sidetracked as time goes by. Naturally, your blogging voice and content will evolve over time, but the heart of your blog, your niche, should always remain the cornerstone of your content. That's what readers will grow to rely on. As long as you stay true to your core niche, your readers will be likely to follow you on your journey as a blogger.

Always remember that to be a successful blogger, your relationship with your readers is a vital part of your blogging experience. Keep them happy by providing the kind of content they expect and enjoy from you. If you fail to meet their expectations, they might just look elsewhere for a blogger who does.

This chapter helps you find your focus as a niche blogger, grow your niche blog audience, and establish yourself and your blog as the go-to place online for information and commentary about your niche topic. You find out how to leverage relationships with other bloggers and your own readers to catapult your niche blog to success. Read on and get ready to be a niche blogger!

Finding Your Focus and Keeping It

All bloggers wake up on some days and feel less motivated than they do on other days. You can find out how to get over blogger's block in Chapter 2 of Book I, but the challenge of staying focused and inspired can be even more challenging for niche bloggers. It's an inevitable part of writing about the same subject day in and day out. Because niche bloggers write about highly specific topics, there might appear to be less room for creativity in your writing. Some bloggers erroneously think that niche blogging is too confining or limiting, but that assumption couldn't be further from the truth.

Niche bloggers zero in on the specific subtopic of a broader subject, but that doesn't mean they need to become prisoners of their self-selected niches. Don't believe me? Take a trip around the blogosphere and start reading niche blogs on a wide variety of targeted subjects. Analyze what those bloggers are writing about and determine how you can creatively use similar ideas to enhance your own niche blog content.

One way to get creative while remaining focused on your niche is to categorize the types of information you want to share on your blog related to your niche. Blogging lends itself well to categorization through the categories and labels functions built into common blogging applications such as WordPress, Blogger, and TypePad.

For example, ReelSEO (`www.reelseo.com`), shown in Figure 2-1, is a blog dedicated to online video marketing news, tips, and trends. The niche is a subtopic of a broader subject — online marketing. Rather than trying to cover all aspects of online marketing, the ReelSEO blog focuses on a growing trend in online marketing — video opportunities. The blog is very successful as one of the few blogs dedicated to this very specific topic that's growing in popularity. As you read the posts on ReelSEO, the passion of the bloggers for their subject matter shines through.

Figure 2-1: ReelSEO focuses on the specific niche of online video marketing.

Looking at the Topics tab in the right sidebar of the ReelSEO blog reveals a *tag cloud* (a grouping of keywords used to identify posts by topic), shown in Figure 2-2, which provides a deeper look into the content on the ReelSEO blog. At the time of this writing, popular tags include *advertising, Google, research, SEO,* and *YouTube,* representing five subtopics within the blog's niche. The lesson is this: Instead of trying to think of broad topics to fit your niche blog, think of smaller topics and write posts about those smaller topics. For the online video marketing niche, ReelSEO does this by writing posts that focus on advertising, Google, research, SEO, YouTube, and more.

Figure 2-2:
The
ReelSEO tag
cloud.

**Book II
Chapter 2**

Benefiting from
a Niche Blog
Approach

Staying focused on your niche doesn't have to be a challenge if you break your niche into the smallest areas of concentration possible and then make sure you're delivering content related to each of those areas.

Generating Traffic and Capturing an Audience

Bloggers who have aspirations to be successful are usually overly concerned with traffic early in the lives of their blogs. To build *real* traffic to your blog (meaning, traffic that lands on your blog for the right reasons and turns into loyal readers), you need to be prepared to invest time and remain patient. However, you can take steps to speed up the process of building an audience for your blog.

Search engine optimization

Niche blogs offer negatives and positives when it comes to search engine optimization:

✦ **The bad news:** It's difficult for niche bloggers to compete for high search rankings for common, broad search terms (although not impossible). The problem is that broad search terms are very competitive. A small, beginner blogger has a hard time fighting for high search rankings for common keywords when so many strong, established Web sites and blogs are fighting for the exact same thing.

✦ **The good news:** Niche blogs can rank very high for very specific search terms. Such traffic is said to come from *long-tail* search engine optimization benefits, and many bloggers work diligently to capitalize on that long-tail traffic by optimizing their posts with very specific keyword phrases in mind.

Think of it this way: If you can't compete for a search term like *Hawaii,* you might be able to compete on more even footing for a specific search string such as *restaurants in Kaanapali Hawaii.* And there would be your niche! Instead of writing a blog and posts about Hawaii in general (a topic that's covered over and over across the Web and blogosphere), why not corner the market on the topic of dining in one of the most popular tourist cities on the island of Maui? Suddenly, your competition for that specific phrase is much smaller than it would be for the broader term, and that's how long-tail search engine optimization (that is, optimizing your site for very specific keywords that attract a highly targeted audience) can benefit a niche blog's traffic growth exponentially.

Link benefits

As you publish more and more posts on your blog, your archive of content will grow; and as you spend more time networking with other bloggers, leaving comments on other blogs, and optimizing your blog posts for keyword phrases, your blog traffic will grow. More traffic means more people reading your content who might like it enough to mention it on their own blogs where they can link to it and drive more traffic to it. Alternatively, people who read your blog might share links to posts they enjoy through their social networking profiles, such as LinkedIn, or via microblogging (publishing short posts, typically of 140-characters or less) through such sites as Twitter.

Each link to one of your blog posts could mean more traffic to your blog.

Furthermore, with each new link to your blog, your blog's Google search rankings could get a boost. Google takes incoming links to your blog seriously within its page ranking algorithm, so when your blog attracts a lot of incoming links (particularly from popular Web sites and blogs), your blog's

Google page rank goes up. A higher Google page rank can deliver benefits in terms of higher search rankings and more traffic to your blog as well as higher rates advertisers are willing to pay for space on your blog.

Not all incoming links are equal. Search engines, such as Google, weigh incoming links from popular sites high, but links from spam sites and links that are paid for can actually get your blog removed from Google search rankings entirely. Organic, real growth is far more valuable to your blog's success than quick, manufactured growth.

Organic growth

Organic growth is a long-term blog-traffic-growth strategy that happens naturally as your blog content gets more expansive and your efforts at engaging in conversations across the blogosphere boost your online exposure. The key to achieving organic growth is to continually publish great content, particularly content that no one else is writing about. Use your unique voice and become a vocal, contributing member of the blogosphere by networking and building relationships with other bloggers and blog readers. In time, your blog traffic will grow slowly but steadily as a result of your efforts. You can find out more about the methods of increasing organic growth through the section "Networking with Other People in Your Niche," at the end of this chapter.

**Book II
Chapter 2**

Benefiting from
a Niche Blog
Approach

Establishing Yourself as an Expert

As a niche blogger, you have the opportunity to become recognized as an authority on your subject matter. This is particularly true if you have credentials such as an education or work experience related to your niche blog topic. However, a passion for and deep knowledge of your subject could be enough to establish you as an expert. That level of expertise depends on the content you publish on your blog as well as the tone in which you write it. Even a blog that's based completely on opinion could become an online go-to place for information on a specific subject. Again, it depends on your writing style and the type of information or opinion you publish on your blog.

Consider these two blogs: a blog about California state politics written by a person who works for a member of the state government versus a blog about California state politics written by an unhappy citizen who publishes little more than personal rants and complaints. Which blogger is likely to become known in the online community as an expert in his particular niche and become the go-to person for information related to California state politics? Of course, the answer is the former example — the blogger who works within the California state political scene every day. Alternatively, the opinion blogger *could* become considered an expert if his blog was written in a more inviting tone, rather than rants and complaints. A personal opinion blogger can be recognized as an expert but the tone needs to match that of an expert rather than a complainer. Similarly, satirical and humorous blogs that are fully intended to take a specific ranting tone can be popular, but again, it's important to match your content to your audience's expectations.

The bottom line is that blogging provides a unique opportunity for people to become recognized as knowledgeable within their fields of expertise or interest. However, not every blogger earns the reputation of being an expert people can rely on for great information. If you want to become known as an expert in your niche blog topic, your content needs to match that intent.

Gaining Online Exposure

You can boost your online exposure and drive traffic to your blog in many ways. Networking and building relationships are discussed in the next section, but you can also pursue other online tactics to boost your online exposure. Take a look at the following list to get some ideas:

✦ **Write articles.** Many Web sites (such as Associated Content, EZineArticles, Squidoo, HubPages, and more) offer repositories of articles and content written by people from all walks of life. Some sites even offer a form of payment for the content you contribute, and all offer ways for you to link that content back to your blog for added exposure and traffic.

Be sure to read the terms and conditions of article sites to ensure the copyright and payment terms match your current and future goals.

✦ **Create videos.** Video is growing in popularity and offers a great way to boost traffic to your blog through the use of another medium. Create videos and upload them to popular video sites such as YouTube, Viddler, Vimeo, TubeMogul, Dailymotion, and more.

✦ **Create podcasts.** Audio is another medium that people enjoy online, and it provides another way to drive traffic to your blog. You can start an online radio show on a site, such as Blog Talk Radio (www.blog talkradio.com), or create podcasts, which you can publish on your blog as well as on audio sites such as Blubrry or iTunes (www.blubrry. com and www.apple.com/itunes).

✦ **Share presentations.** SlideShare (www.slideshare.net), shown in Figure 2-3, offers a great way for people to upload and share presentations — a perfect way to further establish yourself as an expert and provide links to your blog.

✦ **Share pictures.** If you write a niche blog that lends itself to visuals, upload them to picture sharing sites such as Picasa (http://picasa. google.com) or Flickr (www.flickr.com) with links back to your blog.

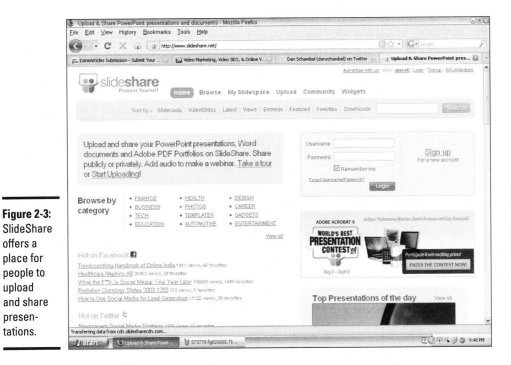

Figure 2-3: SlideShare offers a place for people to upload and share presentations.

The opportunities for increasing your online exposure and driving traffic to your blog are virtually limitless. Don't be afraid to get creative, test new tactics, and find the right mix for you and your blog.

Networking with Other People in Your Niche

Perhaps the best way to increase niche blog traffic and attract loyal readers is networking both on and off your blog. You can use both formal and informal methods to network and build relationships with people online in order to grow your blog. Take a look at some of the following suggestions to get started on your journey to boost your blog's readership:

✦ **Respond to comments on your blog.** Take the time to respond to all comments left on your blog. Doing so shows your readers that you value their opinions and provides the opportunity to get to know them better and build relationships with them.

   Relationships lead to loyalty, and loyalty leads to increased blog readership over time.

✦ **Leave comments on other blogs in your niche.** Visit other blogs in your niche and take the time to leave useful comments on posts you enjoy. Ask questions and follow up to keep the conversation going. Be sure to include your blog's URL in the appropriate field of the blog comment form to drive traffic back to your blog. The blogger will get to know you, and a relationship will develop naturally. Once you're on other blogger's radar screens, they're more likely to follow your blog, leave comments on your posts, and link to your blog, thereby driving traffic to it.

✦ **Connect with people on social networking sites.** Take the time to find and connect with people who write and work in your niche on Facebook, LinkedIn, and other social networking sites. Then share content with them and build relationships with them, and as a result, your blog traffic might just grow organically over time.

✦ **Get on Twitter and be active.** Start a Twitter account and update your Twitter profile with useful tweets, sharing links to your best content when it's appropriate. Follow other bloggers and people in your niche and start conversations with them. Twitter is a phenomenal tool for building relationships with people around the world who are interested in the same niche as you. Branding expert Dan Schawbel of the Personal Branding Blog (`www.personalbrandingblog.com`) provides a great example of someone who uses Twitter effectively for building relationships and sharing useful information, which translates into increased blog traffic. Check out Dan's Twitter profile page (`http://twitter.com/danschawbel`) in Figure 2-4.

Figure 2-4:
Dan Schawbel's Twitter profile stream includes useful information and links related to his niche of expertise, including links to his own blog.

✦ **Use social bookmarking sites.** Start accounts on popular social book-marking sites such as Digg (`http://digg.com`), StumbleUpon (`www.stumbleupon.com`), and Reddit (`www.reddit.com`). Share content from your blog and other sites that you enjoy and follow links other users share to content related to your niche. Leave comments and start conversations with people in your niche, and they just might start shar-ing your content, too!

✦ **Write guest posts for other blogs in your niche.** Reach out to other bloggers who write about your niche or write about broader subjects related to your niche and offer to write guest posts for them. Busy blog-gers are likely to welcome a guest post from you, and it's a great way to not only build relationships with those bloggers but also get your name in front of their established audiences. (Be sure to include a link to your blog in your guest post.)

✦ **Send e-mails to other bloggers in your niche.** Find other blogs about your niche or about a broader subject related to your niche and reach out directly via e-mail to the bloggers who write them.

✦ **Attend blogging conferences or events related to your niche.** You'd be amazed at the number of people you can meet and the networking you can do at conferences and events related to blogging or your niche topic. For example, the annual Blog World Expo conference (shown in Figure 2-5) is one of the biggest events for bloggers where you can learn, network, socialize, and have some fun with other bloggers from around the world.

✦ **Join forums and groups related to your niche and get involved.** Because so many online forums and groups are available online, one is bound to be related to your blog's niche. Take some time to find them and then join and start posting comments, questions, and answers to other members' questions. Forums are a great way to build relationships with other people who are interested in your niche topic and to lead them to your blog for more information and conversation.

You can find out much more about growing your blog in Book VI, but do take the time now to consider how you can follow some of the suggestions provided in this chapter to find people who are likely to be interested in your specific niche blog topic. Then start engaging them where they already spend time online. Lead them to your blog with *useful* links, but don't over-promote. You don't want to be viewed as someone who is only looking for traffic to your blog. The key to blogging success is marrying great content with strong relationships. The combination is unstoppable.

Chapter 3: Choosing Your Niche

In This Chapter

✔ Setting your niche blogging goals

✔ Finding niches that work for you

✔ Reading niche blogs

✔ Analyzing audience potential for niche blogs

✔ Checking out ways to make a niche blog pay

Choosing your niche can be a challenge. When there are so many subjects that you can write a blog about, how do you know which is the right subject for you? How do you narrow that subject down into a niche you can write passionately about? And how can you determine which niche will help you meet your blogging goals for exposure, traffic, and monetization?

Fear not! This chapter gives you the information and tools you need to confidently select a niche topic for your blog.

The biggest mistake you can make as a blogger is choosing a topic that you have no business writing about. Doing so offers far more chances for failure than success. Remember, blogging success comes from a combination of the fantastic content you publish on your blog coupled with your unique voice and perspective on your blog's subject. If you don't know enough about a subject to write well and often about it and you don't feel strongly enough about it to write with passion, you need to select a different niche topic.

Determining Your Niche Blogging Goals

Choosing your blog's niche topic is dependent on your goals for your blog. Naturally, if you're writing your blog for pleasure, with no aspirations to become a successful blogger or to make money from your blog, you can choose any niche that interests you. It doesn't matter how much time you dedicate to writing your blog or the tone you use, if you're writing it only for yourself or perhaps for the enjoyment of your friends and family.

However, if you have objectives for your blog that include growing your readership, becoming recognized within the larger audience of your blog's topic, or making money, the niche topic you choose is absolutely essential to increasing your chances of attaining those objectives. The remainder of this section teaches you about five of the most common objectives niche bloggers strive to achieve to help get you started in creating your own goals for your niche blog.

Don't choose your blog's niche topic until you determine your short- and long-term goals for your blog. Those goals could greatly affect the niche topic that you ultimately write about on your blog. You can find out more about setting blogging goals in Chapter 2 of Book I.

Building your expertise

Many people start blogging because they view it as a low-cost way to build their online platforms and establish themselves as experts across a wide audience they can't otherwise reach. The blogosphere attracts readers from around the world and from all walks of life. If you want to establish a reputation as an expert in some area, you can do so through blogging. This is particularly true of niche bloggers who focus their content on specific topics and become the go-to sources on their areas of expertise for other bloggers and Web site owners. Over time, bloggers who earn reputations as experts often find themselves called upon for national news media coverage, book writing, and more.

As you might expect, your success in establishing yourself as an expert in a specific area comes from the content you write on your blog. In a crowded blogosphere, the bloggers who focus on niche areas can fill the gaps left by the jack-of-all-trade bloggers and corner the market on their topics.

For example, rather than writing a blog all about blogging, Lorelle VanFossen knew her area of expertise was in the WordPress blogging application, and she created a niche blog where she continues to write with knowledge and passion for her subject. Her blog, Lorelle on WordPress (http://lorelle. wordpress.com), is shown in Figure 3-1.

Today, Lorelle is known across the Web as one of the key people for information, tips, and education about using WordPress. She has written books on the subject and contributes to other high-profile blogs about blogging in general. What started as a niche blog has not only established Lorelle as an expert in her field but also opened new doors of opportunity to her.

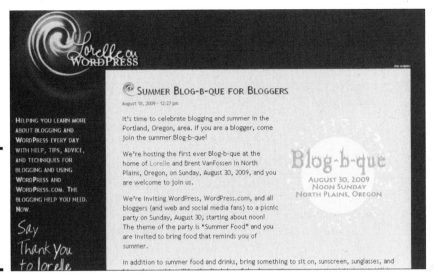

Figure 3-1:
Lorelle
VanFossen
writes
a niche
blog about
WordPress.

Of course, you can't expect to start a blog on any specific subject and become known as the expert in the subject matter automatically. A niche blogger can attract and retain readers only if he writes about a topic he has both experience in and knowledge of. Readers can see through a blog written by a person who lacks knowledge or experience. In simplest terms, don't just repurpose content that can be found elsewhere online or offline. The mark of a successful niche blogger is a thorough understanding of his subject matter based on first-hand experience, which enables him to speak intelligently and authoritatively.

Think of it this way: If you need to find information about raising an autistic child, would you feel more comfortable visiting a blog of a doctor who is raising an autistic child herself or a blog written by someone who is interested in the subject but has never experienced it firsthand or studied it? Certainly, the former blogger would provide more authoritative content and could more easily establish herself as an expert in her blog's niche topic than the latter blogger.

The same principle holds true for your own niche blog. When you contemplate niche topics, consider why you should be *the* person writing a blog on that subject. Determine what makes your blog stand out from others on the same or similar subjects. Decide what unique content or perspectives you have that can attract readers and make them want to build relationships with you and turn into members of your loyal blog community. As such, your standing as an expert in your blog's niche topic will grow organically.

Sharing your passion

The best niche blogs are written by people who are passionate about the subjects they write about. That passion shines through their writing and grabs the attention of readers. A dull blog doesn't attract or retain readers any better than a dull book does. If readers have a hard time getting through a single post without being bored, your blog has little chance for success.

Niche blogs are different from broader topic blogs because the authors behind them typically have made conscious decisions to focus on a topic they love. Think of it this way — when you watch a movie, would you prefer to watch an actor who seems bored with his role and has little emotion or enthusiasm or would you prefer to watch an actor who is passionate about his role and provides a captivating performance? The same principle holds true for bloggers, particularly niche bloggers. Don't let your words die a quick death on the computer screen because they're torturously boring. Instead, let your passion for your niche subject shine through, and readers will get caught up in your enthusiasm, too.

As an example, one of my favorite blogs about branding (`www.perezfox. com`, shown in Figure 3-2) is written by a young twenty-something blogger, Prescott Perez-Fox, whose experience is varied despite his young age. He provides a keen insight into his subject matter that extends beyond his years. His passion for his subject shines through his blog posts, and he always offers a unique perspective. Is he the head of the top branding company in the world? No, but his passion for his subject and his adequate experience and knowledge make his blog stand out from the crowd of blogs about branding.

Figure 3-2:
Prescott
Perez-Fox's
blog about
branding is
insightful
and unique.

In other words, if you're very passionate about a topic, that could be the perfect subject for your niche blog! At the very least, that topic offers a great place for you to start your quest to select a niche blog topic.

Offering your opinion and sharing your knowledge

If you're educated or experienced in a specific subject, or even if you just hold strong opinions about that subject, it could be a good choice for your niche blog topic. Niche bloggers who are very knowledgeable in their subject matter provide authoritative content and can easily become recognized across the blogosphere as experts. Alternatively, people with strong opinions on a specific subject can gain reputations as pundits, as long as their opinions are expressed as authoritative commentary rather than mere complaints or rants.

Readers look for blogs written by people with both experience and knowledge as well as by people who simply have strong opinions. Both types of bloggers can find audiences across the blogosphere. The trick is to understand which type of blogger you are (or want to be), choose a topic that matches your level of experience or opinion, and then stick to it.

For example, many bloggers write about topics related to their line of work. I write a number of blogs about business, marketing, and branding, which are my areas of expertise and where I have a deep level of experience. Alternatively, I could write a blog about a subject I don't have vast experience or knowledge in but have strong opinions about. I don't have time to write another blog, but I could if I wanted to, because the blogosphere is open to anyone with thoughts and ideas to share regardless of their skills, education, or experiences.

Crafting a Green World (`http://craftingagreenworld.com`), shown in Figure 3-3, is an example of a blog that mixes expertise with opinion. The blog is dedicated to sharing ideas for craft projects that use recycled materials. The bloggers that write for Crafting a Green World share both their experience in testing crafts and their opinions related to environmentally friendly crafts and craft-related products.

In fact, many hobby bloggers write niche blogs based on their love of a particular activity. They may not be experts in that activity, and they may not have even been participating in that activity for very long. However, they feel passionately about it and want to share their opinions and thoughts about it with a wider audience. Strong opinions for a specific subject can translate into a successful niche blog just as easily as vast experience or knowledge can.

Figure 3-3:
Crafting a Green World focuses on a very specific niche topic.

What do you love? That could be your blog's niche topic!

Networking and building relationships

Many bloggers start their blogs to find other people with similar interests for personal or professional networking. The blogosphere provides a place for you to interact with people from across the globe and forge relationships with them that can be helpful in terms of sharing ideas and learning from each other as well as boosting your online exposure and driving traffic to your blog.

Networking and building relationships start with writing great content on your own blog that invites comments and discussion. By responding to comments left on your blog *and* leaving comments on other blogs about your niche, you can start to create your own network of online relationships. Many bloggers find great success thanks to the community that forms around their blogs as well as the relationships that they make with people across the social Web on other blogs, social networking sites, forums, and more. For example, the many online forums and groups are dedicated to more topics than you could possibly imagine. From Harley Davidson owners to work-at-home moms (see Figure 3-4 for a popular work-at-home mom's forum at `www.wahm.com/forum`) and everything in between, there's probably a forum or group for it.

Breaking into blogging cliques

I've often heard the blogosphere be compared to high school in that it's a large group of people divided into cliques based on interests, experience, knowledge, and so on. That's true to an extent. However, I'd like to think that the cliques of the blogosphere have looser entry requirements than high school cliques do. In other words, any blogger with a strong voice who has something valuable to contribute to the online conversation is invited to the party.

Figure 3-4: WAHM.com is a popular forum for work-at-home moms.

Basically, you should fully leverage every opportunity you have to interact with your peers and audience. There is perhaps no other medium that allows *anyone* to become a vocal, contributing member as easily as blogging. Use it to your advantage and build strong relationships that boost your online exposure *and* create loyal readers of your own blog.

Growing your niche blog is easier if you already have relationships and networking contacts related to that niche topic that you can tap into to build an early audience and start conversations on your blog.

A true story of matching ads to expectations

At one point in my blogging career, I wrote for a blogging network that handled selling ad space for my blog. During the 2008 U.S. Presidential election, strong political ads started appearing on my blog. My blog was not even remotely related to politics, and I actually made an effort to steer clear of politics on this particular blog, not wanting to invite off-topic and often heated discussions. Therefore, when the strong political ads began displaying on my blog, I realized they ran counter to the user experience I had created on my blog and might not be well received by my audience. Fortunately, the blogging network was willing to remove them from my blog in order to ensure my blog continued to meet reader expectations. Long story short, irrelevant ads can confuse and even anger your readers who have specific expectations for your blog's content. Don't let irrelevant ads destroy the work you've already done to build your blog. Instead, focus your money-making efforts on relevant opportunities.

Making money

The number of people who start blogs with high aspirations of making lots of money grows every day. Unfortunately, making money from your blog can be challenging and often takes a lot of time and patience. However, you can speed up the process, or at least increase your chances of success, by choosing a niche topic that's easier to monetize. You can find out more about choosing a niche to make money later in this chapter. For now, it's important to understand that it's very possible to make money from a niche blog.

When you choose your niche topic, you need to be sure there are money-making opportunities available that are at least somewhat related to your blog's subject matter. Irrelevant ads are unlikely to be useful to your audience, and that means fewer clicks and possibly less traffic. (People don't like blogs that are cluttered with useless ads.) Fewer clicks and less traffic equate to fewer advertisers interested in purchasing ad space on your blog. Less competition for ad space coupled with low traffic volumes reduces the income you can expect to collect for the ad space on your blog.

Bottom line, if you want to make money from your blog, you need to choose a niche that has a built in audience, but you also need to be certain relevant advertising programs and opportunities are available for your niche. If making money is important to you, be sure to read Book VII for all the details about monetizing your blog that you need to get started on the right path to success.

Identifying Niches That Might Work for You

The best way to choose your blog's niche topic is to start broad and slowly narrow your topic down until you end up with a list of possibilities. The following steps can help you get your thought process flowing:

1. **Think of a broad topic that you're passionate and knowledgeable about.**

   Here's an example: After much thought, you determine that you're both passionate about and knowledgeable about writing, but a lot of blogs and Web sites are dedicated to the broad topic of writing already.

2. **Narrow down the broader topic into smaller categories.**

   You can divide writing into categories such as book writing, article writing, copywriting, freelance writing, writing for pleasure, fiction writing, nonfiction writing, screenplay writing, and much more.

3. **Choose a few of those categories that you're interested in and break them into even smaller segments.**

   Using the category of fiction writing, you can break it down by genre or audience as fantasy writing, memoir writing, children's writing, young adult writing, and many more.

4. **Select some of those subcategories and break them down even further.**

   For example, the young adult writing segment could be broken down into writing how-to's, reviews, specific genres, and more.

5. **When you have your categories broken down to small enough segments, choose the ones that interest you the most and which you think you can write about passionately, intelligently, and frequently for a long time to come.**

   You might choose a niche category for your blog, such as young adult fiction, and focus your content on the strategies, trends, success stories, reviews, how-to's, and so on as they all relate to writing young adult fiction.

Keep in mind that you want a subtopic that's broad enough to attract an audience of more than a handful of people. You also want a subtopic that fills a gap in the online world or allows you to add your unique perspective to differentiate it from everything else that's already out there.

**Book II
Chapter 3**

Choosing Your
Niche

After you select a blog topic niche, take some time to write out a list of blog post ideas. Find other blogs, Web sites, or forums related to your niche topic and determine whether there's an existing audience of readers interested in the topic and peers that you can build relationships with. You can find out more about determining the audience potential for your niche blog topic at the end of this chapter. In the following section, you do some preliminary research to make sure you have enough to say about the niche topic you choose and get a general idea of what else is going on across the Web as it relates to your niche topic.

Researching Existing Niche Blogs

There are two primary reasons for researching existing niche blogs as part of your process to choose your own niche topic:

✦ You can learn from other niche blogs. Even if they're written about a topic unrelated to anything you're familiar with, you can still learn from them in terms of content, conversation, and community.

✦ You can research both the potential audience and existing competition when you seek out and read other blogs related to your niche topic.

The following sections cover great sources for doing your research.

Technorati search

Technorati is one of the oldest and most recognized blog search sites. Although the search results found in Technorati are never perfect, you can get started there. Complete instructions for finding blogs via Technorati are in Chapter 1 of Book I.

Google blog search

Google offers a blog search tool that's somewhat useful in finding niche blogs. It's imperfect at best, but it can point you in the direction of content related to your niche blog topic. You can get complete instructions for finding blogs through Google's blog search tool in Chapter 1 of Book I.

Google Alerts

Google offers a great tool called Google Alerts that provides a way for you to keep track of what's being published online related to your niche blog topic. When you set up a Google Alert for a specific search term, you receive an e-mail notifying you (at the times you choose) when new content is published online with that search term. To set up your own Google Alert, follow these steps:

1. **Visit Google Alerts at www.google.com/alerts.**

The Google Alerts page, shown in Figure 3-5, opens.

2. **Enter your search term in the Search Terms text box.**

This step tells Google Alerts that you want to be notified anytime a blog or Web site uses that search term.

3. **From the Type drop-down list, select the Comprehensive option.**

This step configures your alert to notify you of all results from multiple sources (news, Web, blogs, video, and Google groups) rather than just specific types of results.

4. **Using the How Often drop-down list, specify how often you want to receive updates.**

You can choose to receive updates as they happen, once per day, or once per week.

5. **Enter your e-mail address in the Your Email field.**

The e-mail address you enter in this box is where your Google alerts are sent.

Google Alerts are helpful but not perfectly accurate. It is very possible that not all mentions of your search term online will be delivered to you via Google Alerts. In other words, it's a useful tool, but not an exact science.

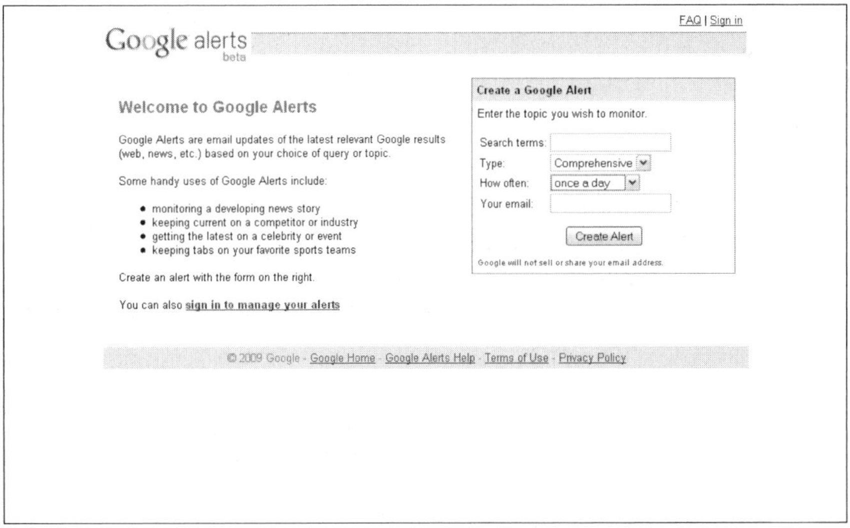

**Book II
Chapter 3**

Choosing Your Niche

![Google Alerts page screenshot]

FAQ | Sign in

Google alerts
beta

Welcome to Google Alerts

Google Alerts are email updates of the latest relevant Google results (web, news, etc.) based on your choice of query or topic.

Some handy uses of Google Alerts include:

- monitoring a developing news story
- keeping current on a competitor or industry
- getting the latest on a celebrity or event
- keeping tabs on your favorite sports teams

Create an alert with the form on the right.

You can also **sign in to manage your alerts**

Create a Google Alert

Enter the topic you wish to monitor.

Search terms:
Type: Comprehensive
How often: once a day
Your email:

Create Alert

Google will not sell or share your email address.

© 2009 Google - Google Home - Google Alerts Help - Terms of Use - Privacy Policy

Figure 3-5:
The Google
Alerts page.

Twitter searches

Twitter is a microblogging site that allows users to publish short, 140-character-or-less snippets, which appear in a reverse chronological stream on their Twitter profiles and within the Twitter streams of other users who sign up to *follow* a user's updates. I discuss microblogging and Twitter in great detail in Book VIII. Right now, follow these steps to search Twitter to find mentions of search terms related to your niche blog topic:

1. **Visit Twitter at www.twitter.com.**

   The Twitter home page opens, as shown in Figure 3-6.

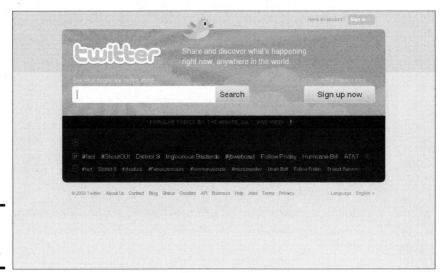

Figure 3-6:
The Twitter
home page.

2. **Enter your search term in the Search text box.**

   This step tells Twitter the specific word(s) you want to find within current Twitter users' posts.

3. **Click the Search button.**

   A new page opens showing a list of Twitter posts that include your search term.

The Twitter search feature is not reliable because it's not as thorough in terms of delivering *all* related results, but it does provide a place for you to start your research into what is being said about your niche blog topic. Also, the Twitter search function returns updates only from the previous few weeks.

Determining the Audience Potential for a Niche Blog

A niche blog's success depends on the potential audience size for that niche. For example, no matter how much a person might love the topic of teaching parrots to do tricks, only so many people in the world are also interested in that topic. Therein lies the struggle for a blogger who wants to be successful or make money from her blog.

With that in mind, you need to determine the audience potential for your niche blog topic. Of course, if your only goals are to blog for fun with no plans to build your online exposure or make money, it won't matter to you how many other people are interested in your niche blog topic. However, the vast majority of bloggers *do* want to build an audience of readers, establish themselves as experts, or make money from their blogs. If you're one of those bloggers, you need to do some research before you make your final niche topic choice.

You can start your research by finding and spending time on other blogs that are either broadly or specifically related to your potential niche blog topics, as discussed earlier in this chapter. This is how you'll get a good idea of what people are interested in and talking about, and you'll have a chance to find any gaps or unique angles on the topic that you can bring to your own blog. Next, you need to do some keyword and monetization research. These steps help you identify the potential traffic your blog could draw over time and the potential ad dollars you can earn.

Nothing is guaranteed with blogging. The research you do now only tells you the *potential* for your niche blog; it doesn't guarantee success. Instead, success comes from your hard work, dedication, and passion for blogging.

Performing keyword searches

The first thing you need to do after you narrow down your topic selections is to do some keyword research to find out what people in the broader audience related to your topic are actually searching for. This step is critical to determine whether the niche you want to write about is something that people are actually looking for through search engines. The reality of blogging is that a lot of your blog's traffic comes from search engine keyword searches. If you have goals to draw a lot of visitors to your blog, you need to be sure that not only are people looking for keywords related to your niche, but also that your content is optimized for those keywords.

Most of your blog's traffic will come from Google searches, particularly in the early life of your blog.

Google AdWords, Wordtracker, and Keyword Discovery

The first place to go for keyword search analysis is the free Google AdWords tool. If you're really serious about your blog's success, you might want to consider paying for an account with a more thorough keyword analysis tool such as Wordtracker or Keyword Discovery. I discuss each of these tools in depth in Chapter 1 of Book V and also give step-by-step instructions for performing keyword search analysis.

Google search

Another option is to conduct a traditional search on Google using keywords you would use if you were looking for the type of content you plan to publish on your blog. Think like a reader would and use the keywords she would be likely to use. After you conduct your keyword search, scroll to the bottom of the first page of search results provided by Google (as shown in Figure 3-7) and notice the list of keyword phrases to the right of Searches Related To. That's a list of other popular search terms that Google identifies as being similar to your search term, and they can give you great ideas of the ways people are searching for the type of content you provide on your blog!

Google Trends

Google Trends (`www.google.com/trends/hottrends`) is a tool provided for free by Google that shows a list of the most popular search terms on Google at any given time. If your niche blog topic is particularly timely, Google Trends just might be a good place to get an idea of exactly how people are searching for your topic right now. For example, Figure 3-8 shows the top search terms according to Google Trends at the moment I'm writing this chapter.

Figure 3-7:
Additional keyword suggestions from a Google search.

Book II
Chapter 3

Choosing Your
Niche

Figure 3-8:
Google
Trends
provides
a glimpse
into popular
keyword
searches at
any given
moment.

Understanding Monetization Opportunities for Niche Blogs

If you want to make money from your niche blog, you need to be sure monetization opportunities are available to you before you even start publishing content. Fortunately, Google AdWords Traffic Estimator and Google AdWords Keyword Tool both can help you get a basic idea of the earning potential your niche blog topic presents through pay-per-click advertising programs such as Google AdSense. (I discuss AdSense in depth in Chapter 2 of Book VII.)

Using the Google AdWords Traffic Estimator

Google AdWords is a tool that advertisers use to bid on keywords and place ads on Web sites and blogs that publish content related to those keywords. This is a form of contextual advertising that many bloggers use because it's easy to implement on a blog through programs such as Google AdSense (the publisher side of Google's AdWords program). Using the Google AdWords Traffic Estimator tool, you can enter keywords related to the niches you're considering starting a blog about to get a general idea of how popular they are based on the amounts advertisers are willing to pay for those keywords.

Typically, keywords that are more popular sell for higher amounts. Although you get paid more when visitors to your blog click those ads, there is a lot more competition for those ads and the audience that is likely to click them; you might actually end up making *less* money by focusing on keywords and niche topics that drive high cost-per-click prices through ad programs such as Google AdWords.

Follow these steps to research potential niche blog topic keyword phrases using the Google AdWords Traffic Estimator tool:

1. **Visit the Google AdWords Traffic Estimator at `https://adwords.google.com/select/TrafficEstimatorSandbox`.**

   This step opens the Google AdWords Traffic Estimator page, as shown in Figure 3-9.

2. **Enter the keywords or keyword phrases you want to search for in the Enter Keywords text box.**

   To search for multiple keyword phrases, so you can compare results, enter each phrase on a new line in the Enter Keywords text box.

3. **Skip to number 4, Select Targeting, and select the language you want your search to use from the list box.**

   You can customize your search, but to get an idea of the popularity of keywords that advertisers are bidding on, leave this search option as general as possible unless your niche blog topic is tied to a specific geographic area.

4. **Select the area you want to search from the list in the Available Countries and Territories list box.**

   You can refine your search or keep it more general to get the best overview of the popularity of your chosen keywords.

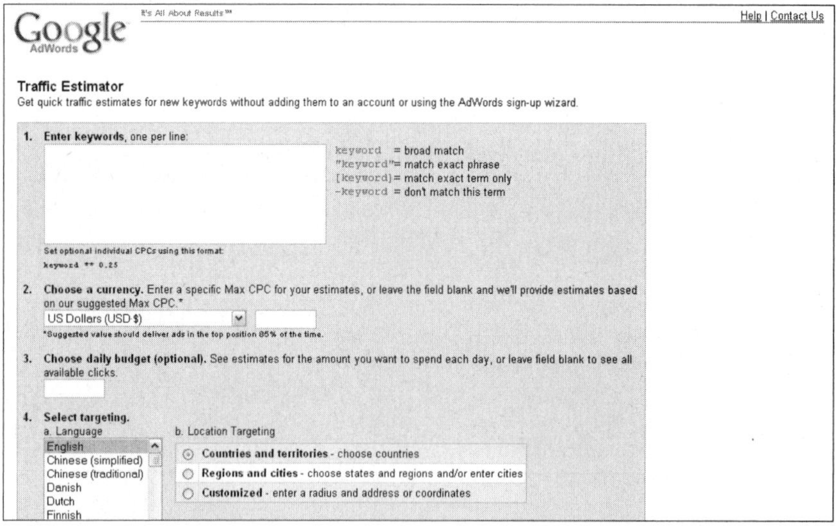

Figure 3-9:
The Google
AdWords
Traffic
Estimator.

5. **Click the Continue button.**

   A new page opens, showing your results.

6. **Take a close look at the Search Volume and Estimated CPC columns, as shown in Figure 3-10.**

   The Search Volume column gives you a comparison of the popularity of a search term versus others in your search list, and the Estimated CPC column (CPC stands for cost-per-click) tells you the amount advertisers are typically paying for clicks on ads served for those keywords.

Focusing on keywords and phrases for your blog that have estimated CPCs greater than $3 (which means they are very competitive) might not deliver the volume of clicks that you need to make money. A better strategy is to choose a niche based on keywords with estimated CPCs between $1 and $2. Stay away from keyword phrases with CPCs that are extremely low. You'd need massive amounts of traffic to make your blog profitable, which is hard to do with a niche blog — at least it's hard to do it quickly.

Using the young adult writing example from earlier in this chapter, the results of the keyword search shown in Figure 3-9 tell you that the estimated CPC rates for those keywords are not as high as you might like. However, all hope is not lost. Read the next section to find out how you can get more ideas to breathe new life into your niche blog topic idea or determine whether you need to find a new niche entirely.

**Book II
Chapter 3**

Choosing Your Niche

Figure 3-10:
The results of a keyword search using Google AdWords Traffic Estimator.

Notes about these estimates for your keywords and targeting:
- Estimates are based on general system-wide performance information. You'll see better estimates with an existing account that has built up a performance history. Newer accounts may still show less accurate results. Sign in to AdWords

Traffic Estimator
« Revise settings | Download as .csv
All estimates are provided as a guideline, and are based on system-wide averages; your actual costs and ad positions may vary. To view estimates based on your keywords' performance history, use the Traffic Estimator within the appropriate ad group. Learn more

Average CPC: **$0.88** (at a maximum CPC of $2.53)
Estimated clicks per day: **47 - 68** (at a daily budget of $70.00)

Estimates are based on your bid amount and geographical targeting selections. Because the Traffic Estimator does not consider your daily budget, your ad may receive fewer clicks than estimated.

Maximum CPC: [   ] Daily budget: [   ] [Get New Estimates]

Keywords ▼	Search Volume	Estimated Avg. CPC	Estimated Ad Positions	Estimated Clicks / Day	Estimated Cost / Day
books for teens		$0.52 - $0.69	1 - 3	9 - 12	$5 - $9
books for young adults		$0.49 - $0.73	1 - 3	2	$1 - $2
fiction writing		$0.74 - $1.00	1 - 3	13 - 22	$10 - $30
nonfiction writing		$0.73 - $1.01	1 - 3	1	$1 - $2
writing for children		$0.94 - $1.24	1 - 3	11 - 17	$20 - $30
writing for teens		$0.90 - $1.25	1 - 3	3 - 4	$3 - $5
writing for young adults		$0.82 - $1.07	1 - 3	0	$1
young adult books		$0.47 - $0.62	1 - 3	6 - 7	$3 - $5
young adult fiction		$0.48 - $0.61	1 - 3	1 - 2	$1 - $2
young adult novels		$0.42 - $0.53	1 - 3	1	$1
Search Network Total		**$0.71 - $0.95**	**1 - 3**	**47 - 68**	**$40 - $70**

« Revise settings [Download as .csv]

Researching with the Google AdWords Keyword Tool

The Google AdWords program offers yet another tool you can use for free to get a basic idea of the kind of traffic niche blog topic keyword phrases receive. The Google AdWords Keyword Tool allows you to find the popularity of a keyword phrase in terms of monthly volume of ad clicks and the estimated cost-per-click that advertisers are paying for those keywords. Furthermore, the tool provides a list of related keyword phrases along with their volumes and estimated cost-per-click numbers. With a simple search, you end up with a wealth of great information to help you pick a profitable niche blog topic!

Take a look at these steps to use the Google AdWords Keyword Tool:

1. **Visit the Google AdWords Keyword Tool at `https://adwords.google.com/select/KeywordToolExternal`.**

   This step opens the Google AdWords Keyword Tool page, as shown in Figure 3-11.

2. **Enter your keyword phrase in the Enter One Keyword Phrase Per Line text box.**

   You can enter multiple keyword phrases for comparison, or you can enter a single phrase if your goal is to find a variety of alternative keyword phrases for ideas.

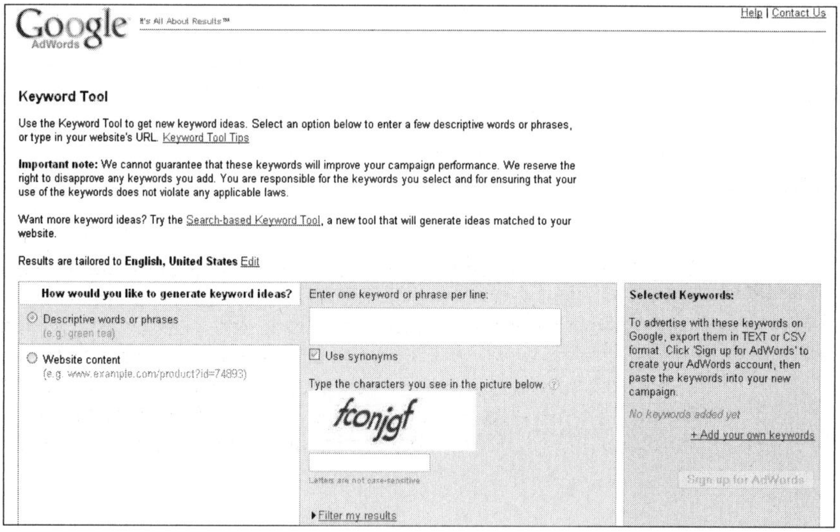

Figure 3-11:
The Google AdWords Keyword Tool.

3. **Enter the security characters in the text box provided.**

   The letters you enter in this text box are not case sensitive.

4. **Click the Get Keyword Ideas button.**

   Your results are provided on a new page, as shown in Figure 3-12.

5. **Using the Choose Columns to Display drop-down list, make sure the Estimated Avg. CPC column, Local Search Volume column, and Global Monthly Search Volume column are visible within your results.**

   These are the three primary columns you should look at when you're researching niche blog topics. You can also play around with the other columns and get a feel for the information they provide.

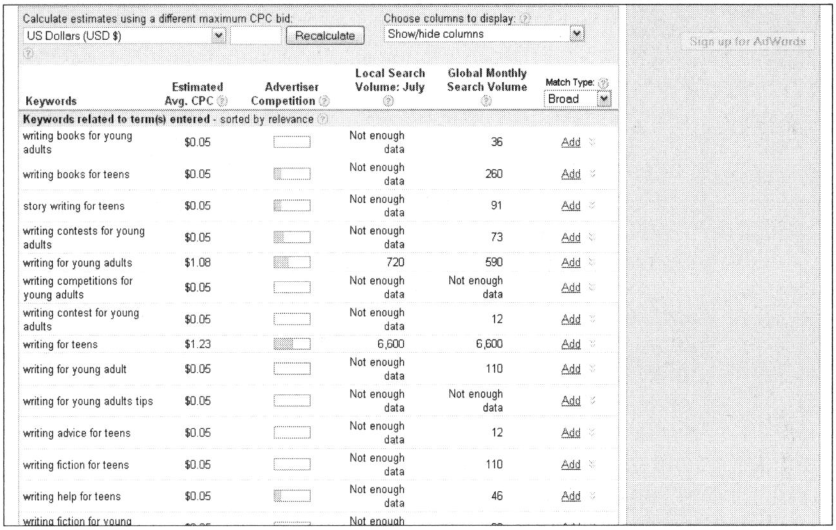

Figure 3-12: The Google AdWords Keyword Tool results page.

Using the young adult writing example from earlier in this chapter, the results of the keyword search for *writing for young adults* and *writing for teens* aren't that inspiring until you scroll down to the phrases listed under Additional Keywords to Consider, as shown in Figure 3-13. Here you find a number of keyword phrases that get a significant amount of traffic *and* have decent Estimated Average CPC rates attached to them. For example, the *books for young adults* result has local search traffic for the previous month of 27,000 and an estimated CPC of $0.71. The page also provides a *books for teens* result (not shown in Figure 3-13), which has search volume from 49,500 locally up to 60,500 globally, with Estimated Average CPC of $0.70.

Figure 3-13: Additional keyword ideas provided by the Google AdWords Keyword Tool.

Additional keywords to consider - sorted by relevance					
youth adults	$0.05		Not enough data	1,300	Add
writing literature	$1.04		49,500	49,500	Add
short stories	$0.57		550,000	1,220,000	Add
literary agent	$0.91		135,000	90,500	Add
writers market	$1.11		22,200	18,100	Add
writers	$1.02		1,830,000	1,830,000	Add
literary agents	$1.15		110,000	90,500	Add
writing fiction	$0.96		90,500	74,000	Add
writing contests	$1.31		74,000	49,500	Add
writing	$1.11		11,100,000	11,100,000	Add
book for young adults	$0.05		Not enough data	1,600	Add
nonfiction for young adults	$0.05		Not enough data	260	Add
novels for young adults	$0.62		2,400	1,600	Add
books for young adults	$0.71		27,100	18,100	Add
reading for young adults	$0.05		Not enough data	390	Add
fiction for young adults	$0.05		Not enough data	1,600	Add
authors for young adults	$0.05		Not enough data	720	Add
literature for young adults	$1.10		1,300	1,300	Add
fiction for teens	$0.75		5,400	6,600	Add
novels for teens	$0.55		4,400	4,400	Add
nonfiction for teens	$0.05		Not enough data	720	Add
fantasy for young adults	$0.05		Not enough data	590	Add

Next, take a look at the statistics for the *novels for young adults, books for young adults, literature for young adults, fiction for teens, novels for teens, writers for young adults,* and *book for teen* results. When you combine the search traffic and estimated CPCs for these similar search terms, you get a monthly search volume of over 100,000 with CPCs up to $1.02. That's not bad for a very specific niche. The analysis could lead you to start a niche blog about writing for young adults and teens with a focus on book reviews. Doing so could marry your passion for writing and learning about writing for a young adult audience with the monetization opportunities related to *books* for teens and young adults.

Keep in mind that the keyword analysis described in this chapter only tells you what's happening online right now. It's possible your niche might be starting to grow in popularity and you could be one of the first bloggers to stake a claim in that niche. It's also possible that a topic that is hot right now might decline in popularity in the future.

The key to this exercise is to look through the list of provided keywords and keyword phrases and find the ones (or groups of similar keywords) that drive a significant amount of traffic (look for numbers in the thousands at the very least) *and* have Estimated Average CPC numbers that are neither too low nor too high. As discussed in the previous section, look for keyword phrases with Estimated Average CPC rates between $1 and $3 to maximize the monetization opportunities for your niche blog. Of course, the rates you're willing to accept depend on your overall monetization goals.

Chapter 4: Writing for Your Niche

C reating content for a niche blog isn't very different from writing for a broader topic, but niche blog content does need to stay focused on the specific topic of the blog. Readers visit a niche blog for targeted content about a subject they're interested in. If your niche blog content steers off course significantly with irrelevant content, readers become confused and look elsewhere to find the targeted content they want and need.

Consider a blog about classic rock that suddenly contains content about country music. How do you think the blogger's audience of classic rock enthusiasts would react to this type of inconsistency in content? It's unlikely that they would be happy about it. In fact, they might feel so confused or even betrayed that they'll turn their backs on the blogger and seek another source for the information, opinions and conversations they're looking for about classic rock music.

Writing about a niche topic doesn't mean you need to limit yourself, but it does mean you need to find creative ways to expand your subject while sticking to your niche. You can find ways to tie unrelated subjects to a niche blog, but it takes a bit of ingenuity. This chapter helps you find ways to write content for your blog without feeling imprisoned by your niche topic.

Creating Content

A phrase used often among bloggers is "content is king," meaning the content you publish on your blog is far more important than anything else you do during your life as a blogger. This is absolutely true. No one is going to read your blog if the content is terrible. But how many times can you talk about the same subject before your niche blog becomes repetitive and boring? Keep reading for tips and suggestions about the type of content you can create on your niche blog and how to keep that content interesting by getting creative.

But wait! You claim that you're not creative? It doesn't matter. The creativity you need to produce great content for your niche blog comes from thinking outside of the box and stretching the limits of your subject matter, which is something you can do with a bit of direction and thought.

Writing different types of posts

The easiest way to breathe life into a niche blog is by varying the types of posts you publish. Although you need to create your own unique style that readers can associate with your blog, that doesn't mean you need to adhere to a stringent style guide. Sometimes you can even present the exact same idea in a different way using a different type of blog post, and appeal to a different segment of your audience without sounding repetitive.

As an example, consider a blog post on a young adult fiction blog about writing dialogue that teens actually believe. You can write a post called *Young Adult Dialogue: The Good, The Bad, and The Ugly,* where you provide examples of good and bad dialogue to help readers learn the difference. Alternatively, you can publish a post called *10 Tips for Writing Great Young Adult Dialogue* where you provide ten very specific tips to help your blog readers learn to write compelling dialogue for their intended audiences. Both posts focus on the same aspect of writing for young adults but with very different approaches, making them unique and able to add value to your readers' experiences on your blog.

Following is a short list of types of posts you can write on your niche blog to keep the content fresh without straying too far from your niche topic. (Keep in mind that these types of posts work on a broad topic blog as well, as discussed in Chapter 2 of Book I, but when written about highly specific topics for a niche blog, they can be very effective.)

- ✦ **Lists:** Everyone loves lists. From *Top 10 Tips* to *10 Steps* and everything in between, lists are always popular blog posts for any blog, niche or not. For niche bloggers, the key is to create very specific lists that tie directly to your niche topic.

- ✦ **How-to:** If you can provide step-by-step tutorials to teach your readers how to accomplish a task, you have another way to present your content that people love. How-to posts work very well on niche blogs because you can provide very detailed instructions about a specific topic your audience is certain to be interested in already.

- ✦ **Don'ts:** Just as people like to read tips and how-to's, they also like to know what they should avoid. Tell them in a blog post and be specific!

- ✦ **Videos:** Online video is becoming more popular all the time. Create your own videos or embed videos other people create, so you can share them with your readers and provide your opinions related to them in order to enhance your own content. Remember to stay relevant to your niche topic to meet reader expectations.

✦ **Polls:** Everyone likes to give their opinion. Invite them to do so in a poll that you publish in a blog post. People who read niche blogs typically have strong opinions on the narrow topic and are highly likely to jump into the conversation if they're asked to do so.

✦ **Reader questions:** Often your blog readers might e-mail questions to you or leave questions within the comments section of your blog posts. Those questions can become great blog posts where you provide the answers! For niche bloggers, this is particularly helpful because the content of your blog is very focused. Chances are good that if one person has a question about the niche topic, a lot of other readers do, too.

✦ **Reviews:** Online reviews are very popular these days, so help your readers by providing your own reviews of products and services that are very closely related to your niche topic. Although it might be tempting to review unrelated products and services (particularly if you're being paid to do so), niche bloggers need to pay close attention to meeting reader expectations. Unhelpful reviews are not likely to meet those expectations. In fact, they can confuse and even annoy your readers.

**Book II
Chapter 4**

Writing for Your Niche

✦ **Links:** Publishing blog posts that include links (sometimes called *link roundups*) of posts from other blogs that you enjoy is a great way to grow your online network, and drive traffic back and forth between your blog and other blogs that you like or recommend. For niche bloggers, link roundups are like mining gold. Find the best bloggers in your niche or up-and-coming bloggers and link to them to start a relationship. Bloggers understand that helping each other through sharing content, linking, and so on can help both blogs grow. You can even link to popular blogs in an effort to begin establishing yourself as the expert in your niche and eventually migrating some of that traffic from the other blog to yours.

✦ **News:** What's going on in the world related to your niche blog topic? You can write about it on your niche blog. Don't just report the news though. Be sure to add your own opinion, knowledge, or experience to your posts to ensure readers get added value from your blog beyond the information they can find elsewhere online. Take the opportunity to demonstrate your knowledge or expertise in your niche within your commentary.

✦ **Trends:** If you know of new or interesting trends happening related to your blog topic, write about them on your blog and start discussions about what those shifting trends might mean to your topic, to you, and to your audience. Again, trend posts are a great way to further establish your expertise, passion, and knowledge in your niche topic.

✦ **Success stories:** Research other people who have achieved great success in some way related to your niche topic. Such stories can be both educational and motivational to readers. Offer links and request quotes when possible, which helps you build relationships with influential and interesting people as well as further build your reputation in your niche area.

✦ **Interviews:** Contact successful individuals who can share useful knowledge about your niche topic and interview them. Then publish the interviews on your blog so your readers can learn from them. Again, this is a great way to build relationships with key influencers and further establish your own reputation within your niche.

✦ **Guest blog posts:** Contact successful people who have knowledge of your topic and ask them to write a guest blog post for you. Your readers are likely to enjoy hearing a different perspective from time to time, and it's a great way to get a conversation going on your blog as well as put you on the radar screens of influential people and bloggers. Guest blogging is a win-win for you and the interviewee. Not only does the interviewee get exposure on your blog, but you also have an opportunity to build a relationship with that person.

Any blog post topic can become the subject of multiple blog posts without becoming repetitive or boring. For example, think of a topic for a blog post you could write about and then take a look at the types of posts listed in this section. How can you take that post topic using those types of posts and morph it into multiple posts? After you answer that question, you can publish the posts together as a series or separately over time.

Choosing your voice and style

Whether you write a broad topic blog or a niche blog, your blog's voice and style make it unique and set it apart from other blogs and Web sites about your niche topic. In fact, this is particularly true of niche blogs that are highly focused on a specific topic.

No matter how great your content is, no one will want to read your blog if it's written in an unappealing voice and a style that's disconnected from the topic. I've stumbled across many blogs over the years that appear to offer great content, but the writing style, grammatical errors, and ineffectual voice have caused me to click away and look for an alternative source for the same kind of information. You don't want that to happen to your blog, so take the time to determine what your voice should be on your blog and then stick to it. Also, brush up on your writing skills to ensure your content is well written. Most importantly, remember your niche, from your topic to your content to your voice, and stick to it!

One of the best parts about blogging is that bloggers don't have to be trained writers to publish a blog. This fact holds true for niche bloggers just as much as it does for broad topic bloggers. Most blogs are written in a conversational tone rather than a strictly professional or academic tone. That's because the blogosphere is rooted in conversations and relationships. If blog readers wanted to find an institutional, formal writing style, they would turn to text books and professional Web sites, not independent blogs. Even the most professional blogger can write in an informal and inviting voice that encourages conversation and relationships. The last thing you want to do on your niche blog is intimidate your readers by writing with a voice that doesn't match your topic, and because niche blog topics are always very specific, your voice needs to be equally specific and on target with your topic.

After you determine the niche topic for your blog, you need to choose the specific voice that will dominate your blog posts. By staying consistent in terms of your writing tone and style, your audience will feel comfortable visiting your blog and interacting with you, which leads to loyalty and relationships — the goal of many bloggers.

For example, political blogger Michelle Malkin has grown to celebrity status thanks to her highly conservative blog shown in Figure 4-1 (`http://michellemalkin.com`). Her tone matches her topic, and her loyal readers respond strongly to her. Alternatively, Perez Hilton's celebrity gossip blog (`www.perezhilton.com`) became popular in part thanks to his sarcastic and biting commentary. Both bloggers stay consistent in terms of the voices they use in their blog writing, and over time, readers have developed expectations for their blog content. If Michelle Malkin suddenly began writing about and touting liberal politics, her core audience would be not only shocked, but also revolt! Similarly, if Perez Hilton started to be kind to celebrities in his posts, his existing audience, who *like and expect* his extreme style that defines his niche, would turn their backs on him quickly. That's simply not the Perez Hilton they want, and as a result, Perez leaves the more politically correct side of celebrity gossip blogging to others.

Figure 4-1: Michelle Malkin's blog has a conservative political voice.

Linking

Links are an extremely important component of any blog if you have goals to grow your blog's readership and money-making potential. Following are the two primary reasons for the importance of incoming links:

✦ **Traffic from search engines:** More incoming links (particularly from popular blogs and Web sites) translate into a higher ranking on search engines. Higher search engine rankings lead to more incoming traffic and higher advertising rates. Sites such as Google rank pages with more incoming links from real sources higher because the automated algorithm used to find and return search results assumes pages with more incoming links are better than those without incoming links. The theory is that no one would link to an inferior page, but many will link to a great page.

✦ **Traffic from the links themselves:** More incoming links means more potential traffic to your blog from the blogs and Web sites that publish those links.

In short, incoming links provide more entry points for people to find your blog, so writing great content that other Web site owners and bloggers want to link to is very important to the success of your niche blog, particularly because niche bloggers don't have the manpower or funds to invest in search engine optimization, advertising, and so on. But how do you get people to link to your blog? No matter how much great content you write, no one will link to your blog if they don't know it exists. That's where creating content with outgoing links can be helpful to growing your blog's audience.

When you write a blog post, be sure to link to your sources, provide links to additional information, and so on. Turn on the trackback or backlink function in your blogging application (described in detail in Chapter 3 of Book I), so other bloggers are notified when you publish a post on your blog that links to their blog via the ping functionality. Also, click the links in your blog posts to make sure they work. As your readers click those links, the Web site owners or bloggers that you link to will see those links within their own blog traffic statistic reports (Chapter 2 of Book V discusses traffic analytics), which puts you on their radar screens. This situation sets the ball in motion for you to start a relationship with those other site owners and bloggers. When they visit your blog and see the great content you publish, they're likely to use your blog as a source for their own posts, which can lead to more traffic to your blog in the future.

It only takes a few seconds to provide links to sources and additional information within your blog posts. Be sure to do so, because outgoing links can lead to indirect blog traffic just as incoming links can lead to direct blog traffic.

Finding inspiration for new content

Expanding the post possibilities for your niche topic can sometimes take additional work in terms of reading and researching. That's because it's easy to have blogger's block when you're writing about a very specific and narrow topic like you do on a niche blog. You won't be motivated to write great posts every day, but for your blog to grow, you need to publish content frequently. With that in mind, take a look at the following suggestions to get your creative juices flowing and come up with new post ideas. You can also find out more about avoiding blogger's block in Chapter 2 of Book I:

✦ **Read other blogs and Web sites.** Visit other blogs and Web sites that publish content related to your niche topic and find out what they're writing about.

✦ **Check Google Trends.** Using Google Trends, you can find the search terms that are currently the most popular on Google. If people are searching for a term related to your niche topic, not only could it make for an interesting blog post, but you could get some of that search traffic! The process of using Google Trends is described in detail in Chapter 3 of this minibook.

✦ **Check your Google Alerts.** Set up a Google Alert for keywords related to your blog's niche topic using the steps in Chapter 3 of this minibook. Then check your Google Alerts messages to find the recent related content people are publishing on other Web sites and blogs.

✦ **Conduct a Twitter search.** If people are talking about your niche blog topic on Twitter, you might find ideas for posts there! Follow the steps in Chapter 3 of this minibook to search Twitter for keywords related to your niche.

✦ **Conduct searches on social bookmarking sites.** Sites such as Digg, StumbleUpon, and Reddit are used by people who want to share links to pages online that they like. Do a search on these sites to find links to content related to your blog's niche topic. You can find out how to use social bookmarking sites in Chapter 4 of Book VI.

✦ **Conduct a YouTube (www.youtube.com) search.** You never know what kinds of videos people are uploading to YouTube, the most popular video sharing site online. Conduct a search on YouTube using keywords related to your niche topic and see what comes up. You just might find an interesting video that you can either embed or link to in your own blog post or that gives you inspiration for a new blog post.

Never republish content on your blog that you find on another Web site or blog. This is a violation of copyright laws (if you don't obtain permission to do so first). It can also hurt your search traffic over time because search engines such as Google downgrade sites that lack original content and might even blacklist them as spam.

Branding Your Blog

After you choose your blog's niche, and if you have aspirations to be a successful blogger, you should consider the branding of your blog. In simplest terms, your blog's *brand* is a representation of your image, message and promise to your readers. You can create tangible representations of your blog's brand by giving it a unique header, *favicon* (the image that appears in your browser toolbar to the left of the URL), and logo as well as a specific color scheme, font, and overall design aesthetic. Consistent visual elements can go a long way when it comes to building your online brand.

Although a corporate blog has a built-in brand to create a blog around, a niche blogger has to create her own brand from scratch. Don't be intimidated. Building a brand is fun! Start by thinking of what you want your blog to represent. What will your blog's content communicate to readers on a high-level? Will your blog be professional or fun? Will your audience be made up primarily of men or women, teens or senior citizens? Consider your message and your audience members and what you want to provide to them on your blog. In other words, what can you promise your audience that they can be sure to find on your blog every time they visit? That's your brand promise. Then choose the unique design, header, colors, and voice that best represent and communicate that brand promise to your audience and stick to it!

The Cake Journal blog (`www.cakejournal.com`), shown in Figure 4-2, provides a great example of a well-branded niche blog. Warning: Visit this blog at risk of making yourself very, very hungry for cake!

Figure 4-2:
The Cake
Journal
is a well-
branded
niche blog.

First, the colors and images are fun and feminine, which immediately create an expectation for readers. Next, a slogan in the header immediately communicates what this blog is about, "Passionate about cake decorations, techniques, delicious cake recipes and sugarcraft creations!" The assumption after reading the slogan is that the blog is written about someone who *loves* cake decorating and wants to share her passion. By adding in words like *techniques* and *sugarcraft creations,* the expectation is set that the blogger knows more about cakes then how to make a Betty Crocker instant box mix.

When the reader clicks the About link in the right sidebar, those assumptions are validated. The blog is written by Louise Winther Dueholm, a self-taught cake artist who has been decorating cakes for the past five years. She also offers a link to her cake decorating e-book in her bio. (You can find out more about using e-books to promote yourself as a niche blogger later in this chapter.)

Also, in the blog's sidebar, you can find links to How-To's, Tutorials, and a Gallery showing that the blog offers useful information and is backed up with actual photos of results. There's also an extensive blogroll, showing the blogger's networking efforts, and links to her Twitter page and the blog's subscription, and more. The content is friendly, conversational, and easy to read and includes images to support each post. It's a great example of a small niche blog that has grown to have a nice following with nearly 7,000 people subscribed to the blog's feed.

It's important to understand that much of successful brand-building comes less from the tangible symbols of a brand and more from the intangible elements. For example, no one cared much when Walmart changed its logo in 2009, but they would care if Walmart shifted its brand promise from low prices to something like luxury shopping. That's a change consumers would be unlikely to accept, because they have expectations for the Walmart brand, which they have come to rely on. When Walmart consistently meets those consumer expectations, the company's brand value grows, and consumers feel a sense of security with it. That security leads to brand loyalty, repeat business, and word-of-mouth marketing from a powerful group of consumer-brand advocates.

The same process holds true for your blog. Your content, your voice, your style, and your visuals should consistently communicate your brand message, image, and promise. If you fail to do so, your readers will become confused and might abandon you and your blog in lieu of another that meets their needs time and again. There are a lot of blogs out there, and even the smallest niche blog has competition within the blogosphere. Don't let your readers get away by disappointing them. Remember, your blog's brand extends beyond your blog design. It's inherent in your content as well. Be consistent.

The rule of brand consistency applies to your online activities that occur off of your blog as well. From the comments you leave on other blogs and in forums to the guest posts you write for other blogs, and everything in between, successful bloggers develop an online persona (or brand) that follows them everywhere they go and in everything they do. That's how you build a powerful online brand that helps you build your online presence, establish yourself as an expert, drive traffic to your blog, and build relationships.

To truly understand branding, pick up a copy of *Branding For Dummies,* by Bill Chiaravalle and Barbara Findlay Schenck, and start to familiarize yourself with the tools and techniques experts use to create powerful brands.

Networking and Commenting

You might be surprised to find out that you can directly *and* indirectly find ideas for content to publish on your own blog by networking with other bloggers and commenting on their blogs, particularly blogs related to your niche topic. First, reading other blogs is one of the best ways to keep up with the online conversation about your niche topic. By reaching out to the bloggers who write blogs about similar topics to your own, you can interact in a dialogue that might spark creative ideas for your own blog. It's very possible that those other bloggers might begin sending tips to you and sharing news, opinions, and more, which can provide further content for your blog.

Networking is critical to niche blogging success because you're writing about a very narrow topic and competing against much larger blogs and Web sites. Without deep pockets and extensive manpower, the typical niche blogger has to rely on building relationships to grow their blogs. That's not a bad thing. In fact, it's probably a very good thing, because relationships can far outlast short traffic boosts that ads and promotions can deliver to larger blogs.

Writing great content for your niche blog comes from your ability to write interesting, original content, but it also comes from networking, joining conversations, and finding out what people want from your blog and your niche topic in general. As your reputation grows in relation to your blog topic, other bloggers will turn to you for your opinions as the expert in your niche. This is another way you can find more content for your blog.

Much of a blog's success comes from the open community and the relationships built within that community among people who share each other's content, talk about it, and drive traffic to it. Don't underestimate the power of online relationships and conversations in terms of growing your blog. Instead, create content that enhances those conversations and relationships.

Of course, a lot of your blog content will be related to your personal opinions, experiences, knowledge, and so on, but it's equally important to understand *all* the content your potential audience is looking for related to your topic. If you want your blog to grow, your job is to deliver a balance of content that matches your needs for your blog as well as your audience's. After all, a blog is nothing more than a one-man show if there's no audience reading it and starting dialogues around it.

Creating Off-Blog Content for Your Niche Blog

As discussed earlier in this chapter, the most successful bloggers (even broad-topic bloggers) don't hide out on their own blogs. Instead, they're active, participating members of the larger blogging community. In other words, if your goal is to become a successful blogger, you need to spend as much time participating in activities off of your blog as you do on your blog. Remember, blogging is part of the social Web. It's a social media tool. Notice the word *social*? If you want to grow your blog, particularly a niche blog that caters to a narrower audience by definition, you need to be social.

A lot of the time you spend off of your blog is in participating in direct and indirect promotional activities and relationship-building efforts. Commenting on other blogs and on forums related to your blog's niche are both off-blog activities that can help you build relationships and drive traffic to your blog. Additionally, you can pursue specific promotional efforts to grow your blog, which are discussed in detail in Book VI.

Niche blogs are the perfect type of blog to grow through off-blog content — the content you create and share using other tools than your blog. Take a look at the examples in the following sections and start thinking how you can apply them to your own niche blog. Depending on your niche topic and the audience you build around it, targeted off-blog content tactics can work very well in helping you to meet your blogging goals.

E-mail campaigns

Many niche bloggers conduct their own publicity campaigns by creating a list of bloggers and influential people with strong online presences related to their topics and e-mailing information to them as appropriate. For example, bloggers e-mail updates, guest post submissions, articles for republishing, interview submissions, invitations to webinars, and more in an effort to further build relationships using content published outside of their blogs. If you send information that is truly useful to the people on your e-mail list, they're more likely to appreciate receiving it.

Try to make sure your e-mails are personalized. Bloggers don't like to receive mass e-mails from people who don't take the time to get to know them and build relationships with them. That's the technique spammers use, and bloggers call it *blog blasting*. You don't want to be grouped in the same category as spammers!

Think like a public relations professional and create e-mails that are valued by the people you send them to. The last thing you want to look like is an e-mail spammer. If you don't inundate your e-mail list with messages and only send useful information, you should get positive feedback.

Newsletter subscriptions

As you read more and more blogs, you're likely to find many that offer links in their sidebars inviting readers to sign up for their newsletters. Many bloggers send formal newsletters to their subscribed readers on a weekly, biweekly, or monthly basis. Your newsletter can include content that isn't on your blog as well as links to content that is published on your blog. The key to creating a useful newsletter is not simply republishing the content that readers can already find on your blog. Including links to that content is fine, but your newsletter content should be original and enhance the content on your blog.

Blogging Tips (`www.bloggingtips.com`), shown in Figure 4-3, provides a good example of promoting a blog newsletter in the blog's sidebar.

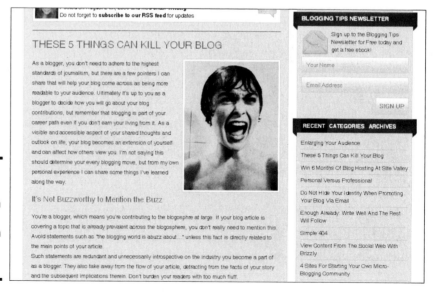

Figure 4-3:
Blogging Tips offers a newsletter subscription in its sidebar.

You can use a number of e-mail tools that are available online to create and send newsletters. For example, Constant Contact (`www.ConstantContact.com`), which is shown in Figure 4-4, is one of the most popular tools for creating standardized e-mail campaigns such as newsletters. Other options include Emma (`http://myemma.com`), MailChimp (`www.mailchimp.com`), iContact (`http://icontact.com`), and VerticalResponse (`www.verticalresponse.com`). Each tool offers similar features. Be sure to compare the current offerings on each site before you commit to using a particular tool.

Most e-mail tools offer free trials or free services to people who need to send small volumes of e-mails. Be sure to look for these offers.

E-books

E-books are digital books that anyone can write. Readers download them from the Internet, and they've become one of the hottest promotional tools that a blogger can add to his marketing arsenal. Of course, you need to write a great e-book, with content your audience actually finds useful, or it won't be successful. You can check out the nearby sidebar for tips on writing and promoting an e-book, but first you need to determine your objectives for writing an e-book. Some bloggers use e-books as a way to further establish themselves as experts in their fields, but others use them solely to earn money by charging a price for them. These are two very different e-book strategies, but both can work depending on your goals for your niche blog.

**Book II
Chapter 4**

Writing for Your Niche

Figure 4-4:
Constant
Contact
is one of
the most
popular
e-mail tools.

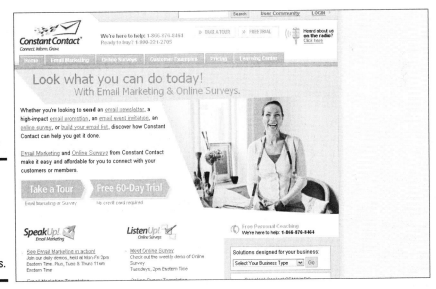

Tips for writing and promoting e-books

E-books are a unique form of writing that has exploded in popularity in recent years. When you sit down to write an e-book, you need to follow a few basic guidelines to ensure your final product will meet readers' expectations. For example, your e-book shouldn't look like a typical document typed in a common word-processing application such as Microsoft Word. Instead, you need to make sure your e-book is visually appealing. Use images and diagrams to break up text-heavy pages and write in short paragraphs as well as bulleted lists to add white space to your pages. Because many people read e-books on their computer screens, use a larger font as well as a font that is easier to read onscreen than the common 10-point or 12-point Times New Roman.

Your e-book should offer information that is truly useful to readers. Consider their needs and create an e-book that addresses them just as you would if you were developing a new product — that's what your e-book is after all. Write in an inviting tone rather than a highly professional one. Your e-book should be easy to read yet packed with meaningful information.

To promote your e-book, contact the bloggers you have relationships with as well as others who blog about topics related to your niche. Offer to send them a copy of your e-book, telling them they can feel free to offer a link to it on their blog. Offer to write a guest post or provide an excerpt for them to publish on their own blogs. Talk about your e-book on social networking sites and through microblogging using tools such as Twitter. Include a link to your e-book in your e-mail signature and anywhere else that you can provide a link. Most importantly, make sure your e-book is available without requiring information from your readers, such as asking for an e-mail address before the download is available. Offer your e-book for free with a Creative Commons license that invites people to share it across the Web, if your goal is to boost your online exposure, blog traffic, and status as an expert in your niche topic.

If your blogging goal is to broaden your online presence or establish yourself as an expert in a field related to your niche topic, an e-book can help. E-books have a reputation for going viral, meaning people like to share the best ones. They talk about great e-books and pass them on to their friends. This viral tendency works perfectly to support a strategy of growing your online presence and establishing yourself as an expert. As more people get their hands on your e-book, more people will recognize your name and your blog and associate them with being sources for authoritative information on your niche subject.

If those are your goals, your e-books should be made freely available to anyone who wants to download them to ensure maximum sharing and exposure. Provide a Creative Commons license on your e-book so people know they can share it freely with proper attribution. (Chapter 4 of Book I provides details about Creative Commons licenses and copyrights.) Furthermore, for maximum exposure of your e-book, don't put a gateway in front of it. In other words, don't require people to provide their e-mail addresses or any other information to access your e-book. If you want to maximize exposure, putting up a deterrent before a person can even see the contents of the e-book will ruin your hard work in writing a great e-book. For example, the Newstex blog shown in Figure 4-5 (`http://newstex.com/publishers/free-ebook-the-truth-about-blog-syndication`) offers a free e-book with no gateway or registration process required for access. As a result, the e-book has been downloaded and shared thousands of times.

Figure 4-5:
Newstex
offers a free
e-book.

E-books that are free and available for sharing are downloaded significantly more often than e-books that require e-mail address submission or payment prior to a person downloading them.

If your goal for your blog is to make money, then you probably care less about how much your e-book is shared and more about how you can maximize earnings from it. If that's the case, then you should charge a fee for people to access your e-book with the understanding that the number of people willing to pay for your e-book could be very small unless you have already established yourself as an expert in your niche topic with something very unique and useful to say. Set a reasonable price for your e-book ($4.99–9.99 is a common price range, depending on your expertise and how well known you are within your niche), and include copyright and disclaimer information indicating that the content of your e-book may not be shared.

Promote your e-book through links and images in your blog's sidebar, within your blog posts, e-mails, newsletters, and so on. The key to generating downloads of your e-book is to raise awareness of it and make people understand why it will be useful to them.

Don't feel like you have to stop with e-books. Although e-books are an amazing promotional tool in terms of establishing your expertise and growing your blog audience, many bloggers, particularly niche bloggers who successfully establish themselves as experts in their fields through their blog content and activities, are able to pursue other opportunities as well. For example, many bloggers branch out into writing and publishing printed books either through established publishers or through self-publishing using a Web site such as Lulu.com (www.lulu.com). Don't be afraid to think big!

Social networking and content sharing

The social Web offers a variety of ways that niche bloggers can share content both on and off of their blogs to gain exposure and traffic. Depending on your blog's niche topic, some opportunities might work better than others in helping you reach your blogging goals. The similarity between the various methods of sharing content off of your blog through social sites is making your content freely available for others. That's where the term *viral* comes from — when a piece of online content spreads across a wide audience through sharing from one person to the next. It's a powerful thing that you can leverage for your blog's success. The following sections highlight a few easy tools you can use to share the off-content material supporting your blog in order to give that content, you, and your blog added exposure and recognition, which just might lead to more traffic and money-making opportunities.

YouTube videos

YouTube (www.youtube.com), shown in Figure 4-6, is the most popular Web site for uploading and sharing videos with people from around the world. Get a YouTube account and start uploading your own videos. Be sure to include a link back to your blog in your videos or YouTube profile and video description areas. Make sure you upload your videos so they're available for the public to both view and share by linking and embedding them into their own blogs and Web sites. That's the only way a video can truly go viral — if there are no barriers to sharing it. You can find out more about creating and uploading videos in Chapter 7 of Book V.

Facebook and LinkedIn groups and pages

Facebook (www.facebook.com) and LinkedIn (www.linkedin.com) are two of the most popular social networking sites online. Facebook has a global audience of hundreds of millions of people who come from all walks of life. You can create a personal profile on Facebook as well as a Facebook group and fan page for your blog brand or business. As an example, Figure 4-7 shows the Facebook fan page for About.com.

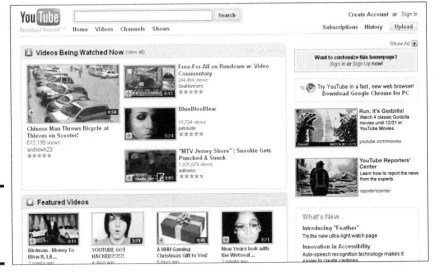

Book II
Chapter 4

Writing for Your
Niche

Figure 4-6:
The
YouTube
home page.

Figure 4-7:
A Facebook
fan page.

The audience of LinkedIn users is typically focused on more professional, business-related people and networking opportunities. With LinkedIn, you can share content by answering questions and setting up your profile notifications to let your connections know when you upload new content to a wide variety of social sites such as SlideShare (discussed in the next section). You can find out more about social networking in Chapter 3 of Book VI.

SlideShare presentations

SlideShare (www.slideshare.net) is a Web site where you can upload PowerPoint and PDF presentations to share with the online audience around the world. It's particularly useful for people who write niche blogs related to business or academics because they can upload additional content that their readers are likely to be interested in and further establishes them as experts in their subjects. You can see an example of content uploaded to SlideShare in Figure 4-8.

Figure 4-8: You can upload and share presentations using SlideShare.

Be careful when you create and upload content such as videos and presentations where you use images or audio. You should be certain you have permission to use all images and audio in your content, unless you can clearly claim that the content used is protected under the terms of fair use, which are described in detail in Chapter 4 of Book I.

Flickr and Picasa

Flickr (www.flickr.com), shown in Figure 4-9, and Picasa (www.picasa.com) are two of the most popular sites for uploading and sharing images. Whether you want to share a photograph or an image of a diagram, flowchart, or cartoon, you can do so on a photo-sharing site such as Flickr or Picasa. Be sure to apply a Creative Commons license to your uploaded content and upload only images that you own. A large audience of bloggers and Web site owners search photo-sharing sites everyday looking for royalty-free images that they're allowed to use on their blogs. Depending on your blog's niche topic, image sharing can be an effective way to drive traffic to your blog, build relationships, and expand your online exposure.

Embed your blog's URL in your uploaded images as a watermark to ensure your blog is always referenced as the copyright owner and source. You can find out about image editing in Chapter 3 of Book V.

Figure 4-9:
You can
upload
and share
images with
Flickr.

Book III

Corporate and Business Blogging

The 5th Wave   By Rich Tennant

"I'm sorry. I'm answering e-mail right now.
And since when does the Taco Bell
Chihuahua have a blog anyway?"

Contents at a Glance

Chapter 1: Starting a Business Blog

In This Chapter

✔ Understanding why companies blog

✔ Discovering which companies to emulate

✔ Enjoying the benefits of business blogging

*B*usiness blogging has become more popular than ever in recent years, with huge corporations, solo entrepreneurs, and every business in between recognizing the power of the blogosphere and the online conversation in boosting both customer relationships and sales. However, to many business owners, blogging can still seem like an unnecessary and foreign tool. These business owners can't make the connection between traditional marketing and the opportunities blogging provides. This chapter helps you understand why companies blog, which companies are blogging well, and how a business blog can benefit you.

Any business can benefit from a company blog in some way. I built my entire post–corporate America career from the idea of starting a blog to sell my first business nonfiction book about copywriting. Today, I have a thriving business, and it's all thanks to the power of blogging and the online conversation that happens on the social Web. My story is not unique. Many business owners around the world have already realized blogging offers a potential opportunity to build their businesses, and many have achieved great success from that knowledge and a lot of effort. The best part about blogging is that you can do it, too.

Of course, business blogging isn't like personal blogging. You have to deal with more unwritten rules and do's and don'ts related to business blogging simply because what you publish on your business blog has a direct impact on your company's brand and future sales. Don't worry. You find out all the do's and don'ts in Chapter 5 later in this minibook. Right now, focus on the why's and why not's and save the do's and don'ts for later, when you have a better understanding of business blogging overall.

Don't start a business blog out of a sense of obligation or because everyone else is doing it. A successful business blog requires deep commitment in terms of time and passion. Set your goals and understand what you're getting yourself into before you jump into business blogging.

Revealing Why Companies Blog

Companies large and small start business blogs for dozens of reasons. Most frequently, those companies have goals to generate sales directly or indirectly from their Web presence, and a blog appears to be a natural extension of reaching those objectives. Following are several reasons why companies blog (note that this list is not comprehensive):

+ To build brand awareness

+ To network with other businesses, experts, and so on

+ To build relationships with existing and potential customers

+ To boost sales

+ To communicate marketing messages and promotions

+ To learn more about their customers

+ To manage their reputation by debunking rumors, nudging conversations in the desired direction, and so on

+ To seem real and human in consumers' eyes rather than as an untouchable entity

There's much more to business blogging than trying to boost sales. In fact, a business blog that focuses entirely on marketing and promotion is unlikely to be successful. Instead, the secret to publishing a business blog that has a chance for success is to write content that's truly useful and meaningful to the consumers who are likely to want and need your products and services. Successful business blogs are written for consumers, *not* for companies. That's the first shift in thinking you need to make before you can start planning your business blogging strategy.

With that in mind, companies blog for more reasons than just to generate sales. Perhaps the most powerful thing a business blog can deliver is a chance to build relationships with consumers both locally and around the world. In the 21st century, companies are realizing that the most powerful brands and businesses are those that have built strong relationships with consumers. Relationship brands, such as Apple and Harley Davidson, which allow consumers to experience the brands in their own ways or with larger groups and develop deep loyalty to them, are some of the strongest brands in the world, thanks primarily to the loyal group of consumers that band together in support of those brands. A business blog offers a perfect way for companies to do more than just talk *at* consumers. By using a blog, companies can talk *with* customers and build the powerful relationships that brand managers covet.

Furthermore, business blogs provide the opportunity for companies to start conversations about their products, services, and brands. They can nudge those online conversations in the right direction and then let them flourish. Loyal consumers who have built relationships with your company and brand will talk about it and defend it, particularly in the online community. Leverage that conversation by providing a place for it to take place and by getting involved to keep it going. You can do it with a blog.

A business blog is an incredible marketing tool for several reasons. It allows you to establish your business as *the* source for information related to the types of products and services you provide. It lets you offer special offers and discounts to thank your loyal readers, and it allows you to listen to and respond to their comments. The best part about publishing a business blog is that the monetary investment is negligible in comparison to traditional marketing initiatives. You can't beat it! My response to clients who ask me whether they should have blogs for their businesses is always the same: "The question isn't why should you have a business blog, but why *shouldn't* you have a business blog?"

Unfortunately, the blogosphere contains a lot of spam and highly personal blogs, which can give some people a skewed interpretation of what blogging can actually do for a business. The truth of the matter is that spam is just a fact of life on the Internet. As much as everyone online wishes spam would go away, that's not going to happen anytime soon (or ever). In terms of personal blogs, they're also a fact of life in the online world because the blogosphere is open to just about anyone. To counter the stereotype that blogs are for personal reasons only, you need to make sure your business blog is well-designed, written in a professional tone, and is distinctly different in design and content from a personal blog. You can find out more about designing a business blog and creating content in Chapters 2 and 4 of this minibook, respectively.

Finding Companies That Do It Right

A lot of companies have blogs, but the vast majority of them aren't fully leveraging the opportunities that the blogosphere offers because they're not publishing the kind of content they should be, and they're not engaging their readers. The strength of a blog comes from interesting, unique content written in a voice that captivates an audience and makes them want to join the conversation. If your business blog posts read like press releases or corporate rhetoric, no one is going to feel compelled to return after the first visit.

Before you get to know the do's and don'ts of writing great content for your business blog, take some time to peruse the blogosphere and start reading company blogs. Read business blogs from large and small companies and blogs within your industry and outside of it. Find blogs from businesses you're actually interested in and start reading and leaving comments. What do you like about those blogs as a consumer? What do you dislike?

Chances are good that if you don't like something about a business blog, you're not alone, and the same concept holds true for your own business blog. You can discover more about finding business blogs to bookmark and understanding your blog's audience in Chapter 2 of this minibook. In the meantime, take a look at the examples of blogs that follow to understand what business blogging is truly about. These companies each offer great content that consumers are interested in and *believe.* And that's where successful business blogging begins.

Southwest Airlines

Southwest Airlines is known as one of the first companies to publish a blog from the employees' perspectives — Nuts About Southwest (`www.blog southwest.com`), shown in Figure 1-1. The Nuts About Southwest blog's debut was revolutionary because it gave employees an opportunity to engage the consumers they work for everyday. Naturally, employees have some rules they have to follow, but the free flow of information and conversation between Southwest bloggers and the consumers who read the Nuts About Southwest blog made a significant difference in helping the airline grow and develop relationships with its consumers.

Figure 1-1:
The
Southwest
Airlines blog
is a bit nutty,
in a good
way.

You can see exactly how much the leaders of Southwest Airlines understand the power of the blogosphere as a tool to build relationships and share information by reading the blog's About page at `www.blogsouthwest.com/about` (shown in part in Figures 1-2 and 1-15). Within the text, the company makes this knowledge very clear by saying, "We want to build a personal relationship between our Team and you, and we need your participation. Everyone is encouraged to join in, and you don't need to register to read, watch, or comment." The About page also succeeds in setting reader expectations related to the interaction between Southwest bloggers and readers by stating, "Some of our bloggers are Flight Crew Members, so they may delay a response for a few days while they are 'on the road.' (Actually should we say 'in the air'?)" Finally, the About page provides the company's comment policy and provides contact information for customer service problems, again, setting expectations for the experience people will share on the blog. Overall, it's well done and shows exactly how much the people at Southwest Airlines understand how a blog should work and how the content within it should be written.

As the Nuts About Southwest blog has grown and evolved over the past few years, the company has added links to the company's social networking, media sharing, and Twitter accounts, as shown in Figure 1-2, so people can connect and interact with the company elsewhere as well. The power of a relationship brand comes from creating branded experiences that allow consumers to self-select how they want to connect with the brand. Southwest Airlines achieves this by providing multiple ways that members of the online community can engage with its primary brand.

Figure 1-2: Southwest Airlines includes social networking, media sharing, and Twitter links on the company's blog.

If you want your employees to write your business blog, take a look at the content on the Southwest Airlines blog to get ideas for the types of posts that make an employee-written blog interesting.

Walmart

The Walmart employee-written blog shown in Figure 1-3 (www.checkout blog.com) is called Check Out and uses the clever slogan, "Where the lanes are always open." What makes the Walmart Check Out blog unique is the fact that it's written by a team of employees who the company refers to as experts in the subjects they write about on the blog. People write about gadgets, gaming, lawn and garden, music, movies, family, and more. Although some of the posts read a bit more like sales pitches than I'd like to see in a business blog, the Check Out blog is still a good example of an employee-written blog that provides useful information to readers. For example, some posts include information about sales, new products, reviews, and so on.

Comments are encouraged (as they should be), but the bloggers aren't as responsive as they should be to make the blog stand out as a great business blog. Still, you should take a look at it as a tool to learn from if you run a retail business online or offline. You can get excellent inspiration, post ideas, and more from reading the Walmart Check Out blog.

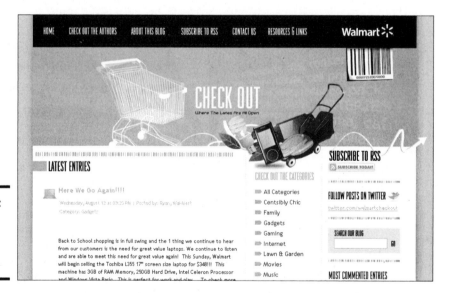

Figure 1-3:
The
Walmart
Check Out
Blog

Dell

Dell offers several company blogs, each with a slightly different purpose. For example, Direct2Dell (www.direct2dell.com), shown in Figure 1-4, is one of the most consumer-focused blogs in the Dell network. The blog has a much stronger professional tone to it, making it a far more corporate-like blog than a blog such as Nuts About Southwest.

Dell had some blogging troubles in the past, though. After being caught in an attempt to squash a blog post that painted Dell's sales process in a negative light, when an employee shared secrets of getting discounts at Dell with the popular blog The Consumerist (`http://consumerist.com`), Dell has since put a lot of effort into using the blog as a more effective social-media tool. Dell received a huge amount of negative press and backlash for trying to bury this negative conversation about its brand and business. Since then, the company has made a conscious effort to revamp its social-media strategy, including its blog content, in order to encourage online conversations rather than stop them. The new Dell blogs, Twitter profiles, Flickr profile, and so on are intended to be more transparent and offer more customer service and meaningful content than they did in the past.

Figure 1-4: The Direct2Dell blog.

Google

As you might expect, Google is a great example of a company that understands the power of the online community and takes advantage of that strength by publishing dozens of company blogs. From blogs dedicated to specific products to blogs written by individual employees who provide their perspectives on their fields of expertise and their industry in general, Google has a blog for it. Check out Figure 1-5 to see the Google blog dedicated to news and information about its Blogger application (`http://buzz.blogger.com`).

Many employees even write popular blogs that are not affiliated with Google, but unlike the position most companies would take on these blogs, Google encourages them. Matt Cutts' blog (`www.mattcutts.com/blog`), shown in Figure 1-6, provides a perfect example of Google's stance on allowing employees to write blogs related to their work and Google in general. Matt Cutts is the head of Google's Webspam team, and he's known across the Web as the go-to guy for information related to Google's search engine algorithm secrets. Although he doesn't divulge any of those secrets on his blog, he does offer a wealth of information related to search engine optimization, Google, and more. His online voice is respected and valued as an asset to Google. His blog is a must read!

Figure 1-5:
The Blogger Buzz blog.

Figure 1-6:
Matt Cutts' blog about Google and SEO.

Zappos

Zappos is an excellent example of a company that understands business blogging. Zappos publishes a number of blogs written by employees, and each blog speaks to a specific audience. The main Zappos blog talks about Zappos, the company, and another blog is all about what it's like working inside Zappos. (See Figure 1-7 for the Inside Zappos blog found at `http://blogs.zappos.com/blogs/inside-zappos`.) Other blogs are written about niche subjects that Zappos customers might be interested in, such as outdoors, parents, health and fitness, fashion, and more.

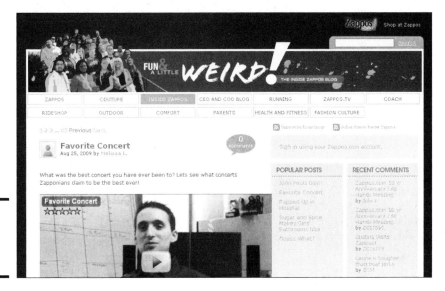

Figure 1-7: The Inside Zappos blog.

To make things even better, the Zappos CEO and COO write a blog (`http://blogs.zappos.com/blogs/ceo-and-coo-blog`), shown in Figure 1-8, which is interesting; written in a personable, relatable voice; and fun to read. How many CEO-written blogs do you think you could say that about? Trust me when I tell you the answer to that question is *not many*.

Zappos even publishes a blog called Zappos.TV, found at `http://blogs.zappos.com/blogs/zappos-tv`, which is shown in Figure 1-9. Zappos. TV includes all video blog posts, and they're very entertaining! For example, a recent video post was called *Well, I'm Your Ice Cream Man,* and the video was all about an ice cream party at the Zappos office. After you read some of the Zappos blogs, you just might find yourself saying, "I want to work there!"

Figure 1-8:
The Zappos
CEO and
COO blog.

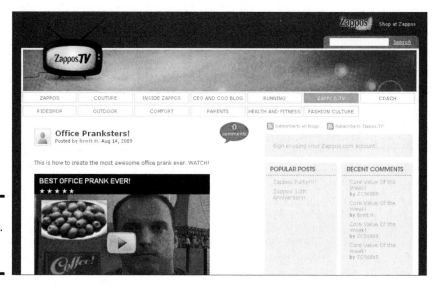

Figure 1-9:
The Zappos.
TV video
blog.

In short, Zappos does an excellent job of engaging consumers, creating interesting content, and being real — three of the most important characteristics of a successful business blog.

Benefiting from a Corporate or Business Blog

The benefits to publishing a business blog can be as big and wide as you want them to be. The truth is that you're in control of creating your success and the benefits that go with that success as a blogger, and that holds true for business blogs just as much as, or more so than, personal blogs. Success comes from commitment and time. If you have those two things, there's no reason that you can't derive some benefits and success from a business blog.

The first step is to determine what your goals are for your business blog. You can find out all about creating a business blog marketing strategy and goals in Chapter 2 of this minibook. When you fully understand what you want to achieve through your business blogging efforts, you can target the necessary steps to help you reach them. However, before you get that far, you need to understand some of the most common benefits of business blogging. For many business owners, the first objective that comes to mind is to increase sales, and a blog can certainly help both directly and indirectly in that area with links to your online store, special promotions and discounts, and so on. But business blogging is about so much more than increasing sales. In fact, if you look at business blogging as simply a tool to boost sales, you're missing out on immeasurable opportunities to grow your business in the long term.

As an example, consider Gary Vaynerchuk of Wine Library TV, at `http://tv.winelibrary.com` (shown in Figure 1-10), who grew his father's wine store in Springfield, New Jersey, to a $50 million per year business, with half of those sales coming from online orders, all thanks to a video blog he created to share his passion for wines. His personality and content proved to be infectious, and he soon found himself called upon to speak at events and appear on national television shows as a social media expert. Recently, he signed a multimillion dollar book deal to share his social media experience and knowledge. If you think a business blog can't help you grow your business, think of Gary Vaynerchuk and get inspired by the possibilities business blogs offer.

Although you can certainly use tactics to boost sales in the short term on your blog, the power of a business blog comes from the long-term benefits your company can derive from it. The remainder of this chapter explains what some of those benefits are so you can get a better understanding of the potential that a business blog can offer to your company.

**Book III
Chapter 1**

Starting a Business Blog

Figure 1-10:
Gary Vayner-chuk's Wine Library TV blog helped him grow his business to $50 million per year.

Building an online presence

Blogging opens the doors for businesses to build online presences that are more expansive than anyone could have dreamed 10 or 20 years ago. With a blog, even the smallest business owner can create a low-cost, professional looking Web site and provide an online destination for consumers to find out about the company and products. By publishing frequent blog posts to that site, the business owner can build relationships with consumers, boost search engine optimization and search traffic, provide customer service, publicize promotions, establish the business and employees as experts, and so much more. Truly, the opportunities are limited only by your own creativity.

For example, the ClickEquations Web site (www.clickequations.com), shown in Figure 1-11, is built on the WordPress blogging platform. You'd be surprised at how many business Web sites are powered by a blogging application. Gone are the days of investing tens of thousands of dollars on Web design and maintenance. Today, business owners can handle most of the technical aspects of their Web sites by themselves if those sites are built on an easy-to-use blogging platform.

By clicking the Blog tab in the top navigation bar of the Click Equations Web site, you're taken to the ClickEquations blog shown in Figure 1-12. The site provides a perfect example of using a blogging application as the foundation for a Web site *and* an associated blog. It's a powerful combination.

Figure 1-11:
The Click-
Equations
Web site is
built on the
WordPress
blogging
platform.

Figure 1-12:
The Click-
Equations
blog.

Hiring a blog designer to help you create your business Web site and blog typically costs a lot less than it does to hire a Web designer and developer to create a traditional Web site. For a custom blog design, you can expect to pay anywhere from $1,500 and up, depending on the depth of your site and scope of the project. To reduce costs to approximately $500 and up, you can opt for a design that's built on a predefined template (called a *premium* template), which is personalized with your branding and content. (You can find out about finding templates for your blogging application in Book IV.) When your blog and Web site are designed, you'll save money in the long run because, unlike a traditional Web site, you need very little technical knowledge to maintain and modify a Web site built on a blogging platform.

Because a blog is updated frequently, your business blog offers you more chances to connect with consumers both on and off your Web site because you always have something new to point people to and talk about. Unlike a static Web site that offers little to no fresh content for conversational purposes, blogs allow businesses to reach out to consumers and create a new way to interact with them that offers significant value over the one-sided informational and transactional Web sites that dominated the Web in the past.

Marketing and publicity

A business blog is an amazing marketing tool. It's not so far in the past that the Internet didn't exist and even less far back that the social Web didn't exist. Today, companies take for granted the ease of using the Internet to promote their businesses. Gone are the days of relying on Yellow Pages and newspaper ads to market your business. In fact, those types of marketing tactics are getting closer to obsolescence every day. In the 21st century, the majority of consumers turn to the Internet to find information about businesses, products, and services. That's why it's critical that your business has a Web site, even if you don't actually sell any products online. Today's Internet is an informational, transactional, and social place, and your business needs to be represented accordingly.

However, a fine line exists between publishing promotional content on your business blog that is useful and valued by readers and publishing so much promotional content that your blog is viewed as all marketing and no substance. At the core of your blog should be substance. Using the classic 80–20 rule, wherein it's estimated that typically 80 percent of a company's business comes from just 20 percent of its customers, you can apply the same percentages to your business blog content. Try to write 80 percent content that's useful, interesting, and meaningful to readers (substance) and 20 percent about discounts, publicity, and so on (promotional).

Gauge your readers' reactions to your content mix over time and adjust as necessary to ensure you're meeting their expectations for your business blog. Remember, interaction is the key to business blogging success!

A company that does a good job of providing substance in its business blog is Logo Design Works, which offers the Logo Design Blog at www. logodesignworks.com/blog (shown in Figure 1-13). Logo Design Works offers logo design services, and the Logo Design Blog provides interesting posts about logo design, hiring designers, analyzing well-known logos, and more. In other words, the company's blog provides excellent substance to support its business and meet customer needs with information that can actually help them.

Figure 1-13:
The Logo
Design
Works blog.

The most powerful aspect of business blogging is the potential to generate word-of-mouth marketing from the content you publish. If you can engage your audience members and get them talking about your business, products, and services *outside* of your Web site, you've hit marketing gold. Blogs are a perfect tool to achieve that goal because they're conversational in nature. They're also filled with personality (at least the good ones are) that encourages readers to participate and build relationships with the bloggers and businesses behind them. Relationships drive customer loyalty and create vocal brand advocates who want to talk about the brands they love and are willing to defend those brands from criticism. When that conversation moves off of your business blog and turns into an online buzz, you've achieved another goal that marketing managers dream of.

The power of the social Web comes from the conversations and buzz that occur on it. With a business blog, you have a chance to start those conversations, nurture them, and let them grow. As a marketer by profession, I think we live in the most incredible time because the power of the social Web and blogging provides more opportunities for businesses to connect with consumers and drive word-of-mouth marketing wider and louder than ever!

Start thinking about the types of promotions and public relations posts that you can publish on your own business blog that would actually help your readers and put smiles on their faces. You don't want to bore them with promotional information. Instead, you want to make them feel like they're special because they take the time to read your business blog. For instance, you can thank them for their loyalty by publishing exclusive discounts for blog readers only, and further connect your business and blog to them. Following are some suggestions for how you can use your business blog as a marketing tool:

✦ **Share sale information.** Your blog is a great place to share sale and discount information with consumers. Over time, they'll learn to *expect* to find this type of information on your business blog, and they'll come looking for it.

✦ **Link to your online catalog or store.** If you mention your products in your blog posts and have an online catalog or store, be sure to link to it!

✦ **Offer tips and advice.** It's possible that consumers might have questions about how to use your products, so it's always helpful to publish blog posts that not only offer tips but also provide suggestions for new ways to use your products.

✦ **Publish referral program details.** Get the conversation going by offering an incentive for referrals.

✦ **Hold a contest.** People love to win prizes. You can take advantage of that by holding contests on your blog. For example, hold a contest on your blog and offer a gift card for a future purchase from your business as the prize, or offer products as prizes. When you send the product to the winner, ask whether she'd like to write a review of the product for your blog or whether you could interview her about her experience using it. You can find out more about blog contests in Chapter 6 of Book VI.

✦ **Answer questions.** Engage your blog readers by asking them to send questions and answer them on your business blog. If one person has a question, chances are good that they're not the only one.

✦ **Solicit customer stories.** People love to see their names and photos in lights, so to speak. Ask your customers to send in stories about their use of your products and publish them on your blog. It's likely each person you talk about on your blog will want to share the post with their friends.

✦ **Include Share This links on your posts.** Be sure to include a link or button that allows readers to share posts they enjoy through social networking sites, social bookmarking sites, Twitter, and e-mail. It's an easy way to foster an online buzz.

✦ **Respond to all comments.** Make sure your readers feel valued! Respond to every comment left on your blog and keep the conversation going.

The possibilities are practically endless. Don't be afraid to think outside the box and be creative about using your business blog as a marketing tool. You can find out more about writing content for your business blog in Chapter 4 of this minibook.

Brand building

A *brand* is the message, image, and promise that your business, product, or service consistently, persistently, and repeatedly communicates to consumers.

A business blog is an amazing tool for building your brand. Not only does it give you the opportunity to put a voice to your brand, which allows you to develop and meet customer expectations for your brand, but it also allows you to extend your business' Web presence exponentially. Each new blog post you publish on your business blog becomes another entry point, and with each new entry point comes the potential for more traffic. As the traffic to your business blog increases, so will the number of loyal readers your blog attracts, the number of incoming links your blog receives, and the extent of your business' online presence. That increased traffic leads directly to building the awareness of your brand to a wider audience who could talk about it, link to your content, tell friends about it, and so on.

Much of the power of a business blog as a marketing tool comes from the long-term brand-building effects that blog presents. For example, a Google search on my name a few years ago would have yielded a small handful of results. Today, a Google search on my name yields tens of thousands or hundreds of thousands of results (as shown in Figure 1-14) depending on how recently Google updated its search index, and that increase in links came entirely from my blogging efforts on both my own company blog and other business blogs that I write for other sources. I went from a nonexistent Web presence to a sizeable one in a relatively short amount of time, thanks to the power of the social Web. There is no secret to achieving that kind of success. It's just a matter of investing time and sweat into writing great content, interacting with people both on and off the blog, and keeping focused on the long-term benefits of blogging as a tool to build a brand and business.

Book III
Chapter 1

Starting a Business Blog

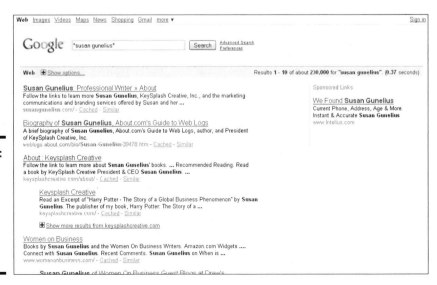

Figure 1-14: A search for "Susan Gunelius" on Google yields 230,000 results.

Your business blog content must offer the same level of brand consistency as all of your other marketing communications do. From your content to your voice and everything in between, a strong brand is one that is consistently presented to consumers. Inconsistency leads to confusion.

Another critical element of brand building is persistence. You need to give consumers the opportunity to develop expectations for your brand, which happens organically through persistent (and consistent) brand communications and experiences. After those expectations develop, you must continue to communicate your brand's messages, images, and promises in order to keep satisfying consumers. You can't give up. The unfortunate truth is that consumers are fickle, and they won't hesitate to leave you if you can't meet their expectations. By building a brand and consistently and persistently meeting consumers' expectations for it, you develop a relationship with them that translates into brand loyalty and brand advocacy, which are both essential to developing effective online marketing communications.

Online conversations about your brand can have far-reaching effects. The goal of building your online brand is to start those conversations and keep them going so there are more and more opportunities for people to find your brand online. After all, there isn't much point to maintaining a Web presence if no one can find it. That's like paying for advertising space in a magazine that no one buys. Why waste your time and money unless you're willing to commit to the long-term brand-building benefits that a business blog can provide? Instead, focus on the long term when you develop your business blog marketing strategy (discussed in detail in Chapter 2 of this minibook) and use short-term marketing tactics to enhance that strategy.

Customer relations versus customer service

A blog is an excellent tool to enhance customer relationships. I caution against publishing a blog for the sole purpose of answering individual customer service-related questions because each individual customer service issue is personal and unique. It's hard to appeal to the members of a wide audience when they have to scroll through a lot of content that doesn't apply to them. Also, you don't want your business blog to become a complaint destination. That isn't the type of content that helps you build relationships with your readers, network across the social Web, and boost your business. However, publishing some customer service-related posts can be helpful to your readers and provide a good forum for conversations that affect broad consumer groups.

The Southwest Airlines employee blog, Nuts About Southwest (`www.blog southwest.com`), offers a great example of steering the dialogue on a business blog from responses to personal complaints and problems to a broader conversation. Southwest provides a number of standard disclaimers about the conversation that occurs on the blog, but the company also offers this disclaimer, shown in Figure 1-15: "Nuts About Southwest is not the forum to address personal Customer Service issues. All of us have 'day jobs,' and we simply don't have the resources through Nuts About Southwest to resolve individual concerns. Even though this is not the forum, Southwest is eager to resolve your concerns." The text then goes on to provide specific customer service contact information. With two simple sentences, the expectation is set that personal issues should be discussed in a more personal setting, because the Southwest Airlines bloggers aren't the right people nor do they have the time to answer these types of questions.

Figure 1-15: The Nuts About Southwest blog provides details about the types of customer service comments that are not appropriate for the blog.

> Southwest's Cofounders got together in 1967 to discuss their idea for a new airline that would bring the Freedom to Fly to America, and when Rollin King finished sketching out the idea on a cocktail napkin, Herb Kelleher told him, "Rollin, you're crazy. Let's do it!" Much the same thing happened when we presented the idea for this blog to Southwest's Leaders. They thought we were crazy—but hey, we are nuts, and we're doing it! The same thing happened when we decided to expand our initial blog into the current version of Nuts About Southwest that you see now. So, from deep in the heart of Texas, we say "Howdy" and welcome you to Southwest's homestead in the blogosphere. (By the way, in case you stumbled upon this site by accident and were looking for our regular web site, southwest.com, this link will take you there: www.southwest.com.) Our goal with the new Nuts About Southwest remains to give our visitors the opportunity to take a look inside Southwest Airlines and to interact with us. This is as much your site as it is ours, and we have expanded our Emerging Media Team to represent an even more diverse cross-section of our Company.
>
> We want to build a personal relationship between our Team and you, and we need your participation. Everyone is encouraged to join in, and you don't need to register to read, watch, or comment. However, if you would like to share photos or videos or rate a post, among other things, you will need to complete a profile.
>
> Southwest Employees try to Live the Southwest Way by displaying the Warrior Spirit, acting with a Servant's Heart, and embracing a Fun-LUVing Attitude. We will try to do our best to ensure that this site displays those qualities, and we want our home to be a fun place to learn about what we hope is your favorite airline—Southwest, of course. You are the "other half" of this blog, and our Team can't wait to communicate with you, so get busy posting.
>
> This is the point where we insert the "fine print" and discuss the guidelines for posting. Nuts About Southwest is a moderated site because we want to ensure that everyone stays on topic—or at least pretty close to it. We would LUV for you to post your thoughts, comments, suggestions, and questions, but when you post, make sure that they are of general interest to most readers. Of course, profanity, racial and ethnic slurs, and rude behavior like disparaging personal remarks won't be tolerated nor published.
>
> Even though Nuts About Southwest is moderated, we pledge to present opposing viewpoints as we have done since our blog first went "live" several years ago, and we will strive to keep posts interesting, diverse, and multi-sided. Our Team wants to engage in a conversation with you, but not every post will receive a response from us. However, we encourage you to respond to our bloggers and to the comments of other individuals. We also ask that you be patient with our Team for a response. Some of our bloggers are Flight Crew Members, so they may delay a response for a few days while they are "on the road." (Actually should we say "in the air"?) Don't forget, the fact that they are on the frontlines ensuring that our Customers get to their destinations safely and comfortably is the very reason that our Crew Members' posts are interesting.
>
> One final disclaimer—Nuts About Southwest is not the forum to address personal Customer Service issues. All of us have "day jobs," and we simply don't have the resources through Nuts About Southwest to resolve individual concerns. Even though this is not the forum, Southwest is eager to resolve your concerns. Our Customer Relations/Rapid Rewards folks want to assist you, and you can contact them through one of the means listed at our Contact Page. For reservations, please visit southwest.com or call our Customer Support & Service (formerly Reservations) folks at 1-800-I-FLY-SWA (1-800-435-9792).

I suggest placing a similar type of disclaimer on your business blog in a place where it can be seen easily. Don't just delete personal customer service questions and complaints. Instead, answer them if the topic would be helpful to the general blog audience. If not, take the time to direct the commenter to the proper place to get an answer to his personal questions or problems. The worst thing you can do on a business blog is try to stop the conversation or hide the negative comments people leave. Although it's perfectly acceptable to delete hateful comments or edit comments to remove profanity, you don't want to be accused of trying to cover up negative conversations. (See the earlier section, "Dell," for the story about what happened when the company tried to quash an online conversation that painted the company in a negative light.)

Of course, as with any tool that allows people to voice their opinions, some people (trolls) will leave comments on your business blog strictly to start arguments and say rude things. It's an unfortunate reality of publishing a blog. As long as you're honest, forthright, and transparent in your writing and commenting, your loyal readers and the majority of new visitors can tell the difference between a *troll* (someone deliberately trying to cause social friction) and a person who is commenting for the right reasons. (You can find out more about responding to negative attacks on your business blog in Chapter 5 of this minibook.)

The success of your business blog as a customer service tool is to set reader expectations so they know what kinds of customer service discussions are appropriate for the blog. In other words, although your blog is not the forum for discussing personal customer service issues, it's a fine place to discuss topics that your customer service team would usually talk to consumers about, such as new payment options, recalls, and so on, which help you build *relationships* with your customers. Provide information that's useful and helpful to them related to customer service issues rather than individual problems.

Give your readers the credit they deserve. In time, you'll find them coming to your defense for you when attacks do occur. That's because blogs are truly a better customer *relationship-building* tool than a customer *service* tool. Building relationships with customers is where a business blog can become a vital part of your marketing plan.

Employee retention

When most people think of a business blog, they often think of only the external blogs that companies publish to promote their products and services. Business blogs offer a lot more than a promotional opportunity, but they can also boost employee morale and retention, particularly when employees are given the chance to write blogs for and about the company and their areas of expertise in their own voices.

Of course, if employees have to write adhering to a stringent set of guidelines and if every post has to be approved by a dozen departments and lawyers, you can forget the part about boosting morale and retention. When that happens, business blogging becomes another annoying item on employees' annual reviews, and it's more of a burden than something they can feel passionate about. Instead, make sure your business bloggers are given the opportunity to express themselves, inject their personalities, and converse with readers as themselves, not as a spokesperson from the public relations department. Readers can tell the difference, and they're unlikely to enjoy the corporate rhetoric that comes when employee bloggers are not given the opportunity to write from their hearts. You can find out more about setting blogger guidelines in Chapter 3 of this minibook.

Take a look at the Womenkind blog (http://womenkind.net/blog) shown in Figure 1-16. This blog is a great example of injecting employee voices into the content of the blog. The content isn't even close to being all marketing-related. In fact, most of the content isn't about the company at all. (Womenkind is an advertising agency that focuses on the female audience.)

Instead, the majority of the content focuses on issues, news, and commentary relevant to Womenkind's core audience: women. The passion of the bloggers for their subject matter shines through and makes readers want to return again and again to learn more and join the conversation. That freedom to write with their hearts undoubtedly makes Womenkind's employee bloggers feel valued and satisfied, leading to employee retention.

Figure 1-16:
The
Womenkind
blog.

**Book III
Chapter 1**

**Starting a Business
Blog**

Employee referrals and new hiring

Business blogs are useful tools not only for existing employees but also for potential employees. Consider using your business blogs to publish open job announcements. For an internal business blog, include referral bonuses in job postings. In other words, get the readers of your business blogs actively involved in helping you find great talent. As your business blog grows, your job postings are likely to get noticed by other bloggers in your industry, who will link to your postings and share them on their social networking and bookmarking profiles as well as on sites such as Twitter. You should do the same to help spread your posts to the widest audience possible. You'd be amazed at the incredible talent out there that's actively participating in the social Web.

Remember, many people use the social Web as a tool to build their online presences and establish themselves as experts in their fields. Don't wait for them to actively look for and find your job posting on sites such as Monster.com. Instead, blog about it, too, and give your job posting the chance to spread to audiences you never dreamed possible.

Staff Only! Using internal blogs

Business blogging for employee retention doesn't stop with a company's external (public) blogs. Instead, companies can also publish internal blogs that are available to employees only, to share company information, news, employee stories, and more with staff members. Internal blogs are a great way to boost the communication process with employees and make them feel like they're in the know rather than just another number on the employee roster. The key to writing a successful internal business blog is to get employees involved. Allow them to publish posts, share their opinions freely, and then respond to them. Transparency is vital on an internal blog when it comes to using it for employee retention purposes. Make your employees feel valued and essential to your company's team by inviting them to participate, listening to them, and giving them the information that they want.

You can also reach out directly to other bloggers in your industry and ask them to help spread the word about your job openings. It's likely that other bloggers would be happy to share the news about a great job opportunity with their own audiences. And keep in mind that each incoming link to your job postings means more incoming links to your blog overall, which translate into more entry points for people to find your business blog and a boost in Google search rankings (discussed in detail in Chapter 2 of Book II).

Knowledge, experience, and expertise

If your employees are knowledgeable in your industry and capable of writing coherent sentences, blogs offer another incredible opportunity. Millions of people publish blogs as a tool to boost their online presences and establish themselves as experts in their fields. Many of them become the go-to people for their subject matters. With that in mind, a business blog written by your expert employees can link your company closely with topics related to your industry and put your company on the map. Suddenly, your business blog can attract a wider audience than ever because people seeking thought leadership content might be very different from your typical consumer blog readers. By offering different ways for people to experience your brand and interact with you online, you expose a more diverse audience to your brand, business, products, and services, which can lead to an indirect boost in sales over time.

Many CEOs and presidents of small and mid-size businesses write blogs and establish themselves as experts in topics related to their companies. For example, one of my favorite small-business blogs is written by Drew McLellan, Top Dog at McLellan Marketing Group, a marketing company he owns in Iowa. Through his blog, Drew's Marketing Minute (www.drews marketingminute.com), shown in Figure 1-17, Drew has established himself as a marketing thought leader who writes in a personable voice that draws in both marketing novices and marketing pros. As a result, the conversations on his blog are lively, and he has developed relationships with a broad audience around the world. Undoubtedly, his business blog has led to new business and repeat business for McLellan Marketing Group as he became known across the blogosphere as one of the go-to guys for marketing and branding expertise.

Figure 1-17:
The Drew's Marketing Minute blog.

 Think of the kinds of information your consumer audience would be interested in learning about from an expert from your company as well as the content wider audiences would look for from an expert. Then find the right person with the necessary knowledge and experience within your company to write a blog that delivers the information that people want and need.

Search engine optimization

Blogs provide a unique and measurable way to boost your company's search rankings on search engines such as Google, because with each new post, you create a new *entry point,* or way for search engines to find you. If you write those posts with keywords in mind, as discussed in Chapter 1 of Book V, you can boost your search rankings even higher. That means when people conduct a search on Google (or their preferred search engines) using the keywords that your posts are optimized for, your blog posts are likely to appear higher on the list of results returned for those searches.

But that's not all! Blogs that are updated frequently with amazing content are often linked to by other Web site owners and bloggers who like the content and want to share it with their own audiences. Great blog posts are also likely to be shared on social networking sites, social bookmarking sites, and Twitter. All of that sharing means more and more incoming links to your blog. Google uses a proprietary algorithm to rank the results it finds for keyword searches, and that algorithm ranks pages with many incoming links higher than pages without incoming links. The reason is because Google believes that people will want to link to great content, so a page with lots of links is assumed to include great content and therefore to be worthy of a higher ranking than a page with few or no links. If you publish interesting content on your business blog that people want to share or talk about, your blog will get more incoming links, which boosts traffic directly through clicks and indirectly through higher search rankings. What's not to like about business blogs?

You can check how many incoming links are pointing to your blog at any time by visiting Google and typing **link:www.*YOURBLOGNAME*.com** into the search bar (inserting your blog's domain). Then click the Search button and a list of all links to your blog is returned to you, as shown in Figure 1-18 for www.drewsmarketingminute.com.

Be careful about paying for incoming links to your blog or Web site. Google sees paid text links as a tool that artificially inflates a site's search ranking and may downgrade your site if you pay for text links, or it may even remove your site from search results entirely.

Figure 1-18:
Checking
the number
of incoming
links to a
blog using
Google.

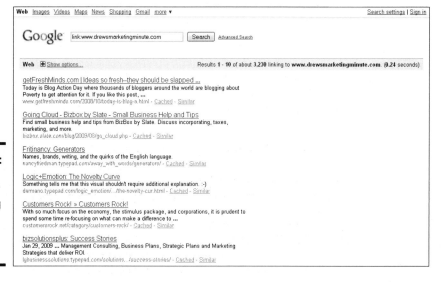

Chapter 2: Developing a Business Blog Marketing Plan

In This Chapter

✔ **Finding and analyzing your competition**

✔ **Differentiating your business blog**

✔ **Getting to know your audience and their needs**

✔ **Defining your business blog marketing strategy**

✔ **Setting goals for your business blog**

Creating a business blog marketing plan is a similar process to creating any marketing plan. You need to know who your competitors are and what they're doing in the same online space where your blog will live, and you need to know who your audience members are and what they want from your blog. You can't create a strategy until you do some research. Only then can you create goals that are focused and attainable. In other words, you need a well-crafted plan before you can leverage the full potential of the social Web.

This chapter shows you how to create your business blog's marketing plan before you launch your new online presence. Joining the blogosphere can be exciting, but don't rush into anything. Launching a blog that's poorly designed, written, and developed can do more harm than good for your business. In short, you don't want people to find your blog, be disappointed in what they find there, and never return again. Do the prep work first!

As you read through this chapter, remember that the most successful business bloggers are creative, not just in the design of their business blogs but also in the content, conversations, and promotions related to those blogs. Because the blogosphere is constantly changing, you never know what might work. Also, you need to be able to continually provide content that your audience likes. Certainly, doing the same thing everyday can get boring very quickly. The same is true of your blog content. If you publish the same type of information every day, advertise on the same sites all the time, and your marketing plan never evolves, your blog will quickly get stuck in a rut.

Researching the Competition

You can find a lot of business blogs out there, and your competition might be stiff. You need to find out whether you're creating a business blog that will not only attract an audience but also lure them away from your competitors' blogs.

Keep in mind that your list of competitors' blogs isn't limited to business blogs published by companies in your industry or offering the same products and services that your business offers. Depending on the type of information you decide to publish on your business blog, competition can come from a wide variety of blogs. Think of it this way: If you own a local hardware store, your business blog competes with all of the following:

✦ Blogs written by big corporations such as home improvement chain stores, Walmart, and more

✦ Local business competitor blogs

✦ Blogs written by builders, handymen, home improvement enthusiasts, and so on

With that in mind, the hardware store's business blog strategist should research *all* of these types of blogs and bloggers to determine what makes them unique and what drives conversations. Then you can use your discoveries to craft a business blog strategy in order to provide valuable content that is different from what's already out there.

As you research your blog's competition, be sure to analyze the designs of those blogs. Your design must not only match your blog's position, but also compete with your competitors' designs. If your competitors' blogs are highly professional and look amazing, you might want to invest in hiring a blog designer to ensure your blog looks as good or even better!

Finding business blogs to benchmark

The first step in developing your business blog's marketing plan is to find other blogs that are delivering the type of information that your target audience is interested in reading. This is a time-consuming task if you're thorough about it, and being thorough is essential to developing a blog marketing strategy. You need to not only find business blogs related to your industry, but you also need to read them, keep track of the comments and conversations happening on those blogs, and analyze the types of content and posts that pique readers' interests and dialogue.

Following are several tips for finding business blogs to benchmark:

✦ **Visit your competitors' Web sites.** As a business owner, you undoubtedly have a list of your primary competitors. Find their Web sites and look for links to associated blogs.

✦ **Conduct a Technorati blog search.** Using the blog search tool on `http//technorati.com`, you can search for blogs related to your business using keywords. You can find the steps to search Technorati to find blogs in Chapter 1 of Book I.

✦ **Do a Google blog search.** You can search blog content on `www.google.com` to find blogs that mention keywords related to your business as described in Chapter 1 of Book I.

✦ **Follow post links.** As you find blogs related to your business through Technorati and Google searches, take a look at the links included in the blog's posts. Many of them just might lead you to *more* blogs related to your business.

✦ **Follow blogroll links.** Visit blogs related to your business' subject matter and look for a section included in many blogs' sidebars called *Blogroll, Useful Links,* or something similar. Bloggers include links to other blogs they like and recommend in their blogrolls, which may lead you to more content for research and benchmarking.

Start a notebook and jot down notes as you spend time on business blogs that will compete with your own. What do you like about them? What do you dislike? What content sparks conversation? What kind of information does the blogger focus on? What information is missing? Find the gaps and opportunities, which you can use to create your own blog marketing plan.

Furthermore, you can seek out blogs that are indirectly related to your business. These blogs provide the opportunity for you to offer additional value to those bloggers' audiences through link exchanges, guest posts, and so on. Indirect marketing is an important part of a successful business blog plan. Using the hardware store example I mention earlier in this chapter, you can partner with a business blog published by a landscaping company. Although the landscaping company is not your business' direct competitor, your companies have an indirect relationship because consumers have expressed an interest in home improvement by hiring a landscaping company, and they're likely to need hardware supplies now or in the future. Thinking outside the box like this can help you better understand how your business blog can fit into the online community while adding value and drawing in readers.

Differentiating your business blog from the competition

When you know who the competition is for your business blog, you need to analyze the content and conversations on those blogs as I mention earlier in this chapter. That's the only way you can accurately find gaps and weaknesses and develop a blog marketing plan that capitalizes on those opportunities. Conducting this competitive research allows you to position your blog in consumers' minds just as well-known brands position themselves against their competition.

**Book III
Chapter 2**

**Developing a
Business Blog
Marketing Plan**

You want your business blog to own a space in your target audience's minds just as brands own a space, such as a word or phrase, in consumers' minds.

A business blog that's exactly like every other blog published about a similar line of business is a fairly useless effort. Why should people leave a blog that they're already reading to get the exact same information elsewhere? Readers have no incentive to visit your business blog if it doesn't add new value to an audience's online experience. After you research competitor blogs and fully understand what they publish and what works for them, you can determine which parts of their strategies you want to emulate and which you want to change or add to.

For example, if Joe's Hardware Store focuses on providing content related to product reviews and new product trends, your hardware store blog might also include that type of information, but your greater focus should be on another niche topic such as providing tutorials and videos showing readers *how* to use those products and accomplish specific tasks. Naturally, there will be some overlap in content between your blog and your competitors' blogs. That's why you're called *competitors.* However, just as you need to position your products and services against your competitors' in consumers' minds, you also need to position your business blog as being different and better than your competitors' blogs.

If your blogging application and host allow it, get your own domain name for your blog. Doing so helps not just in brand building and search engine optimization, but also in making your blog seem more professional than a generic domain name with a hosted extension (such as `wordpress.com`, `blogspot.com`, or `typepad.com`).

Understanding Your Readers and Delivering Content They Want

Your business blog has no chance for success if it doesn't provide information that your target audience wants and needs, just as a product will fail if no one wants or needs it. Of course, you can create a perceived need for your business blog as marketers often do with products and services. However, it's a lot easier to take the time to discover what your audience actually wants and needs from your business blog and then deliver that information consistently.

Your business blog is another tool in your marketing toolbox. It's an excellent place to provide marketing messages, build relationships, and create brand loyalty, but none of that will happen if you're not publishing the right messages. That's why your marketing plan development process needs to include audience research.

Your business blog's audience can be made up of consumers, distributors, business partners, and more. Naturally, it's difficult to provide content that interests diverse readers who want and need very different information from you. That's where focus becomes key to your business blog's success. Remember, your business blog can't be all things to all people. Instead, you need to do your research and determine which audience to build your business blog for. That's not to say you can't publish content on your blog that will interest segments of your target audience. However, you do need to choose your core audience — the one that will help you achieve your business blogging goals — and focus the majority of your blogging efforts around that audience.

For simplicity's sake, the remainder of this chapter focuses on consumers as your business blog's primary audience. Although that may not be the case for *your* business blog, it is for the majority of companies who join the blogosphere in order to grow their businesses.

Finding your customers online

Before you can begin researching the kind of information your audience members want from your business blog, you need to find them where they already spend time online.

Finding your audience is easy if you put yourself in your customers' shoes and search the Web just as they might. Conduct blog searches just as you did for your competitor research discussed earlier in this chapter, in the section "Finding business blogs to benchmark." For example, blogs with a lot of comments might be places where your audience is spending time. Next, search social networking sites, such as Facebook, for groups and fan pages related to your business, as discussed in Chapter 3 of Book VI. You can do the same thing on Twitter and microblogging sites, as described in Book VIII.

Furthermore, search for online forums, Ning groups, and Google Groups related to your business. Active forums and groups often represent online destinations where customers like to ask questions and help one another.

Follow the steps below to find groups on Ning:

1. **Visit www.ning.com, shown in Figure 2-1, and enter your keyword or keyword phrase in the search box that's prefilled with the text What are you interested in?**

Try to be as specific as you can with your keywords to find the most relevant results.

Book III
Chapter 2

Developing a
Business Blog
Marketing Plan

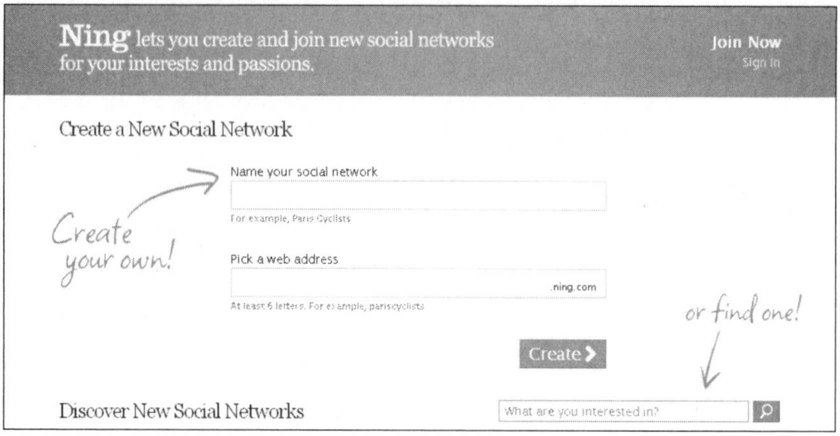

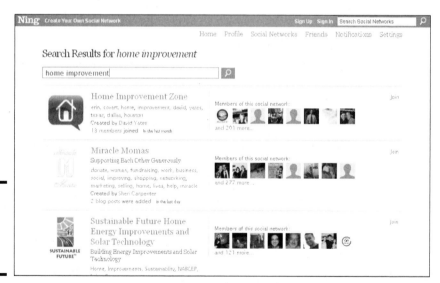

Figure 2-1:
The Ning
home page.

2. **Click the magnifying glass button (or press your Enter key).**

   Ning groups that match your keywords are returned to you on a new page, as shown in Figure 2-2.

Figure 2-2:
The results
of a Ning
keyword
search.

You can perform a similar process using Google Groups, as follows:

1. **Visit www.groups.google.com (see Figure 2-3) and enter your keyword or keyword phrase in the search box at the top of your screen.**

Try to be extremely specific with your keywords. There are a lot of Google Groups!

**Book III
Chapter 2**

**Developing a
Business Blog
Marketing Plan**

Figure 2-3:
The Google Groups home page.

2. **Click the Search Groups button.**

A new page opens with your search results listed, as shown in Figure 2-4.

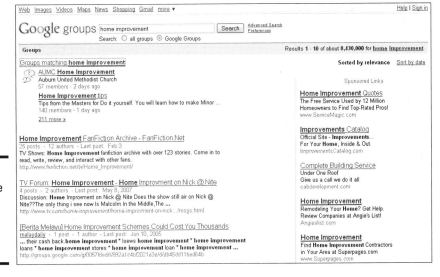

Figure 2-4:
The Google Groups search results page.

3. **You can narrow your results by selecting the Google Groups radio button under the search text box and clicking the Search Groups button again. Alternatively, you can click the link that appears at the top of your results list that reads Groups Matching [Your Keyword].**

In the example shown in Figure 2-4, the search term used is *home improvement.*

When you click the Groups Matching [Your Keyword] link at the top of your results list, a new page opens displaying the Google Groups directory listings that match your keywords, as shown in Figure 2-5. This feature not only narrows your search, but also makes it easy to display the results using more specific criteria such as topic, number of members, language, and more.

Figure 2-5: Narrow your Google Groups search by displaying the Google Groups directory page for your keywords.

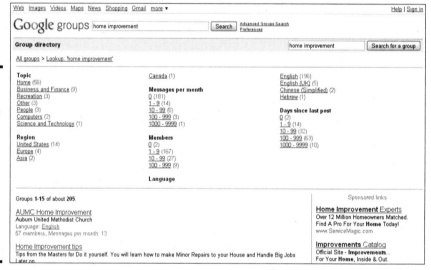

Don't be discouraged if you can't find any Facebook, Ning, or Google groups related to your business. None of the search functions are perfect. However, they do provide one more tool that can help you find out more about the kind of information your target audience wants and needs, or the results might give you ideas for different target audiences entirely!

Just because the relationships that you develop with your readers through your blog occur online doesn't mean they should be different from your offline relationships. Treat your audience members the same way that you would if they were standing in the same room as you and you were having a conversation with them face-to-face. Then take a look at your blog content and promotional efforts and evaluate them as a consumer would if he were standing right in front of you as your relationship with him evolves. Would that person be bored? Would he want to get away from you and avoid you in the future? Or would he be entertained by you and learn from you? And would he seek you out in the future so you could talk more? That's the kind of relationship you want to create and foster on your business blog.

Researching what consumers talk about and want from your business blog

You can begin doing some research about your customers by following their conversations and discovering what matters most to them after you've successfully found where they spend their time online. In other words, you can begin researching the type of content your audience wants and needs by analyzing your competitors' blogs first, as discussed earlier in this chapter, and identifying the types of posts that generate a lot of comments and buzz. Next, take some time to search on social bookmarking sites, such as Digg, StumbleUpon, and Reddit (discussed in Chapter 4 of Book VI), using keywords related to your business, and see what content comes up. If people are interested enough in content to share it through social bookmarking sites, you can safely assume that's the type of content they want and need. You can also conduct keyword searches on sites such as Twitter to find current conversations related to your business.

If you're lucky enough to find forums, Ning groups, and Google groups related to your business, join them and get involved. The conversations that occur on these social sites can be very indicative of the type of information your customers would be happy to find on your business blog. Look at the questions being asked and the answers users provide on these sites. Then consider ways that you can take those questions and answers a step further on your blog so it earns a reputation as being *the* place online for that kind of useful content. For example, if you're in the travel business, you might want to join and participate in forums related to Disney travel, such as the forum at `http://wdwmagic.com`, shown in Figure 2-6.

Don't forget the possibilities that offline customer research can provide you. There may be an audience of consumers who don't realize they can get great content on a business blog. Ask your existing customers what kind of information they'd like to read. After all, no one knows better than your customers! Hand out a survey or send one by e-mail asking your customers to provide their opinions. That's one way to be certain you know exactly what your audience wants and needs.

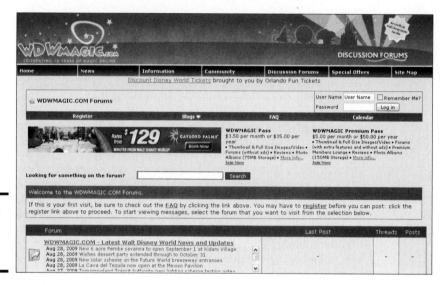

Figure 2-6:
The forum
at WDW-
MAGIC.

Getting involved in the online conversation

After you find the target audience for your business blog online, you need to begin connecting with them and engaging in conversations with them. That's where the power of the social Web comes from, and it's the conversations that happen through the social Web that drive traffic to your blog, help you build relationships that lead to customer loyalty, and boost your business. Successful bloggers get to know their audience members and build relationships with them both on and off their blogs. The same rule holds true for business bloggers. Think of the rule as it applies to personal relationships — you can't always expect everyone to come to the party at *your* house. Unless you have the coolest house around, you have to visit them at their own homes or hang out spots sometimes, too. That's what makes it a two-sided relationship. Now replace *house* with *blog* in the previous scenario because the rule applies to online relationships, too.

Building from the steps I discuss earlier in this chapter, it's easy to get involved in the online conversation related to your business. Visit the blogs, forums, groups, Twitter profiles, and so on where topics related to your business are discussed, and join in! It's that easy. The social Web is typically a very open place where anyone with intelligent commentary to add is welcome to the conversation. If you provide useful answers and interesting information, you'll be very welcome on most blogs and in most groups and forums.

Don't leave your audience hanging. Turn on the comments feature within your blogging application and let the conversation begin! If the dialogue slows, put on your thinking cap and get it going again just as if it were an awkward moment of silence in a face-to-face conversation.

Answering consumer demand with meaningful content

As you get to know more members of the online community, you'll get a better understanding of the kind of content they want and need from you and your business blog. Remember that your business blog should not be about you. Instead, the content has to be written for and about your consumers. You must deliver the information they want and need to make them want to visit again and again and build a relationship with you and your business.

Every post you publish on your business blog should add some type of value to your target audience or there's little reason for them to return. Of course, you can be creative when writing your posts (as discussed in detail in Chapter 4 of this minibook), but first you need to take the fundamental step to develop a business blog marketing plan by fully understanding the type of content that will be meaningful and useful to your target audience. Take your time in doing the necessary competitor and consumer research before you start blogging to ensure you're heading down the path to success.

Driving consumers to your business blog

Business blog traffic-building techniques are very similar to personal blog traffic-building techniques. First, you need to publish amazing content. When you have a repository of great blog posts, you need to start spreading the word about your blog. Following is a brief list of blog promotion tactics to get you started, but for more details be sure to read Book VI.

✦ **Leave comments on related blogs.** One of the best ways to start driving traffic to your business blog is by leaving useful comments on other blogs related to your business. Be sure to include your blog's URL in the appropriate comment form field, so readers who like your comments can follow the link to your blog to read more.

✦ **Link to great content on other blogs.** When you link to content on another blog from one of your blogs, the other blogger can be notified via a trackback or backlink or through his or her blog analytics tools. Getting your blog on the radar screens of other influential bloggers in your niche is a great way to prompt them to check out your blog and to build relationships with them.

✦ **Include your blog's URL everywhere you can.** Put your blog's URL on your business cards; e-mail signatures; Facebook, LinkedIn, and Twitter profiles; invoices; receipts; promotional items; and anywhere else you can think of.

✦ **Syndicate your blog content.** You can syndicate your blog content for publishing on your Facebook or Twitter profiles or through online syndication services such as BlogBurst (http://blogburst.com). Alternatively, you can syndicate through a licensed syndication provider such as Newstex (`http://newstex.com`). Each type of syndication offers another way to expand the audience of people who might find your blog. For example, Figure 2-7 shows the footer of my blog at `www.womenonbusiness.com`, where I include the feeds for two of my other blogs.

Figure 2-7: Include your blog's feed on other blogs and Web sites.

✦ **Use search engine optimization techniques.** Be sure to write each of your blog posts using keywords and search engine optimization tips discussed in Chapter 1 of Book V to increase your rankings for keyword searches via search engines such as Google.

✦ **Share your content on social bookmarking and networking sites.** Publish links to your best content on sites such as Digg, StumbleUpon, Facebook, LinkedIn, and so on.

✦ **Use Twitter to highlight your best content.** Post links to great content on your blog on your Twitter profile.

✦ **Hold a contest.** People love contests. You can hold blog contests to boost comments, increase subscribers, build incoming links, and more!

The opportunities to increase traffic to your business blog are limited only by your imagination and time constraints. Just be careful not to cross the fine line between useful promotion and over-promotion, which can get you blacklisted as a spammer by members of the blogosphere and by search engines.

Creating a Business Blog Marketing Strategy

After you do your competitor and audience research, you can begin thinking about your larger blog marketing strategy. Remember, the online world moves quickly, and what makes sense for your business blog today may be very wrong for it tomorrow. You must be flexible enough to change your business blog marketing strategy as new opportunities arise and existing opportunities fall out of favor. With that said, be prepared to continually review and revise your blog's marketing strategy. No one has the recipe for blog marketing success mastered yet. That means you need to be willing to test new tactics and strategies and learn from them, even if they don't meet your expectations.

Don't get sucked into experimenting with every new blog tool. Instead, pick and choose the ones that get great reviews and seem to be capable of truly adding value to your blog. Consistency is key in building a business blog, and that rule holds true for functionality just as much as it does for content.

Setting long-term goals

A business blog is most effective in helping you achieve long-term goals for your business for the simple reason that it's rare for a blog to become popular quickly. It takes time to generate awareness of your blog, recognition of it, and eventually traffic. You can speed up the process by investing time in short-term marketing tactics to boost growth of your business blog, but more often than not, business blogging success comes from patience and persistence.

Your long-term goals for your business blog should include

+ Developing relationships with your audience and building brand loyalty (the most important goals!)

+ Achieving specific traffic volumes

+ Reaching specific numbers of published posts

+ Achieving specific numbers of subscribers

Notice that besides the first item, these long-term goals are tangible and measurable. Setting measurable goals will help you stay on track in terms of publishing great content and growing your blog organically over time.

The majority of your long-term goals for your business blog are easier to achieve if you publish amazing content frequently and engage in the conversations that occur on your blog.

Developing short-term promotional campaigns

After you set your long-term goals for your blog, you can develop short-term marketing tactics to help you reach those long-term goals. For example, to help you reach your one-year traffic goals, you can hold a blog contest that provides each person who subscribes to your blog's feed with an entry to win a prize from your business such as a discount or product. Alternatively, you can publish guest posts on other blogs to build your incoming links, which typically leads to an increase in blog traffic. You can learn more about blog promotional tactics, such as blog contests, carnivals, guest blogging, and more, in Book VI.

If an initiative doesn't help you reach your short- or long-term goals, you need to think long and hard about whether it's worth your while. The amount of time you spend on initiatives that don't help you meet your goals for your business blog takes away from the time you could be spending creating great content and engaging with your audience — both of which are guaranteed ways to help you build your blog and your business.

The marketing rule that tells us it's cheaper to retain existing customers than it is to find and attract new ones holds true for blogging, too. Don't waste time on short-term tactics that simply inflate your traffic artificially with people who are not likely to return. Instead, focus on targeted initiatives that attract and retain the audience that wants and needs the information found on your business blog.

For example, don't hold a blog contest strictly to boost your blog's traffic in the short term. With proper promotion, a blog contest for a great prize can generate a lot of traffic, but the important consideration for a business blog is how much of that inflated traffic is likely to return to the blog after the contest is over. If the answer is "not many," you should reconsider investing time and effort into that particular promotional tactic.

Advertising opportunities

You can pursue many low-cost opportunities to grow your business blog's readership. Always keep in mind, though, that it's very possible to grow your blog's audience without spending a penny on advertising. However, doing so takes time, and your business might not have the time to wait for organic growth. If that's the case for your business, following are a few cost-based advertising opportunities that you can pursue to find and attract your blog's target audience:

✦ **Place Google AdWords ads.** You can join the Google AdWords (www.adwords.google.com) advertising network for free and create contextual ads that are published on blogs and Web sites, which contain related content.

✦ **Try Facebook ads.** Facebook offers a low-cost advertising program that you can use to drive targeted traffic directly to your blog, as shown in Figure 2-8.

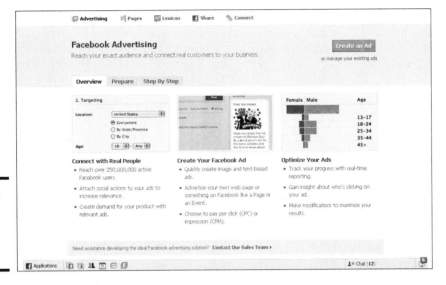

Figure 2-8: The Facebook Ads setup page.

✦ **Use traditional image and text ads.** You can contact other blogs and Web sites where your audience spends time and discuss advertising rates for image and text ads.

Beware! Paying for text link ads could be considered spam by Google, who might downgrade your blog or eliminate it from search results entirely.

✦ **Obtain reviews.** Reach out to other bloggers or publish review opportunities on sites such as SocialSpark (`http://socialspark.com`). Be certain to require that reviews include a link back to your blog.

✦ **Join ad networks.** There are many affiliate programs and ad programs that bloggers can join and use to drive traffic to their business blogs. Read Book VII for specific examples and details.

The most important thing about growing your business blog is getting the word out and motivating your target audience members to visit for the first time. If your content is useful to them, they're likely to return again or tell someone else about your blog. Your goal as a business blogger is to seek out and leverage every opportunity available to you to increase the awareness and recognition level of your blog among your primary audience. Then you can motivate the audience to take action, just as you would with any other marketing initiative.

Chapter 3: Choosing Business Bloggers

In This Chapter

✔ Looking internally for bloggers

✔ Finding external bloggers

✔ Defining rules and guidelines

✔ Training bloggers

After you define your blog's marketing plan and strategy, you need to find someone to write content for it on an ongoing and frequent basis. If you'll be the only blogger publishing content on your blog, then you're in charge, and you can get started right away. However, if you're not satisfied with your writing skills or you don't have enough time to invest in publishing content frequently, responding to comments, and creating an active community on your business blog, you should look for help.

Fortunately, several avenues are open to you to find great blogging talent. In fact, you might already have someone working for you who not only would be happy to write your business blog, but would also do a great job at it because he writes well and understands how the social Web and blogosphere work. Alternatively, many people around the world blog for a living. You can hire a blogger to become your employee or as a contractor. This chapter helps you find bloggers, pay them, and set guidelines for them.

Knowing When You Need Outside — or Inside — Help

Writing a blog is a unique form of writing, and hiring a professional blogger can give your blog an immediate leg up on the competition. That's because professional bloggers who are very knowledgeable and experienced know how to write content that people want to read. They know how to start online conversations and how to use multiple tactics to drive traffic to your blog. In fact, the difference in hiring a professional blogger to write your blog rather than an employee with no blogging experience is significant.

Depending on the type of content you want your business blog to contain, the learning curve a professional blogger has to get over in order to understand your business may be minimal, but the learning curve a social Web novice would have to get over is long and filled with tricks that only experienced bloggers know. I'm not saying the tricks and techniques can't be learned. They absolutely can be, and reading this book is an excellent place to start! However, it takes time to figure out all the do's and don'ts of the blogosphere. An experienced, knowledgeable blogger already knows how the social Web works and can dive into creating great content and driving traffic to your business blog.

Your budget, your existing depth of employee talent, and your short- and long-terms goals for your blog are the factors that help you determine whether you can use a current staff member to write your business blog or whether you need to seek external help.

The blogosphere is a popular place, and it's very likely that one or more people who already work for you might be very well versed in the details of the social Web. They might write personal blogs or spend a lot of time on social networking sites such as Facebook. Regardless of exactly where they spend time online, finding a person who understands how the blogosphere works and *already* knows your business is like finding a golden needle in a haystack. If you can find that person, you've hit the jackpot!

Following are two main reasons why finding an internal candidate who understands the social Web is great for your business blog:

✦ They already understand the importance of building relationships online.

✦ They know how your company works, its products, services, and so on.

You just need to identify who the right people are. Send out an internal communication asking employees if they would be interested in writing your business blog. Make sure you look at any blogs they already write, their social networking and bookmarking profiles, and so on to ensure they actually know their stuff and can write well. The best blogger you can find has a passion for the subject matter *and* your business. She'll understand that her goal is to connect with your audience, and she'll be happy to do so.

The most important thing you need to keep in mind when you recruit an existing employee to write your business blog is that it takes a significant time investment to create a successful blog. Although your employee might not have to spend eight hours per day working on your business blog at first, the time commitment will grow as your blog grows. Also, the more time the blogger invests into creating content, engaging in conversations, and promoting the blog, the faster it will grow. With that in mind, you need to determine whether taking the employee away from other tasks so she can work on your blog makes sense financially and in terms of meeting your overall business goals.

On the other hand, you can recruit a team of internal bloggers to write your business blog, which can help spread the workload. For example, the Whole Foods Whole Story blog (`http://blog.wholefoodsmarket.com`), shown in Figure 3-1, is written by employees who create posts in addition to their regular roles on the Whole Foods Market staff. However, the blog has evolved and grown to include over 30 employee contributors.

Figure 3-1: The Whole Story blog from Whole Foods Market.

Having multiple writers can be a good thing and a bad thing. Remember, many people return to a blog again and again because they like the voice and personality of the person writing that blog. The overall voice of a blog can get confusing when multiple authors contribute content. However, multiple authors can work together cohesively, and readers often find the specific bloggers within the larger team whose content they enjoy the most. Think of your blogger team as an ensemble cast that works together to provide individual perspective with a common focus. Walmart's employee bloggers do this effectively on the company's Check Out blog (`www.checkoutblog.com/authors`), shown in Figure 3-2. Each blogger focuses on his or her area of expertise in the posts. You can use the same technique on your business blog to ensure content is interesting and not repetitive.

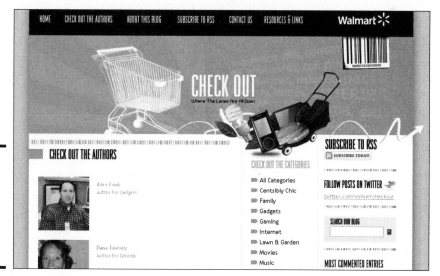

Figure 3-2: Over a dozen employees author the Check Out blog.

Knowing the Skills to Look for When Hiring a Blogger

When you make the decision to recruit a blogger, you need to make sure your candidates have a strong understanding of not just the technical aspects of using blogging tools, but also of how the social Web works. Of course, you can hire someone strictly to write content for your blog, and you can handle the promotion yourself or internally. That way you can cut some costs while ensuring your content will be well written, search engine optimized, and written in a voice that's likely to attract and retain visitors and incoming links.

When you know your budget, you can determine the type of blogger you need to hire and the skills and qualifications she needs to bring with her. The following sections discuss several skills a professional blogger should have.

Blogging experience

Writing content for a blog is unlike any other type of writing. The best bloggers know how to marry great content, a personable voice, and traffic-building techniques in the posts they publish for you. Have candidates provide you with links to blogs they currently write or have written in the past, and take the time to read the content they published, the comments and conversations that related to those posts, and the linking and search engine optimization used within those posts. In addition, analyze the frequency with which they published new content and the depth of that content in terms of longevity, diversity, and interest.

Ability to use blogging applications and tools

Experienced bloggers know how to use the tools of the blogosphere, including blogging applications such as WordPress, Blogger, TypePad, or Moveable Type. They know how to perform tasks such as inserting videos and images, and they understand how to name and link those files to boost search engine optimization. Typically, they know enough HTML and CSS to ensure your blog posts publish correctly and are visually appealing, and they know how to use functionality within blogging applications that can improve your blog's performance, boost the reader experience, and drive traffic.

Writing skills

The blogger you hire must be able to write coherently using proper grammar rules. Furthermore, she needs to be able to write in a tone that's appropriate for the conversational style that the blogosphere is known for. If her posts all sound like press releases, marketing pitches, or corporate rhetoric, and if they're filled with grammatical and spelling errors, you don't want her to write your business blog. After all, your business blog is one of the faces of your business and brand. It's an online destination that can create a first impression *and* reader expectations for your business and brand. If consumers arrive on your blog and find content that's difficult to read; sounds like a commercial; or is overloaded with jargon, misspellings, and grammatical errors, it's unlikely they'll return, which may translate into lost sales.

Social personality

A key component of successful blog promotion and growth is the conversation that happens on your blog through the commenting feature. If the blogger you hire needs to build relationships with consumers and people on and off your business blog, she needs to bring a social personality with her. A good blogger is happy to be a part of online discussions both on and off your business blog.

Understanding of search engine optimization

Search engine optimization (SEO) is essential to driving traffic to your blog. For most blogs, the majority of their traffic comes from search engines. The best bloggers know how to write posts using keywords, embed links, and create content that organically helps your blog's search rankings without violating any of the unwritten rules of the blogosphere and algorithms of search engines such as Google. Most professional bloggers have enough SEO knowledge and experience to be capable of publishing content on your blog that leverages the opportunity to increase search traffic to your business blog. You can find out more about search engine optimization in Chapter 1 of Book V.

Existing social networking, social bookmarking, and other social sharing sites presence

Experienced bloggers should have established presences on social networking sites, such as Facebook and LinkedIn, as well as on social bookmarking sites such as Digg and StumbleUpon. Ask for their usernames on these sites, and connect with them so you can take a look at their profiles and find out how they're already using these tools. The best bloggers also have presences on other sharing sites such as YouTube, Flickr, Picasa, and so on.

Active participation on Twitter

Most bloggers can be found on Twitter. Although activity levels on Twitter can vary greatly, experienced bloggers know how to use Twitter. Ask for their profile IDs and follow them on Twitter. Then read through their Twitter stream and find out what conversations they start or participate in there.

A quick test to gauge a blogger's knowledge of how to use Twitter is to ask her what her favorite URL shortener is, which you can find out more about in Chapter 2 of Book VIII.

Knowledgeable about finding and attracting visitors to your blog

Good bloggers know how to find people who might be interested in the content on your blog and entice them to visit your blog to get that information. It will take them time to build an audience, but experienced bloggers know how to do it. Ask candidates what steps they would take to drive traffic to your blog and then read Book VI and compare their answers with the techniques in that minibook. At the very least, an experienced blogger will list the techniques presented in Book VI.

Self motivated and dependable

Most bloggers work virtually and without supervision. That means the blogger you hire must be self-motivated and dependable, so the content you and your audience need is published consistently and your requirements for the blogger are met.

Understands your business or industry

Although it's not essential for a blogger to understand your business, it does shorten the learning curve and make for more compelling content faster if the blogger you hire already understands your business, industry, products, customers, and so on.

Publicizing Your Open Blogger Job

Next, you need to spread the word about your open blogger job. Fortunately, there are a number of blogs and Web sites that allow you to publish blogger job postings. Some require that you pay a small fee, but others are completely free. When you publish your blogger job opening on some of the more popular sites and blogs, people will share the link to your job posting on other blogs, social networking sites, Twitter, and more. In fact, if you publish your blogger job opening on some of the most popular sites that bloggers use to find positions, you may get hundreds and hundreds of responses, many from very qualified bloggers.

The following list includes some of the most popular sites to publish your blogger job posting along with fees published at the time of this writing, but be sure to check each site before you submit a job posting to confirm the current fees:

✦ **The ProBlogger Job Board:** (`http://jobs.problogger.net`) The ProBlogger Job Board, shown in Figure 3-3, is the most popular place for bloggers to seek work. You have to pay a fee required to publish a job posting on this blog job board, but you're guaranteed to get a lot of qualified applicants when you do.

**Book III
Chapter 3**

**Choosing Business
Bloggers**

Figure 3-3:
The
ProBlogger
Job Board.

✦ **About.com Web Logs Forum:** (`http://weblogs.about.com`) The About.com Web Logs Forum includes a folder where anyone can register for free and post a blogger job opening.

✦ **Freelance Writing Jobs:** (www.freelancewritinggigs.com)
Freelance Writing Jobs is one of the most popular blogs for freelance
writers, including bloggers. One of the reasons the blog is so popular
is its job postings. You can publish an open blogger job posting on
Freelance Writing Jobs for free.

✦ **Blogger Jobs:** (www.bloggerjobs.biz/get-featured) Blogger Jobs
is owned by Splashpress Media, the same company that owns the long-
standing and respected blog Performancing. You can publish a blogger
job posting there for $20 per week, which gives you a featured position
in the blog's sidebar. Alternatively, you can report your open blogger
job, and it could be published as a blog post on Blogger Jobs. To report
an open blogger job, visit www.bloggerjobs.biz/report-a-job and
complete the form provided.

✦ **Freelance Web sites:** Many Web sites allow companies to publish job
postings. Freelancers visit these sites and conduct searches to find open
positions that match their qualifications, and then they submit bids for
those projects. Alternatively, you can search for freelancers who have
created profiles on these sites to find someone whose skills match your
needs and then invite her to submit a bid for your project. Most freelance Web sites charge fees — either membership or flat fees *or* a percentage of the freelancer's pay goes directly to the Web site. Examples
of freelance Web sites where you can post open blogger jobs are: oDesk.
com, Elance.com, iFreelance.com, GetaFreelancer.com, and Guru.com.
Be sure to read all the terms and conditions on these sites before you
publish a job posting on them.

Hiring a Blogger

After you decide to hire a person to write and manage your business blog,
you need to consider some personnel-related issues. For example, you need
to define the requirements the blogger has to meet and the skills he needs
to have in order to meet those requirements successfully so you can write a
detailed job description. You also need to review your budget to determine
how much you can pay a blogger that you hire. The following sections highlight some of the most important factors you need to consider before you
start your search for a business blogger.

Employment status

First, you need to determine whether the blogger should be an actual
employee of your company or whether you plan to treat him as a contractor or vendor. Each employee status warrants a slightly different payment
and taxing structure. You should consult with your accountant to determine
which employee status and payment method is best for your business.
Following is a brief overview of the three most common employee statuses
that bloggers typically hold:

✦ **Employee:** Many bloggers are full- or part-time employees of the companies they blog for. In the United States, they're paid as W-2 employees with taxes and other withholding deducted from their paychecks.

✦ **Contractor:** The majority of bloggers are paid as independent contractors. In the United States, that means they aren't considered employees of the companies for which they provide services for. As such, taxes are not withheld from their pay, and they're taxed as 1099 contractors.

✦ **Vendor:** Some bloggers provide services through their own companies, in a vendor-client relationship, with payment and taxes flowing through the vendors' companies and taxed as company income.

Pay model

After you determine the employment status that your blogger will hold, you need to determine how much you can pay him for his work. The pay structure you choose depends on the tasks and responsibilities the blogger will have to perform. For example, a blogger who is only required to publish posts would be paid differently from a blogger who is required to publish posts, respond to comments, and promote the blog through other Web sites.

Following are some of the most popular blogger pay structures to give you a place to start as you develop your own pay plan:

**Book III
Chapter 3**

✦ **Pay per post:** Many bloggers are paid a flat amount for each post they publish. Depending on the experience of the blogger you hire, you may pay anywhere from $5 per post to $50 and up. As you might expect, the best bloggers charge rates in the $50-and-up range.

✦ **Flat monthly rate:** Some bloggers are paid a flat rate each month and are required to perform certain tasks in order to earn that pay such as publishing a specific number of posts, answering a specific number of comments, creating a certain number of links to the blog from other sites, and so on. The payment amount varies greatly depending on the requirements the blogger must meet.

✦ **Pay per post or flat monthly rate *plus* traffic bonuses:** Some bloggers are paid either per post or a flat monthly rate and have the opportunity to earn bonuses if they exceed certain goals, such as the number of page views, comments, incoming links, and so on. As such, the payments these bloggers earn vary significantly.

✦ **Page views or traffic only:** Some bloggers are paid a specific amount based on the traffic or page views a blog receives each month. For example, a blogger may earn a specific amount for every 1,000 page views the blog receives each month.

✦ **Revenue sharing:** Some bloggers are paid only when the blog owner makes money based on ad impressions, clicks, affiliate ad purchases, and so on.

Choosing Business Bloggers

Publishing ads on a business blog can make your blog appear less professional and damage the user experience.

✦ **Combination or pay models:** Some bloggers are paid using a combination of pay models, such as pay per post *plus* a page views bonus *plus* revenue sharing when a sale is made or ads are clicked.

The pay model you choose to follow or reinvent in order to pay your business blogger is up to you and depends very much on your goals for your blog and your budget. For example, if you want to hire a blogger who can write great content *and* drive traffic to your blog, and you're willing to pay him to invest time and energy into promoting your blog to the fullest extent, you need to be willing to pay significantly more than if you only need a blogger to publish posts on your blog.

Most freelance bloggers wear many hats. Unless you hire a freelancer on a full-time basis and with full-time pay, it's very likely that the blogger you choose to write your business blog has other projects and clients as well. In fact, the best candidates *should* have existing clients. As such, bloggers tend to work unusual hours that fit their hectic schedules. Keep this in mind when you set expectations for your new blogger. You might have to be flexible in terms of the times a blogger actually performs work for you.

Many freelance bloggers are able to receive payment for their work through PayPal (www.paypal.com).

Defining Blogger Guidelines

It's important that you create written *blogger guidelines* that tell bloggers what they can and can't do on your business blog. At the same time, it's essential that your business bloggers have the opportunity to write from their hearts and with passion so their unique voices and personalities shine through. That's how bloggers build relationships with readers, and relationships lead to purchases, word-of-mouth marketing, and loyalty.

The first step you can take to create blogger guidelines is to read Chapter 5 of this minibook and discover some of the ways you can promote a business blog while ensuring your company stays out of trouble at the same time. Then communicate those dos and don'ts to your bloggers. Also, take the time to get specific in your guidelines. For example, if bloggers shouldn't mention your competitors in a negative way, make sure to include that in the guidelines. If you don't want bloggers to mention certain prices or talk about certain employees, you need to tell them that.

Following are a few suggestions for blogger guidelines to get you started on creating your own:

✦ Don't mention customer names without written permission.

✦ Don't discuss individual customer service issues. Instead, direct specific questions to the customer service phone number or contact form.

✦ Don't write negative information about your competitors or their products. Remain professional at all times.

✦ Always use brand names correctly. (This is particularly important for companies that have specific capitalization or punctuation requirements related to their trademarks.)

✦ Personal anecdotes and commentary is welcome but remain professional in your language and content at all times. We don't want to offend anyone, but we do want your personality to shine through.

✦ If you're not sure whether it's okay to post something, ask your supervisor. Once something is published online, it can spread faster and wider than you can imagine and then there's no taking it back!

Don't worry about creating a comprehensive list of guidelines right away. Instead, it's better to understand that your blogger guidelines will change over time as new situations occur on your blog and you learn from them.

Don't try to control the conversation that happens on your business blog. Instead, allow readers to take control while your bloggers gently nudge the conversation in the direction you want.

Training Bloggers

It's absolutely imperative that you take the time to train your bloggers. If they're internal employees, you need to make sure that they understand how to use the tools of the social Web in order to meet the goals you set for them and your blog. If they're freelancers, you need to make sure that they understand your business, your customers, and your competitors.

It's your job to provide your bloggers with rules and guidelines as discussed in the previous section. Don't assume they know what you want them to do. Every blog owner has different objectives for their blogs and styles they prefer for the content that's published on their blogs. You need to communicate your objectives and preferences to your bloggers.

Create an electronic training manual (be sure to include your blogger guidelines discussed earlier in this chapter) that your bloggers can refer to at any time for direction and that you can update on the fly whenever it's necessary (and it will be).

If you have specific requirements for your business blog, you should have your bloggers submit posts to you for review during the first month or so that they write for your blog. This way, you can work with the blogger to revise posts to meet your vision for the blog's content *before* those posts are published for the world to see. In time, your blogger will get a better understanding of what you want and need from the blog's content, and you'll become more confident that the blogger can meet your expectations.

Most professional bloggers expect each of their clients to have varied and sometimes very specific likes and dislikes in relation to the content published on their blogs. They expect you to provide them with feedback and guidance so they can better meet your objectives. Don't be afraid to give them some direction. You'll both be happier and more satisfied in the end if you communicate well from the beginning.

Chapter 4: Writing a Business Blog

In This Chapter

✔ Understanding types of blog posts for business blogs

✔ Turning a business blog into a sales tool

✔ Following success tips

✔ Avoiding things customers don't like

✔ Engaging your audience

Your business blog has no chance at success if it's not well-written, but that applies to more than just the grammatical correctness of your blog's content. It also applies to the *kind* of content that you publish on your business blog. To be successful and attract and retain an audience, your business blog posts have to be interesting, entertaining, informative, and conversational. Think of it this way: If you were standing in front of another person and speaking with him, would you want to continue speaking with him if the conversation was dull and boring? Probably not, and the same thing holds true for your business blog. If your content is horrible, no one will want to hang out with you.

This chapter focuses on the actual writing of your business blog posts, so you can find out how to write content that your audience members want and that can motivate them to join the conversation. Remember, the power of your blog as a business tool is building relationships with readers. You can't build a relationship with someone unless you use your blog as an interactive location for two-way conversation.

Discovering the Types of Business Blog Posts

The only limit in terms of the types of posts you can publish on your business blog is your own creativity. By thinking outside the box, you can create a wide variety of blog posts to keep your content fresh and unique. By writing with your own voice and allowing your personality to shine through, your blog posts are innately unique.

To get started on your path to creating excellent business blog content, take a look at the short list of types of posts you could publish as follows (you can read more about these post types and more in Chapter 2 of Book I):

✦ **New product information and reviews:** If you have a new product, talk about it on your blog!

✦ **How-to's:** Teach your readers how to use your products.

✦ **Trends:** Discuss trends related to your industry. What's changing? What are the latest predictions for the future? Add your own insight to your posts to remind readers that you're knowledgeable and trustworthy.

✦ **Answer questions:** Your blog is a great place to answer consumer questions related to your products and services.

Make sure you steer clear of highly personal questions, or your blog might turn into a customer service tool rather than a marketing tool.

✦ **Interviews:** You can interview happy customers, distributors, employees, industry experts, and more.

✦ **Videos and podcasts:** Mix things up by publishing video and audio posts. Publish a video demo of your product in action or film a behind-the-scenes video that shows your employees doing their jobs to make your business seem more human to your blog audience. Interview a customer or employee and publish it on your blog as an audio post. Get creative and have fun!

✦ **Photos:** Take pictures around your office or at company events and share them in a blog post so people can see what's happening behind the scenes.

✦ **Contests and discounts:** Make your audience feel special by holding contests and announcing special discounts for your products and services on your blog before anyone else hears about them, or make the contests or discounts for your products and services exclusive to people who find them on your blog.

✦ **Insider perspectives:** A great way to build relationships with your audience members is to give them an idea of who is behind the company and what it's like to work at the company. As such, publish posts that talk about the daily activities of your employees.

✦ **Tips, secrets, and lists:** People love list posts, and you can create a list about almost any topic. For a business blog, you can publish helpful lists that give people ideas about how to use your products. You can also get creative and publish entertaining posts such as *10 Things You Never Knew about the CEO.* The key is to offer useful information about your business and build relationships by letting your audience get to know you, your employees, and your business a bit better.

✦ **Guest posts:** Invite industry experts and customers to write guest blog posts and offer new perspectives for your audience.

✦ **Polls and questions:** Ask questions and publish polls on your blog for informal market research and information sharing. People love polls!

✦ **Industry news:** Give your audience an education about your industry by talking about it on your blog. Add your own commentary to news about current events to help your readers understand how it applies to them and can affect their lives.

✦ **Company news:** Share exciting news about your company but don't write the news so that it reads like a press release. Keep it conversational.

Don't always publish the same types of blog posts. Mix up your content for variety, or your audience will lose interest.

Landor Associates is one of the leading branding companies in the world. The company maintains a blog (`http://landor.com/index.cfm?do=thinking.blog`) called *What's up below Deck?,* where the writers talk about a wide variety of topics, but those posts are all cleverly tied back to Landor's core purpose — branding. Take a look at the post from Landor's blog in Figure 4-1, which was written by Landor's New York Managing Director Allen Adamson. In his post, Allen discusses the television show *Mad Men* and ties it back to branding and his own company by comparing how the office look, functions, and politics depicted in the television show compare to modern offices and strategies like those of his own company. It's a clever way to connect a current topic to his company's blog and provide interesting content without confusing his audience.

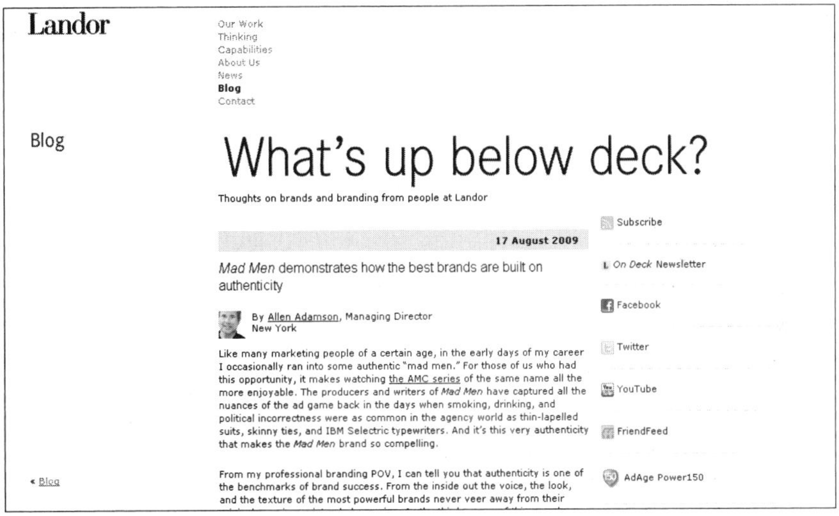

Book III
Chapter 4

Writing a Business Blog

Landor

Our Work
Thinking
Capabilities
About Us
News
Blog
Contact

Blog

What's up below deck?

Thoughts on brands and branding from people at Landor

17 August 2009

Mad Men demonstrates how the best brands are built on authenticity

By <u>Allen Adamson</u>, Managing Director
New York

Like many marketing people of a certain age, in the early days of my career I occasionally ran into some authentic "mad men." For those of us who had this opportunity, it makes watching <u>the AMC series</u> of the same name all the more enjoyable. The producers and writers of *Mad Men* have captured all the nuances of the ad game back in the days when smoking, drinking, and political incorrectness were as common in the agency world as thin-lapelled suits, skinny ties, and IBM Selectric typewriters. And it's this very authenticity that makes the *Mad Men* brand so compelling.

From my professional branding POV, I can tell you that authenticity is one of the benchmarks of brand success. From the inside out the voice, the look, and the texture of the most powerful brands never veer away from their

Subscribe
On Deck Newsletter
Facebook
Twitter
YouTube
FriendFeed
AdAge Power150

« <u>Blog</u>

Figure 4-1:
The Landor Associates blog.

Turning a Business Blog into a Direct Sales Tool

Your business blog can be an effective tool in driving sales both directly and indirectly. The first thing that probably comes to mind when thinking about using your blog as a sales tool is publishing posts that hype your products and services. This is absolutely something you should do on your business blog, but you need to exercise restraint. You don't want your business blog to read like one marketing pitch after another. Remember, your business blog is not an advertising medium but rather a medium for interaction, building relationships, and driving word-of-mouth marketing. However, you can apply short-term marketing tactics to your business blog strategy by occasionally publishing new product announcements, reviews, special discounts, and so on.

Many small business owners do this very well on their company blogs by mixing useful, informative posts with announcements of events they'll be speaking at or attending. That's a great way to establish yourself as an expert in your industry and offer people places where they can network with you in person. Long story short, if your promotional posts are useful and interesting to your blog's audience, then by all means publish them.

As an example, Joe Pulizzi of Junta42 (`http://blog.junta42.com`), shown in Figure 4-2, published a blog post that includes a video of a speech he made at an event related to his area of expertise — content marketing. This is a great way to share useful information *and* remind your readers of the expertise you offer through your business.

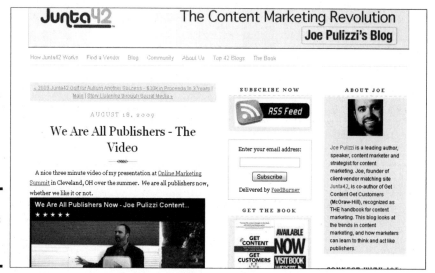

Figure 4-2: Joe Pulizzi's blog for Junta42.

You can turn your business blog into a sales tool in a number of specific ways. Some suggestions follow, but remember, your business blog is *always* an indirect catalyst to sales because it provides you the opportunity to build your brand, engage your target audience members, and develop relationships with them in a manner that wasn't possible a decade ago. Use that ability to connect with consumers to your advantage, but don't abuse it. (I tell you how to avoid abuses in the later section, "Avoiding Things Blog Readers Don't Like.")

✦ **Publish exclusive discounts and promotions.** Your blog audience should be rewarded for taking the time out of their busy schedules to read your content. Make them feel special and valued by providing exclusive discounts and information on your blog that no one can hear about *unless* they read your blog.

✦ **Provide links to your online catalog.** Don't be afraid to get creative in order to publish links to products you want to push on your blog posts. For example, publish product demonstration videos or tutorials and tips related to one of your products, and be sure to include links to that product in your online store to make purchasing it as easy as possible.

✦ **Send newsletters with links to your blog.** E-mail newsletters to your customer e-mail list with links to your useful blog content. Make sure some of those links lead to posts that hype a product or offer an exclusive discount to entice readers to make a purchase.

✦ **Ask consumers to write reviews.** Publish consumer reviews as blog posts (with your consumers' permission) and then provide links to the reviewed products in your online store to make ordering easy.

✦ **Link to your online marketing promotions.** If you have online marketing promotions going on outside of your blog, tell your audience about them and provide links to them. Your blog's audience members should always feel like they're in the know.

If your business operates offline aside from your Web site and blog, you can still write blog posts that lead to direct sales. Instead of seamlessly linking to your online catalog so consumers can make an immediate purchase, you can link to a contact form, your e-mail, or your telephone number. The process consumers have to follow might be more cumbersome, but it can work for businesses that don't have online stores, particularly service businesses. The contact form used by 10k Webdesign (`http://www.10kgroup.com/10kwebdesign/contactus.php`) provides a good example, as shown in Figure 4-3.

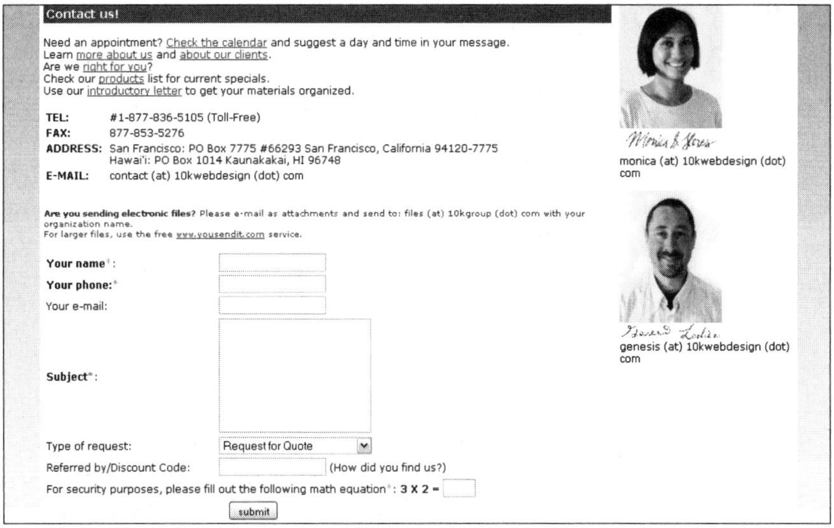

Figure 4-3:
A sample contact form from 10k Webdesign.

Contact us!

Need an appointment? Check the calendar and suggest a day and time in your message.
Learn more about us and about our clients.
Are we right for you?
Check our products list for current specials.
Use our introductory letter to get your materials organized.

TEL: #1-877-836-5105 (Toll-Free)
FAX: 877-853-5276
ADDRESS: San Francisco: PO Box 7775 #66293 San Francisco, California 94120-7775
Hawai'i: PO Box 1014 Kaunakakai, HI 96748
E-MAIL: contact (at) 10kwebdesign (dot) com

Are you sending electronic files? Please e-mail as attachments and send to: files (at) 10kgroup (dot) com with your organization name.
For larger files, use the free www.yousendit.com service.

Your name :
Your phone:
Your e-mail:

Subject :

Type of request: Request for Quote
Referred by/Discount Code: (How did you find us?)
For security purposes, please fill out the following math equation : 3 X 2 =
submit

monica (at) 10kwebdesign (dot) com

genesis (at) 10kwebdesign (dot) com

Finding Out the Tips for Business Blog Success

You can do many small things when you write your business blog posts to position your blog for success. Most of them don't take long to implement but can have a big impact on your blog's growth. Many of these tips apply for personal blogs, too. Take a look at the following list to put your blog on the path to success:

+ **Write often.** Each new blog post represents a new entry point for search engines to find your blog. The more you post, the more potential search visitors you can attract.

+ **Write well.** No one wants to read a blog that is poorly written and filled with grammatical and spelling errors. Furthermore, great content will pull in traffic over time.

+ **Be social.** Show your audience members you value them by responding to comments and e-mails and making them feel like they're part of the community.

+ **Use links.** Link out to great content on other blogs. Don't just hyperlink words like *look here.* Instead, use keywords for linking to boost your search engine rankings.

+ **Get incoming links.** Visit other blogs and start leaving comments. Offer to write guest blog posts for other bloggers, and be sure to include links back to your blog.

+ **Remember your brand.** Blogs are powerful brand-building tools. Be sure to present your brand consistently and persistently.

+ **Write for your audience.** Your biggest priority is writing content that will help your readers. Put yourself in their shoes and then create the kind of content they want and need.

+ **Don't fall for get-traffic-quick schemes.** More often than not, people who guarantee big traffic in a short amount of time are using techniques that could get you banned from Google search.

+ **Don't buy text links.** Google doesn't like them because they artificially increase the number of incoming links that a site gets, which Google uses to rank search results. If Google catches you paying for text links, your blog may be removed from Google searches entirely.

+ **Don't be a hermit.** For your blog to be successful, you need to spend time outside of your blog networking and promoting your amazing content. The blogosphere doesn't work like *Field of Dreams.* If you build it, they *won't* necessarily come.

Avoiding Things Blog Readers Don't Like

Your blog is an interactive tool based on personality and conversation. Blog posts that sound like your legal department wrote them won't attract or retain visitors. In fact, they'll drive visitors away. Instead, your blog content has to be inviting and devoid of the corporate style that many businesses use in their customer communications. Blog posts should be easy to read, highly scannable, and interesting, as opposed to being excruciating to read, so complex they require a legal dictionary to understand, and utterly boring. Again, put yourself in your target audience members' shoes and publish the type of content they want and need written in a friendly voice that invites them to hang out for a while.

Take a step back from your blog and read the content as if you were attending a party and the blog posts are stories that another party guest is telling you. Would you want to keep talking to this person, or would you want to escape and avoid him for the rest of the night? The answer to that question should tell you whether or not you're writing the kind of content that attracts and retains visitors to your blog.

It can take time for your blogging style and personality to evolve, but you can help the process by avoiding some of the fundamental don'ts of the blogosphere. The following sections tell you how to avoid doing some of the things that blog readers don't like. Commit these wrongs at your own risk.

A blog that reads like an employee manual

Your business blog shouldn't be written like an employee manual, a press release, a legal document, a technical paper, a training guide, or anything similarly boring. Instead, it should sound conversational and like it's coming straight out of a real person's mouth. Would you rather read a manual from your company's human resources department or personable blog posts written in a conversational and inviting tone? With any luck, you answered the latter, because that's what the vast majority of blog readers want.

The team from the WooThemes blog (www.woothemes.com/blog), shown in Figure 4-4, offers a great example of writing business blog posts in a human voice that's conversational and inviting.

An impersonal tone

This tip goes along with the "Be human" tip. Your blog posts must be written in a conversational tone that allows your personality and unique voice to shine through. Often a blogger's passion for her subject and personal view point is what keeps readers coming back to read more. Yours might be a business blog, but that doesn't mean it has to be written like a business communication. Instead, inject your personality into every post.

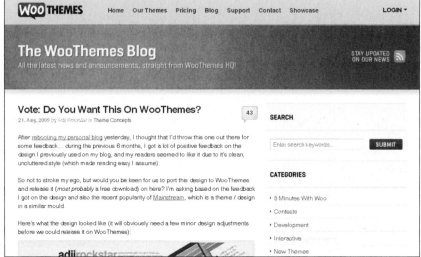

Figure 4-4:
The
WooThemes
blog.

A blog that lacks transparency

In today's world, transparency is more important than ever. Companies that are honest and forthcoming with information are valued higher in consumers' minds than those that try to hide information or tell only part of a story. With that in mind, your blog posts should be written with honesty and candor without giving away any company secrets. People can see through a blog that's written in half-truths and will leave your blog with the perception of your company being untrustworthy if that's the only kind of content they find. That's a reputation you don't want to spread!

Corporate rhetoric

Jargon and buzz words have no place in a business blog unless your target audience is business-to-business readers who understand those words and phrases. Consider your audience before you use an acronym in your blog posts. Following are just ten of the many words that the online community often refers to as *gobbledygook* because they do nothing to enhance writing. Try to avoid these words unless they truly are appropriate for your specific audience:

✦ Scalability

✦ Best in class

✦ Methodology

✦ Paradigm

✦ Value proposition

✦ Synergy

✦ Organic

✦ Grassroots

✦ Best practices

✦ Next generation

You can analyze your blog post content for gobbledygook by using HubSpot's Gobbledygook Grader tool shown in Figure 4-5. The tool was created with marketing expert David Meerman Scott. You can simply copy and paste your content into the text box at www.gobbledygook.grader.com to determine how saturated your writing is with clichés, overused words, and jargon.

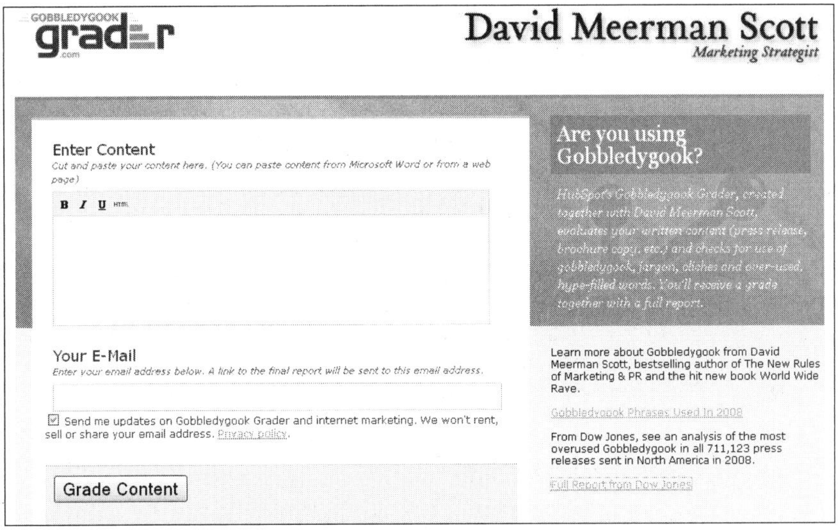

Figure 4-5:
The Gobble-
dygook
Grader tool.

**Book III
Chapter 4**

**Writing a Business
Blog**

PR posts with no real content

If your blog includes one promotional post after another, there isn't much reason for readers to come back. You have to add value to their experience on your blog by educating them, sharing with them, conversing with them, and building relationships with them as opposed to just speaking *at* them by publishing one PR pitch after another. Would you want to watch television if all you saw was one commercial after another? The same question can be asked about your blog. Would you want to read a blog that includes one promotional post after another? Your business blog should include at least 80 percent useful posts and 20 percent promotional posts to strike a good balance that will keep readers interested without frustrating them.

Engaging with Your Audience

The power of a business blog comes from the interactivity it provides between the company publishing the blog and the consumers reading it. It's an opportunity to build relationships with consumers that every business owner can leverage because the barriers to entry into the blogosphere are negligible. Keep in mind that the way your audience engages with you through your blog can often coincide with the types of blog posts you write, as discussed earlier in this chapter. In other words, your content can often prompt and steer the ongoing conversation that happens on your blog. The following sections review some of the ways you can interact with your audience to create conversation and build relationships with them.

Providing content the audience wants

The best way to strike up a conversation is to talk about something other people are actually interested in. If your side of the conversation is boring, chances are good that no one else will join in. However, if your side of the conversation is informative and interesting, other people are much more likely to join in.

Encouraging comments

Remind readers that they're invited to join the conversation by asking for their opinions. Ending your blog posts with a simple sentence, such as, "Leave a comment and tell us what you think," can do wonders in terms of prompting people to join the conversation. Check Figure 4-6 from the Corporate Eye blog (`www.corporate-eye.com`) for an example of how to ask readers to leave comments on your blog posts.

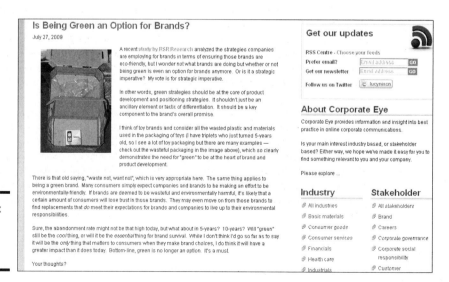

Figure 4-6: The Corporate Eye blog.

Making the audience feel special or exclusive

As I mention earlier in this chapter, there are many ways you can create blog posts that make your audience feel special or exclusive. For example, you can publish special discounts for your blog audience only. The goal is to thank your audience for reading your blog and show them how much you value them. If you ignore them, they're not likely to stay loyal to you. Instead, make sure you remind them how important they are to you by publishing unique posts that make them feel special.

Creating relationships with key influencers

One of the best things you can do for your business blog is find and connect with key online influencers. These influencers might be other industry bloggers, consumers, journalists, industry experts, and so on. The key is to find people who can be your vocal brand advocates and spread the word about your products and blog by creating an online buzz.

For example, if you sell technical equipment, connecting with gadget bloggers who have large and loyal audiences of their own would be a major coup for you. When those influencers know your blog exists and you publish great content, they might link to your content. Alternatively, you can approach them to write product reviews, or write a guest blog post for their blogs. But first, you have to build relationships with them or your requests are likely to get lost in the e-mail clutter popular online influencers have to sort through everyday.

Leveraging word-of-mouth marketing

After you find online influencers, you can leverage their reach to boost word-of-mouth marketing about your blog, business, products, and services. Additionally, you can tap your own blog audience members and ask them to write about your business or share your best posts with the larger online community through Twitter, social bookmarking, social networking, and so on. The key is to jump-start the online sharing process, so the online buzz and word-of-mouth marketing have a chance to grow and spread.

Furthermore, take time to interact with people outside of your blog. You can start an online buzz through conversations that happen on other blogs and Web sites just as easily as you can start them on your own blog. The key is to be patient and persistent. In time, your efforts *will* pay off, but blogging success very rarely happens overnight. For most bloggers, it can take months or years to build a successful blog. Be prepared to invest your time and energy into achieving long-term success with short-term boosts along the way.

Book III
Chapter 4

Writing a Business Blog

Chapter 5: Keeping Yourself and Your Company out of Trouble

In This Chapter

✔ Following the rules of the blogosphere

✔ Staying within the law

✔ Keeping private information private

✔ Responding to negative attacks

✔ Leveraging search engine reputation management

*B*ecause your business blog can be seen by anyone with Internet access, you must follow both the rules of the blogosphere *and* the rules of law in order to avoid trouble. Although a blog might seem more casual and flexible than traditional business publications, and it should be, that doesn't mean you can violate established rules and laws. This is particularly true for public companies that are subject to strict insider trading regulations. The best path to follow is one of caution. It's better not to publish something you're unsure of than it is to risk getting in trouble for something you publish on your business blog.

Trouble isn't restricted to the content you publish on your business blog. It can also come from the *conversation* that happens on and off your blog. Unfortunately, some people travel around the blogosphere trying to incite arguments and stir up trouble by publishing comments for the sole purpose of igniting passionate responses. That's just one more area for potential problems that you need to be aware of when you publish a business blog, and you should have a plan to avoid or deal with that negative publicity when the time comes.

This chapter provides an overview of the primary areas where business bloggers can find themselves at the center of trouble as well as specific rules and guidelines you need to follow to avoid attracting a negative buzz and unwanted turmoil related to your business and brand.

Learning Rules and Laws

You've undoubtedly heard of copyright infringement and privacy laws. Both can be applied to the content you publish on your business blog. Furthermore, you're probably familiar with terms such as *spam* and *attribution*. All of these terms represent rules and laws you need to be aware of and adhere to as you publish content on your blog. Just because you're hiding behind your computer as a blogger doesn't mean that you're above the law. The rules still apply to you.

Many rules and guidelines apply to all bloggers, and you should familiarize yourself with them by reading Chapter 4 of this minibook. You also need to take time to consider how your online behavior and activity affect your business based on the industry you're in, who your customers are, and where and what you sell. It's very possible that you need to follow industry-related rules in addition to the blanket guidelines and laws that apply to the blogosphere and online publishing.

When in doubt, either don't publish questionable content or consult with an attorney to ensure that you can safely publish that content on your business blog. It's always better to be safe than sorry because, in the eyes of the blogosphere or in a court of law, you can't simply claim ignorance and walk away unscathed when you do something wrong.

Following blogosphere rules

The rules of the blogosphere deal primarily with ethics. In other words, the blogosphere simply asks you to publish content in an ethical manner. Following are some of the primary rules you need to adhere to as a blogger:

✦ **Publish original content.** Don't copy content and republish it as your own.

✦ **Provide attribution.** Always link to your sources. You can do this in any way that you choose. For example, you might include a text link within your blog post or at the end of your blog post, as shown in Figure 5-1, which is from the taxgirl blog (www.taxgirl.com). As long as the link to your source is included, you should be safe.

✦ **Don't publish spam.** Don't leave comments on other blogs that are filled with links and viewed as spam.

✦ **Play nice.** Don't attack other people or businesses on your blog in a hateful manner.

In other words, act politely.

Figure 5-1:
Provide attribution to your sources within your blog posts.

Remember to attribute your sources

Staying within the law

Many laws apply to online publishing, and most personal bloggers don't know what they are. You can't afford *not* to fully understand those laws and apply them to your business blog. The last thing you want to elicit from your blog is a legal entanglement. With that in mind, it's a good idea to publish a Terms and Conditions document on your blog so your audience understands the legalities surrounding their participation on your blog. You can see a sample Terms and Conditions document in Chapter 4 of Book I.

To be safe, always publish content on your business blog with the following legal issues in mind:

✦ **Copyrights:** Every piece of published content is owned by the person who created it under copyright law. That means you can't simply find an image on the Web and republish it on your business blog. Don't violate copyright laws. Either create original content or seek written permission to use someone else's content before you publish it on your blog.

Read Chapter 4 of Book I for more blogging rules and details about Creative Commons copyright licenses and fair use.

✦ **Plagiarism:** Simply republishing content that someone else created is considered to be plagiarism and is punishable by law. Instead of republishing someone else's words, link to your source and then write about the content and inject your own voice, opinions, and expertise to make it your own.

✦ **Permissions:** Don't use images, graphs, charts, texts, or any other content on your blog unless one of these exceptions apply:

- You have written permission to do so.

- You know the content is copyrighted under a Creative Commons license.

- You know it's appropriate for you to use that content under the laws of fair use.

You can communicate to your readers that content is republished with permission by including a simple phrase such as "used with permission" (as shown in Figure 5-2) and linking back to your source as appropriate.

Figure 5-2:
Include a "used with permission" disclaimer with content that does not belong to you.

A "used with permission" disclaimer

✦ **Citations:** Always, always, always cite your sources and link to them if possible.

✦ **Libel:** Avoid publishing content on your business blog that can be construed as libelous. In other words, don't publish content that is malicious or can damage another person's or business's reputation, credibility, and livelihood.

✦ **Insider information:** If your company is public, you must adhere to laws related to insider trading and sharing information that might affect the company's stock price. Be sure that any content you publish on your business blog is information that is freely available to the public.

✦ **Confidentiality agreements:** If your company has signed confidentiality agreements with any business partners, your blog content must adhere to the restrictions listed in those agreements.

Maintaining private information

As a business owner, you have access to personal information about your customers, employees, and business partners. Privacy laws get stricter every day. Don't risk violating them. Instead, avoid publishing personal or private information on your business blog unless you get written permission to do so first. This applies to written content, quotes, pictures, and anything else that might violate either a person or a business's privacy.

Don't share private information about your blog's audience unless you get explicit permission to do so.

It's a good idea to publish a privacy policy on your blog, so visitors understand what information you collect from them during their visit (such as the path they travel as they navigate your blog — accessed via your Web analytics tool, as discussed in Chapter 2 of Book V). You can see an example of a privacy policy in Chapter 4 of Book I.

Consider hiring an attorney to write your business blog's privacy policy and Terms and Conditions document to ensure you and your business are fully protected.

Knowing when to hold your tongue

Because the blogosphere is an open medium, people will stumble upon your content and might leave irrelevant, erroneous, or hateful comments on your business blog. It's important that you understand that these types of comments are inevitable and prepare for responding to them. The worst thing you can do is react to negative online conversations about your business or blog. Instead, act professionally and represent your business the best way you can by deleting hateful comments, communicating in a professional tone, and trying to steer conversations back on track without arguing.

The same theory holds true for the content you publish on your blog. Always make sure the topics you write about are relevant and useful to your audience. Although it's important to inject your personality into your business blog posts, don't write your business blog like it's your personal blog. In other words, although there are some topics you can write about freely on your personal blogs, those topics might not be appropriate for your business blog.

For example, most business bloggers steer clear of writing about religion and politics on their blogs because they know those topics can affect their brand and can incite passionate conversations that often turn into arguments and

Book III
Chapter 5

Keeping Yourself and Your Company out of Trouble

become irrelevant to the business behind the blog. It's up to you to determine which topics and conversations are relevant to your blog and then write content that's appropriate for those topics.

If someone leaves an irrelevant comment on one of your blog posts that isn't spam but also isn't helpful, you can try to steer the conversation back on track by responding with a new comment pointing readers back to the topic at hand.

Responding to Negative Comments and Attacks

The day will come during the lifespan of your business blog that you or your business will become the subject of negative comments or the target of attacks. This negative publicity can happen on or off your blog, so it's important that you keep track of what's being said about your business and brand online by implementing a strategy for search engine reputation management (SERM), as discussed later in this chapter. At the same time, you need to have a strategy in place to respond to negative comments and attacks.

You can employ a number of tactics to respond to a negative buzz about your business online. Each situation is unique, and each business has its own goals for its online presence that can affect its response strategies. Take the time to prepare yourself for the inevitable negativity that will come as a result of your business blog so you can react in a timely and professional way when that day comes.

Bloggers must be thick-skinned. There will come a time when someone will say something online that is particularly cruel about you as a person. Don't take it personally, and try to remember that people forget their manners when they're hiding behind their computers. Don't feed into their power delusions by spending any time thinking about them.

Ignoring the negative

Believe it or not, sometimes responding to negative comments just adds fuel to the fire. In time, your loyal blog audience might come to your defense, so you won't have to participate in a negative conversation at all. I caution against ignoring negative comments on your business blog though. Remember, transparency and honesty are essential elements of a successful business blog. By professionally responding to negative comments, your audience is likely to respect your forthrightness and like you more for it.

However, you can take a different approach to handling highly negative comments that address personal complaints and add little to the conversation on your business blog. By responding with a comment that directs the visitor to the appropriate source for answers to their personal problems or questions, you can keep private conversations off of your business blog while being responsive and showing you value *all* visitors at the same time.

Don't be afraid to delete hateful or off-topic comments that detract from the conversation on your blog. You can also edit comments to remove profanity. Just be sure to publish a comment policy on your blog to set visitor expectations, as discussed in Chapter 4 of Book I.

Defending the business

The natural response to negative comments and attacks is to defend yourself and your business. Naturally, you should defend your company against false statements, but be careful. You don't want to come off as completely defensive. Instead, you need to *listen to* and *acknowledge* what people are saying in their comments — even if those comments are negative. Doing so demonstrates to your audience that you value all your visitors and understand that their thoughts, opinions, and experiences matter to you and your company.

When you defend your business against negative comments and attacks, do so in a professional manner. Be open to opposing viewpoints and allow debates and discussions to happen on your blog, knowing that your role is to provide accurate information and a forum for dialogue while reeling in conversations that veer off topic. Instead of jumping up and saying, "That's not true!" in response to a negative comment, ask the commenter why he feels that way or what happened to give him that perception so you can work to make things right or help clarify the issue for him.

Blogging is all about building relationships. Even if you disagree with someone, his opinion is valid and should be acknowledged accordingly. Chances are good that if one person feels negatively about an aspect of your business, he is not alone. Rather than telling him he's wrong, discuss the issue with him, and your larger audience will respond positively to your openness, honesty, and willingness to listen to and work with your customers. In short, don't try to squash the negative. Instead, try to turn negatives into positives through the social conversations that blogs offer.

Engaging the source and audience

Often negative comments are made about you or your business off of your blog. You need to be aware of those conversations and reach out to the people who start them to set the record straight. Proceed professionally so the originating blogger or commenter understands you're not defensive or attacking him in return. You want to extend an olive branch and try to work with him to resolve problems and correct wrongs. Point him in the direction of accurate information online, offer to follow up via e-mail or phone, or provide him with the accurate contact information where he can get the help he needs.

The same process holds true on your own blog. Over time, you'll notice that your loyal audience will do some of the talking for you both on and off your blog. As your loyal brand advocates, they'll jump to your defense, sometimes better than you can do yourself!

Understanding Search Engine Reputation Management (SERM)

Search engine reputation management (SERM) is tied to online brand building. When you search Google or your preferred search engine for your business or brand name, what comes up? Are the results you find the kind of results that you want your customers to find? Those links are the ones people will click to find out about you, your business, and your brand, so the content found through those links will define your online reputation. Search engine reputation management is the process of working to make sure that search engine results related to your business offer links that accurately reflect your brand.

As an example, look at Figure 5-3, which shows the Google search results for the keyword phrase *target blog*. The second result on the page is a blog written by a disgruntled consumer. In fact, official Target business pages don't appear at all within the first page of results.

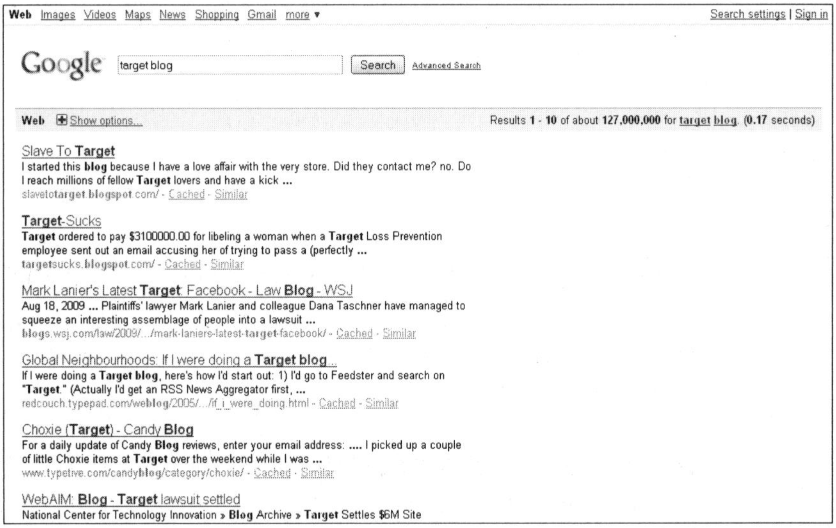

Figure 5-3:
The Google search results for *target blog*.

A similar thing happens when you enter the keyword phrase *Levitt and Sons* into the Google search bar, as shown in Figure 5-4. The top result is a blog written by a highly disgruntled consumer. Today, Levitt and Sons is defunct, having gone bankrupt after the housing market collapsed in 2007. However, this blog came up at the top of search results *before* Levitt and Sons closed its doors. I performed this search in 2007 when I was looking at new home construction and builders, and after finding this result, I admit that I did not pursue purchasing a home from this builder. Of course, it's just one person's experience, but the content published on his blog was compelling and greatly tarnished the company's brand.

You do *not* want this to happen to your business, and that's why ongoing search engine reputation management is absolutely vital.

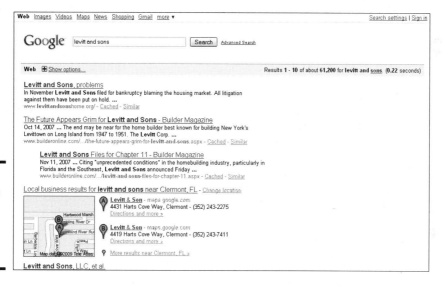

Figure 5-4: The Google search results for *Levitt and Sons.*

Book III Chapter 5

Keeping Yourself and Your Company out of Trouble

Hiring an SERM expert is a great way to analyze and perfect your online reputation, but if hiring a consultant to help you is out of your budget, don't worry. The following sections show you how to conduct SERM initiatives in order to ensure your brand and business are positioned accurately in Google keyword searches.

Responding to and acknowledging mistakes

One of the first things you can do to preserve your search engine reputation is to respond to negative comments and attacks where they happen. For example, if someone writes a negative comment about your company on another blog, leave your own comment in response to offer help or provide accurate information. People who find the negative comment via search engines are likely to also see your proactive and helpful response.

You don't want people to read only one side of a story, particularly when that story paints your business in a negative light. Get involved at the source, engage the original publisher, and redeem yourself and your business where conversations are happening.

Burying the untrue or reputation threats

One of the best ways to control your search engine reputation is to publish great content constantly. The more great content you publish, the more quickly and deeply negative or untrue content published by other people gets buried. Unless that negative content appears on a blog or site that's better search engine optimized for relevant keywords than your own blog, you should be able to bury negative content by flooding the Web with your own content.

With that in mind, don't spend a lot of time responding to negative comments and attacks. Acknowledge them and set the record straight as appropriate, but remember that the more content you publish related to that negative attack, the more chances it has to rise to the top of search rankings. The last thing you want is for the buzz to spread about that negative content, which may draw a lot of incoming links to it, making it harder to bury.

Building an audience of brand advocates and brand guardians

Over time, your blog readers will become loyal to you, your business, and your brand. As such, they'll become vocal brand advocates who want to talk about your business. They represent a powerful form of word-of-mouth marketing that can give your business a significant boost. Furthermore, they're likely to become brand guardians who will defend your business against negative comments and attacks.

There's no stronger form of word-of-mouth marketing than consumer brand advocates who talk about the brands they love, defend them, and try to convert people into brand advocates just like them. Leverage their willingness to talk about you and your business and let the online conversation flow.

Don't be afraid to give up control. Although it's important that you stay aware of what's being said about you and your business online, you shouldn't try to stop conversations. Instead, try to guide them in the right direction, correct inaccuracies, and make yourself available to the wider online community. That's how your blog, as a marketing tool of the social Web, can drive your online reputation and your business to new heights.

Using SERM techniques

To keep track of what's being said online about you, your business, and your brand, you need to stay on top of the conversations taking place on the Web and the content being published. You can keep track of your online reputation in a number of ways. Following are some of the free techniques you can use:

+ **Google Alerts:** Set up Google Alerts (www.google.com/alerts) for your business and brand names as well as keywords people are likely to use to search for your products and services. You can find instructions to set up a Google Alert in Chapter 3 of Book II.

+ **Google search:** Conduct a daily Google search using the Advanced Search feature (www.google.com/advanced_search?hl=en), shown in Figure 5-5, so you can look for specific search strings found within a specific time period, such as within the past 24 hours.

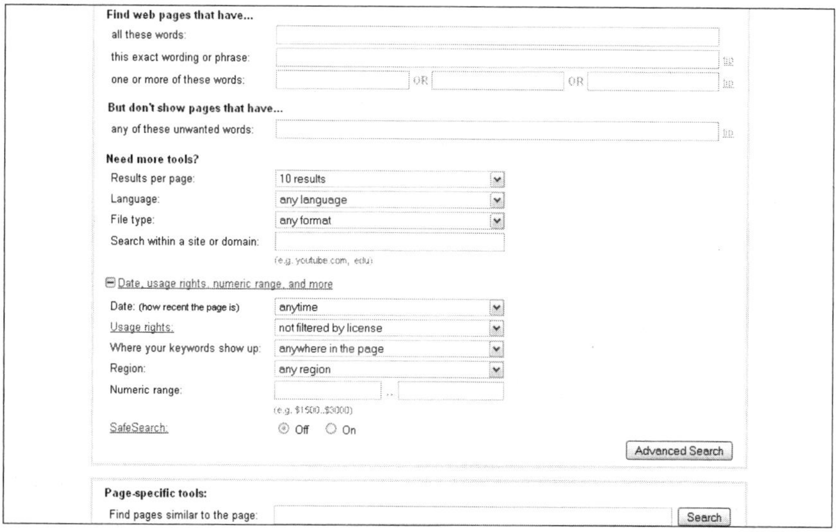

Figure 5-5:
The Google advanced search page.

Find web pages that have...
all these words:
this exact wording or phrase:
one or more of these words: OR   OR

But don't show pages that have...
any of these unwanted words:

Need more tools?
Results per page: 10 results
Language: any language
File type: any format
Search within a site or domain:
                           (e.g. youtube.com, .edu)

⊟ Date, usage rights, numeric range, and more
Date: (how recent the page is)   anytime
Usage rights: not filtered by license
Where your keywords show up: anywhere in the page
Region: any region
Numeric range:
                           (e.g. $1500..$3000)
SafeSearch: ⊙ Off   ○ On

                                    [Advanced Search]

Page-specific tools:
Find pages similar to the page: [Search]

+ **Blog searches:** Conduct blog searches using your business name and relevant keywords via blog search tools such as Google Blog Search (www.blogsearch.google.com), IceRocket (www.icerocket.com), and Technorati (http://technorati.com/search?advanced), as discussed in Chapter 3 of Book II.

Be sure to try the tag search function available through Technorati's search tool (shown in Figure 5-6). Many bloggers identify keyword tags that go along with their posts from within their blogging application, such as WordPress, which Technorati indexes, making them a unique and often relevant way to search for blog content about your business.

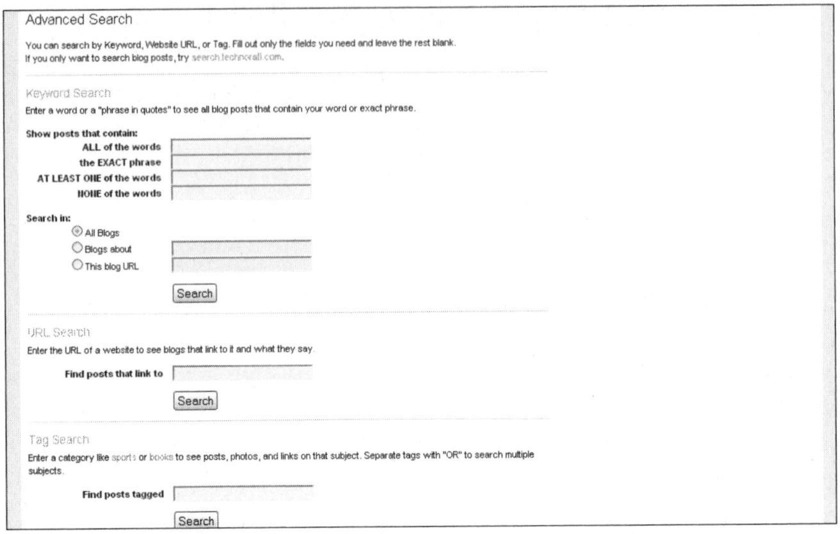

Figure 5-6:
Technorati's
tag search
box.

✦ **Incoming links to your blog:** Using your Web analytics tool, follow incoming links to your blog and read what those publishers are saying about you. You can find out more about Web analytics in Chapter 2 of Book V.

You can also find incoming links to your blog by using Google as follows:

1. **Visit `www.google.com`, as shown in Figure 5-7, and enter** link:www. *yourdomainhere*.com **into the text box, substituting your domain name where it says** *yourdomainhere.*

Change the URL extension if necessary (for example, `.com`, `.net`, `.org`, and so on).

2. **Click the Search button.**

A list of pages that link to your blog is returned to you, as shown in Figure 5-8.

The key to managing your search engine reputation is persistence and consistency. The more amazing content you publish that's optimized for your target keyword search phrases and your business or brand name, the more control you'll have over your online reputation.

Figure 5-7:
Searching
Google for
incoming
links to your
blog.

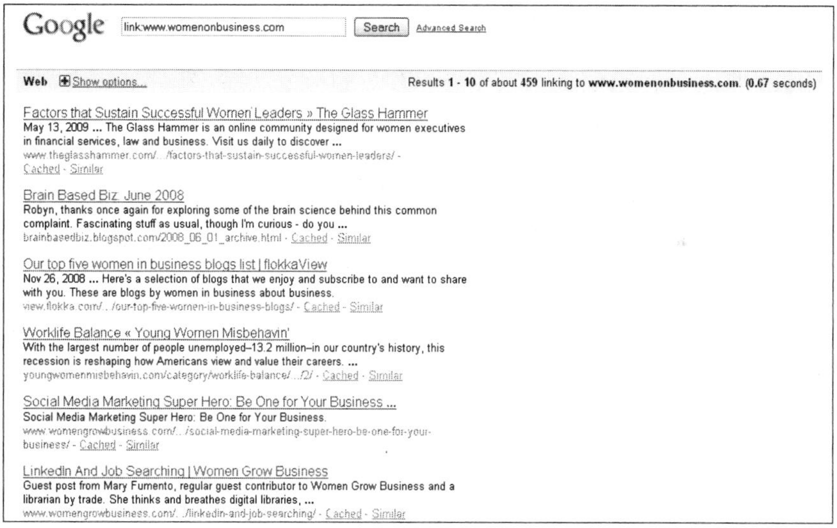

Figure 5-8:
A list of
Web pages
that link to
the blog.

Book IV

Choosing a Blogging Application

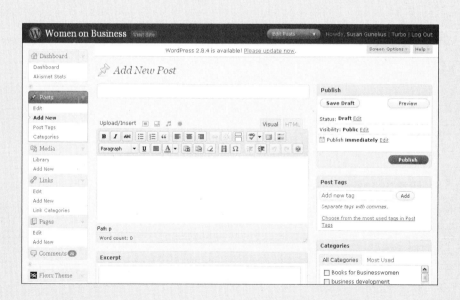

Contents at a Glance

Chapter 1: Choosing a Blogging Application

In This Chapter

✓ Finding out what blogging applications can do

✓ Discovering hosting options

✓ Considering types of blog hosts

✓ Finding and choosing a Web host for your self-hosted blog

Choosing a blogging application that allows you to meet your goals for your blog is critical to your long-term success in the blogosphere. Each blogging application offers similar functionality, but the nuances that exist among applications can have a significant impact on what you can and cannot do with your blog. For example, if your goal for your blog is to increase your Web presence or make money, you need to take time to do some research up front to make the best choice to achieve that goal.

This chapter introduces you to what blogging applications can do for you and defines the types of hosts available, so you can begin your research with an educated base of knowledge about the primary tools of the blogosphere.

Getting Familiar with How Blogging Applications Work

The primary function of all blogging applications (also called blogging software) is the same: to provide users with a way to create a Web presence. In essence, blogging applications are Web-based content management systems (read the sidebar for more information about content management systems) that allow users to create and publish content without a knowledge of Hypertext Markup Language (HTML) or other programming or markup languages.

When blogging applications launched in the 1990s, the online world changed. Suddenly, anyone could have a Web site. Today, many of the most trafficked and popular Web sites are built using a blogging application as a content management system.

What are content management systems?

A content management system (CMS) is an application used to store and publish documents. Content management systems typically offer archive functionality as well as collaborative functionality for creating and editing content.

Document management systems are used to manage documents such as news articles, company documents, financial and legal documents, manuals, and more. These documents can be in digital or printed form. When companies use a document management system,

it is often referred to as an enterprise content management system.

Web content management systems are used to manage the content published online. Most Web content management systems do not require users to have online programming knowledge such as HTML, Extensible Markup Language (XML), or cascading style sheets (CSS) coding abilities. WordPress, Joomla!, and Drupal are examples of popular Web content management systems.

Blogging applications offer several consistent features:

+ **Blog posts:** This is the content that is published on the blog.

+ **Blog comments:** Comments are the conversation that happens around each blog post.

+ **Easy integration of images:** Simple What You See Is What You Get (WYSIWYG) editors, as shown in Figure 1-1, are the hallmark of most blogging applications because that's what allows users to publish posts through an interface similar to word processing software, rather than through extensive coding.

+ **Archives:** The older content that is stored for easy online access is referred to as a blog's content archive.

+ **Feeds for syndication:** Really Simple Syndication (RSS) feeds provide a way for blog content to be delivered to people in multiple ways rather than requiring people to visit a blog to read content.

Blogging applications are amazing tools for Web publishers because they use WYSIWYG editors and drag-and-drop widgets to help nontechnical users create professional-looking Web sites and blogs. Although it can be helpful to know programming languages such as HTML and CSS to leverage the full functionality of a blogging application, it isn't necessary to do so. Take a look at the sidebar to find out more about how HTML and CSS are used to create blogs.

Figure 1-1:
The
WordPress
WYSIWYG
post editor.

Blogging applications also automate a number of useful functions that Web site owners had to do manually in the past. For example, when a new post is published using a blogging application, that post is automatically included in the blog's archives and feed. Additionally, search engines are pinged, notifying them that new content is available. You just have to hit the Submit or Publish button within your blogging application, and everything else is done for you!

Naturally, as you get more advanced in your use of a blogging application, you can find out more about it and do more with it. However, blogging applications are extremely popular because they are easy to use, free or inexpensive, and highly automated.

Understanding HTML, XML, and CSS for blogs

Blogs are created and displayed on your computer screen using a combination of programming and markup languages as follows:

✔ **Hypertext Markup Language (HTML)** is the code used to define the online display of page content, including blog pages.

✔ **Extensible Hypertext Markup Language (XHTML)** is a type of Extensible Markup Language (XML) that is used to write Web pages in a manner that is considered to be better formed and more controlled than HTML provides.

✔ **Cascading style sheets (CSS)** are used to define the presentation of the content on a Web page, such as color, fonts, and layout.

By separating online content from the presentation elements through HTML and CSS, the design and maintenance of blogs become more flexible and easier to manage.

Defining Hosted and Self-Hosted Solutions

Your blog content has to be *hosted* somewhere, meaning it has to be stored somewhere. Most blogging applications support two types of blog hosts: hosted blogs (which are stored online by the blogging application developer who hosts your content for you, often for free) and self-hosted blogs (which you store online, with the help of a Web host of your own choosing that typically requires you to pay a fee for that space). Both options have benefits and drawbacks. The following sections provide an introduction to both forms of hosting.

Hosted blog

Many blogging application developers, such as WordPress, Blogger, and TypePad, offer an option for you to host your content on the developer's server. Some blogging application developers provide hosting services free of charge while others require you to pay a fee (typically a monthly fee, which could be based on the amount of content the developer is hosting for you). Blogs hosted through a developer usually include an extension on the blog's URL such as .wordpress.com, .blogspot.com, or .typepad.com.

By hosting your blog on the blogging application developer's server, you benefit from a consistently high up-time (meaning your blog will be live and functional when people look for it), lower costs, and fewer maintenance hassles. Of course, even developer-hosted blog content can have problems, but going this route significantly reduces the potential for issues *and* makes it incredibly easy for a nontechnical person to have a Web presence.

Self-hosted blog

Rather than hosting your blog content on the blogging application developer's server, many people choose to use a separate Web host to store their data. This is referred to as *self-hosting* your blog. A *Web host* is a company that provides Internet connectivity and makes space on its servers available to individuals and organizations for a fee, where those people can store data for their Web sites, blogs, and so on. The self-hosting option is best for people who aren't afraid of technology and are willing to pay a bit more for greater flexibility and functionality for their blogs.

By self-hosting your blog, you benefit from complete control of your blog in terms of design, content, and functionality. If you self-host your blog, you must find and pay for your own domain name as well. Domain names are inexpensive and provide consistency for people to find your site in the long term as well as unique branding for your blog.

Depending on the blogging application you choose, the hosting options and features vary. Read Chapters 3, 4, and 5 of this minibook for more details about the three most common blogging applications.

Considering the Types of Blog Hosts

The two primary hosting options are discussed in the previous section of this chapter, but the subject isn't quite that cut and dried. The types of blog hosts can actually be split up even more, which can also affect your choice of a blogging application. Take a look at the types of blog hosts that follow to ensure you understand the various options available to you:

✦ **Free:** Everyone loves things that are free, and free blog hosts actually offer a great deal of functionality. Free blog hosts, such as WordPress and Blogger, provide both the blogging application *and* the online space to store your blog content. However, there are typically restrictions related to the amount of space your blog can take up on the developer's servers, the amount of advertising you can publish on your blog in order to make money, and your ability to customize your blog's appearance. With that said, free blog hosts are a good choice for beginner bloggers who have minimal goals for their blogs other than to have fun.

✦ **Shared:** A shared blog host is one where space on a server is shared by multiple users. A shared blog host generally has the lowest price tag attached to it, next to the free option. If you use a shared blog host, your blog content is stored on the same server as other customers of the blog hosting company. That means your costs are kept down, but you have to fight for space, up-time, and the speed of loading your pages. Also, shared blog host accounts usually have storage space limitations, but you can upgrade your account for a higher fee and access more storage space when you need it. Shared blog hosts are used by the majority of bloggers and small business owners because the offerings are fairly comprehensive despite the reasonable costs.

✦ **Reseller:** Some people, known as *resellers,* buy server space from a blog host or company and then rent that space to bloggers. It's essential that you research a reseller before you commit to hosting your blog through one. It is *very* likely that you can get the same features, functionality, and pricing (or more) if you work directly with a blog hosting company.

✦ **Dedicated server:** Blogs that get a lot of traffic and/or need consistent up-time are often hosted on a dedicated server, meaning they don't share server space with any other blogs or Web sites. That means the price tag is higher, but storage space and transfer speed are also higher. Typically, you receive little benefit by paying for a dedicated server host rather than a free or shared server host unless your blog is extremely large and trafficked. WiredTree (www.wiredtree.com), shown in Figure 1-2, is an example of a company that focuses entirely on providing dedicated server hosting for blogs and Web sites.

**Book IV
Chapter 1**

**Choosing
a Blogging
Application**

Figure 1-2:
WiredTree
provides
blog hosting
services on
dedicated
servers.

The vast majority of blogs are hosted for free or on shared servers.

Finding and Choosing a Web Host for a Self-Hosted Blog

Now that you know the primary functions of blog hosts and the most common types of blog hosts, you need to decide which option (free, shared, or dedicated) is best to help you meet your blogging goals.

Changing from one blog host to another rarely works seamlessly. To avoid problems later, take the time to choose the best blog hosting option for you now!

Comparing Web hosts

You can use the following five comparison points to evaluate third-party blog hosts apples-to-apples:

✦ **Fees:** Review the features available from different types of blog hosts described in the previous section (free, shared, or dedicated) and then determine whether or not investing in a third-party blog host can benefit you in the long run.

Web hosting prices and packages change frequently. Be sure to review pricing right before you commit to purchasing Web hosting services, so you're not surprised by a sudden price change.

+ **Space:** It's important to know whether or not a Web host provides enough space to meet your needs at a price you're willing to pay.

  Don't be tempted by hosting discount offers that provide huge amounts of space. Most bloggers don't need terabytes of space.

+ **Transfer speeds and limits:** You need to know that the Web host you commit to using provides a data transfer rate that is fast enough *and* can accommodate all the content on your Web that is viewed by every person who visits.

  You can upgrade your Web host account to include higher transfer limits as your blog grows in popularity and traffic. Don't overpay for features and functions you don't need when you're first starting your blog.

+ **Up-time:** If the Web host you're considering has a reputation as one that does not provide consistent *up-time* (meaning people can access your blog online without getting error or unavailable messages), look for alternative hosting! You need a blog host that provides reliable up-time, so people can always read your content.

+ **Support:** This is the area where some Web hosts excel and others fail. The blog host you use should have a reputation of providing excellent customer service and support. If you have a problem with your blog at any time during the day or night, you need to know you can pick up the phone, send an e-mail, or start an online chat session and get help quickly and easily.

Identifying popular Web hosts for self-hosting your blog

Web hosts come and go all the time, which is why it's important to choose a Web host that has an excellent reputation and staying power. The following list offers several of the most popular Web hosts to get you started on your research into finding the best blog host for you (you can find more Web host reviews at `http://weblogs.about.com/od/choosingabloghost/Choosing_a_Blog_Host_Software_Provider.htm`):

+ **BlueHost:** (`www.bluehost.com`) I currently host my blogs through BlueHost, and I've been happy with their cost, up-time, features, and support.

+ **Go Daddy:** (`www.godaddy.com`) Go Daddy has been in business for a long time and has a reputation as a reliable source for blog hosting.

+ **Host Gator:** (`www.hostgator.com`) Host Gator has a reputation for reliability and great support.

+ **HostMonster:** (`www.hostmonster.com`) Host Monster is gaining popularity due to its affordable prices as well as its features and up-time.

✦ **Just Host:** (www.justhost.com) Just Host, which is shown in Figure 1-3, is a newer blog hosting company, but the company has been getting a lot of praise for its pricing, reliability, and support.

Figure 1-3:
Just Host is gaining popularity for shared blog-hosting services.

Selecting a Web host

After you've compiled the facts about the features, price, and support offered by several hosting companies, look at them side by side and determine which offers the functionality you need for the best price.

You can always upgrade to a package that provides more space and speed as your blog grows. It's an easy process to upgrade from one package to another from the same hosting company, but it can be a hassle to move from one hosting company to another.

That's not to say it's impossible to move from one hosting company to another. It just takes a bit more technical knowledge to make sure everything transfers without any glitches. However, transferring from using a free host to self-hosting your blog on a Web host creates its own set of problems. Foremost, it's very likely that you'll have to change your domain name (for example, to drop the .wordpress.com, .blogspot.com, or .typepad.com extension) when you move from a free host to a Web host. This can hurt your search engine rankings and cause you to lose your search engine traffic.

Bottom line: It's absolutely critical that you set your goals, do your research, and choose the best blog hosting service that will help you over the long term, rather than selecting the quick and easy short-term option.

Chapter 2: Finding the Right Blogging Application

In This Chapter

✔ Setting your goals

✔ Introducing popular blogging applications

✔ Comparing popular blogging applications

✔ Reviewing other blogging application options

✔ Choosing the best blogging application for you

*I*f you have goals for your blog beyond personal enjoyment, choosing the right blogging application is an important decision for you. Although it's true that the popular blogging applications, such as WordPress, Blogger, and TypePad, offer similar functionality, the nuances among them are great enough that you need to do some research and thinking before you start your blog, in order to ensure you pick the right tool.

For example, if you use the WordPress-hosted blogging application at WordPress.com, you can't display ads on your blog. If making money from your blog is important to you, WordPress.com wouldn't be a good choice for your blog. The less-obvious differences like this one can greatly affect your blog in both the short and long term. This chapter helps you understand the blogging applications that are available to you so you can make the best decision possible.

Determining Your Goals and Needs

As with all aspects of joining the blogosphere, the blogging application you choose depends on your goals and needs for your blog. Each blogger has unique goals and needs, and the same blogging application isn't right for everyone. Yes, you can publish blog posts, allow comments, and store archives using any blogging application, but there's more to blogging than writing blog posts.

If your plans for your blogging experience extend beyond publishing written entries, you must consider the factors included in the following sections before you choose your blogging application.

Growing your blog

If you have dreams of growing your blog into a popular, highly trafficked online destination, you need to choose a blogging application that offers enough storage space and bandwidth to ensure the user experience is both streamlined and fast. As your blog traffic grows (or if your blog includes a lot of photos and images), your blog needs enough storage space to hold all the new content you create as well as a higher bandwidth to ensure pages load quickly.

Customizing your blog

Not all blogging applications are equal when it comes to customizing your blog's design and functionality. Specifically, some blogging applications provide significantly limited customization and functionality in comparison with an application such as WordPress.org, which offers you maximum customization and control.

Branding your blog

Branding is the message, image, and promise of your blog, and it encompasses both tangible (color palette, logo, header image, that sort of thing) and intangible (your voice, content, style, and so on) elements, which together create audience expectations for your blog. A well-branded blog typically uses a custom design that differentiates the blog from its competitors. Personalized domain names and customization options are less flexible in some blogging applications than others. Furthermore, blogs that use personalized domain names devoid of the standard extensions that free blogging applications append to them are instantly viewed as more professional. Visitors look at this personalized domain name and recognize that the blogger actually invested money in the blog.

Maintaining your blog

Different blogging applications require different levels of technical knowledge in order to maximize the potential they offer. Although you can publish content easily using any blogging application, modifying design and functionality is more detailed, and some blogging applications offer more options than others.

Personalizing your blog e-mail addresses

If you want an e-mail address with an extension that matches your blog's domain name, your blogging application choice is limited to those that allow you to use your own domain name.

Investing money into your blog

Some blogging applications (such as TypePad) require that you pay a monthly fee to use them and provide limited functionality and customization. Others are offered for free (such as WordPress.org) but require you to pay to store your blog's content through a Web host, such as BlueHost or Go Daddy, which offers maximum functionality and customization. And other blogging applications are offered completely for free but offer limited functionality and customization. The amount of money you're willing to invest in your blog directly affects your choice of blogging applications.

Making money from your blog

Not all blogging applications allow you to include ads and other monetization initiatives on your blog. If you want to make money from your blog, you need to be certain that you choose a blogging application that allows you to use your blog as a money-making tool.

Taking a Look at the Most Popular Blogging Applications

Over the past decade, certain blogging applications have become the dominant players — WordPress.com, WordPress.org, Blogger, and TypePad. The reasons are simple: These applications are well-developed and quick to integrate new updates and functionality as the blogosphere evolves. They're also easy to use and offer excellent support resources.

That's not to say that other blogging applications aren't good. In fact, you can find out about some blogging application alternatives later in this chapter. It just means that the reputations and reliability of the applications listed here have driven their popularity.

WordPress.com

(www.WordPress.com)

WordPress.com, shown in Figure 2-1, is the free blogging application provided by Automattic, Inc. Blogs published through WordPress.com are hosted by WordPress and include the domain extension .wordpress.com, unless you pay a premium fee, in which case you can use your own domain name. WordPress.com bloggers are limited in terms of the functionality they can add to their blogs. For example, you aren't allowed to display ads on a WordPress.com blog, and the design templates (called *themes* in WordPress) you can use to customize your blog are limited unless you pay a fee to access premium features.

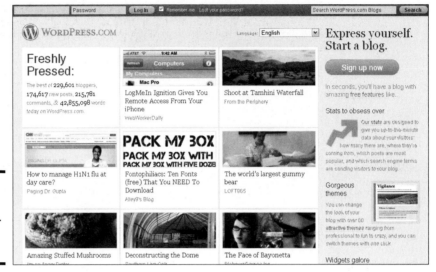

Figure 2-1:
The
WordPress.
com home
page.

On the other hand, WordPress.com is very easy to use, and you can have a blog up and running within minutes. WordPress.com does offer some useful features, such as automatic pinging of sites such as Technorati and Google as well as a comment spam–blocking plug-in (Akismet), post labeling, categorization, trackbacks, and more.

You can find out more about the WordPress blogging applications in Chapter 3 of this minibook.

WordPress.org

(www.WordPress.org)

WordPress.org, shown in Figure 2-2, is offered by Automattic, Inc. for free. However, you need to purchase your own domain name and hosting through a Web host. (You can find out more about Web hosts in Chapter 1 of this minibook.) Additionally, WordPress.org requires some technical knowledge or, at the very least, a lack of fear of technology. That's because to use WordPress.org, you need to be able to upload the application to your Web hosting account and customize it yourself. This isn't hard to do, particularly because most Web hosts offer tools that make installing WordPress very simple. However, it's a process that some bloggers prefer to avoid.

When you use WordPress.org as your blogging application, you have complete control and maximum flexibility. Developers around the world create tools, called WordPress plug-ins, that make it easy to add new features to your blog, and custom designs are simple to create. Additionally, you can use any kind of money-making tools on your WordPress.org blog that you want.

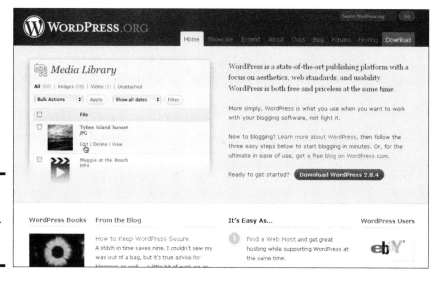

Figure 2-2:
The
WordPress.
org home
page.

Of all the popular blogging applications, WordPress.org is the most flexible and works closest to a true content management system without being technologically overwhelming.

Blogger

(www.blogger.com)

Blogger, shown in Figure 2-3, is owned by Google. It was one of the first blogging applications to gain widespread appeal and continues to be the most popular blogging application for several reasons. First, it's completely free to use, and second, it offers enough customization that many small and mid-size blogs work very well on the platform.

In recent years, several new features have been added to Blogger that make it more competitive with WordPress.org, such as the ability to host a Blogger blog through a Web host of your choice. Also, Blogger blogs always included the .blogspot.com extension until recently when new functionality was integrated allowing users to use their own domain names. However, what sets Blogger apart from other blogging applications is its free price tag coupled with the lack of restrictions related to monetization. In other words, you can publish ads and make money through a free Blogger blog.

Blogger offers the most functionality of the free blogging application choices.

You can get details about Blogger in Chapter 4 of this minibook.

**Book IV
Chapter 2**

**Finding the
Right Blogging
Application**

Figure 2-3:
The Blogger
home page.

TypePad

(www.typepad.com)

TypePad, shown in Figure 2-4, is owned by Six Apart and remains somewhat popular as a blogging application despite the fact that users are limited in functionality and are required to pay a monthly fee. That's not to say that TypePad isn't a good blogging application. Many users are very happy with it because TypePad makes design and maintenance very easy. However, users have to forego extensive customization and features unless they upgrade to more expensive user packages.

TypePad blogs include the .typepad.com extension, but users can purchase and use their own domain names. TypePad also allows users to include ads and other monetization programs on their blogs.

Be sure to check the features offered for each TypePad package on the TypePad Web site to ensure you're willing to pay the required amount to get the functionality your blog needs.

You can find out more about TypePad in Chapter 5 of this minibook.

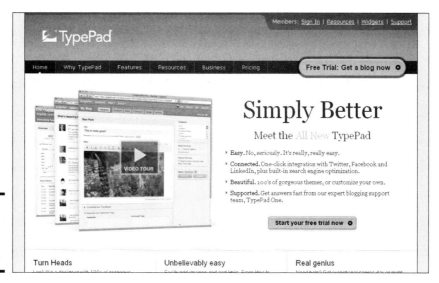

Figure 2-4:
The
TypePad
home page.

Comparing Popular Blogging Applications

WordPress.com, WordPress.org, Blogger, and TypePad all offer similar basic features, but each has its own nuances that can affect your decision in terms of which blogging application will suit you over the long term. Remember, changing from one blogging application to another can be done, but it can cause problems discussed later in this chapter. Position yourself for success from the start by comparing the most popular blogging applications before you join the blogosphere.

Table 2-1 provides a visual comparison of the most popular blogging applications.

Table 2-1   **Comparing Blogging Applications**

Feature	WordPress.com	WordPress.org	Blogger	TypePad
Price	Free (Premium features are available for a fee.)	Free (Web hosting and domain are required, which include fees.)	Free	Tiered structure based on features, number of blogs and authors, and more
Functionality	Limited (Additional functionality is available for a fee.)	Extensive	Limited	Limited (Additional functionality is available based on fee structure.)
Monetization	No (Monetization is available for users who pay a premium fee.)	Yes	Yes	Yes
Technical Knowledge Required	Little	Moderate	Little	Little
Branding	Limited (Additional features, such as personal domains, are available for a fee.)	Yes	Yes	Yes
Customization	Very limited (Additional customization options, such as CSS and HTML modification, are available for a fee.)	Extensive	Limited	Limited
Author and Blog Quantity Limits	Limited number of authors, unlimited number of blogs	Unlimited number of authors, unlimited number of blogs	Limited number of authors, unlimited number of blogs	Limited number of authors, limited number of blogs (The option to have multiple blogs and authors is available based on fee structure.)

An additional note on functionality: WordPres'
ality, although many of those features come '
require a bit of technical knowledge to inst
amount of functionality given its free pric
functionality for a fee.

Also keep in mind that WordPress.org provides the n.
tomization. Blogger users also have a lot of customizatio.
open-source community of developers who create plug-ins an.
WordPress.org users put it above any other blogging application .
customization. TypePad users who pay higher fees for more extensiv
ages get more customization options.

Visit the Web sites for each blogging application you're considering using to
check the most recent information about features and functionality as well as
pricing. Blogging applications are updated frequently, so you need to review
the most current offerings before you choose your blogging application.

Considering Other Blogging Applications

Although WordPress, Blogger, and TypePad are by far the most popular
blogging applications, you have other options. No two bloggers are alike,
nor are two blogging applications. That's why there are many platforms to
choose from and happy users of each. Following is an overview of some of
the less-popular-but-still-common blogging applications.

Movable Type

(www.movabletype.com)

Movable Type, shown in Figure 2-5, is owned by Six Apart, the same company that owns TypePad. The primary difference between Movable Type
and TypePad relates to the management of multiple blogs — something
that Movable Type was built to do and does very well. Also unlike TypePad,
Movable Type blogs are self-hosted, so you store them online through a Web
host, which offers you personal domain selection and greater customization.
However, there is a fee to use Movable Type if you want your blog to have
multiple authors or extensive features, which users must pay in addition to
Web hosting and domain fees.

b2evolution

(http://b2evolution.net)

b2evolution, shown in Figure 2-6, is a free blogging application that users can
install to their Web hosting accounts with their own domains. b2evolution is
popular for people who want to create multiple blogs through a single installation. It's often compared with Movable Type in terms of functionality, but

b2evolution is written in PHP, which has grown to greater acceptance in the blog development community in recent years over Perl, which Movable Type is written in.

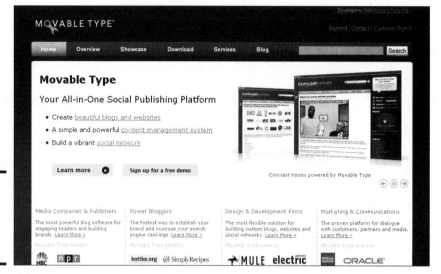

Figure 2-5:
The
Movable
Type home
page.

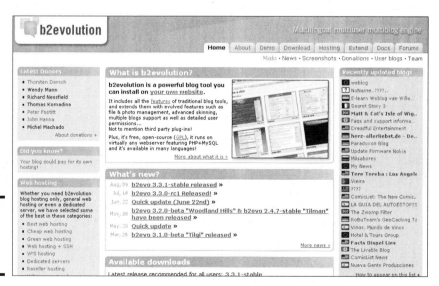

Figure 2-6:
The
b2evolution
home page.

WordPress.org has become more popular than Movable Type, b2evolution, and other multiuser, multiblog applications with the introduction of WordPress MU (which has since been rolled into WordPress.org).

Xanga

(www.xanga.com)

Xanga, shown in Figure 2-7, is an online destination that operates more like MySpace or a social networking site than a standalone blogging application. Xanga members automatically receive space to publish text, photos, audio, and video content in blog form. The site relies heavily on interaction between members.

Figure 2-7:
The Xanga
home page.

ExpressionEngine

(http://expressionengine.com)

ExpressionEngine, shown in Figure 2-8, is owned by EllisLab, Inc. and is advertised as a complete content management system (CMS) rather than solely a blogging application. In fact, ExpressionEngine does come with a variety of CMS tools and features, which you can gain access to by paying a fee. That fee increases based on the amount of functionality you need.

LiveJournal

(www.livejournal.com)

LiveJournal, shown in Figure 2-9, operates more like an online community — where members maintain blogs as part of the user experience — than a standalone blogging application. Anyone can join and publish content for free, but the social nature of the LiveJournal community makes it quite different from the popular standalone blogging applications.

Figure 2-8:
The
Expression-
Engine
home page.

Figure 2-9:
The
LiveJournal
home page.

MySpace

(www.myspace.com)

MySpace, shown in Figure 2-10, is owned by News Corp. and was one of the first social networks to allow users to create profiles and attach blog content to those profiles. Therefore, it's quite different from popular standalone blogging applications because so much of the MySpace experience comes from the social networking aspects of the site.

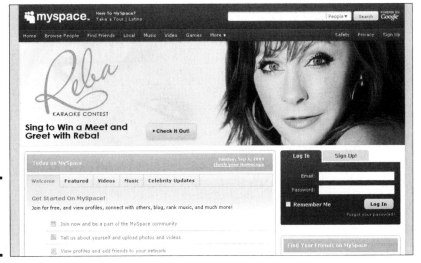

Figure 2-10:
The
MySpace
home page.

Vox

(www.vox.com)

Vox, shown in Figure 2-11, is owned by Six Apart and differs from the company's other blogging applications, TypePad and Movable Type, in that it's more of a social networking tool than a standalone blogging application. However, unlike Xanga and MySpace, which are known first as social networking sites that include blogging features, Vox is known first as a blogging tool supported by its community of users. Therefore, Vox is different from popular standalone blogging applications such as WordPress, Blogger, and TypePad.

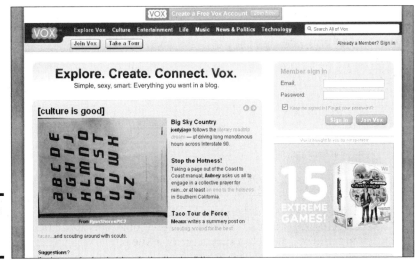

Figure 2-11:
The Vox
home page.

Drupal

(http://drupal.org)

Drupal, shown in Figure 2-12, is a true Web content management system that allows users to create a wide variety of Web sites such as blogs, communities, ecommerce, podcasting, networking, and more. As such, Drupal has a more challenging learning curve than popular standalone blogging applications such as WordPress, Blogger, and TypePad.

Figure 2-12:
The Drupal
home page.

Joomla!

(www.joomla.org)

Joomla!, shown in Figure 2-13, is a Web content management system like Drupal, and it allows users to create simple to elaborate Web sites with complete flexibility and control. Therefore, it is far more challenging to learn Joomla! than it is to learn how to use standalone blogging applications such as WordPress, Blogger, and TypePad.

Figure 2-13:
The Joomla!
home page.

Choosing the Right Blogging Application for You

With all these blogging application choices, how do you know which is the right one for you? It's actually quite simple if you define your goals for your blog, as discussed earlier in this chapter. When you know your goals, you can select the blogging application that you're technically adept enough to feel comfortable using and that helps you reach those goals at a price you can afford.

The most important factors to consider are price, ease of use, and functionality. If you're a beginner blogger joining the blogosphere for fun and have minimal goals for your blog aside from personal enjoyment, then a free blogging application is all you need. WordPress.com or Blogger should work well for you. If you want to be able to monetize your blog as well, Blogger is a good choice.

Alternatively, if you have plans to grow your blog significantly or need complete customization control over your blog for business branding or other purposes, you need a more flexible blogging application. WordPress.org is an excellent choice for people who want to grow their blogs or create blogs for business purposes. If you aren't afraid to learn a bit of technology (or invest a bit of money to hire a blog designer or developer to help you get past the technical steps), WordPress.org is the way to go.

However, if you're less interested in creating a true standalone blog and more interested in publishing content to your user profile in an online community, an option such as MySpace or Xanga might work best for you.

You can move from one blogging application to another, but doing so may cause problems. For example, you may lose content, your formatting may change, your links may be lost, and you may lose your search engine rankings (if your blog's domain has to change).

To avoid problems and headaches in the future, take the time to evaluate the current offerings of all blogging applications and choose the one that will not only help create the perfect blog for you, but also position it for long-term success.

Chapter 3: Taking a Look at WordPress

In This Chapter

✔ Getting to know WordPress

✔ Comparing WordPress.com with WordPress.org

✔ Creating a free WordPress.com blog

✔ Using WordPress.org

✔ Configuring and designing your blog

✔ Publishing posts with WordPress

✔ Understanding WordPress plug-ins

✔ Getting help

When you're ready to join the blogosphere, WordPress is an excellent blogging application choice. The platform offers the flexibility bloggers need to start a blog without a lot of technical knowledge as well as the features to grow and customize it in the future for the ultimate blogging experience. In recent years, WordPress has grown in popularity, particularly for people who have big goals for their blogs. But before you choose to use WordPress, beware: The WordPress blogging application comes in more than one form, which can be confusing. It's important to understand the differences between them before you start your WordPress blog.

This chapter shows you what WordPress can do, the differences between the two forms of WordPress, and how to start your blog and publish posts using WordPress. For more detailed information and advanced instruction about WordPress, be sure to read *WordPress For Dummies,* by Lisa Sabin-Wilson.

Finding Out What WordPress Is

In simplest terms, WordPress is a blog publishing application that makes it incredibly easy for anyone to start a blog without any programming knowledge. WordPress uses What You See Is What You Get (WYSIWYG) editors that allow you to enter and publish posts similarly to how you create documents using word-processing software such as Microsoft Word. Additionally, WordPress uses widgets to make the addition of features to your blog as easy as pointing and clicking or dragging and dropping. WordPress is also known for its flexibility in terms of customization. You can find a myriad of free and premium WordPress themes (offered for a fee, usually between $50 and $100) online, which anyone can use to give his or her WordPress blog a more personalized look.

Furthermore, with WordPress, you can have ultimate control over the function and design of your blog. In fact, WordPress can even be used as a content management system (CMS) to create Web sites, which is particularly useful for small businesses and nonprofit organizations with limited budgets, such as the small horseback riding business site shown in Figure 3-1. However, many of the most popular blogs and many Web sites are created using WordPress, including Mashable (`www.mashable.com`) and the *New York Times* blogs (`http://www.nytimes.com/ref/topnews/blog-index.html`).

Figure 3-1:
A
WordPress
blog can
look like a
Web site.

Understanding the Two WordPress Options

WordPress comes in two different forms: WordPress.com and WordPress.org. The two forms have many differences, and you need to be certain that you understand them before you start your blog. Both options allow users to create blogs, but the features, functionality, and technical skills required for the options differ significantly.

Checking out the differences

The confusion between WordPress.com and WordPress.org is commonly felt by new bloggers. Typically, the nuances are explained in technical language that doesn't help sort out the differences unless you're a seasoned blogger. This section describes the differences between WordPress.com and WordPress.org in layman's terms.

✦ **WordPress.org** launched in 2003 and is known as an open-source application, meaning developers can create tools (which have come to be known as plug-ins) that users can integrate seamlessly into WordPress to enhance functionality. Open-source application code is freely available to anyone who wants to create enhancements and modify it to meet their needs. As such, WordPress.org requires some technical knowledge to use but offers great flexibility in terms of adding functionality and customization.

WordPress.org is free, but users have to upload the application to their own, separate Web hosting accounts to be able to use it. This requires an investment in Web hosting and a domain name as well as additional technical knowledge. Although the technical skills required to use WordPress.org are minimal (unless you plan to handle your own extensive customization), people who are not comfortable with technology might find this path challenging.

✦ **WordPress.com** is also free, but WordPress.com blogs are hosted by WordPress. That means there are no hosting or domain name fees. The technical knowledge requirements are minimal, so if you can use a word-processing application and navigate the Internet, you can use WordPress.com. The features and functionality available to WordPress.com users are limited, but you can purchase premium services to enhance your blog.

Table 3-1 provides a breakdown of the primary differences between WordPress.com and WordPress.org.

Table 3-1	WordPress.com versus WordPress.org	
	WordPress.com	*WordPress.org*
Price	Free, but you have to pay for premium features.	Free, but you have to pay for hosting through a third party as well as for a domain name.
Technical Skills Required	Easy to use if you know how to use a word-processing application and can navigate the Internet.	Requires more technical skills or a willingness to learn because you need to obtain your own Web host, upload and configure the application to your host, and so on.
Functionality	Offers limited functionality, but you can pay for additional features.	Offers maximum functionality through the use of plug-ins and themes that you can add to your blog.
Domain names	Uses the .wordpress.com domain extension, but you can pay a fee to be able to use your own domain that you purchase separately.	Use domains that you purchase separately.
Customization	Offers limited customization, but you can pay for additional customization such as HTML and CSS modifications.	Offers nearly unlimited customization.
Monetization	Does not allow advertising on blogs unless you pay a fee.	Allows monetization of any kind.
Authors	Limits the number of authors for each blog.	Has no author limits.
Storage	Offers limited storage space (though enough for most beginner and intermediate level bloggers).	You can get as much storage as you're willing to pay a Web host for.

Choosing between WordPress.com and WordPress.org

With those differences in mind, you need to review your blogging goals and determine which version of WordPress will help you reach those goals. The biggest considerations are cost, functionality, monetization, customization, and technical skills.

Changing from WordPress.com to WordPress.org at a later date can be done but may cause problems such as lost data, lost links, or formatting issues. Also, if your domain name has to change, you'll lose incoming link traffic and search engine traffic.

If you plan to create a blog for personal enjoyment with limited long term goals, WordPress.com should work well for you. If you want to create a blog that has a chance to become popular and you want to make money from your blog, WordPress.org is a better choice. Alternatively, if you want to use WordPress to create a business or nonprofit Web site, WordPress.org is an excellent choice.

The technical skills required to use WordPress.org aren't difficult to learn. Additionally, many freelance blog designers and developers offer help at reasonable prices, and many blogs and forums are dedicated to helping people with WordPress.org, as discussed later in this chapter in the section "Getting Help and Finding Resources."

Creating a Free Blog at WordPress.com

If starting a free blog with limited functionality is all you need to meet your blogging goals, WordPress.com is a good choice for your blogging application. In fact, creating a blog with WordPress.com takes a matter of minutes. As soon as your blog is live, you can publish posts using the simple WYSIWYG post editor. It just couldn't get any easier!

Creating a new account and blog using WordPress.com require only a few steps:

1. **Visit www.wordpress.com and click the Sign Up Now button on the right side of your screen.**

   This step takes you to the new account creation page.

2. **Complete the sign up form on the Get Your Own WordPress Account in Seconds page, shown in Figure 3-2, and click the Next button at the bottom of the form.**

   Be sure the radio button next to Gimme a Blog! (Like username. wordpress.com) is selected. You arrive at the next page of the signup process.

3. **Complete the form shown in Figure 3-3 by entering your new blog's domain name and title and choosing a language. Then click the Signup button at the bottom of the page.**

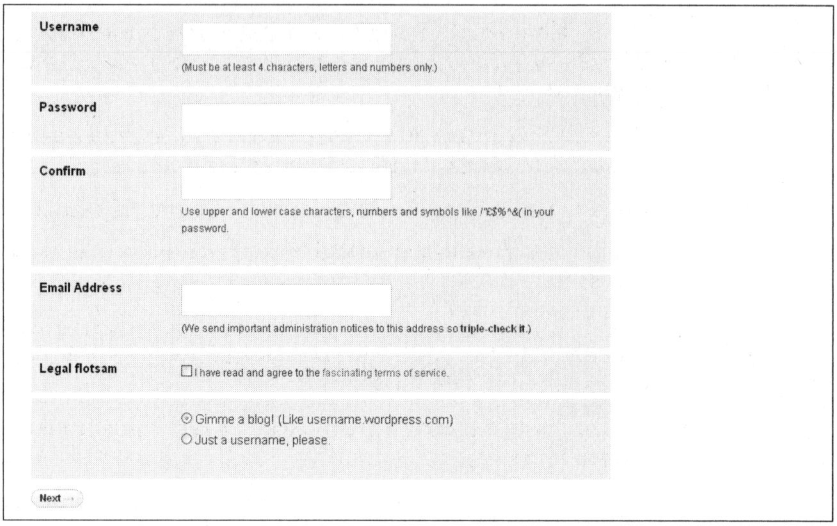

Username

(Must be at least 4 characters, letters and numbers only.)

Password

Confirm

Use upper and lower case characters, numbers and symbols like !"£$%^&(in your password.

Email Address

(We send important administration notices to this address so triple-check it.)

Legal flotsam ☐ I have read and agree to the fascinating terms of service.

⦿ Gimme a blog! (Like username.wordpress.com)
○ Just a username, please.

[Next →]

Figure 3-2:
The WordPress account creation page.

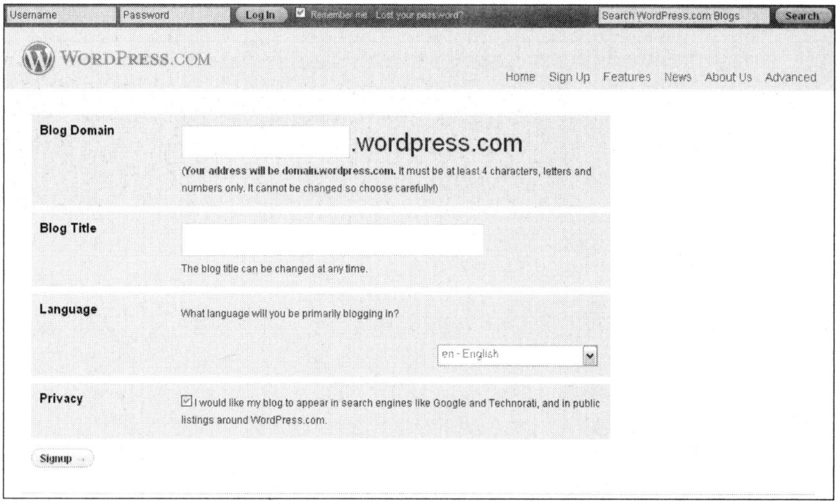

WORD**P**RESS.COM

Home   Sign Up   Features   News   About Us   Advanced

Blog Domain

⬚.wordpress.com

(Your address will be domain.wordpress.com. It must be at least 4 characters, letters and numbers only. It cannot be changed so choose carefully!)

Blog Title

The blog title can be changed at any time.

Language   What language will you be primarily blogging in?

[en - English   ▼]

Privacy   ☑ I would like my blog to appear in search engines like Google and Technorati, and in public listings around WordPress.com.

[Signup →]

Figure 3-3:
Enter your blog's domain name and title.

Keep in mind, your first domain name choice might already be taken. Also, you can change your blog's title later, so don't stress about that now.

Be sure the check box in the Privacy section is selected if you want your blog to be included in search engines to drive search traffic.

4. **Check your e-mail inbox for a registration confirmation message from WordPress, which includes a link that you must click to complete your registration.**

   You should receive your registration confirmation e-mail very quickly. If you don't, check your e-mail spam folder.

5. **Click the link in your registration confirmation e-mail.**

   A new page opens in your Web browser, telling you that your account is active.

   If you forgot the username and password you used to create your account, another message will be sent to you from WordPress with that information, so don't fret!

6. **On the Your Account Is Now Active! page, click the link that is your blog's domain name.**

   Your live blog opens, as shown in Figure 3-4, using the default WordPress theme and content.

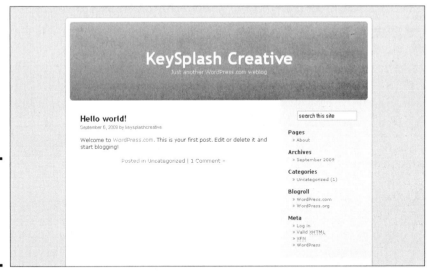

Figure 3-4: The default appearance of a new WordPress blog.

7. **In the right sidebar, under the Meta heading, click the Log In link.**

   This step opens the WordPress.com login page for your blog account, as shown in Figure 3-5.

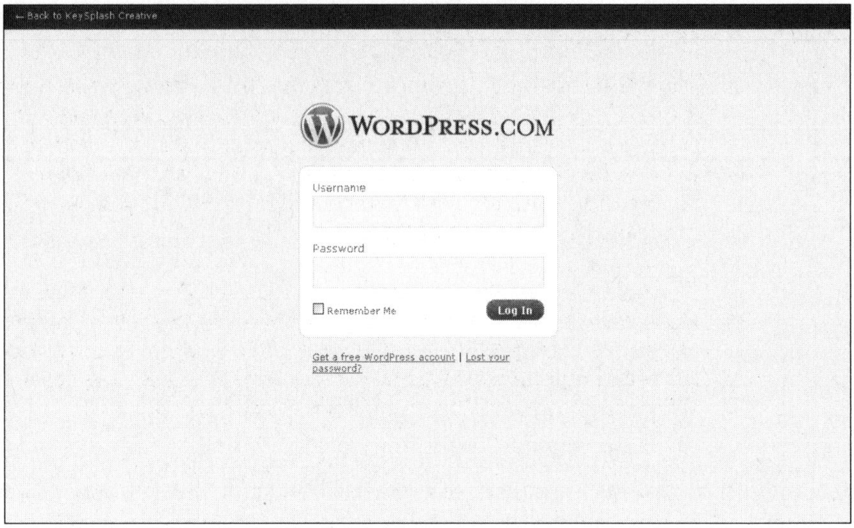

Figure 3-5:
The
WordPress
login
page for
a specific
blog.

8. **Enter the WordPress username and password you used to create your new blog account and then click the Log In button.**

This step opens your WordPress account dashboard, as shown in Figure 3-6, so you can begin configuring your blog settings and publishing content, as described later in this chapter in the section "Reviewing the WordPress Dashboard."

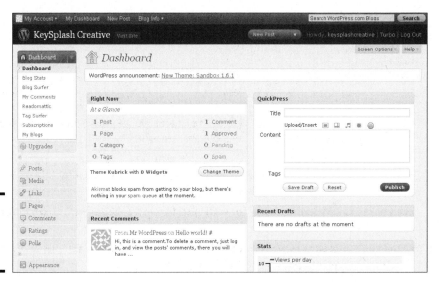

Figure 3-6:
The
WordPress
dashboard.

Installing WordPress.org

WordPress.org requires more work up front to create a new blog than WordPress.com does. First, you need to obtain a Web hosting account to store your blog's data. There are many Web hosting companies, and some are described in Chapter 1 of this minibook. After you obtain a Web hosting account, you need to purchase a domain name for your new blog, which is described in Chapter 3 of Book I.

When you have a Web hosting account and a domain name, you can upload WordPress to your Web hosting account, associate it with your domain name, and start your new blog. This section walks you through the steps to create, customize, and publish content to a new blog created using WordPress.org with BlueHost as the Web host.

Some Web hosting companies make it easier to install WordPress.org than others do, which is an important factor to consider when selecting your Web hosting service. For example, some Web hosts require that you manually download the WordPress.org application from the WordPress Web site and upload all the files to your Web hosting account. This can be a cumbersome and challenging process if you're not technologically savvy.

Fortunately, many Web hosting companies offer WordPress installation through an easy-to-use *cPanel* (short for control panel) and one-click install tools such as Fantastico. With the simple click of your mouse on an icon in your Web hosting account cPanel, you can install WordPress to your chosen domain in seconds.

If you're not technically adept, be sure to choose a Web host that includes a user cPanel and offers one-click installation of WordPress through Fantastico or Simple Scripts.

Following are the simplest steps to install WordPress to a new domain that has already been purchased using BlueHost:

1. **Log in to your Web hosting account cPanel and click the Fantastico De Luxe icon to software installation.**

   As shown in Figure 3-7, the Fantastico icon is located about half-way down the cPanel main page. Clicking this icon takes you to the Fantastico page shown in Figure 3-8.

2. **Click the WordPress link in the left sidebar or in the center of your screen.**

   Both WordPress links lead you to the same place: the WordPress installation page shown in Figure 3-9.

**Book IV
Chapter 3**

**Taking a Look at
WordPress**

Fantastico De Luxe icon

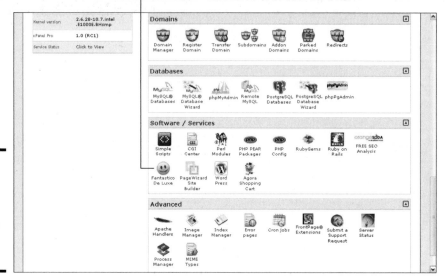

Figure 3-7:
The
Fantastico
De Luxe
icon on the
BlueHost
cPanel.

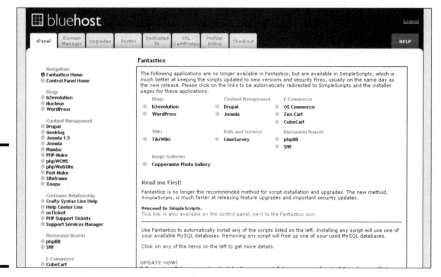

Figure 3-8:
The
Fantastico
page
within the
BlueHost
cPanel.

3. **Click the New Installation link in the center of the page.**

This step allows you to begin the process of installing WordPress to your new domain. You arrive at the WordPress installation configuration page.

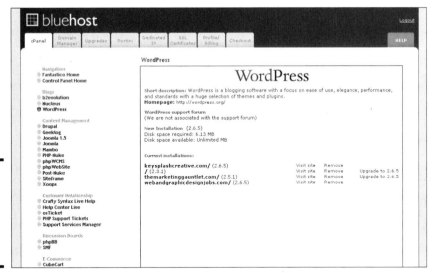

Figure 3-9:
The
WordPress
installation
page in
Fantastico.

4. Select the domain that you want to install WordPress to from the drop-down list, fill in the text boxes, and then click the Install WordPress button.

You must also enter a username and password to access your new WordPress account as well as your nickname, e-mail address, site name and description to complete the base configurations for your new blog.

After you click the Install WordPress button, you're taken to the confirmation page.

5. Review the confirmation details related to your installation and click the Finish Installation button.

Read the information provided in the confirmation details to ensure accurate information is shown.

When you click the Finish Installation button, a page displays with your login information as well as an option to have your installation details e-mailed to you.

6. Click the link to view your new WordPress site.

Your new blog is now live using the default WordPress theme and information, as shown in Figure 3-10. You can log in to your WordPress dashboard by using the link provided to you upon completion of your WordPress installation or by clicking the Log In link under the Meta heading in the right sidebar of your new blog.

**Book IV
Chapter 3**

Taking a Look at
WordPress

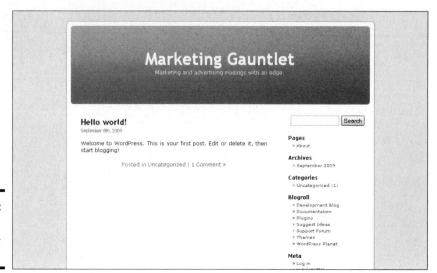

Figure 3-10:
A new
WordPress.
org blog.

Notice that after initial installation, the WordPress.org blog looks just like the WordPress.com blog shown in Figure 3-4.

Reviewing the WordPress Dashboard

The WordPress.com and WordPress.org dashboards work very similarly. However, the WordPress.org dashboard offers more options and controls. The remainder of this chapter uses the WordPress.org dashboard for reference, but note that some of the features shown are not available on the WordPress.com dashboard. If you use WordPress.com, you can skip the features listed in the remainder of this chapter that don't apply to you. In short, if you don't see a feature discussed in this chapter on your WordPress.com dashboard, it's either not available to you or available only if you pay for premium features.

Depending on your blog host and the manner in which you install WordPress to your account, you might be using a different version of WordPress than version 2.8.5 shown in the figures within this chapter. Note that the majority of the functionality is the same, but the layout of your WordPress dashboard might look a bit different than the images shown in this chapter.

When you log in to your WordPress account, your WordPress dashboard opens, as shown in Figure 3-11. This is where you can access all the features and functions to create content and customize your blog.

Figure 3-11:
The
WordPress.
org
dashboard.

The majority of your screen is taken up by boxes that make accessing commonly used features quick and easy. For example, you can see recent comments, incoming links, and so on. To access all features available to you in WordPress, click each item listed in the left sidebar to expand each menu, as shown in Figure 3-12. You can also return to the WordPress dashboard at anytime while you're logged into your WordPress account by clicking the Dashboard link at the top of the left sidebar.

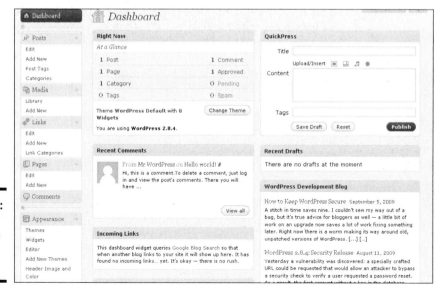

Figure 3-12:
Expanded
WordPress
dashboard
sidebar.

**Book IV
Chapter 3**

**Taking a Look at
WordPress**

The expanded WordPress dashboard sidebar provides the following links to do anything and everything you want or need to do with your blog:

- ✦ **Posts:** The links under the Posts heading allow you to edit existing posts, add new posts to your blog, and add new tags and categories (although you can add tags and categories when you create a new post). You can get instructions for creating a new post later in this chapter.

- ✦ **Media:** The links under the Media heading allow you to view all images and media that you've already uploaded (that's your media library) or add new images. You can also add images directly from within a new blog post.

- ✦ **Links:** The links under the Links heading allow you to edit links that are already included in your account. By default, new WordPress blogs include the links shown under the Blogroll heading in the sidebar displayed in Figure 3-16. You can delete these links if you want by using the Edit link from the WordPress dashboard or add new ones by using the Add New link from the WordPress dashboard. You can also create new categories for your links if you want to separate them and display them under different headings on your blog.

- ✦ **Page:** The links under the Pages heading allow you to edit existing pages on your blog and create new ones. For example, you can create an About page or use WordPress to create a more traditional Web site with the Pages feature. Adding pages works just like adding posts, as described later in this chapter, except that instead of tagging and categorizing pages, you select where they should be published based on your site's page hierarchy using a simple drop-down list in the sidebar of the page editor.

- ✦ **Comments:** The Comments link allows you to view and moderate comments left on your blog posts. From the Comments page, you can approve, delete, edit, and respond to comments as well as mark comments as spam that the built-in comment spam plug-in, Aksimet, misses.

Creating posts and pages, adding media and links, and moderating comments are made extremely easy using the simple WordPress interface. Just fill in the text boxes and select options using the provided drop-down menus, and you're done! For specific details on using WordPress, be sure to read *WordPress For Dummies,* by Lisa Sabin-Wilson.

Configuring Settings

Because the first thing you should do when you start a new blog is configure its settings, the following sections walk you through some of the most important settings you need to consider before you begin publishing content on your blog.

Take the time to look through all the pages and options available through the WordPress dashboard. Although the configuration suggestions included in this section are considered to be the most important, you should review all options to ensure your blog works exactly the way you want it to.

Profile

The Profile Settings page is where you can configure the settings that define and describe you and your blog as follows:

1. Click the Your Profile link on the WordPress dashboard.

The link is located under the Users heading in the left sidebar of your WordPress dashboard, as shown in Figure 3-13. Clicking this link takes you to the Profile configuration page shown in Figure 3-14.

Figure 3-13:
The lower half of the WordPress dashboard with sidebar menus expanded.

**Book IV
Chapter 3**

**Taking a Look at
WordPress**

2. Enter the requested information into the Profile fields, shown in Figure 3-14.

The first check box should remain unselected as this is what allows you to type posts using the WYSIWYG visual editor rather than using HTML coding. Scroll through the remainder of the page and enter the requested information in the boxes provided. Also, update your e-mail address, Web site, biographical information, and password if necessary.

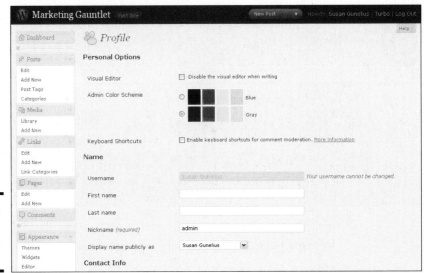

Figure 3-14:
The Profile
configura-
tion page.

3. **Click the Update Profile button at the bottom of the page to save your changes.**

   A User Updated message appears highlighted in yellow near the top of your screen when your data is saved.

You can change these settings at any time, but it's a good idea to configure them up front.

General Settings

The General Settings page is where you can configure the broad settings that affect your entire blog as follows:

1. **Click the General link under the Settings heading in the left sidebar of your WordPress dashboard.**

   This step opens the General Settings configuration page.

2. **Make changes to any information that's inaccurate or needs to be updated.**

   You can change your blog's title, *tagline* (a short phrase that describes your blog in more detail than the title does), e-mail address, new users' default roles (for example, author, editor, and so on), your time zone, the way you want the date and time to appear on your blog, and the day that you want new weeks to start on.

3. **Click the Save Changes button at the bottom of the page to save your changes.**

   A Settings Saved message appears highlighted in yellow near the top of your screen when your changes have been saved.

Reading settings

The most important settings you need to configure for your new blog are related to your blog's front page and post settings as follows:

1. **Click the Reading link under the Settings heading in the left sidebar on the WordPress dashboard.**

   The Reading Settings page opens.

2. **Select one of the two options next to the Front Page Displays heading.**

   Here are your choices:

   - *Your Latest Posts:* Select this radio button if you want your blog posts to appear on your blog's home page.

   - *A Static Page:* Select this radio button if you want a static home page to be your blog's front page so it looks more like a traditional Web site. Then select the page you want to use from the drop-down lists.

     If you want to use a static page for the main page of your blog, the page must already be created so you can select it from the drop-down lists.

3. **Next to the Blog Pages Show at Most heading, enter the number of posts you want to appear on your blog's home page.**

   Most blogs show five to seven posts per page to reduce scrolling.

4. **Click the Save Changes button at the bottom of the screen.**

   A Settings Saved message appears highlighted in yellow near the top of your screen when your changes have been saved.

The Reading settings page also includes configurations for syndication and feeds. It's not necessary to set up your blog's feed when you originally create your blog. You can find out more about blog syndication and feeds in Chapter 4 of Book V and return to configure these settings in your WordPress account at a later time.

Discussion settings

The discussion settings are very important because this is where you determine how comments are handled on your blog posts as follows:

1. **Click the Discussion link under the Settings heading in the left sidebar of your WordPress dashboard.**

The Discussion Settings page opens.

2. **Review the preconfigured discussion settings and make any changes to ensure the comment moderation system is set up the way you want it to be.**

For example, you might not want to moderate comments at all, or you might want to disallow comments entirely (which I don't recommended, if you want to grow your blog).

3. **Click the Save Changes button at the bottom of the screen.**

A Settings Saved message appears highlighted in yellow near the top of your screen when your changes have been saved.

The predefined discussion settings are the ones most bloggers use, but you're free to make any changes you want. For example, when your blog gets popular, you might not want to receive an e-mail every time someone leaves a comment on your blog, or you would be inundated with e-mail! You can find out about using comments to grow your blog in Chapter 2 of Book VI.

Following are some details on a few of the most common settings:

✦ **Default Article Settings:** The settings in this section are important for growing your blog. They're used to notify other bloggers that you linked to their content and to notify you when another blog links to yours. Furthermore, they allow visitors to leave comments on your blog posts. Ensuring these settings are enabled helps your blog to grow by allowing conversations to flow and relationships to develop.

✦ **Other Comment Settings:** These settings control how people can leave comments on your blog posts. If you want your blog to grow with a strong community behind it, the best option is to ensure it's as easy as possible for people to leave comments. For example, you can select the option that requires visitors to enter an e-mail address and name in order to submit comments, in order to reduce spam, but asking readers to register and login to leave a comment, as the second configuration in this section does, will reduce the number of legitimate comments, too. Depending on your goals for your blog, that might not be something you want to do.

✦ **E-Mail Me Whenever:** The settings in this section are intended to help you keep track of the conversations happening on your blog, and you can configure them in the manner that suits your preferences best.

✦ **Before a Comment Appears:** These settings affect how much control you have over publishing comments on your blog. You can choose to approve *all* comments manually before they can be published, or you can choose to only have to approve comments when a new user writes one; after a user's initial comment has been approved by you, any further commenting by this user will be approved automatically. This is entirely up to you.

✦ **Comment Moderation:** The comment moderation section allows you to automatically hold comments that meet your specified criteria for moderation. For example, you can configure your blog so comments with more than two links are always held for moderation or so comments that are flagged as potential spam are always held for moderation.

✦ **Comment Blacklist:** Just as you can configure your blog so comments are held for moderation if they contain certain words, you can also blacklist specific words and automatically relegate them to your comment spam folder.

The Discussion Settings page in your WordPress dashboard also includes an area where you can configure avatar settings. An *avatar* is a small image that people use to identify themselves online and can appear next to comments they leave on avatar-enabled blogs. For example, you can use a photograph of yourself as your avatar.

If you'd like to allow avatars to appear along with comments that people leave on your blog, you can configure that option within the Avatar Settings section of the Discussion Settings page. You can also configure settings for the types of avatars that are allowed on your blog (using a simple ratings scale that determines audience-appropriateness levels), and you can choose the images to publish when a commenter doesn't have a preconfigured avatar.

Privacy Settings

To access the Privacy Settings page, click the Privacy link under the Settings heading in the left sidebar of your WordPress dashboard. The Privacy Settings page is where you can set up your blog to be visible and included in search engine indexing or invisible to search engines. By removing your blog from search engines, you're significantly reducing the amount of traffic your blog can get. Therefore, if you have goals to grow your blog beyond an audience of your friends, family, and people you tell about it, leave the radio button next to I Would Like My Blog to Be Visible to Everyone selected.

Permalink Settings

A *permalink* is the permanent URL to a blog post. The Permalink Settings page is overlooked by most beginner bloggers, but configuring the settings on this page is actually very important because they can greatly affect the amount of search engine traffic your blog gets. Follow these steps to adjust the settings:

1. **Click the Permalink link under the Settings heading on the WordPress dashboard.**

   The Permalink Settings page opens.

2. **Select the radio button next to Day and Name or Month and Name.**

   Selecting one of these permalink structures adds your post title to your blog posts links, giving them better search engine optimization opportunities because your post names might include useful keywords that search engines look for in their indexing algorithms.

3. **Click the Save Changes button at the bottom of the page.**

   A Settings Saved message highlighted in yellow appears near the top of your screen when your changes have been saved.

Understanding Widgets

Widgets can be found by clicking the Widgets link under the Appearance heading in the left sidebar of your WordPress dashboard. They are used in WordPress to make adding features and functions easy. Rather than rewriting HTML or CSS code to alter your blog's appearance, widgets are built into most WordPress themes, including the default WordPress themes, which allow you to simply drag and drop widget boxes to your blog's sidebars. Looking at Figure 3-15, you can see that the default WordPress.org template includes a number of widgets that you can simply click and drag to the right of your screen to add to your blog's sidebar. Similarly, you can remove widgets by dragging them from the right side of your screen back to the Available Widgets (to reset them) or Inactive Widgets (to save them for later) area of your screen.

Figure 3-15: The WordPress Widgets configuration page.

After you drag a widget to your blog's sidebar using the WordPress dashboard Widgets page, you might be given the option to click a drop-down arrow to the right of the widget's name to further customize the content in the widget.

Don't be afraid to play around with the widgets available to you. You can't break anything, and if you don't like a change, you can simply drag the widget out of your sidebar from the widgets configuration page to remove it.

Personalizing Your Blog

The best part about using WordPress.org as your blogging application is the wide variety of customization options that are available to you. Even if you use WordPress.com, you can choose from a number of themes, and you can modify colors and other settings, but WordPress.org truly leads the pack in terms of customization.

Header image and color

When you click the Header Image and Color link under the Appearance heading in the left sidebar of your WordPress dashboard, you access the Header Image and Color page, as shown in Figure 3-16. Here you can make changes to the colors used in your header and upload an image if the theme you're using allows you to do so.

Figure 3-16: The WordPress Header Image and Color page.

Most of the appearance customization changes you can make on your blog depend on the theme you're using because some themes offer more customization options than others.

Themes

You can access the Manage Themes page by clicking the Themes link under the Appearance heading in the left sidebar of your WordPress dashboard. Here you can access the themes that are preloaded with WordPress and change your blog's appearance on the fly simply by activating one of the new themes listed on this page. You can even preview your blog using the new theme with the Preview link provided.

Add new themes

You can access the Install Themes page by clicking the Add New Themes link under the Appearance heading in the left sidebar of your WordPress dashboard. This is where you can find the true flexibility of WordPress design.

Using WordPress.org, you can access a wide variety of free themes directly from this page (try the Search, Featured, Newest, and Recently Updated links near the top of the page to help you find themes you like), or you can upload one of the many free themes available online. You can also purchase a premium theme and upload it to your WordPress account. Using a premium theme requires a small investment, but free themes are typically well-tested and provide a more unique look for your blog than frequently used free themes do. I tell you where you can find WordPress themes later in this chapter, in the section "Finding themes."

Editor

You can open the cascading style sheets (CSS) editor shown in Figure 3-17 for your active WordPress theme by clicking the Editor link under the Appearance heading in the left sidebar of your WordPress dashboard. If you know CSS, this editor is extremely powerful and allows you to modify any part of your WordPress theme.

Cascading style sheets is the programming language used to create Web page presentation, including blogs. CSS tells the Web browser how to display the Hypertext Markup Language (HTML) elements that make up the page content. In broad terms, HTML is used to create the page content and CSS is used to create the presentation, layout, and design of that content.

Always copy the content of the editor text box and paste it into another document before you make any changes. If something doesn't work the way you want it to after you make your edits, you can simply copy and paste the original CSS code back into the editor text box as if nothing was ever changed.

Figure 3-17:
The
WordPress
theme
editor.

Choosing a theme

You can find a wide variety of themes for WordPress.org blogs. Some themes are free, but others, called *premium* themes, are available for a fee. The primary differences between free and premium themes are as explained in Table 3-2.

Table 3-2	Free versus Premium Blog Themes	
	Free Themes	*Premium Themes*
Price	They're, well, free!	They typically cost between $50 and $100.
Reliability	Anyone can create free themes, so you can't be completely sure that they work well until you try them (unless you know the reputation of the developer).	Premium themes from respected developers are far more likely to work the way they're supposed to and typically offer more functionality.
Support	Free themes usually come with no support.	Premium themes often offer support for a fee or through a community forum.
Originality	Free themes can be used by anyone, so your blog might not look unique if you select a popular free theme.	Premium themes offer greater customization and because they have a cost associated with them, fewer people use them, giving your blog a better chance of looking unique.

**Book IV
Chapter 3**

Taking a Look at
WordPress

Finding themes

A variety of sites offer free WordPress themes submitted by people from around the world. Following are a few of the popular sites to find free WordPress themes:

✦ **eBlog Templates:** (www.eblogtemplates.com) This site offers a huge selection, including reviews, statistics, and more.

✦ **WordPress Themes:** (www.wpthemesfree.com) This site has over 3,000 free WordPress themes to choose from.

✦ **Free WordPress Themes:** (www.freewordpressthemes.com) This site includes a wide selection of free WordPress themes editorially selected for usability.

✦ **Performancing:** (http://themes.performancing.com) A number of well-coded, free WordPress themes are offered by the team behind one of the oldest blogs about blogging.

✦ **Blogging Tips:** (www.bloggingtips.com) This site offers several free WordPress themes that are well-coded and backed by a support forum.

Premium themes are also abundant online, but you shouldn't invest in a premium theme unless the developer has a reputation within the WordPress community for creating usable, well-coded themes. Following are several sites that offer reliable premium WordPress themes:

✦ **iThemes:** (http://ithemes.com) iThemes offers a variety of easy-to-use WordPress themes and has an active user forum for help.

✦ **StudioPress:** (www.studiopress.com) StudioPress offers one of the most respected WordPress themes — Revolution.

✦ **WooThemes:** (www.woothemes.com) WooThemes offers a great selection of creative WordPress themes developed by talented designers.

✦ **DIYthemes:** (http://diythemes.com) The well-known Thesis theme created by Chris Pearson is offered by DIYthemes.

✦ **Headway Themes:** (http://headwaythemes.com) The Headway theme takes a bit more technical knowledge and time to set up than other premium themes, but it offers extensive customization options.

Publishing a Post

Publishing a post using WordPress is extremely easy:

1. **Click the Add New link under the Posts heading on your WordPress dashboard.**

The Add New Post page opens, as shown in Figure 3-18.

2. **Enter a title, the body text, post *tags* (keywords to help with search engine optimization), and a category.**

   Select the Add New Category link if you need to create a new category for your post.)

3. **Click the Publish button on the right side of your screen.**

   Your new blog post appears as the top entry on your blog. It's that easy!

Figure 3-18:
The
WordPress
Add New
Post page.

Take some time to hover your mouse over the various icons in the visual editor box to see the pop-up text explaining what each icon does. Most of these tools work the same way in WordPress as they do in word-processing applications. You can add bold to text, create links, and insert images using these icons.

Create a test post and play with the various icons in the visual text editor to see what they do. You can use the Preview button on the right side of your screen to see the results or publish the post. (You can delete it right away by clicking the Edit link under the Post heading on your WordPress dashboard.)

Making Sense of WordPress Plug-Ins

WordPress plug-ins are created by individual developers who want to add functionality to WordPress.org. You can install plug-ins to your WordPress account, activate them, and then use them on your blog. For example, some plug-ins allow you to create online forms and site maps, add social networking icons to your blog posts for sharing, and more.

You can search for plug-ins from your WordPress dashboard or visit `http://wordpress.org/extend/plugins` to search the official repository of WordPress plug-ins.

To install a plug-in, simply download it from the site where you find it, and then upload it to your Web hosting account as follows:

1. **Click the Add New link under the Plugins heading on the right side of your WordPress dashboard.**

    The Install Plugins page shown in Figure 3-19 opens.

    From this page, you can find plug-ins to install or install a plug-in you already downloaded to your computer's hard drive.

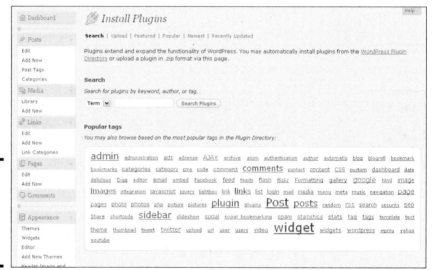

Figure 3-19:
The
WordPress
Install
Plugins
page.

2. **Select the Upload link at the top of the page and follow the steps to upload the plug-in.**

    After the plug-in files have been uploaded to your hosting account, the plug-in appears in the Manage Plugins page on your WordPress dashboard (shown in Figure 3-20), which you can access by selecting the Installed link under the Plugins heading on the right side of your WordPress dashboard.

3. **Click the Activate link to activate the plug-in.**

    After the plug-in is activated, you can use it, configure its settings, and so on as applicable for the specific plug-in.

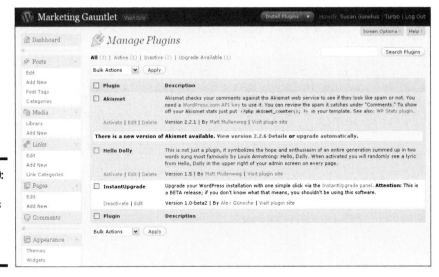

Figure 3-20: The WordPress Manage Plugins page.

 You can install as many plug-ins as you want to your WordPress.org account.

Getting Help and Finding Resources

A number of Web sites, blogs, and books can help you find out more about WordPress.com and WordPress.org. Following is a short list of some of the best places to find WordPress help:

✦ ***WordPress For Dummies:*** Lisa Sabin-Wilson wrote this guide to WordPress.com and WordPress.org, which is available through most book sellers.

✦ **WordPress.org Codex:** (http://codex.wordpress.org/Main_Page) This is the online guide to everything and anything WordPress.org-related.

✦ **WordPress.com Support:** (http://en.support.wordpress.com) You can find online support for WordPress.com here.

✦ **WordPress.com Forum:** (http://en.forums.wordpress.com) This is the online forum for WordPress.com users to ask questions and discuss their blogs.

✦ **Lorelle on WordPress:** (http://lorelle.wordpress.com) This is one of the best blogs about WordPress.

**Book IV
Chapter 3**

Taking a Look at WordPress

Chapter 4: Using Google Blogger

In This Chapter

☑ **Getting to know Blogger**

☑ **Creating a free blog at Blogger**

☑ **Configuring settings**

☑ **Customizing your blog**

☑ **Understanding Blogger gadgets**

☑ **Publishing posts with Blogger**

☑ **Reviewing advanced features**

☑ **Getting help**

*B*logger was originally launched by Pyra Labs in 1999 as one of the first dedicated blogging applications. In 2003, Google purchased Blogger, and since then, the application has grown more popular as new features have been introduced and other Google applications have been seamlessly integrated into the Blogger user interface. Today, Blogger is the most popular blogging application, and it remains free to use.

This chapter teaches you what Blogger can do, how the basic functions work, and where you can find more help. Joining the blogosphere can be overwhelming, but Blogger remains the most popular blogging application for several reasons — it's easy to use, feature-rich, and free. That's all many bloggers need, and Blogger delivers.

Discovering Blogger

Blogger is a free blogging application that you can use via the Internet to write and publish content in your own space on the Web — your blog. Blogger uses a What You See Is What You Get (WYSIWYG) editor that makes writing and publishing content on your blog as easy as it is to type a document using your preferred word-processing software (such as Microsoft Word).

Blogger also provides gadgets that make adding enhanced functionality and features to your blog as easy as pointing and clicking your mouse. Although Blogger started out as a fairly limited blogging application, recent enhancements make it easy for bloggers to accomplish common blogging tasks such as scheduling posts for the future, adding videos to your blog, and more.

That's why many of the top blogs online are powered by Blogger, including all of the blogs published by Google. Even the highly popular Post Secret blog (`www.postsecret.blogspot.com`), shown in Figure 4-1, runs on Blogger.

Figure 4-1:
The Post Secret blog runs on Blogger.

One of the primary benefits to using Blogger as your blogging application is that it allows you to monetize your blog. Not only can you add multiple revenue streams such as direct ads, pay-per-click ads, pay-per-impression ads, affiliate ads, sponsored reviews, text ads, and more to your blog, but also Blogger makes it extremely easy to integrate one of the most popular monetization opportunities for bloggers: Google AdSense. You can find out more about making money from your blog in Book VII.

Creating a Free Blog at Blogger.com

If starting a blog using a blogging application that offers a huge bang for the buck (in other words, a lot of functionality for free), Blogger is an excellent choice. Starting a new blog using Blogger takes just a few minutes, so you can publish content and start monetizing your blog (if making money is one of your blogging goals) almost instantly. And when you're ready to take your blog to the next level, Blogger offers a number of more advanced features to help you reach your goals.

Google adds new features and functions to Blogger all the time. You can stay on top of Blogger news by reading the Blogger Buzz blog at `http://buzz.blogger.com`.

To create a new blog using Blogger, you need to have a Google account, which you'll use to sign in, manage, and access your blog content.

If you already have a Google account, that's great and saves time. Just go to www.blogger.com and click the Create a Blog Link, which opens the Create a Google Account page. Click the Sign In First link in the first paragraph at the top of the page (above the form) and enter your *existing* Google account username from your Gmail, Google Groups, or other Google account, and you can create a new blog immediately.

If you don't have a Google account, follow these steps to start your new blog with Blogger:

1. **Visit the Blogger home page.**

Enter **www.blogger.com** into your browser, and the Blogger home page opens.

2. **Click the Create a Blog button.**

The Create a Google Account page opens, as shown in Figure 4-2.

3. **Enter the requested information into the text boxes provided and click the Continue button.**

The Name Your Blog page opens, as shown in Figure 4-3.

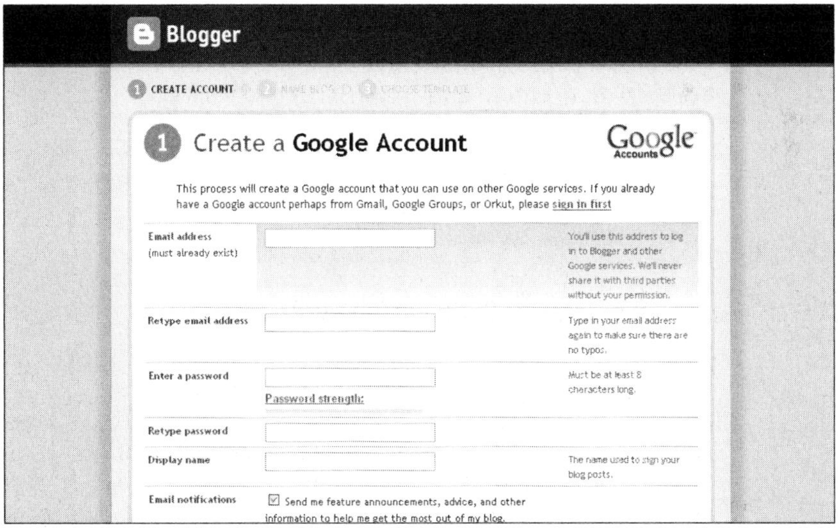

Figure 4-2: The Create a Google Account page.

Figure 4-3:
The Name
Your Blog
page.

4. **Enter a title for your blog (you can change it later) and a domain name and click the Continue button.**

   The Choose a Template page opens, as shown in Figure 4-4.

   It's highly likely that the first domain name you choose won't be available, meaning someone else is already using it for an active or inactive blog. If your desired domain name isn't available, keep trying different domains until you find one that you like and is available.

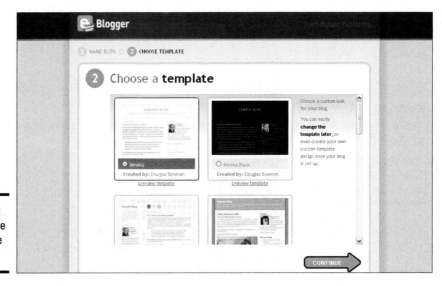

Figure 4-4:
The Choose
a Template
page.

5. **Click the template you like in the template list and then click the Continue button.**

To see all the template options, scroll through the list. You can click the Preview Template button to view a larger image of each.

You can change your blog's template at any time, so don't stress about choosing the perfect template right now.

After you click Continue, the Your Blog Has Been Created page opens.

6. **Click the Start Blogging button.**

Your Blogger account opens with your new blog's New Post page, shown in Figure 4-5, displayed on your screen, where you can enter and publish a new post as detailed later in this chapter.

Figure 4-5:
The New
Post page.

Click the View Blog link in the top navigation bar of the New Post page to view your blog live online. Your blog doesn't have any content in it yet, but you can see that it exists, and all you have to do is provide the content to turn it into a full-fledged blog.

Reviewing the Blogger Dashboard

The Blogger dashboard is where you access all the functions, features, and controls for your new blog. You can add new posts, edit old posts, add enhancements to your blog, change your blog's design, and much more from your Blogger dashboard.

Don't rush into creating content on your blog until you take the time to click through the many pages accessible through your Blogger dashboard. Reviewing each page helps you find out more about what you can do to personalize and configure your blog so it looks and works exactly how you want it to.

Review the following sections to see what kinds of tools are available from the various navigation tabs available through your Blogger dashboard.

The Blogger dashboard main page

Log in to your Blogger account, or click the Dashboard link in the upper-right corner of any page within your Blogger account, to access the main page of your Blogger dashboard, as shown in Figure 4-6.

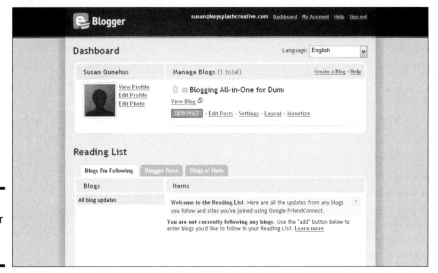

Figure 4-6:
The Blogger
dashboard
main page.

For in-depth instructions to use each feature accessible through your Blogger dashboard, read my book, *Google Blogger For Dummies*.

From the Blogger dashboard main page, you can

✦ Create a new blog.

✦ Create a new post.

✦ Edit existing posts.

✦ Configure your blog's settings.

✦ Change your blog's layout and design.

✦ Add money-making features to your blog.

✦ View and edit your profile.

✦ Edit your photo.

✦ Access your Google account.

✦ View blog posts from blogs in your reading list.

Using the tabs in the top navigation pane, you can also access each of the pages provided on the Blogger dashboard main page from any page within your Blogger dashboard.

Posting tab

From the Posting tab within your Blogger dashboard (refer to Figure 4-5), you can add a new post, edit an existing post, or manage your blog post comment moderation settings. The New Post tab is likely to be the page you use the most often, particularly if you publish content frequently on your blog.

Settings tab

The Settings tab is where you can access all the configuration options for your blog, including basic publishing, formatting, comments, archiving, site feed, e-mail and mobile, OpenID, and permissions settings. Some of these features are described later in this chapter.

Layout tab

The Layout tab provides access to all of the design elements for our blog. From this tab, you can add functionality to your blog through the use of point-and-click and click-and-drag gadgets. You can also change your blog's fonts and colors, edit the HTML code for your blog (if you're versed in HTML), and choose a new template for your blog to give it a completely different look.

Monetize tab

If you want to make money from your blog, you should definitely spend time reviewing the options in the Monetize tab on your Blogger dashboard. From this tab, you can easily add Google AdSense ad units to your blog.

Configuring Settings

Before you publish a new post on your blog, you should configure a number of settings to ensure your blogging experience goes as smoothly as possible and your readers enjoy the best possible experience when they visit your blog. The following sections walk you through some of the most important settings you should configure before you publish your first blog post.

Your blog is yours, which means you can configure its settings any way you want to meet your blogging goals. The suggestions included in the following sections are the settings most bloggers who want to grow their blogs use, but you can choose your own settings. Also, you can change your blog's settings at any time, so you're not locked into the settings you choose when you start your blog.

Profile

Your blog's profile is where you describe who you are and why you're writing your blog. Take the time to write a complete profile so your blog's readers can get to know you and understand why you're the right person to be writing a blog on your chosen subject. Follow these steps to create your blog's profile page:

1. **Click the Edit Profile link on the main page of your Blogger dashboard, shown earlier in Figure 4-6.**

   The Edit User Profile page opens, as shown in Figure 4-7.

2. **Make sure the Share My Profile check box is selected and select the Show My Real Name check box if you want to include your real name in your profile.**

   There are very few anonymous popular bloggers. If you want to grow your blog, the best choice is to tell your audience who you are in your blog's profile.

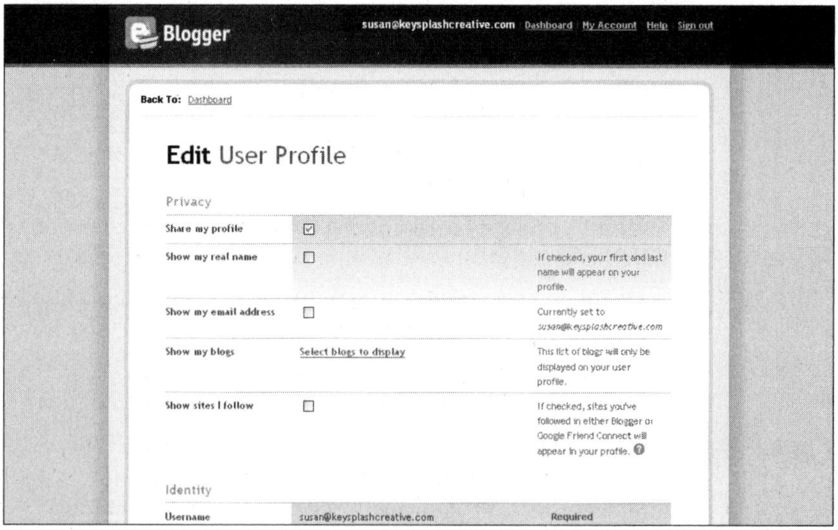

Figure 4-7:
The Edit User Profile page.

3. **Deselect the Show Sites I Follow check box.**

   This setting is active by default, but unless you're certain that you want to promote every blog you follow, leave this setting deselected until you have time to make that decision.

   Only blogs published with Blogger can appear in your Sites I Follow list.

4. **Scroll through the remainder of the text box fields on the page and enter your personal information as appropriate.**

   The more information you include in your profile, the more your readers will learn about you. While you might not want to get too personal, it's a good idea to share enough information about yourself to establish why you're qualified to write your blog.

5. **Click the Save Profile button.**

   Your information is saved, and a message that says Your Settings Have Been Saved appears at the top of your page.

6. **Click the View Updated Profile link at the top of the page to review your profile.**

   You can click the Edit Profile button on your new Profile page if you need to make additional changes.

Basic settings

The Basic settings page is where you can configure the core settings for your blog, such as the title, and a number of post-related settings as follows:

1. **Click the Settings link on your main Blogger dashboard, shown earlier in Figure 4-6.**

   The Basic settings page opens, as shown in Figure 4-8.

2. **Enter a new title in the Title text box and a description of your blog in the Description text box.**

   This is where you can change your blog's title and add a description to tell visitors what your blog is about, in 500 characters or less.

3. **Make sure the Add Your Blog to Our Listings and Let Search Engines Find Your Blog settings are set to Yes.**

   Configuring these settings to Yes means your blog appears in lists from Blogger, and it's included in search engine indexes.

   If you want your blog to grow and attract more visitors, it needs to be visible within Blogger and by search engines. Most blog traffic comes from search engine keyword searches, so you're missing a huge opportunity to expose new visitors to your blog if you exclude your content from search engine indexing processes.

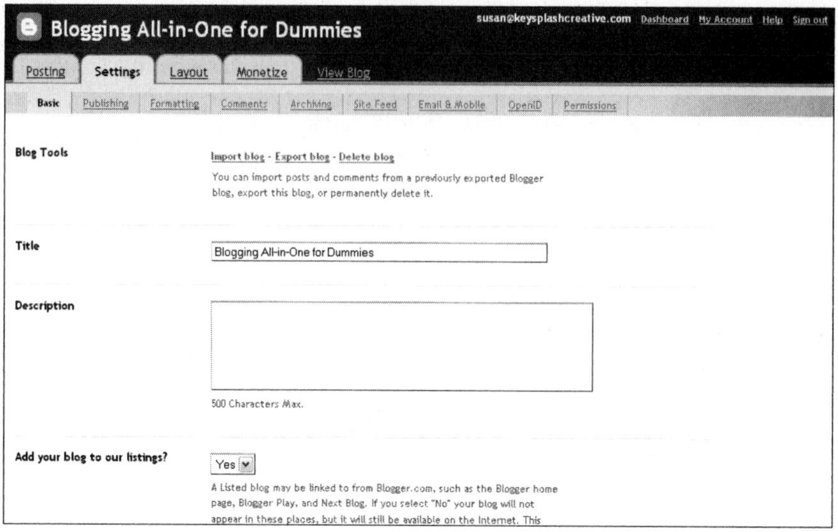

Figure 4-8:
The Basic
settings
page.

4. **Set the Show Email Post Links option to Yes.**

   Make it easy for people to share your blog posts that they enjoy by including an Email Post option with each of your posts.

5. **In the Select Post Editor section, select the radio button next to Updated Editor to ensure you're using the most feature-rich visual post editor.**

   If you know HTML and want to write your posts using HTML rather than the WYSIWYG post editor, select the radio button next to Hide Compose Mode.

6. **Click the Save Settings button.**

   Your configuration settings are saved and immediately affect your entire blog.

Formatting settings

The Formatting settings page is where you can configure a number of settings that affect your blog posts. Following are some of the most important settings to configure before you start publishing content on your new blog:

1. **Click the Settings link on your main Blogger dashboard, shown earlier in Figure 4-6.**

   The Basic settings page opens, as shown earlier in Figure 4-8.

2. **Click the Formatting link on the navigation bar near the top of your screen.**

   The Formatting settings page opens, as shown in Figure 4-9.

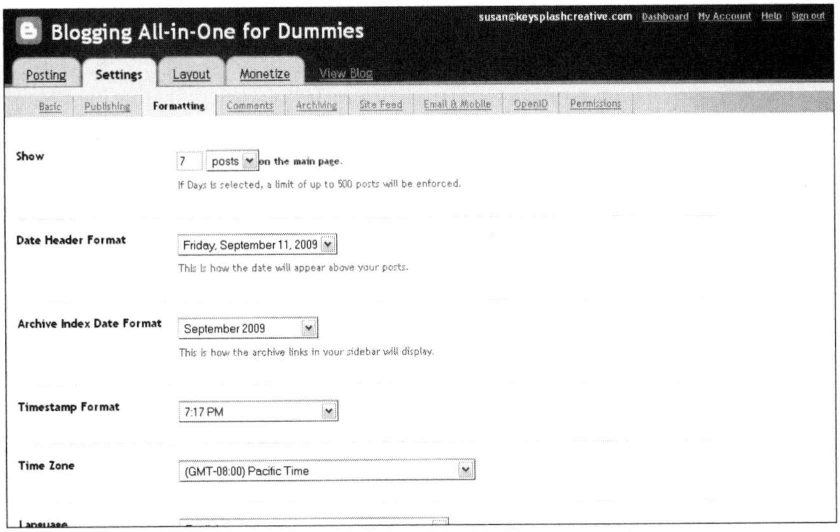

Figure 4-9:
The
Formatting
settings
page.

3. **Next to the Show heading, type the number of posts you want to show on your blog's main page.**

   Most bloggers choose to show five to seven posts on their blog's main page to reduce the need for excessive scrolling.

4. **Using the drop-down lists, select the format you want to use for your post dates, your blog's archives, your post times, your time zone, and your language.**

   These settings are based on your personal preferences.

5. **Click the Save Settings button.**

   Your configuration settings are saved and immediately affect all of your blog posts and archives.

Comments settings

Configuring your blog post comment settings before you begin publishing content on your blog is very important. The conversation that takes place on your blog through the comments that visitors leave on your posts is what gives a blog a sense of community and helps it grow. Following are some of the most important comment settings, which you should configure as soon as possible:

1. **Click the Settings link on your main Blogger dashboard, shown earlier in Figure 4-6.**

   The Basic settings page opens, as shown earlier in Figure 4-8.

2. **Click the Comments link on the navigation bar near the top of your screen.**

   The Comments settings page opens, as shown in Figure 4-10.

3. **Next to the Comments heading, make sure the radio button for Show is selected.**

   This sets up your blog posts so comments left on existing and new blog posts are visible to visitors.

4. **Next to Who Can Comment, select the radio button for Anyone.**

   Opening your blog posts up to accept comments from anyone will help it to grow.

5. **Next to Comment Form Placement, make sure the radio button for Embedded Below Post is selected.**

   This configuration has become the standard most blog visitors are used to and most comfortable with.

6. **Next to Comments Default for Posts, make sure the New Posts Have Comments setting is selected.**

   This setting ensures all new posts include the commenting option.

7. **Next to Backlinks, select the Show radio button.**

   Backlinks are published on one of your blog posts anytime another blog published on Blogger links to that post. Backlinks are a great way to find out about new blogs, drive traffic to other blogs, and build relationships with other bloggers — three important things you need to do if you're trying to build a successful blog.

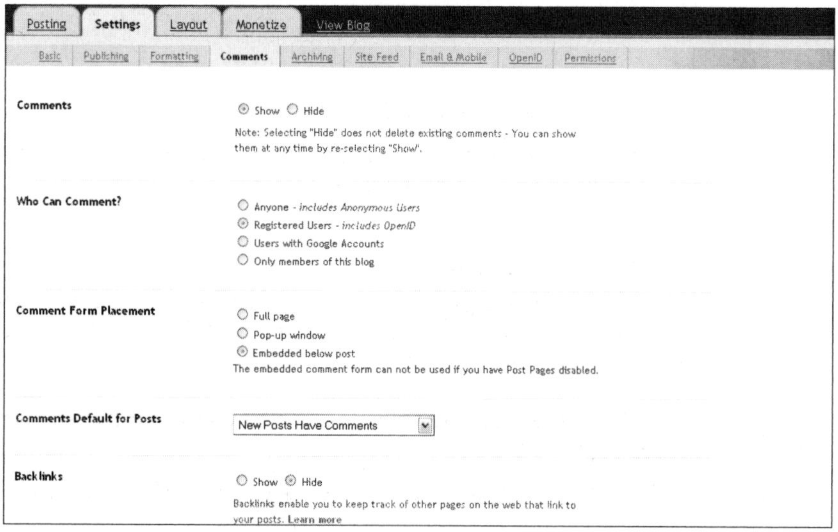

Figure 4-10: The Comments settings page.

8. **Next to Backlinks Default for Posts, make sure the New Posts Have Backlinks option is selected.**

   This setting ensures all new posts include the backlink option.

9. **Select the date and time format you prefer from the Comments Timestamp Format drop-down list.**

   This setting can be configured to meet your personal preferences.

10. **Enter a message to appear above the comment form on your blog posts in the Comment Form Message text box.**

    If you want to include a personal message above your comment form on all of your blog posts, you can enter it here.

11. **Select the radio button next to Always in the section titled Comment Moderation and enter the e-mail address where you want your comment notification messages to be sent.**

    It's a good idea to monitor all the comments that are left on your blog to remove spam, delete offensive comments, and ensure the conversation that happens on your blog adds value to your readers. When comments are waiting in your moderation queue, you receive an e-mail notifying you.

    As your blog gets more popular and comments become more than you can handle, you can adjust this setting to only moderate comments older than 14 days (or the timeframe of your choosing). This is effective because older posts typically attract far more spam comments than new ones.

12. **Select the Yes radio button in the Show Word Verification for Comments section.**

    To reduce the amount of spam comments that clutter your e-mail notifications, you can add an extra step for people to complete before they can submit a comment on one of your blog posts. In this step, people are asked to enter text that matches a text string shown in the comment form before they can submit their comments.

13. **Click the Save Settings button.**

    Your configuration settings are saved and immediately affect all comments left on your blog posts.

Archiving settings

The Archiving settings page is where you can choose how you want your blog posts archived, so your old posts are easier to access. You can configure your archives as follows:

1. **Click the Settings link on your main Blogger dashboard, shown earlier in Figure 4-6.**

   The Basic settings page opens, as shown earlier in Figure 4-8.

2. **Click the Archiving link on the navigation bar near the top of your screen.**

   The Archiving settings page opens, as shown in Figure 4-11.

3. **From the drop-down list next to Archive Frequency, select the way you want your old posts to be saved.**

   You can choose to archive your old posts on a daily, weekly, or monthly basis.

4. **Make sure Yes is selected next to Enable Post Pages.**

   This setting makes each blog post publish as its own page with its own unique URL, which is very helpful for search engine optimization, linking, and growing your blog.

   When you select Yes for Enable Post Pages, your most recent posts still appear on your blog's main page, but readers can click on each post and view it on its own page. Note that the embedded comment form option discussed in the Comments settings section of this chapter only works on blogs that have the Enable Post Pages setting configured to Yes.

5. **Click the Save Settings button.**

   Your configuration settings are saved and the changes affect your blog immediately.

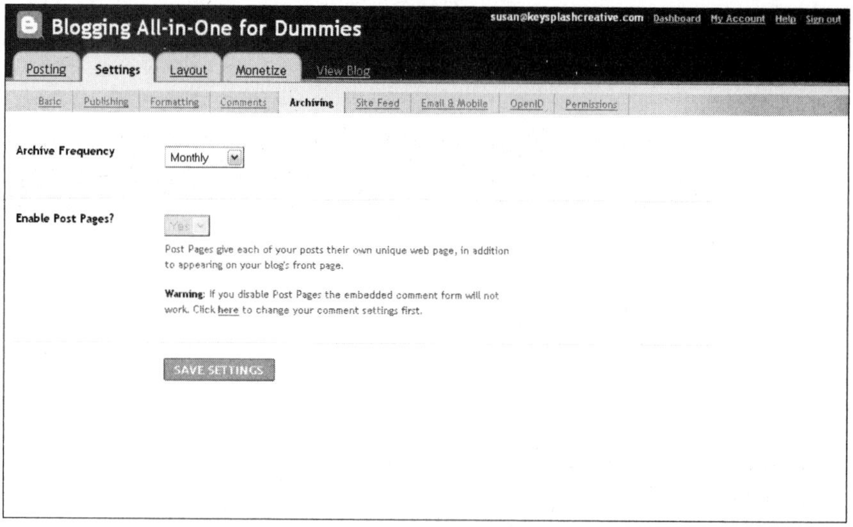

Figure 4-11: The Archiving settings page.

Permissions settings

The Permissions settings page is where you can add new authors to your blog and choose who can view your blog as follows:

1. **Click the Settings link on your main Blogger dashboard, shown earlier in Figure 4-6.**

   The Basic settings page opens, as shown earlier in Figure 4-8.

2. **Click the Permissions link on the navigation bar near the top of your screen.**

   The Permissions settings page opens, as shown in Figure 4-12.

3. **In the Blog Authors section, click the Add Authors button to give additional people access to your Blogger dashboard.**

   Each person you add as an author to your blog can write and publish posts and content on your blog. You only need a person's e-mail address to add him or her as an author on your blog.

4. **In the Blog Readers section, make sure the radio button next to Anybody is selected.**

   This setting means anyone who has Internet access can view your blog. If you're creating a private blog that you want only specific people to view, select the radio button next to Only People I Choose. If you're creating a blog that you only want yourself and other authors that you add to your blog to be able to view, select the radio button next to Only Blog Authors.

**Book IV
Chapter 4**

Using Google Blogger

Figure 4-12:
The Permissions settings page.

Personalizing Your Blog

The many free Blogger templates that are available can give your blog a more personalized look, depending on your tastes. You can access many free templates through your Blogger dashboard, or you can download templates from a variety of Web sites, some of which are listed later in this section.

If you're happy with your blog's template but just want to change the fonts and colors used in your blog, you can do that through your Blogger dashboard, too, and the best part is that you don't have to know HTML to do it!

Changing the fonts and colors used on your blog

Click the Layout link on your main Blogger dashboard page and then click the Fonts and Colors link on the navigation bar near the top of the page to access the Fonts and Colors configuration page shown in Figure 4-13.

Figure 4-13: The Fonts and Colors page with a color element selected.

From the Fonts and Colors page, you can select the various elements that you want to customize within your blog's template from the list on the left side of the screen. (Scroll to see all the options.) After you select an element, you can use the color buttons on the right to choose the color you want to use for that element on your blog. You can even see how your edits will look on your blog on the bottom part of your screen.

If you don't like a change that you make, just click the Clear Edits button. If you want to put your blog back to the way it looked before you started changing colors, just click the Revert to Template Default link to the right of the color palette. When you're satisfied with your color edits, click the Save Edits button and your changes are immediately made on your live blog.

Changing fonts is just as easy as changing colors. Just scroll down the list on the left until you get to a text element, such as Text Font, shown in Figure 4-14, and select it. The configuration settings on the right of your screen change from color selections to font selections. Just select the font family, style, and size you want to use (view your changes on your blog on the bottom half of your screen) and then click the Save Settings button to save your changes (or the Clear Edits button to remove the changes you made).

If you change your blog to a different Blogger template, your font and color changes will be overridden with the default settings for the new template.

Finding and choosing templates

It's easy to change your blog's entire color scheme and layout simply by choosing a different template to use as the skeleton of your blog. To change your blog's template, just click the Layout link on your main Blogger dashboard, shown earlier in Figure 4-6, and then click the Pick New Template link from the navigation bar near the top of your screen to open the Select a New Template for Your Blog page, as shown in Figure 4-15.

Figure 4-14:
The Fonts and Colors page with a font element selected.

Figure 4-15:
The Blogger
Pick New
Template
page.

The Select a New Template for Your Blog page includes thumbnail images of the various free templates available for you to use on your blog without leaving your Blogger dashboard. Just use the scroll bar to the right of the images to scroll through the list and view your options.

Notice that many of the images include lists with radio buttons beneath them. These list items represent variations of the theme shown in the corresponding thumbnail image. Just select one of the radio buttons, and the thumbnail image changes to the new version of that template. Select the Preview Template link under the template you select to see how your blog looks with the new template before you commit to using it.

After you find the template you like, select it and click the Save Template button. Your live blog immediately takes on the layout of the new template.

You can also access a wide variety of free Blogger templates from sources across the Internet. Following are a few popular sites for finding free Blogger templates:

✦ **eBlog Templates:** (www.eblogtemplates.com) This site offers a wide variety of free Blogger templates and includes user ratings.

✦ **BTemplates:** (http://btemplates.com): This site offers many free Blogger templates, and it's easy to search by number of columns, colors, and more.

✦ **Blogger Buster:** (www.bloggerbuster.com) The free templates offered by Blogger Buster are very well designed and coded.

✦ **Blog Flux:** (www.themes.blogflux.com) This site offers over 100 free Blogger themes and includes ratings, demos, and profiles of designers.

✦ **pYzam:** (www.pyzam.com) This site offers more than 1,000 free Blogger templates, which you can search using predefined categories or keywords.

Many blog designers create premium and custom Blogger templates at reasonable prices. For example, you can find premium Blogger templates at www.bloggerbuster.com and http://themeforest.net.

Understanding Blogger Gadgets

You can personalize your Blogger blog and add enhanced functionality to it through the handy gadgets available through your Blogger dashboard. Each Blogger gadget represents a different feature you can add to your blog, such as a list of links, text, a video, a poll, and more. Adding gadgets to your blog is as simple as pointing and clicking.

To add a gadget to your blog, click the Layout link on your main Blogger dashboard, shown earlier in Figure 4-6, which opens the Page Elements layout page, as shown in Figure 4-16.

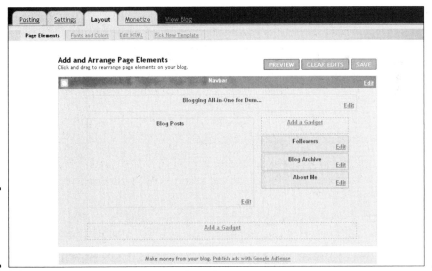

Figure 4-16: The Page Elements layout page.

The Page Elements layout page shows a *wireframe* image (a visual representation without content) of your blog's layout with each element already included in your blog's layout represented as a box — your header, your blog posts, your footer, and your sidebar boxes. You can drag and drop each of these elements to a different position by using your mouse. You can delete elements by selecting the Edit link within a box and following the instructions provided. (Note that not all elements can be deleted from your blog's layout.) Additionally, you can edit the configuration of any element included in your blog by selecting the Edit link within a box and following the instructions provided.

You can also add additional elements to your blog by clicking the Add a Gadget link, which opens the Add a Gadget page shown in Figure 4-17.

Take your time selecting the link for each gadget and reviewing the options included for each to determine which you'd like to add to your blog. Most gadgets are added to a blog's sidebar. For example, you can use the Search Box gadget to add a handy search tool to your blog, which helps visitors find posts related to specific keywords. Alternatively, you might like to add a list of links to other sites and blogs you own or recommend, which you can do in just a few steps by using the Link List gadget.

One of the most popular Blogger gadgets is the Labels gadget, which allows you to add a list of the labels you use to identify your blog posts. Blog readers can use labels to find content related to subjects they're interested in. You can use labels as a very loose blog post categorization system.

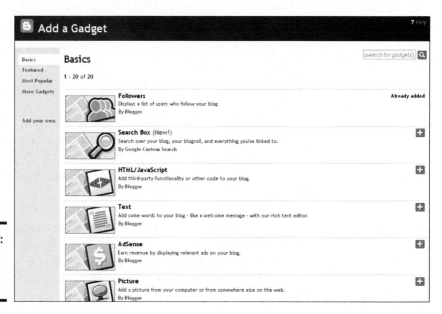

Figure 4-17:
The Add
a Gadget
page.

When you write your blog posts, be sure to take the time to add relevant labels so your post can be found using the Labels list added to your blog.

Following are simple steps to add the Labels gadget to your blog's sidebar:

1. **Click the Labels gadget link (or the + sign to the right of the Labels heading) on the Add a Gadget page, as shown earlier in Figure 4-17.**

   The Configure Labels page opens.

2. **In the Title text box (see Figure 4-18), enter the title you'd like to use for your labels list.**

   This title appears as a heading above your labels list and is helpful because not everyone who visits your blog knows what a Blogger label is.

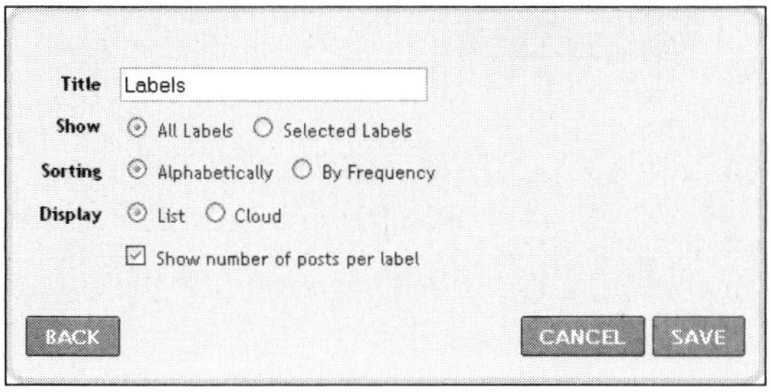

Figure 4-18: Type a title for your labels list here.

Title	Labels
Show	⊙ All Labels ○ Selected Labels
Sorting	⊙ Alphabetically ○ By Frequency
Display	⊙ List ○ Cloud
	☑ Show number of posts per label

BACK   CANCEL   SAVE

3. **Next to Show, select the radio button for All Labels or Selected Labels depending on your preference.**

   You might have some posts saved with labels that you don't want to appear in your labels list. If that's the case, you can exclude those labels by using the Selected Labels option.

4. **Select the radio button next to Alphabetically or By Frequency depending on how you want your labels list to be sorted.**

   This option is completely up to your personal preference, but Alphabetically is the most common.

5. **Next to Display, select the radio button next to List if you want your labels to appear as a list, or select Cloud if you want your labels to appear as a tag cloud.**

   This option is completely up to your personal preference. The list format is traditionally more common, but the cloud option is gaining popularity. Figure 4-19 shows an example of each.

**Book IV
Chapter 4**

**Using Google
Blogger**

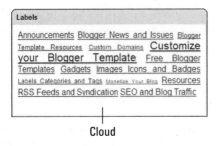

Cloud

Figure 4-19:
You can
choose the
List or Cloud
format.

List

6. **Select the Show Number of Posts Per Label check box if you want to show how many posts in your archives were saved with each specific label.**

   This option is completely up to your personal preference, but until you have a deep archive, you might not want to show the number of posts per label.

7. **Click the Save button to save your changes.**

   Your Label list immediately appears in your blog's sidebar. You can click and drag it on the Blogger Page Elements layout page (refer to Figure 4-16) if you want to change its position on your blog.

The process to add other gadgets to your blog works the same, although the instructions and options for each gadget vary. You can always delete a gadget after you add it, so don't be afraid to test out the gadgets available to you!

Publishing a Post

After you configure your blog to work the way you want it to and you set up your blog's layout and functionality to meet your preferences and needs, you're ready to publish your first post. Don't worry! Publishing posts using

Blogger is a snap if you already know how to use a word-processing application such as Microsoft Word. That's because the visual editor available in Blogger works extremely similarly to a word-processing application. Even the icons in the visual editor toolbar are similar to the ones you're probably already familiar with from your word-processing application!

To publish a post on your new Blogger blog, here's what you do:

1. **Click the New Post button on your main Blogger dashboard page (shown earlier in Figure 4-6) to open the New Post page (shown earlier in Figure 4-5).**

Take some time to hover your mouse over the icons in the visual editor toolbar to see what they do.

2. **Enter a title for your post in the Title text box and type the body of your post in the large text box in the middle of the page.**

3. **Enter labels into the Labels for This Post text box.**

4. **(Optional) If you want to schedule your post to go live at a future time, click the Post Options link above the Publish Post button to expand the window, as shown in Figure 4-20.**

From here, you can change the date and time when you want your post to go live. You can also disallow comments on a specific post from here.

5. **(Optional) You can click the Preview link to the right of the visual editor toolbar to see how your post will look when it's published.**

6. **When you're done, just click the Publish Post button for your post to instantly appear on your live blog.**

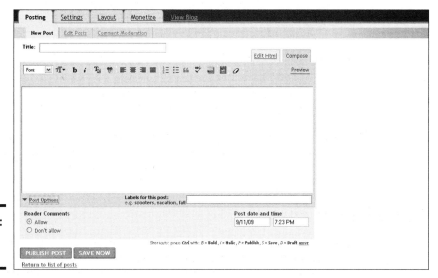

Figure 4-20:
The New
Post page.

If you're interrupted while writing a blog post and need to finish it later, just click the Save Now button and your post will be available for you to access using the Edit Posts link from your main Blogger dashboard. You can also edit or delete a post at anytime from the Edit Posts page.

Getting More Advanced

Blogger has earned a reputation as a beginner's blogging application, but in recent years, many new features have been added, making it a suitable choice for advanced bloggers, too. Two of those features are the ability to use your own domain and host your blog through a Web host.

Using your own domain

Many bloggers don't like having the .blogspot.com extension appended to their blog's domain names. Instead, they want to brand their blog with a personal domain name, and they're willing to invest some money to do so. If you want to purchase your own domain and associate it with your blog, you can, and Blogger makes it easy to do right from your Blogger dashboard, as follows:

1. **Click the Settings link on your main Blogger dashboard, shown earlier in Figure 4-6.**

The Basic settings page opens, as shown earlier in Figure 4-8.

2. **Click the Publishing link on the navigation bar near the top of the page.**

The Publishing settings page opens, as shown in Figure 4-21.

Figure 4-21: The Publishing settings page.

3. **Select the Custom Domain link.**

   The Publish on a Custom Domain page opens, as shown in Figure 4-22.

Publish on a custom domain

Switch to: • blogspot.com (Blogger's free hosting service)

Hint : If you want to publish to an external FTP server, you will need to Set 'Blog Readers' to 'Anybody' and use a Classic Template

Buy a domain for your blog

Already own a domain? Switch to advanced settings

What address would you like your blog to have?   http://www. [   ] .com ☑

CHECK AVAILABILITY

Google Checkout ⚡

VISA · Mastercard · AMEX · DISCOVER

Domains are registered through a Google partner and cost $10 (USD) for one year. As part of registration, you will also get a Google Apps account for your new domain.

We won't leave your readers behind!

http://bloggingallinonefordummier.blogspot.com will redirect to your custom domain.

Word Verification

swise

[   ] ♿

Type the characters you see in the picture.

4. **Enter the domain name you want in the text box and click the Check Availability button.**

   Don't be surprised if it takes many tries to find a domain name that's available.

5. **After you find an available domain, follow the payment instructions and enter the word verification text into the provided text box to purchase your new domain.**

   Your `.blogspot.com` domain will automatically redirect to your newly purchased domain name.

   If you purchased your domain through a third party, you can associate that domain to your Blogger blog by selecting the Switch to Advanced Settings link from the Publish a Custom Domain page, shown in Figure 4-22, and following the instructions provided.

Using a Web host

It is possible to host your blog through a Web host, which gives you greater control over your content and blog's functionality. If you're comfortable with technology, you might want to invest in Web hosting services for your blog, but keep in mind that not only is there a cost associated with Web hosting, but there's also a technical learning curve that's sizeable for beginner bloggers.

**Book IV
Chapter 4**

**Using Google
Blogger**

First, you need to open a Web hosting account with a company such as www.bluehost.com, www.godaddy.com, or www.hostgator.com. Then you need to work with that company to configure your account to be able to receive, store, and publish your blog correctly. After that's done, you need to set up your blog to be able to publish content to it via an FTP (File Transfer Protocol) connection.

The processes to host your blog through a Web host and use your own domain for your blog (which is done as a redirect) are just workarounds. In other words, neither is streamlined, and neither is done as well as power bloggers would like. For example, redirected domains can affect search engine optimization efforts. With that in mind, it's important to understand that most power bloggers choose WordPress.org as their blogging application because it offers the most features, functionality, and customization. Always consider your long-term blogging goals before you choose your blogging application.

Getting Help and Finding Resources

You can take advantage of many resources to find out more about using Blogger. Some of the most popular follow:

✦ **Google Blogger For Dummies:** I wrote this guide to using Blogger for beginners with some advanced functions included. It's available through most book sellers.

✦ **Blogger Help:** (http://help.blogger.com) The official Blogger help site offers a lot of information to help you create your blog.

✦ **Blogger Buzz:** (http:/buzz.blogger.com) The official Blogger blog provides updates about new Blogger features, problems, and more.

✦ **Blogger Help Group:** (http://groups.google.com/group/blogger-help) The official Google Group is dedicated to providing Blogger help. You can join the group and then ask and answer questions.

✦ **BloggerHelp channel on YouTube:** (www.youtube.com/BloggerHelp) The official BloggerHelp channel on YouTube offers several helpful videos that show you how to use a number of Blogger features, including setting up a custom domain.

✦ **Blogger Buster:** (www.bloggerbuster.com) Amanda Fazani writes the Blogger Buster blog and includes many step-by-step tutorials and help on just about every Blogger function and feature you can think of.

Chapter 5: Understanding TypePad

*T*ypePad is a blogging application from Six Apart Media. It's a popular blogging platform despite the fact that you have to pay a monthly fee to use it, and that fee increases if you want added functionality. For example, your blog content is hosted by TypePad, so your blog includes a `.typepad.com` extension unless you pay for an upgraded account as well as for a domain name. To compare apples to apples among the three blogging applications discussed in this book, WordPress, Blogger, and TypePad, this chapter focuses on the capabilities offered through the least expensive, basic TypePad account.

In this chapter, you find out how to start a new blog using TypePad, configure the most important settings, personalize your blog, and publish content to it. Keep in mind, this chapter merely presents an overview to using TypePad. For detailed instructions, check out *TypePad For Dummies,* by Shannon Lowe and Melanie Nelson.

Finding Out about TypePad

TypePad offers an easy-to-use What You See Is What You Get (WYSIWYG) post editor, so publishing content is as easy as creating a document in your preferred word-processing application. Furthermore, it's easy to customize your blog's appearance and functionality through the tools offered via your TypePad dashboard. Many popular bloggers use TypePad, such as celebrity blogger Wil Wheaton (www.wilwheaton.typepad.com), marketing guru

Seth Godin (`www.sethgodin.typepad.com`), and all the blogs published for the Orlando Sentinel news organization (`www.orlandosentinel.com`), as shown in Figure 5-1.

Figure 5-1: The Orlando Sentinel blogs are powered by TypePad.

Understanding TypePad Fees

Most bloggers who use TypePad are happy with the features and services the application provides, but to truly be able to customize your blog and access enhanced functionality, you do need to pay for a more expensive account. Be sure to review the current pricing published on the TypePad Web site (`www.typepad.com/pricing`) to see what you can get at different price points above the basic package.

TypePad users can choose from four types of accounts based on their needs and the costs associated with them as follows:

✦ **Basic:** The least expensive option is the Basic account that lets you create a blog and monetize it. Also, the Basic package is the only account option that does not allow you to schedule blog posts to publish at a future date and time, which is a feature many bloggers rely on when they're on vacation and want to continue publishing content.

✦ **Plus:** The next package costs almost twice as much as the Basic package per month and adds features such as domain mapping to your personal domain (to drop the .typepad.com from your blog's URL) and the ability to create two more blogs tied to your existing account.

✦ **Pro:** The most expensive personal TypePad package, called the Pro package, costs nearly twice as much as the Plus package. With the Pro package, you get even more features, such as the ability to create an unlimited number of blogs and give an unlimited number of authors access to those blogs, as well as enhanced design customization options.

✦ **Business:** The Business package costs about six times as much as the Pro package but adds a great deal of functionality that businesses need such as annual billing and the ability to give more than one person administrative privileges on your blog.

The amount of storage space and bandwidth allocated to your blog differ significantly from one TypePad package to another. Be sure to check the current offerings to ensure the package you choose offers enough space to store your content as well as a high enough bandwidth to ensure your blog pages load quickly in visitors' Web browsers. You can always upgrade your account in the future, so don't overbuy.

TypePad offers a free trial, so you can start a blog using TypePad and determine whether you're happy with it before you have to pay anything. Just be sure to cancel your account before the trial period is over, and you won't be charged.

Creating a Blog with TypePad

If you choose TypePad as your blogging application, you can follow the instructions included in this section to create your new blog and join the blogosphere. Remember, the details included in this chapter refer to the Basic TypePad account, so the features available to you might be different depending on the package you choose.

Follow these steps to start your new Basic TypePad blog:

1. **Visit the TypePad home page.**

Enter the URL **www.typepad.com** into your browser, and the TypePad home page opens, as shown in Figure 5-2.

**Book IV
Chapter 5**

**Understanding
TypePad**

Figure 5-2:
The
TypePad
home page.

2. **Click the Free Trial: Get a Blog Now button or the Start Your Free Trial Now button.**

   Both buttons take you to the Create Your Blog in Minutes page.

3. **Select the radio button for the package you want to sign up for.**

   In this chapter, the Basic package is selected.

4. **Click the Continue button.**

   The Get Started with a TypePad Account page opens, as shown in Figure 5-3.

5. **Enter the information requested in the text boxes.**

   Take some time to choose a Blog URL that you like and don't be surprised if the first one you choose is unavailable.

6. **Click the Create Account button.**

   The Billing Information page opens.

7. **Enter your billing information into the text boxes.**

   Be sure to select the payment plan that works best for you.

8. **Click the Continue button.**

   The Confirm Your Information page opens.

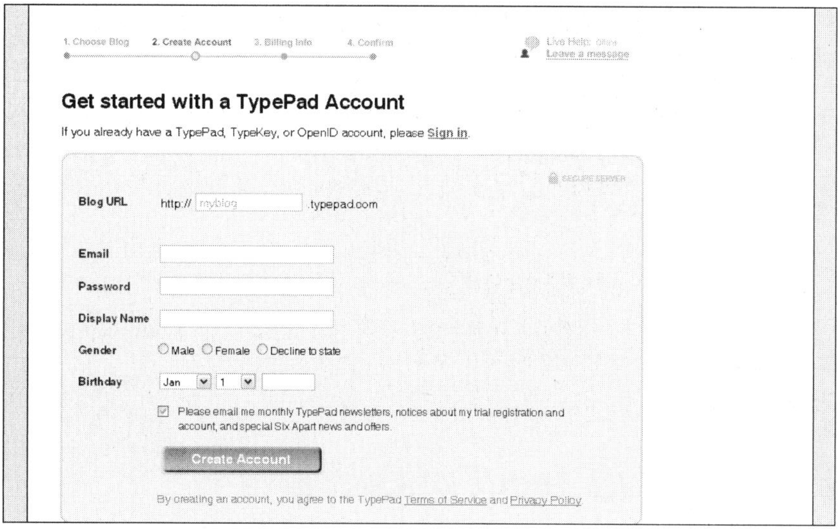

Figure 5-3:
The Get
Started with
a TypePad
Account
page.

9. **Review the information for your new account, and make any necessary changes. Then click the Continue button.**

   The Congratulations, You Have a TypePad Blog! page opens, as shown in Figure 5-4.

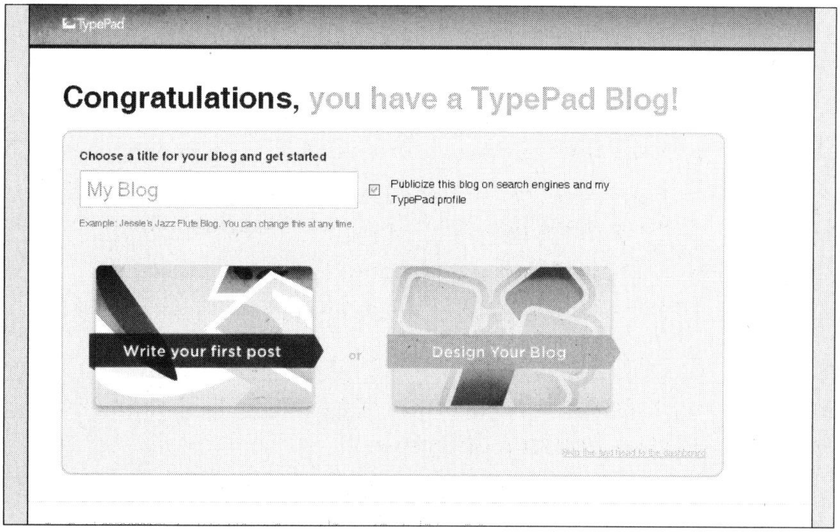

Figure 5-4:
The
Congrat-
ulations,
You Have
a TypePad
Blog! page.

10. **Enter a title for your blog and make sure the check box next to Publicize This Blog on Search Engines and My TypePad Profile is selected.**

    If you don't want search engines to index your blog, and you don't want your blog to appear in your TypePad profile, deselect this check box. However, this isn't recommended if you want your blog to grow and attract search traffic.

11. **Click the Skip This and Head to the Dashboard link beneath the Design Your Blog image on the right side of your screen.**

    This step takes you to your main TypePad dashboard page, where you can configure the settings for your blog to ensure it works the way you want it to, including personalizing the design and publishing posts.

Reviewing the TypePad Dashboard

The TypePad dashboard is where you can access all the tools and features available to you to publish content and enhance your blog. To get started, just select your blog from the Blog drop-down list in the top navigation bar or from the sidebar on the right of your main dashboard page. This action brings you to your dashboard for the specific blog you chose from your account, as shown in Figure 5-5.

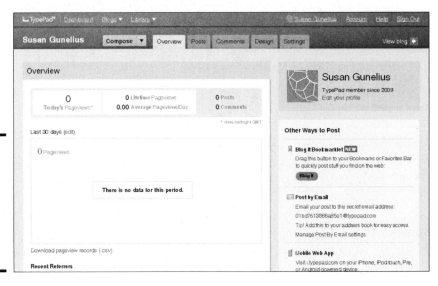

Figure 5-5:
The
TypePad
dashboard
for a
specific
blog in an
account.

The first thing you notice on your TypePad dashboard for your blog is recent activity, which displays in the largest area in the center of your screen. Beneath your recent activity, you can see recent sites that referred traffic to your blog, and across the top of your screen are the navigation bars that allow you to access all the parts of your blog. Take some time to review the information included on each tab. Following is an overview of the features accessible from each of the tabs on the navigation bar:

+ **Posts:** From the Posts tab, you can write new posts and pages, and edit existing posts and pages.

+ **Comments:** From the Comments tab, you can manage the comments left on your blog posts as well as your trackbacks. You can also create and manage a Block List of visitors whose comments you want automatically rejected using their IP addresses or by adding keywords that should trigger comments to be rejected.

+ **Design:** From the Design tab, you can choose a design theme for your blog, organize your content, and adjust your blog's layout.

+ **Settings:** From the Settings tab, you can modify most of the broad settings that affect your blog to ensure it works exactly the way you want it to.

Across the very top of your dashboard is the primary navigation bar. From here, you can access your main dashboard, your blogs, your image library, and your Account, where you can modify your profile, e-mail, password, billing information, and more. In other words, every feature you can possibly modify is accessible from the tabs and links on your blog's dashboard, so poke around and get an understanding of the capabilities available to you before you dive in and publish your first post.

Configuring Settings

After you create your new TypePad blog, be sure to take some time to configure several settings that can greatly impact your blog, especially if you have goals to grow your blog's traffic over time. The following sections show you suggested ways to configure the most important settings for your blog, but remember, they are just suggestions. It's your blog, and you can configure it to work exactly the way *you* want it to. Also, these are just the most important settings, but do take the time to review all configuration options.

Only the most important configuration settings are discussed in this chapter with suggested settings that most bloggers use. However, your blog is your own, and you can configure the settings in the way you want.

Profile

Your blog's profile is where you can provide visitors an overview about your blog. Follow these steps to create your profile for your TypePad blog:

1. **On your blog's dashboard, shown earlier in Figure 5-5, click the Edit Your Profile link in the right sidebar.**

   The Profile page opens, as shown in Figure 5-6.

2. **Enter a word or phrase in the Profile URL text box provided.**

   The lengthy default URL for your blog's profile is cumbersome and useless for search engine optimization. Change it to something that's easier to understand and better describes your profile.

3. **Enter a brief bio in the One-Line Bio text box provided.**

   Keep it short and simple.

4. **Click the Browse button to locate an image on your computer's hard drive to attach to your profile.**

   Follow the instructions provided to attach the image.

5. **Click the Save Changes button.**

   A message in a yellow box appears at the top of your screen saying Your Changes Have Been Saved along with a View Your Profile link. Click the link to view your profile and make sure it looks the way you want it to.

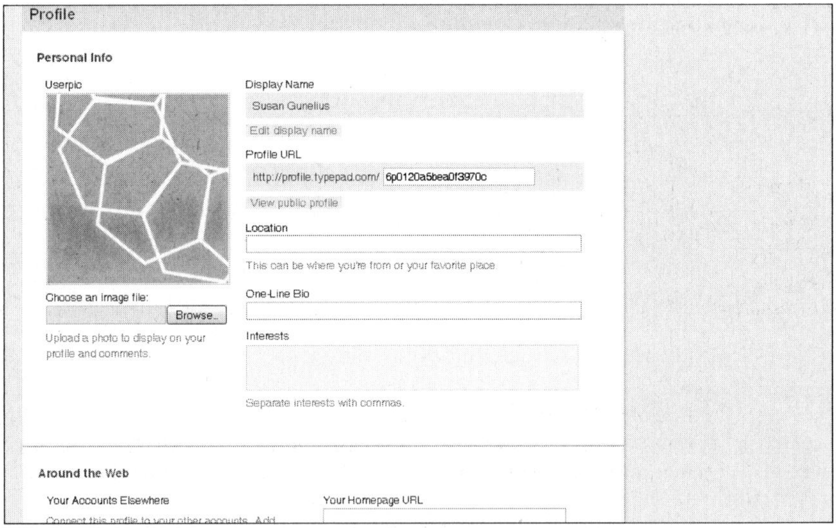

Figure 5-6:
The Edit Your Profile page.

About Me page

You can add an About Me page to your blog. Your About Me page is where you tell visitors why you're qualified to write your blog and what they can expect to find on your blog. It's your first step in building a relationship with your blog readers, so put some thought into crafting an interesting and informative profile. Follow these instructions to create your blog's About Me page:

1. Click the Account link on the top navigation bar on your blog's dashboard.

The Summary Page for Your Account opens.

2. Click the About Me Page tab on the left navigation bar.

The About Me page opens, as shown in Figure 5-7.

3. Enter additional information about you to create a complete profile and click the Save and Publish button when you're done.

Your new About Me page is immediately visible on your blog.

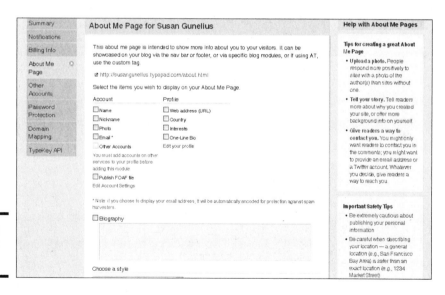

Figure 5-7:
The About
Me page.

Book IV
Chapter 5

Understanding
TypePad

Notifications

You can set up your blog e-mail notifications from the Account link in the top navigation bar on your blog's dashboard as follows:

1. Click the Account link on the top navigation bar on your blog's dashboard.

The Summary Page for Your Account opens.

2. **Select the Notifications tab from the left navigation bar.**

   The Notifications page opens, as shown in Figure 5-8.

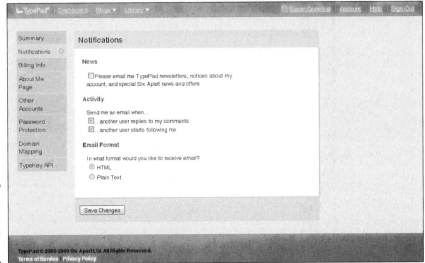

Figure 5-8:
The
Notifications
page.

3. **Make any changes to your notifications that you want.**

   Note that the default notifications settings are the most commonly used, but if you want to reduce the number of e-mails you receive, you can deselect one or both of the check boxes under the Activity heading.

Basic settings

The Basic settings for your blog can be modified at any time. The first thing you should do is add a description of your blog as follows:

1. **Click the Settings tab on the navigation bar on your blog's dashboard, shown earlier in Figure 5-5.**

   The Basics page opens, shown in Figure 5-9.

2. **Change your blog name and enter your blog description in the text boxes provided.**

   Put some thought into what you want your blog name and description to say, and enter it here.

3. **Enter the text you want to appear at the end of the URL for your blog folder in the Blog Folder text box.**

   Note that after you decide on the URL for your blog folder, you should not change it, or links will be lost.

Figure 5-9:
The Basics
page.

4. If you want your blog to be private, select the Password check box.

Do not select this check box unless you want only people with your blog's password to see it. This is uncommon because most bloggers want their blogs to grow and therefore need their blogs to be visible to everyone.

5. Click the Save Settings button.

A Your Configurations Have Been Saved message appears in a yellow box at the top of your screen.

SEO settings

Your blog's SEO settings affect the search engine traffic that comes to your blog. Follow these steps to configure the SEO settings for your TypePad blog:

1. Click the Settings tab on the navigation bar on your blog's dashboard, shown earlier in Figure 5-5.

The Basics page opens.

2. Click the SEO tab on the left navigation bar.

The SEO page opens, as shown in Figure 5-10.

3. Select the Yes, Publicize This Blog check box.

This option makes your blog visible to search engines and allows them to index your content in order to send search traffic to your blog.

**Book IV
Chapter 5**

**Understanding
TypePad**

Figure 5-10:
The SEO
page.

4. **Enter keywords that describe your blog into the Meta Keywords text box.**

   Metadata is extra information about a Web page that does not display on screen but can be viewed or read within the HTML coding of the page. Although metadata is not as important to SEO as it once was, it takes only a few seconds to type in some Meta Keywords, and it certainly can't hurt your blog to do so!

5. **Enter a description of your blog in the Meta Description text box.**

   Keep your description short — one or two sentences.

6. **Click the Save Changes button.**

   Your changes affect your blog immediately.

Posts & Pages settings

Most of the default configurations in the Posts & Pages settings are the ones that are most commonly used by bloggers. However, you should take a few minutes and follow these steps to review them to ensure they work exactly the way that you want them to on your blog:

1. **Click the Settings tab on the navigation bar on your blog's dashboard, shown earlier in Figure 5-5.**

   The Basics page opens.

2. **Click the Posts & Pages tab on the left navigation bar.**

   The Posts & Pages page opens, as shown in Figure 5-11.

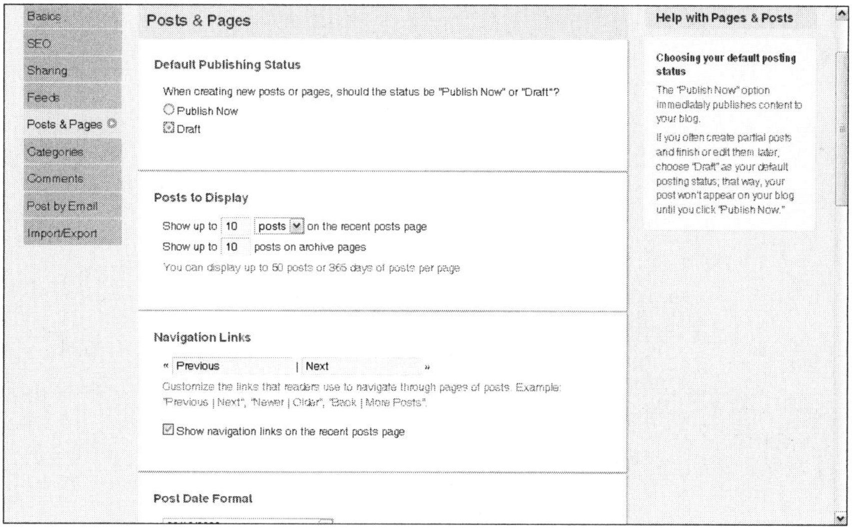

Basics
SEO
Sharing
Feeds
Posts & Pages ⚙
Categories
Comments
Post by Email
Import/Export

Posts & Pages

Default Publishing Status

When creating new posts or pages, should the status be "Publish Now" or "Draft"?

○ Publish Now
☒ Draft

Posts to Display

Show up to 10 [posts ▼] on the recent posts page

Show up to 10 posts on archive pages

You can display up to 50 posts or 365 days of posts per page.

Navigation Links

« Previous | Next »

Customize the links that readers use to navigate through pages of posts. Example: "Previous | Next", "Newer | Older", "Back | More Posts".

☑ Show navigation links on the recent posts page

Post Date Format

Help with Pages & Posts

Choosing your default posting status

The "Publish Now" option immediately publishes content to your blog.

If you often create partial posts and finish or edit them later, choose "Draft" as your default posting status; that way, your post won't appear on your blog until you click "Publish Now."

Figure 5-11:
The Posts &
Pages page.

3. **Select the radio button next to Draft under the Default Publishing Settings heading.**

   By changing this setting to Draft, you can save unfinished posts in draft form and return to publish them later. You can also save posts as you're writing them and publish them only when you're 100 percent certain they're final.

4. **Under the Posts to Display heading, select the number of posts you want to display on your blog's home page and archive pages.**

   Most bloggers display five to seven posts on the home pages of their blogs to reduce the need for excessive scrolling.

5. **Under the Navigation Links, Post Date Format, and Post Time Format headings, make any changes you want.**

   These modifications are strictly based on your personal preferences.

6. **Under the Front Page heading, you can choose to show your most recent posts on your blog's home page so it looks like a traditional blog, or you can show a static page as your blog's home page so it looks more like a traditional Web site.**

   This setting is up to you and depends on how you want your blog to look and function.

7. **Using the drop-down list, select the way you want your blog's list of Recent Posts to display.**

   This setting depends on what posts you want to display in your recent posts list and is entirely up to you.

**Book IV
Chapter 5**

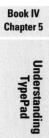

Understanding
TypePad

8. Click the Save Changes button.

Your changes immediately affect your blog.

Categories settings

Your blog post categories are important because they make it easy for your blog's visitors to find content related to topics they're interested in. It's particularly important to modify these settings before you start publishing content on your blog because many of the default categories won't apply to your blog. The following steps walk you through modifying your blog's Categories settings:

1. Click the Settings tab on the navigation bar on your blog's dashboard, shown earlier in Figure 5-5.

The Basics page opens.

2. Click the Categories tab on the left navigation bar.

The Categories page opens, as shown in Figure 5-12.

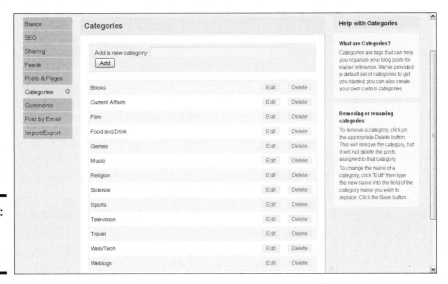

Figure 5-12:
The Categories page.

3. Review the list of default categories and use the Edit and Delete links to the right of each category to modify the list.

Make sure the categories you choose are relevant to the type of content you plan to write on your blog.

4. Enter descriptions of new categories in the Add a New Category box and select the Add button to add it to your list of categories.

You can also add categories as you write new posts, so don't worry too much about adding categories now. You can add them later as needed.

Comments settings

In the Comments settings page of your TypePad blog, you can configure who can leave comments on your posts, whether you want to moderate posts before they're published on your blog, and more, as follows:

1. **Click the Settings tab on the navigation bar on your blog's dashboard, shown earlier in Figure 5-5.**

The Basics page opens.

2. **Select the Comments tab from the left navigation bar.**

The Comments page opens, as shown in Figure 5-13.

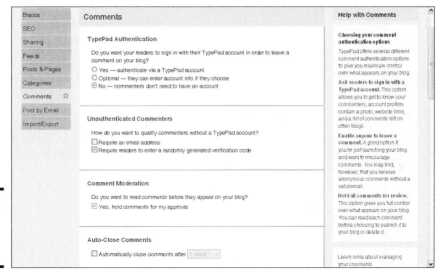

Figure 5-13: The Comments page.

3. **Under the TypePad Authentication heading, select the radio button next to No — Commenters Don't Need to Have an Account.**

Changing this setting opens your blog up to conversation between all visitors without barriers. This is the best setting to use if you want to grow your blog.

4. **Under the Unauthenticated Comments heading, deselect the check box next to Require an Email Address and select the check box next to Require Readers to Enter a Randomly Generated Verification Code.**

Of the two options, this one will reduce more spam comments from publishing on your blog or making it to your moderation queue.

5. **Under the Comment Moderation heading, select the Yes, Hold Comments for My Approval check box.**

   By moderating comments, you can delete spam and irrelevant or inappropriate comments before they're published on your blog and negatively affect the user experience.

6. **Under the Comment Formatting heading, select the Yes, Allow Limited HTML check box.**

   This setting gives more flexibility to people who leave comments on your blog.

7. **Scroll down to the By Default, Accept Trackbacks heading and select the On New Posts check box.**

   Accepting trackbacks on posts is a great way to grow your blog by sending reciprocal traffic to a blog that links to your post and starting a relationship with the other blogger.

8. **Click the Save Changes button.**

   Your changes are applied to your blog.

Personalizing Your Blog

TypePad offers numerous personalization options, even if you're just using the Basic account package as described in this chapter. Unfortunately, you can't use themes created by third-party designers unless you upgrade your account and get access to advanced templates options. However, enough themes and design options are offered with the Basic TypePad account to satisfy most beginner bloggers and some advanced bloggers, too.

Choosing a theme

The first step to customize your blog's design is to choose a theme, as follows:

1. **Click the Design tab on the navigation bar on your blog's dashboard, shown earlier in Figure 5-5.**

   The Design Your Blog page opens.

2. **Click the Choose a Theme button.**

   The Themes page opens, as shown in Figure 5-14.

Figure 5-14:
The Choose
a Theme
page.

3. **Click the links in the right menu and scroll through the theme options available to you until you find one that you like. Then select the radio button below the theme you like and click the Save Changes button.**

Your new theme is immediately applied to your blog.

You can click the Preview button on the Choose a Theme page to see what your blog will look like using different themes before you commit to using one.

Selecting a layout

You have two primary options for TypePad blog layouts: Classic and Mixed Media. Classic layouts allow you to choose a one-, two-, or three-column layout for your blog, and Mixed Media layouts allow you to choose from a variety of layouts to display different media elements such as calendars, images, and more. You can select a layout for your blog as follows:

1. **On the Design Your Blog page, click the Select a Layout button.**

The Layouts page opens, as shown in Figure 5-15.

2. **Select the radio button beneath the layout you prefer and then click the Save Changes button.**

Your new layout is immediately applied to your blog.

Book IV
Chapter 5

Understanding
TypePad

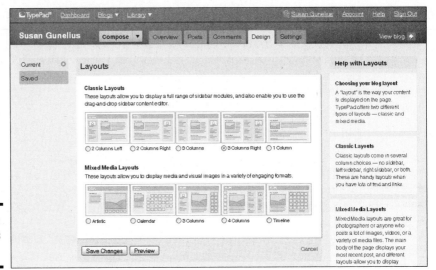

Figure 5-15:
The Layouts
page.

Take some time to test the various layout options available to you by selecting the radio buttons beneath each and then clicking the Preview button to see how your blog looks with each layout option.

Organizing content

TypePad makes it very easy to move content around in your blog's layout with a simple menu and drag-and-drop system. Follow these steps to modify the placement of your content on your blog:

1. **On the TypePad Design Your Blog page, click the Organize Content button.**

The Content page opens, as shown in Figure 5-16.

2. **Scroll through the Modules list at the top of the page and click a feature you want to add to your blog. Then click the Add This Module button.**

The module appears in the wireframe layout of your blog shown in the lower part of your screen.

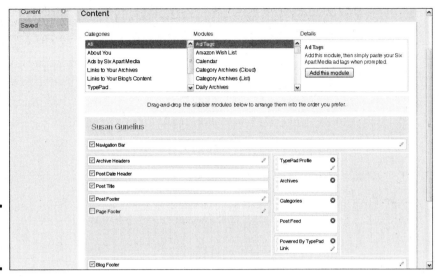

Figure 5-16:
The Content
page.

3. **To move a module within your blog's layout, just click it and drag it to a new location.**

   Your changes don't show up on your blog until you click the Save Changes button. You can use the Preview button to see what your changes will look like on your blog before you commit to saving them.

4. **To delete a module from your blog, just click the red X in the upper-right corner of that module or deselect the check box in the left side of the module as applicable.**

   The module disappears from your wireframe.

5. **Click the Save Changes button when you're done.**

   Your edits are immediately applied to your blog.

Modules that include a pencil image on the right side can be edited. Click the pencil to open the edit window where you can make changes to those modules.

Publishing a Post

TypePad makes it very easy to publish posts on your blog as follows:

1. **Click the Posts tab on the navigation bar in your blog's dashboard, shown earlier in Figure 5-5.**

   The Posts page opens.

2. **Click the New Post link.**

   The New Post page opens, as shown in Figure 5-17.

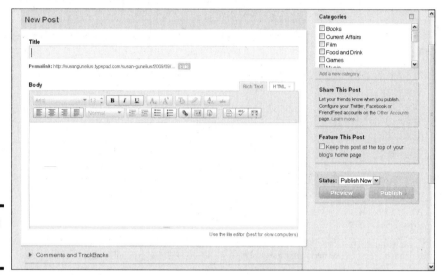

3. **Enter a title and body text for your post in the boxes provided.**

   Take a minute to hover your mouse over the icons above the post editor to see what they are for. Notice that most work similarly to icons used in word processing applications.

4. **From the Categories menu on the right side of your screen, select the check box next to the appropriate category for your post.**

   You can add a new category if an appropriate category is not already in your list, and you can select more than one category for your post as applicable.

5. **Scroll down to the Comments and Trackbacks section under your post editor and click the arrow to expand the section. Make sure the Open radio button is selected under both Comments and Trackbacks.**

   This setting means visitors can leave comments on your post, and any trackbacks to your post will be displayed on your post.

6. **Scroll down to the Keywords and Technorati Tags section and enter relevant keywords and Technorati tags in the boxes provided.**

Often your keywords and Technorati tags will be the same, so you can copy and paste them. Take the time to enter both because they help increase search engine traffic.

7. **Click the Preview button to view your post before you actually publish it. When you're satisfied with your post, click the Publish button.**

Your post is immediately available on your blog.

Using Advanced Features

TypePad offers a variety of advanced features to users with upgraded accounts. For example, you can add functionality with widgets, which are accessible through the Design Your Blog page shown in Figure 5-18 or at `www.sixapart.com/typepad/widgets`. You can also access more themes and use third-party themes and designs when you upgrade your account.

Additionally, you can use your own domain name for your blog if you pay for any account above the Basic TypePad package, as follows:

1. **Click the Account link on the top navigation bar on your blog's dashboard.**

The Summary Page for Your Account opens.

2. **Click the Domain Mapping tab on the left navigation bar.**

The Domain Mapping page opens.

3. **Read through the Important Requirements to ensure you have everything you need to map a new domain to your blog (such as the advanced DNS, domain name system, and settings, which you can get from your new domain registrar). Then click the Begin Here: Map a Domain Name button.**

The Domain Mapping configuration page opens, as shown in Figure 5-18, and you can follow the instructions to map your domain to your blog.

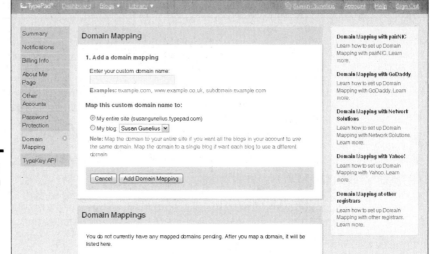

Figure 5-18:
The Domain
Mapping
config-
uration
page.

Getting Help and Finding Resources

You can take advantage of a number of excellent resources to get additional help to start and enhance your TypePad blog. Following are some of the most popular TypePad resources:

✦ **TypePad For Dummies:** Shannon Lowe and Melanie Nelson wrote this guidebook to using TypePad.

✦ **TypePad Knowledge Base:** (`http://help.sixapart.com/tp/us`) This site is where all the documentation on TypePad provided by Six Apart Media can be found.

✦ **TypePad Help:** Click the Help link on the top navigation bar of your Type-Pad dashboard. A new page opens where you can search the TypePad Knowledge Base for help or submit a New Ticket for help from the TypePad support staff.

✦ **The Official Everything TypePad Blog:** (`http://everything.type pad.com`) This blog offers tips, advice, and help from the TypePad community.

✦ **TypePad User Forums:** (`http://getsatisfaction.com/sixapart/ products/sixapart_typepad`) This is the official TypePad user forum where users can ask questions and help each other.

Book V

Blogging Tools

The 5th Wave   By Rich Tennant

HORNER BROS.
MAKERS OF PREMIUM
BELLS & WHISTLES

"As a blog designer I never thought I'd
say this, but I don't think your blog has
enough bells and whistles."

Contents at a Glance

Chapter 1: Search Engine Optimization

In This Chapter

↙ **Understanding SEO basics**

↙ **Using keywords and doing keyword research**

↙ **Demystifying long-tail SEO**

↙ **Writing SEO-friendly blog posts**

↙ **Building relationships to boost search rankings**

↙ **Understanding Google Page Rank**

↙ **Avoiding SEO don'ts**

↙ **Using the NoFollow tag**

↙ **Considering search engine reputation management**

Search engine optimization (SEO) is an elusive subject because the exact recipe for success is a secret known only by a select group of Google and other search engine company employees. With that said, SEO can be challenging, but it's not impossible to boost your blog's traffic from search engines with a bit of understanding and commitment. The best way to get the hang of SEO techniques is to invest time into researching everything you can about it and testing different techniques to determine which work best for your blog. That's because each blog's content is different, and each blog's audience is different. Both of these factors significantly affect the search traffic that has the potential to come to your blog.

This chapter introduces some of the commonly accepted SEO techniques, so you can begin blogging with confidence that your content has a chance to be found through keyword searches on popular search engines such as

Google. However, the information in this chapter is just the tip of the iceberg in terms of discovering SEO techniques. For more detailed information about SEO, read *Search Engine Optimization For Dummies,* by Peter Kent, or the more comprehensive *Search Engine Optimization All-in-One For Dummies,* by Bruce Clay and Susan Esparza.

Understanding SEO Basics

When most people hear the term SEO, they think of keywords, which are discussed in the next section of this chapter, but there's actually a lot more to SEO than using targeted keywords that match people's search engine queries. Although keywords are the starting point for your blog's SEO strategy, they can take your blog only so far. You also need to focus on other SEO techniques to truly grow your blog's search engine traffic.

For example, did you know that the number of incoming links to your blog, particularly incoming links for popular blogs and Web sites, are very important when it comes time for search engines to *rank* your site in comparison with similar sites for search results? In other words, your blog can stand on its own, but it will be very lonely. Boosting the number of incoming links to your blog is discussed later in this chapter, in the section "Increasing your blog's Google Page Rank."

Perhaps the most important aspect of SEO is relationship building. It's definitely not what people first think of when they hear the term SEO, but it's probably the most important. Why? Because the relationships that you build with other bloggers and your own audience help to spread your content across the Web.

On the other hand, some SEO techniques can actually get you in trouble and cause your blog's search traffic to plummet or disappear entirely. In other words, you need to avoid some SEO don'ts at all costs, unless you want to risk having your blog dropped from search results.

And when it comes to SEO, you need to be flexible. Just when SEO experts think they have another aspect of Google's proprietary search algorithm figured out, Google changes it. If you're serious about SEO, be sure to visit sites like SEOmoz (`www.seomoz.org`), shown in Figure 1-1, and stay abreast of the trends and tips related to SEO.

Figure 1-1:
SEOmoz is
a popular
blog and
community
dedicated
to search
engine
optimization.

Interpreting Keywords

Keywords are the first stop on the SEO train because you can use them
to choose a blog topic and optimize your content with those keywords.
Focusing on targeted keywords helps search engines find your content and
rank it accordingly in keyword search results.

Doing keyword research

The first step to using keywords to boost your blog's traffic from search
engines is to find the best keywords to include in your content. That
means you need to do keyword research using tools such as Wordtracker,
KeywordDiscovery, Google AdWords Keyword Tool, and Google AdWords
Traffic Estimator. Both of the tools provided by Google are offered for free
and can give you a good idea of popular keywords. You can find out more
about both Google tools and find step-by-step instructions for using them in
Chapter 3 of Book II.

The goal for keyword research is to find keywords to target in your posts
that are relevant to your blog's topic and neither too popular (because
there's too much competition from powerful sites for those keywords)
nor too unpopular (because there's no sense in focusing on keywords that
no one is searching for).

Wordtracker

Wordtracker is one of the most popular keyword research tools, but it has a price tag attached to it. Fortunately, you can sign up for a free trial to test it before you commit to opening an account. Follow these steps to get started with Wordtracker:

1. **Visit www.wordtracker.com.**

The Wordtracker home page opens, as shown in Figure 1-2. From here, you can start your free trial, review pricing, and take a tour.

Figure 1-2: The Wordtracker home page.

2. **Click the Take the Free Trial Button.**

The Wordtracker 7-Day Free Trial page opens, as shown in Figure 1-3.

3. **Enter your information into the text boxes and click the Continue button to start your free trial.**

A Wordtracker account is not cheap. If you don't want to be automatically charged for your account, you must cancel your account before your 7-day trial ends.

To begin your keyword research using Wordtracker, be sure to review the current tour at www.wordtracker.com/tour.html, where you can find out how to use the tools available to you.

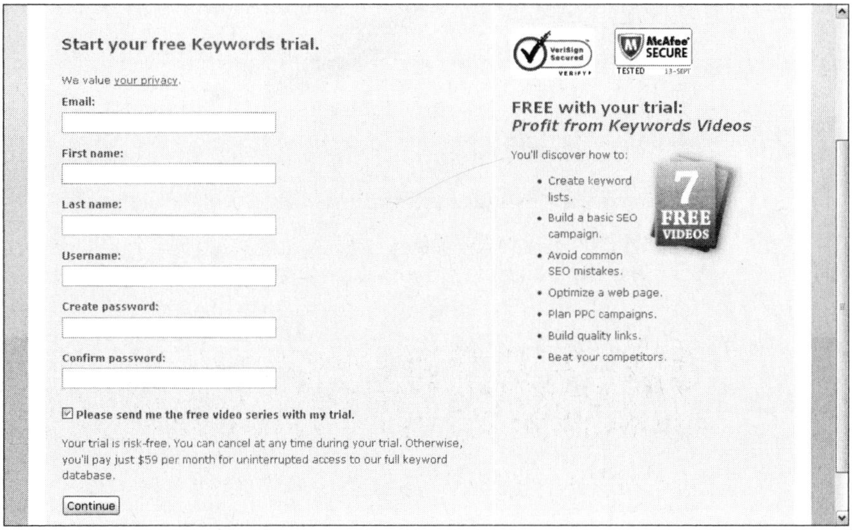

Figure 1-3:
The
Wordtracker
7-Day Free
Trial page.

Keyword Discovery

Keyword Discovery works similarly to Wordtracker and has a price tag associated with it, which is quite steep for beginner bloggers. Fortunately, you can sign up for a free trial. To get started using Keyword Discovery for your keyword research, follow these steps:

1. **Visit www.keyworddiscovery.com.**

The Keyword Discovery home page opens, as shown in Figure 1-4.

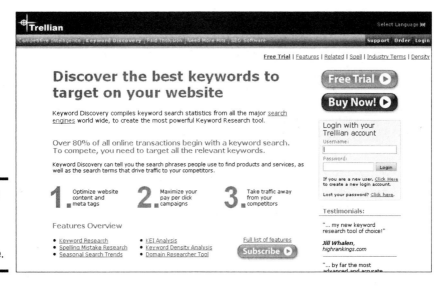

Figure 1-4:
The
Keyword
Discovery
home page.

2. **Click the Free Trial button.**

The Create New Account page opens, shown in Figure 1-5.

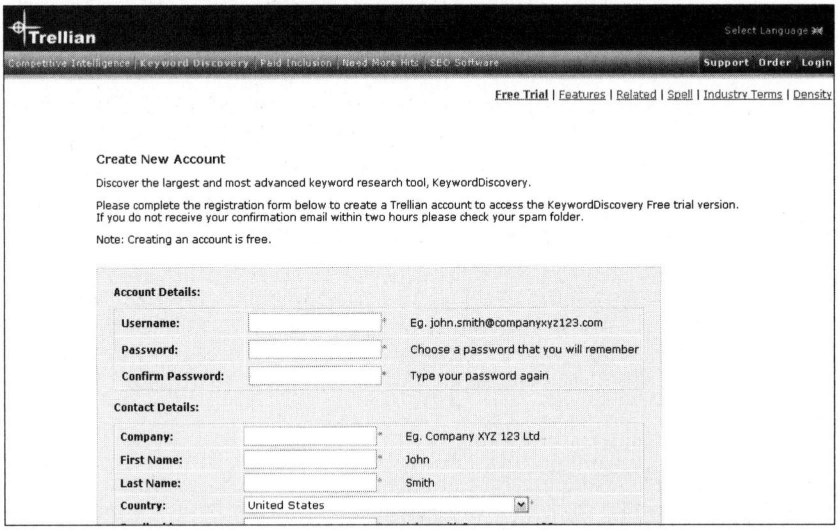

Figure 1-5:
The
Keyword
Discovery
Create New
Account
page.

3. **Enter the requested information and click the Submit button.**

You can begin your keyword research as soon as you provide all the personal information needed to set up your account.

Keyword Discovery offers an excellent Quick Start Guide (`http://www. keyworddiscovery.com/quick-start-guide.html`) and a comprehensive User Manual (`http://www.keyworddiscovery.com/kd-manual. html`), which you can access anytime. You can even print out PDF versions of both documents.

A Keyword Discovery account is not cheap. If you don't want to be automatically charged for your account, you must cancel your account before your free trial ends.

Using keywords

After you identify the keywords you want to target on your blog, you need to use them appropriately or they won't help your blog at all. There are strategic places to use your keywords (such as in your post titles, headings, in bolded text, and within and near links) to help ensure they're picked up by search engines (or at least given more weight in search engine algorithms) and your content is ranked appropriately for them. You can boost your search engine rank for targeted keywords by following these tips:

✦ **Focus on one keyword phrase per post or page.** A good guideline is to focus each blog post that you write on one (or two at most) keyword or keyword phrase.

✦ **Choose keyword phrases that are short.** Statistics show that nearly 60 percent of keyword searches include just two or three keywords. That's where you want your keywords to be!

✦ **Be specific.** This applies to the concept of going after the long-tail SEO, which is discussed in detail in the next section of this chapter.

Although these are broad keyword tips that you can use to boost your search engine traffic to your blog, you can use many more techniques within your blog writing to enhance your SEO. You can find out more on that subject later in this chapter, in the section "Writing SEO-Friendly Blog Posts," but first, long-tail SEO.

Demystifying Long-Tail SEO

Long-tail SEO is a hot topic in the online world as the landscape gets more and more cluttered and the competition for keyword traffic grows exponentially every day. A small blog has little chance of competing with top sites for broad and popular keyword traffic. Imagine you're starting a blog about travel, and then imagine how many other sites are competing for broad related keywords such as *travel* or *vacations.* There's little hope for your new blog to appear high in search engine rankings for those broad terms. However, you can target very specific keyword phrases, called long-tail SEO, and attract very targeted traffic to your blog with far less competition.

Long-tail SEO is the process of targeting very specific keyword phrases that are too narrow for big Web sites to feel threatened by but broad enough to get a decent amount of searches on them each day. For example, rather than targeting a broad term like *travel,* you could target a more specific keyword phrase such as *singles resorts.* This is where keyword research can be extremely useful.

As discussed in Book III, niche bloggers often find great success going after the long tail. It makes sense. These bloggers focus on attracting visitors who are looking for specific information, and niche bloggers make sure they deliver that information. Ultimately, that's the key to long-tail SEO success, but first, you have to drive that specific traffic to your blog. However, you also need to satisfy them when they get there by writing content that's relevant and useful to them, so they talk about your blog, share your content, and visit again.

Writing SEO-Friendly Blog Posts

You need to understand how to use keywords in your writing so they actually help your search rankings. The following suggestions are commonly accepted techniques to use to ensure search engines find your keywords and rank your content accordingly:

+ **Use keywords in your post titles.** Make sure your keywords are included in your blog post's title.

+ **Use keywords in your subtitles and post headings.** Include a subtitle with your blog post or break your post into sections with a heading for each section. Use the headings attributes, H1, H2, H3, and so on (or bold or italics) to format your subtitle and headings.

+ **Use keywords at the beginning and end of your post content.** Use the same keyword as well as variations of that keyword (plural, different verb tense, and so on) at least two times within the first 100 words or so of your blog post as well as at the end of your blog post.

+ **Use keywords in and around links in your posts.** If possible, make your keywords link to another page or include your keywords around links within your post.

Make sure the keyword links you use in your blog post are relevant, or they can do more harm than good. Google might view them as spam if they're abundant and aren't relevant to your post content.

+ **Use keywords to name your images and in ALT tags:** If possible, name the images used in your post with your keywords and include them in the ALT tag of your image's HTML code. However, make sure it's relevant to do so, or Google might view your efforts as *keyword stuffing,* which is a form of spam discussed later in this chapter in the section "Avoiding SEO Don'ts."

What is the HTML ALT tag for images?

The ALT tag for an image in HTML could be configured as follows:

```
<img src="http://www.example.com/uploads/image.jpg" alt="Image Name Goes Here" />
```

When an image is missing or can't be displayed in a visitor's browser, the text in the ALT tag (your designated alternative text) is displayed in place of the image.

Building Relationships to Boost Search Rankings

Perhaps the most critical step to boosting the search engine traffic to your blog is the time you spend building relationships with other bloggers and your blog's readers, because that's how you can increase the number of links to your blog content. Search engines, such as Google, highly value incoming links (particularly links from popular and authoritative sites) in determining how to rank search results. The more time you spend cultivating relationships online, the more your search rankings will rise organically.

Following are some relationship-building tips that can help your SEO efforts:

✦ **Leave comments on other blogs.** Start reading blogs written about subjects similar to your blog and then leave useful comments on posts you enjoy. Commenting is the first step to building a relationship with another blogger and that blogger's existing audience.

✦ **Use the same link phrase everywhere.** When you leave comments on other blogs, always use the same phrase for the link back to your blog. This not only helps your branding efforts, so people begin to recognize you, but it also helps with search engine optimization.

✦ **Link to content you enjoy from your own blog posts.** When you read something you like on another blog, mention it on your own blog and provide a link to the source. Your link shows up as an incoming link for the other blogger, and your own audience is likely to be happy to read more great content that you recommend. Just be sure that you don't copy content from another source verbatim. You don't want to be accused of plagiarism or scraping content, which is described in more detail in the "Avoiding SEO Don'ts" section later in this chapter.

✦ **Share content you like through social bookmarking, social networking, and Twitter.** Use Digg, StumbleUpon, Facebook, and Twitter to share links to content you enjoy, thereby driving traffic to other blog posts that you like. It's possible someone will reciprocate and share your content, too.

✦ **Respond to comments left on your blog.** Don't ignore the people who take the time to leave comments on your blog posts. Instead, make them feel valued by writing a meaningful response to their comments.

These are just a few tips to start building relationships across the blogosphere, which should help your blog's traffic and search rankings over time. Remember, the relationships you build are likely to outlast any search engine algorithms, so make sure you take the time to cultivate them.

Understanding Google Page Rank

After you discover how to increase your search engine rankings, you need to understand what Google Page Rank means and how it can affect the amount of search traffic your blog receives. In simplest terms, Google's search algorithm indexes online content and ranks it in terms of relevancy, usefulness, and authoritativeness. Relevancy is primarily determined contextually and relies heavily on keywords, whereas usefulness and authoritativeness rely more heavily on incoming links.

Google views sites and blogs with a lot of incoming links higher than those with few incoming links. The thought process is that sites with a lot of incoming links must have great content on them or other sites wouldn't want to link to them. Furthermore, sites that are updated frequently with a lot of fresh content have more chances to attract incoming links, driving their Google page ranks up higher.

It's important to understand that Google claims not to use the page ranking system in determining how search results are delivered, but even if the formal Google Page Rank system is no longer used, the *process* behind the system is still valid. In other words, the steps that people took to increase their Google Page Rank are still effective in terms of increasing the ranking of your pages within relevant Google searches, regardless of whether or not the official Google Page Rank system is still in effect.

Increasing your blog's ranking in Google searches

With the factors discussed in the previous section in mind, your blog's ranking in Google search results is dependent on a number of factors (which are tightly guarded by Google), but SEO experts do agree that the following factors affect your blog's ranking in Google search results:

✦ **Incoming links:** People want to link to great content, and they like to link to content written by bloggers with whom they have established relationships.

✦ **Posting frequency:** The more content you write, the more incoming links your blog gets.

✦ **Quality of content:** The better the content is that you write, the more incoming links your blog gets.

✦ **Quality of incoming links:** The more authoritative sites that link to your blog, the higher your blog's page rank.

✦ **Relevancy:** Content that includes relevant keywords (without keyword stuffing) is ranked higher than content without those keywords.

Checking your blog's Google Page Rank

Many sites provide tools for you to check your blog's Google Page Rank. Although the ranking might mean less to Google these days, it still holds weight for advertisers and others who want to get an idea of how popular your blog is. Therefore, it can't hurt to check your blog's Google Page Rank, so you know how it's perceived by others.

PRChecker is free and easy to use. Follow these instructions to check your blog's Google Page Rank using PRChecker:

1. **Visit `http://prchecker.info`.**

   The Check Page Rank page opens, as shown in Figure 1-6.

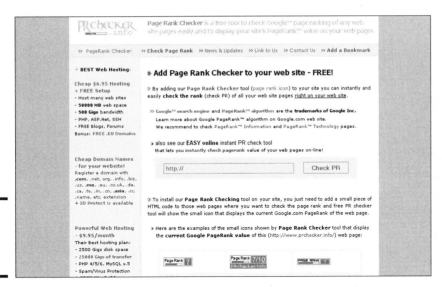

Figure 1-6:
The Check
Page Rank
tool.

2. **Enter your blog's domain name in the text box in the middle of your screen after the http:// text and click the Check PR button.**

   The page expands, as shown in Figure 1-7, revealing an antispam text step.

Figure 1-7:
The PRChecker antispam verification page.

3. **Enter the antispam text string in the text box provided and click the Verify Now button.**

   Your blog's Google Page Rank appears on your screen as shown in Figure 1-8.

Figure 1-8:
A blog's Google Page Rank from PRChecker.

It could take several weeks for your blog to receive a page rank after you launch it. Google recalculates page ranks at unannounced and irregular times, so don't be surprised to find your Google Page Rank change suddenly.

Avoiding SEO Don'ts

Just as there are steps you can follow to increase your blog's search traffic by appropriately using keywords, links and techniques to boost your blog's ranking in Google (and other search engine) searches, there are also things you can do that can hurt your blog's search engine rankings. In fact, there are even things you can do that can get your blog eliminated from Google search entirely. If you want to grow your blog, then you do not want to get caught doing any of the things in the following list:

✦ **Don't pay for text links.** Google views text link advertising as a way to artificially boost search engine rankings. If you're caught paying for text links to your blog, your blog could be removed from Google search entirely, and your Google Page Rank could drop.

✦ **Don't publish links that have been paid for.** Google punishes both the site that pays for text links *and* the site that publishes paid text links in the same way — by dropping both sites from search rankings and dropping both sites' Google Page Ranks.

✦ **Don't keyword stuff.** Keyword stuffing is the process of overloading a Web page with keywords for the sole purpose of increasing search engine rankings. For example, you might find a long list of keywords at the top or bottom of a Web page. They may or may not be set up as links. Use your keywords strategically as suggested earlier in this chapter.

✦ **Don't hide keywords.** Don't try to hide keywords in a very small font or a color that matches your blog's background. Google looks for sites that do this and considers them to be spam, which means no search traffic and no Google Page Rank for sites that are caught hiding keywords.

✦ **Don't scrape content.** Never copy content from another site and republish it as your own on your own blog — called *scraping* content. Although it's okay to copy a quote or small section of content from another site, you should never plagiarize content and republish it on your site. First, to do so without permission is illegal. Second, Google gives credit only to the first site that publishes that content and might penalize sites that are found copying content, regardless of whether or not you link to the original source.

✦ **Don't publish content that is nothing more than links.** Your blog must contain far more original content on it than links. Google views pages that include little more than links as spam. Your blog will be downgraded if you're caught publishing pages full of links, particularly if those links are ads.

Using the NoFollow Tag

The NoFollow tag is a snippet of HTML code that can be added to your links so they're invisible to Google and not included in Google's search rankings. Many bloggers have started using the NoFollow tag on all outgoing links on their blogs, so there's no chance that their links could be considered paid text links, which can cause problems with their Google rankings. However, using the NoFollow tag on all links on your blog also eliminates any link-love that legitimate commenters can get from leaving comments on your blogs.

The format for the NoFollow tag is as follows:

```
<a href="http://www.example.com/" rel="nofollow">link text goes here</a>
```

It's up to you to decide whether you want to use the NoFollow tag on your blog, but at the very least, use it in any text link advertising links and in any sponsored review posts. You can find out more about blog monetization through text link ads and sponsored reviews in Book VII.

Considering Search Engine Reputation Management

Search engine reputation management (SERM) is the process of making sure the search engine results for keywords related to yourself, your blog, your business, your brand, and so on are the ones that you want people to see. For example, you wouldn't want someone to type your name or the keyword phrase related to your blog into Google and find that the top results returned provide negative information about you. That's where SERM comes in handy: You can directly affect the search results that people find with time and commitment.

First, you need to stay on top of what people find when they search for the keywords related to your blog, so you always know where you stand. Conduct daily Google searches on your chosen keywords and keep track of the results. The more great content you flood the online world with that's optimized for your keyword phrases, the farther down other content will fall in search result listings. You can also sign up to receive e-mail alerts using Google Alerts (www.google.com/alerts) and TweetBeep (http://tweetbeep.com) whenever your chosen keywords are mentioned online or within Twitter updates.

Furthermore, the relationships that you build online can help your SERM efforts because the other bloggers that you have relationships with are typically happy to help you get new content online that tells the story you want to share.

Ultimately, the key to SEO success comes from two things: a lot of great, original content and relationships. You can find out more about SERM in Chapter 5 of Book III.

Chapter 2: Measuring Blog Performance

*P*ublishing great content is only the tip of the iceberg when it comes to developing a successful blog. To truly understand which of your blogging efforts is delivering the biggest bang for the buck in terms of boosting traffic, comments, subscriptions, and more, you need to track your blog's performance over time.

By analyzing your blog's traffic patterns, you can quantify your successes as well as test new features, tools, and content. Alternatively, you can determine which of your blogging efforts is not delivering the results you want and need, tweak those elements, or stop them completely. Your goals for your blog greatly affect how committed you need to be to tracking your blog's statistics.

Fortunately, a number of Web analytics tools are available to help you easily track your blog statistics. In this chapter, you find out about popular Web analytics tools, what to track, and how to use the information you collect.

Making Sense of Web Analytics

You can easily gather statistics related to your blog's performance by using a Web analytics tool, such as the tools discussed later in this chapter, but your efforts won't help much if you don't understand what the data you collect means. Furthermore, Web analytics tools can provide *a lot* of data, but all that data isn't helpful to you if you don't know what to focus on.

Each blogger has different goals for his or her blog, and that means each blogger has different data that is meaningful to him. This section focuses on the most commonly tracked data. For more details about Web analytics, read *Web Analytics For Dummies,* by Pedro Sostre and Jennifer LeClaire.

Defining Web analytics terms

Before you can start tracking your blog statistics, you need to understand what the terminology used by Web analytics tools means. Following are descriptions of some of the most commonly used terms:

✦ **Hits:** A *hit* is counted by Web analytics tools every time a file downloads from your blog. Each page on your blog can have multiple files on it. When a person accesses a page on your blog, every file on that page downloads and counts as a hit. For example, if a page includes a blog post with multiple images in it, each of those images downloads when a visitor accesses that page, which gives an inflated view of the popularity of your blog. Therefore, hits are not commonly used to evaluate Web traffic trends.

✦ **Visits:** Each time your blog is accessed, a visit is counted by your Web analytics tool, meaning a person who accesses your blog more than once is counted multiple times. Therefore, visits give an inflated view of your blog's overall popularity and are not typically used to determine Web traffic trends.

✦ **Visitors:** There are three forms of visitor statistics:

  • *Visitors:* Anyone who visits any page of your blog is a visitor, so a person can be counted more than once if she visits multiple times.

  • *Return visitors:* Anyone who visits your blog more than once is a return visitor.

  • *Unique visitors:* Each individual visitor is counted once regardless of how many times they visit your blog.

The most important data is unique visitors because that statistic demonstrates a blog's reach. However, unless visitors register and sign in to access your blog's content (which is not recommended), it's nearly impossible to ensure repeat visitors to your blog are counted one time only.

Web analytics tools use *cookies* (small pieces of text or code that are stored in your Web browser when you visit a Web page) to reduce the number of visitors who are counted twice, but if people clear their cookies from their Web browsers, the Web analytics tool has no way to identify them as repeat visitors. That is, if a visitor comes to your blog, clears the cookies from her Web browser, and then returns to your blog, she's counted as a new visitor (meaning she's counted as two visitors, when in fact, she's just one).

The opposite is true in terms of tracking return visitors. If people clear the cookies from their browsers, they won't be tracked accurately. Therefore, tracking visitors is more accurate than tracking visits, but it's still far from perfect.

✦ **Page views:** The page views statistic is the most common one for bloggers to track because it provides the clearest picture of how popular a blog is. Each page viewed on your blog, regardless of who views it, counts as a page view. Online advertisers use page views as the standard of measurement to calculate advertising rates. More page views equals more people seeing an ad and potentially clicking it or acting on it.

✦ **Top pages viewed:** Web analytics tools typically provide a report that shows your blog's most viewed pages (including post pages). This statistic is also referred to as Top Content. Monitoring top pages viewed can help you focus your content creation and marketing efforts.

✦ **Top paths taken:** Paths represent the way visitors navigate through your blog — the links they follow, the content that's most interesting to them, and the features that keep them on your blog longer.

✦ **Top entry pages:** Top entry pages represent the pages that people most frequently land on when they visit your blog. This statistic is helpful in terms of finding where visitors are coming from. Using the Top Paths Taken data with the Top Entry Pages data can provide valuable information.

✦ **Top exit pages:** Top exit pages represent the last pages that people view before leaving your blog. This statistic can help you identify content that is underperforming.

✦ **Bounce rate:** The bounce rate tracks the percentage of people who leave your blog immediately after landing on it. The bounce rate represents people who did not find what they were looking for when they were led to your blog. The lower this number is, the more effective your marketing and search engine optimization efforts are, meaning the people who are finding your blog are the ones that you want to find it. In other words, your SEO and marketing efforts are reaching your blog's target audience.

✦ **Referrers:** One of the most useful statistics you can find using your Web analytics tool is referrers, which identifies the Web sites, blogs, and search engines that lead visitors to your blog. Often the referrers statistic is broken down further into a category for search engines only and another for non–search engines. You can find where traffic is coming from and determine where to focus your marketing efforts going forward by analyzing referrer statistics.

✦ **Keywords and keyword phrases:** Using your Web analytics tool, you can learn which keywords and keyword phrases people are typing into their preferred search engines that are leading them to your blog. Search engines can drive large amounts of visitors to your blog. By analyzing the keywords and keyword phrases that people type into search engines, which lead them to your blog, you can focus your future SEO and content creation efforts to target those keywords.

Knowing what to track

In addition to the most commonly tracked statistics listed in the preceding section, Web analytics tools provide the ability to track a myriad of other statistics, such as the browsers your blog visitors use, their countries, and more. The sheer volume of available data can make narrowing down that data into usable chunks of information overwhelming.

To make blog traffic analysis a less daunting task, take the time to review the data available to your through your Web analytics tool to determine which statistics are most useful to you in terms of helping you reach your blogging goals. Focus your analysis on those data points and then enhance your analytics from there. Starting small and working your way up as you get more comfortable with the data you collect, makes the process of understanding your blog's performance more manageable. Suggestions for putting the data you collect to work for you are included later in this chapter.

Depending on your blogging application and host, you might not be able to access a full complement of Web analytics. Self-hosting your blog through your chosen Web host, as discussed in Chapter 1 of Book IV, gives you maximum control and provides access to the widest array of Web analytics data.

Choosing a Web Analytics Tool

Various Web analytics tools are available to bloggers, offering different levels of data and at varying price points. Most bloggers start with a free Web analytics tool, and as their blogs grow, they might consider moving to a fee-based tool. Take the time to research the various Web analytics tools to find the one that integrates with your blogging application and offers you the functionality you want at a price you're willing to pay.

Several free Web analytics tools provide sufficient data and functionality for the majority of bloggers, such as Google Analytics.

Most Web analytics tools are easily integrated into your blogging application. Simply sign up for an account for the Web analytics tool you choose, copy the HTML or Javascript code provided to you, and paste it into your blog's footer, sidebar, or other location as directed by the Web analytics tool provider.

Some of the most popular Web analytics tools are discussed in the following sections.

Be sure to evaluate your blogging goals before you invest in a fee-based Web analytics package. It's very likely that a free tool, such as Google Analytics, can provide the data you need.

Google Analytics

www.google.com/analytics

Google Analytics, shown in Figure 2-1, has become one of the most popular Web analytics tools for four reasons:

+ It's easy to integrate into your blog.

+ It provides comprehensive results.

+ It provides reasonably accurate results.

+ It's free.

Figure 2-1:
The Google
Analytics
home page.

Google Analytics provides a variety of reports, including custom reports, so you can easily track your blog's statistics. You can also track advertising and promotional campaigns. Figure 2-2 shows a snapshot of some of the information available through Google Analytics.

To use Google Analytics, you must create a free Google account (if you don't already have one through another Google application such as Blogger, Gmail, Google Reader, Orkut, and so on).

Figure 2-2:
The Google
Analytics
overview
page.

StatCounter

www.statcounter.com

StatCounter, shown in Figure 2-3, offers a free and paid Web analytics tool. As you would expect, the free tool provides rudimentary statistics (although enough for most beginner bloggers). If you really want to delve into the analytics behind your blog, the paid version provides far more details.

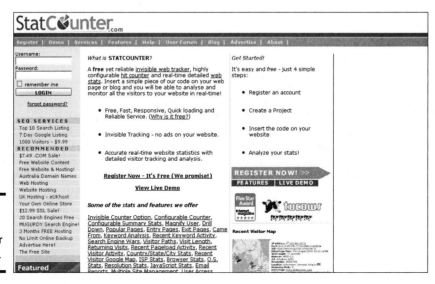

Figure 2-3:
The
StatCounter
home page.

The StatCounter Web site offers a table that breaks down the tiered fee structure for the various packages offered based on monthly page loads and log size. In other words, the free tool provides only details on the most recent 500 page loads (which make up the log size) and is recommended for sites with fewer than 250,000 page loads per month. This is a big limitation if you want to track data on more page loads than the most recent 500 at any moment, because your statistics will never provide a truly accurate picture of your blog's performance over time. While a variety of statistics are offered, as shown in Figure 2-4, you should take the log-size limitation into consideration before you rely too heavily on the statistics provided by StatCounter.

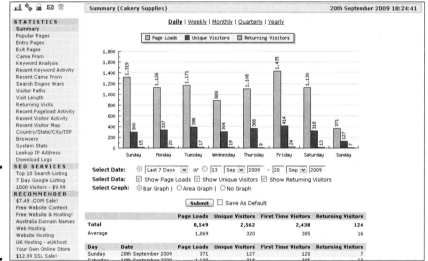

Figure 2-4:
The StatCounter summary page.

Site Meter

http://sitemeter.com

Site Meter, shown in Figure 2-5, provides a basic amount of statistics for free but only the information from the last 100 visitors to your blog is included in those statistics. You can pay a fee to use the premium Site Meter features, which allow you to access more data and track the last 4,000 visitors to your site.

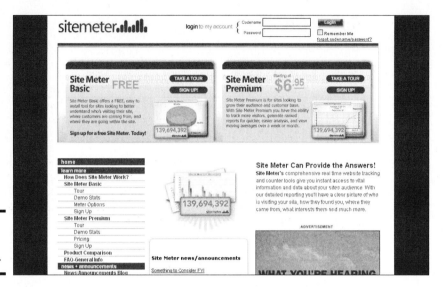

Figure 2-5:
Site Meter
home page.

Depending on your blogging goals and metrics requirements, Site Meter
might not provide the data you want at a price point you're happy with. Be
sure to research the current offerings before you make your decision. You
can see a summary of Site Meter statistics in Figure 2-6.

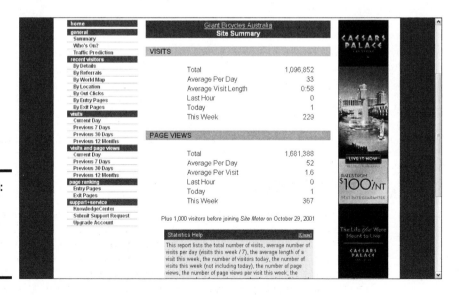

Figure 2-6:
The Site
Meter
summary
statistics
page.

Omniture

www.omniture.com

Omniture's SiteCatalyst, shown in Figure 2-7, is the Web analytics tool often used by corporations and very popular Web sites that depend on the most accurate and in-depth statistics possible. As such, pricing is not available unless you speak directly with a sales representative about your individual needs for a custom solution.

With that in mind, you can imagine how much higher the Omniture SiteCatalyst price tag is than the other Web Analytics tools mentioned in this chapter. However, if your business or income is highly dependent on the success of your blog, you might want to consider investing in the depth and accuracy of the Omniture SiteCatalyst Web analytics tool.

Figure 2-7:
The Omniture SiteCatalyst home page.

Using Your Blog Data

Now that you know the most common data to analyze and the most common Web analytics tool options, you need to know what to do with the data you collect about your blog. The more content you publish on your blog, and the longer your blog exists, the more useful your data will become in terms of trend analysis. The date ranges you select to analyze depend on your individual blogging goals. However, you can start using the data you collect sooner rather than later in a variety of ways. Some common uses for blog data are included in the following sections.

Always be sure to set the date range you want to track within your Web analytics tool.

Harnessing the power of referrer statistics

One of the best ways to grow your blog is by building relationships with other bloggers and people across the social Web. Your blog statistics offer a unique way to do exactly that. By visiting the sites that refer traffic to your blog, taking the time to comment or participate in the conversations on those sites (or e-mailing the site owner if commenting is not available on the site), you not only acknowledge the other site, but also start a new relationship that can grow and be beneficial to both parties.

Publishing content similar to popular content

Review your blog statistics to figure out what posts on your blog are getting the most traffic and then publish more content like those original posts. Chances are good that if those posts are popular, that's the kind of content your audience wants (or at least, that's the content that's driving people to your blog). If it worked once, it just might work again!

Timing post publishing for high traffic days

If you have posts that you want to be certain a large audience sees, use your blog statistics to determine which days of the week your blog gets the most traffic by analyzing page view trends over time. You can then publish the posts that you think have the best chances for being shared and sparking conversation to go live on those days for maximum exposure.

Identifying keywords

By analyzing the top keywords that are driving traffic to your blog from search engines, you can determine which keywords are performing well, which are not, and which are misused. You can then use that analysis to revise existing content and create new content that focuses on the keywords that drive the best traffic to your blog.

Finding underperforming content

Using the Bounce Rate and Top Exit Pages statistics, you can determine which content on your blog is not enticing people to stay on your blog longer. You can try to revise that content to make it more useful and appealing.

Calculating online marketing results

If you publish content on your blog for marketing purposes, such as an e-book, a press release, an announcement, a presentation, and so on, you can determine how frequently that content was accessed and when it was accessed using your Web analytics tool. This allows you to determine how well your promotional efforts are working to drive targeted traffic to those specific pages or content on your blog and use those results to tweak your current or future campaigns.

Keeping Perspective

Don't expect to understand and effectively use Web analytics tools immediately. It takes time to not only understand how to read your blog's data, but also to figure out how to use it effectively to reach your individual blogging goals. In fact, you might want to try more than one Web analytics tool and compare the data provided by each to find the one that you're most comfortable with. No two Web analytics tools are alike, so don't be surprised if two tools tell very different stories about your blog.

Understanding Web analytics limitations

Unfortunately, no Web analytics tool in existence can provide completely accurate data about any blog or Web site. It's unfortunate, but true. The best you can do to analyze your blog's performance is to choose a Web analytics tool and stick with it in order to analyze trends over time.

The problem lies in a lack of standards related to Web analytics. There simply are no rules in place, so each Web site is different, browsers are different, users are different, and analytics tools are different. With so many variables, it's no wonder that no single Web analytics tool is 100 percent accurate.

The first thing you need to understand is that no two Web analytics tools are going to provide the same statistics. That inconsistency is just something Web analysts accept as a limitation they have to deal with. Typically, Web analysts test more than one tool and choose the one that provides the level of detail they need and rely more on trend analysis than specific numbers.

For example, if you use the same Web analytics tool for six months and suddenly see a significant jump in your blog visitors, such as the one shown in Figure 2-8, you can feel confident that a catalyst, such as a link to your blog from a very popular Web site, caused the jump. However, if you switched back and forth between multiple tools that provide varying data from one day to the next, you might not detect a traffic jump.

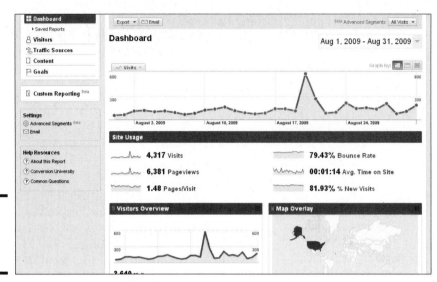

Figure 2-8:
A blog statistic anomaly.

Although Web analytics is an inconsistent and imprecise science, you can create a semblance of consistency by choosing a tool and sticking with it over time.

Remembering not to sweat the numbers

It can be easy to get caught up in your blog's statistics, but try not to do so. It will drive you crazy, and it can take up a lot of time that could be better invested in creating great content and building relationships across the social Web. Try to refrain from checking your blog's statistics every day, at least during the first few months of your blog's lifespan. Instead, focus on publishing content and check your blog statistics once a week. Over time, trend analysis will help you refine your blogging strategy more so than daily traffic fluctuations.

However, throughout your blog's lifecycle, you will undoubtedly test different techniques to boost traffic, and you should analyze those tactics more closely using the statistics provided in your Web analytics tool. How else will you know whether those efforts produced positive results?

The key to blogging success is developing a strong, loyal community around your blog. Short-term traffic jumps are nice, but if those visitors don't come back, short-term jumps don't help your blog much overall. Try to focus on long-term growth rather than short-lived jumps.

You can find out much more about growing your blog in Book VI.

Chapter 3: Editing and Finding Images

In This Chapter

- ✔ Changing image size and format
- ✔ Finding resources for image editing
- ✔ Understanding image hosting issues
- ✔ Determining if you can use an image
- ✔ Finding images that are safe to use

*I*mages are an important part of a blog because they add visual interest and visual relief by breaking up what would otherwise be very text-heavy pages. Images can also help to illustrate a point and even boost search engine rankings, as discussed in Chapter 1 of this minibook. However, you need to be aware of some rules related to using images on your blog. Additionally, a few handy formatting tips and editing tools can make the process of adding images to your blog very easy.

This chapter shows you how to edit images you want to use on your blog with easy-to-use, and sometimes free, editing tools. You also find out some of the do's and don'ts of using images on your blog, so you can avoid getting into legal trouble.

Changing Image Size

One of the first things you need to understand about adding images to your blog is that the larger the file size, the more room that image takes up in your Web hosting account, and the longer it takes to load on your live blog. If you're using a Web host to store and share your blog, the former consideration can affect you, and if you don't want visitors to get annoyed waiting for your blog to load in their browser windows, the latter should affect you.

The smartest course of action is to save the image that you want to use on your blog to your computer hard drive and then resize it using an image-editing tool, such as one of the tools discussed later in this chapter. Save the image at the size you want it to appear on your blog. (You might need to do some tests to determine the size you like for images on your blog.) Then upload it to your Web hosting account and insert it into your blog post, sidebar, blog page, and so on, as appropriate.

Resizing images before you upload them to your blog is particularly important for blogs that use a lot of images. Each image takes up storage space in your blog or Web hosting account. You don't want to run out of space and have to find another blogging solution or upgrade your Web hosting account simply because images that could have been stored in smaller sizes and used less storage space were not.

After you upload an image to your blog, you can shrink it from your post editor without affecting the resolution. However, if you try to enlarge the image from your post editor, the image will become pixilated and blurry.

Changing Image Format

When you include images on your blog, they should be saved in a Web-friendly format, which compresses the file size for speedy page loading, and ensures images will appear correctly onscreen. The preferred image file formats for online use are

+ **JPEG:** JPEG files end in a `.jpg` extension. JPEG files can be saved at high or low resolution.

+ **PNG:** PNG files end in a `.png` extension. These files are typically very small in size but display well on screen.

+ **GIF:** GIF files end in a `.gif` extension. They're very small, with low resolution, and work very well for line art and simple images.

The best resolution choices for online images are 72 dpi to 150 dpi.

When you find an image you want to use on your blog, check the file format to determine whether it's Web-friendly. For example, TIFF (`.tif`) and Bitmap (`.bmp`) files are usually very large, and they slow page load times significantly, thereby reducing the overall user experience on your blog. If you need to change the file format, use one of the image-editing tools listed later in this chapter to save the file as a `.jpg`, `.png`, or `.gif`.

Finding Resources for Changing Image Size and Format

You can use a variety of online sources for free or for a fee to modify image files. Alternatively, many higher-priced software products such as Adobe Photoshop offer extensive image-editing options. However, unless you plan to pursue extensive design projects and have the time to learn a more complicated, in-depth software, one of the freely available online image-editing solutions should do everything you need for your blogging purposes.

The most important and common functions you need to be able to accomplish are changing your image sizes and switching formats. Both of these functions are offered in the free tools described in the following sections.

Picnik

www.picnik.com

Picnik, shown in Figure 3-1, offers a free online image-editing tool as well as premium tools, which are offered for a fee. However, most bloggers find that the free tools offered by Picnik provide all the capabilities they need. You can sign up for a free Picnik account and upload your image files for editing. When you have your images uploaded, you can change file formats, sizes, and much more and then save the new image to your hard drive in a matter of seconds. Because Picnik runs online, you need to have an active Internet connection to use it.

Even the free version of Picnik offers some advanced tools such as red-eye removal and custom effects. The best part about Picnik is that it's extremely easy to use. Even the most technically challenged people should be able to use Picnik without any problems. If you do have trouble, check out the active forum on the Picnik Web site, where you can ask questions and get help.

Figure 3-1:
The Picnik
home page.

Paint.NET

www.getpaint.net

Paint.NET, shown in Figure 3-2, is completely free and completely great! You can download Paint.NET to your Windows computer, and use it to modify images in many of the same ways that expensive image-editing software such as Adobe Photoshop provides. The capabilities offered in Paint.NET are more advanced than those offered by Picnik, but it does take a bit more technical savvy to use it. However, for saving images in new formats or at new sizes, Paint.NET is easy to use.

Paint.NET offers many tutorials and an active forum, so help is never far away. Furthermore, the developers behind Paint.NET continue to improve it and free upgrades are released as they come available. Unlike packaged photo-editing software that require you to pay for upgraded versions every year or so, Paint.NET upgrades are always free.

Figure 3-2:
The Paint.
NET home
page.

GIMP

www.gimp.org

GIMP, shown in Figure 3-3, is free image-editing software that you can download and use on a variety of systems, including Windows and Mac. It offers robust features, similar to those offered through expensive image-editing software programs such as Adobe Photoshop. Resizing images and saving them to different formats are easy tasks to do, but GIMP offers far more advanced photo-retouching and -manipulation tools, too.

Of the tools discussed in this section, GIMP is the most challenging to figure out if you aren't technically savvy. However, if you invest the time to learn how to use it, you'll love what it allows you to do with images. The GIMP Web site offers a user manual and a number of tutorials to help you bypass the learning curve quickly.

Figure 3-3:
The GIMP
home page.

Shrink Pictures

www.shrinkpictures.com

If you're looking for a rudimentary tool that allows you to resize images and save them in `.jpg` format, Shrink Pictures, shown in Figure 3-4, is a viable option for you. Shrink Pictures is free to use. It runs online, so you need to be connected to the Web to use it. Just upload a `.jpg`, `.png`, or `.gif` file of 6MB or less to the Shrink Pictures Web site, select the size and quality you want your new image to be from the list of options provided, add a grayscale or sepia effect if you want, and click the Resize button. Your image is saved in `.jpg` format using the settings you selected.

Shrink Pictures is one of the easiest image-resizing tools you can use, but the capabilities are also extremely limited. However, those capabilities are enough for many bloggers.

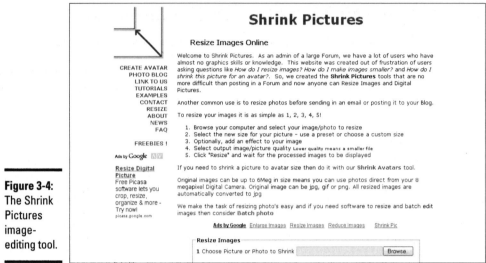

Figure 3-4:
The Shrink
Pictures
image-
editing tool.

Using Images on Your Web Host, Not Others'

The concept known as *stealing bandwidth* affects bloggers, particularly where images are concerned. Each image that you publish on your blog needs to be stored in a hosting account that makes it accessible to every person who has access to the World Wide Web. Storage space costs money to people who host their blogs and Web sites through Web hosts, so each image they publish costs a bit of money to live online.

Stealing bandwidth happens when other sites publish the same image on their sites without uploading the image to their own Web hosting accounts first. Instead, they simply insert the HTML code into their blogs or Web sites that tells Web browsers to display the image from its original location. Each time the image loads on sites that simply copied HTML code rather than uploading the image to their own hosts, the originating site's bandwidth is used to serve that image. Depending on the originating site's hosting account and depending on the frequency the image is loaded on various sites, the person who's paying the originating Web host may suddenly find herself with a hefty bill from her Web host for exceeding her account limits.

Don't steal bandwidth. Unless someone specifically provides you with the HTML code to publish an image on your blog that is stored on another site's Web hosting account, always save the image you plan to publish on your blog to your computer hard drive first. Then upload it to your own Web hosting account, and insert it using the HTML code that serves it from *your* Web host.

Determining Whether You Can Use an Image

Before you publish an image that you find online on your blog, you must be certain that it's okay for you to do so. Images are protected under copyright law, and it's very likely that an image you find from a Google search or while surfing the Net is not freely available for you to republish on your blog without violating copyright laws.

Remembering copyright, fair use, and attribution laws and rules

First, there are copyright laws, which are discussed in detail in Chapter 4 of Book I, that protect images of any kind, and violating those laws can get you into a lot of trouble. There is such a thing as fair use, which makes copyright laws fuzzy because fair use suggests that you can republish images and other content for editorial commentary, academic purposes, and the like. However, you should err on the side of caution. If you don't have permission to use an image on your blog, don't use it. It's that simple.

Even if you do have permission to use an image or know that the copyright license attached to that image allows you to use it, you should always provide proper attribution by citing and linking to the source.

Creative Commons licenses

Creative Commons licenses are discussed in detail in Chapter 4 of Book I. In simplest terms, Creative Commons licenses were created to provide copyright alternatives for people who didn't want the tight restrictions of traditional copyright law to apply to their original work.

There are several types of Creative Commons licenses that people can apply to their work, ranging from the most lenient use, which requires nothing more than attribution, to the most restrictive use, which requires the work be used as is (no derivatives), only for non-commercial purposes, and only with the same Creative Commons license applied to the new work. When you use an image with a Creative Commons license on your blog, make sure you understand which type of Creative Commons license the image uses and follow the steps to comply with those rules when you republish it.

Creative Commons licenses make it a bit easier to find images to use on your blog, but you still need to be sure that the person who licensed the work is the original creator.

Asking permission

The safest course to follow is to ask permission to use any image on your blog before you do so. However, this isn't realistic, because asking permission is time-consuming, and finding the original owner is often impossible. If you can obtain permission to use an image owned by someone else on your blog, be sure to mention it on your blog.

Obtaining permission is particularly important for blogs that publish images of people or events, such as celebrity bloggers, because the owners of images used by those bloggers are typically paid to take and distribute those images. Republishing those images might cause the owner to lose money, and that's when bloggers often find themselves in trouble. Although a cease and desist letter from the image owner or his attorney is typically as far as the incident goes, you certainly don't want to be the blogger that is made an example of and find yourself in the middle of a court battle or facing criminal charges for copyright violation.

Finding Images That Are Safe to Use on Your Blog

Fortunately, a number of freely available and low cost sources make images available for you to safely use on your blog. Although the usage restrictions might vary from site to site or image to image, as long as you check the requirements and follow them, you can quite easily find many images available. Following are several sources to get you started.

Flickr

www.flickr.com

Flickr, shown in Figure 3-5, is a photo-sharing site where anyone can create a free account and upload images. When a person uploads an image to Flickr, she can set the usage restrictions related to that image, so people who find it know what they can or cannot do with it. For example, she might apply a Creative Commons Attribution license to the image, meaning anyone can use the image in any other work as long as the original owner of the image is cited as such.

To conduct a search on Flickr for images with Creative Commons licenses attached to them, follow these steps:

1. **Visit www.flickr.com/creativecommons.**

   From this page, shown in Figure 3-6, you can select the link for the type of Creative Commons licensed images you want to find.

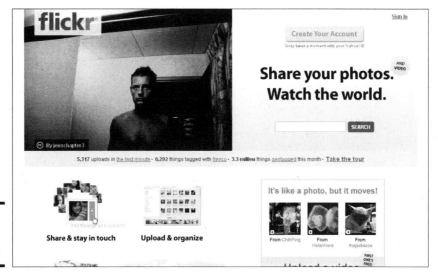

Figure 3-5:
The Flickr
home page.

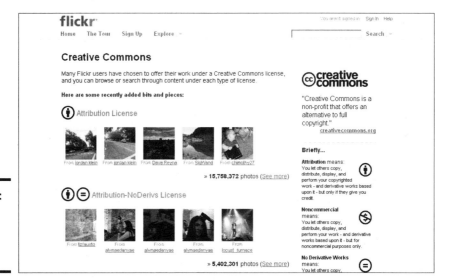

Figure 3-6:
The Flickr
Creative
Commons
page.

2. **Click the See More link under the images displayed under your chosen license heading. (This example uses the Attribution License.)**

   The Creative Commons Attribution image archive opens.

3. **Enter the keyword you want to search for in the text box and click the Search button.**

   Images matching the license and keywords you selected are returned to you.

4. **Click the image you want to use on your blog.**

    The image detail page opens, as shown in Figure 3-7.

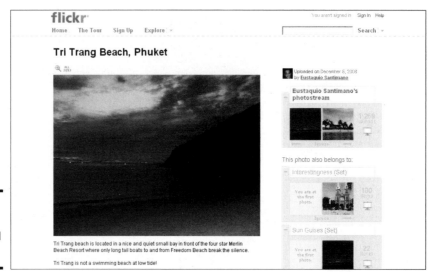

5. **Click the All Sizes link above the image to open the image download page.**

6. **Click the link to Download the image at the size shown or click the appropriate link above the image for the size you do want to download.**

7. **When the size you want is displayed, click the Download link for that image size and save it to your computer's hard drive.**

Just because someone uploads an image to Flickr doesn't guarantee that person owns the image. Use your best judgment when you republish images uploaded to Flickr of celebrities or events that might be owned by a professional organization or source other than the individual who uploaded them to Flickr.

Stock.XCHNG

www.sxc.hu

Stock.XCHNG, shown in Figure 3-8, is an image-hosting site. You can register for a Stock.XCHNG account, so you can download images to your computer that you want to use in your blog. People upload images to Stock.XCHNG, and apply rules for use of those images. Some images simply require that you attribute the owner, but others require that you contact the owner for permission to use them. As such, you have to read the image restrictions for each image you consider using on your blog and follow the specific instructions provided.

Image Categories drop-down list

Figure 3-8:
The Stock.
XCHNG
home page.

Search text box

There are many free images available on Stock.XCHNG that you can use as long as you follow the usage requirements, but there are also many images that you can pay a fee to use. Images with a fee attached to them are typically listed at the top of your keyword search results and are labeled as Premium Results.

To find images you can use on your blog for free with Stock.XCHNG, follow these steps:

1. **Visit www.sxc.hu and enter your search keyword into the search text box on the left side of your screen, as shown in Figure 3-8.**

Alternatively, you can search all images in a category by clicking the arrow in the Image Categories drop-down list at the top left of your screen and then clicking the category of your choice from the list that appears.

2. **Click the orange button with the magnifying glass in it (below the search text box) to start your search.**

   Your results page opens.

3. **Click the image you want to use.**

   The image detail page opens, as shown in Figure 3-9. In the Usage section to the right of the image and in the Availability section beneath the image, be sure to check the license and options links to find out how you can use the image and what you have to do to use it.

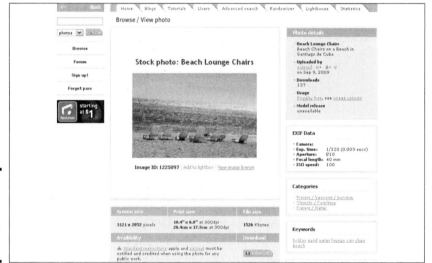

Figure 3-9: Stock. XCHNG image detail page.

4. **Click the Download button to save the image to your hard drive.**

   You're prompted to log in or create a new account before you can complete the image download process. After you log in, you can save the image to your computer's hard drive.

morgueFile

`http://morguefile.com`

You can find many images available on morgueFile that you can freely use on your blog. The standard morgueFile license allows users to adapt and republish the free images found on the site without attribution, however, many image owners do include their email addresses or personal notes asking to be notified when their images are used.

Read the current morgueFile license language at `http://morguefile.com/license/morguefile`.

To find a free image to use on your blog from morgueFile, follow these steps:

1. **Visit www.morguefile.com and enter your keyword in the search text box on the right side of your screen.**

   Make sure Free Photos is selected in the Search drop-down list.

2. **Press your Enter key.**

   Your results are returned to you, as shown in Figure 3-10.

Figure 3-10:
A
morgueFile
search
results
page.

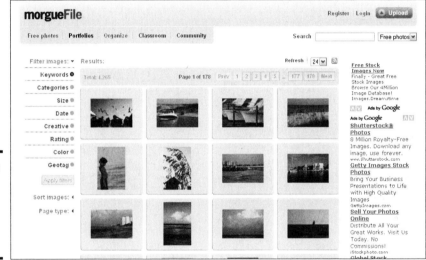

3. **Click the image you want to use.**

   The image detail page opens with license information and a Download button, as shown in Figure 3-11.

FreeFoto.com

`www.freefoto.com`

FreeFoto.com offers over 100,000 images that are free to use as long as you follow the link and attribution requirements for each image. You can find the current requirements at `http://test.freefoto.com/browse/99-05-0?ffid=99-05-0`.

Figure 3-11: The morgueFile image detail page.

Follow these steps to find images you can use on your blog using FreeFoto.com:

1. **Visit www.freefoto.com, and enter your keyword in the search text box in the upper-left corner of your screen. Click the Search button to begin your search.**

   Your image results are returned to you grouped into categories, as shown in Figure 3-12.

Figure 3-12: A FreeFoto. com image search category results page.

2. **Click the link for the category that you want to view.**

   The images saved in that category are displayed on your screen.

3. **Click the image you want to use on your blog.**

   The image detail page opens, as shown in Figure 3-13.

Figure 3-13:
A FreeFoto.
com image
detail page.

4. **Click the License button to read the image license details, and click the Download button to save the image to your computer hard drive.**

   As long as you follow the current usage instructions for that image, you can freely use the downloaded image on your blog.

Dreamstime

www.dreamstime.com

Dreamstime offers both free images and images available for a fee. The images are uploaded by their owners, and many talented photographers offer images for free as a way to get more exposure for their work. Even the images offered for a fee via the Dreamstime Web site are reasonably priced.

To find free images on the Dreamstime Web site, follow these steps listed:

1. **Visit www.dreamstime.com/free-photos, shown in Figure 3-14, and enter your keywords into the search box in the top right of your screen. Click the Search button to launch your search.**

Figure 3-14:
The
Dreamstime
free photos
landing
page.

Your search results are returned to you.

2. **Click the image you want to use.**

The image detail page opens, as shown in Figure 3-15, and there you can log in (or register if you don't already have a Dreamstime account) and save the free version of the image to your computer's hard drive, or you can purchase credits to download high-resolution versions of the image or variations of the image.

Figure 3-15:
A
Dreamstime
image detail
page.

PicApp

http://picapp.com

PicApp works differently from the other image sources discussed in this chapter. PicApp images come from professional sources such as Getty Images, Corbis, and more, and the owners of those images expect to get paid royalties anytime their images are republished.

Although you can use the images available on PicApp for free (and you're not required to register on the site to do so), there's a catch. Each image displays on your blog with an ad component. That's how the image owner is paid. If you can live with the ad component appearing with the image on your blog, PicApp is a great source for celebrity and current event photos.

Follow these steps to find and use images from PicApp on your blog:

1. **Visit http://picapp.com (see Figure 3-16) and enter your keywords into the search box on the left side of your screen. Then click the Go button.**

Your results are returned to you.

Figure 3-16:
A PicApp home page.

2. **Click the image you want to use.**

The image detail page opens, as shown in Figure 3-17.

Figure 3-17:
A PicApp
image detail
page.

3. **Select the radio button next to the size of the image that you want to use on your blog, and then copy the Embed code provided in the text box.**

4. **Return to your blogging application and paste the Embed code into the HTML editor of your blog post.**

Fee-based image sources

The many fee-based image sources online offer a wide range of images and price tags. Even if you pay to access an image, you still need to be certain that you're aware of and follow the licensing requirements for that image. Images with a Royalty Free license are most commonly used by bloggers, but fees can vary significantly depending on the source, resolution, and more. You can reuse Royalty Free stock images in your works as many times as you want, and you can manipulate those images to suit your purposes after you pay a one-time fee.

iStockphoto (www.istockphoto.com) and BigStockPhoto (www.big stockphoto.com) are two sites that offer many images at very reasonable prices. If you have a big budget, you can look into using images from some of the big players such as Getty Images (www.gettyimages.com) and Corbis Images (www.corbisimages.com).

Chapter 4: Understanding RSS, Blog Feeds, Subscriptions, and Syndication

In This Chapter

✔ Defining RSS

✔ Making sense of feed subscriptions

✔ Setting up your blog feed

✔ Sharing your feed

✔ Tracking feed statistics

✔ Increasing your blog subscribers

✔ Understanding other forms of syndication

*B*log subscriptions and syndication can be confusing subjects for bloggers because there are actually several forms of both. However, all forms of blog subscriptions and syndication help bloggers achieve the same end goal: getting their content in front of more people and boosting page views.

The thought process behind blog subscriptions is that they make it easier for audience members who are interested in your blog's content to find and view any new content you publish. If you want to grow your blog, taking the time to understand RSS, blog feeds, subscriptions, and syndication is essential to meeting your blogging goals. This chapter covers not only what these terms mean, but also how to configure your blog's feed and find more syndication opportunities.

Defining RSS

RSS (Really Simple Syndication) is the most commonly used Web feed format. In simplest terms, RSS is the technology used to standardize Web content and feed it to people so they can read it in the manner of their choice — by e-mail or by feed reader. A *feed* is simply a data format used to make it easy for people to subscribe to your blog content through a *feed reader*, which is a tool that ingests feeds from multiple sources (such as blogs) and makes it easy for a person to view all of that content in one place.

While the technology behind the scenes configures your blog content using a standardized XML file format, as shown in Figure 4-1, your blog's feed is delivered to subscribers in a readable format similar to the format used on your blog with font styles, images, and so on intact. (Figures 4-2 and 4-3 demonstrate blog feeds viewed in a feed reader and e-mail, respectively.)

In other words, people can view your blog content in three ways:

✦ **On your blog:** People can visit your blog directly to read the content you publish. Feeds and subscriptions are not necessary to view blog content this way.

✦ **By e-mail:** People can subscribe to your blog's feed and request to receive an e-mail each time you publish a new post. The e-mail can include either a summary (partial feed) of your new blog posts with a link for subscribers to click to read the rest of the post, or it can include the complete posts (full feed).

✦ **By feed reader:** People can subscribe to your blog's feed and read it via their preferred feed readers. Again, your blog's feed can include partial or full content from your blog posts.

Blog feeds and syndication make it very easy for people to read the new content on your blog, because instead of having to visit your blog at multiple times throughout the day to find new content, that content is delivered directly to them (along with the content from other blogs they subscribe to).

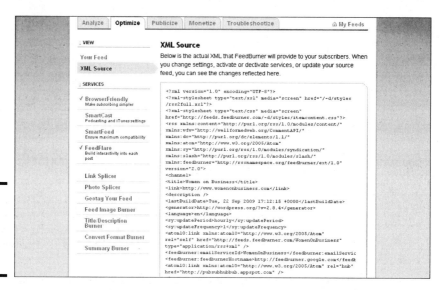

Figure 4-1:
The XML format of a blog's RSS feed.

Making Sense of Feed Subscriptions

People can access your blog's content by subscribing to your blog's feed in one of two ways: feed reader or e-mail. For people who subscribe to your blog's feed in their feed readers of choice, your content is aggregated, along with the content from other blogs they subscribe to, and pulled into the feed reader periodically throughout the day. An example of blog feed subscriptions using Google Reader is shown in Figure 4-2. Check out the nearby sidebar to find out more about popular feed readers.

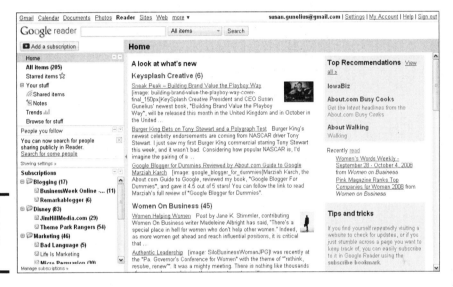

Figure 4-2:
Blog feeds
via Google
Reader.

For people who subscribe to your blog's feed via e-mail, they receive an email with your new content included within the message at the times you determine when you originally configure your blog's feed. An example of a blog feed subscription delivered by e-mail is shown in Figure 4-3.

Of the two types of feed subscriptions, more people subscribe to blog content via feed reader than e-mail, for a few reasons:

✦ **Convenience:** People who subscribe to multiple blogs would spend a lot of time checking each of those blogs every day for new content. They can save time and energy by logging in to their feed readers once or twice a day to find all new content for all the blogs they subscribe to in one place.

✦ **E-mail clutter avoidance:** E-mail inboxes fill up quickly, and receiving e-mails for all the blogs a person subscribes to can be overwhelming and time-consuming.

✦ **Organization:** Feed readers allow users to categorize the feeds they subscribe to, making it easy to check for new content related to specific topics.

Visitors to your blog can subscribe to your blog's feed with a couple of clicks of the mouse as long as you provide a link to do so somewhere on your blog, as described later in this chapter.

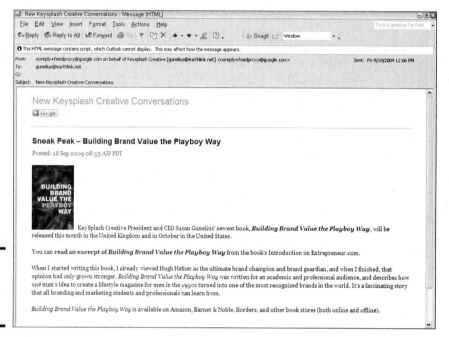

Figure 4-3:
A blog feed
delivered
via e-mail.

Popular feed readers

You have many feed readers to choose from. Some are Web-based tools, which you can access only through an Internet connection, and others are desktop-based, meaning you download the application to your computer and use it offline. Following are some of the most popular Windows and Mac feed readers.

Google Reader: (www.reader.google. com) A free Web-based feed reader available to Windows and Mac users.

Bloglines: (www.bloglines.com) A free Web-based feed reader available to Windows and Mac users.

NewsGator: (www.newsgator.com) NewsGator offers Web-based, mobile, and desktop feed readers for Windows and Mac users. Some tools are offered for free, but others require you to pay a fee in order to use them.

Setting Up Your Blog Feed

Depending on the blogging application you use, the steps you need to follow to integrate your blog's feed into your blog differ slightly. However, the process to create your feed (often referred to as *burning your blog's feed*) is always the same, and it's very easy. In fact, it takes only a few minutes to create your blog's feed using a tool such as FeedBurner, which is owned by Google.

Discovering FeedBurner

FeedBurner, shown in Figure 4-4, is a free online tool that allows users to create a unique feed URL for their Web sites and blogs, which they can publicize and invite readers to subscribe to via e-mail or their preferred feed readers. FeedBurner also provides metrics that allow Web site owners and bloggers to track statistics related to the overall use of their feeds by subscribers.

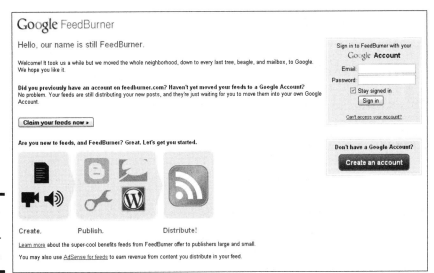

Figure 4-4:
The
FeedBurner
home page.

FeedBurner offers easy integration of Google AdSense ads into a blog feed. This is particularly helpful to bloggers who want to monetize their blog feeds.

Even though FeedBurner is owned by Google, when you burn your blog's feed using FeedBurner, visitors to your blog are still given the option to subscribe to the feed via e-mail or through a variety of feed readers, not just Google Reader (Google's free feed-reader application).

Using FeedBurner to create your blog's feed

To use FeedBurner to create your blog's feed, you need a Google account. If you use another Google service such as Gmail, Google Groups, and so on, you probably have a Google account already, and you can use that account to log in to FeedBurner to create your blog's feed.

Follow these steps to create your blog's feed using FeedBurner:

1. **Visit `www.feedburner.com` and enter your Google account information in the Sign In box on the right side of your screen, as shown in Figure 4-4, and click the Sign In button (or click the Create an Account button to create a new Google account so you can log in to FeedBurner).**

   The Welcome page opens, as shown in Figure 4-5.

Figure 4-5:
The
FeedBurner
Welcome
page.

2. **Enter the URL of your blog into the Burn a Feed Right This Instant text box and click the Next button.**

   The Identify Feed Source page opens.

3. **Select the radio button next to the option that says RSS Feed and click the Next button.**

The Welcome! Let Us Burn a Feed for You page opens, as shown in Figure 4-6.

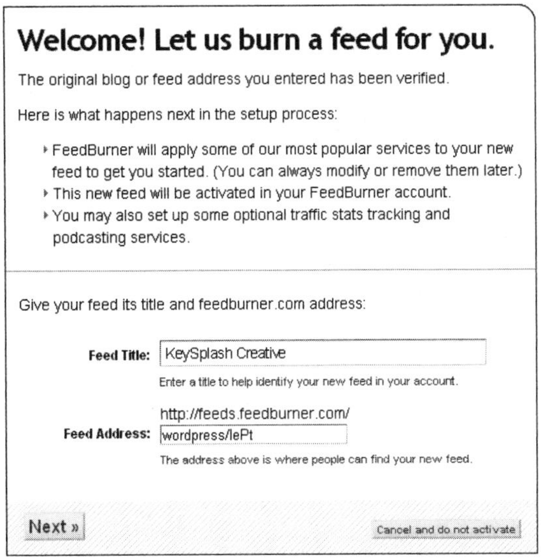

Welcome! Let us burn a feed for you.

The original blog or feed address you entered has been verified.

Here is what happens next in the setup process:

▸ FeedBurner will apply some of our most popular services to your new feed to get you started. (You can always modify or remove them later.)
▸ This new feed will be activated in your FeedBurner account.
▸ You may also set up some optional traffic stats tracking and podcasting services.

Give your feed its title and feedburner.com address:

Feed Title: KeySplash Creative

Enter a title to help identify your new feed in your account.

http://feeds.feedburner.com/
Feed Address: wordpress/lePt

The address above is where people can find your new feed.

Next »   Cancel and do not activate

Figure 4-6: Choose your blog feed format.

4. **Edit your feed's title and address to suit your preferences (or make no changes and use the automated title and feed address) and click the Next button.**

The Congratulations page opens.

5. **Click the Next button.**

The Get More Gusto From Your Feed Traffic Statistics page opens, shown in Figure 4-7.

6. **Select the check boxes next to any additional items listed that you want to track and click the Next button.**

The Your Feed is Ready for the World page opens, offering you options to publicize your feed.

7. **Click the icon for your blogging application.**

Follow the instructions provided to publicize your new feed on your blog.

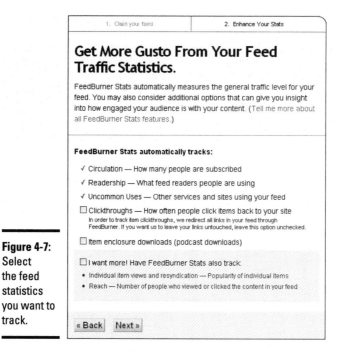

Get More Gusto From Your Feed Traffic Statistics.

FeedBurner Stats automatically measures the general traffic level for your feed. You may also consider additional options that can give you insight into how engaged your audience is with your content. (Tell me more about all FeedBurner Stats features.)

FeedBurner Stats automatically tracks:

✓ Circulation — How many people are subscribed

✓ Readership — What feed readers people are using

✓ Uncommon Uses — Other services and sites using your feed

☐ Clickthroughs — How often people click items back to your site
In order to track item clickthroughs, we redirect all links in your feed through FeedBurner. If you want us to leave your links untouched, leave this option unchecked.

☐ Item enclosure downloads (podcast downloads)

☐ I want more! Have FeedBurner Stats also track:
- Individual item views and resyndication — Popularity of individual items
- Reach — Number of people who viewed or clicked the content in your feed

« Back   Next »

Figure 4-7:
Select the feed statistics you want to track.

Making Your Feed Available

After you create your blog's feed, you need to make it available to your blog readers. In other words, you need to publicize your blog's feed and make it easy for readers to subscribe to it. During the FeedBurner feed configuration process described in the preceding section, you're given the opportunity to select your blogging application and follow the steps provided to publicize your feed on your blog. Typically, this involves copying and pasting some HTML code into your blog's template or within a widget or gadget (depending on your blogging application).

 The RSS logo, shown in the margin, is usually used to draw attention to the subscription area on a blog. It's a universal symbol that online publishers and visitors recognize as representing content subscription options.

The most common way to publicize a blog feed is by adding a subscription link and information to your blog's sidebar. Figure 4-8 shows what a subscription widget can look like in a blog sidebar.

Subscription widget

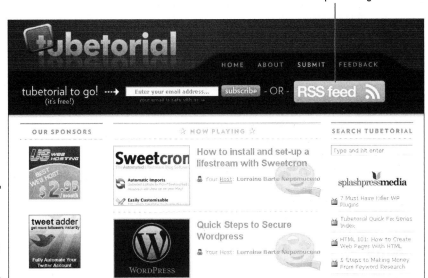

Figure 4-8:
A well-
placed blog
subscription
widget.

Tracking Feed Statistics

To get to the FeedBurner Feed Stats Dashboard, shown in Figure 4-9, log in
to your FeedBurner account at `www.feedburner.com` and click the link
that corresponds with the feed you want to analyze (if you have more than
one feed) from the My Feeds page. A new page opens with all the statistics
related to that feed available to you.

Analyzing your feed statistics through FeedBurner can provide valuable
insight beyond the number of subscribers your blog has. For example, you
can find out what your loyal subscribers like and don't like about your blog
content. To figure this out, you can analyze the click-throughs from your
feed to the content on your blog in order to determine which content most
interests your readers and which content is underperforming. You can also
find out how many feed reader and e-mail subscribers your blog has and
which countries they live in.

Figure 4-9:
The
FeedBurner
Feed Stats
Dashboard
page shows
a summary
of statistics.

You can view your feed stats for specific days or time periods, which is particularly helpful if you launched new efforts to boost subscribers and you want to track the success of those efforts. Furthermore, you can easily download your FeedBurner statistics report and save it as an Excel or CSV file so you can sort data and manipulate it to best meet your analysis needs.

The number of subscribers to your feed can change significantly from one day to the next. Don't be as concerned with daily overall subscriber statistics as you are with growth trends over time.

Increasing Your Blog Subscribers

If you want to grow your blog's audience, an important concern should be increasing the number of people who subscribe to your blog's feed. Subscribers are often your most loyal audience, and increasing the number of loyal readers of your blog content is always beneficial. The steps in the following sections can help you boost your blog subscribers.

Avoid gimmicks to boost blog subscribers, which often end up driving short-term subscription rates up, but those subscribers either unsubscribe soon after or end up ignoring your content within their feed readers entirely. The goal is to attract and retain loyal readers through blog subscriptions.

Publish useful content frequently

The more great content you publish on your blog, the more people will want to read it. Think of it this way: No one feels motivated to return to a blog that's updated sporadically with uninteresting content. However, if your blog content is always fresh, useful, and meaningful, people are more likely to want to return and read more of it.

Make subscribing easy

You need to make it extremely easy for people to subscribe to your blog. Publish your subscription link in an obvious location on your blog such as at the top of the sidebar or within the header on every page of your blog. A subscription option should always be visible and require nothing more than a simple click of the mouse.

Ask people to subscribe

Sometimes increasing the number of subscribers to your blog requires nothing more than asking people to subscribe. Add a sentence to the end of your blog posts that says something like, "If you enjoyed this post, subscribe to have future content delivered to you by feed reader or e-mail." Be sure to include a link to your blog's subscription sign-up page.

If you use WordPress.org as your blogging application, you can use the Subscribe-Remind plug-in (`http://wordpress.org/extend/plugins/subscribe-remind`), which adds text to the bottom of each of your posts that invites readers to subscribe to your blog, or the What Would Seth Godin Do (`http://wordpress.org/extend/plugins/what-would-seth-godin-do`) plug-in that uses cookies to identify new and return visitors and displays a customizable message box above your blog post, which you can use to suggest that new visitors subscribe to your blog.

Offer something in return to subscribers

Providing something of value to entice people to subscribe to your blog's feed can be effective, particularly if the giveaway is relevant to your blog topic and useful to subscribers. For example, offer a free e-book, a weekly e-mail newsletter, 15 minutes of your consulting time, a free gift, or another meaningful item to new subscribers to not just entice the general public to subscribe but to entice your *target* audience to subscribe.

Show off your popularity

FeedBurner offers subscriber buttons, called *FeedCount chicklets,* that show how many people subscribe to your blog's feed. You can find and configure your own FeedCount chicklet by logging in to your FeedBurner account, selecting the appropriate feed link from your list of feeds, and clicking the Optimize tab near the top of the page. Next, click the FeedCount link in the left sidebar to open and configure your blog's FeedCount chicklet, as shown in Figure 4-10. After you've configured your settings, you can simply follow the directions provided for your blogging application to add the FeedCount chicklet to your blog.

After your subscriber list starts to grow, incorporating a FeedCount chicklet into your blog shows visitors that your blog has a large number of subscribers and creates the perception that your blog must be good, because a lot of people are subscribing to it.

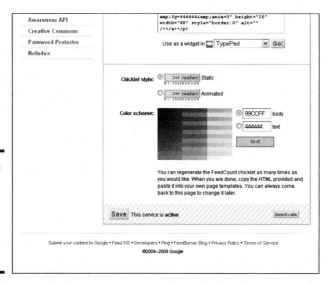

Figure 4-10: You can choose the design of your blog's FeedCount chicklet.

Discovering Other Forms of Syndication

The most common form of blog syndication is direct syndication, meaning you create your blog's RSS feed and publicize it on your blog, inviting people to subscribe to receive your blog's new content via feed reader or e-mail. However, there are other ways you can syndicate your blog's content, such as through partnerships with third-party aggregation and syndication companies. This type of syndication allows your content to be simultaneously published through multiple sources. There are three primary methods of blog content syndication, which are described in the following sections.

Free or bartered

When a blogger enters into a free or bartered syndication agreement, they're allowing another entity, such as a Web site, to republish their content on the open Web without compensation. Free or bartered syndication can help you as a blogger by getting your content in front of a larger audience. With that added exposure, you can drive more traffic to your blog and possibly boost your other endeavors such as selling more products, booking speaking engagements, and so on.

Although several free and bartered syndication companies have come and gone in recent years (such as BlogRush and ScriptWords), a few remain, including Seeking Alpha (for the financial industry — www.seekingalpha. com) and paidContent (which allows bloggers to republish individual posts — www.paidcontent.org). Furthermore, bloggers can share their feeds and republish them on other blogs and Web sites through direct relationships with those Web site owners and bloggers.

Ad-supported

Ad-supported licensing agreements allow bloggers to republish their syndicated content on other Web sites and publications. In return, the bloggers are compensated in the form of a portion of the revenue generated from ads served with that content. Typically, content syndicated through the ad-supported model is distributed on the open Web, and the advertising revenue is small. Companies such as BlogBurst (www.blogburst.com) offer ad-supported syndication to highly trafficked and established blogs. Smaller blogs can join BlogBurst but are not included in ad revenue–sharing.

Licensed

Licensed content syndication works very differently from free, bartered, and ad-supported syndication. First, it's harder to have your blog accepted into a licensed syndication agreement because content that is licensed for syndication is typically provided to professional end-user customers through top distributors, alongside content from well-known news organizations. Furthermore, content delivered through licensed syndication is usually distributed via closed systems rather than through the open Web, which means that content is exposed to new audiences rather than competing with the same online audience.

Bloggers who syndicate their content through licensed agreements are usually paid royalties each time their content is accessed by end-user customers. Bloggers who create a lot of great content that end-user professionals want and need can earn some money and increase their exposure to key professional audiences through licensed syndication with a company such as Newstex (www.newstex.com). Even podcast, video, and Twitter content can be syndicated through a licensed syndication agreement with Newstex.

Before you sign up to syndicate your blog content through a third party, make sure the opportunity truly helps you reach your blogging goals. Read all the fine print and sign an agreement only if it suits your needs.

Chapter 5: Using Offline Blog Editors

In This Chapter

✔ Discovering the offline blog editor

✔ Benefiting from using an offline blog editor

✔ Finding Windows-compatible offline blog editors

✔ Finding Mac-compatible offline blog editors

✔ Finding multiplatform offline blog editors

*O*ffline blog editors offer a lot of benefits to bloggers that can save them time and reduce frustration. Although most offline blog editors offer the same features that common blogging applications do, some provide additional functionality that allows you to enhance your posts easily as well as providing the accessibility and security that comes from working without the need for an Internet connection.

How many times have you been working on your computer when suddenly the electricity went out, your Internet connection was lost, or another event caused you to lose all your work? That's a reality that nearly every blogger has faced at one time or another, and offline blog editors help solve those problems.

In this chapter, you find out how offline blog editors work and what they can do for you. Additionally, you find out about some of the most popular offline blog editors, so you can choose which tools you want to try.

Meeting the Offline Blog Editor

An *offline blog editor* is a tool that enables you to type and create your blog posts (and pages, depending on the functionality of your blogging application) without accessing the Internet until you're ready to actually publish a post online. You can download an offline blog editor to your computer, configure it to recognize your existing blogs, and publish posts to your blogs without leaving the offline blog editor tool.

Gone are the problems of losing your Internet connection and all your work. With an offline blog editor, you create your posts independent of the Internet. Furthermore, offline blog editors typically offer a What You See Is What You Get (WYSIWYG) post editor that's even closer to traditional word-processing tools than the visual editors found in most blogging applications. That means tasks such as importing images, resizing them, formatting text, and so on are very easy to do with an offline blog editor.

Most offline blog editors offer similar functionality. Following are some of the most important features to look for when you choose an offline blog editor:

+ **Cost:** Many free offline blog editors are available (particularly for PC users). Don't pay for an offline blog editor until you try some of the free tools first.

+ **Drafts:** Make sure the offline blog editor you choose allows you to save a draft of a post before you actually publish it on your blog. If you're called away from your computer, you don't want to risk losing the work you've already done.

+ **Tags:** Your offline blog editor should let you add tags (keywords) to your posts to identify them and help search engine optimization.

+ **Pinging:** It's very important that you choose an offline blog editor that includes a ping function, meaning when you publish new content from your offline blog editor to your live blog, Technorati, search engines, and so on are notified of the existence of that new content with a ping. Pings are discussed in detail in Chapter 3 of Book I.

+ **Time stamps:** Your offline blog editor should allow you to change the dates of your posts and schedule them for publishing at specific times. This feature is particularly helpful when you know you'll be away from your blog for an extended time but want to ensure that fresh content is published on your blog during your absence.

+ **Image editing:** Make sure the offline blog editor you choose allows you to easily insert and edit images.

+ **Categories:** Depending on the blogging application you use, it might be important for your offline blog editor to allow you to categorize your posts so they appear in the appropriate category archives on your live blog.

+ **HTML editor:** Even if you don't know HTML today, in time, you'll undoubtedly learn some basic HTML code, and it will help you as a blogger. Sometimes simple HTML tweaks can fix all kinds of problems in a blog post. Make sure the offline blog editor you choose allows you to view and edit the HTML code for your posts.

Benefiting from an Offline Blog Editor

You can get a variety of benefits from using an offline blog editor to create and publish your blog posts. Although most offline blog editors provide similar features and functionality, no two offline blog editors are exactly alike. That's why it's important to visit offline blog editor Web sites, check out the offerings in the current versions, and then choose the one that meets your needs.

TIP

Don't be afraid to try more than one offline blog editor. In fact, this is probably the best way to compare them, particularly the free options, to determine which you like the most. It won't hurt your blog if you test more than one offline blog editor.

Following are some of the top benefits bloggers derive from using offline blog editors:

✦ **Peace of mind:** Because you don't need an Internet connection to use an offline blog editor, you don't have to worry about online availability or a sudden loss of connectivity.

✦ **Speed:** Offline blog editors respond to your commands quickly, unlike online editing within your blogging application, which is dependent on the speed of your Internet connection.

✦ **Multiple blog posting:** When you use an offline blog editor, you can easily publish a post to multiple blogs. Just associate each blog to your offline blog editor and select the ones you want your post to publish to with your mouse. It's that easy.

✦ **Fewer code problems:** If you've ever tried to copy content from a Microsoft Word document and paste it into the visual editor of your blogging application, you've probably noticed that when you publish that post, the formatting of the text is a complete mess. That's because extra HTML code is added when you copy and paste from Word or another word-processing application to your blogging application. You can avoid that problem by using an offline blog editor that accepts text copied and pasted from Word without any problems or additional code appended to it.

✦ **Easy image and video inclusion:** Adding images and video to blog posts can be challenging for some bloggers. Those problems are solved when you use an offline blog editor.

Fortunately, many blogging applications have been upgraded in recent years to now include auto-save functions and other features that once made offline blog editors essential to bloggers. However, offline blog editors can still benefit bloggers, particularly those who are new to the blogosphere and are not completely comfortable with the editor available through their blogging applications.

Finding Windows-Compatible Offline Blog Editors

You can choose from a number of offline blog editors if you use a Windows-based computer. The following sections focus on two of the most popular options: Windows Live Writer and BlogDesk. Both are completely free to use and offer similar functionality.

If you test more than one offline blog editor, you'll find that they work very similarly. If you figure out how to use one, you can use any offline blog editor, and because they work very similarly to common word-processing tools and blogging applications, the learning curve is negligible.

Windows Live Writer

www.windowslive.com/Desktop/Writer

Windows Live Writer, shown in Figure 5-1, is offered for free by Microsoft. As you might expect, it is compatible only with Windows platform computers. However, you can use it with most blogging applications, such as WordPress, Blogger, TypePad, Movable Type, LiveJournal, and more.

Figure 5-1:
The
Windows
Live Writer
home page.

To get started using Windows Live Writer, first you have to download the program to your computer by visiting www.windowslive.com/Desktop/Writer and clicking the Download link. Follow the instructions provided onscreen to install the program as you would any downloadable program.

Be sure to deselect the check boxes for additional programs offered for download with Windows Live Writer during the download process. If you want only Windows Live Writer, that's the only program you need to download, regardless of how many other programs are offered with it.

When Windows Live Writer is installed on your computer, you can open it from your Windows Start menu.

You can easily associate your blogs with Windows Live Writer by clicking the Edit tab from the top menu bar and then clicking the Add Blog Account link. Adding blogs is a simple process, and after a blog is added to Windows Live Writer, you can select it and publish content to it. You can also preview content on your blog before you publish it, save drafts, easily insert images, video, tags, categories, and more.

For Windows users, Windows Live Writer is one of the most comprehensive, easy-to-use offline blog editors available.

BlogDesk

www.blogdesk.org

BlogDesk, shown in Figure 5-2, is another popular and free offline blog editor for Windows users. It offers features that are nearly as comprehensive as Windows Live Writer, with a simpler interface. BlogDesk is compatible with WordPress, ExpressionEngine, Movable Type, Drupal, and Serendipity blogging applications.

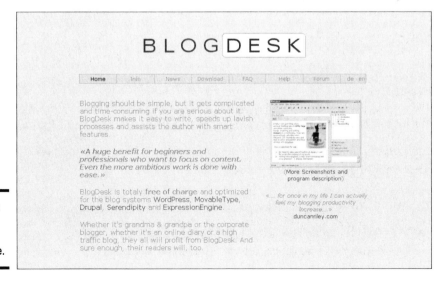

Figure 5-2:
The BlogDesk home page.

To install BlogDesk on your computer, select the Download link from the top navigation bar on the BlogDesk home page, shown in Figure 5-3. The Download page, and here you can click the Download BlogDesk link. Then follow the instructions to download BlogDesk as you would any other program.

During the BlogDesk download process, be sure to select the check box to install a BlogDesk icon on your desktop when prompted to. Having an icon handy makes it quick and easy to launch BlogDesk in the future.

When BlogDesk is installed on your computer, you can launch it, and associate your blogs to it by selecting the File tab from the top menu bar and then select the Manage Blogs link. Just follow the instructions provided to add more blogs to BlogDesk. It's easy to switch between blogs (they're listed on the right side of your BlogDesk window), and you can use the top menu items to add images, tags, and more.

Finding Mac-Compatible Offline Blog Editors

Unfortunately, there are fewer Mac-compatible offline blog editors than Windows-compatible ones, and the best Mac-compatible offline blog editors have fees attached to them. Some of those options for Mac users are discussed in the following sections and later in the "Finding Multiplatform Offline Blog Editors" section.

MarsEdit

www.red-sweater.com/marsedit

MarsEdit, shown in Figure 5-3, is the most comprehensive Mac-compatible offline blog editor, but it's not free. You can sign up for a free 30-day trial before you have to pay to use it, but after that 30-day trial is over, you need to purchase the software in order to continue using it. The price tag isn't high, but if a free alternative suits your needs, why pay for MarsEdit?

If you decide to give MarsEdit a try as your offline blog editor, simply visit www.red-sweater.com/marsedit and click the Free 30-Day Trial Download Now link. Install the software on your computer as you would any other downloadable software and then launch MarsEdit to associate your blog with the application.

MarsEdit is compatible with WordPress, Blogger, Tumblr, TypePad, Movable Type, LiveJournal, Drupal, and Vox blogging applications. It's easy to use and offers a clean interface.

Figure 5-3:
The
MarsEdit
home page.

ecto

`www.illuminex.com/ecto`

Another popular offline blog editor for Mac users is ecto, shown in Figure 5-4. Like MarsEdit, ecto is available for a fee, and it offers functionality that is very similar to MarsEdit.

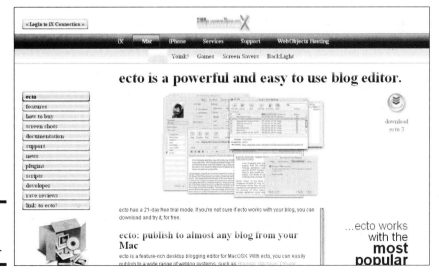

Figure 5-4:
The ecto
home page.

Because ecto is compatible with most blogging applications, such as WordPress, Blogger, TypePad, Movable Type, ExpressionEngine, Drupal, and more, you can easily associate your blogs and publish new posts with it.

Finding Multiplatform Offline Blog Editors

If single-platform offline blog editors don't meet your needs, you can test a multiplatform offline blog editor such as those described in this section. These offline blog editors can work on your PC or your Mac and offer some unique features of their own.

Qumana

www.qumana.com

Qumana, shown in Figure 5-5, started out as a popular offline blog editor, because it's very easy to insert ads into blog posts with it. If that feature is important to you, Qumana is certainly worth looking into, particularly if you're not comfortable editing HTML code yourself in order to insert ads from other providers before, after, and within your blog posts.

Figure 5-5:
The Qumana home page.

You can download Qumana for free by clicking the Download button on the Qumana home page. Just follow the instructions provided on your screen to download the version of Qumana that's appropriate for your system — Windows, Mac, or Linux.

Qumana is compatible with all the common blogging applications such as WordPress, Blogger, TypePad, Movable Type, LiveJournal, and more. As with most offline blog editors, it's very easy to associate your blogs with Qumana, and the post editor is streamlined and easy to use.

ScribeFire

www.scribefire.com

ScribeFire, shown in Figure 5-6, is unique because it's not a true offline blog editor (you have to be online to use it), but you don't have to be logged in to your blogging application account to use it. However, it's become fairly popular as a blog editor, so it warrants mention.

ScribeFire is an extension to the popular Mozilla Firefox Web browser. You can use ScribeFire with WordPress, Blogger, TypePad, Movable Type, LiveJournal, or other popular blogging applications to edit and publish content to your blog. For example, if you come across a Web page or article that you want to blog about while you're surfing the Internet, you can simply click the ScribeFire toolbar (available from Firefox after you download the ScribeFire add-on), and an editor opens so that you can immediately create your blog post. When you're ready to publish your post to your blog, you can do so without leaving ScribeFire.

Figure 5-6:
The
ScribeFire
home page.

To install ScribeFire to your computer, simply click the Install ScribeFire Now link in the right sidebar of the ScribeFire home page shown in Figure 5-6. The Firefox Add-Ons page for ScribeFire opens, and you can click the Add to Firefox button to access ScribeFire.

The ScribeFire functionality is a bit more stripped down than what offline blog editors provide, but its ease of integration with Firefox makes it a worthwhile option for testing to determine whether it meets your needs.

Chapter 6: Creating a Podcast

In This Chapter

✔ **Finding out about podcasts**

✔ **Discovering why podcasts are popular**

✔ **Determining whether podcasting is right for you**

✔ **Planning your podcast**

✔ **Finding the equipment you need**

✔ **Preparing to record your podcast**

✔ **Finding an online home for your podcast**

✔ **Publicizing a podcast**

*M*any bloggers begin publishing podcasts as an extension of their blogging experience. In simplest terms, podcasts are audio files delivered online. Video blog posts are also technically considered podcasts, but they're treated separately in Chapter 7 of this minibook. As such, this chapter focuses entirely on the creation and publication of audio podcasts as they relate to enhancing or extending a blog.

Creating a podcast can seem intimidating to beginner bloggers, but there are many free tools available that make becoming a podcaster easier than you might imagine. This chapter tells you how to start a podcast, publish it, and promote it so you can determine for yourself whether podcasting is right for you and your blogging goals. For complete details about beginner podcasting, pick up *Podcasting For Dummies,* by Tee Morris, Chuck Tomasi, Evo Terra, and Kreg Steppe; and for more advanced help, read *Expert Podcasting Practices For Dummies,* by Tee Morris, Evo Terra, and Ryan Williams.

Getting the Scoop on Podcasts

A traditional podcast is an audio recording that you publish online using an RSS feed that allows people to subscribe to receive new episodes of the podcast, which are pushed to them through their preferred podcast services. Unlike radio programs that are broadcast at specific times and on specific radio stations, people can access and download podcasts anytime after they're published, and then they can listen to the podcast as many times as they want.

In recent years, the term *podcasting* has become a bit diluted and now represents a variety of online audio publishing methods. In this chapter, I bypass semantics and reference podcasts in the broader sense: online audio publishing that extends or enhances a blog. Therefore, for the purposes of this chapter, a podcast does not have to be a traditional ongoing broadcast; there are many options available to bloggers these days for publishing and promoting audio content through their blogs, many of which are collectively referred to as podcasts, regardless of whether that label is technically correct.

Here are two common methods for getting a podcast out there to the public:

✦ **Bloggers can upload their audio files to their own Web hosting site and publish them directly within a blog post.** Although that's not the traditional definition of podcasting, many people refer to this method of publishing audio files as podcasting, simply because it represents a method of online audio publishing.

✦ **Bloggers can get accounts with radio and podcasting sites.** Bloggers can sign up for accounts with online radio and podcasting sites where they can not only upload their podcasts and create media RSS feeds for those podcasts, but also bypass traditional recording methods if they choose. For example, it's possible to create audio files by telephone thanks to new Web sites that offer easier solutions for the less technically savvy individuals who want an online radio show, a podcast, or an audio presence.

Bottom line: Podcasting might technically mean subscribable, broadcast-online audio publishing, but the lines between online audio have blurred. That's actually a good thing though, because the shift has opened the doors to online audio publishing wide. Anyone can develop an online audio presence these days.

Most of the concerns podcasters face are related to copyright laws. Always consult your attorney for legal advice, but the basic issues facing podcasters involve using music in a podcast without permission. Furthermore, you have to be careful what you say in your podcasts to avoid being accused of slander.

The best way to avoid trouble is to use music in your podcasts only if you own it or have written permission to use it. Alternatively, some podcast-recording applications, discussed later in this chapter, provide music options that you can use freely in your podcasts. In terms of what you say during your podcast, make sure you provide attribution to anyone you quote, and don't say anything that can be viewed as defamatory or malicious toward another person or entity. Editorial commentary is perfectly acceptable as long as it doesn't cross the line into slander territory. The best choice is to always err on the side of caution.

Discovering Why Podcasts Are Popular

Podcasts have grown more and more popular as the technology to create and publish them online has gotten easier to use, and the technology used to download and listen to podcasts has gotten less expensive and more accessible to a wider audience.

Podcasts are an excellent way to extend a blog, particularly if they're published through an online radio or podcasting site, where they can be advertised and shared to a broader audience. Similarly, podcasts present a great opportunity to enhance your blog. By including a link to your podcast or the audio file directly within one of your blog posts, blog readers have a new, more personal way to interact with you. Podcasts tap into the readers' sense of hearing, which adds a new layer to your online content and may even appeal to some visitors more so than written posts.

In other words, podcasts help to draw attention, attract new audiences, and build relationships. They're just one more way you can deliver meaningful, useful content and connect with your audience.

Determining Whether Podcasting Is Right for You

Podcasting offers a variety of positives and negatives to bloggers. Take the time to consider your blogging goals before you dive into the world of podcasting, so you don't waste your time. Following are some of the reasons you may decide to become a podcaster, too:

✦ **Grow your audience.** When you publish podcasts, you can host them through sites designed specifically for sharing and promoting audio content. (Some of those sites are discussed later in this chapter.) Doing so opens your content up to new audience members who might not find your blog otherwise. They might simply prefer audio content or stumble upon it while searching for something else. Either way, as more people find your podcast, more people can be led to your blog.

✦ **Entertain or educate your existing audience in a new way.** Reading blog post after blog post can get boring for some people. Adding an audio component to your blog with a podcast creates a new element of interest.

✦ **Expand on your blog posts.** Sometimes it just takes too long to type a detailed blog post, and more often, people won't read a lengthy blog post if it's not riveting. Podcasts help solve that problem. If your podcasts are entertaining and interesting, they might hold an audience's attention longer than a 1,000-plus-word blog post does.

+ **Communicate with like people.** Podcasts can be highly interactive depending on the format you choose and the provider you use to publish them online. For example, you can interview people in your podcasts and publish them online at a later date for people to listen to. They can leave written comments but can't vocally participate. Alternatively, if you record your podcasts through a radio or podcasting site that allows listeners to call in and participate, similar to an online radio show, then they can join the conversation, too. It's a great way to make your listeners feel valued and important.

+ **Make your content more convenient to consume.** Podcasts can be downloaded and listened to at any time, making them easy to consume. For example, a person can download a podcast from iTunes to his iPod and listen to it while he's working out, driving to work, and so on. It's a convenient medium to spread your messages and connect with people in ways a blog doesn't provide.

Podcasting can be fun and help you reach your blogging goals, but there are also negative aspects. For example, it's time-consuming to plan, create, edit, and publish a podcast. Also, podcasting might require a monetary investment in equipment such as microphones, editing software, and more. Consider your goals and make sure that shifting to podcasting matches those goals before you dive into the world of audio blogging.

Your podcasts can only be as successful as you make them. That means publishing one podcast and never publishing another won't work. To be a successful podcaster, you need to publish new audio content on a consistent basis that's relevant to your overall blog topic, and you need to commit to promoting your podcasts by talking about them on your blog, through social networking, and so on. Just as blogging success is a long-term strategy, so too is podcasting success. Promotional suggestions are provided at the end of this chapter.

Finding the Equipment You Need

There are two common ways to create a podcast: with your own digital recording and editing equipment or through a Web site that allows you to record your podcast via your telephone, such as BlogTalkRadio and Blubrry, which are discussed in the "Finding an Online Home for Your Podcast" section, later in this chapter. If you choose the latter option, all you need to become a podcaster is your computer, an Internet connection, and a telephone. If you choose the former option, the equipment you need gets a bit more complex. Don't be overwhelmed though. You don't need a state-of-the-art recording studio to create a podcast.

You can use several free audio-recording programs to create your podcasts. There are also many audio-recording programs that cost money, some with high price tags. However, before you invest in expensive software, try a free alternative. You might find it serves your purposes quite well. The following sections describe two of the most commonly used free audio-recording programs.

Audacity

http://sourceforge.net/projects/audacity

Audacity, shown in Figure 6-1, is available for Windows, Mac, and Linux users and can be downloaded for free from the SourceForge Web site. It's a simple program that allows you to create audio files with basic effects such as introductions. Many podcasters use Audacity because it offers plenty of features to create professional audio files, and it's free!

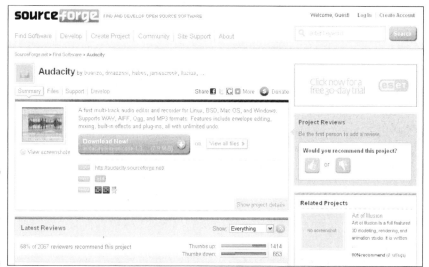

Figure 6-1: Audacity is a free audio-recording program.

GarageBand

www.apple.com/ilife/garageband

GarageBand, shown in Figure 6-2, comes preinstalled on all newer Mac computers. It offers easy-to-use audio-recording capabilities, which you can use with the microphone built into your Mac or with an external microphone plugged into one of your Mac's USB port. GarageBand also has a large library of music that podcasters can use freely and without violating copyright laws. Furthermore, GarageBand makes it easy to share your podcast online through iTunes.

Figure 6-2: GarageBand offers audio recording to Mac users.

Strategizing and Creating Your Podcast

Before you sit down at a microphone and record your first podcast, you need to do some planning, and not just technical planning. First, you need to create a strategy for it. Don't worry. You don't have to create a list of strategic imperatives and action items. A podcast isn't a business plan. However, you do need to consider some of the fundamental decisions that have the greatest impact on your podcast's success. The following sections help you focus on the building blocks of your podcasting venture.

Setting goals for your podcast

Before you start creating podcasts, you need to set your goals. It can take longer to prepare, record, edit, and publish a podcast than a written blog post, so before you invest that time, make sure you have a goal in mind. Take a look at the reasons why people create podcasts earlier in this chapter to help you define your own objectives. What do you hope to achieve by adding audio content to your blog? For example, podcasts are a great way to build relationships, particularly if you record your podcasts that allows listeners to call in and participate verbally.

However, if you're simply creating podcasts for fun, goal-setting is not as essential. The important thing is to always have fun. If you sound bored and indifferent during your podcast, no one will listen and it can reflect poorly on your blog, too.

Don't start your podcasts with unrealistic goals, or you set yourself up for failure. It takes time to create podcasts. For example, if you start with a one-hour format, you might become overwhelmed quickly and abandon your podcast entirely. Instead, start small and grow as your comfort-level and audience grow. For example, begin with a 5-minute podcast and work your way up to longer podcasts as you get more comfortable.

Picking your podcast subject matter

For a podcast related to your blog to be successful, you need to make sure that your podcast content is relevant to your blog's content. That means the first step to planning your podcast is defining your podcast's primary topic. More than likely, this topic should mirror your blog's topic, or it should be a niche within your blog topic that can be effectively discussed in audio format.

Considering your audience

After you determine your podcast's topic, you need to take some time to consider your existing blog audience as well as the new audience you want to attract with your podcast.

Podcasts are part of an integrated blog marketing strategy, meaning your blog and podcast should work seamlessly together to help you achieve your broader goals. The two media should not be disjointed but rather work cohesively. That means your podcast content should benefit and meet the needs of your existing audience as well as the new audience you're trying to attract to your blog.

If your podcast and blog don't work cohesively, then either your existing audience or your new audience is going to be disappointed. In other words, your existing blog audience won't want to listen to your podcasts if the content is meaningless to them, and your new podcast audience won't want to visit your blog if the content you write does not interest them. Consistency is key to overall online publishing success.

Selecting your voice

Depending on your subject matter and your audience, you need to decide the tone of your podcast. Will it be humorous and fun or serious and business-like? Should it be purely entertaining or educational? The way you speak has a significant effect on your podcast in terms of how you and your podcast connect with your guests and audience as well as how you handle the topics you discuss during your podcast. Your voice should be consistent with your blog voice in order to cohesively integrate them into your overall online presence.

Think of it this way. If you write a blog about providing expert stock market advice and education and then you start a podcast to enhance and extend your blog, the topics and your voice used in your podcast should mirror those in your blog. For example, if your podcast is a satirical look at the stock market filled with dark comedy and commentary that doesn't offer helpful advice to investors, your existing blog audience is unlikely to be interested in your podcast, and the new audience that finds your podcast is unlikely to be interested in your blog. Certainly, you may get some audience crossover, but not even remotely close to the crossover that could exist if your blog and podcast provide a consistent brand message, image, and promise that meet your audience's expectations of you and your content.

Most importantly, be expressive and show passion for your subject in your podcast. Make your audience care as much as you do.

Of course, if you're starting a podcast that you plan to have live completely separate from your existing blog or Web presence, then consistency in voice and content aren't an issue for you.

Identifying your podcast format

Just like radio shows have formats that they stick to, your podcast should have at least a loose format that includes a professional introduction and closing. For example, use music (with copyright permission) and a scripted introduction and closing statement before and after *every* one of your podcasts for consistency. Once your podcast attracts an audience, you might want to invest in hiring a company to help you create a show introduction and closing similar to those you hear on radio shows.

Furthermore, select a length for your podcast and don't deviate from that length. Just as television and radio shows don't deviate in length from one day or week to the next, neither should your podcast. It's important to set audience expectations and consistently meet them in order to gain loyalty. If your podcast exceeds your allotted time, consider splitting it up into multiple parts and promote the continuation to drive interest and excitement just as television shows do with multipart episodes.

If you record your podcast through a Web site that allows you to take listener calls, determine when you'll take those calls during your show (for example, as they come in or at the end of the podcast) and stick to that format for all of your podcasts. Again, consistency is key to creating listener expectations — be sure to deliver on those expectations every time. That's how audience loyalty develops.

Recording your podcast

When the time comes to record your podcast, you need to have a microphone and audio-recording software. (Popular options are discussed later in this chapter.) Make sure you have a quiet location to record from and test your equipment before you begin. Most importantly, prepare your podcast content and practice what you're going to say. Although it's not necessary to have a written script, and in fact, in some cases scripted podcasts can be very dull, you do need to have a basic structure in mind before you get started. Stick to your time guidelines, and have fun! Your audience will know if you're overly nervous or utterly disinterested.

Editing your podcast

After your podcast is recorded, you can use your audio-recording software to make any necessary edits. Of course, if you produce a live podcast, editing isn't an option. However, for recorded podcasts, editing is extremely important. Not only can you add music, introductions, closings, and so on during the editing process, but you can also delete dead air, clean up "ums," and fix any errors. No podcast is perfect, and that's part of what makes online audio interesting and real. Your goal should be to create a professional-sounding podcast but not so perfect that you seem inhuman.

Testing, analyzing, tweaking, and learning more

The world of podcasting continues to evolve and new tools for podcast recording, publishing and analyzing results are hitting the Internet all the time. After you determine your podcasting goals, take the time to research some of the current recording, publishing, and hosting options available to you, and select the tool that helps you meet those goals. Your choice might come down to selecting the tool that requires the least technical knowledge to use, and that's absolutely fine. Fortunately, there are podcasting tools available today that enable anyone to create online audio content quickly and easily.

Also, take the time to figure out what kind of metrics you can get from the publishing and hosting site (or sites) you choose, and then track those statistics. You might be able to determine topics that drive significant traffic or promotional efforts that cause a boost in listeners. By analyzing your podcast's performance over time, you can identify areas for improvement or opportunities for continued success.

Most importantly, don't get complacent with your podcasts. Not only will your audience notice, but you might miss opportunities for improved technology or analysis that can ultimately save you time or money. In short, you never know what podcasting advance will launch next week, next month, or next year. If you're serious about podcasting, the next great tool may be exactly what you need to take your podcast to the next level of success!

Take some time to listen to other podcasts to get an idea of what works so you can apply similar techniques in your own podcasts. Following are several great podcasts to get you started:

✦ **Small Business Trends Radio:** (www.smbtrendwire.com) A small business podcast

✦ **The Engaging Brand:** (www.blubrry.com/engaging) A branding podcast

✦ **Jaffe Juice:** (www.jaffejuice.com/across_the_sound) A social media podcast

✦ **Duct Tape Marketing:** (www.ducttapemarketing.com/blog/category/podcast) A marketing podcast

✦ **CBS Sports Netcast:** (http://www.cbssports.com/xml/podcasts) A sports podcast

✦ **CNN Politics Daily:** (http://edition.cnn.com/POLITICS/podcast) A political news podcast

Finding an Online Home for Your Podcast

Many Web sites allow you to upload your podcast for sharing or distribution. Some of those sites also host your audio file for you, and some even create an RSS feed of your podcasts for you, which you can use to upload your podcast to more sites. To choose the site where you want to upload and host your podcasts, you need to determine your distribution objectives and your overall strategic goals for your podcast.

Following are three of the most popular sites to upload and distribute your podcasts. Review each in detail and be sure to check the current offerings on each site before you dive into uploading your first podcast. Some are easier to use than others, and each one offers different features. You can't really go wrong with any of the options discussed in this chapter, but doing a bit of research up front can help you make the best decision for you, your podcast, and your blog.

BlogTalkRadio

www.blogtalkradio.com

BlogTalkRadio, shown in Figure 6-3, burst onto the online scene when it launched in 2006. Within a year, word had spread about the site that made creating your own online radio show or podcast easier than ever. Suddenly, anyone could have an online radio show or be a podcaster, and the site grew very quickly. One of the unique things about BlogTalkRadio is the strong community of users that grew around it (both publishers and listeners). You can find a podcast about almost any subject on BlogTalkRadio.

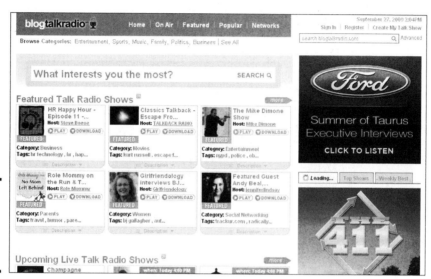

Figure 6-3:
The BlogTalk Radio home page.

Although anyone can publish podcasts or listen to BlogTalkRadio for free, a tiered pricing structure is available for publishers, allowing them to choose to pay for more functionality.

Start with a free account to be sure you're comfortable using BlogTalkRadio before you invest in a premium account.

What sets BlogTalkRadio apart from other Web sites that provide podcast uploading and hosting is the ease of use the site offers. To be a podcaster through BlogTalkRadio, you simply create an account, create a show page, and call in to a provided telephone number to record the audio portion of the podcast. You can see a sample BlogTalkRadio show page in Figure 6-4. You choose the date and time of your podcast, and when it's over, people can still access it through the BlogTalkRadio Web site archives at any time. You can also create an RSS feed of your BlogTalkRadio podcast, which you can upload to iTunes, a popular podcast download site from Apple, which is discussed in the "iTunes" section a little later on.

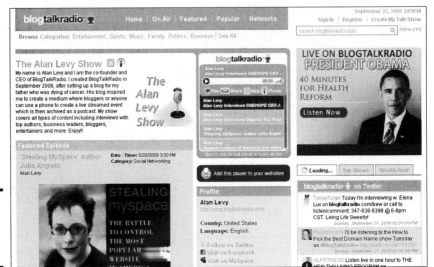

Figure 6-4:
A BlogTalk Radio show page.

BlogTalkRadio offers a number of helpful videos that make it even easier to use the site and become a podcaster, which you can access at `www.blog talkradio.com/faq.aspx`. There's even a video that shows you how to submit your BlogTalkRadio podcast to iTunes.

If technology isn't your strength but you want to be a podcaster, BlogTalkRadio is a perfect solution for you!

Blubrry

`www.blubrry.com`

Blubrry, shown in Figure 6-5, offers two options for podcasters. First, you can create your podcast, and then you can upload it to Blubrry for hosting, creating your RSS feed (to make your podcast available through iTunes), and sharing. Alternatively, you can host your podcast through a separate Web host and simply use Blubrry as another distribution point to make your podcast available to a wider audience. The method you choose depends on your technical ability. If creating audio feeds is something you aren't prepared to handle, the Blubrry hosting option is the better choice for you.

Figure 6-5:
The Blubrry
home page.

Blubrry offers a convenient WordPress plug-in called PowerPress that allows WordPress.org users to upload audio files to Blubrry with a few mouse clicks. Even if you don't use WordPress, you can use Blubrry, which offers ways for you to easily publicize your podcast on your blog, Twitter, and more as well as a way to make it available through iTunes.

When you start a free account with Blubrry, you can create a show page for your podcast, and then start creating audio content and uploading it to Blubrry for hosting and publishing. A sample podcast show page on Blubrry is shown in Figure 6-6.

A unique feature that Blubrry offers to podcasters is an advertising mechanism that enables you to earn advertising revenue from your podcasts. Advertisers select the Blubrry podcasts they want to place ads in, and the podcast publishers earn a percentage of the revenue from those ads. That means you aren't guaranteed to get an advertiser who wants to publish ads on your podcast, but if you publish great content on a subject that advertisers' audiences are interested in, you just might be able to earn some money from your podcast.

Blubrry offers a number of helpful video tutorials as well as a useful help section on its Web site, which you can access at `http://help.blubrry.com`, and a Blubrry Beginner Podcaster Guide, which you can view at `www.scribd.com/doc/242029/Blubrry-Beginning-Podcaster-Guide`. Both resources make it very easy to get started with Blubrry.

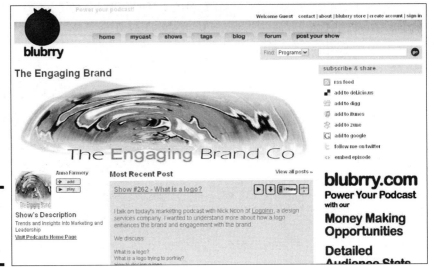

Figure 6-6:
A Blubrry
podcast
show page.

iTunes

www.itunes.com

iTunes, shown in Figure 6-7, is owned by Apple, and it's one of the most popular sites for people to find and download podcasts (both audio and video) to listen to on their MP3 players, such as an iPod. Making your podcast available for free download through iTunes is an excellent way to boost your audience. Not only do a lot of people actively search iTunes for podcasts, but downloading podcasts to iPods allows people to listen at their leisure.

iTunes is owned by Apple, but it's compatible with both Windows and Mac computers.

To make your podcast audio files available through iTunes, you need to have a place to host your audio file online, and you need to be able to create a media RSS feed for your podcast. There are Web sites that can help you create a media RSS feed, such as FeedBurner (www.feedburner.com) and MyRSSCreator.com (www.myrsscreator.com). For more on creating a media RSS feed, check out *Podcasting For Dummies,* by Tee Morris, Chuck Tomasi, Evo Terra, and Kreg Steppe. Alternatively, you can use a Web site such as BlogTalkRadio or Blubrry to host and publish your podcast. Both sites make the process of uploading your podcast to iTunes very simple.

Figure 6-7:
The iTunes
home page.

Publicizing Your Podcast

After you create your podcast and make it available online, you need to promote it and drive traffic to it. Don't be afraid to get creative with your promotional efforts. The key is to drive targeted traffic to your podcast (people who are likely to be interested in the topics you discuss during your podcast) and to make sure your content, voice, and style are interesting enough and useful enough to ensure they'll want to come back to listen to your next podcast and share it with other people.

Making your podcast available through several distribution points is a great start to publicizing your podcast. For example, make your podcast available on BlogTalkRadio or Blubrry *and* iTunes, but don't stop there. To make your podcast successful, you need to do more to spread the word about its existence than simply uploading it to a couple of podcasting sites.

Following are several ways you can begin promoting your podcast:

✦ **Blog about it.** Write a post about your upcoming podcast and entice your blog readers to listen. Don't be afraid to remind them with another post as the date and time of your podcast gets closer!

✦ **Tweet it.** Twitter is a great place to hype your podcast, and your Twitter followers might just retweet your podcast post for you!

✦ **Talk about it on Facebook, LinkedIn, and other social networking sites.** Mention your podcast on all your social networking profiles. Don't forget to create a Facebook fan page for your podcast, too! And if you use a Web site such as BlogTalkRadio or Blubrry to host and publish your podcasts, be sure to get involved in the social communities on those sites, too!

✦ **Share it on social bookmarking sites.** Share your promotional podcast post on Digg (www.digg.com), StumbleUpon (www.stumbleupon.com), Reddit (www.reddit.com), and any other social bookmarking sites you use.

✦ **License your podcasts for syndication.** License your podcast content for syndication through a company such as Newstex (www.newstex.com) to get it in front of professional audiences.

✦ **Hype it in your newsletter.** If you send a newsletter to your blog subscribers or another audience, be sure to mention your podcast!

✦ **Link to it in your e-mail signature, forum signatures, and so on.** Include a link to your podcast with a blurb of promotional copy to generate interest and click-throughs in your e-mail signature, online forum signatures, and anywhere else you can think of. You can even publish the link offline on your business cards, ads, invoices, and so on.

✦ **Send an e-mail.** Use an e-mail service such as Constant Contact (www.constantcontact.com) or Emma (www.myemma.com) to create and send a newsletter to your e-mail address list that hypes your podcast.

Creating podcasts takes time, and your first attempts aren't likely to be perfect. Don't give up. Keep creating and publishing podcasts, and you'll get better and better at it. Continuously promote your podcasts, and your audience will continue to grow. As long as your podcast content is interesting, meaningful, and useful, and your voice and tone are entertaining, your podcast efforts are not for naught.

Chapter 7: Creating a Vlog

*O*nline video is growing in popularity by leaps and bounds, and adding video blog posts to your blog, called *vlogs* — a fusion of the words *video* and *blogs* — is an excellent way to enhance and extend your blog. Just as audio podcasts can help you grow your blog in new directions and attract new audiences, so can vlogging. Studies show the number of online videos increasing exponentially in the near future, and many people already spend as much or more time watching online video as they do reading online content.

However, jumping into the world of vlogging isn't something one should do without planning. It takes time and effort to create quality videos that people want to watch and share. This chapter helps you determine whether vlogging is right for you and shows you how to get started on a successful path as a vlogger. For more details about vlogging, read *Videoblogging For Dummies,* by Stephanie Cottrell Bryant.

Understanding Vlogs

Video blogs, or *vlogs,* are technically a form of podcasting, meaning they're serial broadcasts of online video content. However, in recent years, online video podcasts have come to be known simply as vlogs, and audio podcasts have come to be referred to as podcasts. Although there's still some overlap in reference, the two are separated more often these days than they are lumped together in the broader definition of podcasting. (Audio podcasts are discussed in Chapter 6 of this minibook.)

A vlog is not a standalone video uploaded to a video-sharing or -hosting site and republished within a blog post on your blog. A true vlog is identified as serial video broadcast. That means you need to publish videos serially for your video content to truly be considered a vlog. You can publish your vlog content daily, weekly, biweekly, or as often as fits your schedule and goals, as long as it's an ongoing effort. True vlogs include a media RSS feed, which people can subscribe to through sites such as iTunes or through video syndication providers such as Newstex.

Understanding why vlogs are popular

Vlogs have become increasingly popular as the availability of broadband, high-speed Internet connections has grown and as the technology for creating, uploading, and sharing online video has become more accessible. Today, uploading and viewing streaming video content is simple thanks to such Web sites as YouTube (www.youtube.com), the most popular online video site, and thanks to connection speeds that make watching online video seamless — just like watching television but with fewer commercials. The variety of online video content coupled with the on-demand nature of online video viewing makes it a convenient medium for just about anyone with high-speed Web access to enjoy. These days, people can even watch online video on their mobile phones!

Following are some popular vlogs, which you can use to get ideas for your own videos:

✦ **Wine Library TV:** http://tv.winelibrary.com

✦ **Daisy Whitney's New Media Minute:** http://newmediaminute.blip.tv

✦ **SBTV:** www.sbtv.com

✦ **Zack's Investment Research:** www.zacks.com/video

✦ **ProBlogger:** www.problogger.net/archives/category/video

The process of creating videos for the Web has become less overwhelming thanks to technological advancements. For example, Mac users can create videos with the microphone, camera, and software that come preinstalled with their computers. PC users can purchase an inexpensive webcam and digital microphone or a Flip Video camera for under $150 and start creating videos the same day. What was once an intimidating and expensive process is now so easy a child can do it — and if you search YouTube for video content, you can find many videos created and uploaded by kids!

Leveraging the video trend opportunity

With the number of online videos growing every day and the number of people watching those online videos and actively searching for online video content growing even faster, many bloggers understand the potential that vlogging presents to connect with new audiences and offer new content to their existing audiences.

Because bloggers can upload and share their vlog content through video sites such as YouTube, TubeMogul, and more (video Web sites are discussed in detail later in this chapter), their content is immediately available to a wider audience that might not find their blogs otherwise. Furthermore, by embedding their vlog content into their blog posts, vloggers have another way to tap into their audiences' senses through sight and hearing. Video also provides a new way to connect with your existing and potential audience in a way that written text cannot because it's an innately interactive medium.

As the demand for online video continues to grow, bloggers who enter the world of vlogging set themselves up to build an audience and benefit from the world of online video while it's still in its growth phase. It's a great opportunity for bloggers who are committed to continually creating meaningful, useful, and entertaining video content.

Determining Whether You Should Vlog

Before you dive into vlogging, take some time to consider your overall goals for your blog and building your online presence. Vloggers are exposed in ways that bloggers are not, simply because they appear on camera for the world to see and judge. You need to have a thick skin to be a blogger and a thicker skin to be a vlogger, because negative comments are inevitable. However, vlogging can also help you build your online presence and brand in ways that blogging alone cannot. Again, your long-term online goals are an important factor in determining whether or not you should vlog.

Furthermore, vlogging takes time. Not only do you need to determine what you're going to vlog about, but you need to record your video; possibly edit it; add introductions, closings and music if you're trying to create a professional video; save and compress it for the Web; upload it to a host or video-sharing site; name, tag, and describe your video; and promote it. That's a lot more steps than typing and publishing a blog post. However, the potential exposure vlogging offers bloggers is something they might not be able to get through written posts alone.

Ultimately, your decision to become a vlogger depends on three primary factors:

✦ Your comfort level in putting yourself and your thoughts on camera for the world to see.

✦ Your commitment to creating and uploading quality videos continually.

✦ Your desire to grow your online presence.

When you know how you feel about each of the above factors, your decision to enter the world of vlogging (or not) should be easier to make.

Finding the Equipment You Need

To create videos that you can upload to the Web, you need to have appropriate equipment. At the very least, you need a microphone and video camera that are compatible with your computer. If you hope to create quality, professional-looking videos, you also need video-editing software. Your goals for your vlog dictate the equipment you need.

Audio and video

The first thing you need to begin creating a video to publish online is a microphone and video camera that are compatible with your computer. Most Macs come with microphones and video cameras built in, so if you're recording your video directly from your Mac, you can try using the built-in microphone and testing the quality. If you don't have a Mac or want to create a higher-quality video, you can purchase a webcam or a digital video camera such as the popular Flip Video Camera, which is inexpensive, very portable, and easy to connect to your computer (Mac or PC) to upload your videos. For the highest-quality videos, you should invest in better microphones (one for each participant in the video) and a higher-quality video camera that allows you to record in high-definition.

Editing software

If you want to be able to add music, transitions, an introduction and closing to your video, or if you simply want to delete mistakes, you need to use video-editing software. For example, Mac users can use iMovie, which comes preinstalled on newer Macs, and Windows users can download Microsoft's free Movie Maker software at www.download.live.com/moviemaker. For more advanced video editing, software companies such as Adobe, Corel, and Sony make packaged programs with higher price tags.

Planning and Creating a Vlog

When you have your equipment ready, you can put together your plan to record your first video. That's right — it's important to create a vlogging strategy and plan before you get started as a vlogger. The following sections provide an overview of the process you can follow to enter the online video-publishing world.

Picking a topic

If you're vlogging to extend your blog audience or to enhance your blog content for your existing audience, your video topics should relate to your overall blog topic. The two should coexist and work together to market your overall Web presence. Of course, if your vlogging efforts are unrelated to your blog, you can choose any topic for your videos that you want, but if your goal is to create an integrated marketing plan through your online content, your strategy should be one of consistent branding. With that in mind, your vlog should mirror and enhance your blog in terms of content and tone and vice versa.

Planning the video

Don't just pick up your video camera and start recording. Chances are good that the result won't be as professional or high-quality as your potential audience would like. Instead, take the time to structure your video, create a loose script or outline of what you'll do and say in the video, and stick to it. Determine whether your videos will include a consistent introduction, music, and closing, and pick the tone your videos will adhere to. In other words, decide whether your videos should be highly professional, educational, entertaining, or humorous, and then stay true to that voice. By setting expectations for your content with your audience, and then delivering on those expectations in every one of your videos, you can build audience loyalty.

Lighting considerations

Make sure the location for your video shoot has sufficient lighting and that the lighting is positioned correctly. For example, if the light source is behind the person in your video, the person's face will be shadowed and difficult to see in the video. Practice with your lighting in a test video to make sure it's adequate and translates well on a computer screen.

Setting up sound

Record your video in a quiet location or be certain that the microphone you're using is adequate to pick up the sound of your voice rather than background noise. No one wants to watch a video that's difficult to hear. Test your sound and listen to it on your computer before you record your final video.

Editing the video

Few videos are perfect without some editing, and this is particularly true for vlog content. If you want people to return to view your videos week after week (or whenever you publish them), you need to take the time to edit out mistakes and remove dead space or other problems. Also, adding a consistent introduction and closing that play in all of your videos can give your vlog a professional boost without a lot of effort. Videos from MediaBytes with Shelly Palmer offer a great example of a vlog with a professional and consistent introduction and closing. You can view those videos at `http://shellypalmer.blip.tv`.

Saving your video

When your video is done, you need to save it in a Web-friendly format (such as `.wmv` for Windows Media Viewer for Microsoft Windows, `.avi` for Windows, `.mov` for Mac, `.mp4` for iPod or Sony PSP, `.mpeg`, or `.3gp` for cell phones), and compress it to meet the restrictions of the site where you plan to upload it. Each video-publishing and -sharing site (several are discussed in detail later in this chapter) has different requirements and restrictions. Be sure to read all the requirements of the publishing and sharing site you plan to use to host your vlog so you compress and save your videos correctly.

Remembering laws and rules

Copyright and slander laws apply to vlog content just as they apply to blog and audio podcast content. Don't use a piece of music in your videos unless you own it or have permission to do so. Similarly, don't use photos or images in your videos unless you own them or have permission to do so. And just as you can't say defamatory comments in person or in your podcasts, you can't do so in your videos either, or you could be accused of slander, which is punishable by law. Always err on the side of caution to be safe.

You should also be sure to read all of the terms and conditions and user agreements for any sites that you upload and share your videos through. Most importantly, make certain that you retain all rights to your video content after you upload it to a video Web site.

Uploading and Sharing a Vlog

After your video is recorded, you need to get it online! That means you need to upload it to a host that provides a video player, which allows people to view it. The Internet offers many video-uploading and -sharing sites for you to choose from. Some of the uploading capabilities and requirements vary from site to site, but if you're truly looking to boost your audience and grow your online presence with your vlog, the best strategy is to ensure that your videos are available through multiple distribution points. The reason for this is simple: Online video search capabilities are disappointing at best.

There are *a lot* of videos online, and that means your videos face a lot of keyword competition. For maximum exposure, offering your vlog content through multiple sites and promoting it well are very important to your success. You can find out more about vlog promotion later in this chapter. Right now, take a look at some of the most popular video-uploading and -sharing sites discussed in the following sections.

The online video world is growing quickly. As such, online video sites are continually working to improve their capabilities. Make sure you take the time to research the current offerings and restrictions offered by the video sites you consider using to publish and share your vlog to ensure those sites meet your goals.

YouTube

www.youtube.com

YouTube is owned by Google, and it's the biggest and most popular online video uploading and sharing site by far. Statistics show that the vast majority of online video viewing is done on YouTube.

YouTube offers many advantages. It's easy use, and you can easily embed YouTube videos into your blog posts. YouTube offers media RSS feeds of your videos, allows tagging, and uses a video player that works very well. Figure 7-1 shows an example of a YouTube video page with tags and a description.

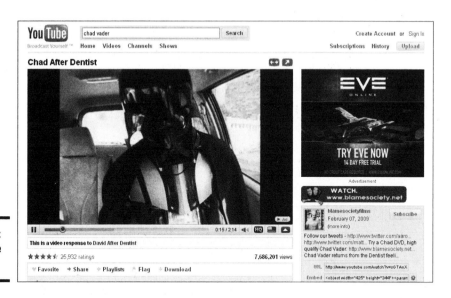

Figure 7-1: A YouTube video.

You can also create a branded YouTube channel, such as the one shown in Figure 7-2, to store all your videos, making it very easy to point people in the direction of your vlog archives.

Figure 7-2:
A YouTube
channel.

However, using YouTube also has some drawbacks. If you're relying on
the YouTube keyword search mechanism to drive traffic to your blog, you
might be disappointed. There are *a lot* of videos on YouTube, and many of
them are simply created for entertainment. That means your vlog has a lot
of search competition on YouTube. Furthermore, YouTube has uploading
restrictions that make it difficult to upload lengthy videos.

Regardless of the drawbacks, YouTube continues to be the go-to place for
online video.

Viddler

www.viddler.com

Viddler is a free video-uploading and -sharing site that even offers a way
for you to record your video via webcam directly to the site. The site offers
nearly unlimited storage space as well as RSS feeds and iTunes-sharing capabilities for extended distribution.

Viddler offers single video or batch video uploading, and you can customize
the Viddler video player to link to your blog, include comments, insert your
logo, change the colors, and more.

Unfortunately, you can't create a channel page on Viddler, but you create
a group where you can display your videos, as shown in Figure 7-3 for the
Wine Library TV group page.

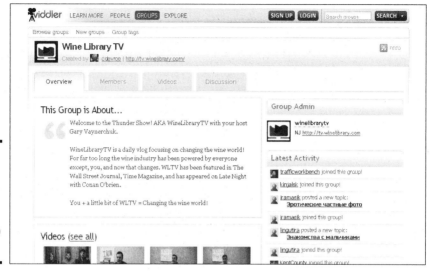

Figure 7-3:
The Wine
Library
TV group
page on the
Viddler Web
site.

You can also add tags and titles to your videos to make it easier for people
to find them in keyword searches. A sample video page is shown in
Figure 7-4.

Figure 7-4:
A video on
Viddler.

Vimeo

`www.vimeo.com`

Vimeo is a bit different from other video-uploading and -sharing sites because it was created by filmmakers as a place to share original, creative videos. That means there are strict uploading guidelines that prohibit any commercial videos. Also, you can upload only videos that you participated in creating, and there are advertising restrictions as well.

These restrictions might rule out Vimeo as a source for publishing your vlog, but for the right vlogger, it could be the ideal place to share his or her content. You can find complete and current Vimeo upload guidelines at `http://vimeo.com/guidelines`. Take the time to read them to ensure Vimeo offers the capabilities you need before you start uploading content to the site.

On the positive side, Vimeo offers video channels (a sample is shown in Figure 7-5) and a customizable video player as part of a free account. Furthermore, there is an upgrade Plus account that Vimeo users can pay a fee to access, and it offers higher-quality video, more storage space, additional video player customization, and the ability to create multiple channels.

Figure 7-5:
The White House channel on Vimeo.

Dailymotion

www.dailymotion.com

Dailymotion, allows users to upload and share videos for free. You can add titles and tags to make it easier for people to find your videos in keyword searches, and you can upload high-definition videos, too.

You can also create a user page (see a sample Dailymotion user page in Figure 7-6) to promote your videos, and you can even customize the video player colors and features when you embed Dailymotion videos into your blog posts.

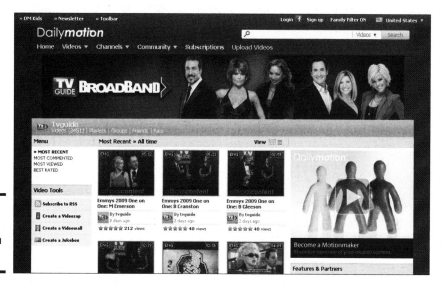

Figure 7-6:
TV Guide's Dailymotion user page.

Some of the biggest user complaints about Dailymotion are the intrusive ads found on the site and the cumbersome search feature that can make it difficult for smaller video publishers' content to be discovered.

blip.tv

www.blip.tv

blip.tv is unique in that it promotes its site as an online destination for people to start their own online television programs. On blip.tv, your series of videos, which you call a vlog, is referred to as a *show*.

blip.tv offers both free and paid accounts. Both make it easy to upload your videos, share them, and embed them using the blip.tv video player in your blog posts. However, the paid account offers a feature that may potentially be important to your vlog distribution and promotion efforts in the future, such as the ability to make iPod and MP3 versions of your uploaded videos automatically, which you can upload to iTunes and distribute through other syndication methods easily. If changing the format of your videos and creating media RSS feeds is something you don't want to tackle, but you want your videos available on iTunes and through other syndication outlets, then you might want to consider the paid version of blip.tv.

blip.tv offers a useful Learning Center that walks users through how to create, upload, distribute, share, and promote their videos, which you can access at `www.blip.tv/learning`.

When you upload videos to blip.tv, you can add titles, descriptions, and tags to make it easier for people to find your content through keyword searches, and all blip.tv users get a show page. A sample show page is shown in Figure 7-7. Additionally, your uploaded videos could be distributed to a variety of sites in the blip.tv distribution network, including YouTube, Vimeo, and more.

Figure 7-7:
A blip.tv
show page.

TubeMogul

`www.tubemogul.com`

TubeMogul, shown in Figure 7-8, is a newer player in the online video-uploading and -sharing world, but the site offers a number of advantages that other sites do not. TubeMogul is not a site that hosts and plays your videos, but rather you can distribute your videos to multiple publishing sites through TubeMogul.

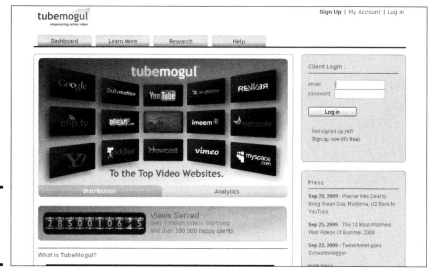

Figure 7-8:
The
TubeMogul
home page.

First, TubeMogul distributes your videos to multiple sites when you upload it. With one upload, your video is distributed to sites such as YouTube, Viddler, Dailymotion, blip.tv, Break.com, and more. TubeMogul also offers video analytics to track the performance of your vlog, and you get unlimited storage.

However, there are tiered use packages for TubeMogul users, which limit the number of video distributions, type of analytics, and other features you can access. The free package is adequate for beginners, but if you're very serious about distributing and analyzing your vlog content, be sure to check the current prices and packages available to you on the TubeMogul Web site.

Promoting Your Vlog

With so many online videos available, it can be very difficult to acquire search traffic to your vlog content. Although it's essential that you take the time to name, describe, and tag your online videos when you upload them in an attempt to attract search traffic, it's equally or more important to promote your videos in every way that you can. Following are a number of suggestions to help you promote your online videos:

✦ **Blog about it:** Before your new video is published, write a blog post telling your blog readers what they can expect in your upcoming video.

✦ **Embed your video in a blog post:** After your video is published, embed it into a new post on your blog.

✦ **Include your vlog content in your blog's sidebar:** Most blogging applications provide easy ways to add a widget or gadget to your blog's sidebar where you can republish your vlog content.

✦ **Tweet about it:** Hype your upcoming videos on Twitter, and post the link to your new videos on Twitter when they're published.

✦ **Mention it on social networking sites:** Share the link to your new vlog content on Facebook, LinkedIn, and other social networking sites that you belong to. Create a Facebook Fan Page or Group to further promote your vlog.

✦ **Add your content to social bookmarking sites:** Submit the link to your new vlog content on Digg (`www.digg.com`), StumbleUpon (`www.stumbleupon.com`), Reddit (`www.reddit.com`), and any other social bookmarking sites that you use.

✦ **Send e-mails:** Use a service such as Constant Contact (`www.constantcontact.com`) or Emma (`www.myemma.com`) to send a professional e-mail to your e-mail address list with a link to your new vlog content.

✦ **Place online ads:** A great way to promote your vlog is to purchase ad space on blogs that cater to a similar audience as your target audience. You can also try to barter an ad exchange with those blogs.

✦ **Pursue multiple distribution opportunities:** Upload your vlog to iTunes, publish your videos on multiple video sites (or use a site like TubeMogul to broaden your online video distribution), participate in licensed video syndication with a company like Newstex, and so on. The more places people can find your video content, the more exposure it gets and the more your audience can grow.

✦ **Promote it anywhere and everywhere:** Include the link to your vlog on your business cards, in your e-mail and online forum signatures, on your invoices, and anywhere else you can think of.

If you create great video content consistently and continually, your audience will grow in time. Just don't give up too soon.

Book VI

Promoting and
Growing Your Blog

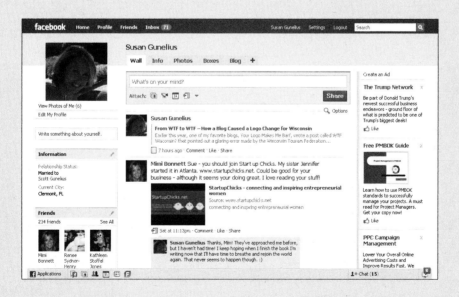

Contents at a Glance

Chapter 1: Secrets to Blogging Success

In This Chapter

✔ Writing well and often

✔ Link building and link baiting for traffic

✔ Using Google Trends

✔ Committing time to your blog's success

✔ Building community

✔ Realizing the importance of patience

Taking your blog from launch to success is a process not unlike growing a plant from seed to flower. It takes time, focus, and patience to build a successful blog. Without the necessary commitment in all of those areas, your blog can only grow so far. Just like you must water and nurture a plant, modifying its food and sun intake to ensure it thrives, you must nurture your blog with great content, promotion, and discussions in order for it to grow and thrive.

Blogging success comes directly from the time you spend *on* your blog as well as the time you spend *off* of your blog, meaning your blog needs great content but also continual promotional efforts by you to ensure that awareness, recognition, and repeat traffic follows. Blogging success depends on more than a site-centric marketing approach. This chapter introduces you to the fundamental secrets that position you for blogging success.

Writing Well

The best bloggers write well. Does that mean you need to be a professional writer or hold an advanced degree in writing or literature to become a successful blogger? Absolutely not! In fact, the vast majority of popular bloggers are not trained writers. However, they do have several traits in common that are vital to a blog's success, too:

✦ **Grammar knowledge:** To be a successful blogger, you need to know how to structure sentences. Does your grammar have to be perfect? No. But you do need to be able to use a grammar checker within your word-processing software or purchase a grammar text book to help you learn the rules.

✦ **Ability to spell or use spell check:** *Don't* be ashamed if you can't spell well. That's common. *Do* be ashamed if you don't take the time to consult a dictionary and use spell check to ensure your blog posts are free of spelling errors.

✦ **Succinct style:** Blog posts are traditionally short. It's difficult to read long text online, so bloggers who are capable of writing succinctly without sacrificing their messages have an advantage over long-winded bloggers. Try to keep your blog posts under 800 words and delete extraneous words and phrases that don't help make your point or move the post along. If readers get bored, they'll click away. If you want to write a long post, consider splitting it up into a series of posts.

✦ **Clear communication:** Always edit your posts for clarity. A sentence might seem perfectly understandable to you as you're typing it, but it might make little or no sense to readers. Take a step back from your post and look at it from an unbiased perspective to ensure people will understand you without question.

✦ **Engaging style:** Your blog posts should be written in a style that engages your audience. Let your passion for your subject and your personality shine through your writing. That's what will draw readers in and make them feel like they know you, and that's how relationships and a community develop around your blog.

Always proofread your blog posts before you click the Publish button! Blog posts laden with spelling and grammatical errors do not retain an audience. (Of course, there are exceptions to every rule, so your content should always mirror the expectations of your intended audience.)

Writing Often

Popular blogs are updated frequently — often multiple times each day. The reason is simple. The more posts you publish on your blog, the more entry points there are for people to find your blog through links, keyword searches, and so on. The amount of new content you publish and when you publish it is dependent on your goals for your blog. The more great content you publish, the better chance your blog has of growing quickly.

However, the quality of your content cannot suffer due to an aggressive publishing schedule. It doesn't matter how many posts you publish per day if they're all terrible. No one will return to your blog if the content they find on their first visit isn't satisfactory, but if they find great content that has been published recently, they're likely to return.

Quality of posts trumps quantity of posts.

Following is a rough guideline to help you determine how frequently you should publish new content on your blog to reach your blogging goals:

✦ **Rapid growth:** For accelerated blog growth, publish new content on your blog at least three times per day. Allow at least two hours between publishing posts.

✦ **Moderate growth:** For moderate blog growth, publish new content on your blog at least one time per day.

✦ **Slow growth:** For slow blog growth, publish new content on your blog at least three times per week. Try to leave no more than two days in a row without publishing new content.

✦ **Very slow growth:** If blog growth is not important to you, feel free to publish content anytime you want.

Just because you publish great content on your blog doesn't mean it will grow. That's just the first step to creating a successful blog. You also need to spend time building your blog's community and promoting it. The remainder of this chapter provides the fundamentals you need to get started.

Building Links

One of the best ways to boost your blog traffic is through incoming links — links on other blogs and Web sites that lead *to* your blog. If you write great content on your blog, the commonly accepted theory is that other bloggers and Web site owners will want to talk about it and attribute your blog as the source for their own posts through links back to your original post.

Each incoming link to your blog from legitimate blogs and Web sites helps your Google search page ranking, meaning your blog can get more search traffic. At the same time, those links provide direct traffic to your blog from people who want to learn more about what you have to say.

Link baiting

Although generating incoming links is a goal of all bloggers who want to grow their blogs, there is another tactic called *link baiting* that works a bit differently. In short, link bait blog posts are typically written about hot, buzzworthy topics that people are actively searching for online. You can write a post on a hot topic in an attempt to not only drive short-term traffic from those searches but also to encourage other bloggers and Web site owners to link to your post.

Link baiting can be a great way to boost short-term traffic to your blog, but unless the subject of the post with the link bait is related to your blog's topic, the short-term traffic will disappear as soon as it arrives simply because it's unlikely the rest of the content on your blog will interest those visitors. Consider how well link bait posts fit into your overall blogging plan before you use them, particularly because they can dilute the overall experience on your blog for users who are confused by the inconsistency they can present.

Using Google Trends for short-term traffic boosts

Google Trends provides a great way to find current buzz-worthy topics to blog about. Just visit www.google.com/trends/hottrends, shown in Figure 1-1, to find a list of the top 20 keyword phrases people are searching for at any time. Use those keywords to write your own blog post in an attempt to attract some of that search traffic.

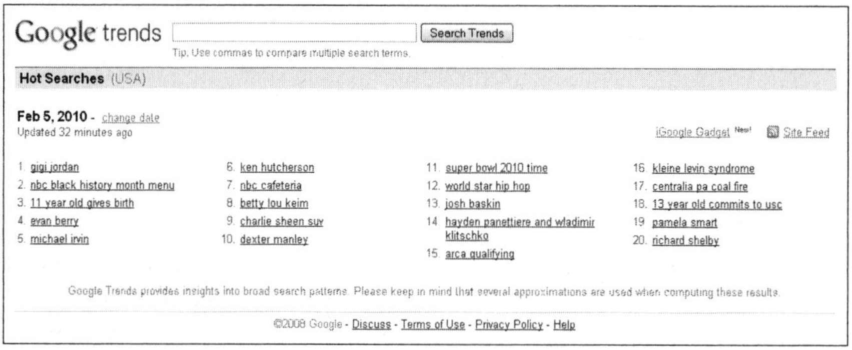

Google trends [   ] [Search Trends]
Tip: Use commas to compare multiple search terms.

Hot Searches (USA)

Feb 5, 2010 - change date
Updated 32 minutes ago

iGoogle Gadget New! Site Feed

1. gigi jordan
2. nbc black history month menu
3. 11 year old gives birth
4. evan berry
5. michael irvin

6. ken hutcherson
7. nbc cafeteria
8. betty lou keim
9. charlie sheen suv
10. dexter manley

11. super bowl 2010 time
12. world star hip hop
13. josh baskin
14. hayden panettiere and wladimir klitschko
15. arca qualifying

16. kleine levin syndrome
17. centralia pa coal fire
18. 13 year old commits to usc
19. pamela smart
20. richard shelby

Google Trends provides insights into broad search patterns. Please keep in mind that several approximations are used when computing these results.

©2008 Google - Discuss - Terms of Use - Privacy Policy - Help

Figure 1-1:
Pay a visit to Google Trends.

Using Twitter to find hot topics to blog about

Twitter offers another easy way to find buzz worthy topics to blog about in an attempt to boost short term traffic. Just visit www.twitter.com, shown in Figure 1-2, and take a look at the three rows of hot topics displayed beneath the search bar. They are

✦ **Popular topics right now:** These are popular topics Twitter users are actively tweeting about at any given moment.

✦ **Popular topics today:** These are popular topics Twitter users were tweeting about during the past 24 hours.

✦ **Popular topics this week:** These are popular topics Twitter users were tweeting about during the past seven days.

Figure 1-2:
Take a
look at the
popular
topics on
Twitter.

Click through links that interest you and relate to your blog topic to get a
better understanding of what is being said. If it's a good fit for your blog, you
can write a blog post using related keywords to try to capture some of that
active traffic.

Committing the Time

Building a successful blog takes a big time commitment. Although the monetary investment is nonexistent or at most negligible, the time commitment
is often more than bloggers bargained for when they joined the blogosphere.
Don't be misled. Creating content and promoting a blog in order to grow it
takes a lot of time, and you can't take a break or much of the results from the
work you did prior to your break will disappear.

Think realistically about how much time you have to invest in growing your
blog, and then develop a plan that not only helps you reach those goals but
also fits your schedule.

Having Passion

A boring blog and a bland blogger do not make a great blog. For your blog
to grow, you have to love your topic and let that passion show in everything
you do related to your blog. Make your passion for your subject contagious.
Readers will feel that passion and be moved by it in a way that makes them
want to return to your blog again and again.

It's your passion and personality that make your blog unique. Certainly, the
content you write is unique, but throughout your life as a blogger, you'll
learn that there are many, many bloggers out there who are likely to write
about the same topic that you write about. What sets you apart from all
those other bloggers is your unique perspective, voice, and passion.

Socializing

The most successful bloggers are usually very active in the online community. They're happy to respond to every comment left on their blog posts and every e-mail they receive, and they do so with a personal touch. Of course, time constraints might make that level of personal attention impossible for you, so the goal is to be as active and social on and off your blog as you can.

The best bloggers respond to, acknowledge, and validate their readers, making them feel important.

Not only should you be sure to respond to comments and e-mails on your blog, but you should also leave comments on other blogs related to your blog topic, join forums and social networking groups, start a Twitter profile, and more to become active across the social Web. You need to get to know people online just as you would offline to build a successful blog. That's how you build a community around your blog, and that community will ultimately include your most loyal readers who will discuss your blog, link to it, share your content, and more!

Reading More than Writing

The most successful bloggers read a lot. Not only do you have to read to get blog post ideas, but you should stay on top of what's going on in the world as it relates to your blog topic in order to respond to questions published through the comments on your blog or through e-mails to you.

Furthermore, you need to read all the comments and correspondence you get through your blog. The longer you blog, the more this correspondence will grow. Even owners of low-traffic blogs can get a lot of correspondence on a day-to-day basis. Successful bloggers get massive amounts of correspondence, which means they have to read a lot.

If you're not willing to read to find blog post ideas, build your blog community, improve your network, and continually learn about blogging *and* your blog topic, your blog will face limited growth potential.

Being Comfortable with Technology

You don't have to have a degree in computer science to be a successful blogger. You just need to be willing to learn. If you can use the Internet and a word-processing program, you can use common blogging applications such as WordPress, Blogger, and TypePad.

The best bloggers do more than simply the bare minimum with the technology that powers their blogs. They take time to learn some HTML and CSS, how to obtain and use a custom domain name, how to use a Web host to store and share their blogs, how to install add-ons and plug-ins to enhance their blogs, and more. Most bloggers don't know how to use any of these tools until they dive in and get started. In fact, most bloggers are self-taught when it comes to using the tools of the blogosphere.

With this book in your hand and some practice, you can get over any fears you have of technology and start testing new tools as your blog grows.

Having Patience

If patience is a virtue, then bloggers are very virtuous because blogging success requires *a lot* of patience. Blogging success also takes time. First, you need to build up a repository of great content. At the same time, you need to get involved in the online community of the social Web by joining the conversation and building relationships with other bloggers. Next, you need to promote your blog content and leverage many of the common blog promotional tactics to boost your blog traffic.

The remainder of this minibook provides many suggestions for how you can get started in growing your blog through promotion. None of the tactics require monetary investments, but they do require time commitments. Consider your own blogging goals as you read through this minibook and begin creating your own blog promotion plan.

Chapter 2: Building Community

The most successful blogs have a powerful community of readers who join the conversation on the blog, advocate the blog, protect the blog against incorrect critiques or negative publicity, and promote it. Building a community around your blog takes time and commitment, but if you can do it, your blog will grow exponentially at the hands of your loyal community.

The commenting feature inherent in blogs makes it a powerful tool for interaction and conversation. The Web that was once dominated by one-sided narrative and exposition turned into a two-way dialogue with active participants when Web 2.0, the social Web, evolved. Blogs are a place where like-minded people can share information, ask questions, and learn thanks to the commenting feature.

This chapter shows you how to leverage the comments feature both on and off your blog to grow your blog community. Your blog's success starts with great content followed by the loyal community of readers who are affected by that content and motivated enough by it to actively respond to it. Read on to find out how to spark the conversation and community on your blog.

Responding to Comments

If blog posts are the heart of a blog, then comments are the veins pumping blood to the heart. In short, they're the lifeline of a blog because the conversation that occurs on your blog is where a community develops. Conversations create relationships, which lead to loyalty. That means the comments left on your blog posts are extremely important, and you should treat them as such.

To be a successful blogger, you need to be accessible and responsive. That means you should respond to every comment left on your blog to acknowledge the commenters and attempt to engage them further. People need to feel valued when they take the time to read your posts and leave comments on those posts. Show them they matter to you by responding to them through the comment feature on your blog. Mention them by the names they provided in the blog comment form so they know your response is directed at them.

One of your most important jobs as a blogger is to create compelling content that motivates people to comment on that content. However, after they comment, you can't abandon them. Make your readers feel comfortable in expressing their thoughts and opinions on your blog, and the conversation will grow in time. Subsequently, a sense of community will evolve organically as you continue to keep the community entertained, interested, and comfortable.

It's okay to delete off-topic comments or redirect comments that stray off-topic. Read Chapter 4 of Book I to find out about creating a blog comment policy to set expectations for conversations on your blog.

Posting Comments on Other Blogs

Your efforts to build a community and grow your blog don't end when you log out of your blogging application. To truly be successful in your blogging efforts, you need to read more than you write, meaning you need to spend a lot of time reading posts on other blogs related to your blog topic, leaving comments on those posts, and networking with those bloggers and their readers.

Whenever you leave a comment on another blog, be sure to use the same keyword phrase in the Name field of the comment form and provide the URL to your blog in the URL field of the form. Doing so helps your search engine optimization and branding efforts.

When you leave comments on other blogs, make sure the comments you leave are insightful and truly add to the conversation. Don't be afraid to ask questions, respond to questions left by other readers, and engage the blogger or other readers. This is another form of networking that can help you establish yourself and your blog as a go-to place online for information about your blog's topic.

Avoid getting involved in comment wars, where two or more readers move from healthy debate to arguing through the comment feature on a blog post. Getting tangled up in such a comment war, especially if it becomes personal, could potentially damage your brand and your blog.

Handling Comment Moderation

A common question that beginner bloggers have is whether they should moderate the comments left on their blogs. Unfortunately, comment moderation is essential if you want to ensure the conversations on your blog are relevant and appropriate. Spam is more prevalent than ever, and even the best spam blockers let some spam comments get through and publish on blogs. The only way to ensure that spam and inappropriate comments aren't published on your blog, thereby negatively affecting the user experience on your blog, is to moderate them.

Book VI Chapter 2

Building Community

Most blogging applications offer customizable comment moderation settings, which you can configure to best suit your needs. The most effective setting is one that requires moderation only the first time a visitor leaves a comment on your blog. After a person has a comment approved on your blog, she can comment anytime in the future and her comments will publish instantly.

If your blogging application allows it, set up your comment moderation to mark comments with two or more links as spam automatically. This setting doesn't count the link provided in the URL field of the comment form as one of the two links, so readers can leave two additional links within their comment before it is identified as spam. As an example, Figure 2-1 shows the comment moderation settings page in a WordPress.org account dashboard.

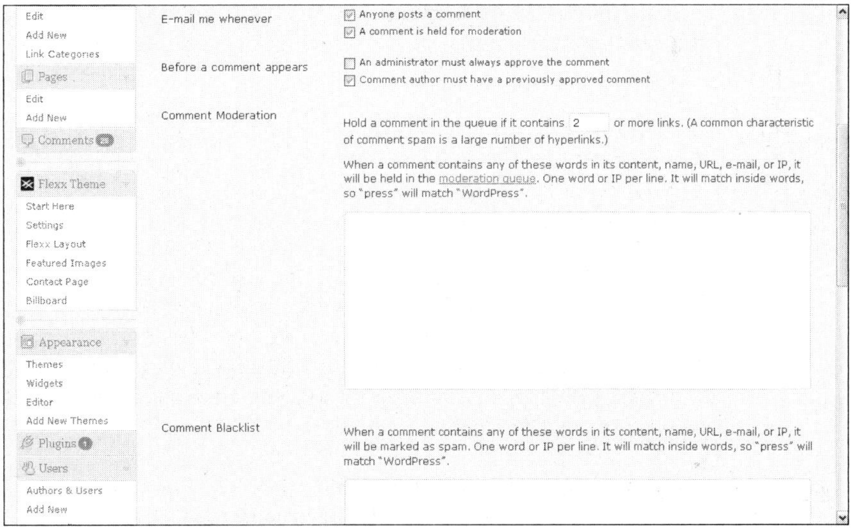

Figure 2-1: The WordPress comment moderation settings.

Similarly, you may be able to block comments from specific IP addresses or comments that include specific words, depending on the blogging application and comment spam blocker you use. Most spam blockers catch comments with profanity and other common spam words, but if you see comments with words you want to block coming through for you to moderate, add those words as words to block within your comment spam settings.

The bottom-line is that spam, inappropriate comments, and irrelevant comments can offend your readers and disrupt the experience on your blog. In the early days of your blog, your moderation queue is likely to be manageable. As your blog grows and you receive more comments to moderate, you can reevaluate your comment moderation settings and adjust them as necessary.

Linking and Creating Trackbacks and Backlinks

Including links within your blog posts to other blogs is a great way to get on the radar screens of those bloggers and drive traffic to your own blog through the trackback or backlink functions offered in some blogging applications.

For example, if you use WordPress, TypePad, or Movable Type as your blogging application, you can use the trackback function incorporated into your blog post editor to provide the URL where you want to send a virtual shoulder tap, which lets another blogger know that you linked to his or her content within your blog post. Your link appears within their blogging application dashboard as well as on the post page for the URL you tracked back to. Readers of that blog can see the link to your blog and follow it to read more from you.

You can see how incoming links look on a WordPress account dashboard in Figure 2-2.

Trackbacks are automatically sent between WordPress blogs without the blogger taking any additional steps.

Trackbacks left on TypePad blog posts are easy to identify and follow as shown in Figure 2-3.

Alternatively, if you use Blogger, a backlink is automatically sent to other Blogger-hosted blogs that you link to within your blog posts. Backlinks display above the comments section in a Blogger blog post, as shown in Figure 2-4. The feature is more limited for Blogger users, but it does help generate some traffic and awareness of your blog.

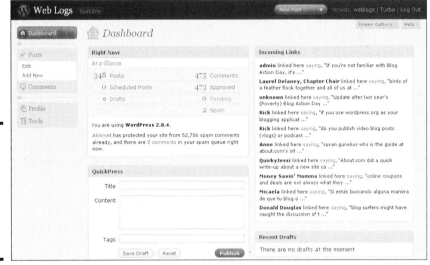

Figure 2-2: Incoming links displayed on a WordPress account dashboard.

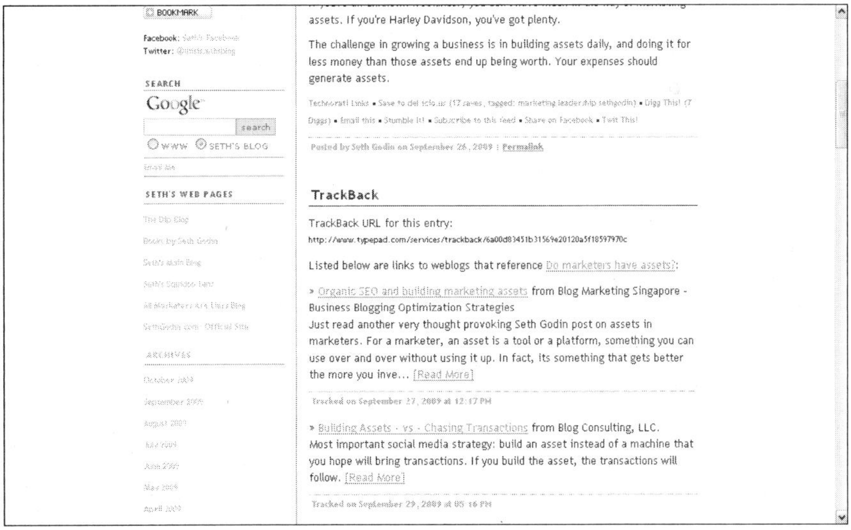

Book VI Chapter 2

Building Community

Figure 2-3: Trackbacks on a TypePad blog post.

Figure 2-4:
Backlinks
on a
Blogger
post.

Inviting Guest Bloggers

Opening your blog up to guest bloggers is a great way to build the community around your blog because it can make readers feel valued when you allow them to participate in this seemingly formal way. Sometimes a guest blogger's post can spark a new conversation and breathe new life into a blog, too. You can find out more about guest blogging in Chapter 5 of this minibook.

Going on Beyond the Blogosphere

Community building can be done outside of the blogosphere in a variety of ways. Don't be afraid to get creative in your efforts to connect with people, network, and build relationships across the social Web. For example, you can join forums related to your blog's topic, Facebook groups, Google Groups, and answer questions on LinkedIn.

You can also think outside of the box and build your online presence in an effort to reach out to a broader audience. For example, you can create video content or podcasts for sharing on YouTube.com and iTunes, or you can upload presentations or images to SlideShare.net, Flickr.com, or Picasa.com. Social sharing sites offer a great way to connect with more people than you can do on your blog alone. Always include a link back to your blog and mention it when you can without sounding overly promotional, and your blog audience and community will grow.

Chapter 3: Social Networking

In This Chapter

- ✔ Understanding social networking
- ✔ Finding social networking sites
- ✔ Using social networking to boost blog traffic
- ✔ Avoiding social networking don'ts
- ✔ Starting your own social network

The evolution of the Internet from a navigational tool to a transactional tool and eventually to a social tool has opened up the world of communication in ways no one expected. Through the social Web, people from across the globe can easily interact and share thoughts, news, photos, videos, and more at anytime. Like-minded people whose paths might never have crossed 20 years ago can now find each other on blogs, forums, and a variety of social sites.

Social networking is just one of the tools of the social Web that people from all walks of life have embraced, and it's an excellent tool to build relationships and grow your blog. This chapter explains what social networking is and how you can use social networking to drive traffic to your blog or even create your own social network.

Defining Social Networking

In simplest terms, social networking is networking done via the social Web. It's exactly like in-person networking, but instead of doing it face-to-face, you do it from the comfort of your own home through your computer. There are no barriers to entering the world of social networking. Anyone with a computer and a Web connection is invited to the party.

As the social nature of the Web evolved, innovative people saw an opportunity to provide online destinations for those interactions to take place. Thus, social networking Web sites were born. Today, various social networking sites allow you to register for an account, create a profile, interact with other members, share content, and develop relationships. Some sites even enable you to create your own social networking destination.

Any networking done online via the social Web is considered social networking, but there are also specific social networking Web sites that exist as central destinations for social networking activities between users. Facebook, LinkedIn, Orkut, Friendster, and MySpace are just a few examples of social networking Web sites, some of which are discussed in detail in this chapter.

Social networking can be a formal or informal activity. Unlike offline networking, which is typically associated with business networking, online social networking sites are open to formal and informal networking uses. Bloggers, business people, journalists, and more use social networking sites to promote products and services, provide customer service, and so on. At the same time, friends, families, and peers use social networking sites to converse, share personal stories and photos, and so on.

As the social Web grows, the world gets smaller and smaller. Friends and families that once had trouble communicating across long distances can now communicate in real time and share far more than just spoken words. Business people who once shared ideas through e-mail can now collaborate through social networking.

Finding Popular Social Networking Sites

There are many social networking Web sites, but some have grown more popular than others. Each offers slightly different capabilities, and some are preferred by niche users. For example, Orkut (`www.orkut.com`), which is owned by Google, is most popular in Brazil and India, whereas Friendster (`www.friendster.com`), which was once very popular in the United States, has lost market share in the western world and is now preferred in Southeast Asia.

There are even social networking sites dedicated to specific topics. For example, Classmates.com (`www.classmates.com`) is popular among people looking to reconnect with classmates. There truly is a place for everyone on the social Web!

By far the most popular social networking sites are Facebook, LinkedIn, and MySpace. Each offers slightly different features and appeals to a slightly different audience. In recent years, many people have shifted from MySpace and LinkedIn to focus more heavily on Facebook, which has grown significantly both in the number of users and the capabilities the site offers.

Facebook

www.facebook.com

Facebook is the most popular social networking site, with approximately 300 million users. The site is known for providing a wide variety of features as well as an onsite advertising mechanism. You can create a personal profile, brand page (your blog could be your brand), business page, organization page, or celebrity page, as well as groups through your Facebook account.

Additionally, you can upload photos and videos and update your *wall* (shown in Figure 3-1) with short posts, similar to the way microblogging updates via a site like Twitter (discussed in Book VIII) work. Other users can leave comments on your wall posts, and those comments can include pictures, videos, and so on. You can also send private messages to other users.

Figure 3-1:
A Facebook user's wall.

However, you can't interact with other users on Facebook until you connect with them by sending a *friend* request, which the other person can either accept or decline. That's because Facebook is a closed site, meaning you can only view other users' profiles if you're a registered member. If a member chooses to hide their profile, you cannot view it unless you *friend* that person via Facebook first. If your friend request is accepted, you can view that person's profile, pictures, posts, and more.

To create your own profile in Facebook, simply visit www.facebook.com (shown in Figure 3-2) and begin the sign up process. It's free, and you probably already know a lot of people on Facebook!

When your account is active, take some time to create a complete profile and then start searching for people you know on Facebook. When you find someone you know, send him or her a friend request and start sharing, conversing, and networking via the social Web!

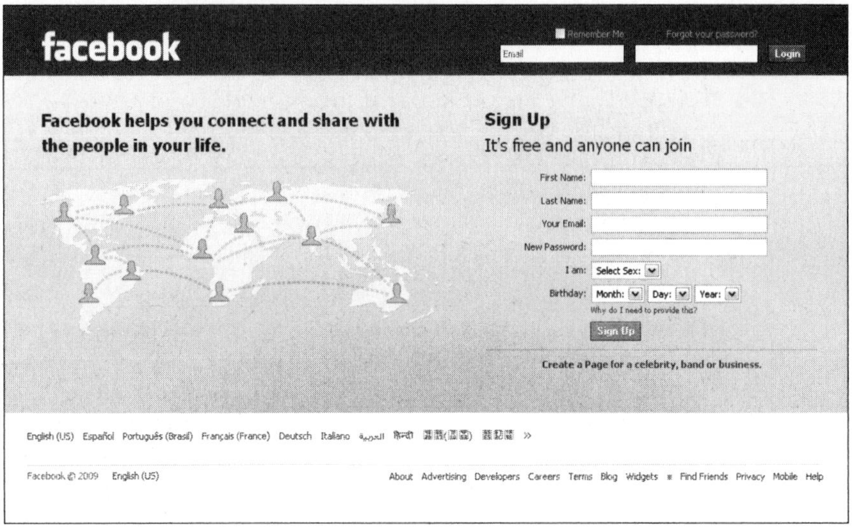

facebook

Facebook helps you connect and share with
the people in your life.

Sign Up
It's free and anyone can join

First Name:
Last Name:
Your Email:
New Password:
I am: Select Sex:
Birthday: Month: Day: Year:
Why do I need to provide this?
Sign Up

Create a Page for a celebrity, band or business.

English (US) Español Português (Brasil) Français (France) Deutsch Italiano العربية हिन्दी 简体中文 繁體中文 »

Facebook © 2009   English (US)

About Advertising Developers Careers Terms Blog Widgets ▪ Find Friends Privacy Mobile Help

Figure 3-2:
The
Facebook
home page.

You can find out more about Facebook in the book *Facebook For Dummies,*
by Leah Perlman and Carolyn Abra.

Reaping the benefits of Facebook

Facebook is a great social networking tool because so many people use it.
Of course, the sheer volume of users can also be a negative because you
can get lost in the clutter. However, you can find a lot of people to meet and
build relationships with on Facebook.

Facebook is active. That means a lot of users are regularly updating their
profiles, sharing photos and videos, posting information, and sharing links
and comments on their own walls and other users' walls. Unlike other
social networking sites where people create a profile and then abandon it,
Facebook users are engaged. That's exactly the atmosphere you need to promote your blog! I explain more about that in the following section.

Facebook also makes it easy to find people who might be interested in the
same topics that you care about (like your blog topic). Simply search for
groups and fan pages that interest you and join those that are open to the
general Facebook user population.

Using Facebook to promote your blog

Facebook is an excellent social networking site to leverage for blog promotion. Although you should refrain from flooding the Facebook community
with promotional information, there's no reason why you can't provide links
to your blog posts or mention your successes, particularly if you do so on

relevant group or fan pages; within your wall posts, where your friends are likely to appreciate and possibly share them; and so on.

Following are suggestions for using Facebook to promote your blog:

✦ **Status updates:** Post status updates to your wall that mention your new blog posts and include links to those posts. You can also publish requests for guest posts. Don't be afraid to get creative!

✦ **Making friends:** Send friend requests to other bloggers and people you want to connect with who can help you promote your blog in the future.

✦ **Adding your blog feed:** You can import your blog's feed by using the Notes application in Facebook, so every time you publish a new blog post, the title, a snippet, and a link to the post automatically publishes as a note on your Facebook wall for all your friends to see and follow. Simply log in to your Facebook account and open your Facebook profile page. Along the top of our profile is a series of tabs where you can view your Wall, Info, Photos, and more. You can add a Blog tab by selecting the + sign to the right of your existing tabs and selecting the Blog tab from the list. (You can search for the tab in the search text box if it does not automatically display in the list of available tabs.) After the Blog tab is added, just follow the steps provided to add your blog to the tab.

✦ **Creating a Facebook page:** Although Facebook profiles are intended to be a place for individuals to create a presence on Facebook, Facebook pages are intended to represent a business, brand, or celebrity. They're meant to give those businesses, brands, and celebrities a presence on Facebook. Facebook pages are a great way to provide information, links, photos, videos, and more related to your blog and build a separate community around your blog's topic. You can also join Facebook pages related to your blog that are created by other people, and then get involved by adding content to those pages and joining the conversation. You can start Facebook page by logging into your Facebook profile and visiting `http://www.facebook.com/pages/create.php`.

✦ **Starting a group:** Facebook groups don't provide as many robust features as fan pages do, but they can be created for any reason. Facebook groups are meant to create a place where people can discuss and share information about a specific topic. They provide one more way you can connect with people and share information about your blog and related topics. You can either start your own Facebook group or join other groups related to your blog. You can create a Facebook group by logging in to your Facebook profile and visiting `www.facebook.com/groups/create.php`.

✦ **Advertising:** Facebook users can place ads that can be very targeted. The cost is minimal, but your ad needs to be compelling to encourage clicks. You can create your own Facebook ad by visiting `www.facebook.com/ads/create`. Sample Facebook ads are shown in the right sidebar of Figure 3-1.

Take the time to read your friends' wall posts and leave comments. Join groups and fan pages that interest you and start conversations that lead back to your Facebook profile and blog. Using Facebook is a 360-degree marketing strategy wherein all parts should work together and always lead people back to your profile or blog.

LinkedIn

www.linkedin.com

LinkedIn is a very popular social networking site, particularly among business people and people looking to further their careers. It's an excellent site for sharing professional knowledge and career development networking. Many companies actively seek new employees through LinkedIn, and many users find new careers through the networking they do on LinkedIn.

You can create a free LinkedIn account at www.linkedin.com, shown in Figure 3-3. Take the time to create a comprehensive profile. Next, start searching for people you know on LinkedIn and send *connection* requests to them. As your network grows, you'll find more and more people to connect with. You can update your LinkedIn profile with interesting information (such as links to your blog posts), join or create groups, and send private messages to other users.

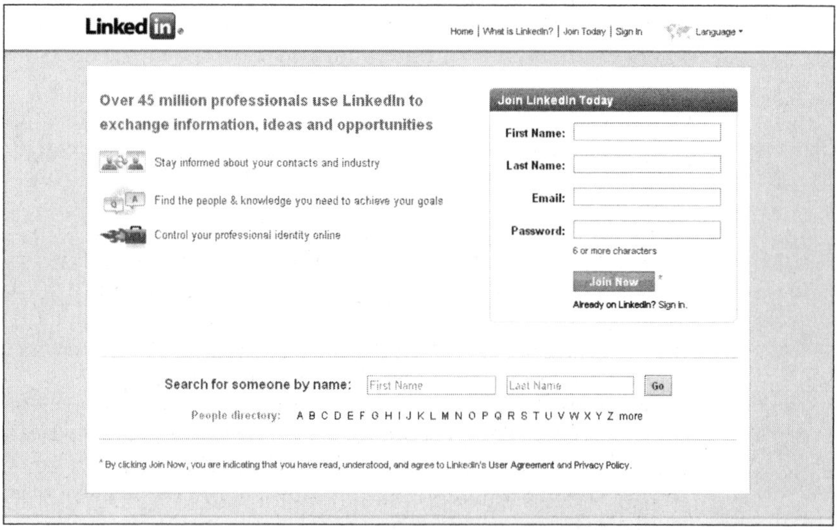

Figure 3-3: The LinkedIn home page.

LinkedIn is very much a closed social networking site. Unlike Facebook where users can send friend requests to anyone, LinkedIn users must identify a prior relationship with another user in order to send a connection request to that user. That means you must be able to identify a company you and the other person worked at together, the other person's e-mail address, or similar personally identifying information.

To find out more about LinkedIn, you can read *LinkedIn For Dummies,* by Joel Elad.

Looking at the benefits of LinkedIn

One of the primary benefits of LinkedIn is its focus. Because most users have some interest in business or career development, LinkedIn offers more opportunities than blog promotion. The networking you do on LinkedIn can open the doors to a lot more than added blog traffic. With that in mind, try to keep the content you publish on LinkedIn professional.

The LinkedIn user audience is made up primarily of adults, which means the site is fairly clear of the clutter that teenage audiences can create on social networking sites. That means the site has a bit more of a premium reputation without the price tag one might expect from a business networking site.

The majority of active LinkedIn members use the site for business networking and career development. If your blog and your social networking goals are not related to business or career development, then LinkedIn is probably not the site where you should invest a lot of your time promoting your blog. However, it's a popular social networking site that can open new doors to people who do use it.

Using LinkedIn to promote your blog

LinkedIn users typically network through the site in a more professional manner than most Facebook users do. With that behavior in mind, you need to adjust your blog promotional efforts on LinkedIn to match user expectations. Following are some suggestions to promote your blog on LinkedIn:

✦ **Making connections:** Search for people you know and then connect with them through LinkedIn. If you read a blog you enjoy, check to see whether the author provides a link to his LinkedIn profile somewhere on his blog. If so, send a connection request. Your LinkedIn connections can receive updates of your LinkedIn activities, which may include updates related to your blog, so the more quality connections you make, the better.

✦ **Answering questions:** The question-and-answer feature in LinkedIn is a wonderful indirect blog promotional tool. By answering questions related to your blog topic, you can mention your blog or specific posts and increase the awareness of your blog and traffic to it. To ask or answer questions on LinkedIn, log in to your LinkedIn profile and select the More link on the top navigation bar. Next, select the Answers link from the drop-down menu to access the Answers section of LinkedIn, where you can ask and answer questions, search for questions, and more.

✦ **Recommending people:** LinkedIn offers a recommendation tool that you can use to write recommendations for people you're connected with, which appear in their profiles. You can write a recommendation for someone and send a request asking her to write a recommendation for you in return. Keep in mind, you can send recommendation requests without making one for the other person, but the polite approach is to reciprocate. Positive recommendations boost your online reputation and credibility as the go-to source for information related to your blog topic or your area of expertise. You can recommend anyone that you are connected to on LinkedIn by visiting their profiles and selecting the Recommend This Person link on the right side of the page.

✦ **Starting a group:** LinkedIn groups provide a great way for people with similar interests to further discuss and share information about a specific topic. You can create a LinkedIn group about your blog topic where you can share links to your blog and develop another online community that should transfer seamlessly into blog traffic. To start a group on LinkedIn, log in to your LinkedIn profile and select the Groups link in the top navigation bar. Next, select the Create a Group link from the drop-down menu and follow the instructions provided. You can also find and join existing groups using the Groups Directory link from the Groups drop-down menu on the top navigation bar.

MySpace

`www.myspace.com`

MySpace was one of the earliest and most popular social networking sites. Although its popularity has waned in recent years as more and more users migrate to Facebook, MySpace retains a large audience and offers another effective way to promote your blog.

MySpace works a bit differently from the sites that have become social networking standards, such as Facebook and LinkedIn. For example, MySpace users can publish complete blog posts on their MySpace pages. Furthermore, MySpace profiles can be public, unlike LinkedIn and Facebook where profiles are closed.

Over the years, MySpace developed a reputation of being *the* site for teenagers, but more and more teens are shifting to Facebook. That means

MySpace, owned by News Corp., had to proactively shift its brand position to remain competitive in the long term. Today, MySpace is reinventing itself as the social networking site for bands, performers, and artists. That doesn't mean the site is closed to other types of people. On the contrary, the site remains free to use and open to anyone.

MySpace still has a reputation of being a social site for teenagers. If your blog is highly professional, you might want to use a social networking site such as LinkedIn instead of MySpace.

You can find out more about MySpace in *MySpace for Dummies,* by Ryan Hupfer, Mitch Maxson, and Ryan Williams.

Checking out the benefits of MySpace

One of the top benefits of MySpace is its open community. The content you publish on MySpace can be viewed by anyone (unless you set your profile as private), which extends its reach significantly. Because you can publish more than snippets of information through MySpace blog posts, you can share far more information.

MySpace profiles are also highly customizable. You can easily link your profile to an online store, your blog, and so on. Additionally, you can use a customized MySpace layout complete with your branded images, designs, and colors. In other words, MySpace provides another way you can further communicate and drive awareness of your online brand.

There's also a MySpace Latino site at `http://latino.myspace.com`.

MySpace even offers groups and forums where you can network beyond your official MySpace page. You can share videos, photos and more through MySpace, too.

To get started with MySpace, just visit `www.myspace.com`, shown in Figure 3-4, and click the Sign Up button to create your free account.

Using MySpace to promote your blog

MySpace offers another online destination where you can spread the word about your blog. The more places you can get the word out, the better. Following are suggestions for using MySpace to promote your blog:

✦ **Creating a profile:** Take the time to create a comprehensive profile, so people know who you are, where to find your blog, and so on.

✦ **Adding content:** Create MySpace blog posts that enhance your existing blog, link to posts in your existing blog, and promote your existing blog. Also, add photos or videos to further enhance your existing blog and be sure to direct visitors to your existing blog for more information.

✦ **Making friends:** Find people you know or want to connect with on MySpace and send friend requests. MySpace is open, so you can send requests to any other user.

✦ **Engaging users:** Begin leaving comments on other MySpace users' blog posts and build relationships with them. Chances are good that they'll reciprocate, and they're likely to want to read more from you. Also, join groups and actively participate. Building relationships through MySpace is critical to using it as a blog promotional tool.

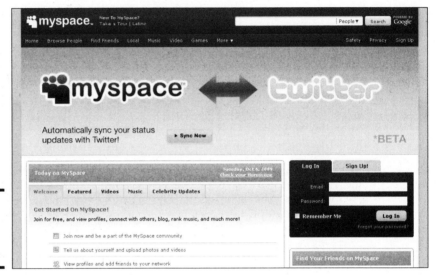

Figure 3-4: The MySpace home page.

Your MySpace page should be a teaser for your blog. However, avoid making your MySpace page completely promotional or there's no reason for anyone to bother visiting it.

Starting Your Own Social Network with Ning

Ning is a unique social networking Web site that enables you to create your own social network related to your likes, interests, business, blog, or any other topic you want. You can register to use Ning for free at www.ning. com, as shown in Figure 3-5. After you're registered, you can either join Ning networks that other users have already created or you can create your own social network within minutes.

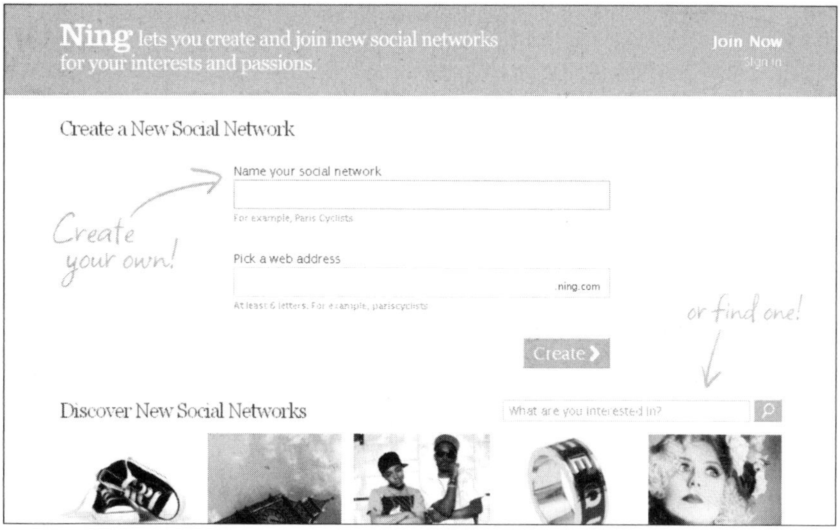

Figure 3-5:
The Ning
home page.

When you create your own Ning social network, you can customize it by
using one of the dozens of free themes available and then change the colors
and features to match your brand. You can add photos, videos, chats,
groups, and more to enhance the user experience on your Ning social network. Furthermore, Ning social networks are search engine optimized and
indexed by Google and other search engines. A Ning network tied closely to
your blog can drive a variety of traffic to your blog through both your networking efforts and organic search traffic. Figure 3-6 shows a sample Ning
social network created by a user.

Keep in mind, creating your own social network takes time and commitment.
Often beginner bloggers start with building social networks through existing
communities on Facebook, LinkedIn, and MySpace before investing the time
and energy into creating and maintaining their own social network on a Web
site such as Ning. The choice is yours. You can find out more about Ning in
the book *Ning For Dummies,* by Manny Hernandez.

Social networking provides an excellent opportunity for you to create
an integrated marketing plan for your blog where all of your efforts work
together cohesively. Using the various tools of the social Web, you can
directly and indirectly promote your blog without spending a penny.

Figure 3-6:
A user-created Ning social network.

Using Social Networking Sites to Boost Blog Traffic

Social networking is a long-term blog growth strategy, but it is possible to get direct bursts of traffic from your efforts. In general, social networking helps your blog growth strategy in three ways:

✦ **Raising awareness:** Social networking could be called free awareness advertising. Just publish announcements or links to your blog and your blog is on the radar screen of all your social networking connections.

✦ **Relationship building:** The time you spend interacting on social networking sites is incredibly valuable. Strong relationships lead to loyalty and future opportunities.

✦ **Generating buzz:** If you publish a link to one of your blog posts that is particularly interesting, timely, or helpful, you're likely to see a bump in traffic.

Social networking is just one tool in your blog marketing toolbox, and it's a long-term strategy. Don't rely on it entirely, or you'll be disappointed in your results.

Avoiding Social Networking Don'ts

As with all online activities, some things you just shouldn't do if you want to remain a welcomed member of the online community. These don'ts range from ethical to legal considerations, and you need to be aware of them and follow them at all times. Think of it this way: If you socialize with another person in public, there are rules of etiquette that you follow, and the same is true of online social networking.

Read and adhere to the terms and conditions and user agreements (if available) for any social networking sites that you join.

Following are several social networking don'ts that apply to all online social networking sites and activities:

**Book VI
Chapter 3**

Social Networking

- ✦ **Don't be 100% promotional.** No one is going to want to read your updates and content if they are entirely promotional. Don't just publish link after link to your blog on your social networking profiles. It's perfectly acceptable to promote your new blog content, but be sure to publish far more nonpromotional content than promotional content on your social networking profiles.

- ✦ **Don't be nasty.** Remember your manners. Don't get involved in online arguments or publish negative comments. Be diplomatic and remember that a lot of people can see what you publish in your social networking activities. Also, keep in mind that content lives online for a long, long time.

- ✦ **Don't spam anyone.** Spam is the kiss of death for social networking. Don't send spam links or participate in spam activities of any kind.

- ✦ **Don't be deceptive.** The social Web community is large, but chances are good that if you lie, you'll get caught. Be honest and stay out of trouble.

- ✦ **Don't forget the law.** Copyright laws apply in your social networking activities just as they do in your blogging activities. Do not copy another person's work (written, video, or photo content) without permission and always attribute your sources.

Once you're identified as a spammer or person who acts inappropriately, it can be hard to repair your online reputation. Don't give anyone a reason to speak negatively about you and tarnish your brand or your blog's brand.

Chapter 4: Social Bookmarking

Social bookmarking is a tool of the social Web that anyone can use to share online content with people around the world. For bloggers, social bookmarking provides another way to spread the word about the amazing content they publish. Various social bookmarking sites are available, and this chapter helps you find them and use some of the most popular options they provide.

Additionally, this chapter tells you about some of the biggest social bookmarking don'ts, and there are several of them. Social bookmarking users feel strongly about their unwritten rules, and you need to be aware of them *and* follow them. Don't get nervous. They're easy to follow, and if you use common sense, you should do just fine.

Getting to Know Social Bookmarking

Social bookmarking is the process of sharing Web pages that you like through the social Web. You sign up for an account with a social bookmarking Web site, and then you provide the URL and other requested information to submit a page that you like to the site. Your submitted page is then shared with all other site users.

Social bookmarking works the same way that bookmarking Web pages through your desktop browser works, but instead of saving your bookmarked Web pages to your computer's memory, you save them online. Additionally, you can make them available for anyone to see. Some social bookmarking site submissions are even indexed by Google, which helps drive search traffic to the submission, and ultimately, to the corresponding Web page.

The Web pages you submit through social bookmarking sites are not only shared with the online world, but also, other registered users of those sites can typically comment on your submissions, rate your submissions, and more. That's how social bookmarking moves from sharing to interactivity.

Most social bookmarking sites are set up so saved links are automatically included in keyword searches that users can perform onsite. For example, you might be able to include keyword tags with your URL submission, and those tags help other users find your submitted content.

Finding Popular Social Bookmarking Sites

Many social bookmarking sites are available, and each follows the same basic rules and processes. However, depending on your blog's topic, you might find that some social bookmarking sites drive more traffic to your blog than others. The key to success is testing several sites and tracking the results using your blog analytics tool (discussed in Chapter 2 of Book V).

Some social bookmarking sites cater to highly niche topics and audiences, but others appeal to much broader audiences and a wide variety of content sharing. So, when looking into a social bookmarking site, find out whether it's specialized and what that specialization is. For example, a social bookmarking tool such as Sphinn (`www.sphinn.com`) is dedicated to sharing content about online marketing, whereas Kirtsy (`www.kirtsy.com`) has a strong female audience.

The following sections focus on some of the most popular social bookmarking sites. Keep in mind that there are positives and negatives to submitting your content to well-trafficked social bookmarking sites. Your content can easily get lost in the clutter because so many links are submitted every day. However, if your content is noticed by many users of the social bookmarking site where you submit it, or if some of the top users take notice of your content, then their comments, ratings, and so on can drive a lot of traffic to your blog.

Don't expect a flood of traffic to come to your blog after you submit one of your post links to a social bookmarking site. Of course, you never know what might happen after you click the submit button!

Social bookmarking is another useful tool in your blog marketing toolbox that combined with your other promotional efforts, can work together to grow your blog over time.

Digg

`www.digg.com`

Digg is the most popular social bookmarking site, but it's actually considered to be more of a social news site than a social bookmarking site. That's because the site's purpose is to enable users to share links to content more so than for bookmarking content online for your personal use.

To share content on Digg, you need to set up a free account through the Digg home page shown in Figure 4-1. Just select the Join Digg link in the top navigation bar and provide the requested information to start using Digg right away.

You can submit content to Digg (or *digg* a link) by clicking the Submit link on the Digg site, and then entering the URL, description, and title for the content you're sharing into the submission form that opens, as shown in Figure 4-2. Digg searches your submission to ensure it's a new link to the site and then asks you to provide additional information such as keyword tags, a category for the link, and more. If the URL has already been submitted to Digg, you're given the option to digg it again.

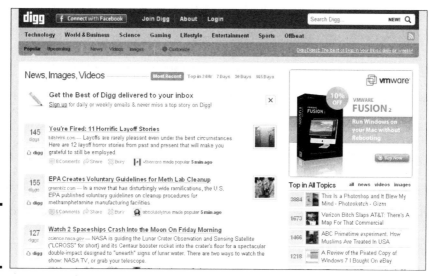

**Figure 4-1:
The Digg
home page.**

Each time a user diggs a submitted link, that link rises in popularity. Conversely, each time a user buries content, that link decreases in popularity. Digg users can find content by newness of the submission, popularity, or category. You can also search by keyword.

StumbleUpon

www.stumbleupon.com

StumbleUpon is another popular free social bookmarking site where you can share (or *stumble*) links to content that you like. The site relies on a voting system that's similar to the one used by Digg. Users can give stumbled links a thumbs-up or thumbs-down to boost or lower the popularity of those links.

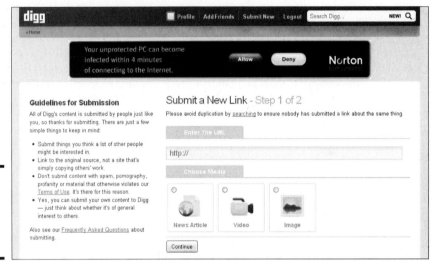

Figure 4-2:
The
Digg link
submission
form.

To join StumbleUpon, just visit www.stumbleupon.com and click the Join StumbleUpon link in the upper-right corner of the page, as shown in Figure 4-3. Complete the online form, and within minutes you can stumble content. One of the best features of StumbleUpon is the StumbleUpon toolbar, which you can add to most browser toolbars to make stumbling content instantly as easy as clicking your mouse button.

Figure 4-3:
The
Stumble-
Upon home
page.

Submitting content to StumbleUpon by using the StumbleUpon toolbar can be done at anytime by simply clicking the thumbs up icon on the toolbar. A window opens, shown in Figure 4-4, where you can add a title, description, keywords, and more to make your submission interesting, which encourages click-throughs. If the page you want to stumble has already been stumbled by another StumbleUpon user, all you have to do is click the thumbs-up icon, and your vote is added to the ranking for that link.

Delicious

`www.delicious.com`

Delicious is useful for both online bookmarking of your favorite Web pages so you can access your personal bookmarks from any computer (just set your account to private) and for sharing links to content you like. Submissions to Delicious are not categorized as those to Digg and StumbleUpon are. Instead, Delicious relies entirely on keywords. In other words, when you submit content to Delicious, be sure to take the time to include highly relevant keywords with your submission or you won't get any traffic from your efforts at all.

Delicious is free to join by clicking the Join Now button in the top-right corner on the site's home page, shown in Figure 4-5. Complete the information requested, and you're ready to go!

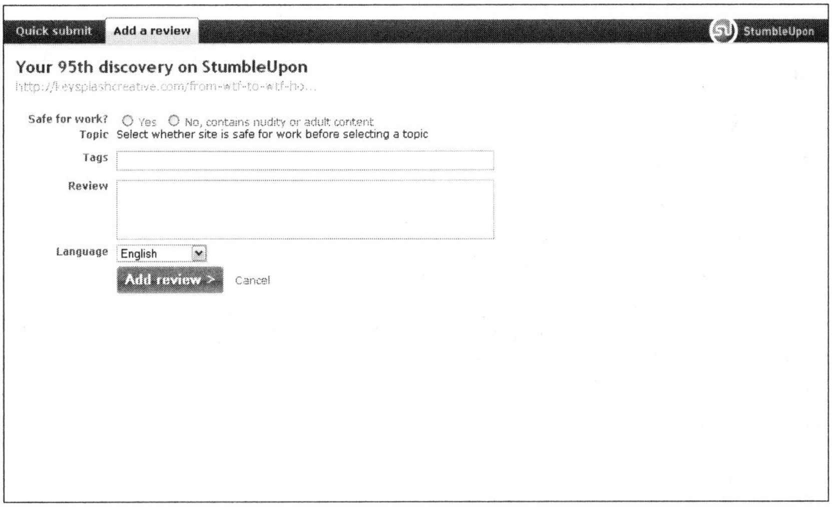

Figure 4-4:
The Stumble-Upon link submission window.

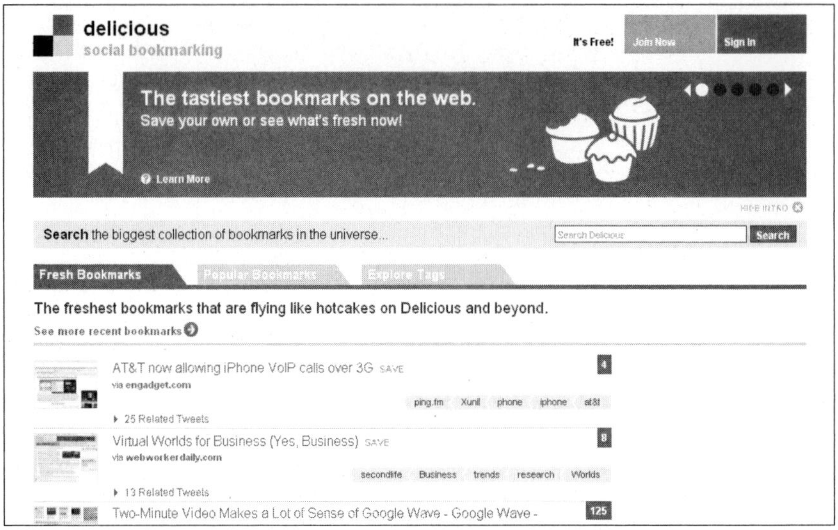

Figure 4-5:
The
Delicious
home page.

Submitting content to Delicious is easy with the Delicious toolbar buttons that you can add to most browser toolbars, which you can find for several different Internet browsers at `http://delicious.com/help/tools`. After you add the appropriate buttons to your browser's toolbar, you can just click the Add to Delicious button on your toolbar, and a Delicious content submission window opens, shown in Figure 4-6, where you can enter keywords to save your content for your future use or for sharing with other Delicious users.

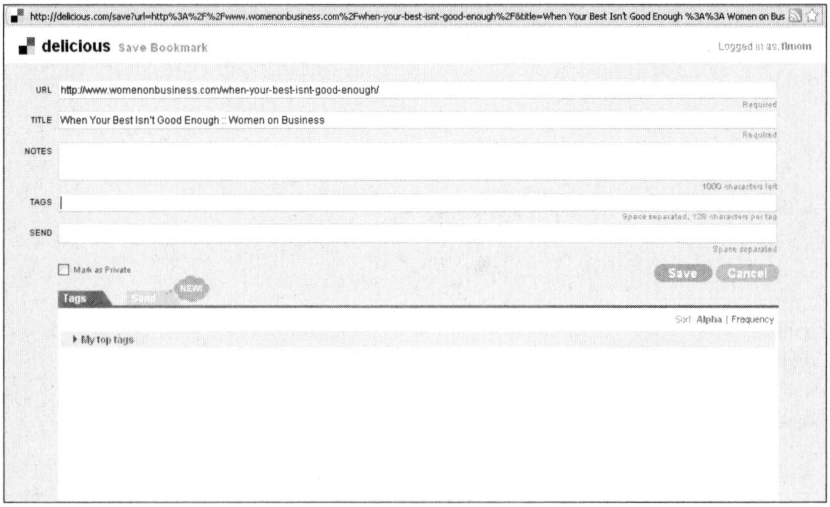

Figure 4-6:
The
Delicious
link
submission
form.

Yahoo! Buzz

`http://buzz.yahoo.com`

Yahoo! Buzz is owned by Yahoo!, one of the most popular search engines. That means, it has a built-in audience, and the content that becomes popular on Yahoo! Buzz can make it to the home page of Yahoo!. Imagine the traffic that could drive to your blog!

Additionally, there's a link to Yahoo! Buzz from the Yahoo! home page at the center of the page alongside the most popular headlines of the moment, as shown in Figure 4-7. That means that it's easy and common for Yahoo! visitors to click that link and arrive at the Yahoo! Buzz home page, where they just might dig deeper to find more content — like yours!

Yahoo! Buzz is free to join with a Yahoo! account, which you can create by selecting the Sign Up link at the top of the Yahoo! Buzz home page as shown in Figure 4-8. When you have an account, you can *Buzz Up* content or submit links that you want to share.

Reddit

`www.reddit.com`

Reddit is a popular social bookmarking site despite its plain appearance, as shown in Figure 4-9. To use Reddit, create a free account by selecting the Register link in the upper-right section of the Reddit home page and provide the requested information. When your account is active, just select the Submit a Link button on the Reddit site to share your links.

Figure 4-7:
The link
to Yahoo!
Buzz on
the Yahoo!
home page.

Click this link to go to the Yahoo! Buzz home page.

As Reddit users vote for the submitted content (choosing to vote up or down), the most popular links make it to the home page of Reddit, which drives a lot of traffic to those blogs or Web sites. It's challenging to get your content to the home page of Reddit, but if it happens, the bump in traffic to your blog is significant.

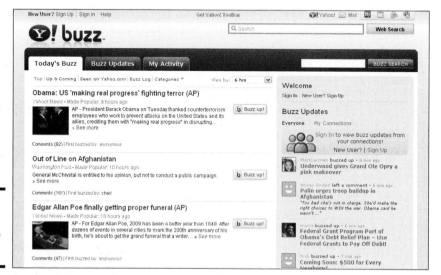

Figure 4-8:
The Yahoo
Buzz! home
page.

Figure 4-9:
The Reddit
home page.

Reddit is open to all content submissions but it does have a reputation of focusing on offbeat news and unique commentary on current news.

Slashdot

www.slashdot.com

Slashdot is niche social bookmarking site, shown in Figure 4-10, that's popular among people looking to share content about technology, science, and science fiction. In fact, the site's slogan tells the story in just six words, "News for nerds. Stuff that matters."

Figure 4-10:
Slashdot offers social bookmarking for technology and science content.

Slashdot works slightly differently from other social bookmarking sites because all link submissions are reviewed by human editors before they are published on the site for the Slashdot user community to view.

Newsvine

www.newsvine.com

Newsvine, shown in Figure 4-11, is a popular niche social bookmarking site for serious business and news content. The site weighs submitted links by popularity (the user community rates submissions), freshness of content, and reputation of the user who submitted the link.

Figure 4-11:
Newsvine focuses on business and news submissions.

If you write a blog about business or news, Newsvine could be an excellent tool for you to share links to your best blog posts.

Propeller

www.propeller.com

Propeller is offered by AOL and works similarly to other popular social bookmarking sites such as Digg. The interface is inviting and well-designed, as shown in Figure 4-12, and it works just as well. The site has a niche focus on news and political content.

Propeller users submit and vote on content to boost or lower its popularity. You can submit content and tag it with relevant keywords to help other users find it in searches, and you can communicate and share links and information in a social setting.

Using Social Bookmarking Sites to Boost Blog Traffic

Promoting your blog through social bookmarking sites can drive small bursts of traffic to your blog, particularly when you share your best posts through these sites. But there's more to using social bookmarking as a promotional tool than simply submitting links to your posts. First, you need to take the time to submit your links with an interesting description and as much detail as possible, and second, you need to become an active member of the communities on each social bookmarking site that you use in order to build a reputation and network of users who are likely to share your submissions further.

Figure 4-12:
Propeller
from AOL.

Following are several tips for submitting links to social bookmarking sites:

✦ **Include a useful description.** It's easy to get lazy with social bookmarking and submit your links without taking the time to write a great description of the content you're submitting to accompany your link. Don't fall into that trap or you're wasting your time. Instead, write interesting descriptions that tease people into wanting to click through to read the complete post or article. Just don't be deceptive in your descriptions or you'll do more harm than good.

✦ **Use relevant keywords and tags.** Take the time to tag your social bookmarking submissions with relevant keywords that other people are likely to use when searching for content like the content you're submitting. Search is a critical component to helping people find your content on popular social bookmarking sites that receive thousands of link submissions everyday.

✦ **Write interesting titles.** The title you use in your social bookmarking submission does not have to match the blog post, article, or Web page that you're submitting. Take a few minutes to craft a title that is likely to intrigue people to click through to read the entire post or article. However, make sure the title you use accurately reflects the content people will find when they click your link.

Submitting links in the best way that you can is very important, but being an active member of the social bookmarking community you submit content to is just as important. Following are suggestions for getting involved beyond simply submitting links:

✦ **Submit other people's content.** Always submit more content written by other people and published on Web sites and blogs that are not owned by you than you submit of your own content. People appreciate your taking the time to share your useful content, but they also notice if the only content you ever submit is your own. Check out the don'ts later in this chapter to find out why too much self-promotion is frowned upon in the world of social bookmarking.

✦ **Leave comments on other users' submissions.** Take the time to leave positive and useful comments on links that you enjoy that are submitted by other users. This is an essential part of networking, building authority, and leveraging the full opportunity that social bookmarking offers.

✦ **Rate other users' submissions positively.** When you find content that you enjoy that another user submits, take a moment to rate it. For example, if you're on Digg, digg that content, or if you're using StumbleUpon, give it a thumbs-up. It only takes a second, and other users notice and appreciate it. Many will even reciprocate!

✦ **Friend or connect with other users who submit content similar to yours.** Don't forget to utilize the networking aspects of social bookmarking sites. Many of these sites enable you to friend or connect with other users to create your own networks of people with like interests who can help share, rate, and comment on each other's content. The efforts of a group are always more powerful than the efforts of an individual.

Avoiding Social Bookmarking Don'ts

Sharing content on social bookmarking sites does not come without rules and etiquette. Always check the guidelines provided on any social bookmarking site that you join and use to ensure you don't violate them, which can lead to account suspension.

Furthermore, be sure to follow the unwritten rules of social bookmarking. It's safe to assume your social bookmarking activities won't raise any red flags among other users as long as you use common sense. However, following are some of the biggest social bookmarking don'ts, so you're fully aware of them. If you're caught breaking these rules, you're likely to be blacklisted, meaning if your account isn't suspended, your content will never rise to the top of social bookmarking sites and your efforts are for naught.

✦ **Don't submit far more of your own content than content that belongs to other people.** Use the classic 80/20 rule of marketing as a guideline. For every two links of your own content that you submit to a specific social bookmarking site, submit eight pieces of content from other sites and blogs. Keep in mind that some social bookmarking sites do not allow users to submit their own content at all. That's why it's essential that you always read the current site guidelines before you dive in and start submitting content.

✦ **Don't submit content from the same site repeatedly.** Even if you don't own the site that you're submitting links to, do not continually submit content from the same site. That's considered a spam tactic, and you'll be viewed as a spammer within the social bookmarking community if you're caught.

✦ **Don't submit recaps or republished posts links.** Instead, submit original source links. Always take the time to submit the original source of a story rather than a republished or recapped version of the story (with a link to the original story) from another blog or Web site. In other words, give credit (and traffic) where credit is due — to the original publisher.

Social bookmarking is unlikely to drive massive amounts of traffic to your site, but with persistence and a focus on building relationships *as well as* sharing your content, you can give your blog a boost and enhance your overall integrated blog-marketing plan.

Chapter 5: Inviting or Being a Guest Blogger

In This Chapter

✔ Understanding guest blogging

✔ Defining your goals

✔ Being a guest blogger

✔ Inviting guests to write for your blog

One of the core components to a successful blog is the networking and community-building that a blogger does in support of his blog. Those efforts not only offer ways to broaden your online relationships but also open opportunities for cross-promotion with other bloggers through guest blogging. Whether you invite another blogger to write a post on your blog or you write a post for another blogger to publish on her blog, the key is sharing great content with audiences who are likely to find value from it.

Guest blogging also provides a great way to inject new life and fresh ideas into a blog. Every blogger faces blogger's block on occasion and has trouble coming up with new posts or putting a creative spin on a topic she has been writing about for a long period of time. A guest blog post can bring new energy and perspectives to a blog, giving it a much needed boost. Not only that, but a guest blog post is a free post for your blog! In other words, it's one less post you have to write!

This chapter walks you through the process of guest blogging — both being a guest blogger by writing for another blog *and* accepting guest blog posts for publishing on your blog. You find out how to get started and make guest blogging work for you in growing your blog and your online network.

Understanding Guest Blogging

Guest blog posts are posts written for a blog by someone other than the blogger or bloggers who typically author the blog. There are two ways you can get involved with guest blogging:

✦ **On your blog:** When you accept guest posts on your blog, it means that you publish posts written by other bloggers who either request permission to write the guest post or whom you invite to write a guest post.

✦ **On another blogger's blog:** When you write a guest post for another blog that you don't own or typically write for, you're submitting a guest post for potential publication on that blog.

Most bloggers accept and publish guest posts on their own blogs as a way to build relationships with other bloggers, add a new perspective to their blog content, or attract new readers that the guest blogger may drive to the post. Alternatively, bloggers write guest blog posts to build relationships, share their expertise or opinions, and get to know a new audience that might follow the blogger back to his blog, thereby boosting his own blog traffic.

Defining Your Goals

Whatever reason you choose to accept or write guest blog posts, take the time to define your guest blogging objectives before you get started. Your goals may greatly affect the guest blogging opportunities you pursue. For example, if you want to introduce yourself to new audiences by writing guest posts for other blogs, take the time to research the blogs where your desired audience already spends time and then submit guest blog inquiries to those blogs. Think of it this way: Writing guest blog posts for five highly trafficked and targeted blogs could be far more effective in driving repeat traffic to your blog than writing 50 guest blog posts for blogs with little readership and about irrelevant topics.

With that in mind, focus your guest blogging efforts to ensure you get the biggest bang for the buck in terms of meeting your short- and long-term objectives. Both writing and publishing guest blog posts take time, and it's essential that you pursue the best opportunities for you and your blog rather than waste time on many activities that are unlikely to help you achieve your goals.

Just because a guest blogging opportunity doesn't drive loads of traffic to your blog doesn't mean it wasn't useful and worthwhile. Much of guest blogging is about building relationships with other bloggers.

Being a Guest Blogger

If you're ready to forge new relationships across the blogosphere, expose your content to new audiences, and potentially, increase traffic to your own blog, then guest blogging is a great option to pursue. Keep in mind, guest blogging takes time. You can't write a sub-standard guest post and expect to have another blogger publish it on his blog or ask you to guest blog for him again in the future. It takes time, patience, and a willingness to follow up after your guest post is published to make guest blogging successful.

Writing a guest blog post

Many of the best bloggers built their blogs by including guest blogging in their repertoire of promotional activities. Writing a guest blog post requires time and thought. You need to determine the best topic to write about for the blog and audience where your guest post will be published, and then you need to think of how you can bring your unique voice, opinion, or expertise to that topic to make your post stand out, get noticed, and coexist with the other content on that blog.

The first step to writing a guest blog post is taking the time to read the blog where your post will be published. Get an idea of the content that has already been covered, the content that gets people talking, and the topics that are inappropriate or best to avoid. This is particularly important when you provide a guest post to a well-established blog where the author has already covered every topic and subtopic you can imagine. Take the time to come up with a unique perspective that makes your post irresistible.

For example, the guest post shown in Figure 5-1 was published on one of the most popular blogs about blogging, Darren Rowse's ProBlogger (www. problogger.net). The guest blogger, Sid Savara, took a topic that's often covered on blogs — WordPress plugins — and provided a highly focused, extremely useful post with *5 Plugins to Make Your WordPress Blog Blazing Fast*. This is just one way to write a great guest blog post — provide immediately actionable and useful information.

It's also important to ensure your tone, writing style, post length, and language match the blog where your guest post will be published. In other words, your post needs to comfortably live next to the other content that's already published on the blog. For example, if you provide a guest blog post to a highly political blog, it's safe to assume your post should probably reflect the views typically published on the blog, or you're likely to be shunned.

When you write your guest posts, you need to strike a balance to ensure your posts stand out from the other posts but aren't jarringly different from them.

Figure 5-1:
A unique
guest blog
post.

Choosing blogs to write guest posts for

The most important part of choosing which blogs to write guest posts for
is to know who your best audience is and find blogs where similar people
spend time. Make sure the content on those blogs matches yours in terms
of view points, tone, and so on to ensure the audience would be comfortable
reading your guest post. Look for blogs that you would enjoy reading if you
were looking for the type of information your guest post would contain.

After you create a list of blogs you'd like to send guest blog pitches to, take
some more time reading the content, including the archives and comments,
to truly understand the audience and the blogger. Get involved in the conversation by leaving comments and informally introducing yourself to the
blogger and her community of readers.

Finally, be sure to check the popularity of blogs you consider sending guest
blog post pitches to in order to ensure it's worth your time. Although you
might have to start pitching smaller blogs until your online reputation
grows, you should at least check to make sure the blog is updated frequently
and some comments are left on recent posts. You can also check the blog's
authority by looking it up on Technorati (`www.technorati.com`) or Alexa
(`www.alexa.com`). For example, Figure 5-2 shows the traffic patterns for
three blogs about blogging to give you an idea of how they compare, which
could affect your choices for submitting guest post queries.

Technorati and Alexa rankings are imperfect and should be used to give you
a general feel for a blog's traffic and popularity.

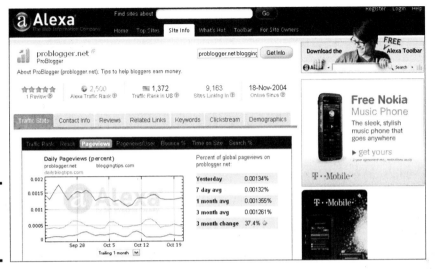

Figure 5-2:
The Alexa
rankings of
three blogs.

Making your pitch

After you identify a blog that you want to provide a guest post for, you need
to contact the blogger behind that blog to make your pitch. You can simply
send an e-mail to the blogger (most bloggers provide their e-mail addresses
or a contact form on their blogs) to introduce yourself and your guest post
idea. To make your pitch stand out and increase the likelihood it will be
accepted by the blogger, follow these suggestions to write a great query note:

✦ **Provide your credentials.** Established bloggers are protective of their
readers and only publish guest posts that are well-written and provided
by people who can demonstrate their expertise or the added value they
bring to the blog. With that in mind, be sure to fully describe yourself,
your credentials, and any other information that directly applies to the
blog and your guest post to ensure the blog owner understands that
you know what you're talking about and have something important to
contribute.

✦ **Offer your blog statistics.** If your blogging statistics are growing or
doing well, provide traffic statistics (such as monthly page views) to the
blogger to show you can send some traffic to the blog when you promote it on your own blog.

✦ **Demonstrate your blogging knowledge.** If you can send a blog post
written in HTML, tell the blogger! It takes a blogger time to copy and
paste a guest post, fix formatting issues, add images, and so on. If you
can do all of that for him, make sure he knows it. He'll appreciate the
time you can save him.

+ **Provide links to your blog and/or online writing.** Show the blogger that you already have an online presence or, at the very least, that you can write well. Guest blog posts should be error free. Demonstrate that you can write the perfect post without any editing on the blogger's part!

+ **Define how you'll promote your post.** If you plan to promote the guest post on your blog, Twitter, Facebook, in a newsletter, and so on, then tell the blogger. All that promotion means more potential traffic for the blogger!

+ **Write unique content.** Tell the blogger the post you plan to write for him is 100% unique and has not (and will not) be published elsewhere in whole or in part. Duplicated content can hurt a blog's Google page rank and traffic, so it's important to demonstrate that you understand this.

+ **Include your guest post with your query.** If you've already written your guest blog post, send it to the blogger with your pitch, making it even easier for him to publish it!

Many bloggers publish guest blogging requirements and guidelines on their blogs. Be sure to search for them before you send your pitch.

Following up after your post is published

When your guest post is accepted and published, that doesn't mean your job is done. Next, you need to promote your guest post, respond to comments left on the post, and make sure both you and the blogger who published your guest post get the most from it in terms of traffic, exposure, and relationship-building.

Many bloggers check their blog analytics to determine the popularity of specific posts, including guest posts. Make yours stand out by promoting it heavily and driving a lot of traffic to it. On the flip side, make sure some of that traffic follows you back to your blog by joining the conversation and forging new relationships with that blog's audience.

Inviting Guest Bloggers to Write Posts for Your Blog

You can open up your blog to guest writers at any time, but until your blog starts to grow in terms of traffic and readership, you're unlikely to get a lot of inquiries. However, it's important to be prepared because you never know when you'll get your first pitch. Also, you can ask other bloggers to write guest posts for your blog at any time. Remember, writing guest blog posts takes time (that's time away from their own blogs), but extending the invitation can never hurt!

Benefits of accepting guest bloggers on your blog

Not only can guest bloggers add new ideas and perspectives to your blog, but they can also bring some traffic with them. Believe it or not, there are benefits to accepting guest bloggers on your blog that go beyond blog traffic. For example, the relationship that you build with a guest blogger may open doors for new opportunities in the future for collaboration or referrals. You never know!

The most obvious and universal benefit of publishing guest posts on your blog is the fact that a guest post equates to one less post you have to write! Take that time off from writing and do some extra off-blog promotion such as commenting on other blogs, social networking, and social bookmarking. Guest posts also add to the frequency of posts on your blog, which helps drive more search traffic to your blog — each new post is a new entryway for Google to find your blog!

Finding guest bloggers for your blog

One of the first steps to opening your blog to guest bloggers is to publish a post announcing it! A *Call for Submissions* post can jumpstart the process by publicizing the news, which you can then share through social bookmarking (discussed in Chapter 4 of this minibook), Twitter (see Book VIII for more about Twitter), and social networking (discussed in Chapter 3 of this minibook).

If your blogging application allows you to create pages, create a page and publish the link in your blog's top navigation bar or another prominent place on your blog. The page should communicate what people should do in order to submit a guest blog post to your blog.

Furthermore, don't be afraid to reach out to other bloggers you like and ask them if they would be interested in writing a guest post for your blog. The worst that can happen is they say no!

Setting guidelines for guest bloggers

Many bloggers publish guest blogging guidelines on their blogs, so the requirements and restrictions are very clear to anyone who considers submitting a pitch. At the very least, you should have text prepared to respond to e-mail inquiries that outline your requirements.

Take some time to visit blogs and look for links that say such things as "Write for Us" or "Post Ideas." Often, bloggers publish guest blogging guidelines on pages labeled in such a way, which you can use to help create your own requirements.

Figure 5-3 shows the guest blogging requirements for Blogging Tips (`www.bloggingtips.com`), which are comprehensive and well-written.

Figure 5-3: Guest blogging guidelines.

Tracking the results

If you want to find out just how much traffic a guest blog post drives to your blog, you need to track the results. You can do this by looking at the number of comments left on the post, the interactivity of the guest blogger in terms of responding to those comments, and using your Web analytics tool, as discussed in Chapter 2 of Book V.

For example, drill down into your blog analytics to determine how many page views the guest blog post received on the first day it was published, the first week, two weeks, and so on. Then check to see where that traffic came from. If you saw a noticeable bump in comments, traffic, and incoming links to the guest post, then that's a guest blogger you want to invite back!

Repaying the favor

If someone writes a guest blog post for you, you aren't obligated to write a reciprocal post for his blog. However, it's definitely something you want to do for bloggers whose blogs are well-trafficked or cater to a niche audience that matches yours very well. It's also a relationship you want to maintain and grow in case new opportunities arise in the future.

Separating spam guest post requests from legitimate ones

Many people send guest post requests for the sole purpose of boosting incoming links to their blogs or Web sites with little or no interest in actually building relationships or real cross-blog promotion. Remember, more incoming links boosts a blog or Web site's Google page rank, so many unscrupulous people online might send you guest blog requests with ulterior motives.

In 2009, I received a lot of spam guest post requests from people working for questionable online education companies. The prior year, there was a rise in these requests from people working for finance companies. These unscrupulous companies hire people to generate incoming links for them. The content is often republished or loosely related to the blog being pitched, and they add no value to your blog. Therefore, be sure to check the source for guest blog post inquiries to ensure they're legitimate and associate your blog only with Web sites and people that you want to be connected to.

Book VI Chapter 5

Inviting or Being a Guest Blogger

You can run guest post submissions through Copyscape (`www.copyscape.com`), as discussed in Chapter 4 of Book I, to determine whether the content is original.

Often, the problem comes from the links within the guest post sent to you. For example, a post with seemingly random and irrelevant links to keyword phrases should jump out at you as a link-buying scam, and you should not publish that guest post. Always use your best judgment and err on the side of caution to protect your blog and your audience from spam.

If the links within a guest blog post submitted to you are spam, don't publish the post.

Although you need to be wary of spam guest blog post inquiries, you're more likely to receive legitimate requests. Do your due diligence to get to know the blogger and where the site links within the post will send your readers before you accept a guest blog post, and you should be safe.

Chapter 6: Hosting Blog Contests

In This Chapter

✔ **Understanding and benefiting from blog contests**

✔ **Getting prizes**

✔ **Writing the blog contest post**

✔ **Setting rules**

✔ **Thinking about traffic**

✔ **Promoting your blog contest**

✔ **Choosing a winner and sending prizes**

*B*log contests are not only a great way to boost blog traffic, but they're fun, too! Who doesn't like to win prizes? Blog contests can even create a sense of camaraderie and community around your blog as readers rally together in anticipation!

Before you get too excited, there are positives and negatives to holding blog contests, and they can cause problems that you need to position yourself to avoid in order to have any chance for success, so I make sure to leave you some warnings to watch your back along the way. This chapter explains how to create a blog contest, promote it, and award prizes so you get maximum bang for the buck.

Understanding Blog Contests

As you might expect, a blog contest is a contest for a prize that is held by a blogger. As a blogger, you can get a prize of your choice and raffle it off to a winner all through your blog! Because you're the contest host, you can set the rules to help the contest benefit your blog in the best way possible. For example, you can choose the entry method, contest duration, prize, and so on.

Blog contests are an excellent way to excite your existing readers and drive short-term bursts of traffic to your blog. The trick is attracting entrants who actually become repeat readers of your blog. Of course, the first step is to promote your contest, so people are motivated to visit your blog to enter.

The other critical component of a blog contest is the investment — both monetary and time. For example, to hold a blog contest, you have to follow these ten steps at a minimum:

1. Get a prize.
2. Set the rules.
3. Publish the contest post.
4. Promote the contest.
5. Moderate entries and comments.
6. Repromote the contest (one-time promotion is not enough).
7. Pick a winner.
8. Contact the winner for shipping information.
9. Ship the prize.
10. Announce the winner.

Depending on the prize you're giving away, a blog contest may be costly, and it's always time consuming.

As always, consider your blogging goals before you jump into hosting a blog contest to ensure the time and money investments are worthwhile to you.

Benefiting from Blog Contests

Blog contests can provide a number of benefits to bloggers. For example, your existing blog audience is likely to be excited by the idea of winning a prize. Additionally, if you take the time to promote your blog contest, you may get a big surge in traffic as people visit your blog to enter the contest. However, most of the traffic that comes from a blog contest is short-lived. The more closely tied to your blog's topic that your prize is, the more likely you'll get entrants who might be interested in reading your blog, too. On the flip side, your contest won't drive a lot of traffic if you don't have a great prize. It's up to you to balance your objectives for the contest to determine the kind of traffic you want it to generate for you.

Take the time to set up your contest so entries, the prize, shipping, and so on work best for *you*. If possible, get someone to donate a prize for you and ship it for you, so you don't incur those expenses. You can also structure the contest in a way that requires entrants to help promote your blog in order to enter. These are just a few of the ideas discussed throughout this chapter to help you create successful blog contests.

Deciding on Prizes to Give Away in a Blog Contest

First, you need to pick a prize. Be certain to choose a prize that people are likely to want, or no one will enter your contest! You can go two different ways with your prize:

✦ **General/popular item:** Pick a prize that appeals to a broad audience. The more exciting your prize is, the more excitement will grow around your contest and the more entries it will receive. Of course, you can always give away a cash prize!

✦ **Targeted item:** On the other hand, prizes closely related to your blog's topic are more likely to drive smaller traffic bursts but more targeted traffic.

Additionally, cost is a primary prize factor. If you have to pay for your prize, your budget might dictate what you can give away. Also, you need to pay to ship your prize. Be sure to check shipping costs before you hold your contest, so you know you can afford to ship the prize to the winner. Of course, you can always give away prizes that don't cost you anything but your time. For example, if you're an artist, you can give away a sketch or portrait, or if you're a business person, you can give away an hour of consulting time.

If possible, find a sponsor to donate a prize for your contest. Many companies donate products or services to blog contests in exchange for the publicity the contest gives them. You can publish your request on sites such as HARO (`www.helpareporterout.com`) or ProfNet (`https://profnet.prnewswire.com`), as shown in Figure 6-1.

Book VI Chapter 6

Hosting Blog Contests

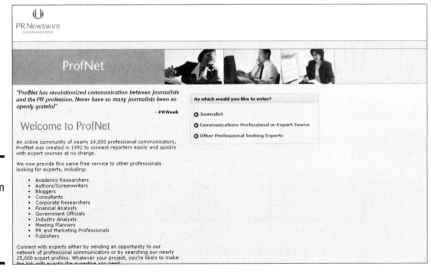

Figure 6-1:
You can turn to ProfNet to request prize sponsors.

If someone donates a prize for your blog contest, ask the donor to ship it directly to the winner rather than to you, so you don't have to pay shipping costs.

Writing a Blog Contest Post

Your blog contest post should provide all the rules and fully describe the prize. It's better to give too much information than not enough information. If possible, include a picture of the prize. Make the contest post exciting and fun. At the minimum, your blog contest post should include the following:

✦ **Prize description:** Be specific and make the prize sound amazing (without embellishing the truth).

✦ **How to enter:** Make it very clear exactly what a reader must do in order to enter the contest. Also, if there are restrictions related to the number of times a person can enter, include them in your contest post.

✦ **Start and end date:** Clearly state the date and time (include your time zone) when the contest officially starts and ends.

✦ **Prize delivery restrictions:** If you have restrictions related to where you're willing to ship a prize, include them (for example, continental U.S. only).

✦ **How a winner will be selected:** Clearly state how winners will be chosen. The safest choice is to randomly select a winner, because complaints can arise from a subjective judging process. (See "Choosing a Winner," later in this chapter, for more info.)

✦ **The rules and restrictions:** Include all rules and restrictions to protect yourself. It's better to discourage a few entries rather than set yourself up for legal problems by not disclosing all rules and restrictions.

Blog contests are meant to be fun, but many people in the world use them as a tool to cause trouble by complaining about unclear rules. Don't leave yourself open to negative publicity or legal action. Instead, hold a fair and honest contest and disclose all rules. The simpler you keep your contest, the better.

Be sure to publish a contest reminder post as the entry deadline approaches to reenergize the excitement and solicit additional entries!

Setting Rules

Your blog contest rules need to be clear and comprehensive. Include the expiration date, the specific entry requirements, details about anyone who may not enter, and so on. For example, a contest post for a copy of this book may list the following rules (adapted from the contest post shown in Figure 6-2):

✦ To enter, leave a comment on this post.

✦ Comments must be left on this post before 11:59 pm on Saturday, April 16, 2010 (Eastern Time) to be entered into the drawing. One comment per e-mail address please. Contest open to entrants with continental U.S. mailing addresses only.

✦ Each comment will be entered into a drawing, and one winner will be selected randomly from those entries. The winner will receive ONE copy of *Blogging All-in-One for Dummies.*

✦ The winner will be contacted via e-mail, so please be sure you leave a valid e-mail address in your comment.

✦ The winner will be notified by April 16, 2010. If the winner does not respond with his or her mailing address within 72 hours of the notification e-mail being sent, he or she forfeits the prize and an alternative winner will be selected (same guidelines apply).

✦ Each winner's prize will be shipped by the publisher after the mailing address is provided. After the prize is claimed, the winner's name will be announced on this blog.

Figure 6-2:
A blog contest post.

 The preceding contest rules are hypothetical and have not been approved by an attorney, but they can be used to help you get started in creating rules for your own blog contest. Most bloggers don't seek legal approval to conduct a blog contest, but I'd be remiss not to mention that the safest path in any business or publishing endeavor is always to obtain legal approval for your actions.

Structuring the Contest for Maximum Traffic

I'm an advocate of keeping blog contests simple by requiring people to just comment on the blog post to obtain an entry and selecting winners randomly to reduce problems and legal entanglements. However, many people prefer to create more complicated contests, particularly entry and winner selection methods, in an effort to increase traffic from the contest.

An easy way to maximize the traffic from your blog contest is to structure the entry method so entrants have to help you promote your contest. For example, you could hold a blog contest and require people to blog about the contest and link to it, link to it on Twitter, or link to it on Facebook in order to get an entry. You could either select the winner from those incoming links randomly or subjectively by judging posts to find the best, most creative, or some other criterion. Keep in mind, this process is logistically challenging because you have to keep track of all the incoming links and so on.

As always, the way you structure your blog contest is entirely up to you. Just be aware of the potential complications and balance them against your objectives to ensure you structure the best contest for your blog.

Promoting Your Contest

Few people will know about your blog contest unless you promote it on sites other than your blog. Begin by publishing links to it on Twitter, Facebook, LinkedIn, and so on. Share the link through social bookmarking, e-mail, and anywhere else you can think of.

In addition to your own efforts in promoting your blog contest across the social Web, several Web sites are set up to help people promote blog contests. A few of the most popular sites are discussed in the following.

If you can, take the time to publicize your blog contest on all these sites for maximum exposure!

Online-Sweepstakes.com

`www.online-sweepstakes.com`

Online-Sweepstakes.com, shown in Figure 6-3, is one of the most popular sites for bloggers to promote their blog contests. To submit your contest to Online-Sweepstakes.com, just register for a free account on the site, select the Add a Sweep button, and provide the information requested in the form. Make sure you have your blog URL, the contest post URL, the prize description, and the start and end dates for your contest available.

Figure 6-3:
Promote
your blog
contest.

ContestBlogger.com

www.contestblogger.com

ContestBlogger.com is an online forum where people can submit links to
online contests. The forum includes a folder dedicated to blog contests. To
submit your blog contest to ContestBlogger.com, simply visit www.con-
testblogger.com/forum/blog-contests (shown in Figure 6-4), register for a free forum account, and then start a new forum post in the Blog
Contests folder that includes all the details about your contest as well as a
link to your blog contest post. Make your contest sound irresistible!

About.com Web Logs Forum

http://forums.about.com/n/pfx/forum.aspx?folderId=4&listMo
de=13&nav=messages&webtag=ab-weblogs

The About.com Web Logs Forum, shown in Figure 6-5, provides a place
where anyone who is holding a blog contest can promote it. Just register
for a free account at the site, and create a new forum post in the About.com
Web Logs Forum in the Blog Contests folder. Don't forget to include the link
to your contest post!

Figure 6-4:
Submit your
blog contest
link.

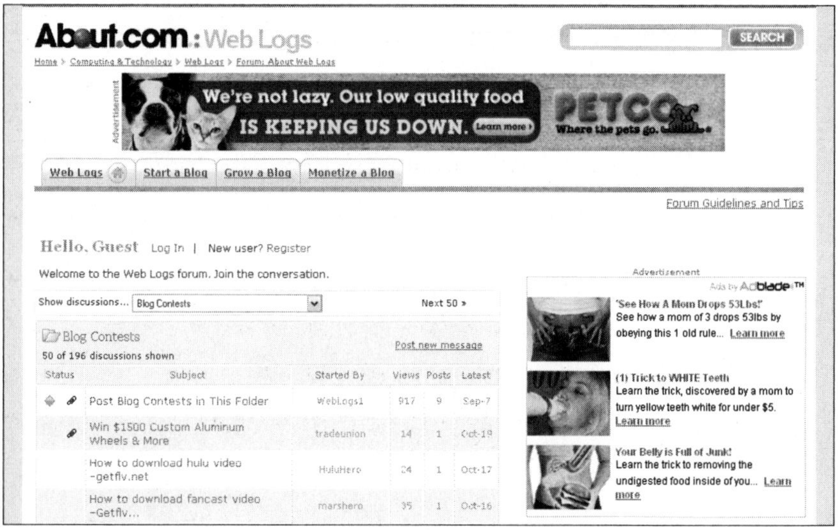

Figure 6-5:
The About.
com Web
Logs
Forum Blog
Contests
folder.

Choosing a Winner

When it comes time to choose a winner for your blog contest, be sure you comply with the rules you published in your blog contest post. Be sure to close your contest by publishing a new blog post that announces the winner and link back to the original contest post stating that the winner was chosen based on the rules outlined in that post.

Random selection

If you need to select a winner randomly, a convenient way to do so is using Research Randomizer. This site randomly selects a number within any given number range you enter, and it can even select multiple random numbers at once if you have more than one winner.

First, you need to number your contest entries. If all individuals who leave a comment on the contest post are automatically entered into your contest, this is particularly easy to do. Just count the comments or visit the comments for that specific post within your blogging dashboard where they might be numbered for you already depending on your blogging application (for example, WordPress numbers all comments within the dashboard). You can either pick those numbers out of a hat to choose your winner or use a tool such as Research Randomizer to select your winners.

To use Research Randomizer, follow these steps:

1. **Visit www.randomizer.org.**

The Randomizer home page opens, shown in Figure 6-6.

2. **Click the Randomize link in the top navigation bar.**

The randomization form opens, as shown in Figure 6-7.

3. **In the How Many Numbers Per Set text box, enter the number of winners your contest should have.**

This is the quantity of random numbers the tool will generate for you.

4. **In the Number Range text boxes, keep 1 for the From text box and enter the number of entries your contest received in the To text box.**

The default values are fine for all other text boxes.

5. **Click the Randomize Now! button.**

Your randomly selected number or numbers are returned to you, as shown in Figure 6-8.

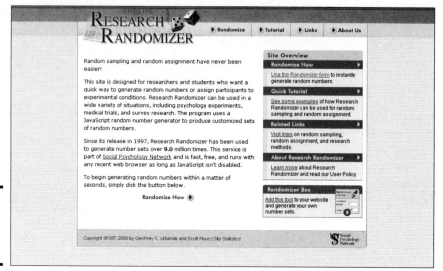

Figure 6-6:
Research
Randomizer
home page.

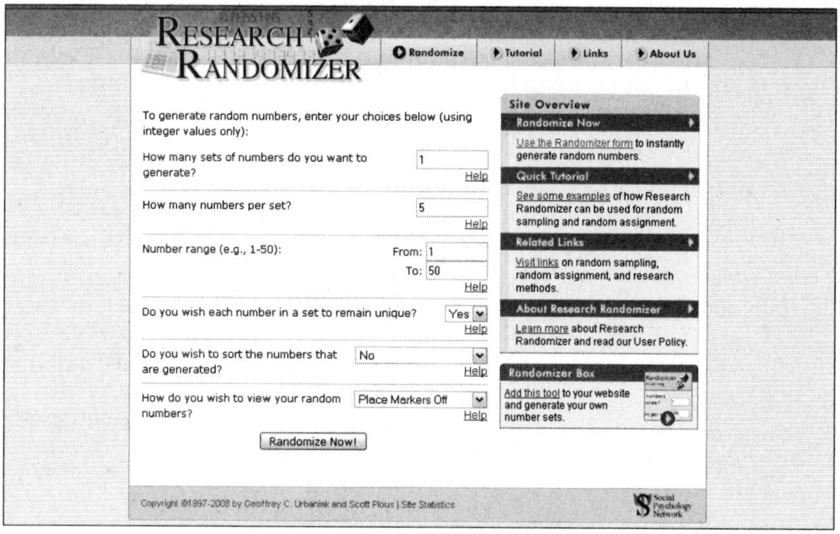

Figure 6-7:
The
random-
ization form.

Figure 6-8:
The
Research
Randomizer
Results
page.

Subjective selection

Blog contest winners can also be chosen using a subjective judging process. Either you can judge entries yourself, or you can ask your readers to vote on submissions and those with the most votes can be named the winners. Because subjective selection is *subjective,* the process is up to you.

Remember, blog contests take time to manage, so a simple entry and winner selection process is preferred. If you do decide to use a subjective process to select a winner, be prepared for someone to voice their displeasure at not being selected as the winner and question the judging process. It's an unfortunate side effect of holding a subjective blog contest that could very well happen to you.

Sending Prizes

After your contest winners have been selected and you obtain mailing addresses, you can ship the prizes (or the sponsor can do so). Make sure you use a trackable shipping method so you can confirm delivery, and if the item is expensive, be certain to insure it. Notify the winner when the item is shipped, the method used, and the expected delivery date.

The last thing you need to do to wrap up your blog contest is announce in a blog post that the winners have been chosen!

Chapter 7: Joining Blog Carnivals

In This Chapter

✔ **Using blog carnivals for promotion**

✔ **Understanding the benefits of blog carnivals**

✔ **Finding blog carnivals**

✔ **Starting a blog carnival**

✔ **Following blog carnival do's**

*I*f you've been wracking your brains in order to come up with a promotional event, you've come to the right chapter. Everyone loves a carnival, and people love blogs, so why not put the two together? When you do, you come up with an event known as a *blog carnival.*

Blog carnivals aren't as popular as they were a few years ago, but they still present a fairly easy and free way to promote your blog and drive traffic to it. They're a great way to boost incoming links to your blog and network with other bloggers, so it's worth considering blog carnivals as a part of your overall blog marketing plan.

This chapter tells you what blog carnivals are, how to find blog carnivals to join, and how to host your own blog carnival. Read on to see whether blog carnivals are right for you and your blogging goals.

Using Blog Carnivals for Promotion and Link-Building

Blog carnivals are promotional events where one blogger acts as the carnival host and other bloggers join as carnival participants. The host announces the carnival topic and date, and then other bloggers commit to writing about that topic on their own blogs on the specified date. Each participant sends the link for the carnival post to the host, who publishes the actual blog carnival post on the date of the carnival with links to all of the participants' posts included in it.

The blog carnival host may or may not write summaries or interesting snippets about each participant's post, but it's up to the carnival host to decide how she wants to publish the links. When the blog carnival post is published by the host, readers will have easy access to a variety of posts about a specific topic.

Each blog carnival participant (as well as the host) is expected to promote the carnival on his or her blog prior to the event. Furthermore, when the carnival post is published on the host's blog, participants are expected to promote that post as well. Sometimes, participants are encouraged to republish the carnival post on their own blogs for reciprocal linking benefits.

Incoming links are weighted heavily by search algorithms such as the one used by Google, which can give your blog a boost from search traffic.

Understanding Who Can Benefit from a Blog Carnival

Blog carnivals are an excellent way to increase the number of incoming links to your blog, thereby boosting search traffic to your blog over time. They're also a great way to get a short-term traffic boost as readers of the host's blog and other participants' blogs click on your carnival post link to read what you have to say about the carnival topic.

Blog carnivals work well for focused, niche topics where readers are actively looking for more information or varied opinions on a specific subject. They provide an excellent way to help participating bloggers build relationships with each other and with the other participating blogs' audiences.

It's unlikely that a blog carnival will drive floods of traffic to your blog, but it's an excellent relationship-building and networking tool, which can lead to indirect traffic and overall blog growth over the long term.

Finding Blog Carnivals

A number of Web sites enable blog carnival hosts to publicize their carnivals and open them for submissions and participation. If you're interested in hosting a blog carnival and finding participants or finding an open carnival that you can join as a participant, Blog Carnival (`www.blogcarnival.com`), shown in Figure 7-1, is one of the most popular sites to do it.

It's easy to register for a free account at Blog Carnival and then search for open carnivals (ones that are ongoing and available for bloggers to join) from the open Carnival List shown in Figure 7-2. You can find the open Carnival List at `http://blogcarnival.com/bc/clist.html` or by clicking the link in the upper-right corner of the Blog Carnival home page that shows the number of carnivals under the Blog Carnival Index heading. To find carnivals that match your blog topic and audience, enter related keywords into the text box or select a carnival category from the Filed Under drop-down list.

Figure 7-1:
The Blog
Carnival
home page.

You can submit your own posts (called *articles* on the site) to open blog carnivals by using the form provided on the site, shown in Figure 7-3. You can
access this form by creating a free Blog Carnival account and selecting the
Submit an Article link from the specific carnival page you want to join.

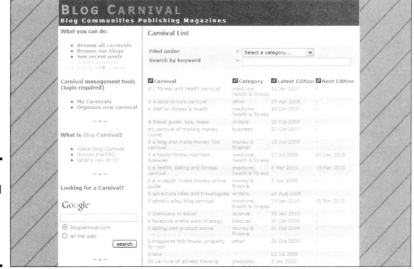

Figure 7-2:
The Carnival
List to
search
for open
carnivals.

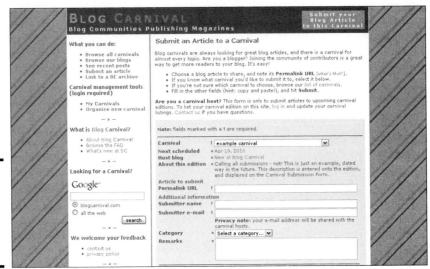

Figure 7-3:
The Blog
Carnival
article
submission
form.

Starting a Blog Carnival

If you decide to start a blog carnival of your own, you can go about it the hard way or the easy way:

✦ **The hard way:** You can start a blog carnival and host it on your blog by simply publishing a call for content and participation on your own blog and promoting it through your social networking and Twitter efforts. You can also contact other bloggers directly and ask them to participate. However, this is a tedious and time-consuming task. Unless you have a tight network of bloggers who would benefit from blogging about the same topic, you'll have better luck with the easy way.

✦ **The easy way:** You can use a site such as Blog Carnival to promote your blog carnival. Simply create a free account at Blog Carnival and follow the easy instructions to create your carnival, publicize an open edition of your carnival (editions are used for ongoing carnivals that happen weekly, monthly, and so on), and publish a call for submissions. An example carnival is shown in Figure 7-4, and an example edition of that carnival is shown in Figure 7-5, so you can see the difference between how Blog Carnival handles them.

If you use the easy way to create a blog carnival, you should still promote it on your blog and through your social Web profiles such as on Twitter, Facebook, and so on. You can find out more about promoting your blog carnival later in this chapter.

Figure 7-4:
An example
blog
carnival.

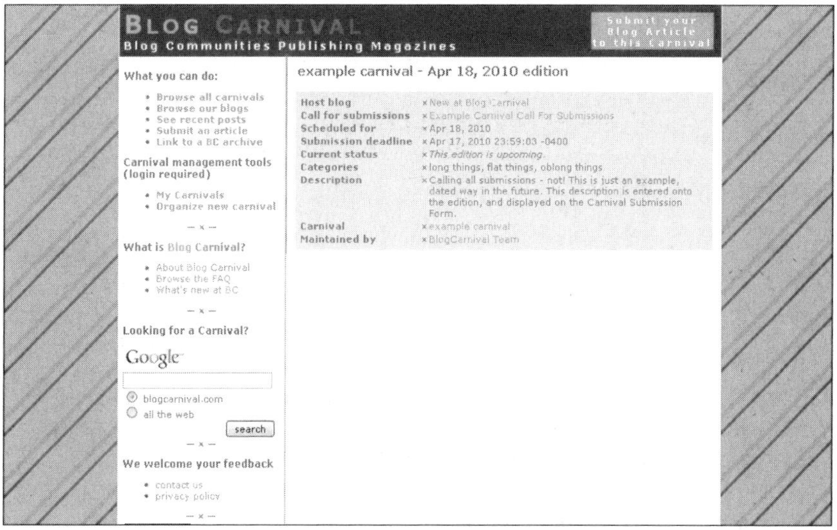

Figure 7-5:
An example
blog
carnival
edition.

Promoting a Blog Carnival

Writing a blog carnival post is just a small part of hosting or participating in a successful blog carnival. Without promotion, a blog carnival can go unnoticed. To drive traffic to your blog carnival, follow these promotional suggestions:

+ Blog about the carnival before, during, and after the final carnival post is published.

+ Ensure carnival participants help to promote it.

+ Tweet about the carnival.

+ Spread the word through social networking sites such as Facebook, LinkedIn, MySpace, and so on.

+ If the blog carnival is ongoing, create a Facebook Page or Group for it.

+ Share links to the carnival on social bookmarking sites such as Digg, StumbleUpon, Reddit, and so on.

+ Leave useful comments on blogs related to the carnival topic and include a link to the carnival post for more information.

+ Share the link to your carnival in the About.com Web Logs forum, at `http://forums.about.com/n/pfx/forum.aspx?folderId=12&listMode=13&nav=messages&webtag=ab-weblogs`.

+ Visit online forums or groups related to your blog carnival topic and share the link to the final carnival post for visitors to find excellent content.

The important thing is to make an effort to promote the blog carnival in any way you can.

Blog Carnival Do's

A blog carnival is only as successful as the quality of content provided by the participants and the promotion done by the host and participants. The most important thing you want to avoid doing when you participate in a blog carnival is dropping the ball. That means if you commit to participate in a blog carnival, you must

+ Be responsible and submit your post on time.

+ Make sure your post is a good one that's well-written, on topic, and interesting.

- ✦ Keep your carnival post free of spam links and self-promotion.
- ✦ Help to promote the carnival by blogging about it and linking to it on Twitter, Facebook, Digg, StumbleUpon, and so on.

The blog carnival host also has responsibilities to ensure the carnival is managed and promoted well so participants get the maximum exposure possible. As a blog carnival host, you should

- ✦ Solicit submissions from reliable bloggers that match the carnival topic.
- ✦ Follow up and make sure you obtain well-written posts on time.
- ✦ Publish a well-written, interesting carnival post with links to all participants' posts.
- ✦ Follow up with participants to ensure they promote the carnival post.
- ✦ Heavily promote the carnival on your blog, via Twitter, through Facebook, and on all other social Web profiles you maintain both before the carnival and once the carnival posts are published.

**Book VI
Chapter 7**

**Joining Blog
Carnivals**

Book VII

Making Money from Your Blog

"Tell the boss you-know-who is talking smack in his blog again."

Contents at a Glance

Chapter 1: Blog Advertising 101

In This Chapter

✓ Setting your goals

✓ Taking a look at types of ads

✓ Setting expectations

✓ Making your advertising venture a success

*B*log advertising can come in many forms and offers an even wider array of monetization options. From text ads to video ads and everything in between, many bloggers dabble in the world of online advertising in an attempt to make money from their blogs, and there is no shortage of advertisers looking for the unique and targeted audiences that blogs already have in place. Why not publish ads on your blog in an attempt to recoup your hosting, design, development, or other costs or as compensation for your time and sweat equity?

Of course, not every blogger feels the same way about advertising, and not every blogging application allows bloggers to monetize their blogs with ads. However, you can't make an educated determination about whether or not you want to publish ads on your blog until you understand how blog advertising works. This chapter explains the basics, and the remainder of this minibook delves into the specifics about the various opportunities the majority of bloggers pursue to make money through blog advertising.

Determining Your Goals

Do you want to make money from your blog? If so, then blog advertising is an easy way to try to do it. Some bloggers shun publishing ads on their blogs believing they reduce the professionalism of the blog. However, the majority of bloggers do pursue some kind of advertising opportunity at some point during the course of their lives as bloggers.

With that in mind, you need to determine what your blogging goals are and then decide whether publishing ads on your blog in an attempt to make some money matches those goals or runs counter to them. You might find that a happy medium that balances a small number of ads with your amazing content is the best mix for you, your audience, and your blogging goals.

Blogs that are covered in ads with little or no original content are typically identified as spam by major search engines such as Google. Make sure your blog includes enough original content!

Deciding to Publish Ads on Your Blog

After you decide that you're interested in publishing ads on your blog, your work begins. If you're serious about making money from your blog, then be prepared to invest a lot of time into trying new advertising opportunities, testing ad placement, and so on to find the best moneymakers for your blog. Just make sure the advertising opportunities you pursue always complement your overall blogging goals.

Take some time to research a wide variety of advertising opportunities and truly understand the requirements of each before you dive in. Every space on your blog could potentially be monetized, but you need to pick and choose the tactics that help you make money without offending your readers. In other words, never allow your monetization efforts to override your efforts to publish great content. Without great content, your blog can't grow, and without an audience, it's nearly impossible to make money from your blog.

Keep in mind that blog advertising doesn't make many people rich. Certainly, there are exceptions, but the vast majority of bloggers don't make a lot of money from their blogs, despite their efforts. The reason is that successful blog monetization requires a lot of time and dedication in terms of growing your blog and then finding the monetization opportunities that best leverage your audience and traffic patterns to drive income. It's a tough nut to crack, but with patience and persistence, you can make more than pocket change and possibly *a lot more* than pocket change.

Darren Rowse of ProBlogger does a great job of chronicling his blog monetization efforts at `www.problogger.net`.

Reviewing Types of Ads

There are a number of different types of ads that you can publish on your blog as well as other online monetization efforts. The three most common advertising models are

✦ **Pay-per-click (PPC):** Advertisers pay the blogger each time a person clicks on the advertiser's ad.

✦ **Pay-per-impression (PPM):** Advertisers pay the blogger each time the ad appears on the blog's page (that is, each time a person loads the page in their browser).

✦ **Pay-per-action (PPA):** The advertiser pays the blogger each time someone clicks the ad and performs an action such as making a purchase or filling out a contact form.

Those advertising models are broken down further into the types of ads that bloggers can publish on their blogs. Following are the most common:

✦ **Contextual ads:** These ads are delivered based on the content on the page where the ad is displayed. The intention is to match ads with relevant content in order to maximize click-throughs.

✦ **Text link ads:** Text link ads are hyperlinked text (usually using specific keywords) within a blog post, list, sidebar, and so on that links to the advertiser's chosen page.

✦ **Image ads:** Banner, button, skyscraper, leaderboard, and any other picture ads qualify as image ads (also called display ads). These are described in more detail later in this section.

✦ **Video ads:** Ads that are displayed within online videos (preroll, postroll, overlay, and so on) are becoming more and more popular.

✦ **Affiliate ads:** Affiliate advertising gives you the opportunity to place ads for specific products, companies, and so on and get paid a predetermined percentage or rate when someone performs an action related to the ad.

✦ **Review posts:** Although review posts on a blog might not be *traditional* advertising, in the online world it's important to mention them here as a monetization opportunity. You can write reviews that are sponsored by a company, person, entity, and so on and receive payment for it.

There are a variety of specific types of image ads that bloggers can publish to make money, including

✦ **Banner ads:** Display (image) ads that appear on a Web site and link directly to the advertiser's landing page are called banner ads.

✦ **Button ads:** Button ads are the most popular form of display advertising on blogs because they fit well in a blog's sidebar and don't take up a lot of real estate space. Button ads are 125 pixels wide by 125 pixels high and are commonly placed in groups of two, four, six, or eight.

✦ **Skyscraper ads:** Ads that are tall and narrow are called skyscraper ads. The most common sizes are 120 pixels wide by 600 pixels high or 160 pixels wide by 600 pixels high. Skyscraper ads fit well in a blog's sidebar.

✦ **Leaderboard ads:** Ads that are short and wide are called leaderboard ads. The most common size is 728 pixels wide by 90 pixels high. Leaderboard ads fit well above or below a blog's header.

✦ **Transitional ads:** Ads that appear as a Web page before, in between, or after a visitor arrives at the Web page he is trying to get to. Transitional ads are often referred to as interstitial, introstitial, or exterstitial, depending on where they appear within a Web site.

✦ **Floating ads:** Floating ads appear to float or move across a Web page in front of the actual page content.

✦ **Pop-up, pop-over, pop-under ads:** Ads that appear in a window in front of or behind the window a visitor is viewing are called pop-up, pop-over, or pop-under ads.

✦ **Peel-back ads:** Peel-back ads appear behind a Web page and look like a corner of the page is lifted up to expose the ad beneath it (like the corner of a page of a book is being peeled back to expose the page behind it). When the visitor clicks the corner, the Web page appears to peel back, and the ad beneath it is fully displayed.

✦ **Expandable ads:** Expandable ads are typically image ads that enlarge when a visitor's mouse pointer hovers over them or when the visitor clicks them.

Most bloggers use a variety of advertising options to monetize your blog. Wired Science (`www.wired.com/wiredscience`) does a good job of mixing a variety of image ads to monetize its home page, as shown in Figure 1-1.

Many bloggers find a mix of ad types and payment models that works best for them through trial and error over time. Don't be afraid to try new programs, but always read the agreements, terms and conditions, and other legal documents before you sign up for a new program to ensure it will help you meet your goals.

Figure 1-1: A variety of ads can work well together.

For each advertising opportunity you pursue, check the payment method, payout threshold, support provided, whether or not you're allowed to publish other ads on your site, placement requirements, and so on. Also, make sure you can cancel at anytime.

Setting Earnings Expectations

If you're a new blogger with little traffic to your blog, you can't expect to make much money. Your earnings will increase as your traffic grows, your content archive grows, and your efforts in testing advertising opportunities allow you to hone in on the best options for your blog.

You're likely to hear stories of bloggers making thousands of dollars each month from their blogs. It's certainly possible for you to do the same. However, don't be tempted to cover your blog with ads.

As you read through this minibook, you find out about a variety of blog advertising options as well as the positives and negatives of each. Be sure you understand the potential pitfalls before you commit to publishing ads on your blog that could do more harm than good.

Set small goals for your monetization efforts and continually boost them as your time as a blogger and your audience grow. For example, set a goal to make $25 per month within three months, and $100 per month within six months. Believe it or not, those goals are aggressive for most bloggers. Again, your goals depend on your overall blogging goals and your commitment to monetizing your blog.

Keeping Ethics and Legalities in Mind

There are many forms of blog advertising, many of which you can learn about in this book. However, you should avoid participating in any advertising opportunities that are illegal or could be deemed unethical by the blogging and search communities. For example, the Federal Trade Commission issues laws and restrictions related to publishing reviews or endorsements online and accepting free products or payments in return for publishing such reviews, which you can review in Title 16 Part 255 of the Code of Federal Regulations (CFR) available at your local library or at www.ftc. gov. The specific URL for Part 255 of the electronic CFR is http://ecfr. gpoaccess.gov/cgi/t/text/text-idx?c=ecfr&sid=9e1feabc52fb3 64fdbde5a1b2b1e6648&rgn=div5&view=text&node=16:1.0.1.2.22& idno=16.

In terms of ethics, the blogosphere frowns upon ads that are not disclosed as such, particularly reviews and text link ads. Search engines, such as

Google, even consider text ads as a deceptive practice that artificially inflates the assumed popularity of the Web page the link leads to. The key is to remember to be honest, disclose ads as such, and follow the law.

Tips for Advertising Success

There is no single recipe for blog monetization success. If there were, everyone would be doing it! Instead, the successful bloggers make money because they do several things well, and you can do them, too. Check out the following tips to boost your advertising success:

+ **Stay focused.** Both your blog content and ads should be highly focused and appeal to your blog's audience in order to drive any interest to them from advertisers.

+ **Test.** Placement, type, size, and so on are all critical components to the success of the advertising you place on your blog. Take the time to test different ways of displaying the ads on your blog as well as the types of ads you publish in order to find the best mix for your blog.

+ **Diversify.** Don't put all your eggs in one basket. Instead, publish a variety of ad models and types to not only make your blog visually appealing and allow each ad to stand out, but also to continually test performance of different opportunities.

+ **Monitor your blog ads.** No matter what advertisements you decide to publish on your blog, always make certain that the ads that actually appear on your blog match what you expected from the advertiser and are appropriate for your blog. It's not uncommon for irrelevant or offensive ads to sneak onto your blog through large advertising networks. Monitor your blog ads to ensure they don't negatively affect the experience visitors have on your blog.

+ **Focus on growth.** Always write great content, work on boosting incoming links, build your community, and grow your audience. Without those things, you'll have a hard time finding advertisers who are interested in placing ads (at least ones that pay well) on your blog.

+ **Track results.** Pay close attention to the performance of the ads on your blog so you can make changes as necessary. If an ad isn't driving revenue, replace it. That's valuable advertising space on your blog. Don't give it away for free, and don't let it go to waste!

Some advertising programs, such as affiliate networks or sponsored review networks, provide tracking reports to ad publishers, so it's easy to analyze how ads are performing on your blog. If tracking is vitally important to you, make sure the program you choose has such a feature.

It's also important to understand that different advertising opportunities have different technical requirements in terms of how you integrate the ads into your blog, how long the ads take to load on your blog, and so on. Some of these requirements could negatively affect your blog.

For example, if an ad causes your blog to load extremely slowly, then that ad is negatively affecting the user experience on your blog. The last thing you want is for someone to click away from your blog because an ad is causing it to load in a browser too slowly. Be sure to read and understand the technical requirements of placing ads on your blog supplied by the advertiser to ensure you can handle them and are comfortable with them.

Chapter 2: Publishing Contextual Ads

In This Chapter

✔ Checking out the context of contextual ads

✔ Benefiting from contextual ads

✔ Exposing the negatives of contextual ads

✔ Finding contextual ad programs to join

Contextual ads are one of the most popular types of online advertising, and many bloggers publish them on their blogs in an effort to derive an income. These ads come in a variety of formats and offer several payment models for bloggers to choose from, making them flexible and easy to implement on your blog.

This chapter introduces you to contextual advertising so you can evaluate contextual advertising opportunities and programs in order to choose the best ones to test on your blog. Not all contextual advertising programs are equal, and none are likely to make you rich. However, they're an important element to test as part of your blog-revenue-generating plan. Several of the most popular contextual advertising programs are introduced in this chapter to help you get started.

Understanding Contextual Ads

Contextual ads are text, image, or video ads that are displayed to your blog visitors based on the content on the page where the ads appear. Because these ads are contextually relevant to your blog's content, visitors are expected to be more likely to be interested in them and click them than they would completely irrelevant ads.

For example, if you write a blog about pregnancy, an ad about smoking products or alcohol would be highly irrelevant and unlikely to generate interest or perform well. If an ad can't generate interest and click-throughs, you won't make any money from it. That's why contextual relevance is so important, and that's why contextual advertising is so popular for advertisers and ad publishers.

Contextual ads typically use the pay-per-click payment model, but pay-per-impression and pay-per-action contextual ads exist as well. (Payment models are discussed in detail in Chapter 1 of this minibook.)

Getting the Most Benefits from Contextual Ads

The best way to boost your earning potential from contextual advertising is to write highly focused content, so the most relevant ads are displayed. For example, the Moms & Dads parenting blog of South Florida (`http://blogs.trb.com/features/family/parenting/blog`), shown in Figure 2-1, displays a highly targeted ad for a school in South Florida that the blog's visitors are likely to be interested in based on the blog's content.

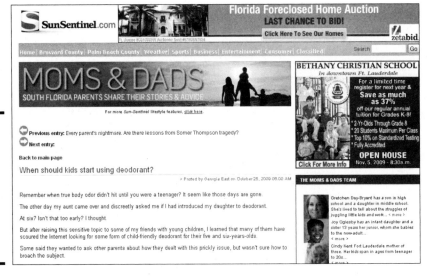

Figure 2-1: Contextual ads are relevant to the content of the page where they're displayed.

Furthermore, it's essential that you spend time growing your blog. The larger your blog's audience of targeted readers, the greater chance there is for people to click the contextual ads placed on your site. As your blog grows, you can also secure higher paying advertising opportunities because advertisers are apt to pay more for exposure to a larger, highly targeted audience.

Often advertisers bid on keywords related to their ad in an attempt to secure placement on Web sites and blogs that have a built-in audience of people who are already likely to be interested in their ads. In other words, they determine the maximum amount they're willing to pay to place ads on sites that match their chosen keywords, and ad space is given to the highest bidder, similar to an auction. For bloggers, that means writing with keywords in mind can give your contextual advertising income a boost. Bloggers who write about topics with popular keywords that many advertisers are actively bidding on are likely to earn more than bloggers who write about topics with less-popular related keywords. That's because as more advertisers bid on specific keywords through the common auction process that contextual advertising programs such as Google AdSense use, the price for those keywords goes up.

It's important to note that focusing on popular keywords might cause you to earn less money than focusing on less-popular keywords. The reason is simple. Popular keywords have a lot more competition for advertisers' dollars. It's difficult for a smaller blog to compete with big, established Web sites and blogs for extremely popular keywords. Imagine competing for a broad, popular keyword such as *politics* with all the other blogs and Web sites related to politics that have significantly bigger audiences than yours? You're unlikely to win.

Therefore, a better strategy might be to focus on highly targeted, less-popular keywords (such as *California local politics,* if your blog is about local politics in California) that draw attention from advertisers who are looking to promote their products and services to your blog's niche audience. The assumption is that your audience will be more valuable in terms of conversions than a broader, less-focused audience would be.

You can find out more about keywords and analyzing keyword popularity in Chapter 2 of Book II.

Unfortunately, there's no written recipe for success that any blogger can follow to earn money from contextual advertising. Instead, the best course of action is to experiment. Test types of ads, payment models, placement, keywords, and so on until you find the recipe that works for you, your blog, and your audience. Every blog is different, and it takes time to determine which ad mix drives the most interest and revenue on *your* blog.

Exposing the Negatives to Publishing Contextual Ads

There's a downside to publishing contextual ads on your blog. Foremost, your contextual advertising earning potential is only as good as the contextual advertising program from which you publish ads.

Most contextual advertising programs such as Google AdSense or Kontera (both discussed later in this chapter) rely on computer algorithms to determine content relevancy and display ads accordingly. If the algorithm is subpar, the ads displayed on your blog may be irrelevant to your content and uninteresting to your audience. That means click-throughs will be lower than they would be for highly relevant ads, and that means less revenue for you.

Irrelevant ads can also damage the user experience on your blog, particularly if ads that are considered to be inappropriate or offensive to your audience are displayed on your blog. (Displaying an ad for fast food burgers on a vegan lifestyle blog might not go over well.) With that in mind, it's essential that you monitor the ads that appear on your blog to ensure they are acceptable and relevant.

Another negative to contextual advertising is the earning potential. You need three things to earn money from contextual advertising:

- **An audience:** Without traffic to your blog, you won't make any money because there are not enough people to click the ads on your blog.

- **A good contextual advertising program:** As mentioned earlier, if the contextual ads that appear on your blog are irrelevant, then your earning potential goes down.

- **Focused content — a lot of it:** The more targeted content you write for the keywords you choose to focus on, the more opportunities there are for relevant ads to display on your blog to an interested audience.

If you don't have these three things going for you, your contextual advertising income is limited. Be patient and persistent. Your earnings should rise over time as you spend more time testing programs, researching keywords, growing your blog traffic, and writing focused content.

Finding Popular Contextual Ad Programs

There are many contextual advertising networks that you can join in order to serve ads and make money from your blog, but the same programs don't always work well for all bloggers. Always research contextual advertising programs that you consider joining to ensure the payout method, payout threshold, requirements, and restrictions match your goals before you join.

Some contextual advertising programs have established requirements that sites and blogs need to meet in order to be accepted into the network. Be sure to review any requirements before you join a program. Of course, as your blog grows, it will qualify to participate in more contextual advertising programs (such as Pulse 360, discussed later), which may perform better than the broad and highly popular programs such as Google AdSense (discussed very, very soon).

Several of the most popular contextual advertising programs are discussed in the remainder of this chapter.

Note: All of the contextual ad programs that I discuss here offer a tracking feature.

Google AdSense

www.adsense.google.com

Google AdSense, shown in Figure 2-2, is the most popular contextual advertising program. It's easy to add Google AdSense ads to your blog, and ads come in a variety of formats. Payments are reliable, and it's rare to see an ad space left open on your blog for long.

With such a big program and the mammoth Google algorithm behind it, Google AdSense is certainly the simplest program to implement. That's why most bloggers experiment with it before they try another ad program. Unfortunately, that also means your earning potential from Google AdSense might be more limited because there are so many blogs and Web sites competing for available ads, and the relevancy of ads served can sometimes be questionable.

Additionally, it's not uncommon for spam ads to be served through Google AdSense. It's up to you to monitor the ads served on your blog to ensure they're appropriate and modify your account settings or notify Google when problems arise.

Google AdSense offers a variety of ad sizes for you to choose from and display on your blog, making it extremely versatile, as shown in Figures 2-3 through 2-6. There are text ads, image ads, video ads, and even ads that can be served within your blog's RSS feed.

Figure 2-2:
The Google
AdSense
home page.

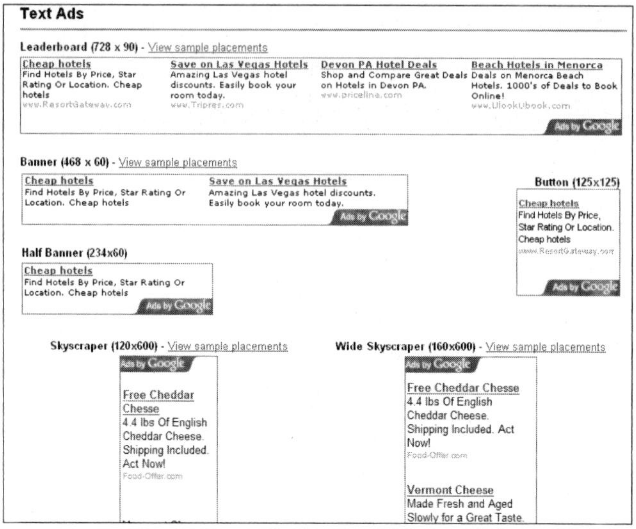

Figure 2-3:
Google
AdSense
text ads.

Figure 2-4:
Google
AdSense
image ads.

After you sign up for a Google account and configure your AdSense settings, you can select an ad unit, copy the provided HTML code, and paste it on your blog where you want ads to appear (often in the sidebar, header, or between posts). Within a couple of days, ads start appearing on your blog. You can log in to your Google AdSense account at any time to track your earnings and modify your ad settings. It's entirely up to you to manage your Google AdSense account. You earn money when visitors to your blog click a Google AdSense ad displayed on your blog.

Figure 2-5:
Google
AdSense
video ads.

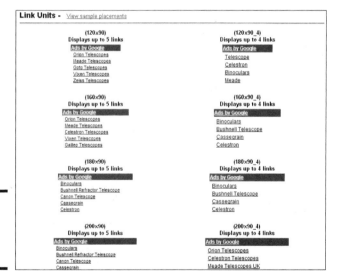

Figure 2-6:
Google
AdSense
link ads.

Kontera

www.kontera.com

Kontera is a contextual advertising program that allows you to publish text link ads (as shown in Figure 2-7) related to your blog's content and earn money each time a visitor to your blog clicks one of those ads.

When a visitor hovers his mouse over the text link on your blog, a small pop-up opens displaying an overview of the ad, as shown in Figure 2-8. When the visitor clicks the text link, he's taken to the advertiser's Web page.

Kontera is extremely easy to implement, and it's free to sign up for an account, create an ad unit, and start earning money from your blog each time a visitor clicks one of the Kontera ads displayed on your blog.

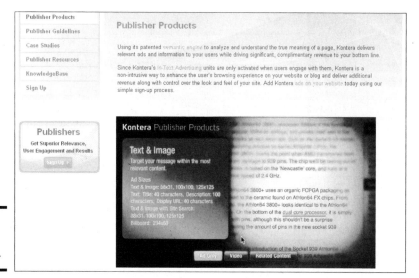

Figure 2-7: A Kontera text link ad.

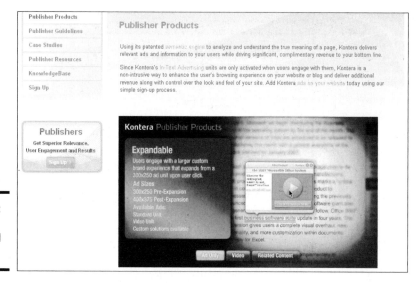

Figure 2-8: A Kontera text link ad pop-up.

Some people associate in-text link ads with a drop in Google page rank, which could negatively affect your blog's traffic over time. That's because Google considers text link ads to be spam. Therefore, proceed with caution. Many bloggers successfully use Kontera to monetize their blogs, but there's a risk associated with it.

Clicksor

www.clicksor.com

Clicksor is a smaller contextual advertising program that's free for you to use on your blog. Just sign up for an account, create your ad unit from the many choices available (shown in Figure 2-9), and you can start earning money each time a visitor clicks one of the Clicksor ads served on your blog.

Clicksor offers ad units in a variety of formats including inline text ads (shown in Figure 2-10), text ads (shown in Figure 2-11), and image ads (shown in Figure 2-12).

Clicksor delivers added value by allowing you to set up some targeting parameters for ads served on your site rather than relying on context alone. For example, you can include geographic parameters for the ads served on your blog. Clicksor uses those parameters in conjunction with its relevancy algorithm to display the best ads possible, which can help maximize click-throughs and boost your earnings.

Figure 2-9:
Clicksor ad formats.

Figure 2-10:
A Clicksor
inline text
ad.

Figure 2-11:
A Clicksor
text ad.

Vibrant

www.vibrantmedia.com

Vibrant Media offers a variety of contextual advertising options for bloggers to make money from their blogs. Unfortunately, the Vibrant Media program has high requirements in terms of the number of page views your blog needs to generate each month in order to sign up for the program, but it's definitely worth putting the program on your radar screen as your blog grows.

Figure 2-12:
A Clicksor
image ad.

Vibrant offers text-based ads that open when a visitor to your blog hovers his mouse over the hyperlinked text (as shown in Figure 2-13), revealing a small pop-up ad. When he clicks the ad, he's taken to the advertiser's site, and you make money.

Pulse 360

www.pulse360.com

Pulse 360 offers pay-per-click contextual ad formats, as shown in Figure 2-14. Pulse 360 differentiates itself by selling the sites where ads are placed rather than just selling keywords. That means the ads that appear on your blog through Pulse 360 should be highly relevant and from well-established advertisers who are looking to communicate with very specific types of audiences.

Pulse 360 boasts a network of well-known publishers, and to join the program, you have to call the company directly. It might not be easy to get accepted, but if you can, Pulse 360 ads can perform very well.

Chitika

http://chitika.com

Chitika premium ads are served based on the keywords entered in popular search engines such as Google. When a person enters a keyword phrase into their preferred search engine and clicks your blog link from the list of search results, Chitika automatically displays an ad based on that keyword phrase on your blog. Ads are only shown to search traffic visitors, not to visitors who come to your blog directly or through a link from another site. Chitika premium ads include pictures and descriptions and come in a wide variety of sizes, as shown in Figure 2-15.

Chitika premium ads follow the pay-per-click payment model, so you make money when a person clicks the ads on your blog. The ads tend to work best on sites that receive a significant amount of search traffic each month and use highly targeted keywords.

Figure 2-13:
A Vibrant Media text ad.

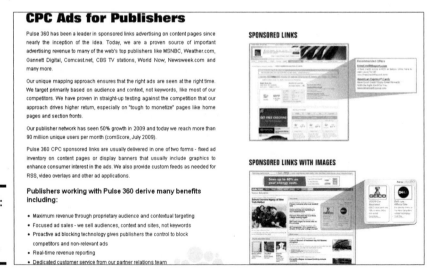

Figure 2-14:
Pulse 360 contextual ad formats.

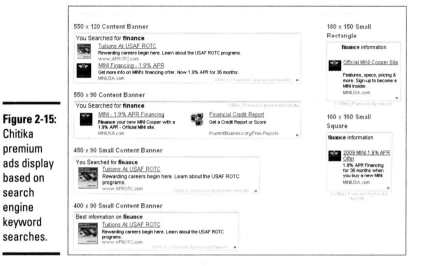

Figure 2-15:
Chitika
premium
ads display
based on
search
engine
keyword
searches.

Chapter 3: Using Text Link Ads

In This Chapter

✔ Understanding text link ads

✔ Knowing the positives of text link ads

✔ Revealing the negatives of text link ads

✔ Finding popular text link ad programs

Text link ads are exactly what the name implies: text links that advertisers pay for, which lead people to the advertiser's Web page. Many companies sell text link ads, and different programs have different publisher requirements in terms of whether or not your blog will be accepted.

Text link ads can generate a nice amount of income from your blog, but they are controversial because search engines view them as a way to artificially inflate the popularity of a Web page. For example, Google's search-results-ranking algorithm includes the number of incoming links to a Web page as assumptive of that page's popularity, believing that the more people that link to a Web page, the better the content must be. Therefore, paying for links skews the assumed popularity of a Web page, and Google punishes both the text link advertiser and publisher for giving an unfair advantage to the advertiser's search rankings. In fact, your blog could be dropped from Google search results entirely if you publish text link ads.

This chapter walks you through an introduction to text link ads so you fully understand the pros and cons of publishing text link ads on your blog. You also find out about some of the most popular text link advertising programs, so you can begin experimenting with them if you choose.

Understanding Text Link Ads

Text link ads may or may not be contextually based, and they can appear inline (within the body copy of your posts) or as standalone links, as shown in Figure 3-1 (notice the text links within the post and in the sidebar under the *Related Resources* heading). Payment models also differ with the most common being the pay-per-click method.

Figure 3-1:
Examples of inline and standalone text link ads.

When you join a text link advertising program, you submit specific pages of your blog into the network's inventory. Advertisers look for inventory pages that are likely to attract visitors who will be interested in their products. When they find pages they want to advertise on, they purchase text link ad space on those pages and an ad from that advertiser appears in that space. You earn money each time someone clicks the text link ad published on your blog. It's that simple!

Blogs with a lot of content that are highly trafficked can make quite a bit of money from relevant text link ads.

Knowing the Positives of Text Link Ads

Text link ads have some great things going for them. They're fairly unobtrusive to the user experience on your blog, and they take up little space (or no additional space in the case of inline text ads). For bloggers who want to make as much money as possible from the limited space on their blogs, text link ads are very attractive.

At the same time, text link ads tend to convert better in terms of generating click-throughs than other types of ads, particularly inline text ads, because readers assume the text link will take them to more useful information. In other words, they might be fooled into thinking the link is not an ad at all. Unfortunately, this misconception is also a negative because it could be considered unethical and a loose bait-and-switch tactic. It's up to you as a blogger to determine the level of transparency you require on your blog to protect the user experience.

One of the biggest positives of text link ads is the simplicity of integrating them into your blog. Most text link ad programs make it extremely easy to sell space on your blog to eager advertisers. The more focused your blog's content is, and the more traffic it receives, the more money you can make from text link ads.

Uncovering the Negatives of Text Link Ads

Text link ads do have some drawbacks, and they're nothing to sneeze at. They can frustrate your blog's visitors who click a link within one of your blog posts and end up getting an ad in return. You certainly don't want to drive traffic away from your blog because your links fail to meet expectations and the user experience becomes frustrating! However, a negative user experience isn't the only drawback of publishing text link ads on your blog.

The biggest problem with text link ads is the potential harm they could do to the amount of search traffic that comes to your blog. Google and other search engines rank Web pages in terms of keyword relevancy and usefulness and return results for keyword searches based on that algorithm, which includes a component related to incoming links. Although no one but the inner circle of Google's employees knows the secrets of Google's page-ranking algorithm, one thing is for certain — Google does not like sponsored links (such as text link ads) because they artificially inflate a site's popularity.

Google believes that the best pages on the Web will get a lot of incoming links because people want to share that content. If someone pays for incoming links, that person is artificially inflating the popularity of the Web pages. As a result, Google has been known to punish both the advertiser and text link ad publisher by dropping both sites' Google page ranks or eliminating them from Google search results entirely. Most blogs generate the bulk of their traffic from Google searches. Imagine the harm that a lowered page rank (which Google uses to weight your blog when returning search results) or even removal from Google search could do to your blog.

Although some text link ad networks claim to have procedures in place to protect advertisers and publishers, unless the link uses the NoFollow HTML tag, which means Google will not include the link in its ranking process, there's no way to be sure publishing text link ads on your blog is safe.

The NoFollow HTML tag can be added to any link to make that link invisible to Google when it counts incoming links to a site for ranking purposes. You can find out more about the NoFollow tag in Chapter 1 of Book V.

Text link ads and the death of a blog network

Know More Media was a popular business blog network founded in late 2005 with nearly 100 highly trafficked blogs by 2008. Know More Media employed business experts to author the blogs in the network and sold ad space to cover expenses. The network grew quickly and derived a large amount of traffic from Google and other search engines until one day in 2008 when Google traffic to all blogs in the network nearly disappeared.

What happened?

It took some investigation, but the definitive answer was that Know More Media published text link ads on its blogs without the NoFollow HTML tag, and it was punished severely for it.

Just a few months earlier, Know More Media had begun displaying text ads on its blogs (see the example on the Know More Media blog *Customers Are Always* in Figure 3-1), and Google dropped all of the Know More Media blogs from its search ranking. After removing the text link ads from all Know More Media blogs and spending a few months trying to work with Google to get the Know More Media blogs included in Google search results again, Know More Media saw no signs of redemption or reinclusion. With no search traffic, the entire network folded, and Know More Media closed its doors in mid-2008.

Only you can decide whether the safeguards used by the text link advertising network coupled with the revenue potential are enough to meet your goals for your blog. Weigh the positives and negatives carefully and proceed with caution. See the nearby sidebar for a real-world case study in the negative effects of text link advertising.

Finding Popular Text Link Ad Programs

There's a big variety of text link ad programs that you can join to publish text link ads on your blog. Each program offers slightly different payouts and requirements. Always read all the terms of the publisher agreement before you join a text link ad program to ensure it matches your goals. Knowing the potential harm text link ads can do to your blog, be sure to stick with reputable companies.

The following sections introduce you to several of the most popular text link advertising programs, so you can research them further and determine whether one works for you.

TextLinkBrokers

www.textlinkbrokers.com

TextLinkBrokers has been around for several years and is very well known. The company claims to have safeguards in place to protect your Google page rank if you publish text link ads on your blog, but be sure to check the current information on the company's Web site before you join. These programs tend to change frequently, and it's up to you to stay up-to-date.

To join TextLinkBrokers, simply sign up for an account and provide the requested information about your blog. If you're blog is accepted into the program, a rate is assigned to links sold on your blog, and your blog is added to the current inventory list on the TextLinkBrokers Web site, as shown in Figure 3-2. Advertisers search the inventory and purchase ad space on sites that meet their requirements. When space is purchased on your blog, the advertiser's ad is displayed on your blog.

1 | 2 | 3 | 4 | 5 | 6 | 7 | 8 | 9 | 10 | 11 | 12 | 13 | 14 | 15 | 16 | 17 | 18 | 19 | 20 | 21 | 22 | 23 | 24 | 25 | 26 | 27 | 28 | 29 | 30 | 31 | 32 | 33 | 34 | 35 | 36 | 37 | 38 | 39 | 40 | 41 | 42 | 43

SITE ID	SITE DESCRIPTION	# of PAGES	SITE AGE	ZONE	OUTBOUNDS	TLB SCORE	DETAILS
9495	Business advice site	62	11 yrs.	1	0	109	DETAILS
2029	Weather Trivia Site	2	14 yrs.	1	0	108	DETAILS
4929	Child Education directory site	21	11 yrs.	1	0	107	DETAILS
3551	World news and expression site	4	10 yrs.	1	10	105	DETAILS
8563	Travel Site	1	12 yrs.	1	11	105	DETAILS
1727	Publication and News Service Site	3	10 yrs.	1	3	104	DETAILS
4963	Computers/Technology Blog Site	9	10 yrs.	2		104	DETAILS
9504	gas price tracker site	33	11 yrs.	1	0	104	DETAILS
3351	Books/Literature news site	1	8 yrs.	1	32	103	DETAILS
3375	Science & biology site	11	5 yrs.	2	0	103	DETAILS
8484	Online video site	3	N/A	2	2	103	DETAILS
9477	internet community site	16	5 yrs.	1	0	103	DETAILS
2246	Steam Locomotive Site	1	11 yrs.	2	2	102	DETAILS
4181	Software Graphics Site	1	12 yrs.	1	2	102	DETAILS
9445	Jefferson airplane music site	41	12 yrs.	1	0	102	DETAILS
9497	Disabilities support website	27	13 yrs.	1	1	102	DETAILS
9500	browser compatibility site	44	12 yrs.	1	0	102	DETAILS
9647	Guitar worship info site	14	11 yrs.	1	1	102	DETAILS
4123	Used books directory	2	9 yrs.	1	11	100	DETAILS
5013	Business phone number directory	2	10 yrs.	2	10	100	DETAILS
7949	Food Site	2	14 yrs.	2	1	100	DETAILS
2240	Military Aviation Photography Site	1	9 yrs.	2	1	99	DETAILS
2243	UFO Phenomenon Site	1	11 yrs.	2	1	99	DETAILS
3671	Leadership/Business site	23	9 yrs.	2	0	99	DETAILS

Figure 3-2: TextLink-Brokers Inventory List.

TextLinkBrokers offers monthly rented links, contextual links, hosted pages of links, and more to bloggers. You can pick and choose the opportunities you want to participate in, and you can approve or deny all text link ad requests that you receive.

Text Link Ads

`www.text-link-ads.com`

Text Link Ads is a popular text link advertising broker that allows you to publish text link ads on your blog, as shown in Figure 3-3.

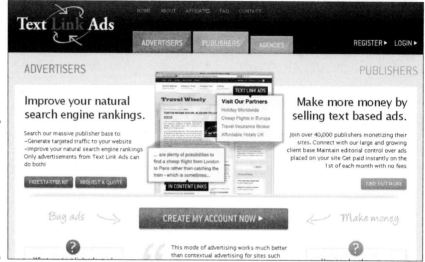

You can sign up to participate in the Text Link Ads network for free. If your blog is accepted into the program, a price is set by Text Link Ads for space sold on your blog, and advertisers can purchase that space from the Text Link Ads inventory. You have the opportunity to approve or deny an ad before it's published on your blog.

LinkWorth

www.linkworth.com

LinkWorth offers a wide variety of text ad formats (shown in Figure 3-4) including standalone, inline, and contextual text ads. LinkWorth publishers (called *partners*) can configure their accounts to use the NoFollow HTML tag with all text link ads, thereby avoiding any problems with a drop in Google page rank.

LinkAdage

www.linkadage.com

LinkAdage is a smaller text link advertising program that is free to join. You set the price you want to charge for ads placed on your blog, and when an advertiser purchases that space, the ad is served on your blog using the special code provided by LinkAdage. You can also customize the design of the text link ads displayed on your site and filter the types of ads displayed on your blog by category.

LinkAdage enables you to sell text links on your blog in several different ways with the broker method shown in Figure 3-5.

Text link ads might seem like easy money, but they can do more harm than good. Do your research first!

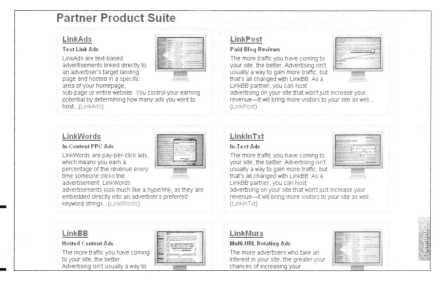

Figure 3-4:
LinkWorth
ad formats.

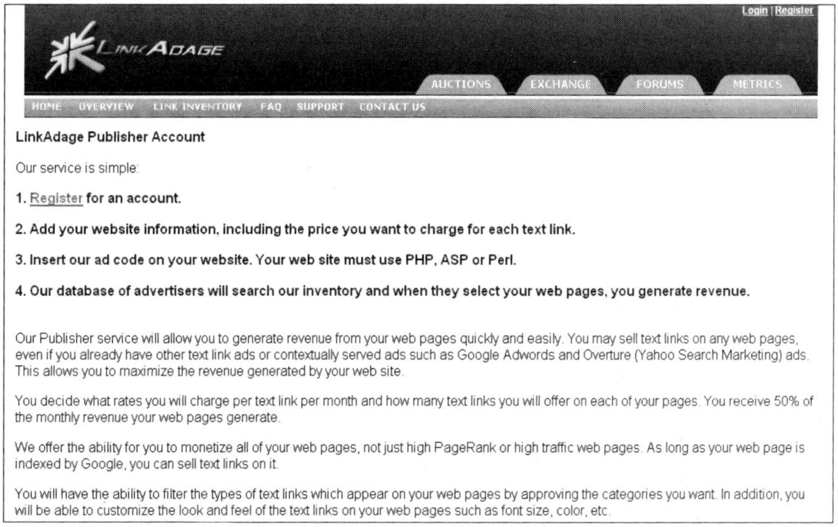

Figure 3-5:
The
LinkAdage
Publisher
page.

Chapter 4: Placing Impression Ads

In This Chapter

✔ **Finding out about impression-based ads**

✔ **Reviewing the problems**

✔ **Finding popular impression-based ad programs**

*I*mpression-based ads pay you each time the page on your blog loads (hence the term *impression*) that the ads appear on, and they offer a great way to monetize your blog. Although many impression-based ad networks have strict requirements for publishers related to traffic levels and content, it's not impossible for beginner bloggers to find programs to join.

This chapter introduces you to impression-based ads so you understand the pros and cons and can make the best decision about testing impression ads on your blog. You also find out about some of the most popular impression-based advertising programs, so you can begin your experimentation.

Understanding Impression-Based Ads

Impression-based ads are popular with bloggers because no action is necessary for you to make money. In other words, each time the ad is displayed on your blog (meaning each time someone loads a page on your blog where the ad appears), you earn money regardless of whether visitors click the ad or notice it at all.

In simplest terms, you're paid based on the number of times an ad is shown on your blog. With each page view where the ad is placed, that ad is delivered to a visitor, which counts as an impression. Advertisers pay bloggers a small fee, such as $0.10 per 1,000 impressions, so you're not likely to make a lot of money from these ads unless your blog is very highly trafficked.

Typically, impression-based ads pay less per impression to publishers than most pay-per-click or pay-per-action ads, but blogs with high traffic levels can earn a nice amount of money from them. In fact, many impression-based ad programs accept only well-trafficked blogs into their networks. The reason is simple: Advertisers want to make sure they're going to get enough exposure (page views) to make their monetary investment worthwhile.

That's not to say that a blogger with a smaller audience can't find an impression-based advertising program that will accept him. The more targeted your blog content is and the more desirable your niche blog audience is to advertisers, the more likely you are to secure impression-based advertising on your blog.

Many bloggers think impression-based ads are the ultimate form of advertising to monetize their blogs, but that isn't always the case. Unless your blog gets a lot of traffic, you won't make a lot of money from impression-based ads. However, it's guaranteed money because no action is required by your audience in order for you to earn an income from impression-based ads.

Reviewing the Problems with Impression-Based Ads

Before you jump on the bandwagon, you should know the downsides to impression-based ads. Aside from limited earning potential, wherein only highly trafficked blogs are likely to make a lot of money from impression-based ads, the format has a few other problems as well. First, you need to be certain that the advertiser or program you join is accurately counting page views. Make sure you join a program that provides detailed reports and match them up to your own site analytics to ensure they're correct.

Furthermore, impression-based ads are a great way for bloggers to monetize the area of their blog below the fold (the *fold* is the area that's visible in a browser window when a page loads), which works very well for publishers but not for advertisers. That's why many advertisers have strict placement restrictions related to their impression-based ads — to ensure their ads aren't hidden in places where no one will see them.

Some impression-based advertisers even have restrictions on where other ads can be placed on your blog when their ads are displayed. For example, an advertiser might require that its impression-based ad be published within the top 720 pixels of your blog with no other ads appearing above the 720 pixel mark. In essence, the advertiser wants its ad to be the only one visible above the fold on your blog. These requirements can severely limit the advertising flexibility on your blog.

Always check the restrictions on ad placement and participation in other advertising programs for the impression-based ad network you join to ensure it doesn't actually reduce your blog's earning potential.

It's important to balance the amount of money you're likely to generate from impression-based ads by placing them in premium locations on your blog against the earning potential pay-per-click or pay-per-action ads could derive from those premium locations. That's why testing and experimenting is so important to finding the best earnings plan for your blog.

Finding Popular Impression-Based Ad Programs

You have many impression-based ad programs to choose from, and it's up to you to read the current requirements of each program in order to determine whether or not a program is right for you to test on your blog. Requirements change frequently! The following sections identify some of the most popular and well-known impression-based ad programs to help you get started.

Carefully read all impression-based advertising agreements before you sign them to ensure you're willing and able to comply with them.

Tribal Fusion

www.tribalfusion.com

Tribal Fusion is a very popular advertising network that offers impression-based advertising opportunities to publishers with established blogs and high daily traffic volumes. To join Tribal Fusion, you need to meet specific page view requirements, your blog must be updated frequently, and it must have a professional design. Be sure to check the Tribal Fusion Web site for current program participation requirements to see whether your blog qualifies.

As a Tribal Fusion ad publisher, you can control the types of ads delivered on your blog by blocking ad categories or specific advertisers. After your application to join the program is approved, you can configure your publisher account settings and begin accepting ads on your blog. Tribal Fusion handles the behind-the-scenes technology that matches ads with publishers for maximum performance for both you and the advertiser.

Tribal Fusion offers image, flash (animated image ads), pop-under, interstitial, video, expandable, and floating ad units, so there's likely to be an ad format that works on your blog. (I explain these types of ads in more detail in Chapter 1 of this minibook.) Advertisers can advertise on specific blogs within the TribalFusion network, which are separated by category, as shown in Figure 4-1, or across the entire network.

ValueClick Media

www.valueclickmedia.com

ValueClick Media offers a popular impression-based advertising program for well-trafficked blogs. The traffic requirements for ValueClick Media are lower than those for Tribal Fusion, making it easier for smaller blogs to be accepted into the program, but always check the Web site for the most up-to-date participation requirements before you submit an application.

**Book VII
Chapter 4**

Placing Impression Ads

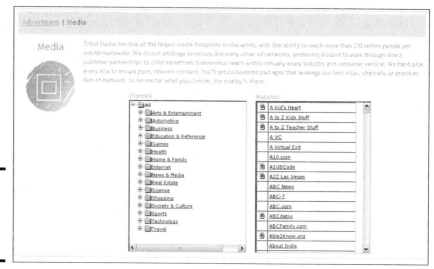

Figure 4-1:
Tribal
Fusion
publishers
list.

After your blog is accepted into the ValueClick Media network, you can
begin displaying ads on your blog in a variety of formats, including banners,
rich-media, pop-unders, and video ads, as shown in Figure 4-2. You can also
approve or deny any ads that ValueClick Media associates with your blog
and set the minimum cost per impression that advertisers must pay in order
to place ads on your blog.

Burst Media

www.burstmedia.com

The Burst Media impression-based advertising program is called Burst
Network. Only well-trafficked blogs are accepted into the Burst Network program, so be sure to check the Web site for the most current requirements for
participation. As a Burst Network publisher, you can choose the ad formats
and campaigns you want to run on your blog. The more formats and campaigns you're willing to publish on your blog, the more money you can make.

You can sign up for an exclusive or nonexclusive agreement with Burst
Network. Exclusive publishers typically get the best ads, but they can't display ads from other networks on their blogs. You must weigh the positives
of displaying higher paying ads on your blog through Burst Network with the
revenue you might lose by putting all of your eggs in one basket and forego-
ing other advertising options.

Burst Media offers an excellent reporting tool, shown in Figure 4-3, so you can keep track of your earnings and ad performance at any time.

Figure 4-2:
A partial list of ValueClick Media ad formats.

Figure 4-3:
The Burst Media reporting tool.

Six Apart Media

www.sixapart.com

Six Apart owns several blogging platforms, including TypePad and Movable Type. Six Apart Media (shown in Figure 4-4) is the advertising arm of Six Apart that connects advertisers with publishers through an impression-based ad network.

The Six Apart Media Advertising Program is managed by Adify (www.adify.com), which is shown in Figure 4-5. Six Apart has fewer requirements for publisher acceptance than some of the other popular impression-based advertising programs, because it has been around for a shorter amount of time and is still growing.

When your blog is accepted into the Six Apart Media Advertising Program, you're instructed to set up an account with Adify to manage your ads. From there, you can set the rates you want to charge for your ad space, control the ads that appear on your blog, and more.

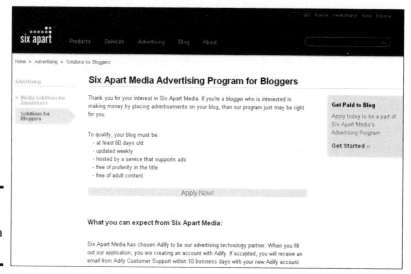

Figure 4-4:
The Six Apart Media site.

Figure 4-5:
The Adify
home page.

Chapter 5: Making Money with Affiliate Advertising

In This Chapter

✔ Understanding affiliate advertising

✔ Benefiting from affiliate advertising

✔ Knowing the problems of affiliate advertising

✔ Making affiliate advertising work on your blog

✔ Finding popular affiliate advertising programs

*A*ffiliate advertising is a form of online advertising where advertisers pay online publishers (such as bloggers) to place ads on their sites and receive a payment in return for some type of action from the publisher's visitors. For example, the publisher (called an *affiliate*) might get paid a determined amount when a visitor clicks the advertiser's ad, visits the advertiser's site, and makes a purchase.

Affiliate advertising is popular among both bloggers and advertisers. Not only does it offer advertisers a way to promote their products and services in front of highly targeted audiences, but it also provides an excellent way for bloggers to make money from their blogs with little additional effort. After an affiliate program is set up, it typically runs on its own!

This chapter explains what affiliate advertising is and how you can use it to derive an income from your blog. I also warn you about problems to avoid and how to find affiliate advertising programs that offer the best chance for you to make money.

Understanding Affiliate Advertising

Affiliate advertisers pay bloggers to promote their products and services on their blogs. In return, the advertiser pays the blogger whenever a visitor to that blog performs some type of action such as clicking the affiliate link and making a purchase.

Both large and small companies use affiliate advertising to promote their products and services. Some manage their affiliate advertising programs internally, and others go through a third-party affiliate directory, which handles all the technology and behind-the-scenes maintenance of each advertiser's program.

Affiliate advertising comes in many forms. You can publish text, image, or video ads that link to the advertiser's Web site, or you can link to that site directly within the content of a blog post. Anytime you link to the advertiser's site, you just include your unique affiliate identification link, so the person's actions can be tracked. That's how you get paid. Without your special affiliate link, there's no way for you to get paid.

Benefiting from Affiliate Advertising

Affiliate advertising can work very well for niche blogs that are directly related to consumer products or services. For example, technology bloggers can easily join affiliate programs that allow them to earn money from affiliate links to computer products and gadgets. Similarly, pregnancy bloggers can benefit from affiliate programs that allow them to earn money from affiliate links to baby gear, books, DVDs, and more!

The more closely tied to your blog topic that your affiliate ads are, the more money you're likely to make.

With that in mind, affiliate advertising is a form of blog monetization that can actually *enhance* your blog. If the products and services advertised through the affiliate ads on your blog are directly related to your blog's topic, your readers are likely to find those links to be useful and helpful. That's not always the case with other advertising opportunities such as contextual ads that offer far less control to bloggers.

Think of your affiliate advertising earnings as a commission paid to you for helping to sell the advertiser's product. Rather than the advertiser paying for ad space on your blog, they pay you when your affiliate link drives the action the advertiser requires from it. Typically, payments from affiliate advertising are higher on a per-action basis than contextual or impression ads are on a per-click or per-impression basis. However, because an action is required in order for you to make money, the frequency of earnings is lower. That's why it's absolutely essential that you test affiliate advertising programs on your blog to identify the ones that your audience members are most interested in and find most useful.

Knowing the Problems with Affiliate Advertising

As mentioned in the previous section, affiliate advertising requires an action for you to make money. The space taken by an affiliate ad on your blog reduces the amount of contextual, pay-per-click, or direct advertising you can place on your blog. It's up to you to evaluate your blogging goals to determine whether you should use that space for pay-per-action affiliate advertising.

Furthermore, affiliate advertising won't help you make money from your blog if your readers aren't interested in the products and services you're linking to as an affiliate. Your efforts are for naught if you're not offering products that appeal to your existing audience.

Many bloggers are turned off by affiliate advertising. Although the payments are higher than many other forms of advertising, they come less frequently (only when a visitor performs the necessary action). Therefore, affiliate advertising tends to work best for niche blogs with large audiences. The reason is two-fold: It's easier to find products readers are interested in when you blog about a highly targeted topic, and more people are statistically likely to click your affiliate link and perform the required action when there's a larger audience that sees it.

Another important point to understand about affiliate advertising is that not all programs are created equal. Be sure to thoroughly research any affiliate advertising program you consider joining before you do so. Read the contracts and agreements, become familiar with the payment terms, and make sure the process works for you and helps you meet your goals for your blog.

Making Affiliate Advertising Work on Your Blog

Affiliate advertising is popular for several reasons. First, it's easy for both advertisers and bloggers to implement. Second, targeted affiliate ads can generate sizeable revenues for both advertisers and bloggers. Third, affiliate advertising can actually be viewed as unobtrusive and helpful to blog audiences, which is something most other monetization opportunities don't provide.

How do you make affiliate advertising work for you, your blog, and your readers? Begin by researching affiliate advertising programs to find ones that offer the best earning potential given the products or services being advertised and the interests of your audience. Following are a number of tips to help you make your affiliate advertising efforts a success:

✦ **Program trustworthiness:** Make sure you choose an affiliate advertiser or affiliate advertising manager that is reputable, meaning it tracks results accurately, pays decent commissions, and pays on time.

✦ **Advertiser reputation:** Only choose affiliate advertisers whose products and brands match your audience's expectations for your blog. If you wouldn't be comfortable buying from the company you're advertising, then don't publish those ads on your blog. They can do more harm than good in terms of how your audience views you and your blog.

✦ **Commissions:** The types of commission structures offered by affiliate advertisers runs the gamut. Make sure you stand to make an adequate amount of money on any affiliate program you join. A good guideline is to look for commission rates above 20 percent.

✦ **Product and service pricing:** If the products or services you're selling on your blog through affiliate advertising are priced very low, then you need to generate a lot of clicks and actions in order to make more than pennies on your effort. Consider how well an affiliate ad can monetize a space on your blog given the product and service pricing and commission rate to ensure it's worth your while.

✦ **Tracking mechanism and accuracy:** The best affiliate advertising programs offer tracking tools so you can analyze your blog's performance and modify your participation as necessary to maximize your earning potential. Furthermore, the affiliate advertising program you choose should be capable of accurately tracking the performance of your affiliate ads and links, so you're certain you're paid correctly.

✦ **Support and help:** Make sure the affiliate program you join offers help when you need it. Online support, e-mail support, or telephone support is adequate — as long as you have some way to contact a human being to work through any problems you encounter related to ads displaying correctly, payments, and so on.

After you choose your affiliate program, there are additional steps you can take to boost the earnings potential of your affiliate ads and links. Following are a some tips to help you:

✦ **Placement:** Where you place your affiliate ads and links on your blog can have a significant impact on conversions. For example, an affiliate link placed within your blog's footer is unlikely to generate as many clicks and actions as an affiliate link at the top of your blog's sidebar could. Place your affiliate ads and links where your blog readers are likely to see them, such as within your blog posts, between posts, in your blog's sidebar, in your blog's header, in your blog's navigation bar, and so on.

✦ **Promotion:** You can drive traffic to your affiliate links and ads with promotion. For example, include them on your Twitter and Facebook profiles and updates, include them at the bottom of your e-mail signature, and anywhere else you can think of.

✦ **Timeliness:** Don't select an affiliate ad and then abandon it. Update your affiliate links and ads so they always lead to products and services that your audience is likely to be interested in at that moment in time. Stale ads don't drive as much attention and traffic as timely, updated ads do. Rotate your ads for maximum awareness and interest.

✦ **Tracking:** Don't just rely on the advertiser to provide you with tracking reports. Instead, set up your own tracking mechanisms to enhance the advertiser's reports by using your Web analytics tool (as discussed in Chapter 2 of Book V).

Finding Popular Affiliate Advertising Programs

With so many affiliate programs available for bloggers, it can be hard to find the right place to start. The following sections provide you an overview of some of the most popular affiliate advertising programs, so you can begin your own research to find the one that best meets your goals and your audience's needs.

Much of your affiliate advertising success comes from testing different products and programs and finding the right mix for your audience, but you can help the earnings come in by following the tips listed earlier in this chapter and experimenting with placement, ad types, products, and more, as well as promoting your affiliate links off of your blog.

Read all the terms and conditions related to any affiliate program you're considering joining before you commit. For example, the last thing you want is to join a program only to find out later that the program is exclusive, meaning you aren't allowed to display any other form of affiliate advertising on your blog. Also, make sure you can drop out of the program at any time if it's not meeting your needs.

Direct affiliate programs

Direct affiliate programs are created and managed directly by the advertiser. You sign up to participate in the affiliate program on the advertiser's Web site, you access reports and tracking through the advertiser, and the advertiser pays you directly. Following are a few popular direct affiliate programs for bloggers.

Amazon Associates

```
https://affiliate-program.amazon.com
```

The affiliate program from Amazon.com is called Amazon Associates. Nearly any online publisher can join Amazon Associates for free and immediately begin publishing affiliate links and ads to any product listed on the Amazon Web site, including books, music, clothing, electronics, and more. Because Amazon sells such a wide variety of products, it's easy for bloggers to find some products that would be useful to their readers.

The Amazon Associates program offers flexibility in terms of both the earnings model and payments. Additionally, Amazon offers a wide variety of ad formats to choose from, several of which are shown in Figure 5-1. You can choose from image ads, interactive ads, video ads, link ads, and more! You can also publish multiple Amazon affiliate ads on your blog.

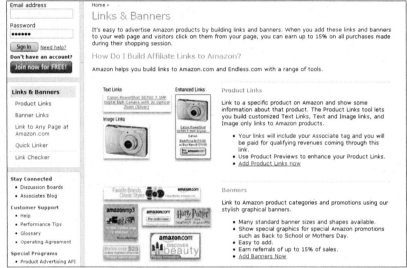

Figure 5-1:
Amazon Associates offers a variety of ad formats.

To become an Amazon Associate, simply visit the Amazon Associates Web site and click the Join Now button. Provide the information requested in the application form, and you're given access to Associates Central, where you can configure your ads and start making money!

It's very easy to add Amazon Associates affiliate links and ads to your blog. The Associates Central site walks you through the process to configure any ad for your blog. After you configure your ad, you're given a bit of HTML code, which you can copy and paste on your blog where you want the ad to appear. It really is that easy.

As an Amazon Associates affiliate, you can either self-select the products you want to link to from your blog or use one of the automated features to link to current popular products, wish lists, and more. You can even set up your own Amazon store front such as the one shown in Figure 5-2, fill it with products your audience is likely to be interested in, and link to it from your blog. If you prefer, you can embed your Amazon store into your blog, so it looks like it's actually part of your blog.

The options for making money with Amazon Associates on your blog are numerous, and because so many people know the Amazon brand and trust shopping with Amazon, your earnings potential goes up.

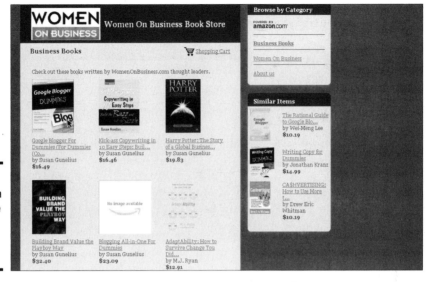

**Book VII
Chapter 5**

Making Money with Affiliate Advertising

Figure 5-2:
The Amazon store for the Women On Business blog.

eBay Partner Network

https://www.ebaypartnernetwork.com/files/hub/en-US/index.html

With the eBay Partner Network, you can earn money by linking to products for sale or up for auction on eBay.com. The eBay affiliate program uses what it calls a Quality Click Pricing (QPC) model, which fuses the pay-per-action payment model with the pay-per-click (EPC) model. In other words, as an eBay affiliate, you make money on an earn-per-click basis depending on the quality of the traffic (in terms of short-term sales and long-term value) that your blog sends to eBay via your link.

According to the eBay Partner Network Web site, affiliates typically earn between $0.06 and $0.21 per click. However, it's difficult to control your eBay Partner Network earnings. Although you can drive traffic to eBay through your affiliate ads and links and motivate people to make purchases boosting your short-term quality rating, it's difficult to control future purchases and activities (that is, your long-term quality rating). You need to test this program extensively to determine whether it's appropriate for your blog, your audience, and your goals.

You can include eBay ads on your blog through image ads, banners, text links, or within your blog's feed. Figure 5-3 provides an example of an eBay Partner Network ad published on a blog.

Figure 5-3:
An eBay
Partner
Network ad
sample.

AllPosters.com

http://affiliates.allposters.com/affiliatesnet

If you write a blog that can be directly related to art, posters, and so on, then AllPosters.com offers an affiliate program that might work well for you and your audience. For example, entertainment bloggers can link to posters of popular celebrities or movies. Similarly, art bloggers could link to artist prints. There are many opportunities to monetize a blog if the blog's audience is interested in products available through AllPosters.com.

The standard commission rate for AllPosters.com affiliates is 20 percent, making it a competitive program. As an AllPosters.com affiliate, you can display image, banner, flash, and other types of ads on your blog. You can even create an AllPosters.com store, complete with search functionality, as shown in Figure 5-4.

Third-party-managed affiliate programs

Third-party-managed affiliate programs are run by companies that handle all of the technical and payment aspects of an advertiser's affiliate program. Bloggers can join a number of advertiser's affiliate programs through the third-party manager's Web site. Reports, payments, and so on are accessed through the third-party manager rather than through the advertiser directly.

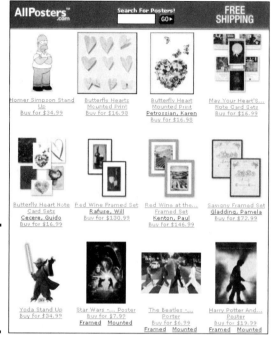

**Book VII
Chapter 5**

**Making Money with
Affiliate Advertising**

Figure 5-4:
An
AllPosters.
com affiliate
store
sample.

LinkShare

www.linkshare.com

LinkShare is a popular third-party affiliate program that allows you to create affiliate links for a wide variety of LinkShare partner advertisers. In fact, many of the companies that advertise through the LinkShare affiliate program are well-known, such as Macy's, PetSmart, Walmart, iTunes, and more. Many of your blog's readers are likely to feel more comfortable clicking links and buying from companies and brands they recognize and trust, which could boost your earnings as a LinkShare affiliate versus other programs.

Unlike other affiliate directory programs that require publishers to have highly trafficked blogs in order to become an affiliate, LinkShare is open to small blogs, too. The site provides an extensive help section, and it's easy to register and start displaying a variety of affiliate ads on your blog, such as the sample contextual ad shown in Figure 5-5.

Figure 5-5:
A LinkShare
affiliate ad.

Not all advertisers in the LinkShare affiliate program pay the same. Be sure to check the requirements and payment method for each advertiser to ensure the terms match your goals.

Commission Junction

www.cj.com

Commission Junction, shown in Figure 5-6, is a popular third-party affiliate advertising program, particularly for established and well-trafficked blogs. To become a Commission Junction affiliate, your application goes through a multistep approval process. After your blog is approved, you can apply to join specific Commission Junction advertiser partners' affiliate programs. Different advertisers use different payment models within the Commission Junction affiliate program.

Commission Junction advertisers are typically well-known companies and brands such as Yahoo!, Expedia, Hewlett-Packard, Home Depot, and more, which your blog's readers are likely to feel comfortable clicking on and buying from. Of course, that trust helps boost your conversions and earnings.

E-junkie

www.e-junkie.com

E-junkie, shown in Figure 5-7, is a popular third-party affiliate program manager for entrepreneurs as well as small and mid-size businesses. Any advertiser can join and implement a robust affiliate program quickly and easily through E-junkie. You can join an affiliate program listed through E-junkie and make money based on the individual advertiser's terms. All payment, tracking, and so on are done through the E-junkie Web site.

Figure 5-6: Commission Junction is a popular affiliate advertising company.

Figure 5-7: E-junkie is popular among small advertisers.

ShareASale

www.shareasale.com

ShareASale, shown in Figure 5-8, is a smaller third-party affiliate manager that is popular among entrepreneurs and small business owners. You can join ShareASale and search for and apply to join affiliate programs that you think would work well on your blog. ShareASale provides all the technical information you need as well as payments and reporting.

Affiliate directories

Affiliate directories are Web sites that list a wide variety of direct affiliate programs. These directories list submissions from companies and individuals and may include reviews and other useful information added by site users. Rather than joining the program through the affiliate directory Web site, links are provided to visit each advertiser's site and join each program directly. Tracking, payment, and so on is handled by the advertiser or a third-party manager depending on the specific advertiser's program. Following are overviews of some comprehensive affiliate directories.

Associate Programs

www.associateprograms.com

Associate Programs offers a directory that includes a variety of affiliate programs for bloggers to join. Both large and small companies' affiliate opportunities are listed through Associate Programs, including some well-known brands such as Amazon.com and Barnes & Noble.

When you visit the Associate Programs Web site, you can search the site to find affiliate programs by category. When you find a program that suits your needs and matches your readers' interests, you can follow the provided link to apply to join that program. For example, if you write a blog about wine, you can search Associate Programs to find affiliate programs related to wine, such as those shown in Figure 5-9.

AffiliatesDirectory.com

http://affiliatesdirectory.com

AffiliatesDirectory.com offers a useful directory of affiliate programs complete with reviews, ratings, and more, as shown in Figure 5-10. Links are provided to each program where you can get more information directly from the advertiser and apply to join a specific program directly through the advertiser or third-party manager's Web site.

Both large and small companies list their affiliate programs on AffiliatesDirectory.com, including well-known brands such as Travelocity and Blockbuster.

Figure 5-8: ShareASale is popular among entrepreneurs.

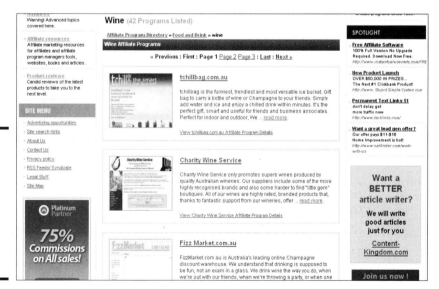

Figure 5-9: Sample wine-related affiliate programs from Associate Programs.

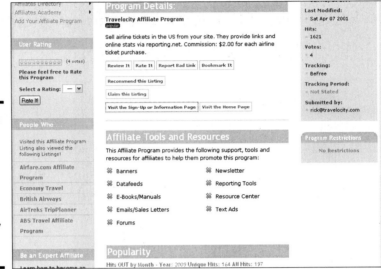

Figure 5-10:
Affiliates-
Directory.
com
provides
affiliate
program
information,
reviews,
and more.

Chapter 6: Publishing Sponsored Reviews and Paid Posts

In This Chapter

✔ Getting the scoop on sponsored reviews

✔ Understanding why bloggers like sponsored reviews and paid posts

✔ Exposing drawbacks of sponsored reviews and paid posts

✔ Publishing sponsored reviews and paid posts safely

✔ Finding popular sponsored review and paid post programs

*P*ublishing posts on your blog that a company or individual pays you to write is a popular way to make money, but sponsored reviews and paid posts do not come without potential problems. In fact, they can bring big problems to bloggers who are not aware of how to publish sponsored reviews and paid posts correctly to meet blogosphere, ethical, and legal requirements.

This chapter walks you through the process of publishing sponsored reviews and paid posts on your blog with extra attention given to the written and unwritten rules related to the practice. You can also find a variety of popular sponsored review and paid posting programs that you can join.

Discovering Sponsored Reviews

In simplest terms, sponsored reviews are reviews of products, services, companies, or anything else that a company or individual (called the *advertiser* in this chapter for simplicity) pays you to write and publish on your blog. A paid post works the same way, but a review is not necessarily part of the post. Instead, you're simply paid to write about a product, service, company, or anything else.

A sample paid post is shown in Figure 6-1. Notice that the paid post in this example includes the phrase "Sponsored Post" as well as an explanation in the first paragraph, so it's very clear that the post has been published in return for some form of compensation.

Figure 6-1:
A sample
sponsored
post.

Sponsored reviews and paid posts typically include links (often using specific keywords provided by the advertiser) to the advertiser's Web site or Web page of choice. Sometimes the advertiser requires that the blogger include specific language within the paid post, and there are even advertisers who require bloggers to write positive reviews in order to get paid.

Advertisers like sponsored reviews and paid posts for several reasons. First, they can spread the word and generate an online buzz among a target audience for a product, service, and so on. Second, they can boost the number of incoming links to the advertiser's site, thereby increasing the advertiser's Web site Google page rank, as discussed in Chapter 1 of Book V. A higher page rank can lead to increased search traffic from Google and other search engines, and of course, more site traffic can lead to more sales for the advertiser.

Bloggers who publish sponsored reviews and paid posts that meet the advertiser's requirements are paid based on the terms set forth in advance. Most often, the payment is a flat fee (or it may come in the form of a product to test), which is paid upon publication of the post.

A blogger with high traffic, Google page rank, Alexa rank, Technorati rank, and so on (as discussed in Chapter 5 of Book VI) can demand higher pay per post payments because advertisers have tangible proof that their ads will get a good amount of exposure — more than a lesser-trafficked blog is likely to deliver. However, small, niche blogs with desirable target audiences can also demand higher pay-per-post fees.

Sponsored reviews and paid posts can also be published on Twitter, Facebook, and other sites, depending on the advertiser's requirements.

Understanding Why Bloggers Like Sponsored Reviews and Paid Posts

Bloggers like sponsored reviews because they are usually easy money. In just a few steps, you can earn anywhere from several dollars to hundreds of dollars depending on the amount of traffic your blog gets and the specific opportunity. Even a small blogger can earn $5–$25 to spend just a short amount of time writing and publishing a sponsored review or paid post. The writing requirements are usually simple, and the time investment for the blogger is minimal. Face it: You're writing posts for your blog anyway, so why not get paid for it?

If a paid post or sponsored review is directly related to your blog topic and you can write honestly about the product, service, or company in the paid post, then that post can actually be beneficial to your audience. For example, if a company sends you a product that your blog audience would be interested in learning about and asks you to test it and review it on your blog in return for a payment, that's a win-win situation for you.

Each paid post or sponsored review opportunity is different. It's up to you to review each opportunity to ensure it not only offers you the chance to earn money but also allows you to meet or exceed your audience's expectations for your blog.

Exposing Potential Drawbacks of Sponsored Reviews and Paid Posts

Sponsored reviews and paid posts are easy money for bloggers and cheap advertising for companies, but there are serious negatives to publishing them on your blog. Be sure you understand the requirements of any sponsored review or paid post opportunity before you commit to publishing the associated post. Some drawbacks of sponsored reviews and paid posts are

✦ **Loss of search traffic:** Publishing sponsored reviews and paid posts can hurt your blog's search rankings, which leads to lower search traffic (or no search traffic at all).

✦ **Legal trouble:** There are legal requirements mandated by the Federal Trade Commission related to publishing sponsored reviews and paid posts that most bloggers are not aware of, which you can learn about in Chapter 1 of this minibook.

✦ **Audience confusion or rejection:** Sponsored reviews and paid posts can hurt the user experience on your blog if readers see them as little more than clutter that adds no value to the blog at all.

If your blog readers believe you're publishing useless paid posts simply to make money, they're likely to be disappointed and leave your blog entirely. Don't risk losing traffic just to make a few dollars.

Publishing Sponsored Reviews and Paid Posts Safely

Despite the drawbacks to publishing sponsored reviews and paid posts, you can take some steps to do so safely. Keep in mind that some advertisers won't want you to take these steps to protect yourself. If that's the case, you shouldn't work with those advertisers.

The following sections provide the most important steps to take in order to publish sponsored reviews and paid posts safely to protect yourself and your blog.

Provide full disclosure

The Federal Trade Commission (FTC) enacted regulations in December 2009 that require bloggers to disclose any "material connection" between themselves and an advertiser that provides money, free products, free services or other compensation in exchange for writing and publishing a post for the advertiser. The FTC regulations also require bloggers to provide accurate reviews about how the product or service would work for an *average* user. Noncompliance with the regulations can lead to fines and penalties.

Be sure to check the FTC Web site, at www.ftc.gov, for the most recent regulations and updated "Guidelines Concerning the Use of Endorsements and Testimonials in Advertising," from the *Code of Federal Regulations* (16 CFR Part 255).

Use the NoFollow HTML tag

Google and other search engines use proprietary algorithms to rank Web pages and return relevant results for keyword searches. Incoming links to a Web site boost that site's Google page rank for those specific keywords used in the link and context of the page. The assumption is that Web pages with a lot of incoming links must include great content or no one would want to link to them.

Google views the practice of paying for incoming links to a Web site as a way of artificially inflating the popularity of that site. Therefore, Google penalizes sites that pay for incoming links and sites (including blogs) that publish paid links. That includes links within sponsored reviews and paid posts. You can make your links invisible to Google by inserting the NoFollow HTML tag within the link code, as discussed in Chapter 1 of Book V.

Stay relevant and useful

Only publish sponsored reviews and paid posts that are relevant to your blog's topic and that your audience is likely to find interesting, meaningful, and useful. In other words, make sure your paid posts and sponsored reviews enhance your blog's content rather than detracting from it.

For example, if you write a blog about protecting the environment, don't publish a paid post for a Hummer or another gas-guzzling vehicle. Instead, your sponsored reviews and paid posts should focus on green products and services to enhance your blog content overall. Writing a paid post about the Toyota Prius would make better sense for your blog, and your audience would be apt to *want* to read your review, finding it useful and helpful.

Finding Popular Sponsored Review and Paid Post Programs

As your blog grows, companies are likely to contact you directly and ask whether you're interested in publishing a sponsored review or paid post to help promote the company's products or services. You can accept these opportunities and charge the advertiser directly if they meet your needs.

If you want to increase the number of sponsored review and paid post opportunities for your blog, you can join a paid post network that connects advertisers with online publishers. Some paid post programs allow you to search for opportunities that you're interested in and apply to publish posts for them. Other programs allow advertisers to search from the participating publisher directory and offer paid post opportunities to publishers of their choice. A third program model automatically matches participating publishers with advertisers' submitted opportunities.

The terms of each opportunity are always unique and determined by the advertiser, so the onus is on you, the publisher, to review the offer and make sure it meets your needs before you apply for it or accept it. After you accept an opportunity from a paid posting program, you're required to publish the post within a specific amount of time. It's important to understand that your published post is likely to be reviewed by the advertiser who may be able to withhold payment or ask you to rewrite your post if it doesn't meet the requirements of the opportunity.

Following are a number of popular sponsored review and paid post programs that you can join for free so that you can start earning money from your blog by doing what you already do — writing posts.

SocialSpark

http://socialspark.com

SocialSpark is owned by Izea and offers a legitimate and fairly safe way for bloggers to make money through sponsored reviews and paid posts. That's because all links published in SocialSpark paid posts must include the NoFollow HTML tag. This protects the advertiser and publisher from potential Google penalties as described earlier in this chapter. Furthermore, SocialSpark mandates that all sponsored reviews and paid posts published through the program must be honest and provide full disclosure as part of the program's Code of Ethics. Therefore, posts that you publish through the SocialSpark program comply with FTC regulations.

Both large and small companies publish opportunities on SocialSpark, which are listed on the SocialSpark Web site shown in Figure 6-2, so you can search through and apply for ones that you're interested in.

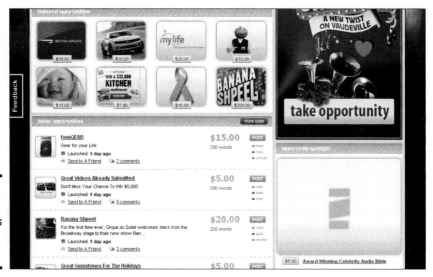

Figure 6-2:
SocialSpark opportunities are easy to search.

SocialSpark has a strict code of ethics that advertisers and publishers have to adhere to, making it one of the safest sponsored review and paid posting networks.

PayPerPost

http://payperpost.com

In 2009, PayPerPost (owned by Izea) launched a new version (4.0) of its sponsored review and paid posts program, shown in Figure 6-3.

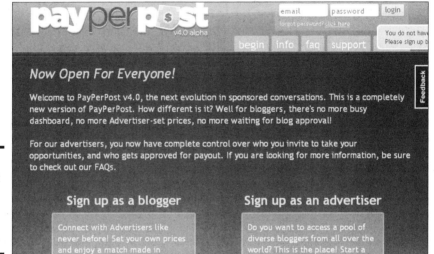

Figure 6-3:
PayPerPost matches bloggers with advertisers.

PayPerPost version 4.0 automatically matches bloggers to opportunities submitted by advertisers. In simplest terms, you can join PayPerPost and provide details about your blog, the minimum payment amounts you're willing to accept, and so on. Advertisers submit opportunities, and PayPerPost returns a list of potential bloggers to the advertisers that are deemed to be appropriate matches for the opportunity. The advertiser then selects the blogger he wants to work with. The blogger is notified about the opportunity and can accept or decline the offer. After an offer is accepted, the blogger must follow the opportunity instructions in order to get paid.

PayPerPost expects full disclosure from publishers as part of version 4.0. This is different from the disclosure requirements mandated in earlier versions of the PayPerPost program.

SponsoredReviews

www.sponsoredreviews.com

SponsoredReviews, shown in Figure 6-4, provides two ways for bloggers to find opportunities. First, you can search for and apply for opportunities, and second, advertisers can search for bloggers and bring opportunities to you. You can negotiate directly with advertisers on rates and terms. SponsoredReviews simply requires that you publish accurate reviews.

ReviewMe

www.reviewme.com

ReviewMe, shown in Figure 6-5, is an easy sponsored-review and paid-posting program to join. Simply provide your blog information, and your blog is added to the directory for advertisers to search. If an advertiser finds your blog and thinks it's a good match for an opportunity, you're notified and given the opportunity to accept or reject the offer.

PayU2Blog

www.payu2blog.com

PayU2Blog, shown in Figure 6-6, is a smaller sponsored review and paid posting program that matches advertisers with participating bloggers. If your blog is accepted into the PayU2Blog program, you will begin receiving opportunities that are matched to your blog, which you can approve or deny. PayU2Blog expects bloggers to publish accurate information and reviews.

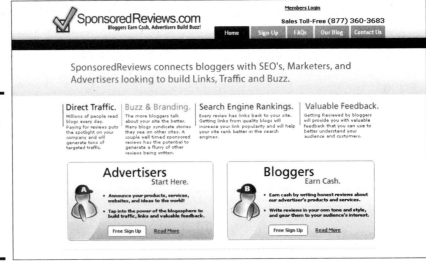

Figure 6-4:
Sponsored-Reviews allows bloggers and advertisers to search for each other.

Figure 6-5:
ReviewMe gives advertisers the chance to find bloggers for paid postings.

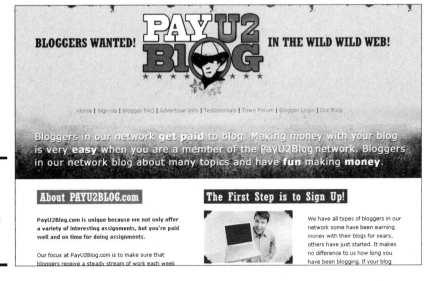

Figure 6-6:
PayU2Blog matches advertisers with bloggers.

Chapter 7: Merchandising for Profit

In This Chapter

✔ Understanding blog merchandising

✔ Benefiting from merchandising

✔ Reviewing considerations before you jump in

✔ Finding popular merchandising programs

Selling merchandise through your blog is a simple way to make money. You can find products to sell that can be tied to nearly any blog topic. Whether you create your own logo or slogan and sell T-shirts with those elements printed on them or you decide to sell products offered through a merchant, you can find a way to monetize your blog through merchandise sales.

In this chapter, you find out about creating and selling your own merchandise as well as promoting and selling merchandise through an established on-demand product-merchandising program.

Understanding Blog Merchandising

Anyone can create and sell merchandise on a blog, but doing so can take time and skill. Fortunately, there are Web sites that make selling merchandise through your blog extremely easy. Want to sell T-shirts with your favorite quote on them? You can do it (as long as you own the copyright to the quote) with very little effort thanks to online merchandising sites.

Most online merchandising programs provide two options for selling merchandise on your blog:

✦ **Create your own designs.** You can create your own digital images and upload them to the merchandising program site. Once uploaded, you can sell merchandise such as mugs, bags, and so on with your image printed on those products.

✦ **Use established designs.** Many merchandising programs offer a variety of art and images that you can choose from to print on merchandise items. This is a great option if you aren't able to create your own digital art. Check out the example of an established design from CafePress (shown in Figure 7-1 and discussed later in this chapter) that you could sell on a variety of items through your blog.

You can design and promote the products you want to sell on your blog. All sales, shipping, and so on are managed by the merchandising program. Because products are printed on demand (when a person orders the item), you don't have to worry about paying for inventory, shipping costs, and the like. Usually, you're given the option to set your own prices, thereby establishing your own profit margin.

Some merchandising programs provide free and paid options. Typically, if you pay a fee, you can create custom stores. If you want to create and sell different types of merchandise to different audiences, then having the ability to create multiple stores is important. For example, you can create a store related to your cooking blog and a store related to your travel blog, which would be likely to carry very different merchandise. The guidelines and capabilities of programs differ, so be sure to research your options and choose the best one for you, your audience, and your blogging goals.

Figure 7-1:
An
established
design from
CafePress
on a
sweatshirt.

Benefiting from Merchandising

Merchandising can be an effective blog monetization tactic, particularly for bloggers who write about topics that can be directly linked to consumer products. However, not every blogger writes about a topic like baking, where selling products such as T-shirts that say "My Buns are Hotter Than Yours" makes sense. The most successful merchandising efforts offer products that the blog's audience members are likely to be interested in at the moment they're reading the blog and see the associated product.

However, most bloggers can find ways to creatively associate some kind of product with their blog topics. For example, I created a tagline for my blog written for and by women working in the field of business (www.womenon business.com) — "Business women — we're not bitches; we're driven." Although I haven't used this tagline on merchandise such as T-shirts, mugs, and so on as a way to monetize my blog, I certainly could. In fact, it could be a successful endeavor. With that in mind, don't be afraid to think out of the box and tie merchandise and consumer products to your blog's topic creatively.

Furthermore, the most effective merchandising efforts are promoted both on and off the blog. You can drive people to your merchandise through your blog, Twitter, Facebook, e-mail signature, and more. No one can buy your merchandise if they don't know where to find it.

Similarly, make sure the links and ads that lead your blog's visitors to your merchandise are placed strategically. For example, don't hide links to your merchandise in your blog's footer or subpages. Instead, include ads in your blog's sidebar, between posts, or in links within your posts. Make sure it's easy for your audience to find your merchandise. If that merchandise is directly related to your blog's topic, which is of interest to them, you stand a greater chance of actually selling that it.

Reviewing Considerations before You Jump In

At first glance, it might seem like there are no negatives to participating in product advertising programs and selling merchandise through your blog. However, there are some pitfalls that you need to be aware of and analyze before you get started:

✦ **Quality:** Before you advertise your merchandise on your blog, purchase a few items from the program site to ensure the quality is acceptable. The last thing you want to do is offer T-shirts that shrink after one washing or bags that aren't strong enough to carry more than a single book.

✦ **Return policy and process:** Make sure that any product advertising or merchandise program you join has a clear and easy-to-follow return process. If people purchase products through your blog and they're dissatisfied, you want to be certain they have an easy way to return the items and get their money back.

✦ **Costs:** Make sure that the cost of the item + shipping + your up-charge does not make the merchandise you sell through your blog too expensive. (An *up-charge* is the dollar amount you add to the product cost and keep as your earnings.) No one will buy your products if they're priced too high.

Review the programs you consider joining to ensure that the costs of the items plus any other fees added to the cost of the product (such as shipping and handling) are not excessive. You need to know what the final cost of any item you sell is, because it's usually up to you to add an additional dollar amount to that cost, which you keep as your profit. If the price is already too high *before* you add your charge to an item, you won't sell anything, making the entire effort a waste of time.

✦ **Relevancy and uniqueness:** As discussed earlier in this chapter, the merchandise you sell through your blog should be relevant to your blog's topic in order to leverage the real-time interest of your blog visitors. At the same time, your merchandise should be unique and representative of your blog. There's little incentive to purchase an item through your blog that a visitor can buy anywhere. Make your merchandise special, and your sales should go up.

✦ **Copyrights and trademarks:** It's absolutely essential that you make sure you own the copyright for (or get permission to use) any image or text that you upload for imprinting on the merchandise you sell through your blog. Otherwise, you could open yourself up to being accused of copyright and trademark violations and legal troubles.

Taking a Look at Merchandising Sites

There are a few popular merchandising sites, which are reliable and easy to use. When selecting a merchandising site, it's a good idea to order some products first, and make sure you're satisfied with the quality, shipping, customer service, and so on. Then determine what you want to sell and make sure those products are available to you before you take the time to set up your store. Following are highlights of some of the most popular merchandising sites.

CafePress

www.cafepress.com

CafePress is one of the most popular online merchandising sites for bloggers to monetize their blogs. You can upload your own designs to print on products through CafePress such as T-shirts, sweatshirts, bags, mugs, posters, and more, or you can sell merchandise with designs offered by CafePress on them. When you sign up with CafePress, you get your own CafePress storefront, which you can link to from your blog, so your blog visitors can view and purchase your items.

CafePress handles all the logistics of the merchandising program. Purchased products are produced on demand and shipped directly from CafePress to the customer. All you have to do is set up your store and promote it, and CafePress takes care of the rest — including returns and customer service. CafePress also handles all payments. Because you determine how much you want the mark-up on items to be, you control your potential revenue stream.

CafePress allows you to set up as many basic stores as you want for free, and each store can include up to 80 items. For a small monthly fee, you can set up a premium shop, as shown in Figure 7-2, where you can offer an unlimited number of products and customize as you wish.

Figure 7-2:
A CafePress premium shop.

Zazzle

www.zazzle.com

Zazzle is an online merchandising program that is free to join. You can set up your own store and sell as many products as you want. Your products can come from the Zazzle marketplace of designs and items provided by Zazzle or created by other Zazzle members. You can also upload your own designs and sell them on products or add your designs to the Zazzle marketplace for other members to sell.

You set your pricing for both your own sales and sales of your designs and items through the Zazzle Marketplace. You can also earn volume discounts based on the dollar amount of products you sell each month.

Through Zazzle, you can sell individual items or link to your custom Zazzle store. A Zazzle store example is shown in Figure 7-3. The choice is yours. Zazzle handles all customer service, production, shipping, payments, and so on. You also get access to a variety of reports to track your progress.

Printfection

www.printfection.com

Printfection, shown in Figure 7-4, is an online merchandising program that you can join for free, upload your designs, and then sell products with those designs printed on them either individually through your blog, in your own Printfection store, or through the Printfection site. You can customize your Printfection store and even integrate it directly into your blog, so it looks like it's part of your blog rather than a separate Printfection site. Also, you can open multiple stores through a single account.

Printfection handles all of the technical aspects of the site as well as production, shipping, returns, customer service, and payments. Although Printfection offers a smaller selection of products than some other online merchandising programs, it's still a popular option for bloggers.

Figure 7-3:
A Zazzle
store.

Figure 7-4:
Printfection
offers
on-demand
merchan-
dising.

Chapter 8: Displaying Ads in Your Blog's Feed

So you're chugging along, monetizing your blog, and everything seems to be going well. Only, there's a catch: Some of your regular readers don't visit your blog page very often because they receive your blog posts via an RSS feed. Wait, wait, don't panic and start hollering just yet. There's a solution: Add advertisements to your feed. There are several programs that make the process of setting up feed advertising easy for you, and once it's set up, it typically works on its own with little intervention by you.

As with all blog monetization opportunities, there are positives and negatives to feed advertising. This chapter explains how feed advertising works and what to consider before you begin displaying ads in your blog's feed to ensure it's the appropriate way for you to meet your blogging objectives.

Understanding What Feed Ads Are

Feeds are described in detail in Chapter 4 of Book V. In short, feeds are distributed using Really Simple Syndication (RSS). They include either full or partial content from your blog. Each time you publish a new post to your blog, it's distributed via your blog's feed to anyone who subscribes to it. Subscribers can access your blog's feed via e-mail or through a feed reader, such as Google Reader, making it easy for subscribers to find new, enjoyable content in one place rather than visiting each blog individually to determine if new content has been published.

Feed advertising enables bloggers to insert ads within their blogs' feeds. For example, an advertisement could appear in between posts within a blog's feed, as viewed in a person's feed reader, such as the Pheedo (`http://pheedo.com`) ad shown in Figure 8-1.

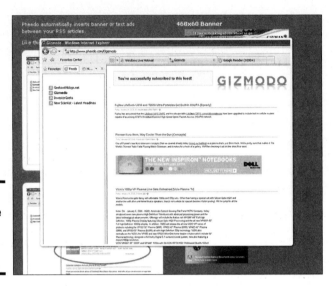

Figure 8-1:
An example
of a feed
ad from
Pheedo.

Most feed advertising programs allow you to choose the type of ads you want to display in your blog's feed, including text or image ads. You may also be able to customize the colors of the ads displayed in your feed and choose the position where ads are placed, such as above or below each post in your feed.

Feed advertising programs usually use the pay-per-click payment method, so you earn money every time a person clicks an ad displayed in your blog's feed.

Benefiting from Feed Ads

Many bloggers view their blog feeds as a lost monetization opportunity because people who subscribe to blogs and read them via e-mail or a feed reader often don't click through and visit the blog where the post was published. This is particularly true for bloggers who syndicate full-text feeds of their blog posts, because subscribers can read the entire content of those posts through their feed reader or via e-mail (depending on their chosen subscription method).

The reason is simple. If people aren't clicking through to your blog, they don't see the ads and other monetization tactics on your blog at all, which means you lose the chance to generate ad revenue from them. Inserting ads in your blog's feed helps offset that lost opportunity.

You can't benefit from feed ads if no one is clicking them. In order to maximize your earnings from feed ads, you need to monitor them to ensure they're relevant to the content of your blog. If they're not relevant, then your blog subscribers are unlikely to be interested in them and less likely to click them. It's up to you to analyze the relevancy of ads displayed in your feed and ensure the program is meeting your needs and goals.

Uncovering the Negatives of Feed Ads

Although many bloggers are proponents of feed ads, there are just as many bloggers who refuse to insert ads into their blogs' feeds. The primary reason is because they believe ads in feeds clutter the actual content of the feed and create a negative user experience (particularly if the ads are irrelevant to the blog's content), making it even less likely that the subscriber will click through to read more from the blogger. Even worse, some bloggers believe that a feed covered in ads turns off subscribers so much that they not only unsubscribe from the blog but also stop visiting the blog all together.

 If you see your blog subscribers decreasing after you add advertising to your blog's feed, take a closer look to determine whether the ads are the reason. Take some time to analyze the amount of money you're earning from feed ads to ensure the benefits outweigh the negatives.

Finding Popular Feed Ad Options

There are two feed advertising options that most bloggers test on their blogs first — Google AdSense for feeds (formerly Feedburner ads) and Pheedo. Both of these programs partner with well-known advertisers, provide excellent customization and reporting, and pay on time and accurately.

Google AdSense for Feeds

www.google.com/adsense

Google AdSense is the most popular feed advertising option for bloggers for a few reasons:

✦ **Ease of integration:** Because many bloggers try Google AdSense for contextual advertising on their blogs (discussed in Chapter 2 of this minibook), it's very easy to try Google AdSense for feeds. The blogger's account is already set up! Also, because Google owns Feedburner (www.feedburner.com), one of the easiest ways to create and manage your blog's feed and subscribers, it's simple to link your feed with your AdSense ad units. Furthermore, Google also owns Blogger, so it's even easier for Blogger users to integrate Google AdSense for feeds into their blogs.

✦ **Customization:** Google AdSense for feeds is easy to customize in terms of picking the location where you want your feed ads to appear, colors, the type of ads you want to publish in your feed, and more. Figure 8-2 shows the Google AdSense for feeds configuration page, which includes a variety of customization options.

✦ **Tracking:** Google AdSense for feeds can track ad performance easily through the Google AdSense dashboard.

✦ **Trust:** Google is a well-known brand that people know and trust working with, particularly because most bloggers already have established relationships with Google.

✦ **No barriers to entry:** Anyone can sign up to participate in Google AdSense for free and publish ads in their blog's feed.

To set up Google AdSense ads for your blog's feed, follow these steps:

1. **Log in to your Google AdSense account at `http://adsense.google.com` and select the AdSense Setup link in the top navigation bar.**

This step opens the AdSense Setup page shown in Figure 8-2.

2. **Click the AdSense for Feeds link.**

The AdSense for Feeds Create Ad Unit page opens, as shown in Figure 8-3.

3. **In the Ad Type drop-down list, select the type of ads you want to display in your blog's feed.**

You can choose to publish text ads, image ads, or both.

Figure 8-2: The Google AdSense Setup page.

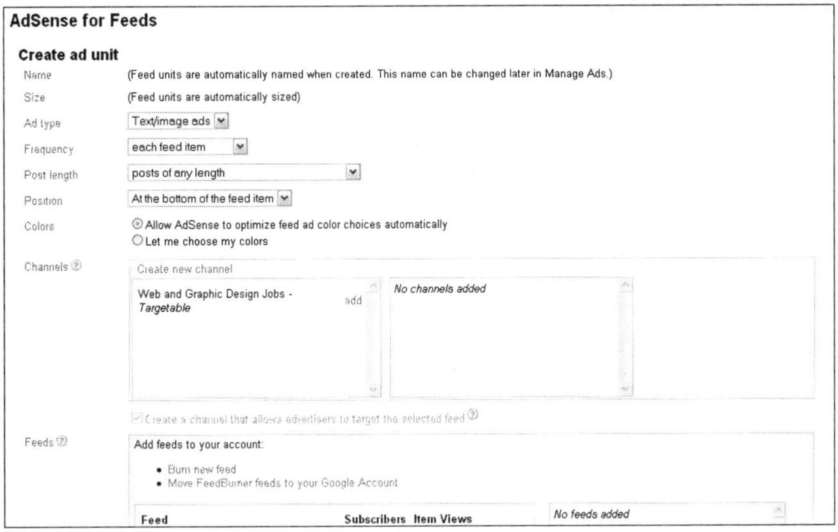

Figure 8-3:
Google
AdSense
for feeds ad
configuration
page.

4. **In the Frequency drop-down list, select how often you want ads to appear in your blog's feed.**

You can choose to have ads appear after every post in your feed, after every second post, after every third post, or after every fourth post.

5. **In the Posts Length drop-down list, select your parameters for how long a post must be in order for an ad to publish with it.**

You can choose to have ads display with posts of any length, longer than 50 words, longer than 100 words, longer than 250 words, or longer than 500 words.

6. **In the Position drop-down list, select where you want ads to appear in relation to your posts within your blog's feed.**

You can choose to have ads appear above or below your posts within your blog's feed.

7. **In the Colors section, select the radio button that reflects how you want colors to be chosen for your feed ads.**

You can choose to have colors automatically set or you can choose them yourself.

8. **In the Custom Channels section, you can create a specific channel for your ad unit.**

With Google AdSense, custom channels help you track your ad unit performance and make it easier for advertisers to target and place ads on your blog.

**Book VII
Chapter 8**

Displaying Ads in
Your Blog's Feed

9. **In the Feeds section, you can select the feed where you want the ads from the ad unit you're creating to appear and then click the Add link to add them to the ad unit.**

If you have not already added your blog's feed to your Google AdSense account, you can do that from this section of the form, too.

10. **Click the Save button.**

This step saves your ad unit so ads can begin appearing within your blog's feed.

Pheedo

www.pheedo.com

Pheedo offers blog feed advertising from a variety of well-known companies, including Verizon, ESPN, Ford, and more. Pheedo ads can be placed above, below, beside, or within your feed posts, or they can be displayed as stand-alone items. Figure 8-4 shows several Pheedo feed ad formats.

Pheedo offers your feed to advertisers who review your blog's traffic, post frequency, and other criteria to determine how much they're willing to pay to reach your feed readers. Therefore, popular, highly trafficked, and frequently updated blogs stand to earn far more money from Pheedo ads than lesser-trafficked blogs can.

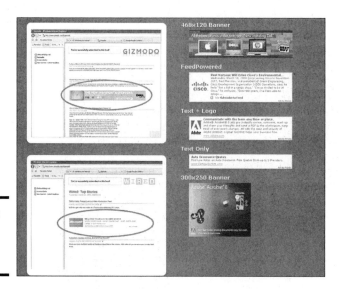

Figure 8-4:
Pheedo
ad format
examples.

You can apply to be a Pheedo ad publisher through the Pheedo Web site. If your application is approved, a representative from Pheedo contacts you to help you get started. Follow these steps to become a Pheedo ad publisher:

1. **Visit `http://pheedo.com/site/pub_get_started.php` to complete the publisher application.**

Complete the application as thoroughly and honestly as you can.

2. **Enter your contact information in the first section of the application as shown in Figure 8-5.**

Make sure that you enter the primary Web site URL for your blog, not your blog's feed address in the Website field.

3. **Enter your fee information in the second section of the application, as shown in Figure 8-6.**

In this section, enter the URL for your blog's feed as well as a count of all the feeds you ultimately want to include Pheedo ads in (if you have more than one feed you want to monetize). Additionally, use the drop-down list to select a category for your blog's feed and enter the number of subscribers and views your feed has in the fields provided.

4. **Enter the requested information in the last section of the application, as shown in Figure 8-7.**

This section of the form is called the Red Tape section because it's where you provide information about who referred you to Pheedo, agree to the Pheedo terms and conditions, and enter any additional information or comments that you want to include in your application.

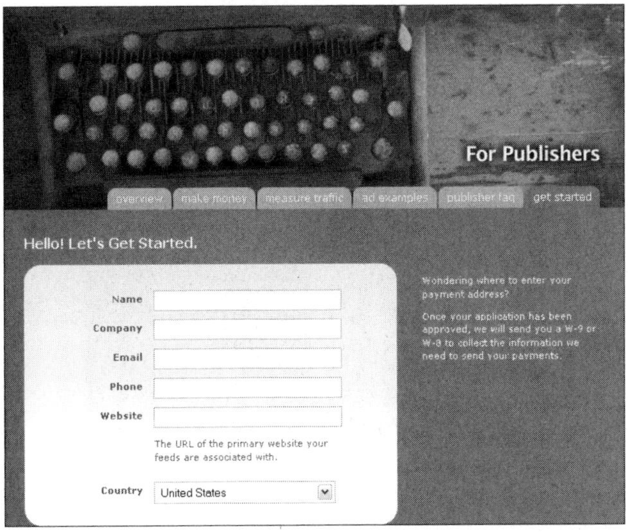

Figure 8-5: Enter your contact information in the Pheedo publisher application.

5. **Click the Submit Your Application button.**

Your application is automatically sent to Pheedo. You will be contacted if your application is approved.

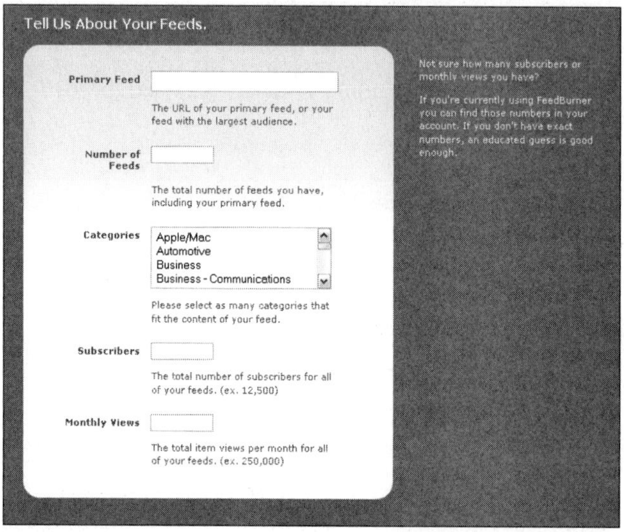

Figure 8-6:
Enter your blog feed information in the Pheedo publisher application.

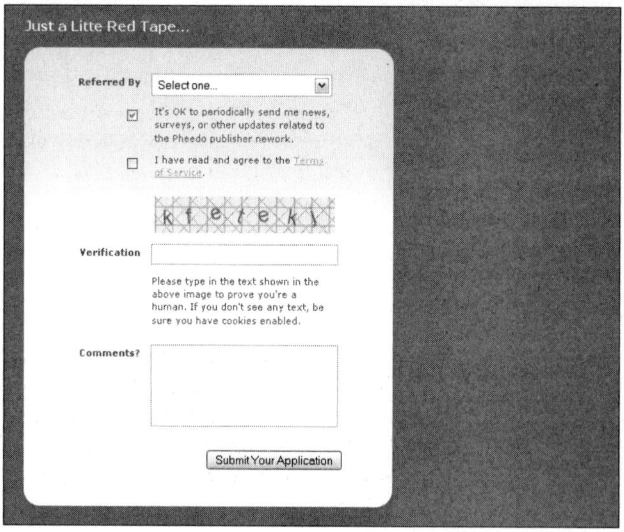

Figure 8-7:
Provide the Red Tape information requested in the Pheedo publisher application.

Chapter 9: Selling Ad Space Directly

In This Chapter

- ✔ Choosing to sell direct ads
- ✔ Selecting types of ads to sell
- ✔ Researching similar blogs
- ✔ Developing a rate sheet
- ✔ Accepting payments
- ✔ Promoting your blog ad space
- ✔ Using a third party to facilitate the process

*A*lthough most people think of selling advertising space through a program like Google AdSense first when they hear of blog monetization, you can also sell ad space on your blog directly or through a third party that can facilitate the process for you. There are advantages and disadvantages to both options, but one thing is for certain: Directly selling ad space on your blog should be a part of your blog monetization plan.

This chapter explains how to sell ad space on your blog, how to price that space, and how to create a rate sheet for potential advertisers. You also find out how to accept payments and how third-party facilitators can help make the process of selling your own ad space easier.

Choosing to Sell Direct Ads

Why share your ad revenue with sites such as Google AdSense? Wouldn't it be better if you could keep 100 percent of the fees charged for ad space on your blog? Those are fair questions to ask. Certainly, if you sell your own ad space, you can set your own prices and keep all your earnings. You can also charge flat fees for your ad space, which guarantees that you make a specific amount of money for that space.

However, selling direct ads has big drawbacks. First, your blog usually has to be well-trafficked and produce high monthly page views and unique visitors to entice an advertiser to solicit and purchase ad space from you. Furthermore, you have to do all the promotion to spread the word about your available ad space and make it seem like *the* place for advertisers to display their ads. In other words, selling your own ad space requires a lot of time and effort. Of course, when your blog is well-established, it's easier to sell ad space directly, but that can take a long time. Therefore, many small bloggers offer ad space for direct purchase but combine those efforts with other contextual and impression advertising.

You certainly have nothing to lose by offering ad space for direct sale on your blog. Create a post or page that provides the details about your ad space opportunities, such as the one shown in Figure 9-1 for the highly popular ProBlogger (`www.problogger.net`). Be sure to include your e-mail address or contact form so interested advertisers can contact you for more information. The worst case scenario is that no one contacts you.

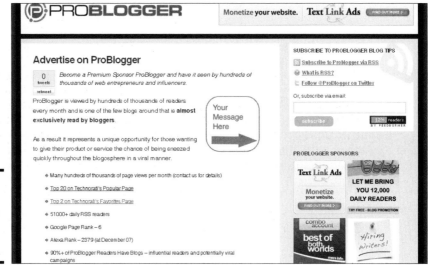

Figure 9-1: The ProBlogger advertising page.

Selecting Types of Ads to Sell

When you sell ad space on your blog, you decide what types of ads you're willing to accept and publish. However, you also need to have the technical ability to insert the ads on your blog. For example, selling text link ads is easy — just insert the text link. Similarly, it's not difficult to place an image ad in your blog's sidebar, particularly if your blogging application allows you to paste HTML code into a widget or gadget easily. On the other hand, inserting ads into your blog's header or between posts is a bit more challenging for beginner bloggers. With that in mind, your technical abilities could dictate the types of ad space you can sell on your blog.

When you sell your own ad space, you can accept or decline any ad space inquiry that you receive, giving you the ultimate control of the ads that appear on your blog and the Web sites those ads lead your audience to. Most bloggers like having this level of control, and it's one more benefit of selling ad space directly.

You can sell ad space in a variety of forms on your blog, including image, text, video, sponsored reviews, paid posts, and more.

Researching Similar Blogs in Size and Topic

How do you know how much to charge for the ad space on your blog? It's simple. Take some time to research other blogs that are similar to yours in size and topic, look at the rates they charge, and price your ad space accordingly. For example, a beginner blogger with a small audience can't expect to charge the same fees for ad space that a well-established blog such as ProBlogger charges. No advertiser would be willing to pay the same amount to place an ad on a site that gets hundreds of thousands of page views per month as they would on a site that gets just hundreds or just thousands of page views per month. Advertisers are willing to pay rates that match the exposure and return they expect to get from their investment, and you need to price your ad space to match the results your blog can deliver.

Finding blogs is discussed in Chapter 1 of Book I. There you can find tips for finding blogs on specific topics.

To find out where your rates should be set, you can inquire about purchasing ad space on blogs that are similar to yours — if the rates are not already published on the blog. Alternatively, you can visit a site such as BuySellAds. com (`http://buysellads.com`), which is discussed in detail later in this chapter, and search for publishers to find out the rates they're charging as well as their traffic levels.

For example, Figure 9-2 shows a list of publishers selling ad space through BuySellAds.com with 10,000–79,000 impressions per month and a traffic rank up to 30,000 in the Web design and development category. You can click on each listing to get additional details such as the detail page for W3Avenue. com (a small blog about Web development), shown in Figure 9-3, which shows the ad rates and details for buying ad space on that site through BuySellAds.com.

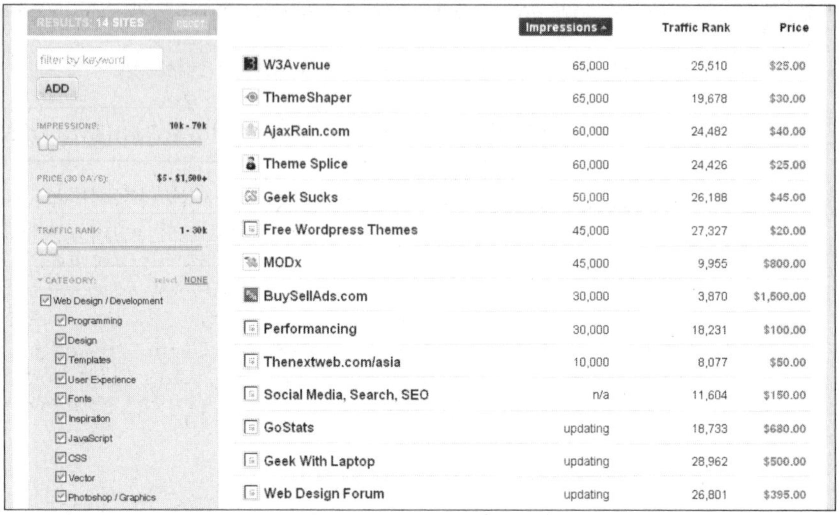

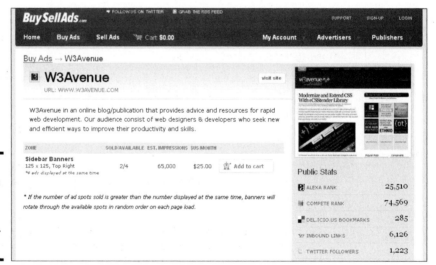

Figure 9-2: A list of direct ads available for purchase through BuySellAds. com.

Figure 9-3: Ad rates for W3Avenue. com via BuySellAds. com.

Developing a Rate Sheet

When you have an idea of what you want to charge for your ad space, you should create a rate sheet that not only provides your ad space rates but also helps to sell your blog to advertisers. You can either publish your rate sheet information on your blog or e-mail it in response to inquiries. Having a rate sheet prepared saves you time later because you won't have to retype the same information again and again each time you get an inquiry.

Be sure to update your rate sheet as your blog traffic and audience change.

Your rate sheet should include the following information:

✦ **Description of your blog:** Try to sell the value of your blog by making it sound appealing.

✦ **Demographic profile of your blog's audience:** Tell advertisers who will see their ad when it appears on your blog. Include any statistics you have about gender, age, location, and so on. You could get this information by publishing a poll on your blog using `www.polldaddy.com`, `www.surveygizmo.com`, `www.surveymonkey.com`, or another Web site that allows you to create free polls, which you can easily insert into a blog post by simply copying and pasting some HTML code. Check out the sidebar later in this chapter to find out more about demographic surveys.

✦ **Traffic statistics and rankings:** Provide your blog's Google page rank, Alexa rank, Technorati rank, monthly page views, monthly unique visitors, number of subscribers, and so on to show advertisers the kind of reach that advertising on your blog can give them.

✦ **Awards and recognition:** List any awards or special recognition that your blog has earned, which could add value to your site and make it more appealing to advertisers.

✦ **Other enhanced value:** List any accomplishments, syndication agreements, and so on that give your blog added exposure.

✦ **Ad specifications:** Provide descriptions of the types of ads you accept and technical specifications for those ads such as size, format, and so on.

✦ **Restrictions:** If you have any restrictions related to the types of ads you're willing to publish on your blog such as no links to pornographic sites, text links must use the NoFollow HTML tag, and so on, be sure to define them.

✦ **Pricing and payment terms:** Provide prices as well as payment guidelines. For example, explain when payments must be made and how they can be made, such as by check or PayPal.

✦ **Custom advertising opportunities:** If you're open to discussing customized advertising on your blog, make sure you mention it on your rate sheet.

✦ **Your contact information:** Make it easy for interested advertisers to contact you to set up their advertising with you or get more information.

Accepting Payments

Selling ad space is only half the job when it comes to monetizing your blog directly. You also need to collect payments, and not everyone is as honest when it comes to paying bloggers as they should be. Make sure your payment requirements and terms are spelled out clearly in your rate sheet, and obtain the advertiser's agreement to your terms in writing via e-mail or a signed contract.

Make sure you provide details in writing about how and when advertisers must pay you. For example, you can require that payments be made up front *before* you place the advertiser's ad on your blog. If an advertiser doesn't agree with those terms, you can certainly refuse to publish the ad. The most important thing is to ensure you're protected.

Also, make it easy for advertisers to pay you. Sign up for a PayPal account at `www.paypal.com`, as shown in Figure 9-4, so you can accept bank account transfers and credit card payments. If you have to accept checks, make sure you cash the check before you place the ad. Again, you need to protect yourself. Of course, you must place the ad in a timely manner and for the time period that you and the advertiser agree upon.

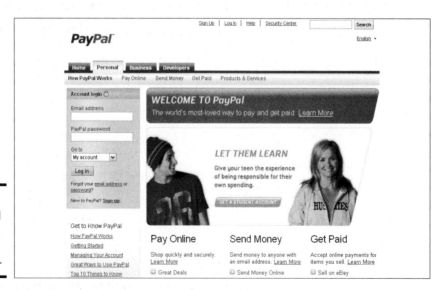

Figure 9-4:
Use PayPal for easy payment processing.

Promoting Ad Space for Sale on Your Blog

After you put together your rate sheet and determine the types of ads you're willing to publish on your blog, it's time to spread the word that the space is available. The key to selling ad space on your blog is to first spend time growing your blog's audience by writing great content and promoting your blog as discussed in Book VII. Then you can tell the online world about your desirable audience and targeted ad space.

Make sure you take the time to learn about your audience. Use a site such as PollDaddy (`www.polldaddy.com`) or SurveyGizmo (`www.surveygizmo.com`) to create and publish demographic polls on your blog. Ask your blog audience where they're from, how old they are, and so on to help you find out more about them.

Check out the survey example from PollDaddy shown in Figure 9-5 to see how a survey or poll can look in a blog post. Sites such as PollDaddy make it easy to create your own survey, copy some HTML code, paste it into a blog post, and collect information from your readers. You can find out more about polls and surveys in the nearby sidebar.

Book VII
Chapter 9

Selling Ad Space Directly

Using surveys to learn about your blog's audience

Fortunately, there are a number of Web sites that allow bloggers to create surveys (or polls) for free. PollDaddy (`www.polldaddy.com`), SurveyMonkey (`www.surveymonkey.com`), and SurveyGizmo (`www.surveygizmo.com`) are three popular options. Depending on your survey needs, you can create single-question or multiple-question surveys to find out more about your blog's audience. Try to create multiple-choice answers, so it's easy to tabulate your survey results. Questions might include the following:

✔ What is your age?

✔ What is your highest level of education?

✔ Where do you live? (Answers could be country, state, or town of residence, and so on.)

✔ What is your gender?

✔ What is your nationality?

✔ What is your income?

✔ What is your profession?

✔ What is your marital status?

✔ What are the ages of your children?

✔ What kinds of pets do you have?

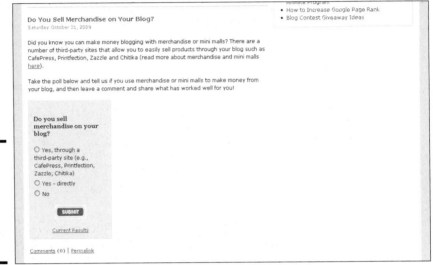

Figure 9-5:
PollDaddy
offers a
great way
to survey
your blog's
audience.

Using a Third Party to Facilitate the Ad Sales Process

For many bloggers, attracting advertisers is difficult. That's where third-party facilitators can be very helpful. Sites such as BuySellAds.com allow bloggers to post their available ad space. Typically, you can set your own rates, and advertisers search these sites to find niche blogs and Web sites that offer great rates for exposure to targeted audiences. It's far easier for an advertiser to search through a site that lists a wide variety of ad space opportunities than it is to find and visit the same number of individual blogs and Web sites to find or inquire about purchasing ad space on those sites.

These third-party sites typically handle the technology and payment process for both the advertisers and the ad publishers. In exchange, the third-party site takes a percentage of the fees charged to the advertiser by the publisher.

You need to consider whether the benefits of getting wider exposure for your available ad space are worthwhile given the loss in revenue taken by the third-party site. Only you can determine through testing whether the amount of ad space sold through a third party is more than you can sell on your own and makes up for the loss in revenue. Of course, you can always increase your advertising rate to make up for the lost revenue.

There are a number of sites that offer ways for bloggers to sell ad space. Some of the most popular sites are discussed in the following sections.

BuySellAds.com

www.buysellads.com

BuySellAds.com, shown in Figure 9-6, is open to nearly any online publisher with ad space to sell. You simply register for free, provide the requested information about your blog, including your ad sizes and fees, and BuySellAds.com takes care of the rest. Your blog's traffic rankings are added to your listing automatically, so you don't have to worry about keeping that information updated.

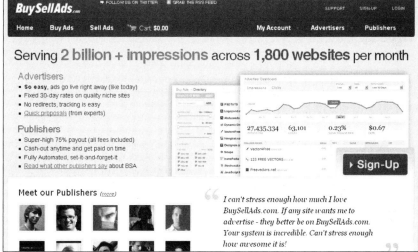

Figure 9-6: BuySellAds.com makes selling ad space easy.

BuySellAds.com provides you with a snippet of HTML code that you add to your blog where you want your ads to appear. That code automatically generates the ads that advertisers purchase on your blog and removes them when they expire. You don't have to do anything other than accept ads as they come to you. In fact, you can even set up your account to automatically approve all ads purchased on your blog, so you don't have to do anything after your account is set up. An example of how ad space sold through BuySellAds.com looks on a blog is shown in Figure 9-7.

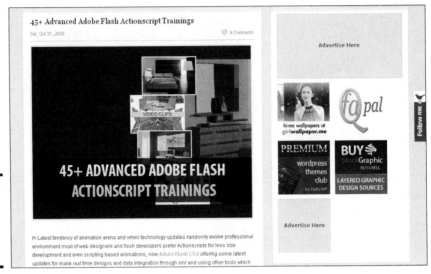

Figure 9-7:
Ad space sold via BuySellAds. com.

BuySellAds.com also handles all payment processing. When your account reaches the payout threshold, you can withdraw your funds.

Blogads

www.blogads.com

Blogads connects many well-known advertisers, such as PBS, PETA, and Budget Rental Cars, with online publishers that are offering ad space for sale. If your blog is consistently updated and gets over 1,000 page views per day, then you can apply to offer your ad space through Blogads.com.

The Blogads.com program is difficult to get into and is not always actively accepting new publishers, but if your blog is popular, it's worth applying.

Blogads.com offers several ad sizes, as shown in Figure 9-8. You can set your own pricing for your ad space, and you always have the opportunity to accept or reject any advertiser's ad. Because all ad space sold through Blogads.com is sold at a flat fee for ads to be displayed for a specific amount of time, you always know how much you'll make. Blogads.com takes a percentage of that fee to cover their expenses for managing the technology, payment processing, and so on.

Book VII
Chapter 9

Selling Ad Space Directly

Figure 9-8:
Blogads.
com sample
ad units.

PerformancingAds

www.performancingads.com

Through PerformancingAds, you can list your blog, and advertisers can publish 125 x 125 pixel ads on your blog. If your site gets 250,000 page views per month, you can work with PerformancingAds to sell ad space on your blog directly through the PerformancingAds Premium program.

Through the basic PerformancingAds program, you can register for an account and provide information about your blog, which is then added to the categorized marketplace of publishers, as shown in Figure 9-9. PerformancingAds takes care of the technology and payment processing. All you have to do is insert the provided code into your blog, and the rest is done for you.

Figure 9-9:
The Performancing Ads
marketplace.

Chapter 10: Benefiting from Indirect Monetization Opportunities

In This Chapter

✓ Requesting guest blogging fees

✓ Booking speaking engagements

✓ Offering consulting services

✓ Writing for other sources

✓ Asking for donations

✓ Using licensed or ad-supported syndication

✓ Accepting job offers

Some bloggers don't like the idea of displaying ads on their blogs or publishing paid posts and sponsored reviews. The concern is that monetizing a blog can damage the blog's brand image by making readers believe the blogger is more interested in making money than providing useful content and building relationships with readers.

For most bloggers, there's both a monetary investment to keep a blog going as well as a significant time investment. Therefore, it's common for bloggers to search for some way to generate revenue from their blogs because blogging takes away from other income-generating activities that help the blogger pay the bills.

This chapter tells you about some of the popular ways bloggers can make money from their blogs without publishing ads, sponsored reviews, or paid posts at all. You can jumpstart the process by actively seeking and pursuing these monetization options, but the longer you blog and the more your blog grows, the more opportunities will find you!

Requesting Payment for Guest Blogging Services

In Chapter 5 of Book VI, you find out all about guest blogging. To review, guest blogging is the process of writing a post to be published on another blogger's blog. You can write guest blog posts for other blogs or you can publish guest posts written for your blog by other bloggers. Guest blogging is a great way to boost your online exposure, build relationships, generate incoming links, and grow your blog's traffic. As your blog and your online reputation grow, you can charge a fee to write a guest blog post for other blogs.

Some of the most popular bloggers charge hundreds of dollars to write a guest blog post for another blog. For example, popular blogger Chris Garrett (www.chrisg.com) offers blog-writing services, as shown in Figure 10-1. It's unlikely that you will earn high fees until you firmly establish your blog and online reputation as an expert in your blog's topic. Consider setting your fees based on the amount of time you anticipate it takes you to write guest posts to ensure it's worth your time investment.

Figure 10-1: Chris Garrett offers blog-writing services for a fee.

You can always continue to volunteer to write guest blog posts for sites that are larger than your own and stand to give your blog extra promotion.

Booking Speaking Engagements

The more well-known you become across the blogosphere and online community, the more you can build your online brand, reputation, and recognition. This effort can help you establish yourself as an expert in your field who has important opinions and ideas to share, which other people can learn from. After you establish that reputation, you can sell your knowledge by making yourself available to speak at conferences and events.

Many well-known bloggers earn significant fees for public speaking. For example, Gary Vaynerchuk of Wine Library TV has become a sought-after social media expert and public speaker as a direct result of his highly successful video blog related to his wine store in New Jersey and his contagious passion for his subject matter. Today, Gary offers his speaking services through his Web site (`http://tv.winelibrary.com/speaking`) as shown in Figure 10-2.

Figure 10-2: Gary Vaynerchuk is a sought-after public speaker.

To offer your public speaking services, add a page or post to your blog that details your expertise, experience, and capabilities. It's up to you if you want to publish your rates or negotiate with each person who inquires about your services separately. Keep in mind, popular bloggers can charge thousands of dollars plus expenses to speak at events around the world. Price your services accordingly and be certain that all your expenses are paid by the group that hires you.

Offering Consulting Services

As your reputation as an expert in your field grows online thanks to your blogging efforts, you can offer consulting services to people and companies that want greater access to your expertise. It's easy to offer consulting services. Just add a page or post to your blog, outline the type of consulting services you want to provide, include information about your experience and expertise, and provide a way for people to contact you for additional information.

Popular blogger Chris Brogan offers a great example of how to create a page on your blog that describes your consulting services on his blog, `www.chrisbrogan.com`, as shown in Figure 10-3.

Figure 10-3: Chris Brogan offers consulting services on his blog.

It's up to you to set your consulting fees. Select a rate that ensures you'll make enough per hour to make consulting worth your time. Top bloggers can charge hundreds of dollars per hour for their consulting services. Price your services to match your level of expertise and your reputation in comparison with other people in your field and the acceptable "going" rates.

Writing for Other Publications

One of the most common ways bloggers who operate blogs of all sizes use to indirectly monetize their blogs is by writing for other publications. Once you establish your online expertise and reputation, you can apply to write for other publications such as blogs, Web sites, article repositories, magazines, and so on.

Various freelancing Web sites are set up to connect writers with people who are actively looking for their services. Examples include Elance (`www.elance.com`) and iFreelance (`www.ifreelance.com`). There are also blogs that list online writing and blogging job opportunities such as ProBlogger (`www.problogger.net`), Freelance Writing Gigs (`www.freelancewritinggigs.com`), and About Freelance Writing (`www.aboutfreelancewriting.com`), shown in Figure 10-4.

Figure 10-4: Find writing opportunities on the About Freelance Writing blog.

Make sure your writing skills are polished and be prepared to provide writing samples for most writing jobs that you apply to.

Asking for Donations

Although it's not common to get a lot of donations to your blog, it doesn't hurt to ask for them. You can make it easy for your readers to donate to your blog by signing up for a PayPal account at www.paypal.com and adding a donation button to your blog, which automates the process by electronically transferring money from the donor's account to yours. An example of what a PayPal button looks like is shown in Figure 10-5.

Get creative with your donation requests. Add a link at the end of your posts that says, "Like my blog? Buy me a cup of coffee." It's just another way to ask for your loyal readers to support your blog and help you cover hosting costs, your time investment, design costs, and so on, which can add up quickly as your blog grows.

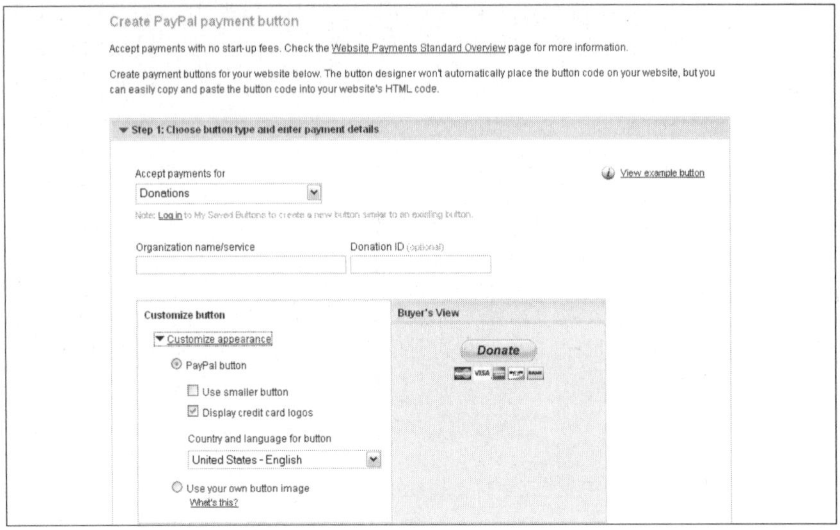

Figure 10-5:
A PayPal
donation
button.

Using Licensed or Ad-Supported Syndication

You can syndicate your blog content and make money. Using a company such as Newstex (www.newstex.com), shown in Figure 10-6, you can license your content for syndication to distributors (such as LexisNexis), who, in turn, provide that content to end-user customers — such as business people, academics, legal professionals, and more — who use it to do their jobs. Alternatively, you can syndicate your blog content through an ad-supported syndication company, such as BlogBurst, and potentially earn revenues.

Figure 10-6:
Make
money by
syndicating
your blog
content
through
Newstex.

Truth be told, most bloggers make very little money from syndication. Instead, syndication is best leveraged for promoting and growing your blog to a wider audience, but if you can make a few dollars, why not?

Accepting Job Offers

One of the most interesting ways to monetize your blog indirectly is by accepting new opportunities that come your way as your online reputation grows. As more people hear of you, read your content, and find out about your expertise, you're likely to receive more and more opportunities for writing, speaking, and so on. Some of these opportunities may come in the form of job offers.

As an established blogger, you may get offers to report on events, provide consulting services, write for new publications, or even join a company in a role related to your expertise. For example, I've gotten clients and speaking gigs for my company, KeySplash Creative, Inc., as a result of my blog content, and I've gotten more than one book deal as a direct result of content from one or more of my blogs. That's just one more way that the power of the social Web and blogging can lead to new opportunities and additional earnings!

Be sure to thoroughly research any opportunity that comes to you to ensure it's legitimate and worth your time investment.

Book VIII

Microblogging with Twitter

Contents at a Glance

Chapter 1: Getting the Short Story with Microblogging

In This Chapter

✔ **Microblogging for beginners**

✔ **Understanding the microblogging craze**

✔ **Choosing a microblogging application**

*M*icroblogging, Twitter, Plurk, Jaiku — these terms were unheard of until 2007, and the world would never be the same afterwards. If you haven't jumped on the microblogging bandwagon yet, get ready for a fun ride! Microblogging is one of the "it" online activities for people to do. In fact, it's become so popular that terms such as *instant messaging* have nearly become *passé*. Everyone is tweeting!

Whether or not microblogging will continue to grow or fade away when the next big fad comes along remains to be seen. For now, it seems like everyone is microblogging, primarily through Twitter, where millions of people publish short messages to each other and the world all day, every day. This chapter explains what microblogging is and describes the most popular microblogging Web sites.

Microblogging for Beginners

What is microblogging? In simplest terms, *microblogging* is the process of publishing short status updates (for example, 140-characters or less through Twitter) on a personal profile through a microblogging Web site. The most popular microblogging sites are Twitter, Plurk, and Jaiku (each is discussed in detail later in this chapter). You can create a profile on a micro-blogging site for free, input some personal information, and start publishing microblog posts. (Twitter users call them *tweets.*) Typically, you can make your account public or private, so you control who can see your updates — any person with access to the Internet or just people you approve.

Microblogging is intended to be a platform to share what you're doing *right now,* and it has transformed the world of online communications.

Tweet tweet

Truth be told, the term *microblogging* has nearly been replaced. Almost as quickly as microblogging was introduced to the world, a dominant player stepped up to the plate and turned the process of microblogging into *tweeting*. Although it's true that Twitter (www.twitter.com) has become the most popular microblogging Web site, there are other options for people who want to publish short snippets online without going through the hassle of starting a blog, sending an e-mail message, or opening an instant messaging application. But more about that later in this chapter.

You can publish updates to most microblogging sites via the Web or a mobile phone, and that ability makes this form of blogging extremely flexible and portable.

Microblogging updates generally appear in reverse chronological order on your profile page. For example, you can easily view the updates for everyone you choose to follow on a single page within your Twitter account, as shown in Figure 1-1.

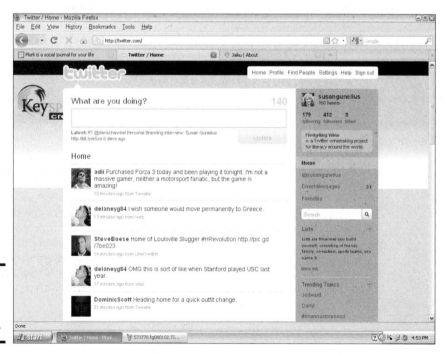

Figure 1-1:
A Twitter account home page.

Of course, microblogging gets a bit more complex than that. For example, you can use special characters and phrases to share information through microblogging. You can send people direct messages, participate in live microblogging events, and more. Although it might seem like microblogging is just one more fad to add to the growing list of online applications and tools that clutter your desktop, many people find great value in it as a tool to connect with friends, meet new people, network, build business relationships, sell products, provide customer service, and much more.

In other words, microblogging is what you make of it. There's no right or wrong way to use microblogging tools. That's not to say there aren't guidelines and unwritten rules of ethics, but not even the creators of Twitter provide a clear explanation of what microblogging is specifically intended to do. The only explanation provided on the Twitter Web site is, "Share and discover what's happening right now, anywhere in the world." Believe it or not, that really is all there is to it.

Don't be intimidated by microblogging! You can't break it, and as long as you act ethically and honestly, you can just dive in and join the conversation!

Understanding the Microblogging Craze

Now that you know what microblogging is, you're probably wondering why it's so popular. Why does it seem like everyone is talking about Twitter? I'm not sure that anyone truly knows the answer to that question. One might argue that it's the current cool online toy. Others might say that it's easy to use. Still others might say that it's free, so why not give it a try? I think the real reason is a bit of all of those answers combined.

The Internet has become a truly social place, where people can connect from around the world at any time. Microblogging made the concept of real-time communication across the globe a reality but with an added bonus. Everyone doesn't have to be online at the same time for it to work. Unlike instant messaging, where both people communicating have to be online simultaneously for it to work, microblogging updates are stored and can be directed to people or easily tied to specific topics, making it simple for people to catch up on conversations and for multiple people to communicate with each other.

As shown in Figure 1-2, Twitter users can connect by tagging each other using the @reply feature or tagging topics using a hashtag feature. (Both features are discussed in detail in Chapter 3 of this minibook.)

Figure 1-2:
A Twitter
stream with
@replies
and
hashtags.

Although many people abandon microblogging because they can't find additional value in it over other forms of communication, there's a large audience of people who love the ability to connect with others from around the world with few barriers to entry and an easy-to-use interface. The bottomline: Microblogging through a site such as Twitter is convenient, far-reaching, and free! I think it's safe to say that many long-distance telephone bills probably dropped after friends and family found microblogging!

Many social networking sites, such as Facebook, include a form of microblogging *within* their systems where users can publish status updates.

Choosing a Microblogging Application

When microblogging first hit the social Web, a number of players jumped on board. Today, a few remain the leaders: Twitter, Plurk, and Jaiku. Although Twitter is by far the most popular microblogging site, its size can make it cluttered. Therefore, Plurk and Jaiku remain viable alternatives for many people.

Because it's free to join each of the most popular microblogging sites, many people open an account with each and test them before they commit to using just one. Take some time to find out where the people you want to interact with spend their time. Look at the functionality provided by each site and then give the ones you're interested in a test run. Some people use more than one microblogging site, but that can become confusing and time-consuming for both you and your audience. Only you can ultimately determine which microblogging site (or sites) will help you meet your individual blogging goals.

Twitter

`www.twitter.com`

Character limit: 140 per message

Tens of millions of people have signed up and created free Twitter accounts since the site debuted in 2006 as a way for people to share quick status updates online. Statistics show that most of those people did not remain active users over a long period of time, and the vast majority of Twitter status updates (called *tweets*) come from a small group of power users. Those people who truly enjoy using Twitter and have built strong relationships with other users find a lot of value in it. Only you can determine whether Twitter is right for you by giving it a try!

Twitter, shown in Figure 1-3, allows anyone to view anyone else's tweets, unless a user sets his account to *Private,* meaning only accepted *followers* can see that user's tweets. When you sign up to follow another user, that person's tweets are displayed within your Twitter stream in reverse chronological order, mixed within all the tweets of the users you follow. It can get cluttered; a wide variety of third-party Twitter applications can make it easier for you to manage your tweets.

Figure 1-3:
Twitter is the most popular micro-blogging site.

**Book VIII
Chapter 1**

**Getting the
Short Story with
Microblogging**

With Twitter, you can also send private direct messages to other users, and you can tag other users within your tweets to notify those users that you referenced them in a tweet. It's easy to share information through Twitter. Therefore, it's not surprising that many individuals and businesses find it useful for promotion and customer service.

The remainder of this minibook tells you the basics about Twitter. For a complete reference guide, check out *Twitter For Dummies,* by Laura Fitton, Michael E. Gruen, and Leslie Poston.

Plurk

www.plurk.com

Character limit: 140 per message

Plurk, shown in Figure 1-4, was introduced in 2008 as a microblogging alternative to Twitter. Plurk offers many similar features to Twitter such as the ability to send private messages and make your updates (called *plurks*) visible only to the people you choose.

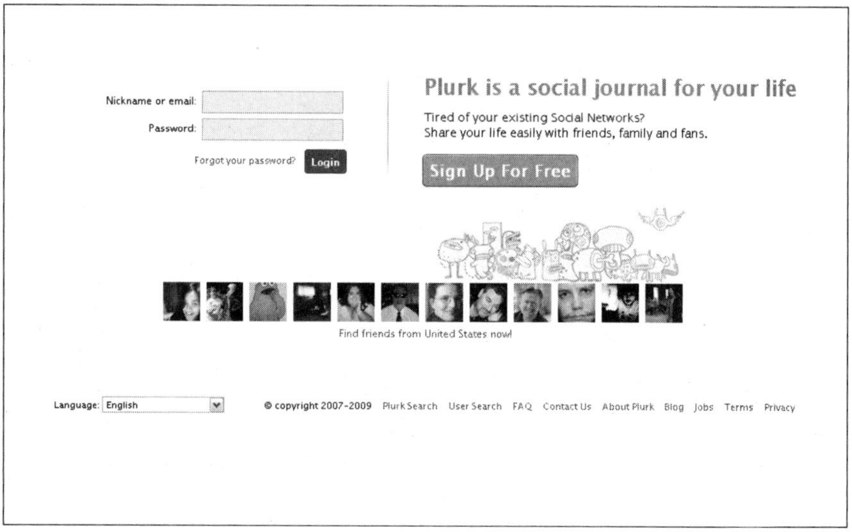

Figure 1-4:
The Plurk
home page.

The site picked up steam quickly after its introduction thanks to some special features that Twitter didn't have and that users liked, including a threaded messaging capability and scrollable timeline visuals. Furthermore, the ability to easily insert video and image content into updates set it apart from Twitter.

One of the features that makes Plurk unique is the ability to create *cliques*. You can create a Plurk clique, so it's easy to keep track of what a smaller group of users are doing. This feature makes Plurk a great choice for creating and growing online communities more so than simply sharing information as Twitter is best known for.

Jaiku

www.jaiku.com

Character limit: 100 per message

Jaiku, shown in Figure 1-5, was founded in 2006 and purchased by Google in 2007. Today, Jaiku is maintained by a group of volunteer engineers. The site was originally created as a way for people to share status updates with groups of friends and acquaintances online. Jaiku works similarly to Twitter, with features such as the ability to keep updates private and send private messages, but Jaiku adds a few enhancements that many users find to be quite valuable.

Figure 1-5:
Jaiku allows users to comment on status updates.

**Book VIII
Chapter 1**

Getting the
Short Story with
Microblogging

Jaiku users can publish updates to their personal status streams (called *jaikus*), or they can join *channels* that are dedicated to specific topics. They can post to channels separately from their own Jaiku streams and even invite other users to join channels of interest. By using channels, Jaiku users can keep their personal streams less cluttered. Furthermore, Jaiku users can comment directly on other users' updates and those messages and comments can be viewed in a threaded mode, making it very easy to follow conversations. This is a desirable feature that Twitter doesn't offer.

Chapter 2: Getting Started with Twitter

In This Chapter

✔ Discovering Twitter

✔ Checking out who's using Twitter

✔ Understanding Twitter drawbacks

✔ Creating an account

✔ Developing your profile

✔ Writing tweets

✔ Finding people to follow

✔ Setting up e-mail preferences

*T*witter is the most popular microblogging Web site by far with millions of people using it for a myriad of reasons. Although Twitter has only been around since 2006 (and has only been widely known since 2007), it has become the go-to place for conversations, information sharing, and even breaking news. The Twitter name has become the new generic name for microblogging, just as BAND-AID and Kleenex became generic names in consumers' minds for bandages and tissues, respectively.

Of course, Twitter does have limitations. Also, the Twitter world is not lawless. That means you need to be aware of the do's and don'ts of microblogging before you get started. Some of these rules are written by Twitter, but most are unwritten guidelines of etiquette and protocol that evolved at the hands of the users.

Although Twitter has yet to turn a profit for the people behind it, businesses and individuals alike continue to support it as a viable communications tool with a long future ahead of it. Whether or not Twitter is just a fad remains to be seen. For now, it's the hot social Web tool, and it seems like everyone knows someone who uses Twitter. This chapter introduces you to Twitter and shows you how to start your own Twitter profile and join the microblogging world with the most popular tool.

Getting to Know Twitter

Twitter (www.twitter.com) is a free microblogging tool that allows you to create your own space online to publish short (140-character or less) status updates called *tweets*. When you create a Twitter account, you can set up your profile so your tweets are visible to anyone with Internet access or only to people whom you choose to allow access to see them.

Unlike social networking sites such as Facebook and LinkedIn that often require you to have established relationships with other users in order to connect with them and view their content, Twitter is far more open. You can *follow* any other Twitter user's tweets, meaning their updates appear within your Twitter account stream along with all the other tweets from users you follow. Likewise, anyone can follow you, and your tweets appear in their Twitter streams (unless you set your account to be private, in which case you must approve followers before they can view your content).

Twitter offers additional functionality such as a direct messaging function that allows you to send private messages to people you follow and receive messages from people who follow you. Thanks to the open source nature of Twitter, there are thousands of applications created by third parties that integrate seamlessly with Twitter to enhance its functionality. Some of the most popular Twitter applications (also called *Twitter apps*) are discussed in detail in Chapter 4 of this minibook.

Twitter provides more than a simple status update tool though. Thanks to features such as @reply and hashtags (discussed in detail in Chapter 3 of this minibook), you can tag other users and topics within your tweets. Doing so makes it easy for users to find out who's talking about them or discover topics of interest to them. You can even search for topics and find links to popular topics on the home page of Twitter, as shown in Figure 2-1.

Figure 2-1:
Search for
topics or
find popular
topics from
the Twitter
home page.

The basic concept of Twitter is very simple. The site provides a place for you to publish short status updates and read status updates from other people. Try not to think too hard about it, and instead, just have fun and get your feet wet. In other words, dive in and start tweeting!

Finding Out Who's Using Twitter and Why

Individuals use Twitter. Celebrities use Twitter. News organizations use Twitter. Businesses use Twitter. Even politicians use Twitter. In other words, Twitter is open to anyone, and it seems like everyone is using it. Of course, the reasons why a person opens a Twitter account vary greatly, and that's what makes it so interesting.

Consider an individual who opens a Twitter account simply to connect with friends and family across long distances. Even if your relatives live near you, Twitter can make it easy to communicate without the formality of picking up the phone or sending an e-mail. Instead of engaging in a lengthy conversation, they can send brief updates. Not only can they send updates to each other, but because Twitter is open to broader audiences, other friends and family members can join the conversation, too! Twitter truly is a social medium.

But what about companies? What value do they find in Twitter? The truth is that no one has discovered the secret to using Twitter for business and marketing success, but a large number of large and small organizations are trying to figure it out. Currently, businesses use Twitter for brand building, self-promotion, publicity, customer service, and more. There's even a third-party site, ExecTweets (`www.exectweets.com`), that provides easy access to business executives' tweets, as shown in Figure 2-2.

Many people use Twitter simply as a way to share information, ideas, opinions, or links to online content. Some people use it to ask questions to a wider audience. It's an excellent networking tool and a great place to find people around the world with interests similar to your own.

Even bloggers can use Twitter to boost their online presences, build relationships, and grow their blog audiences. Using Twitter to grow your blog is discussed in more detail in Chapter 3 of this minibook. Suffice it to say, Twitter can be used for any purpose you can imagine (within the boundaries of the law and ethical considerations of course).

**Book VIII
Chapter 2**

**Getting Started
with Twitter**

Figure 2-2:
Find
business
executives'
tweets on
ExecTweets.
com.

Taking a Look at Twitter Drawbacks

As with most technological tools, Twitter does have limitations that draw user complaints. That's really not surprising when you consider that Twitter really only drew widespread usage in 2007 and still doesn't generate a profit for Google. In other words, Twitter is young, and it's not a cash cow yet. The site might be popular and generate a lot of publicity, but until it drives revenue, enhancements are likely to go only so far. Fortunately, third-party developers create amazing applications to integrate with Twitter and solve some of the problems with limitations that users experience. (Some of these applications are discussed in Chapter 4 of this minibook.)

Be sure to set your expectations for Twitter performance before you create your account. Following are some of the biggest problems users encounter with Twitter:

✦ **Twitter overload causes downtime.** Twitter grew very quickly. As such, the site was often not available during the first two years of its lifecycle. There simply were too many people trying to access the site at the same time and the technology behind Twitter couldn't keep up with the demands. Today, downtime is less frequent, but if a big news story breaks (such as when the death of Michael Jackson occurred in 2009 or the earthquakes in Haiti happened in 2010), you can bet that you'll see the now-famous *over capacity* page, as shown in Figure 2-3.

You can check on the status of Twitter performance at any time by visiting the Twitter Status page at `http://status.twitter.com`, as shown in Figure 2-4.

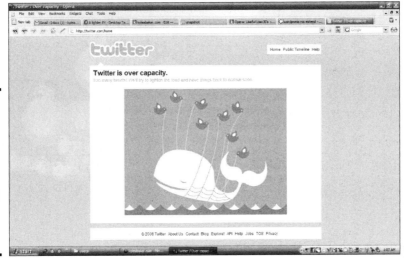

Figure 2-3:
The Twitter over capacity page features a whale being carried by Twitter birds.

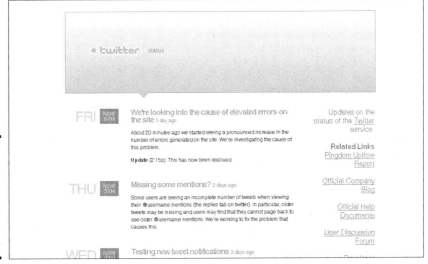

Figure 2-4:
Check for current Twitter problems on the Twitter Status page.

✦ **Twitter is cluttered.** Because all tweets appear in your Twitter stream in chronological order, it can be hard to find the updates you're most interested in, and it's very difficult to follow conversations. Most Twitter users follow a wide variety of people — sometimes hundreds or thousands of people. Following the tweets by all those people listed in a single stream can be difficult to navigate and requires a lot of scrolling. Think of it this way, if you follow 100 people on Twitter and each publishes 10 tweets per day, that's 1,000 tweets per day that you need to scroll through on your Twitter account home page. It can be easy to miss important tweets!

Some third-party Twitter applications can help you manage and sort your tweets, and I discuss those applications in Chapter 4 of this minibook.

✦ **Twitter is filled with spam.** Many people create Twitter accounts for no other purpose but to spam other users. The onus is on you and other Twitter users to block suspicious accounts from following you, so the Twitter team can review and ban those accounts that are found to be spam.

✦ **Twitter provides little support.** Remember, Twitter doesn't generate a profit yet. It's not surprising that support is limited. Although the Twitter Web site does include a frequently asked questions section, a blog, and a support section, it can be difficult to get help when you need it. A commonly cited example is when someone creates a Twitter account posing as another person. This happens frequently with celebrities, companies, and brands. For example, there are many Twitter accounts for top celebrities. Usually, only one account (or no accounts) is actually owned by that person. The others are imposters. Even if you send a message to Twitter notifying the team of a fake account, it can be difficult or impossible to get a response.

✦ **Twitter has storage limitations.** Twitter saves tweets from a Twitter stream only for a specific amount of time. That means if you want to find a tweet published by someone from a year ago, you won't be able to do so.

✦ **Twitter offers few monetization options.** Many Twitter users would like to monetize their Twitter profiles. Although there are some *pay-you-to-tweet* options available through third-party companies and some advertising options, many users would like to be able to generate more revenue from their Twitter activities, particularly bloggers who are used to monetizing their blogs and expect to be able to do so with microblogging, too.

IZEA, a social media marketing company, offers two programs for Twitter users to connect with advertisers and get paid to publish tweets: Sponsored Tweets (www.sponsoredtweets.com), shown in Figure 2-5, and SocialSpark (www.socialspark.com).

Depending on your goals for using Twitter, the limitations may or may not affect you. Furthermore, as Twitter continues to grow, it's inevitable that changes will be made and enhancements will be added. You can always find new information about Twitter on the Twitter blog at http://blog.twitter.com, shown in Figure 2-6.

Figure 2-5:
Sponsored Tweets provides Twitter users with a way to monetize their Twitter activities.

Figure 2-6:
The Twitter blog provides updated information.

Creating an Account

It takes just a few minutes to create a Twitter account and join the world of microblogging. All you need is a valid e-mail address that isn't already connected to another Twitter account.

To create a Twitter account and join the tweeting craze, follow these steps:

1. **Visit www.twitter.com.**

   The Twitter home page opens, as shown earlier in Figure 2-1.

2. **Click the Sign Up Now button near the center of your screen.**

   The sign-up page opens, as shown in Figure 2-7.

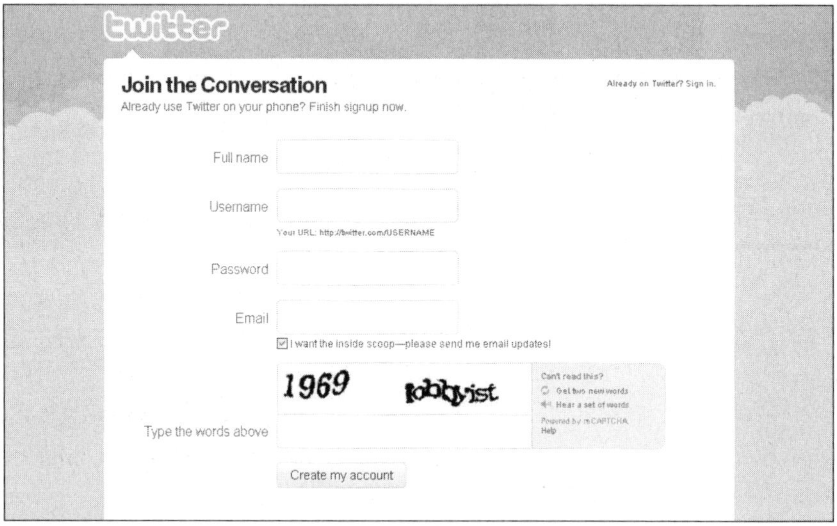

Figure 2-7:
The Twitter sign-up page.

> **twitter**
>
> **Join the Conversation**   Already on Twitter? Sign in.
> Already use Twitter on your phone? Finish signup now.
>
> Full name [   ]
>
> Username [   ]
>   Your URL: http://twitter.com/USERNAME
>
> Password [   ]
>
> Email [   ]
>   ☑ I want the inside scoop—please send me email updates!
>
> *1969*   **lobbyist**   Can't read this?
>   ↻ Get two new words
>   ◀) Hear a set of words
>   Powered by reCAPTCHA
>   Help
> Type the words above [   ]
>
>   [Create my account]

3. **Enter the requested information into the form.**

   Type your full name into the Full Name text box and your desired Twitter username into the Username text box. Next, enter the password you want to assign to your account and a unique e-mail address.

   Your username doesn't need to be the same as your full name. Your username is the name that appears at the end of your unique Twitter URL and is the name used to identify you to other Twitter users. Take some time to choose it carefully.

4. **Enter the provided CAPTCHA code into the Type the Words Above text box.**

   This code identifies you as a human, so Twitter understands a real person is creating the account rather than an automated spam robot.

5. **Click the Create My Account button.**

   By clicking the Create My Account button, you automatically agree to the Twitter Terms of Service, which you can read at http://twitter. com/tos, and your account is activated immediately.

Writing Your Profile Description

After you create your new Twitter account, it's essential that you take a few minutes to create a complete profile description. Writing a comprehensive profile helps build your credibility among other Twitter users because they understand not only that you're a real person but also that you have expertise and opinions to bring to the table.

Naturally, if you're using Twitter only for fun or to communicate with friends and family, the depth of your profile isn't as important as it is for someone who's using Twitter to build an online presence or grow a business. Therefore, it's up to you to determine the information you want to include in your Twitter profile that best helps you meet your goals.

Follow these steps to create a complete Twitter profile:

1. **Visit www.twitter.com and click the Sign In link in the top-right corner of the page.**

   A fly-out window opens, shown in Figure 2-8, and here you can enter your Twitter username and password.

2. **Click the Sign In button once you enter your username and password.**

   Your Twitter account home page opens, as shown in Figure 2-9.

3. **Click the Settings link in the top right navigation bar.**

   Your Account page opens, as shown in Figure 2-10.

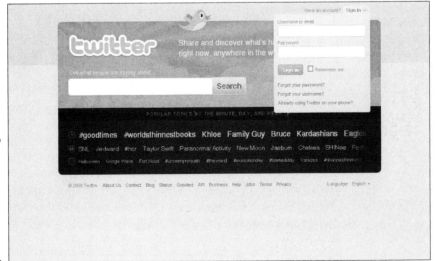

Figure 2-8:
Sign in to
your Twitter
account
from the
Twitter
home page.

**Book VIII
Chapter 2**

Getting Started
with Twitter

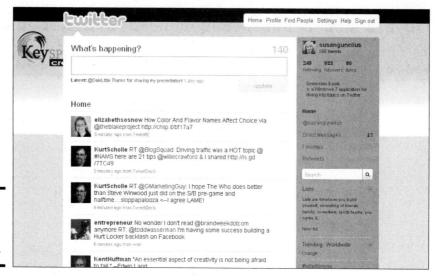

Figure 2-9:
A Twitter
account
home page.

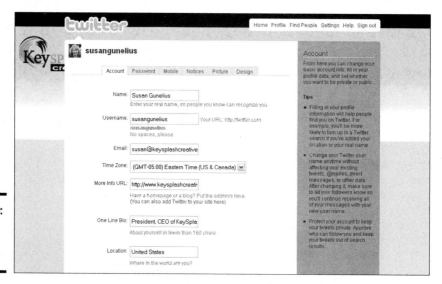

Figure 2-10:
A Twitter
Account
page.

4. Enter the information requested in the boxes provided.

The information provided in this form appears at the top right of your Twitter profile page. Everyone who visits your Twitter profile sees this information, so take some time to enter it and create a compelling biography.

The One Line Bio text box allows you to enter only 160 characters or less. Make sure you write your bio in a manner that allows you to stay within that character constraint.

5. Select the check box next to Protect Your Tweets if you want to keep your Twitter updates private.

By selecting this check box, only people who request to follow you and that you approve can see your Twitter updates. Otherwise, anyone with Internet access can view your tweets.

6. Click the Save button.

Your new profile information is immediately visible in your Twitter account sidebar, as shown in Figure 2-11.

Figure 2-11: A Twitter account profile and bio.

Book VIII Chapter 2

Getting Started with Twitter

Writing Tweets

After you create your Twitter account and complete your profile by adding your bio, a link to your blog or Web site, and so on, you can begin publishing tweets.

You can publish tweets before you update your profile, but if your goal is to connect with a broader audience than your family and friends, the best path is to update your profile *before* you start tweeting.

Remember, there's no right or wrong way to tweet. Depending on your long-term objectives, you might want to stay professional. Alternatively, you might want to keep your tweets very personal. However, even the most professional Twitter users inject their personalities into their tweets. Just like blogging, your Twitter content is very boring if it doesn't have any personality.

Get started by building some content. Publish a variety of tweets telling the world what you're working on; talking about what you like; sharing links to stories, videos, or images; and so on. It's up to you! You can even share links to your own blog posts. Just be careful not to fill your Twitter stream with self-promotional tweets. Unless you're providing meaningful, useful, and interesting content in your Twitter updates, no one will want to follow you.

Take some time to visit other Twitter users' profiles and read what they're sharing to get some ideas of what *you* find interesting. Then implement similar ideas into your own tweets.

Take a look at trending and popular topics on Twitter by looking in your Twitter profile's right sidebar for trending topics (meaning they're growing in popularity right *now*) and check the Twitter home page for links to popular topics. Those are great topics to include in your own tweets if you want to join a larger conversation.

Later in this chapter, you find out how to find other people to follow and connect with on Twitter. To get started, though, focus on building some content. You don't want to connect with other people if your Twitter stream is blank. Instead, wait to follow others until you have some tweets. That's because people typically visit the profiles of anyone who signs up to follow them, and they're likely to reciprocate and follow in return if they find interesting information in that person's Twitter stream. In other words, don't lead them to you until you have something for them to see, so they can determine whether they want to follow you in return.

As you write your tweets, remember that they must be 140-characters or less. Not surprisingly, you can fill up 140-characters very quickly. Twitter users understand that and are forgiving of the use of abbreviations, misspellings, and grammatical errors when it's clearly done to save characters. For example, instead of writing *before* in a tweet, you can use *b4* and save several characters.

There is a third-party application called TwitLonger (www.twitlonger. com) that you can use to write tweets that are longer than 140-characters.

To get started, take a look at the following suggestions for types of tweets you can publish in your Twitter stream. In time, you'll find out what kinds of tweets work best for you in terms of allowing you to meet both your needs and your followers' needs.

✦ **Tell the world what you're doing.** Create a tweet that does exactly what Twitter asks you — What's happening? It might seem boring to you, but it's a great way to share a bit of information about yourself. You can extend this idea to tweet about what you just finished doing or what you're about to do.

✦ **Share content.** Link to online content that you enjoy, don't like, want to get other opinions about, and so on. There's so much to talk about based on the content published across the Web!

✦ **Ask questions.** When you've a group of people following you, publish a tweet that asks a question either to start a conversation or because you truly need the answer.

✦ **Promote yourself, your blog, your business, and more.** Share updates about your achievements, publicity for your business, promotional information, links to your blog content to drive traffic, and so on.

✦ **Participate in Twitter events.** Twitter users often band together to participate in events such as Follow Friday, where users use the #hashtag #FF and list other Twitter users in a tweet (for example, @susangunelius) in order to recommend them as people that their own followers should check out and follow, too.

✦ **Have fun.** Some tweets can be for no other purpose but entertainment.

Reviewing Types of Tweets

Truth be told, you can create any kind of tweet you want as long as your tweets aren't offensive. That's one of the best benefits of using Twitter — you can use it for your own reasons and in your own way. Each Twitter user's experience is unique, and as such, each Twitter user's content is specific to their wants and needs from the microblogging experience.

Whether you use Twitter for personal reasons or professional reasons, the types of tweets you publish will be similar. It's the purpose behind those tweets that varies from one user to the next. Many people create a Twitter account and then have trouble trying to decide what to tweet about. Take a look at the following list of ten popular types of tweets to get started in writing tweets:

✦ **Sharing interesting links:** Include links to interesting articles, blog posts, and so on that you want to share with your followers. Just be sure to include a snippet that explains what the link leads to and why you're sharing it.

✦ **Sharing your own links:** If you write a blog, have an online business, or publish content online, there's nothing wrong with sharing links to that content that your Twitter followers might find interesting.

✦ **Providing your opinion:** You can publish your opinion on any subject through your Twitter stream. Just be sure to match your opinion-based tweets with your target audience, particularly if you tweet for professional purposes.

✦ **Being personable:** You should try to inject your own personality into your tweets, so your followers get to know you better and feel like they're developing relationships with you. Don't be afraid to be yourself and use your own voice in your tweets.

✦ **Asking questions:** Twitter is a great medium to engage your audience by publishing questions, particularly if you have a sizeable group of followers who might be willing to join the conversation.

✦ **Promoting yourself:** Yes, it's acceptable to publish tweets that are self-promotional. Just make sure the majority of your tweets provide useful and meaningful information, so your followers aren't turned off by a Twitter stream filled with self-promotion.

✦ **Having fun:** You can publish tweets for entertainment purposes only. Doing so adds another facet of your personality to your Twitter stream and can be a great way to start discussions and additional sharing between you and your followers.

✦ **Sharing pictures, videos, and more:** With the help of useful Twitter apps such as TwitPic (discussed in Chapter 4 of this minibook), you can easily link to pictures, videos, and more through your tweets, making your Twitter stream multidimensional.

✦ **Joining conversations and participating in activities:** You can publish tweets with hashtags and join tweet chats (both are discussed later in this chapter) to make your Twitter stream more interactive and to build relationships with other Twitter users.

✦ **Replying to other tweets:** You can use the @reply feature in Twitter (discussed later in this chapter) to engage your followers directly and to build relationships with them.

There's no right or wrong way to tweet as long as you're not offensive in your tweets. Make your Twitter profile and your Twitter stream your own!

Following Twitter Etiquette

There are two types of guidelines you should be aware of and follow when you use Twitter. First, you need to read the Twitter Rules on the Twitter Web site. These rules tell you what you're specifically not allowed to do on Twitter and include not impersonating another person, not using trademarked names that you don't own in your username, not publishing other people's private information on Twitter, not threatening anyone, and more.

Be sure to read the most recent Twitter Rules before you start tweeting. You can find them at http://help.twitter.com/forums/10711/ entries/69214.

In addition to the official Twitter Rules, there are also unwritten etiquette rules that other Twitter users expect you to follow. If you want to be a welcomed member to the Twitter community, adhere to the following etiquette tips:

✦ **Attribute your sources.** If you're retweeting another user's Twitter update, be sure to use the RT and @reply features to credit that source for the information.

✦ **Don't spam.** An easy way to get people to stop following you on Twitter is to continually publish tweets that can be deemed spammy. First, don't spam your followers with constant self-promotion and links to your own Web site, blog, and so on. Second, if you're publishing sponsored tweets or ads, disclose them as such. You don't want your Twitter stream to look like one long list of ads and promotional links. Instead, be sure to always add value in your tweets.

✦ **Don't be offensive.** Consider your audience when you write your tweets. Avoid using offensive language or tweeting about subjects that may offend your current or desired audience.

✦ **Keep personal matters out of your Twitter stream.** If your Twitter stream is public, don't get too personal in your tweets. Keep private information to yourself and avoid getting into heated debates that could turn off your followers.

If your Twitter stream is public, anyone with Internet access can view your tweets. Think before you tweet!

Finding People to Follow

After you've some content published on Twitter, it's time to start following other users. Whenever you find someone whose content you like and want to see in your Twitter stream, simply click the Follow button at the top of that user's profile page. His updates immediately appear in your Twitter home page stream.

Most users set up their Twitter account settings so that each time a person becomes a follower, they receive an e-mail with a link to the new follower's Twitter profile. When they view the new follower's Twitter stream, they might decide to follow him in return. That's why it's important to have some content on your Twitter stream before you start following other people.

Use these steps to search for people to follow on Twitter:

1. **Log in to your Twitter account.**

2. **Select the Find People link in the top right navigation bar of your Twitter account, as shown in Figure 2-9.**

The Find Accounts and Follow Them page opens.

You can search for other Twitter users in several different ways using the tabs at the top of the page. By default, the Find on Twitter tab is selected as shown in Figure 2-12.

3. **Enter the search terms of your choice and click the Search button.**

You can search by a person's first or last name, username, brand name, or business name. A list of matches is returned to you, which you can click through to try to locate a specific person or account.

The Twitter search function is not perfect. Don't be surprised if you can't find the person you want easily.

4. **Click the Find on Other Networks tab to find people in your existing Gmail, Yahoo!, or AOL address books, as shown in Figure 2-13.**

Simply click the type of account you have by using the left navigation bar and enter your e-mail address and password to link to your account and search for users who have Twitter accounts associated with the e-mail addresses in your address books.

Figure 2-12: Search for people on Twitter.

5. **Click the Invite by Email tab to send e-mails to people who you want to invite to join Twitter.**

   The Invite window opens, as shown in Figure 2-14, where you can enter e-mail addresses and click the Invite button to send messages asking those people to sign up and join you on Twitter.

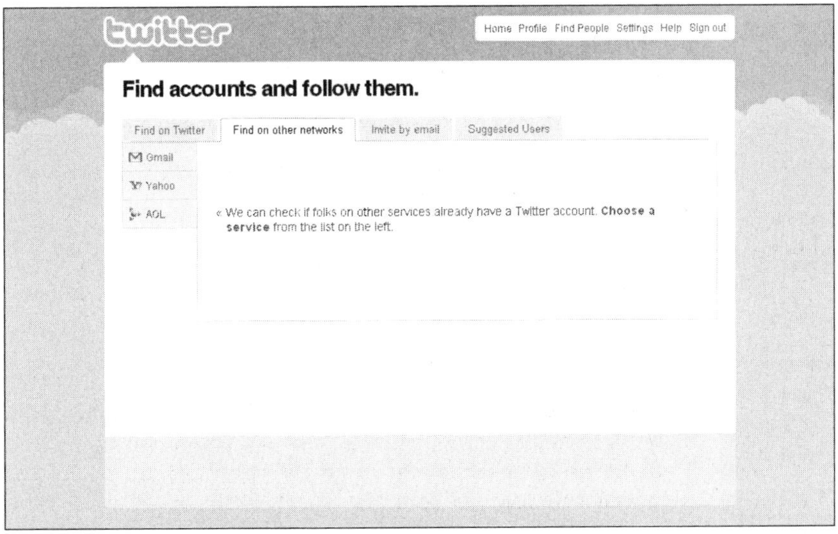

Figure 2-13: Find Twitter users from your online e-mail address books.

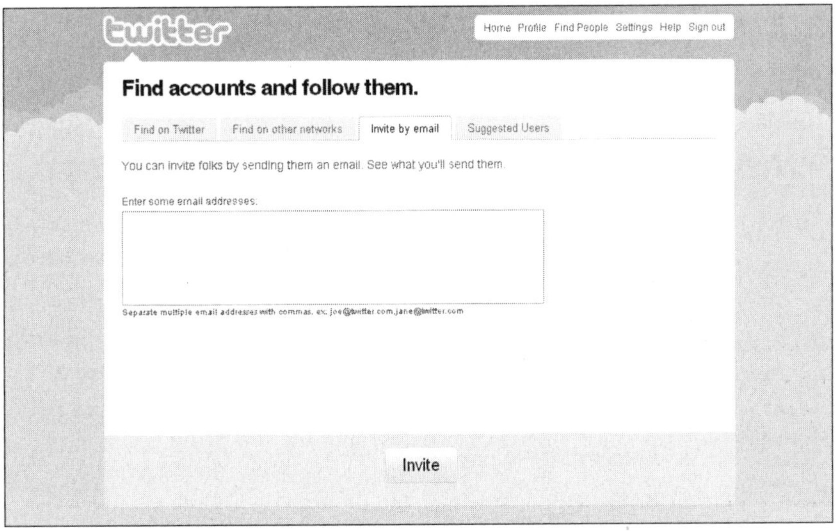

Figure 2-14: Invite people to join Twitter by e-mail.

Book VIII Chapter 2

Getting Started with Twitter

6. **Click the Suggested Users tab to view a list of popular users, as shown in Figure 2-15.**

Scroll through the list. When you find people you want to follow, select the check box to the left of their usernames and avatars, and click the Follow button.

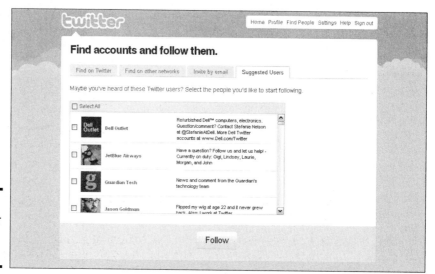

Figure 2-15: Find popular Twitter users.

If you know someone's Twitter username, you can easily find him or her by simply appending that username to the main Twitter URL as `www.twitter.com/username`.

Setting Up E-Mail Notification Preferences

Another important step in creating your Twitter account is to set up your e-mail preferences. You can easily determine when you receive e-mails from Twitter, as follows:

1. **Log in to your Twitter account and select the Settings link from the top-right navigation bar, as shown earlier in Figure 2-9.**

Your Account settings page opens, as shown earlier in Figure 2-10.

2. **Select the Notices tab.**

Your Notices settings page opens, as shown in Figure 2-16.

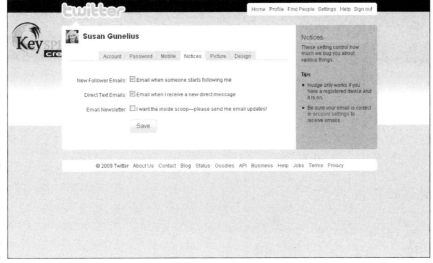

Figure 2-16:
Set up
your e-mail
notification
preferences.

3. **Select the check boxes next to the events when you want to be notified by e-mail.**

   To stay up-to-date with your Twitter activity, select the check boxes next to New Follower Emails and Direct Message Followers.

4. **Click the Save button.**

   You will automatically begin receiving an e-mail at the e-mail address listed in your Twitter account anytime one of the events you selected occurs.

You can also customize your Twitter profile page design and upload a picture to your account from the Settings section of your account. Both features are discussed in detail in Chapter 3 of this minibook.

**Book VIII
Chapter 2**

**Getting Started
with Twitter**

Chapter 3: Getting More out of Twitter

In This Chapter

✔ Customizing your profile

✔ Using URL shorteners

✔ Understanding @replies, retweets, and hashtags

✔ Blocking followers

✔ Sending direct messages

✔ Using Twitter to boost blog traffic

✔ Joining tweet chats

✔ Finding Twitter badges

✔ Following Twitter etiquette

*O*n the surface, Twitter might seem like another form of online chatting, but it actually offers a lot more. In fact, the features and functionality of Twitter can be used in many different ways to meet the needs of a wide variety of users. Some people use Twitter as a way to communicate with friends and family, and others use it to promote their businesses. What makes Twitter so appealing is the fact that it's not a one-size-fits-all tool. Instead, each person molds Twitter into the tool that they want it to be.

This chapter introduces you to the features and terminology of Twitter that help you take your microblogging experience to the next level in terms of building a reputation, leveraging the opportunities Twitter offers, and ensuring you're a welcome member of the Twitter community.

Customizing Your Profile Page

Whether you're using Twitter for personal entertainment or for business, it's a good idea to customize your profile page. If you tweet for entertainment, it's just fun to customize your Twitter profile to make it your own (and less boring than all the other plain profile pages you find). However, if you tweet for professional reasons, then it's absolutely essential that you take the time to brand your Twitter profile page, just as you brand your Web site, marketing materials, and so on.

The more you use Twitter and view other people's profiles, the more you'll notice custom backgrounds. They're often more memorable and can create a perceived image of the Twitterer in your mind before you even read a person's tweets. That's the same goal you should have for your Twitter profile.

For example, take a look at Internet guru John Chow's custom Twitter profile (created by www.custombackgroundsfortwitter.com), shown in Figure 3-1. Notice how much more interesting it is than the standard Twitter profile background shown in Figure 3-2.

Make your Twitter profile stand out from the crowd by customizing it. There are many companies that create custom Twitter backgrounds for a fee, but fortunately, there are also Web sites where you can create your own customized Twitter backgrounds. Check out the nearby sidebar for some recommended Web sites where you can create your own Twitter backgrounds for free or for a small fee.

Figure 3-1: John Chow's customized Twitter background.

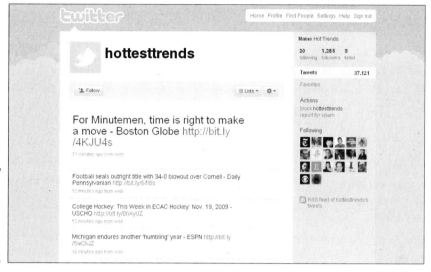

Figure 3-2:
A standard
Twitter
profile
background.

Changing your Twitter profile background image

At the very least, you can modify your Twitter background image and your Twitter profile color scheme with ease. Follow these steps to customize your Twitter profile background using the tools provided within your Twitter account.

1. **Log in to your Twitter account at www.twitter.com.**

Click the Settings tab in the upper-right navigation bar, as shown in Figure 3-3.

Web sites to create custom Twitter backgrounds

A simple Google search for "free Twitter backgrounds" yields a wide variety of Web sites that offer free standard background templates as well as tools to create custom backgrounds. Following are several sites to get you started:

✔ **Social Identities** (www.custombackgroundsfortwitter.com) offers both free and customizable Twitter backgrounds.

✔ **MyTweetSpace.com** (www.mytweetspace.com) offers free custom Twitter

backgrounds as well as premium options for a fee.

✔ **Free Twitter Designer** (www.freetwitterdesigner.com) offers very customizable free Twitter backgrounds.

✔ **TwitBacks** (www.twitbacks.com) offers free Twitter backgrounds, which you can search for based on categorization such as nature, car, photo, and so on. You can also customize those backgrounds for free.

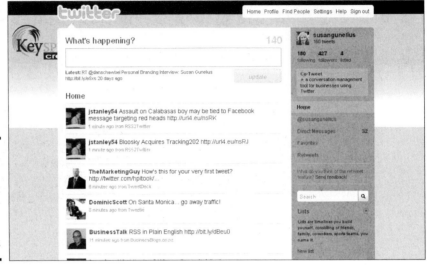

Figure 3-3:
Select the
Settings link
to modify
your Twitter
profile
background.

2. **Select the Design tab from the navigation bar in the center of your screen below your username.**

   The Design page opens as shown in Figure 3-4 with thumbnail images of the available background options to choose from.

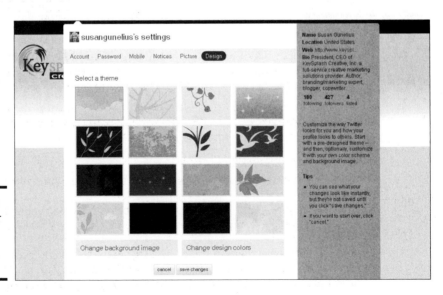

Figure 3-4:
The Twitter
profile
Design
page.

3. **To change the background image of your Twitter profile to a custom image, click the Change Background Image link beneath the thumbnail pictures.**

   The window expands to show a new section where you can make changes to your Twitter profile background image, as shown in Figure 3-5, by uploading a background image of your own.

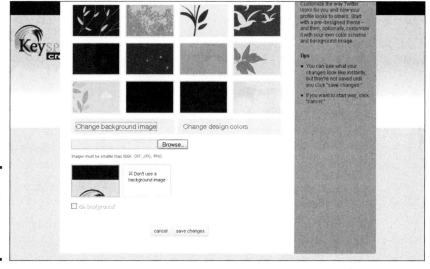

Figure 3-5:
Upload your
own Twitter
background
image.

4. **Either enter the destination path on your hard drive where your Twitter background image is saved into the text box or click the Browse button to navigate to the image on your hard drive.**

   The background image you use should be less than 800 KB and 1,600 pixels wide by 1,200 pixels high to work with most screen resolutions. Your file can be in JPEG, PNG, or GIF format.

5. **Click the Save Changes button.**

   Your new background is immediately applied to your Twitter profile.

If the image you want to use in your Twitter profile background is small, you can select the Tile Background box and the image will repeat in a tiled pattern.

When you create a custom Twitter background, be sure to include your contact information, Web site URLs, and any other information that you want to promote in order to show people more about you, your business, and so on.

**Book VIII
Chapter 3**

**Getting More
out of Twitter**

You cannot create clickable links in Twitter backgrounds, so be sure to include full URLs, e-mail addresses, and so on.

Modifying the color scheme of your Twitter profile

No matter what background image you use in your Twitter profile, you can always change the color scheme of the text that appears in your Twitter stream and sidebar. Changing the text color is particularly helpful if you upload a custom background using colors that don't match the default text color scheme in Twitter.

The following steps teach you how to change your Twitter profile color scheme to make it match your background and preferences.

1. **Log in to your Twitter account at www.twitter.com.**

Click the Settings tab in the upper-right navigation bar, as shown earlier in Figure 3-3.

2. **Click the Design tab on the navigation bar in the center of your screen below your username.**

The Design page opens as shown in Figure 3-4 with thumbnail images of the available background options to choose from.

3. **Click the Change Design Colors link beneath the thumbnail images.**

A new section of the window opens, as shown in Figure 3-6.

4. **Enter codes to change the colors in your Twitter profile or use the color picker to select new colors.**

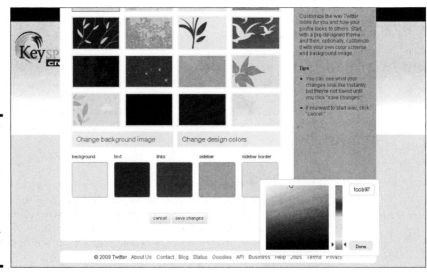

Figure 3-6:
Enter codes or use the color picker to change the color scheme of your Twitter profile.

5. **Click the Save Changes button.**

Your new colors are automatically visible in your Twitter profile.

Make sure the colors you choose work well with your background and are easy to see. Most importantly, make sure it's easy for people to see linked text.

Using URL Shorteners

The more you use Twitter, the more you realize how often people share links to Web sites, videos, images, and information in their tweets. The problem is that many URLs are very long. That means a URL can take up an entire tweet leaving no room for you to explain why you're sharing it. Imagine that you want to share a link to a great blog post you just wrote, but you can't even fit the entire URL into a tweet. What do you do? That's where URL shorteners become an essential tool of microblogging.

Understanding why URL shorteners are useful

Fortunately, some Web sites make it easy to shorten URLs *and* track how many people clicked on those shortened URL links. Using a URL shortener takes just a few seconds. You can create a free account on most URL shortener Web sites, which allows you to track the number of clicks on your published shortened URLs, or you can use some URL shortener Web sites without creating an account at all. (You won't get any additional features, such as click-tracking, though.)

Simply copy the URL that you want to shorten and paste it into the appropriate text box on the URL shortener Web site that you choose. Click a button and a shortened URL is provided to you, which could be as few as ten characters in length. Copy and paste that URL into your tweet, and anyone who clicks it is automatically sent to your original URL to view the content you want to share. That's all there is to it!

URL shorteners offer another benefit to bloggers. Sometimes URLs change. If a URL that you share via Twitter changes, then the URL you publish in your tweet won't work. Using a URL shortener often fixes that problem. After you create a shortened URL, it will always lead people who click it to your original linked page.

Choosing URL shorteners

When choosing a URL shortener, consider your needs. Do you want to track how many times people click your shortened link? Do you want to be able to make URLs as short as possible? Each URL shortener offers slightly different features, and sometimes you need to register for an account in order to access all the features.

Additionally, some URL shorteners allow you to create customized URLs while others only provide an automated short URL for you. Some allow you to post your Twitter updates directly from the URL shortener Web site as you create your shortened URL. There are even URL shorteners that provide a handy toolbar to make shortening URLs easier and faster.

There are a number of URL shorteners available. Following is an overview of several of the most popular sites to shorten URLs for your Twitter updates.

TinyURL

www.tinyurl.com

TinyURL, shown in Figure 3-7, shortens URLs to 25 characters, making it the longest URL shortener. TinyURL is free to use, and you don't have to create an account to shorten your URLs. There's a useful toolbar that you can download to make shortening URLs quick and easy. Many users like the fact that they can create customized URLs with TinyURL, but there isn't a tracking mechanism, which turns off just as many users.

Figure 3-7: TinyURL shortens URLs to 25 characters.

bit.ly

www.bitly.com

bit.ly, shown in Figure 3-8, has grown in popularity significantly. You can shorten URLs to 14 characters and track the number of clicks they get with or without a free account. You can access full history reports, and even add the bit.ly sidebar bookmarklet to your browser toolbar to make shortening URLs and publishing them to Twitter as easy as possible. If you prefer, you can also shorten URLs and publish them to your Twitter account without leaving the bit.ly Web site.

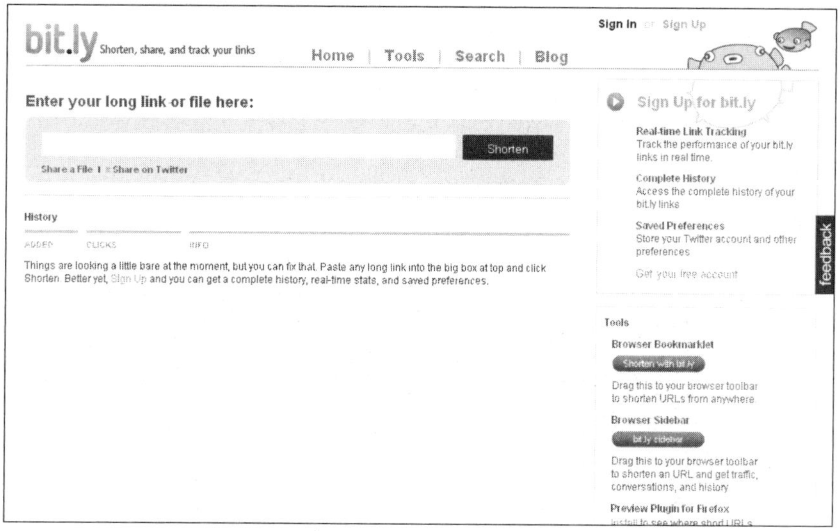

Figure 3-8:
bit.ly is a
popular URL
shortener.

Snurl

www.snurl.com

Snurl, also called SnipURL, (shown in Figure 3-9) allows you to shorten URLs without registering for an account. However, if you do create a Snurl account, you can track clicks on your shortened URLs and customize your shortened URLs. You can also browse through a list of recent *snips* from other users. Snurl shortens URLs to 13 characters.

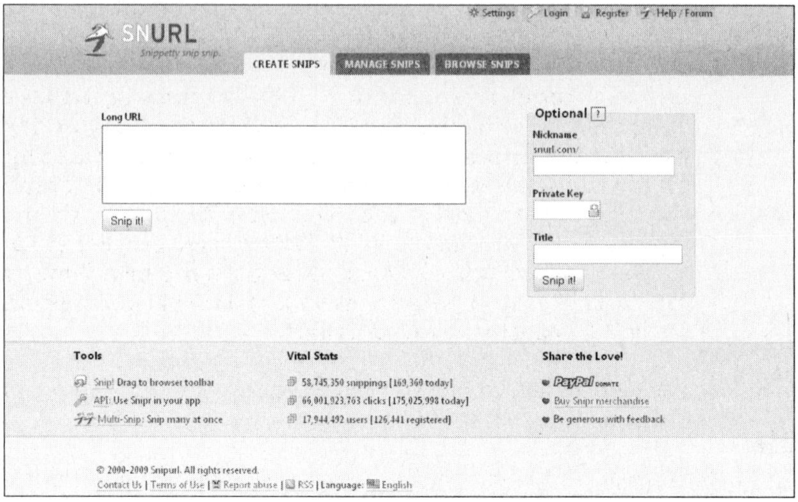

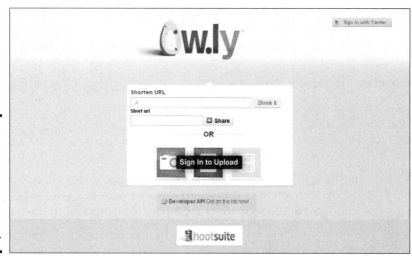

Figure 3-9: Snurl is also called SnipURL.

Ow.ly

`www.ow.ly`

With Ow.ly, which is owned by HootSuite and shown in Figure 3-10, you can shorten URLs to 17 characters with or without an account. Ow.ly allows you to shorten a URL and share it with the click of a mouse not only on Twitter but also on a variety of other social Web sites such as Facebook, Blogger, Digg, and more. If you create a HootSuite account, you can also upload images, videos, MP3 files, and documents. HootSuite stores them and automatically creates a shortened URL for you to share the links to those files. With a HootSuite account, you can also track the clicks on your shortened URLs.

Figure 3-10: Ow.ly integrates with HootSuite for enhanced functionality.

Understanding @replies

To make Twitter a tool capable of publishing two-way online conversations, users reply to each other's tweets directly from their own Twitter streams using the @reply tag. If you come across a tweet published by another person and you want to reply to it through your public Twitter stream, you can do so by starting your tweet with *@username,* where *username* is replaced with the other person's Twitter username. For example, if you want to reply to a tweet that I publish through your public Twitter stream, you can do so by starting your tweet with *@susangunelius* or by selecting the Reply link beneath the original tweet.

You can publish @replies to any Twitter user whether or not you're following them.

You can easily keep track of other users' tweets that include @replies to you because they appear in an @replies list, which is accessible through the @replies link in the right sidebar of your Twitter home page. Likewise, anyone that you include as an @reply in one of your tweets can see that @reply listed in their own @replies list in their home page sidebars. Figure 3-11 shows a list of Twitter @replies.

Figure 3-11:
A list of Twitter @replies.

When @username is used within a tweet (meaning it doesn't appear as the prefix to the tweet), it's considered a *mention,* not a reply. Mentions are also collected and appear in your @replies list in your Twitter homepage sidebar.

Book VIII Chapter 3

Getting More out of Twitter

Retweeting

Retweeting is a way to attribute a tweet to another user using the letters *RT* along with @username to identify the original source. For example, if you read a tweet from me and want to share it with your own followers, you can publish a tweet that begins with *RT @susangunelius* followed by the text of the original tweet that you want to share. Twitter makes the process of retweeting even easier by including a Retweet link beneath all tweets. Just click the Retweet link beneath the post you want to share with your followers, and it's automatically published within your Twitter stream. Figure 3-12 shows an example of a retweet in a Twitter stream.

Figure 3-12: Retweets in a Twitter stream.

The process of retweeting not only gives credit where credit is due (to the original tweeter) but it also provides a tap on the shoulder to the original tweeter through the @reply function. In other words, a retweet tells the original source of the tweet that you appreciate his content and you're sharing and promoting it. It's a great way to get on the radar screens of popular Twitter users or other users that you want to connect with in a deeper way than simply following them provides.

Using Hashtags

Hashtags are used to help Twitter users keep track of ongoing conversations. Hashtags are made up of a keyword preceded by #, and they appear within a tweet. For example, you can create a tweet about the Olympics by including #*olympics* within your tweet. Users can find tweets related to specific hashtags by searching for them using the Twitter search function. Figure 3-13 shows a list of tweets that include the same hashtag.

Figure 3-13: A list of tweets with the same hashtag.

Sometimes, users plan to tweet about specific topics and create hashtags about that topic. They might even set up a tweet chat where a group of users all log in to Twitter at the same time and publish tweets using the predetermined hashtag, creating a real-time conversation. Tweet chats are discussed in more detail later in this chapter.

Blocking Followers

Unfortunately, there are many spam profiles on Twitter. It's important to block those profiles from following you, so Twitter can identify them and delete those accounts. When you block people from following you, they won't see your tweets in their own Twitter streams, and they won't show up on your followers list (nor will you appear on their followers list). They won't be able to send direct messages to you, either.

To block someone from following you on Twitter, just log in to your Twitter account and visit that person's profile page. Click the Block link in the right sidebar. A pop-up opens, confirming that you want to block that user. Click the confirmation button, and that person is immediately blocked.

Sending Direct Messages

Sending direct messages through Twitter is very different from publishing @replies within your tweets. Direct messages are private, whereas @replies are public (if your Twitter stream is public). Think of direct messages as a form of e-mail within Twitter. You can send direct messages to anyone you're following and receive direct messages from anyone who is following you.

You can access your direct messages by clicking the Direct Messages link in the sidebar of your Twitter home page, as shown in Figure 3-14. You can also set up e-mail notifications so you know when you receive a direct message through Twitter, which is discussed in detail in Chapter 2 of this minibook.

Access your direct messages by clicking this link.

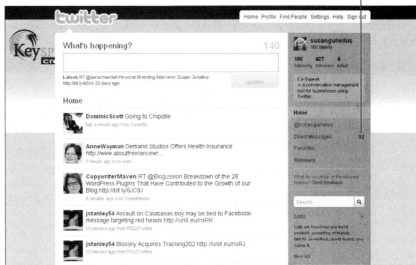

Figure 3-14:
You can address direct messages through the link in your Twitter home page sidebar.

Sending a direct message through Twitter is very easy. Just click the Direct Messages link in the right sidebar of your Twitter home page, find the person you want to send the message to from the drop-down list near the top of your screen, type your message into the text box provided, and click the Send button. Your message immediately appears in the other user's Direct Messages Inbox. He or she can reply to you via a direct message, too.

Using Twitter to Boost Blog Traffic

Don't be afraid to get creative in using Twitter to drive traffic to your blog. There are a number of tools you can use to feed your blog posts directly into your Twitter stream (see Chapter 4 of this minibook for recommendations), but you don't want your Twitter stream to be filled only with automated updates and links to your blog. Instead, get creative and use Twitter as both a tool to directly *and* indirectly promote your blog.

Following are several suggestions for ways you can use Twitter to drive traffic to your blog:

✦ **Tweet links to your blog posts:** If you write a particularly useful blog post, make sure you tweet it!

✦ **Network:** Use @replies, retweets, and hashtags to start and join Twitter conversations, get on other users' radar screens, and show them that you value what they have to say. This is one of the best ways to grow your online presence and boost blog traffic. The power of community is far-reaching. In time, the people you build relationships with will help you promote your content by retweeting it and talking about it, too.

✦ **Answer questions:** Twitter is a great place to establish yourself as an expert and share your knowledge. By answering questions and joining conversations, you can establish yourself as a go-to person for information related to your area of expertise. As more people see you as an expert, more people are likely to visit your blog for additional information from you.

✦ **Live tweet:** If you attend an event or meeting that your Twitter followers would be interested in, tweet about it in real-time. Share your experience, opinions, lessons learned, and more with your followers and make the information valuable for them, too. They'll appreciate your effort.

✦ **Ask for promotional help:** Don't be afraid to ask your followers to help you promote content. For example, tweet about your new blog post and ask your followers to retweet it or share it through social bookmarking sites such as Digg, StumbleUpon, and so on. Just be sure to do the same for them if they ask you!

✦ **Tap into the knowledge base:** Twitter is filled with people from all walks of life and varied expertise. Tap into that knowledge base by tweeting calls for quotes, interview subjects, guest blog posts, and so on. You can also offer your own services through a tweet.

The key to success is publishing a variety of tweets that provide an adequate mix of self-promotional, conversational, useful, and entertaining information. A one-dimensional Twitter stream isn't going to attract followers, engage people, help you build relationships, or grow blog traffic. Most importantly, be personable, and be yourself.

Joining Tweet Chats

A tweet chat can be a prearranged chat via Twitter updates that happens at a specific time and usually about a specific subject. A person who wants to start a tweet chat can invite people to join in advance by tweeting about it or contacting other people in any way he chooses. Participants might communicate through the use of a predetermined Twitter hashtag, or they might use a third-party Twitter application such as TweetChat (`http://tweet chat.com`), shown in Figure 3-15, to make the tweet chat easier to follow. Furthermore, tweet chats can consist of a free-flowing conversation or follow an agenda with one person acting as the leader.

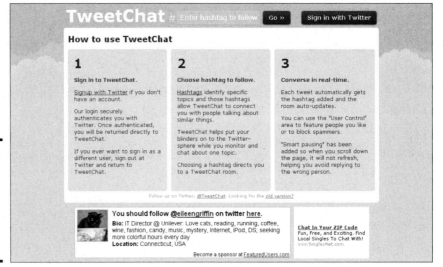

Figure 3-15: TweetChat makes it easy to join chat sessions on Twitter.

Informal tweet chats can happen spontaneously. For example, someone might begin tweeting about a topic using a specific hashtag. His followers might reply or retweet using the same hashtag, and before you know it, a group of people are all communicating via Twitter (in a public forum, which can't happen via other tools such as instant messaging) about the same topic, where anyone can jump into the conversation!

Finding and Using Twitter Badges

You can drive traffic to your Twitter profile from your blog by including links in your blog's sidebar, at the end of your posts, or even in your blog's header. Similarly, another easy and effective way to promote your Twitter content on your blog is by adding a free *Twitter badge* (also called a Twitter button) to your blog's sidebar. These badges often say "Follow Me" or a similar phrase and may or may not include a graphic of the Twitter bird icon.

Depending on the blogging application that you use, the steps to add a Twitter badge to your blog's sidebar vary. However, it's usually as simple as uploading the Twitter badge image file to your blog, adding a text widget or gadget to your blog's sidebar, and pasting the HTML code for the uploaded file into the widget or gadget.

Many Web sites offer free Twitter badges. Following are a few popular sites to search to find a Twitter badge you like:

✦ **Twitter Buttons:** (`www.twitterbuttons.com`) This site offers several pages of free Twitter badges.

✦ **TwitButtons:** (`www.twitbuttons.com`) This site offers both animated and nonanimated free Twitter badges.

✦ **MySocialButtons:** (`http://mysocialbuttons.com`) This site offers free Twitter badges as well as free badges for other social profiles such as Facebook, LinkedIn and more.

✦ **iStockphoto:** (`www.istockphoto.com`) If you're looking for a more unique Twitter badge, this site offers a variety to choose from. Note that you need to sign up for an account and it costs a small fee to download images from this site (you must purchase credits to buy images for download). To find Twitter badges, conduct a search from the home page using the keyword *Twitter*. Figure 3-16 shows a partial list of Twitter badges available through iStockphoto.

Book VIII Chapter 3

Getting More out of Twitter

Some Web sites that provide free Twitter badges offer HTML code that you can copy and paste into your blog. These sites host the badge file for you. It's always best to save the image to your hard drive and upload it to your blog, so you're hosting it rather than relying on another site to host it for you.

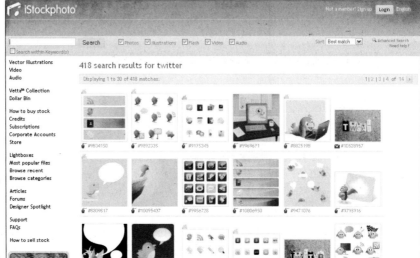

Figure 3-16:
Twitter
badges from
iStockphoto.

Chapter 4: Using Third-Party Twitter Applications

In This Chapter

✔ Understanding what third-party Twitter apps are

✔ Finding Twitter apps

✔ Using popular twitter apps

*T*he Twitter tool on its own doesn't offer a wide range of features and functions, but when you add the power of the many applications developed by third parties to enhance the Twitter user experience, it can be a powerful tool for growing your blog, marketing a business, promoting yourself, building relationships, and much more.

This chapter introduces you to some of the most popular Twitter apps. For more information about Twitter applications, be sure to read *Twitter For Dummies,* by Laura Fitton, Michael E. Gruen, and Leslie Poston. You can also find reviews of various Twitter applications on Laura Fitton's Pistachio Consulting blog and Web site (`http://pistachioconsulting.com`), Darren Rowse's Twitter Tips blog (`www.twitip.com`), and on the About.com guide to Web Logs (`http://weblogs.about.com`).

Understanding What Third-Party Twitter Applications Are

Twitter applications (often called Twitter apps) are developed by third parties (not affiliated with Twitter). They're usually free to use and can be easily integrated into your microblogging activities. Twitter apps enhance the functionality of Twitter, so you can perform additional tasks, track performance, and more. There are even Twitter apps that can help drive traffic to your blog and promote your content. Some Twitter apps function entirely online whereas others require you to download them to your computer and use them from your desktop.

New Twitter applications are introduced all the time, so it can be hard to decide which ones to try. The best course of action is to define your goals for your Twitter experience, and seek out Twitter apps that help you reach those goals. Some apps were designed for Twitter users who tweet solely for fun and to connect with friends and family, and other apps were designed for users who hope to increase business or blog traffic.

When you know your goals, you can test the Twitter apps that seem likely to help you reach those objectives. Take some time to research those applications. Conduct a Google search for reviews and opinions about those apps, and once you decide it's worth your time to try a new app, go ahead and experiment with it. You don't have to commit to using a Twitter app forever, and if it's free to use (as most Twitter apps are), then why not give it a test run?

Finding Twitter Apps

Several Web sites provide lists of Twitter apps, such as the Twitter Fan Wiki (`http://twitter.pbworks.com/Apps`), shown in Figure 4-1, oneforty (`www.oneforty.com`), Twitdom (`www.twitdom.com`), and Twapps (`www.twapps.com`). You can also find reviews and opinions about Twitter apps on blogs about Twitter and blogging in general. Some great blogs to check out are mentioned at the beginning of this chapter. However, most Twitter users agree that the best place to find out about Twitter apps is through your own Twitter stream of people you're following.

Figure 4-1: Find Twitter Apps in the Twitter Fan Wiki.

When Twitter users find an app they like, they usually tweet about it. Similarly, if they find apps they don't like, they tweet about those, too. Don't be tempted to try every new app that you hear about. Instead, remember your goals for your Twitter activities and test the Twitter apps that are likely to help you meet those goals.

New Twitter apps can be as tempting as shiny new toys, but don't lose track of your goals as you play with them. As you read about or test an app, ask yourself, "How is this app going to be helpful to me?" That's where the real value of Twitter is found.

Using Popular Twitter Apps

Trying to create a comprehensive list of the most useful and popular Twitter apps is an impossible task for two reasons. First, the pool of Twitter apps changes constantly, and second, every person has different goals for his Twitter activities, which are best supported with different Twitter apps.

With that in mind, this chapter introduces you to a number of popular Twitter apps to give you a starting point. Most people who try the Twitter apps mentioned in this chapter find value in them and speak positively about them.

New Twitter applications are released all the time, and existing Twitter apps are retooled and updated frequently. Be sure to check for updates for the apps you decide to use, and research new apps to ensure they'll help you meet your goals, before you jump in and invest time experimenting with them.

TwitThis

www.twitthis.com

If you want to drive traffic to your blog, TwitThis is a great Twitter app for you to use. TwitThis is a very simple Twitter app that allows you to include a *TwitThis* button or link on each of your blog posts. It integrates easily with most blogging applications and gives your blog readers the opportunity to tweet your blog posts with the click of a button! You can see what a TwitThis button looks like at the end of a blog post in Figure 4-2.

TwitThis uses TinyURL (http://tinyurl.com) to automatically shorten the URL to your blog post, so there are no extra steps required for the person who clicks the TwitThis link or button on your blog post to tweet it. She simply needs to log in to her Twitter account, add a message if she chooses, and that's it. That person has tweeted your blog post for her entire list of followers to see in their Twitter streams!

Figure 4-2:
The
TwitThis
button at
the end of a
blog post.

TweetMeme

`www.tweetmeme.com`

TweetMeme works similarly to TwitThis but provides a few additional features. For example, when you use the TweetMeme app, you can place a button at the end of your blog posts (or wherever you choose) that people can click to automatically tweet the URL to your blog post. You can see the Retweet button in a blog post in Figure 4-3.

Figure 4-3:
Readers
can click
the Retweet
button to
tweet the
URL to your
blog post.

The Retweet button

The Retweet button can also display the number of times the post has been tweeted, which is particularly useful if your blog is popular and content is tweeted frequently. The perception for your blog audience is this: If a lot of people are tweeting a blog post, it must be good.

You can also put the Retweet button in your e-mails, Web site, RSS feed, and more, making it versatile tool that can help you promote yourself and your blog in multiple places.

TweetDeck

www.tweetdeck.com

If you're following a lot of people on Twitter or if you just like to be organized, TweetDeck should make your life a lot easier. If you get a lot of tweets in your Twitter stream each day, it can be easy to miss important tweets in that clutter. TweetDeck helps to solve that problem.

TweetDeck allows you to create three separate panes in your browser window so you can manage your tweets, @replies, and more, as shown in Figure 4-4. You can customize the panes and group the people you're following into categories of your choice. For example, if you follow some people for fun, you can put them in one category, and if you follow other people for work, you can put them in another category.

TweetDeck is a desktop application that you need to download (along with the free Adobe AIR). TweetDeck uses a lot of memory on your computer, so it can slow down your work.

Figure 4-4: TweetDeck displays three separate panes in your browser window.

Tweetie

`www.atebits.com`

Tweetie is similar to TweetDeck in that its primary benefit is helping you organize your Twitter activities. The application must be downloaded to your computer hard drive to use, and it works on both Macs and iPhones (shown in Figure 4-5).

Figure 4-5: Tweetie for iPhones.

Unfortunately, if you use the free version, ads appear in your Twitter stream. You can remove the ads by paying a registration fee. Tweetie offers a few features that users really like, such as threaded tweet conversations and easily accessible user details.

TwitPic

`www.twitpic.com`

Many people like to share photos and images through Twitter, but Twitter doesn't offer an option to upload and link to images online. That's where TwitPic comes in handy. With TwitPic, you can upload images from your mobile phone, camera, or computer and share them in a tweet. You can even add a description that appears beneath the image.

Figure 4-6:
An image
uploaded to
TwitPic.

When a person clicks the link in your tweet to your TwitPic image, he not only sees that image, but he can also leave comments that display beneath the image, as shown in Figure 4-6.

SocialOomph

www.socialoomph.com

It's important to spread your tweets out so they publish at multiple times during the day. The reason is simple — you never know who's online and using Twitter at any given moment. It's safe to assume that every person following you isn't using Twitter at the exact moment that you're publishing tweets. Therefore, it's very easy for your tweets to get pushed far down in others' Twitter streams quickly, meaning they might not see your tweets at all. If you publish tweets throughout the day, there's a greater chance that more people will see them.

The problem is finding the time to continually tweet during the day. Some people find it easier to write a number of tweets at the same time and schedule them to publish at multiple times in the future. Twitter doesn't offer a scheduling feature, but SocialOomph (shown in Figure 4-7) does.

**Book VIII
Chapter 4**

**Using Third-
Party Twitter
Applications**

With SocialOomph, you can write multiple tweets at the same time and schedule them to publish at multiple times of your choice in the future. Of course, you can always publish spontaneous tweets throughout the day, too. However, with SocialOomph, you can feel confident that more of your followers will have a chance to see some new content from you throughout the day, depending on when they're online and using Twitter.

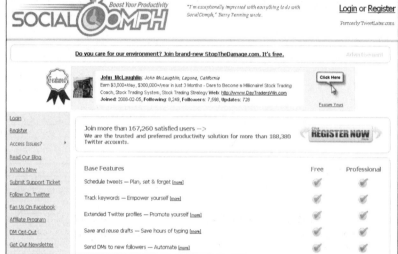

Figure 4-7: SocialOomph lets you schedule tweets to publish in the future.

Twellow

www.twellow.com

It can be hard to find people on Twitter unless you know their real names or usernames. Fortunately, there's a Twitter app that makes it a bit easier to find other people and promote yourself.

Twellow, shown in Figure 4-8, is often referred to as the Yellow Pages of Twitter. You can add your own listing to Twellow for free, so other Twitter users can find you. Similarly, you can search for Twitter users to follow through Twellow. You can search for people and companies as well as by category.

You can also find people with similar interests to your own and in specific locations using the following popular Twitter apps — GeoFollow (http://geofollow.com), Localtweeps (www.localtweeps.com), and WeFollow (http://wefollow.com).

Figure 4-8:
Twellow
is like a
Twitter
Yellow
Pages.

TwitterCounter

http://twittercounter.com

Just as you can promote your blog content through your tweets, you can also promote your Twitter content on your blog with TwitterCounter. This Twitter app enables you to include a widget on your blog that invites readers to follow you on Twitter and shows the number of Twitter followers you have. The perception is that if a lot of people are following you on Twitter, you must be publishing great tweets! It's easy to create and customize your own widget using TwitterCounter, as shown in Figure 4-9.

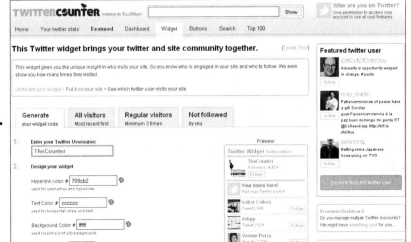

Figure 4-9:
Create
your own
follower
widget with
Twitter
Counter.

**Book VIII
Chapter 4**

Using Third-Party Twitter Applications

You can also access statistics via TwitterCounter related to your Twitter activity as well as the activities of other Twitter users, including some of the most popular Twitterers!

The more ways you can connect with people online, the better. Each connection opens new opportunities for building relationships, driving traffic to your blog, and meeting your goals.

TweetBeep

www.tweetbeep.com

TweetBeep is a third-party Twitter application that alerts you via e-mail when your chosen keywords are found on Twitter. It works similarly to Google Alerts (discussed in Chapter 3 of Book II). You just visit the TweetBeep Web site, shown in Figure 4-10, enter your chosen keywords in the online form, select how often you want to be notified when your keywords are found, and you're done. You'll start to receive e-mails that include links to tweets using your keywords at the times you designated.

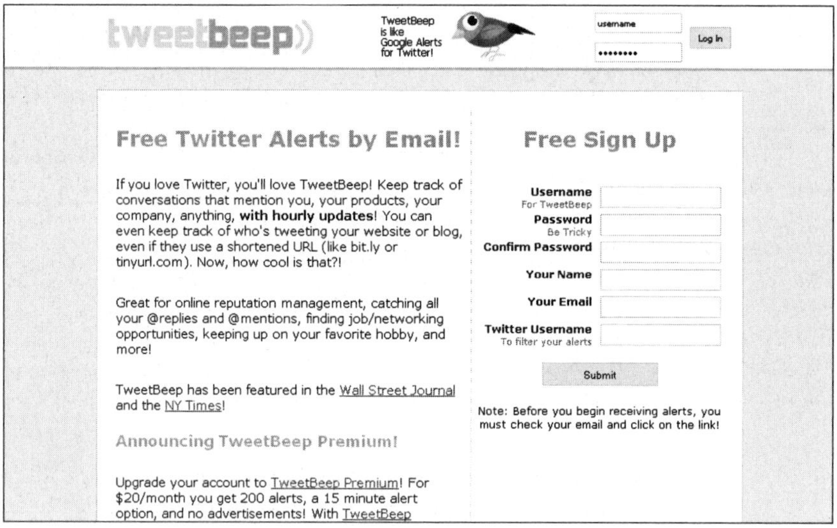

tweetbeep)) TweetBeep is like Google Alerts for Twitter! username ••••••••• Log in

Free Twitter Alerts by Email!

If you love Twitter, you'll love TweetBeep! Keep track of conversations that mention you, your products, your company, anything, **with hourly updates!** You can even keep track of who's tweeting your website or blog, even if they use a shortened URL (like bit.ly or tinyurl.com). Now, how cool is that?!

Great for online reputation management, catching all your @replies and @mentions, finding job/networking opportunities, keeping up on your favorite hobby, and more!

TweetBeep has been featured in the Wall Street Journal and the NY Times!

Announcing TweetBeep Premium!

Upgrade your account to TweetBeep Premium! For $20/month you get 200 alerts, a 15 minute alert option, and no advertisements! With TweetBeep

Free Sign Up

Username
For TweetBeep

Password
Be Tricky

Confirm Password

Your Name

Your Email

Twitter Username
To filter your alerts

Submit

Note: Before you begin receiving alerts, you must check your email and click on the link!

Figure 4-10: The TweetBeep Twitter alerts form.

There are a few limitations to the free version of TweetBeep. For example, you can only set up ten alerts and receive e-mails at specific intervals, and those e-mails can only include up to 50 instances of your keywords. However, that's usually enough for most Twitter users.

TweetBeep is a great way to keep track of conversations about you, your blog topic, and so on. It's also a great way to find people who are tweeting about topics that interest you whom you might want to follow, retweet, and so on in order to build relationships with them.

Twitterfeed

http://twitterfeed.com

Promoting your blog content via Twitter is an effective way to boost your blog traffic. Twitterfeed, shown in Figure 4-11, makes it easy to automatically feed your blog posts into your Twitter updates. After you set up your Twitterfeed account and link your Twitter profile to your blog, a new tweet is automatically published each time you publish a new blog post. That tweet includes a snippet from your blog post and a link to that post.

Figure 4-11: Use Twitterfeed to update Twitter when you publish new blog posts.

You can also use Twitterfeed to update your Facebook profile with your blog posts, and you can track your feed statistics by using Twitterfeed.

Make sure your Twitter stream includes more tweets than the automated updates from your blog via Twitterfeed. Your Twitter stream gets boring when it only includes automated updates.

yfrog

`www.yfrog.com`

If you want to upload and share images or videos via Twitter, then yfrog, shown in Figure 4-12, is a great Twitter app for you. Using yfrog, you can upload images and videos from your computer, a webcam, or another URL. You can also use yfrog from your iPhone, and it integrates with a variety of other Twitter apps such as Tweetie and TweetDeck, discussed earlier in this chapter.

Figure 4-12: Share images and videos via Twitter with yfrog.

The yfrog interface is easy to use. You can upload your image or video, add a message, enter your Twitter login information, and you're done. A new tweet is published in your Twitter stream, which includes a link to your image or video on yfrog. Other users can leave comments on your image or video via yfrog and retweet it.

Another useful Twitter app for sharing webcam videos, photos, pictures, YouTube videos, and URLs is Tweetube (`www.tweetube.com`).

OpenBeak (formerly called TwitterBerry)

`http://orangatame.com/products/openbeak`

OpenBeak, shown in Figure 4-13, is a third-party Twitter application that allows BlackBerry smart phone users to access and post to Twitter directly from their handheld devices. The application isn't as pretty or feature-rich as some other Twitter apps are for other smart phones (such as Tweetie for iPhones, as discussed earlier in this chapter), but it gets the basic job done.

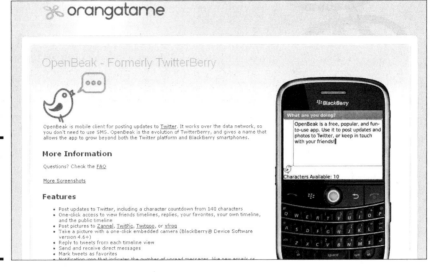

Figure 4-13: OpenBeak allows BlackBerry users to tweet on the go.

CoTweet

`www.cotweet.com`

CoTweet, shown in Figure 4-14, makes it easy for multiple Twitter users to publish tweets to the same Twitter profile. This Twitter app is particularly useful for companies that employ multiple people to publish content to the company's Twitter profile each day. It's also useful for blogs that are written by a team of people who each want to publish content to the blog's Twitter profile.

Figure 4-14: CoTweet is an excellent app for companies and blog networks.

You can manage multiple Twitter accounts with CoTweet, and you can access statistics, assign tweets to colleagues for follow up, schedule colleagues to be "on Twitter duty" at specific times, and more. It's a feature-rich Twitter application that can be used in a variety of ways depending on your needs.

Glossary

@reply: (Pronounced *at* reply.) A Twitter update that begins with @username, which identifies a tweet as being directed at a specific Twitter user. @username used *within* a tweet is considered a mention.

affiliate advertising: Bloggers sign up through advertising programs agreeing to display ads for advertisers. Those advertisers pay the bloggers each time a visitor to their blogs follows an affiliate ad link and makes a purchase or performs a specified action. Popular affiliate advertising programs include Amazon Associates, LinkShare, and Commission Junction.

Amazon Associates: A popular affiliate advertising program for bloggers.

archive: The location on a blog where posts that are not current are stored for easy access by visitors.

Atom: A type of syndication format used to deliver feeds. Also see *feed, feed reader,* and *RSS.*

attribution: Citing the source of a story, quote, or image used within a blog post.

audio blog: See *podcast.*

bandwidth: The amount of data that can be transmitted through a network, a modem, or an online connection. It's typically measured in bits per second (bps).

blog: A fusion of the words *Web* and *log.* Originally dubbed *Weblogs,* the term blog quickly grew to be the preferred nomenclature. Blogs began as online diaries with entries listed in reverse chronological order. As blogging grew in popularity, more individuals, groups, and businesses joined the blogosphere. Blogs are unique in that they provide a two-way conversation between the author and visitors through the comment feature. Blogs are considered one of the first methods of bringing user-generated content to the mainstream.

blog carnival: A blogging promotional event wherein a group of bloggers gather together to write about a predetermined topic. Each blogger submits the link to his or her post, and all links are published in a single carnival round-up post. Each participant promotes the carnival on his or her blog with the intention of driving traffic to all blogs involved.

blog contest: A blogging promotional event wherein a prize is given away in order to drive traffic to the hosting blog.

blog host: A company that provides space on its servers to store and maintain blogs. Also called *Web host* or *host*.

blog marketing: The process of promoting your blog to drive traffic to it. Examples of blog promotion tactics include leaving comments on other blogs with links back to your blog, linking to blogs within your blog posts and sending a trackback to that blog, adding blogs to your blogroll, participating in social bookmarking and networking, and so on. Also called *blog promotion*.

blog posts: Individual entries written by a blogger and published on a blog.

blog promotion: See *blog marketing*.

blog statistics: The data used to track the performance of a blog.

blogger: A person who writes content for a blog.

Blogger: An online application owned by Google that allows users to create and maintain blogs.

blogger's block: Occurs when a blogger cannot think of anything to write a blog post about.

blogging: The act of writing and publishing blog posts or entries.

blogging application: The program used by bloggers to create and maintain blogs, such as Blogger, WordPress, TypePad, MovableType, and LiveJournal. Also called *blogging platform* or *blogging software*.

blogosphere: The online blogging community made up of bloggers from around the world who create user-generated content as part of the social Web.

blogroll: A list of links created by a blogger and published on his or her blog. Links in a blogroll are typically related to the blog topic or other sites the blogger enjoys or recommends.

bounce rate: The percentage of people who leave a blog immediately after finding it.

browser: A program used to surf the Internet, such as Internet Explorer, Firefox, Opera, Google Chrome, Safari, and more. Also called *Web browser.*

business blog: A blog created and maintained by a business for professional purposes.

CAPTCHA: The acronym for Completely Automated Public Turing test to tell Computers and Humans Apart. It presents a challenge or question which a user must complete before submitting data (such as a blog comment) through a Web site.

category: Used in some blogging applications (such as WordPress) to separate similar blog posts so it is easier for readers to find them.

comment: An opinion or reaction by a blog reader to a specific post. Comments can be submitted at the end of blog posts when the blogger has chosen to allow them. Comments are what make a blog interactive.

comment moderation: The process of holding comments for review prior to publishing them on a blog. Comment moderation is typically used to ensure spam and offensive comments are not published on a blog.

comment policy: A set of rules and restrictions published on a blog to set visitor expectations related to the types of comments allowed on the blog and what types of comments are likely to be deleted.

content management system (CMS): A tool for creating and maintaining online content that separates design, content, and interactivity and allows multiple users to easily manage the Web site.

contextual advertising: Ads served based on the content found on the Web page where the ads appear. Popular contextual advertising programs include Google AdSense and Kontera.

copyright: Legal ownership of intellectual property giving the owner exclusive right to reproduce and share that property.

Creative Commons license: Created to give copyright holders more flexibility in allowing reproduction and sharing of their property.

CSS: The acronym for *cascading style sheets,* which is used by Web designers to create blog layouts. In other words, CSS works behind the scenes to configure the look and feel of a blog.

dashboard: The primary account management page of an online software program, such as Blogger or Google AdSense, where users can access the tools and functionality to modify settings, create content, and more.

domain name: The part of a URL that represents a specific Web site. Domain names are typically preceded by www. and end with an extension such as .com, .net, or .org.

fair use: An exception to copyright laws that allows limited use of certain copyrighted materials.

feed: The syndicated content of a blog. Also see *RSS* and *feed reader*.

feed advertising: Advertisements that appear within blog feeds.

feed reader: A tool used to read RSS feeds. Feed readers receive feeds from blogs and deliver them to subscribers in aggregated format for quick and easy viewing in one place.

flash: Streaming animation that appears on Web pages.

footer: The area spanning the bottom of a blog page, which typically includes copyright information and may include other elements such as a contact link or ads.

forum: An online message board where participants post messages within predetermined categories. Other participants respond creating an online conversation between a potentially large group of people.

FTP: The acronym for File Transfer Protocol, which is the process used to transfer files from one computer to another across the Internet.

gadget: A tool used in the Blogger blogging application to make it easy for bloggers to add functionality and features to their blogs.

Google: A company based in California that produces software, programs, tools, and utilities to help people leverage the Internet to accomplish tasks. Popular Google programs include Google search, Google AdSense, Google AdWords, and more.

Google AdSense: A contextual advertising program that's popular with bloggers and online publishers.

Google Alerts: An application offered by Google that provides e-mail updates whenever specified keywords are found online.

guest blogging: The process of writing free posts to appear on another person's blog or accepting free posts from another blogger to publish on your blog with the purpose of networking and driving blog traffic.

hashtag: An informal categorization system for Twitter that helps users identify tweets related to topics of interest. Hashtags include the # symbol followed by a keyword, such as #olympics.

header: The area spanning the top of a blog page where the blog title, graphics, and possibly navigational links or ads appear.

hit: A blog statistic counted each time a file is downloaded from your blog. Each page in a blog or Web site typically contains multiple files.

home page: The first page a visitor sees when he or she enters a root domain name.

HTML: The acronym for Hypertext Markup Language, which is a programming language made up of tags used to create Web sites and blogs.

HTML editor: The blog composition function, wherein the blogger must enter HTML code to create the post.

impression-based advertising: An ad model wherein bloggers publish ads for advertisers and get paid based on the number of times those ads are loaded on a Web page and displayed to visitors. Popular impression-based advertising programs include ValueClick and Tribal Fusion.

keyword: A word or phrase used to help index a Web page, allowing it to be found by search engines.

labels: Keywords used in the Blogger blogging application to informally categorize blog posts.

link: A connection between two Web sites. When selected, a link takes the user to another Web page. Also called *hyperlink*.

linkbait: A post written for the primary purpose of attracting traffic and links. Linkbait posts are typically related to buzz topics that might have nothing to do with the topic of the blog the post is published on.

long-tail search engine optimization: The process of optimizing Web pages for highly focused searches based on specific keywords and keyword phrases.

message board: See *forum*.

microblogging: Short snippets of text (typically 140 characters or less) published through sites such as Twitter and Plurk.

MovableType: A blogging application owned by Six Apart.

multiuser blog: A blog authored by more than one person and accessible through the blogging software by multiple people.

niche: A specific and highly targeted segment of an audience or market. A niche blog is written about a focused topic and appeals to a very specific group of people.

NoFollow: An HTML tag that makes links invisible to Web browsers.

offline blog editor: A tool used to create and edit blog posts from a computer desktop rather than online.

paid post: A blog post written and published in exchange for some form of compensation.

page: Some blogging applications allow users to create pages in addition to posts. Unlike individual post entries, pages are completely separate from the chronological blog post archive and live online similarly to individual Web pages.

page rank: A measurement used to determine a blog's popularity typically based on traffic and incoming links.

page view: A blog statistic that tracks each time a Web page is viewed independent of who is viewing that page.

pay-per-action: An online advertising payment model that pays the publisher each time an ad is clicked and an action is performed (for example, a sale is made or a lead form is submitted). Also called *PPA.*

pay-per-click: An online advertising payment model that pays the publisher each time an ad is clicked. Also called *PPC.*

pay-per-impression: An online advertising payment model that pays the publisher each time an ad is displayed. Also called *PPM.*

permalink: A fusion of the words *permanent* and *link.* A link to a specific page in a blog that remains unchanged over time.

ping: A signal sent from one Web site to another to ensure that the other site exists. Pings are used to notify sites that receive updates from ping servers of updates to a blog or Web site.

plug-in: Tools created by third parties that enhance the functionality of a program or site, such as WordPress.org.

podcast: An audio file that's recorded digitally for playback online. Bloggers use podcasts to create audio blog posts. Also called *audio blogging.*

post: An entry on a blog, typically published in reverse chronological order.

post editor: The blogging software composition function wherein a blogger can type the content for a blog post. Also see *HTML editor* and *visual editor.*

professional blogger: A person who writes blog content as a career.

profile: A blogger's About Me page, which describes who the blogger is and why he or she is qualified to write the blog.

referrer: A Web site, blog, or search engine that leads visitors to your blog.

retweet: A Twitter term used to identify updates that are copied from another user's Twitter stream and republished. Retweets are preceded by *RT.*

RSS: The acronym for *Really Simple Syndication.* The technology that creates Web content syndication, which allows users to subscribe to Web sites and blogs and receive new content from those Web sites and blogs in aggregated format within a feed reader. Also see *feed* and *feed reader.*

search engine: A Web site used to find Web pages related to specific keywords or keyword phrases. Search engines use proprietary algorithms to comb the Internet and return results, which are typically presented in a ranked order. Google, Yahoo!, and Bing are popular search engines.

search engine optimization: The process of writing Web content, designing Web pages, and promoting online content to boost rankings within search engine keyword searches. Also called *SEO.*

search engine reputation management: The process of monitoring the perceived reputation of a person, brand, company, and so on based on the search engine results that are delivered when a person conducts a search using keywords related to that person, brand, company, and so on. Also called *SERM.*

SEO: See *search engine optimization.*

SERM: See *search engine reputation management.*

sidebar: A column on a blog to the right or left of the main column, or two sidebars can flank the main column. Sidebars typically include ancillary content such as a blogroll, archive links, and ads.

social bookmarking: A method of saving, storing, and sharing Web pages for future reference. Popular social bookmarking sites include Digg, StumbleUpon, Reddit, and Delicious.

social networking: The act of communicating and building relationships with other people online. Popular social networking sites include Facebook, LinkedIn, and Friendster.

social Web: The second generation of the World Wide Web, which focuses on interaction, user-generated content, communities, and building relationships. Also called *Web 2.0*.

spam: Comments submitted on your blog for no reason other than to drive traffic to another Web site. Spam also comes in e-mail flavor.

sponsored review: A blog post written for the purpose of being paid by an advertiser who solicits it. Popular sponsored review networks include PayPerPost.com, ReviewMe.com, and SponsoredReviews.com. Also called *sponsored post* or *paid post*.

sponsored tweet: A Twitter update published for the purpose of being paid by an advertiser who solicits it.

subscribe: When a person signs up to receive a blog's feed in his or her feed reader or via e-mail.

tag: Keywords used to identify and informally categorize a blog post. Tags are also read by blog search engines to provide search results to users.

Technorati: A blog search engine.

template: A predesigned blog layout created to make it easy for people with little to no computer knowledge to start and maintain a blog. Also called *theme*.

text link ads: Ads that appear as simple text links on blogs and Web sites. Text link ads are typically used to drive business and to boost the number of incoming links for the advertiser's Web site thereby boosting the advertiser's page rank.

theme: A predesigned blog layout created to make it easy for people with little to no computer knowledge to start and maintain a blog. Also called *template*.

trackback: A reference link or shoulder tap used to notify a blog when another blog has linked to that site. Trackbacks appear as links within the comments section of blog posts.

tweet: A Twitter update.

Twitter: A microblogging application.

Twitter app: A tool developed by a third party to enhance the functionality of Twitter.

TypePad: A blogging application owned by Six Apart.

unique visitor: When a visitor is counted one time regardless of how many times he or she visits a Web page. Also see *visitor*.

URL: The acronym for Uniform Resource Locator. The unique address of a specific page on the Internet consisting of an access protocol (such as `http`), a domain name (such as `www.sitename.com`) and an extension identifying the specific page within a Web site or blog (for instance, `/specificpage.htm`).

URL shortener: A tool used to shorten lengthy URLs for republishing in microblogging updates such as Twitter.

visit: Each time a page on your blog is accessed, a visit is counted.

visitor: A person who views a page (or multiple pages) on your blog.

visual editor: The blog post composition function where bloggers can type posts using a common word processing interface. Also see *WYSIWYG*.

vlogging: A fusion of the words *video* and *blog*. The process of publishing videos rather than written blog posts. Also called *video blogging*.

Web 2.0: See *social Web*.

Web analytics: The data used to track the performance of a Web site.

Web host: A company other than a blogger's blogging application provider that stores blogs (as well as other Web sites) on its server for a fee.

Web log: See *blog*. Also called *Weblog*.

widget: A tool used in the WordPress blogging application to add additional features and functionality to a blog, particularly in the blog's sidebar.

WordPress: A blogging application from Automattic, Inc. There are two versions of WordPress: WordPress.com, which lets bloggers create blogs that are hosted by WordPress, and WordPress.org, which allows bloggers to create blogs that must be hosted through a third-party Web host.

WYSIWYG: The acronym for What You See Is What You Get. The visual editor provided by most blogging software programs that allows users to type blog post content in a form similar to traditional word-processing software, where the format seen onscreen during the editing process looks similar to how the final, published post will appear, rather than using HTML code as required in the HTML editor.

Index

B